A History of Women in the United States:
State-by-State Reference

A History of Women in the United States: State-by-State Reference

VOLUME 1

INTRODUCTORY ESSAYS

ALABAMA–ILLINOIS

Doris Weatherford, General Editor

GROLIER ACADEMIC REFERENCE, AN IMPRINT OF SCHOLASTIC LIBRARY PUBLISHING, INC.

DANBURY, CONNECTICUT

Published by Grolier Academic Reference, an Imprint of Scholastic Library Publishing, Inc. Danbury, Connecticut

Cover image: "Two Kinds," oil painting by Pamela Chin Lee, 24" x 36",
© Pamela Chin Lee/Omni-Photo Communications, Inc.

Library of Congress Cataloging-in-Publication Data

A history of women in the United States : state-by-state reference / Doris Weatherford, editor.
    p. cm.
    Includes bibliographical references and index.
    Contents: v. 1. Alabama–Illinois — v. 2. Indiana–Nebraska — v. 3. Nevada–South Dakota
— v. 4 Tennessee–Wyoming; appendices.
    ISBN 0-7172-5805-X (set : alk. paper)
    1. Women—United States—History. 2. Women—United States—States—History. I.
Weatherford, Doris.

HQ1410.H58 2003
305.4'0973—dc22
                                                                          2003049299

Printed and Manufactured in the United States of America.

1 3 5 4 2

EDITORIAL AND PRODUCTION STAFF

TABLE OF CONTENTS

VOLUME 4

SUPPLEMENTAL MATERIAL

PREFACE

A first of its kind, *A History of Women in the United States: State-by-State Reference* presents detailed histories of the women in each state (plus Puerto Rico and Washington, D.C.) within a national context. Intended for use by researchers at the high school, college, and university levels, as well as by the general public, this set presents national, regional, and local history of women through topical essays, detailed state histories, biographies, and appendices—including a chronology of U.S. women's history, a compendium of historical documents of national importance, and tables of statistics regarding women's status in society.

The first volume of this four-volume set opens with nine introductory essays, which offer a broad perspective on the themes and issues of U.S. women's history. The essays explore chronological periods in women's history across the country, such as women in early America and in the Progressive Era, as well as themes that have spanned women's history in the United States from its beginning, such as feminism, and race and ethnicity. The essays offer a national context for themes and trends that resound in the state articles. For instance, the essay on the Reform and Progressive Era discusses the activism that shaped the history of the country—and women in particular—during the late 19th and early 20th century, while each state article deals with those same progressive trends in the context of regional, state, and local history.

State articles follow the introductory essays and include the following sections:

- **History of Women in the State.** The heart of each state article, this narrative offers an overview of women's history in the state from prehistory to the present day. Political history is the primary focus, but cultural and social history is also discussed. The narrative is arranged chronologically and corresponds roughly to eras outlined in the U.S. history standards. The aim is to allow students to research not just the details of individual states, but to conduct analysis and comparisons across states, thereby investigating regional trends and variations, as well as national trends.

- **Sidebars and Special Features.** These boxed features sprinkled throughout the main narrative spotlight particular events, people, locales, and trends. For example, the main narrative for Alaska mentions the first woman to win the famous Iditarod dog race, while a sidebar describes in more detail the importance of the Iditarod for the history of women in Alaska. Sidebars also track important themes across all states, such as women and work, or the effect of race on women's experiences.

- **Timeline.** A timeline is provided for each state. Located close to the end of each state narrative, the timeline highlights key events in the state's history alongside important national events.

- **Prominent Women.** This section follows the main narrative and offers concise profiles of the most significant women associated with each state. Inclusion in this section is based on important milestones, such as the first women to be elected to the U.S. Congress in their own right, Nobel Prize and Pulitzer Prize winners, the first women to achieve accomplishments in specific fields, and the like. The decision about the states in which to include women was based on their birthplace or hometown, or on the location in which they did a good portion of their training or work. The names of women who are profiled are set in small caps when they are first mentioned in the main state narrative.

- **Prominent Sites.** This next section describes places of historical importance to women. The entries describe the significance of the place to women's history, and contact and location information is included.

- **Resources.** In addition to bibliographic resources, this section offers less traditional sources for further research, such as Web sites and selected organizations and institutions whose work concerns women's history and issues. Web sites have been carefully selected for their authority and content, as well as their longevity.

Also included in each state article are:

- **Literary Quote.** Each state article opens with a quote from a literary work about the state or representing some aspect of the state. Each quote is taken from a work written by a woman.

- **Key Information Chart.** Placed on the first page of each article is a chart of important data, such as the percentage of women in the state legislature and the percentage of female college enrollment.

- **Map of the State.** Also placed on the first page is a locator map that shows the most important cities and locations mentioned in the state article.

- **Primary Documents.** Appearing throughout the article, each state article includes excerpts from primary source material used to convey historical authenticity to the people, events, and trends discussed. These documents frequently appear within sidebars and special features and include extracts from newspaper articles and editorials, political cartoons, diary excerpts, important writings from prominent women thinkers, and so forth.

The last volume includes a set of appendices:

- **Appendix I: Chronology.** An expansion of the timelines included in each state entry, this chronology of achievements and events relating to women in the United States helps readers put the events in each state into a broader national perspective.

- **Appendix II: Primary Documents.** Documents important to the history of women on the national scale are presented here. Examples include Margaret Sanger's "The Case for Birth Control," first published in 1924, and Shirley Chisholm's "Equal Rights for Women," a speech delivered to the U.S. House of Representatives in 1969.

- **Appendix III: Statistical Material.** Included are both state-by-state and national data on women's political participation, population, vital statistics, employment, education, and health.

The set closes with a general bibliography, which presents an extensive collection of resources in U.S. women's history to complement the resources in the state entries, as well as a detailed name, place, and concept index.

During the research and writing of this encyclopedia, the authors and editors often encountered limitations in the historical record that typify the study of women's history. Although this problem varies from state to state, primary historical documents, especially of earlier periods, are sometimes completely silent on the existence of women and their activities and accomplishments. Secondary historical texts can be equally silent. Consequently, even the names of women who participated in important activities—the first settlers in a region, for instance—sometimes cannot be cited. Nevertheless, we have decided to mention women, even when nameless, if the historical record shows that they were involved in notable activities and achieved important milestones. Women's history is, in fact, much more difficult to trace than traditional "male" history simply because it is not unusual for the same woman to have three or more surnames during the course of her life.

Other problems concerning the limitation of the historical record, such as variations in spelling and dates relating to women, also arose. We tried to adjudicate such variations by consulting standard reference sources, but because these sources often exclude women, we were forced to make our own decisions about variations in historical data based on the best research available.

Further, because standard comprehensive histories of women in most states and regions do not exist—a lack we hope to remedy with the publication of this encyclopedia—much of our research was original and synthesized from a wide range of sources. These sources included books, reports, articles, oral histories, and the like, especially the six-volume *History of Woman Suffrage* by Susan B. Anthony and others, which documents the state-by-state struggle for women's voting rights. We also made particular use of histories written and recorded by the New Deal's Federal Writers' Project and the women's electoral information stored in Rutgers University's American Women and Politics database, as well as state archive reports and historical monographs on specific trends that relate, even if in a minor way, to women.

University presses in many states are increasingly aware of the amount of unpublished material on women that is available. A serious gap remains, however, between academia and the public historians who transmit the American past to subsequent generations. We hope this encyclopedia will begin to close that gap.

A History of Women in the United States:
State-by-State Reference

INTRODUCTORY ESSAYS

WOMEN IN EARLY AMERICA

The narrative of American history usually begins with Columbus's voyage of 1492 and the Spanish conquistadores who followed, or with the establishment of the first lasting English settlement at Jamestown in 1607. The first Europeans to arrive in what they called a "New World" were all men—sailors, soldiers, fishermen, priests, and treasure seekers; thus the earliest settlements were all-male frontier outposts. European women arrived later, usually as members of immigrant families or as indentured servants advertised as potential wives for male colonists. New France was so desperate for women settlers that the government sponsored the so-called daughters of the king: between 1634 and 1662, 230 women were recruited to travel to what is now eastern Canada. Nevertheless, in 1662, New France was inhabited by six French men for every French woman.

European women may have been scarce in the early colonial years, but Native American women whose ancestors had lived on the continent for thousands of years were present in every colony. In New Spain, a Native American woman known as Doña Marina, or La Malinche, served as a guide and translator for Hernán Cortés when he captured the Aztec capital in present-day Mexico in 1519. She married another Spaniard, had children, and became known as the Mother of Mexicans (mestizos, or those of American Indian and Spanish background); she is an ambiguous figure who was considered both a cultural intermediary and also a traitor, at least in part, to her people and her culture. She set a pattern for other Native American women not only in Mexico itself but also in California, New Mexico, and Texas. In the French colonies, which came to encompass the area around the Great Lakes and the Mississippi Valley, as well as eastern Canada, Native American women married French traders and created metis (mixed race) family networks that were vital to the lucrative fur trade.

In Jamestown, Virginia, Pocahontas, the young daughter of a powerful chief, learned to speak English and in 1614 married John Rolfe, an English tobacco planter who soon took her to England. She died there before their return voyage, but her descendents founded some of the first families of Virginia. English men did marry Native American women, but these matches were more the exception than the rule. English men preferred to have English wives, and in the colonies that became the United States, Native Americans and whites remained separate for the most part, and the children of Native American–white marriages, known by the derogatory word *halfbreed*, were raised in Native American communities.

Until the 18th century, the Chesapeake region (Virginia and Maryland) continued to have unequal sex ratios, thus immigrant women could easily find husbands and quickly remarry if their husbands died. This made the region attractive to poor, single women in England, where their marriage prospects were not as good. Unfortunately, the Chesapeake also had a distinct disadvantage: the climate was conducive to diseases, especially yellow fever, malaria, and dysentery, that were disproportionately deadly to young children and pregnant women. Women who did travel to Virginia often regretted the move. Elizabeth Sprigs, a young indentured servant, wrote to her father in England that she was "toiling almost day and night, . . . whipped, . . . scarce any thing but corn and salt to eat, . . . almost naked no shoes nor stockings to wear." (Berkin and Horowitz 1998, 107) These conditions kept women from voluntarily immigrating in any great numbers, and the sex ratio remained unequal until children born in the colonies—roughly equal numbers of boys and girls—outnumbered the new immigrants.

In New England, where the first English immigrants came in family groups to Plymouth in 1620 and the Massachusetts Bay Colony in 1630, the balance of the sexes was more nearly equal. The first settlers in New England had immigrated primarily for religious reasons: to raise their children and worship in the way that they believed was right. Called Puritans, Separatists, or Dissenters, they did not have such religious freedom in England. Some families had moved first to the Netherlands, which had a greater degree of religious freedom than the British Isles. Within a few years, though, these families grew concerned that their children were becoming Dutch rather than English; New England represented a place where they could maintain their faith, their nationality, their culture, and their customs.

Settlements in New Netherland (now New York and New Jersey) and New Sweden (Delaware and Pennsylvania) began, as in Virginia, as military outposts with nearly all-male populations. In 1624 the first women arrived in the mid-Atlantic region (now New York, New Jersey, Delaware, and Pennsylvania) when 30 families of Walloons, French-speaking refugees from present-day Belgium, came to New Netherland. Within 20 years, the Dutch colony had a truly international population of Dutch, Swedes, Finns, Germans, English, and women and men from other countries of Europe, as well as enslaved Africans and Native American trading partners.

The much smaller colony of New Sweden fell to the Dutch in 1655; nine years later, the Dutch themselves surrendered to the English, and New Netherland became New York. By that time, the colony had between 9,000 and 10,000 European inhabitants, with roughly equal numbers of women and men. New colonies formed in the region: in the 1670s, East and West New Jersey (which merged in 1702), and the 1680s,

Pennsylvania and Delaware. The official history of these colonies is entirely male: the proprietors, or owners, were all men who received their charters from the English king. But settlement was primarily by families, and so European women were part of the region's history from the beginning. The problem for historians is that the sources are all too often silent about women's activities and even their presence.

THE HISTORICAL RECORD

The written records of all the colonies largely ignored women. A woman's name might appear in public records at her birth, her marriage, her children's births, and her death. From these scanty records, demographers and family historians have constructed histories of women in the aggregate, determining age at marriage, number of children, and age at death. They have done family reconstitutions by tracing families over time to ascertain changing patterns of behavior. Earlier historians often relied on prescriptive sources—documents telling women how to behave—written almost exclusively by men. But these sources—sermons, legal codes, pamphlets, and books of advice for girls or mothers—only described how elite, literate men thought women should act; they did not tell how women actually behaved.

In the last quarter of the 20th century, historians turned to new kinds of sources to uncover the voices of early American women. They used legal records, which not only showed how the laws were applied but also, in women's written petitions and depositions, illuminated areas of everyday life that otherwise would have remained obscure. Divorce records, especially rich for Connecticut, show the actions women took against abusive husbands; they also help answer mundane questions, for example: Who did the housework? Where did people sleep? How did unmarried men and women meet and court? Material culture studies—the use of probate records, estate inventories, and archaeological remains—have allowed historians to explore changes in consumption, production, and technology that affected women's lives. The appearance of multiple spinning wheels in Maryland inventories, for example, is evidence of home production of surplus cloth for sale. Butter churns and other equipment in Pennsylvania show women's work producing butter and other dairy products for market. Urban archaeology has produced evidence of abortion and infanticide, including the skeletons of two infants found in the excavation of a colonial Philadelphia well. This varied evidence has led to much greater knowledge of colonial women's actual experiences, rather than simply their ideal, prescribed behavior.

COLONIAL WOMEN'S EXPERIENCES

Although their sex and gender were strong determinants of women's experience, so were factors like class, race, ethnicity, religion, and geography. A black woman working in slavery in Maryland clearly had a very different life than did a wealthy white woman in New Jersey. Life experience varied for women living in different parts of colonial America. Among white women, life as an indentured servant working on a large dairy farm was quite different from that of a merchant's wife in Philadelphia. Enslaved black women on Jamaica sugar plantations had much shorter lives and fewer surviving children than female slaves on Virginia tobacco plantations. Despite these great variations, women did share some common experiences.

Marriage and childbirth were the defining experiences of most women's lives, and those experiences were, in turn, defined not only by the biological fact of sex, but also by gender, that is, social and cultural ideas about men and women. Biology was destiny for colonial American women. Most women bore five to ten children at two-year intervals, following the predominant pattern of all societies where large families are the ideal, where birth control is virtually nonexistent, and where children are breast-fed on demand.

Modern birth control methods did not exist, but methods of birth control were certainly not unknown. This aspect of women's lives is one of the most difficult to uncover because such information was shared orally among women. From the scanty written evidence that does exist, we know that some women consciously prolonged breast-feeding to lengthen intervals between births. Women used various methods of birth control, some of which they could control themselves, such as herbal abortifacients; others relied on abstinence or withdrawal, which required their husbands' participation. Barrier methods like condoms or pessaries (suppositories) were known, but their main users were probably prostitutes. Abortion was considered a sin and a crime, but only after quickening, the perceptible movement of the fetus in about the fourth month of pregnancy. Given these available means, women could have limited the number of children they had, but usually they did not. Greater use of the available birth control practices and devices only began in the late 18th or early 19th century.

Until about 1800 women did not feel that they had a choice in the matter: pregnancy and childbirth were inevitable. About that time, however, some women began to advocate limiting family size. In 1808 Abigail Adams, wife of one president (John Adams) and mother of another (John Quincy Adams), wrote disparagingly about the older view that women had no control over pregnancy: "I have heard some good women say with respect to children that they must have their Number. This doctrine takes away the free agency of Man, but I believe serves as a consolation to those who can fully assent to it." When Adams heard of a younger woman's miscarriage, she was glad, for, she said, "it is sad slavery to have children as fast as she has." (Norton 1980, 73, 75) Women, and their husbands as well, recognized the potential harm to women from great numbers of pregnancies and childbirths, and began to limit their families. There was also a growing sentiment—called domestic feminism by some historians—that children would benefit from the increased attention possible in a smaller family. Ideology as well as biology determined women's fate.

BIRTH

Children were born at home, usually in the presence of women only, usually the midwife and her assistants, who might be the mother's neighbors or relatives. Childbirth was dangerous for both mother and child—infant and maternal mortality rates were high. Part of the responsibility of midwives was to pray for the life and health of mother and child, and good midwives were often highly successful. Martha Ballard of Hallowell, Maine, and Susanna Mueller, a German Lutheran midwife in rural Lancaster County, Pennsylvania, each delivered more than 1,000 infants, with few deaths.

For Roman Catholics and most Protestants, infant baptism marked a child's formal initiation into the church. When frontier conditions or war prevented ministers from coming to perform baptisms, mothers brought their infants long distances to receive the rite. A Dutch minister reported in 1664 that black parents occasionally requested baptism for their children, but he refused because he thought they were only trying to gain freedom for their children, since by custom of the time Christians could not be enslaved. Isabelle Montour, the daughter of an Algonquin woman and her French husband, lived in the Great Lakes region, where Jesuit priests willingly baptized children in Native American villages. She later married an Iroquois and moved first to New York and then to Pennsylvania, where she interpreted between colonial governors and Iroquois delegations. When the Moravian leader Count Zinzendorf visited, she sought baptism for her grandchildren,

but he said that was impossible until a Moravian church was built in the area.

EDUCATION

Underlying the different life experiences of early American men and women was the belief, nearly universally held, that men and women were fundamentally different by nature. They were suited to different roles and different occupations, and therefore needed different kinds of education and socialization. In colonial America, most boys and girls received their early education from their parents or at dame schools (schools for young children taught by women). Widely used primers inculcated gender roles at the same time that they taught reading.

In their early teens young people might have received vocational training as apprentices. Boys apprenticed more often than girls, who usually learned from their own mothers or other female relatives. Boys were to learn the "art, trade, and mystery" of a carpenter, a shipbuilder, a merchant, or a blacksmith. Although some boys might have been forced into specific trades by their fathers, young men usually had at least a small measure of choice—they could veto specific trades and perhaps even follow a trade of their own choosing. For girls, little choice was possible: apprenticeship records note that they were to be "taught housewifery, sew, knit, and spin, read in Bible, write a legible hand." (Woloch 1992, 79) Occasionally, girls were apprenticed to learn a specific trade, always connected to housewifely skills. Most common were apprenticeships to learn the trade of dressmaking or mantua (cloak) making.

Girls sometimes learned skills by working in a family business. For example, daughters and wives of printers often worked in the print shop; this fit well with the skills girls were taught, since bookbinding involved sewing the pages of a book together. Shoemaking, too, involved women in the work of sewing the soft tops of shoes to their soles.

Although women's work was encompassed in the single word *housewifery*, the work varied widely.

MARRIAGE

A properly ordered society, according to colonial authorities, consisted of a series of hierarchies, based on "the superiority of husband over wife, parents over children, and master over servants in the family, ministers and elders over congregation in the church, rulers over subjects in the state." The most damning accusation Massachusetts civil and religious leaders made against female preacher Anne Hutchinson was that she had acted rather as "a Husband than a Wife, and a preacher than a Hearer; and a Magistrate than a Subject." But the submission expected of wives to their husbands was a different sort than that expected of children or servants. A good husband, according to Puritan ministers, would "make his government of her, as easie and gentle as possible; and strive more to be lov'd than fear'd; though neither is to be excluded." Wives were to "take delight in [their husbands' rule], and not account it a Slavery, but a Liberty and Priviledge." But women were not subservient only; they also shared authority with their husbands over children and servants, "for tho' the Husband be the Head of the Wife, yet she is an Head of the Family." (Morgan 1966, 19, 45–46)

Married women suffered from many legal handicaps. They could not testify in court, serve on juries, transfer land, or sign legal documents on their own. Marriage, in effect, made women invisible or nonexistent, subsumed by law within their husband's identity. Women had so little control over property that they rarely left wills, unless their husbands predeceased them. Their dying wishes usually were conveyed orally and concerned the care of minor children and their own funerals and burial sites.

REVOLUTIONARY WOMEN

In the mid-18th century, religious revivals, known collectively as the Great Awakening, created schisms in many colonial churches and created tensions between daughters and parents, and wives and husbands. Women were on both sides of the disputes over theology and style of worship. While ministers engaged in abstruse theological disputes, women voted with their feet, often choosing more enthusiastic, evangelical preachers such as Methodists, over traditionalists. Barbara Heck, the traditional "Mother of American Methodism," led the campaign to build the first Wesley Chapel on John Street in Manhattan. Women's roles in these religious revolutions prefigured their roles in the political revolution that soon followed.

In the traditional narrative of the American Revolution, men did all the fighting, occasionally joined by heroines like Deborah Sampson of Massachusetts, who dressed as a soldier, and Mollie Pitcher, the legendary figure probably based on a Pennsylvania woman (either Margaret Corbin or Mary Hays) who took her husband's place when he fell in battle. When the war was won, according to traditional history, the Founding Fathers established a new nation. Just one woman played a significant role: Betsy Ross, who sewed (and may have designed) the first flag of the new nation. But these women—whose names became part of the Revolution's history—were highly unusual; most women played less prominent roles.

Some women accompanied the Continental army—as laundresses, as prostitutes, or simply as relatives of the soldiers. Others, the majority, fought the war at home in less visible ways. For example, although men were the primary actors in the Boston Tea Party, women played a vital role in boycotting tea and other newly taxed goods. Women were the principal consumers who bought, prepared, and served tea and other products, and they rebelled by using homemade herb teas or coffee and homespun cloth. Without women's active cooperation in the boycott, the Boston Tea Party would have been a hollow protest.

While most women silently supported the Revolution with their everyday behavior, a few spoke out on the role women should play in the war and in the new nation. In 1776 Abigail Adams asked her husband, John, then a delegate to the Second Continental Congress to "Remember the Laidies" when the Congress met to consider "the new Code of Laws." She was not asking for women's suffrage but for protection for married women. Her letter continues: "Do not put such unlimited power into the hands of the Husbands. Remember all Men would be tyrants if they could." Playfully she warned her husband that "If perticuliar care and attention is not paid to the Laidies we are determined to foment a Rebellion, and will not hold ourselves bound by any Laws in which we have no voice, or Representation." (Cott 1996, 72) Although she was half joking, Abigail Adams had serious concerns about women's legal disabilities.

Mercy Otis Warren, the first historian of the Revolution, admitted that politics was "a subject . . . much out of the way of female attention," but she argued that extremes of war required women's attention: "As every domestic enjoyment depends on the decision of the mighty contest, who can be an unconcerned and silent spectator? Not surely the fond mother, or the affectionate wife who trembles lest her dearest connections should fall victims of lawless power, or at least pour out the warm blood as a libation at the shrine of liberty." (Kerber 1980, 84)

Mercy Warren and Abigail Adams reasoned that women had a right and a duty to political action because republican wives and mothers must necessarily be involved in the public life of the nation. This was the beginning of the foundation for women's participation in reform movements in the 19th century and the rationale underlying the winning of the vote for women in 1920.

—Alison Duncan Hirsch

FURTHER READING

Berkin, Carol. *First Generations: Women in Colonial America*. New York: Hill and Wang, 1996.

Berkin, Carol, and Leslie Horowitz. *Women's Voices, Women's Lives: Documents in Early American History*. Boston: Northeastern University Press, 1998.

Cott, Nancy F., ed. *Root of Bitterness: Documents of the Social History of American Women*. 2nd ed. Boston: Northeastern University Press, 1996.

Kerber, Linda K. *Intellect and Ideology in Revolutionary America*. Chapel Hill: University of North Carolina Press, 1980.

Morgan, Edmund S. *The Puritan Family: Religion and Domestic Relations in Seventeenth-Century New England*. Rev. ed. New York: Norton, 1966.

Norton, Mary Beth. *Liberty's Daughters: The Revolutionary Experience of American Women, 1750–1800*. Boston: Little, Brown, 1980.

Ulrich, Laurel Thatcher. *A Midwife's Tale: The Life of Martha Ballard, Based on Her Diary, 1785–1812*. New York: Knopf, 1990.

Ulrich, Laurel Thatcher. *The Age of Homespun: Objects and Stories in the Creation of an American Myth*. New York: Knopf, 2001.

Woloch, Nancy. *Early American Women: A Documentary History, 1600–1900*. Belmont, Calif.: Wadsworth Publishing, 1992.

WOMEN IN THE ANTEBELLUM, CIVIL WAR, AND RECONSTRUCTION ERAS

Generalizing about women's lives in the antebellum, Civil War, and Reconstruction years is difficult (and even dangerous) since the many differences that separated women—in region, religion, class, race, and age—clearly defined their lives. Yet a young Native American woman on the Great Plains, a French Canadian working girl in Massachusetts, an older slave woman in New Orleans, a middle-aged white Protestant reformer in Illinois, an Irish baby girl carried off a ship in New York City, each experienced significant and specific change because of her sex.

ANTEBELLUM

For most antebellum women—excepting those with significant wealth—daily life was filled with domestic work. Lydia Maria Child, an antislavery activist and writer, outlined her achievements in 1864, which included preparing 360 dinners, 362 breakfasts, dusting her sitting room and kitchen 350 times, filling the lamps with oil 362 times, and dusting the bedroom and stairs another 40 times. What she left out were the clothes she made, washed, and mended; the family and friends she nursed; the buckets of water she carried; the oven fed with wood sometimes chopped by her as well. Daily life was strenuous.

For women who worked on farms, both small and large—and most, during this period, still did—the house opened up into yards and barns. In addition to the tasks mentioned above, women's work often included tending to chickens and hogs, preparing milk and cream, churning butter, and helping with planting and the harvest. With the introduction of the Mason jar in 1858, home-canned fruits and vegetables added flavor, variety, and nutrition to winter diets but caused additional work for already burdened farming women.

Although the work of slave women was not unique to them—field labor was also done by yeoman women of the South, pioneer women in the West, and Native American women—their relationship to that work was definitively shaped by bondage. Even among slave women, however, differences were significant. On large plantations with a relatively stable enslaved population, conditions could be miserable, and yet enough continuity existed to establish networks of support among families. The connections were sustained and solidified by shared African traditions even as slaves adapted traditional American religion, music, and culture for their own use. Women working in white plantation homes and in towns and cities often had greater comfort as well as greater constraints, living and working in the midst of white families.

Yet looming over slave women was the constant fear of family dissolution. The changing economy of slavery meant that throughout the antebellum and Civil War years the slave population was gradually moved south and west, sometimes in family units, but more often as individuals. When one member was sold, it was unlikely that the family would ever be reunited.

During the mid-19th century, industrialization and the many new inventions that resulted from it began improving life for a fortunate minority of women and promised change for most of others.

The factories of New England, which drew young women from surrounding farms, and later, from Canada, Ireland, Germany, and other countries, produced cloth. Women of the North, South, and West made the cloth into clothes for their families and made or had made, in the South, for their slaves. When the production of cloth moved largely outside the home, much changed for women. Although now relieved of this time-consuming task, women became more dependent on the growing capitalist economy both as workers and consumers. In addition new closed stoves cut down on the ever-present soot and gave greater warmth; however, carbon monoxide emissions often made them deadly as well.

Food was still a central occupation and pre-occupation for women. What women cooked and ate differed across regions and within communities. In the Northeast, for example, potatoes were white, meat largely meant pork, and greens were not eaten in great quantities (they spoiled easily). Southern slave women often had very limited diets—corn and pork were staples—and the preparation of that food for themselves and their families generally came after a long day of work.

Children were both a hindrance and help as women went about their domestic lives. Continuing a trend begun at the turn of the 19th century, birth rates gradually fell over the course of the century, owing in part to increased knowledge about contraception. Yet death rates for children, mostly from cholera, typhoid, and flu, remained very high, especially for slave children. Children could and did start working at a very young age, providing another set of hands to care for younger children, tend to farm animals, or toil in fields and in factories.

Immigration patterns changed during the antebellum period, as the pull of opportunity in the United States was augmented by the push of events elsewhere. The Potato Famine in Ireland of 1849–1850 caused a corresponding swell in the population of Irish immigrants, many of whom came in family groups, and most of whom settled in northeastern urban centers. Germans, fleeing the revolution in 1848, came in numbers as well, many moving farther inland and gathering in farm communities. Mostly men but some women arrived on western shores from China and elsewhere in Asia; the men primarily to work in mining camps and on the railroads, the women to run saloons, or to work as laundresses, domestic workers, and increasingly, because of the skewed sex ratio, as prostitutes.

In the far West women's lives were dramatically shaped by the Mexican War, which, by 1848, had added to U.S. territory the areas that would become the states of New Mexico, California, and Arizona. The Mexicans living on this land were now full-fledged citizens, but white Americans swiftly laid claim to much of their land and assets; in California alone the Southern Pacific Railroad appropriated 11 million acres. The Gold Rush of 1849 drew crowds from Europe, South America, Australia, and China, as well as from the eastern United States, with devastating consequences for the Native American communities already in place. The Native American population in these areas fell (from about 150,000 in 1848 to 30,000 in 1860) as the U.S. government moved tribes onto smaller and smaller reservations. For some women the West represented a place free of religious persecution, and thousands of Mormons migrated to what would become the state of Utah in the 1840s and 1850s to escape the intolerance of the Northeast and Midwest.

Working-class women in the antebellum period often took home piecework; women sewed clothes, corsets, and finished shoes while tending small children and cooking for their families. The maturing industrial revolution, however, drew growing numbers of women into factories in the 1860s and 1870s, limiting women's flexibility even as it ushered in the possibility of new forms of solidarity among female workers. These years saw some of the earliest organized protests by women on their own behalf, sometimes alongside their husbands, fathers, and brothers. For the Great Shoemakers' Strike of 1860, for example, 800 women in Lynn, Massachusetts, gathered for a dramatically successful parade in support of the workers.

Perhaps what most characterized this period for women were the new ways in which they chose to come together and act on behalf of what they saw to be the greater good of society. The Second Great Awakening, a movement of religious revivals in the first half of the 19th century that originated on the then southwest frontier and moved north and east, helped inspire a new sensibility in women (and men), encouraging unprecedented activism and outreach. With both positive and negative effects, the Second Great Awakening brought efforts to control poor women's lives and efforts to end slavery. Free black women in the North worked together with men to strengthen their communities and to aid fugitives from the South. Schools, for example Catharine Beecher's Western Female Institute in Cincinnati, Ohio, were established to train women as teachers to help civilize the western frontier.

Women's work also fueled the reform movements of this era, largely, but not exclusively located in the Northeast. Moral reform organizations reached out to prostitutes; temperance reformers worked to control men's drinking, given its costs to women and children; idealistic women sustained utopian communities. Women also were the foot soldiers of the antislavery movement, which gathered strength beginning in the early 1830s: from Nat Turner's rebellion; to the advent of William Lloyd Garrison's radical newspaper, *The Liberator*; to the passionate speeches of the southern-born Grimké sisters; to

the 1852 publication of Harriet Beecher Stowe's best-selling novel, *Uncle Tom's Cabin*. Emerging from this reform work was the women's rights movement, to some extent inspired by the limits and indignities women experienced while working in temperance and antislavery organizations. In 1848, at Seneca Falls, New York, women and men gathered to decry the limits placed on women by law and convention and to begin a movement designed to win suffrage for women—a goal accomplished 72 years later.

CIVIL WAR

The Civil War drew on talents of women across the country, even as it significantly and sometimes permanently disrupted their lives. In the South, most white men between the ages of 18 and 40 went into the Confederate army, leaving virtually no family untouched. Although the percentage of families affected was smaller in the North and West, the war's effects still were felt at home as well as in factories and workplaces. Mary Livermore, an organizer for the northwest branch of the U.S. Sanitary Commission in Chicago, recalled seeing women tending to the fields in Wisconsin and eastern Iowa: plowing, driving the reapers, and loading grain. If the sight at first startled and dismayed her, she soon began to feel pride in women's skills and adaptability.

From the first, women were a major resource for the Union and the Confederacy. Two weeks after the firing on Fort Sumter, 20,000 aid societies, North and South, had been formed to supply their armies with clothing, food, bandages, and reading materials. These societies coalesced into the U.S. Sanitary Commission in the Union, remaining largely local in the Confederacy.

Many women also worked for the war effort more directly. An estimated 300 to 400 women on each side were said to have cross-dressed and fought as soldiers, although the numbers will never be certain. Harriet Tubman, who also nursed and worked for the freedpeople (recently liberated slaves) was a scout and spy for the Union army in South Carolina. A number of Confederate women, among them Rose Greenhow and Belle Boyd, were spies.

Working women were hit hard by the war. Some 300,000 women entered the workforce during the Civil War in the North; however, they found little work that paid a living wage. Seamstresses were both hurt and helped by the invention of the sewing machine (the first U.S. patent for which was granted in 1846). The sewing machine speeded production (previously all clothes, bed linens, and so on were hand sewn); however, workers were forced to buy both machines and thread despite skyrocketing prices.

Some doors did open. U.S. treasurer Francis Spinner began hiring women as "government girls" in the North, and the Confederacy also hired women in small numbers. Those numbers grew throughout the war; by 1875, when Spinner retired, women's access to jobs as clerks in federal offices had been secured. During the war years the numbers of women working as teachers grew as young men enlisted; by the end of the century women would be the majority in the teaching profession, holding positions across the country, especially in the earlier grades.

When the war began, nursing was not deemed a respectable career for women, despite Florence Nightingale's example during the Crimean War (1853–1856). Many Union women struggled against this view from the beginning of the war. Prison reformer Dorothea Dix offered her services to the Union and was named superintendent of U.S. Army nurses on June 10, 1861. By 1865 she had officially appointed 3,200 women as nurses. Another 3,600 women nurses worked independently. Nurses came from various backgrounds; some who volunteered were recruited by doctors; some were relatives of the wounded; others were former slaves who had fled to

military camps. Some working-class women were paid by the government, others were volunteers, few were specifically trained for the work.

Slave women were deeply affected by the war and its outcome. During the war many female slaves were moved by their owners in an attempt to evade occupying armies and the chaos they created. Enslaved women helped to undermine slavery even in areas away from the fighting by staging work slowdowns, talking back to owners (often mistresses, whose husbands and sons were at war), and simply leaving for the front. African American women in the North worked for the freedpeople in a number of capacities; some moved south to Washington, D.C., and the Sea Islands (off the coast of South Carolina) to help them directly, to nurse African American soldiers, or to raise money to help the many refugees swelling the camps around Washington.

RECONSTRUCTION

Historian Eric Foner has dubbed this era the "Unfinished Revolution," and this description was as true for women as well as for the nation at large. A number of the tentative gains of the war years—increased work opportunities for women, along with respect for the skill with which they performed the tasks they took on—were erased by the needs or desires of returning soldiers. However, many soldiers did not return, leaving mothers, wives, and daughters bereft both emotionally and financially.

The hopes of the women's suffrage activists were dashed by 1870, as the states ratified the 15th Amendment, granting the vote to African American men only, despite the patriotic war work of women. Longtime women's rights supporter Frederick Douglass, aware of the political wind and the violence in the South, deemed it the "Negro's Hour," and many activists agreed. Elizabeth Cady Stanton and Susan B. Anthony angrily rejected his position and worked against the amendment. This struggle, and the fault lines it revealed within the antislavery movement, caused a split among the women's rights activists, a split overcome only in 1890 with an almost entirely new generation of activists.

Reconstruction devastated southern women, white and black. White slave-owning women had to adjust to a new economic and social order, which called for domestic skills that many women had not been taught, and the performance of domestic tasks that many women found demeaning. Because the economy was suffering, yeoman women, whose situation was precarious to begin with, were often threatened by the prospect of losing their farms and homes.

For African American women, newly freed from slavery, this period was bittersweet. The time just after the war was characterized by movement. Blacks traveled to reunite their families—often looking for years—and to establish themselves in new environments, sometimes just a plantation or two away. Even such small changes had tremendous significance. African American women often chose, in those first years, to stay home from the fields and tend to their families, a decision that angered former masters. The sharecropping system that emerged in this period had benefits and drawbacks for freedpeople: they were able to better shape their days independently; however, the plantation owner still controlled the resources and often cheated them out of their proper earnings.

These years were marked by white efforts to continue to control former slaves, both physically and economically, with new Black Codes (laws limiting the mobility, political agency, and social customs of former slaves); the rise of the Ku Klux Klan; and the threat to black women of harassment or rape. Despite the early intervention by the federal government to curb overt abuses, the North retreated from this position by the 1870s, sparking some westward migration by a number of African American communities.

During Reconstruction the West changed immensely. Native Americans were more strictly confined to reservations, with corresponding loss of life, both from the disruption of their communities and from their resistance to government force. The 1875 Page Law almost entirely blocked the emigration of women from China, largely in response to fears about prostitution. White women from the East were arriving in the region in greater numbers during this period, bringing with them ideas about respectability and gender conventions, ideas that often constricted and devalued the lives of nonwhite and poorer women.

By the end of the 1870s, women worked in factories in greater numbers, and were more often nurses, teachers, clerks, and lecturers. They had participated in activist organizations that helped to end slavery, even if the social and economic situation that followed was still grim. They had fought in wars, both directly and indirectly, from the Mexican War of 1846 to the Indian wars against government troops to the War between the States. And they had, like Lydia Maria Child, prepared many dinners, mended many shirts, carried buckets of water, and tended the home-fires, both literally and figuratively.

—Lyde Cullen Sizer

FURTHER READING

Boydston, Jeanne. *Home and Work: Housework, Wages and the Ideology of Labor in the Early Republic.* New York: Oxford University Press, 1994.

Chitty, A. B., Priscilla Murolo, and Joe Sacco. *From the Folks Who Brought You the Weekend: A Short, Illustrated History of Labor in the United States.* New York: New Press, 2003.

Clinton, Catherine, and Nina Silber, eds. *Divided Houses: Gender and the Civil War.* New York: Oxford University Press, 1992.

Edwards, Laura. *Gendered Strife and Confusion: The Political Culture of Reconstruction.* Champaign: University of Illinois Press, 1997.

Evans, Sara. *Born For Liberty.* New York: Touchstone Books, 1997.

Faust, Drew Gilpin. *Mothers of Invention: Women of the Slaveholding South in the American Civil War.* Chapel Hill: University of North Carolina Press, 1996.

Fox-Genovese, Elizabeth. *Within the Plantation Household: Black and White Women of the Old South.* Chapel Hill: University of North Carolina Press, 1998.

Ginsberg, Lori. *Women and the Work of Benevolence: Morality, Politics, and Class in the Nineteenth-Century United States.* New Haven, Conn.: Yale University Press, 1992.

Jones, Jacqueline. *Labor of Love, Labor of Sorrow: Black Women, Work and the Family from Slavery to the Present.* New York: Knopf, 1986.

Sizer, Lyde Cullen. *The Political Work of Northern Women Writers and the Civil War, 1850–1872.* Chapel Hill: University of North Carolina Press, 2000.

WOMEN AND THE SETTLEMENT OF THE WEST

"The West" has had different meanings to different women. For women indigenous to the region, the West meant "home." For Spanish American women with roots in New Spain, the West was *El Norte* (the North). For Americans from the eastern United States, the West has been different places at different times. In the 18th century the "Great West" referred to areas like Kentucky and Ohio, what historians now call the trans-Appalachian West. By the 1840s, when waves of migrants began heading west by foot or in wagons, and after 1869 by transcontinental railroad, the frontier had moved to west of the Mississippi River (the trans-Mississippi West). This 19th-century West—from the Great Plains to the American Southwest to the Pacific Coast—has remained the region most strongly associated with the real and mythic American West.

By the middle of the 19th century, people converging from across the globe made the West the most culturally and ethnically diverse region in the United States, ultimately making its history an object study in the racial, class, and gender dynamics of women's encounters across cultural divides. Most scholars agree that these encounters invested white women with significant power as agents of white privilege and cultural conquest. Women's newfound freedoms in the American West—more job opportunity, ability to own land, women's suffrage—often came at the expense of other women and men. At the same time, however, western women of all racial and class backgrounds adapted and persevered—and have continued to shape the land and world they inhabit.

INDIGENOUS WOMEN

Even before European contact, the people in what became the American West were remarkably diverse. Thousands of distinct indigenous cultures organized gender relations in widely different ways: some had strict divisions of gender roles and sexuality, while others had more fluid ideas of acceptable behavior for both sexes. Some cultures offered formal roles for women in community governance; others did not. The origin stories of Ácoma Pueblo in present-day New Mexico, for example, show women's religious significance by balancing the masculine sky with the feminine earth. In everyday life, Ácoma people were matrilineal—tracing their roots through maternal descent—and Ácoma women built, maintained, and headed family households in huge, apartmentlike buildings.

Many indigenous societies cast gender in more complex terms than a simple male–female dichotomy. Plains societies, including the Blackfoot, often characterized brave or assertive female elders as "manly hearted women"—a much-respected status. Among the Navajo of the American Southwest, individuals of both biological sexes could adopt a cross-gender role. Scholars have found at least 113 Native American societies that had such a dual role for biological men, while at least 44 groups, most of them west of the Mississippi, had a roughly equivalent role for those born biologically female. Some cross-gender roles were temporary—adopted for warfare, for example—while others were permanent. As this diversity suggests, the cultural groups of pre-European-contact America did not share a common conception of gender.

The varied colonization strategies of the Spanish, French, and English deepened the differences among western indigenous women. In 17th-century colonial New Mexico, Spanish religious authority and civil authority competed with each other, but both tried to stamp out indigenous cultures. Franciscan friars tried to end Pueblo marriage and sexual practices, and ordered Native American women to cover their bodies from head to foot. Yet the Pueblo people managed to blend their own traditions with those of Spanish Roman Catholicism. Even slave women captured by Spanish soldiers for domestic and sexual labor managed to extract some rights and privileges from their masters and many ran away.

Indigenous women in French America fared better. French colonists and the mostly Algonquian peoples of the Upper Midwest and Quebec created a unique, metis (mixed) society in which indigenous women were of vital importance. In this shared world, which one historian has labeled "the middle ground," 17th-century French traders and local peoples developed a lucrative economy based on hunting and trapping beaver and selling their pelts to the European market. Native American women were vital to the success of French colonization, because trappers and traders relied on their highly specialized skills in preparing beaver skins for market and for translation and other intermediary services. Marriage between fur traders and indigenous women became a central component of many Native American cultures. For many French men, these alliances were literally marriages of convenience. But many other marriages appear to have been loving and lasting partnerships that created strong family bonds. One European man recalled his deceased Native American wife as "a good and faithful partner to me for twenty years" and "a most kind mother to her children." (Van Kirk 1980, 33)

Indigenous women had their own reasons for these marriages. Some were attracted to European men because the women had converted to Christianity. Others valued access to European goods, for example, kettles and woven cloth. Still others no doubt wanted to assume the role of cultural intermediary in the trading economy. Over time, however, both French men and Native American women grew disillusioned with these marriages. Many traders abandoned their "country wives," as these women were known, to marry European women.

Across the West the violence and illness resulting from European colonization ravaged indigenous communities. Many European men used rape and other forms of sexual violence as tools of conquest. In New Mexico the rape of local women became so widespread that, in 1609, concerned Spanish colonial officials relocated their new capital, Santa Fe, farther from Pueblo villages. War between indigenous peoples and Europeans also affected men, women, and children. Hundreds of thousands of Native Americans, who lacked immunities to European infectious diseases, died. Smallpox was the deadliest: an outbreak in 1739 killed nearly half the Cherokee people, while another from 1801 to 1802 killed two-thirds of the Omaha. Infants and young children were the most vulnerable. Their deaths, coupled with a decline in women's fertility, decimated populations. From 1769 to 1848, for example, California's indigenous population fell 50%, from about 300,000 to 150,000.

Population decline accelerated in the 19th century, when gold- and land-seekers poured into the West from around the world. In the peak years, between 1841 and 1866, perhaps 350,000 newcomers arrived, stirring up renewed conflict with indigenous peoples. In the 1850s, at the height of the gold rushes, violence and disease reduced California's remaining indigenous population fivefold, from 150,000 to 30,000. The destruction of Native American communities in California was only the most extreme example of a phenomenon that shaped the American West.

WESTERING WOMEN

In contrast the number of white women in the West began to grow. Many migrants came by way of overland wagon routes like the Oregon Trail, and as the number of trail riders rose, so did the percentage of women among them. The first overland travelers crossed in 1841, followed by increasing numbers until the 1870s, when transcontinental railroads captured most of the migrant traffic. Between 1862 and 1866, some 125,000 migrants—more and more of them women—walked or rode the 2,000-mile trail, a journey lasting between four and six months. By 1857 women made up half of some wagon trains. These women soon put their stamp on western society.

Narcissa Whitman, the first white woman to travel the Oregon Trail, exemplified the aspirations and effects of these newcomers. In 1835 Narcissa Prentiss married an acquaintance, Marcus Whitman. Prentiss had yearned to be a missionary, but the job was not open to single women. In 1836 the Whitmans joined a group headed west from St. Louis, Missouri. With great optimism, the Whitmans founded a mission to the Cayuse in Walla Walla Valley, in what would become the state of Washington. But the Cayuse resisted the Whitmans' evangelizing. Frustrated, the Whitmans began to spend more time aiding new migrants on the Oregon Trail than attempting to convert the Cayuse. In 1847, when an epidemic of measles killed nearly half the Cayuse population, the survivors blamed the Whitmans. In retaliation several Cayuse burned the mission to the ground, killing 14 whites, including the Whitmans. After white militias killed most of the Cayuse, the few survivors joined the nearby Nez Percé and Yakima tribes. Thus the Whitmans' attempts to change the West ended in their own deaths and the cultural death of the Cayuse people.

In the years that followed, white women made the overland journey in greater numbers and safety, but it was still an immense and exhausting undertaking. A few women headed west eagerly, but most had little say in their husbands' decisions to move. The endless work of collecting prairie grasses and buffalo manure for fuel, preparing hasty meals in the blazing sun or pouring rain, and trying to prevent children from drowning or being trampled by horses and oxen pushed many women to the limits of their endurance. In addition to their domestic chores, most overland women also had to accept traditionally "male" jobs, like driving wagons or hunting for food. Some men occasionally did women's work, but only as a temporary measure, when a wife lay ill or was recovering from childbirth. As many as one in five women on the trail was pregnant, and the journey left little time for childbirth and recuperation.

Many men and women traveling overland were looking for land. The Homestead Act of 1862 offered public land to all male citizens as well as to women who were single, divorced, widowed, or heads of household (because of a husband's disability or illness). To gain ownership of land, the homesteader needed to pay filing fees of around $20 on plots of land of up to 160 acres, improve the land (by planting crops and digging a well), build a home, and live on the plot for the majority of a three- to five-year period. Like trail life, homesteading was difficult and dangerous. Married women, although they could not hold their own claims, participated in all aspects of the family homesteading enterprise—engaging in fieldwork as well as continuing their domestic duties.

Some women saw homesteading as their own path to independence, especially after 1900, but most sought that independence with the help of family and kin. In the 19th century, only about 5% of homesteaders were women, but after 1900, the number grew to around 20%. Most were part of families. In 1909 Elinore Pruitt Stewart, a Denver laundress turned Wyoming homesteader, began publishing magazine articles and a book that helped make the single woman homesteader a national icon of female independence. One study of North Dakota, where a high percentage of homesteaders were women, found that only 7% matched the stereotype of the single, unattached homesteader. In her writings Stewart concealed her own marriage to a neighboring landowner. Both male and female homesteaders relied on relatives as they sought western independence. Mormons embraced the merits of cooperation in their new western communities in what would become the state of Utah. The Church of Jesus Christ of Latter-day Saints, as the Mormons are officially known, had been dogged by violent opposition since its founding in upstate New York in 1830. By 1847, three years after an Illinois mob murdered founder Joseph Smith, the Mormon faithful followed new leader Brigham Young to Utah, which they named Deseret. Mormons quickly established successful farming communities that were organized collectively. By 1852, 20,000 Mormons lived in Salt Lake City, and Mormon delegations began creating new agricultural settlements elsewhere in Utah and in the areas that would become the states of Idaho, Arizona, and Nevada.

The Mormon practice of polygamy (men having multiple wives) made them pariahs in the eyes of most Americans. Protestant women reformers and national politicians cast polygamous families as little more than sexual harems for Mormon men. Yet many Mormon women defended polygamy, arguing that their "sister wives" provided companionship and offered cooperative housekeeping and child rearing. Mormon women lived in a patriarchal culture, to be sure, but they could and did see advantages to their own way of life. As the Mormons demonstrated, the reality of women's experience in the 19th- and early-20th-century West was considerably more complex than the mythic images suggested by Elinore Pruitt Stewart's articles or Narcissa Whitman's tragic death.

DIVERSITY OF WESTERN WOMEN

Women from around the world began to settle in the West in sizable numbers. By 1880 some 15,000 African American settlers, known as "Exo-dusters," had moved from the South to Kansas to escape the aftermath of the Civil War. Many other homesteaders were immigrants or first-generation Americans (homestead laws required citizenship but not U.S. birth). In Utah's Salt Lake Valley immigrants who converted to Mormonism made up 70% of the Mormon settlers; in 1890, only one in five North Dakotans was a white native-born child of native-born parents. In the Southwest many Hispano families, guaranteed American citizenship by the Treaty of Guadalupe Hidalgo (1848), which ended the Mexican War, filed homestead claims to supplement old family landholdings. Many were women; unlike the Anglo-American legal tradition known as common law, which did not recognize married women's property rights, Mexican civil law created a Hispano tradition of married women's separate ownership of land and property. Many Hispano women owned and ran their own ranches.

In urban areas of the West, too, a range of women were moving in. African Americans created small communities across the West, most notably in San Francisco. During this period the West was the only part of the United States where a majority of African American teenage girls attended high school. Jewish women also populated western cities and towns, especially mining camps, where anti-Semitism was rare. Jewish American Josephine Marcus grew up in San Francisco and moved to Tombstone, Arizona, where she met and married infamous gunman (and Christian) Wyatt Earp.

For many women, however, the West was not the land of opportunity. Some new westerners came involuntarily. In the winter of 1838–1839, the Cherokee people began to travel on what became known as the Trail of Tears, a forced march from their Georgia homeland to Indian Territory (present-day Oklahoma). Around one in four tribal members, largely women and children, died on the trail. In the Southwest many Hispano women, like their menfolk, could not prove their citizenship or property ownership and lost their land to Anglos. Some immigrant women, especially the Chinese, came to the West as virtual sex slaves. In 1860 two-thirds of Chinese women living in San Francisco were prostitutes. Confined to cell-like rooms and exposed to deadly venereal diseases, these women were objects of sexual violence as well as moral scorn. By 1880 stricter immigration policies—many of them openly discriminatory against Asian peoples—had reduced the proportion of prostitutes among Chinese women to about one in five.

WOMEN REFORMERS

In response to such conditions, many 19th-century white women, like the trailblazing Narcissa Whitman, felt a moral imperative to cleanse the West of its sinful ways and establish or restore its reputation. Some white women reformers on the Pacific Coast created missionary homes to Christianize and "save" Chinese prostitutes. Like their counterparts in the East, confident, reform-minded women lobbied for temperance, Sunday closure of businesses and saloons, improving public education, the creation of welfare systems, and the building of sanitation systems for the hastily constructed western boomtowns.

White women reformers' unshakable sense of superiority was deleterious to their efforts. As symbols of moral betterment, white women—even those who were not actively trying to remake other women into their own image—became the standard against which all western women were judged. As a result many white women's gains came at the expense of men and women of other class and racial backgrounds. In many places, for example, white schoolteachers began replacing African American and Mexican American women. Some white women's successes were nothing short of ironic: while white women reformers lobbied for married women's property rights, the U.S. government was taking away these very same rights from Native American and Hispano women, whose cultural and legal traditions embraced women's control and ownership of property. The first married women's property rights law passed in New York in 1848, the same year that the U.S. takeover of New Mexico ended married women's rights to own property in that region.

CONCLUSION

Women as well as men sought both adventure and opportunity in the American West, but some women—middle-class white women—found these more easily than others. Voting rights offers perhaps the best example: the Wyoming Territory granted women the right to vote in 1869, and by 1912 nine U.S. states—all of them in the West or Midwest—had followed suit, years before the 19th Amendment made women's suffrage a federal law in 1920. Women's suffrage was partly an attempt by male lawmakers to attract white women to sparsely populated western regions, but it was also a product of white women's successful efforts to establish themselves as the moral arbiters of a new western society eager to redeem itself in eastern eyes. In the political arena, especially, the West continued to be amenable to female participation. In 2003 both of California's U.S. senators were women, as were all five of Arizona's statewide elected officials.

However, even as some white women marched triumphantly to western polling booths and statehouses, men and women of different class, religious, and racial backgrounds saw their own rights and sources of authority erode. Mormon women had gained the right to vote in Utah in 1870, but ironically, gentile (non-Mormon) women's rights activists successfully lobbied for the rescinding of this right, arguing that it strengthened support for polygamy. More generally, in the early 20th century, Anglo politicians in the Southwest were creating new barriers like poll taxes and literacy tests to keep black and ethnic Americans from voting. In 1912, for example, Arizona's first state legislature approved both women's suffrage and a bill that required voters to read from the U.S. Constitution in English. Most Native American men and women would not gain U.S. citizenship until the Indian Citizenship Act of 1924. In the decades that followed Chicano (Mexican American), Asian, and Native American women fought—often successfully—for greater say in western politics and society. Whether raising their families, reforming their communities, or fighting for economic equality on the picket line, women have continued to improve their claims in the American West.

—Katherine Benton-Cohen

FURTHER READING

Armitage, Susan, and Elizabeth Jameson, eds. *The Women's West*. Norman: University of Oklahoma Press, 1987.

Faragher, John Mack. *Women and Men on the Overland Trail*. New Haven, Conn.: Yale University Press, 1979.

Jameson, Elizabeth, and Susan Armitage. *Writing the Range: Race, Class, and Culture in the Women's West*. Norman: University of Oklahoma Press, 1997.

Jeffrey, Julie Roy. *Converting the West: A Biography of Narcissa Whitman*. Norman: University of Oklahoma Press, 1991.

Montoya, María E. *Translating Property: The Maxwell Land Grant and the Conflict over Land in the American West, 1840–1900*. Berkeley: University of California Press, 2002.

Perdue, Theda, ed. *Sifters: Native American Women's Lives*. New York: Oxford University Press, 2001.

Ruiz, Vicki. *From Out of the Shadows: Mexican Women in Twentieth-Century America*. New York: Oxford University Press, 1998.

Schlissel, Lillian, and Catherine Lavender, eds. *The Western Women's Reader*. New York: HarperPerennial, 2000.

Schlissel, Lillian, Vicki L. Ruiz, and Janice Monk, eds. *Western Women: Their Land, Their Lives*. Albuquerque: University of New Mexico Press, 1988.

Shoemaker, Nancy, ed. *Negotiators of Change: Historical Perspectives on Native American Women*. New York: Routledge, 1995.

Sigerman, Harriet. *Land of Many Hands: Women in the American West*. New York: Oxford University Press, 1997.

Taylor, Quintard, and Shirley Ann Wilson Moore. *African American Women Confront the West, 1600–2000*. Norman: University of Oklahoma Press, 2003.

Van Kirk, Sylvia. *Many Tender Ties: Women in Fur Trade Society, 1670–1870*. Norman: University of Oklahoma Press, 1980.

WOMEN IN THE REFORM AND PROGRESSIVE ERA

The term *Progressive Era* refers as much to a pervasive national mood as it does to a precisely defined chronological era in U.S. history. Beginning around 1890 and lasting until the early 1920s, a new zeal for reforming the country's social, political, and economic structures emerged on the national scene. Progressivism was a response to the rapid, large-scale, and unregulated growth of industrialization that followed the end of the Civil War in 1865, a period often referred to by historians as the Gilded Age because of the unprecedented wealth and power created by the men who became industrial giants. But only a very few Americans realized immense benefits. For a great many others, the consequences of this unchecked industrial expansion had been unhealthful and dangerous working conditions, overcrowded and unsanitary housing, child labor in factories and coal mines, and brutal economic insecurity. Many of those most severely affected were newly arrived emigrants from the south and east of Europe as well as African Americans migrating from the rural South to work in northern industrial cities. Progressive reformers, the majority of whom were urban, upper middle class, and well educated, sought to ameliorate many of the worst consequences of the Gilded Age industrial boom. They employed the methods of the emerging social sciences, sociology and economics among them, to identify and study social problems, gather abundant evidence, and propose solutions.

The particular causes Progressives championed varied widely, from abolishing child labor, to regulating unhealthful working conditions, to improving health conditions in overcrowded tenement districts, to tackling political corruption. Their strategies differed as well, from exposing political and corporate misdeeds through muckraking journalism, to lobbying elected officials for regulatory statutes, to establishing social welfare programs in urban neighborhoods. What tied these diverse groups of reformers together, however, was their staunch belief that the government—local, state, and federal—was obligated to address and redress the most damaging consequences of industrialization for those who were most vulnerable in American society. The duty of government, Progressives insisted, was to take action on behalf of the public's health, safety, and welfare. But their aim was not purely philanthropic, for Progressives argued that the size and power of government must expand to act as a balance to the control over the nation now enjoyed by those who had achieved extreme wealth. The Gilded Age financier and railroad magnate J. Pierpont Morgan, for example, had amassed a personal fortune that by 1900 actually exceeded the size of the national treasury. Such extreme imbalances between the wealthy and powerful and the poor and powerless threatened the economic competition necessary for capitalism's survival as well as the proper functioning of democratic institutions.

Although many reform activities took place in the private sector, securing reform through laws and government regulation remained a central theme of Progressivism. The movement stretched beyond political party boundaries, involving both Republicans and Democrats; in 1912 the short-lived Progressive party emerged onto the political stage as a third party. Although women could not vote in national elections until the ratification of the 19th Amendment in 1920, they were nevertheless active participants in Progressive Era reforms and in many cases acted as organizers and leaders of reform movements.

WOMEN IN THE PROGRESSIVE MOVEMENT

Like the movement in general, Progressive women activists were more likely to be from the upper middle class and to be well educated. By 1880 the nation had experienced the blossoming of higher education for women as both public and private colleges began to admit them, albeit often in special "women's programs" separate from those programs available to male students. Of equal importance were the elite female-only colleges, such as Mount Holyoke and Radcliffe, which not only provided women with an excellent education but also stressed their duty to make use of their training to improve society. A generation of women, therefore, was very well prepared to engage in useful and productive work for the benefit of American society.

Unfortunately, however, these women found that most professions remained closed to them. Undeterred, they carved a niche for themselves outside of male-dominated occupations. Many reform-minded women, excluded from regular medical practice, helped to develop the emerging field of public health through their work as physicians, nurses, and municipal inspectors. Frances Perkins (1882–1965), for example, began her professional life in New York City as a public health nurse after graduating from Mount Holyoke in 1902. After earning a master's degree at Columbia University, Perkins went on to be appointed by Pres. Franklin D. Roosevelt (1933–1945) as the first female Cabinet member in U.S. history. As secretary of labor, Perkins was instrumental in the creation of the Social Security Act, passed by Congress in 1935. Other women forged career paths by pioneering social welfare work, through activities that included running neighborhood well-baby clinics, distributing pasteurized milk in sterilized bottles to poor families, and teaching English language and Americanization classes in immigrant communities.

Women also were instrumental in pioneering both the theory and practice of the social settlement, a Progressive experiment in addressing urban problems. Located in poor or working-class neighborhoods, settlement houses played multiple roles within the community. Progressive women and men lived and worked in the settlement house, applying the techniques of the social sciences to study problems within the neighborhood and to develop and implement solutions. Settlements acted as social centers, sponsoring classes and speakers, running day nurseries, and providing after-school club activities for neighborhood children. Settlements served the equally important function of gathering places where Progressive thinkers lived and worked together, sharing their analyses of social problems and planning their activities on behalf of reform. In 1889 Jane Addams, a graduate of Rockford Female Seminary in Illinois, along with her partner Ellen Gates Starr, established Hull House on Chicago's Near West Side. Located among Italian, Greek, and Eastern European Jewish immigrant neighborhoods, Hull House was the first American social settlement and became the model for many others in Chicago and in cities throughout the United States. A tireless community activist and social welfare advocate throughout her long public career, Addams made important contributions to the development of social theory as well, publishing numerous works on topics ranging from intergenerational conflict in immigrant communities to the necessity of play for the normal development of all children. Addams took a controversial antiwar stand when the United States entered World War I in April of 1917. She became the first president of the Women's International League for Peace and Freedom, founded in 1919. In recognition of her work on behalf of world peace, Addams received the Nobel Peace Prize in 1931.

Historians have described the contributions made by Progressive women as a kind of "social housekeeping." Although many in this generation of women activists remained unmarried throughout their lives, they took on many of the duties traditionally associated with women's roles in American life, such as looking after the needs of children or taking responsibility for the health and well-being of family members. Progressive activists, however, performed these traditional duties not within the private realm of their own homes and families, but in the public arena on behalf of society as a whole. Through their efforts in both private and public endeavors, Progressive women reformers brought attention to the needs of the underserved in American society and insisted that the problems of the urban poor, working women and children, and immigrant communities were worthy of the nation's attention.

At times relations were strained between reformers and the communities for whom they presumed to speak. Native-born women could be insensitive to cultural and religious distinctions among their immigrant clientele. Public health workers, for example, sometimes condemned immigrant mothers' child care practices (such as displaying a great deal of physical affection) or family food preferences (such as cabbage and coarse breads) as "unhealthy" when they simply differed from their own middle-class preferences. Social welfare activities were sometimes greeted with suspicion among Roman Catholic and Jewish immigrants who confused the secular Progressive reformers with Protestant missionaries or agents of the state. Immigrant women, however, were far from passive observers in Progressive campaigns, for reformers themselves realized that, without their active approval and cooperation, the Progressive vision of an improved society could never be realized. Accordingly, women reformers frequently learned to adapt their strategies to better suit the preferences of the local population.

Over time, Progressive reformers working in local communities established networks that extended throughout entire states and eventually crisscrossed the nation. The story of Florence Kelley provides a good example. Upon completing her studies at Cornell University, the socialist Kelley joined Hull House in 1891, where she worked closely with labor activists and radical reformers to improve conditions for industrial workers. In 1899 Kelley cofounded the National Consumers' League, a powerful organization that used the power of the consumer boycott to pressure businesses into improving working conditions, especially for women and children. The National Consumers' League also successfully lobbied for laws in many states establishing maximum working hours and prohibiting child labor in factories.

Like the National Consumers' League, the Women's Trade Union League (1903–1950) pushed to advance the causes of working women. Founded in Chicago by Hull House–trained William English Walling, working-class activist Mary Kenney O'Sullivan, Jane Addams, and a number of other Chicago Progressives, the Women's Trade Union League consisted primarily of middle-class and upper-class women who provided support for working women's labor union activities at a time when the American Federation of Labor, led by Samuel Gompers, showed very little interest in organizing women and, in fact, was often hostile to their efforts. At times socioeconomic differences impeded the Women's Trade Union League in its endeavors. The league enjoyed its greatest success within the clothing and textile trades, businesses that exploited tens of thousands of women workers through extremely low pay and often dangerous working conditions. During the winter of 1909–1910, the Women's Trade Union League sponsored a major strike of clothing workers in New York City, winning concessions from many clothing factories throughout the city. Tragically the strike failed to improve conditions at the

Triangle Shirtwaist Factory; the following year 143 women and girls and 3 men were killed in a fire that swept through the factory. Triangle's owners had locked the doors on the outside, leaving the workers trapped inside when the fire broke out. The building's rickety fire escape collapsed when the workers attempted to escape the flames, and trapped workers suffocated or were burned to death; several jumped to their deaths on the sidewalk below.

Progressive women continued to make advances. In 1912 Julia Lathrop was appointed by Pres. William Howard Taft (1909–1913) as the first chief of the United States Children's Bureau, a new federal agency within the Department of Labor established specifically to investigate and report on the needs of America's children. Lathrop was another alumna of Rockford Seminary (and of Vassar College as well) and a Hull House resident; her father had been one of the founders of the antislavery Republican party in 1854. Lathrop had been instrumental in the creation of the nation's first juvenile court in Cook County, Illinois, and had also been appointed by that state's governor to the Illinois State Board of Charities. As chief of the Children's Bureau, Lathrop directed many studies of child labor, infant and early childhood mortality, prenatal care, and public education. The Children's Bureau also administered the Sheppard–Towner Act, passed by Congress in 1921 to provide assistance to individual states for establishing maternal and child health education programs.

Not all women who contributed to the Progressive movement did so as paid professionals. Reform efforts depended heavily on the unpaid support of thousands of nonworking women through social and philanthropic organizations. Club women provided financial backing and volunteer services as well as their highly developed interpersonal and networking skills. They labored to establish municipal libraries, playgrounds, and well-baby clinics and lobbied to further Progressive legislation. In 1890 some 200 clubs came together to form the General Federation of Women's Clubs; by 1910 its national membership reached nearly 1 million. The National Congress of Mothers was founded in 1897 as a child welfare advocacy group. (The National Congress of Mothers was the forerunner of the National Parent Teacher Association.) Rural women organized activities to promote measures for the betterment of their lives, including improving roads, bringing maternal and child health care to isolated areas, and establishing school lunch programs. Rural women were also very active in the temperance movement.

By the end of the 19th century, the Women's Christian Temperance Union had evolved into a broad-based women's rights organization. Its dynamic leader, Frances Willard, recognized that alcoholism (usually alcoholic husbands and fathers) and its effects on women would be completely remedied only when women gained legal, political, and economic rights. When the Women's Christian Temperance Union joined forces with the growing movement dedicated to granting women the right to vote, a truly mass movement for female suffrage was born. In cities and rural villages throughout the United States, club women constructed a new place for themselves within the public arena, demonstrating their willingness to shoulder the responsibilities of citizenship at a time when women were still denied the fundamental privilege of voting in national elections. Unsurprisingly the majority of Progressives supported the cause of women's suffrage. In the first decades of the 20th century, a number of states granted women the right to vote. Despite these victories, many women's suffrage activists worked for the passage of a constitutional amendment that would define and protect the vote as a privilege of citizenship for all women.

AFRICAN AMERICAN WOMEN IN THE PROGRESSIVE MOVEMENT

Progressive women's extensive networks for social reform remained largely segregated by race, a reflection of the harsh realities of American life in the Progressive Era. Organizations were segregated not only by custom but also, in many states, by law. African American women established a parallel movement for social reform and, although it shared a number of characteristics in common with white Progressivism, many of the priorities and goals of black Progressives remained distinctly different. Although leaders of black Progressive organizations tended to be middle class and educated, they did not experience the same wide social chasms that separated white Progressives from the poor, working-class, and immigrant communities. Most important, the urgent need to combat white violence against blacks made antilynching crusades the top priority for black Progressives. The incidence of lynching, or executions (hangings) conducted by lawless mobs, had actually increased at the turn of the 20th century. (According to a Tuskegee University study, between 1882 and 1944 reported lynchings of blacks numbered 3,417 in the United States.) This "reign of terror," as it was known among African Americans, reflected whites' hostility to the legal, political, and economic gains blacks had achieved since the abolishment of slavery. White authorities rarely attempted to intervene and, in fact, not uncommonly collaborated with the mobs. An 1892 lynching of three black businessmen in Memphis, Tennessee, spurred the journalist and co-owner of the *Memphis Free Speech* newspaper, Ida B. Wells-Barnett (1862–1931), to launch a fierce campaign to expose the horrors of lynching and put an end to the violence. A graduate of Rust College in Mississippi, Wells-Barnett had taught in black Memphis schools before beginning her career in journalism. Her vigorous efforts against lynching made her the target of white hatred; her Memphis newspaper office was burned and looted, and her life threatened. (Wells was lecturing in Philadelphia on the night of the attack and so escaped harm.)

Like her friend Wells-Barnett, Mary Church Terrell was one of the most prominent national black leaders of the Progressive Era. In 1884 Terrell became one of the first African American women to earn a college degree—from Oberlin College in Ohio. An educator and the wife of a black judge in Washington, D.C., Terrell had experienced the barriers of racism in the nation's capital despite her education and prominent social standing. In 1896 Terrell, along with Wells-Barnett, the underground railroad heroine Harriet Tubman, and a number of Progressive African American women, founded the National Association of Colored Women to crusade for political and educational reform. In 1909 Terrell, along with a group of both black and white Progressives that included Wells-Barnett, William English Walling, and Jane Addams, formed the National Association for the Advancement of Colored People.

PROGRESSIVES AND WORLD WAR I

In 1917 the entry of the United States into World War I posed an acute dilemma for Progressives. Although most eagerly supported the war effort, others opposed the nation's involvement in the carnage overseas. Many Progressives also feared that the new military fervor would divert money and resources from the programs they had worked so hard to establish. Women, however, now possessed the organizational skills, experience, and state and national networks the country needed, and thousands of women applied themselves to numerous home-front activities, including gathering supplies for the Red Cross, launching food conservation drives, and promoting Liberty bonds to finance the war. Under its able leader Carrie Chapman Catt, the nation's largest women's suffrage organization, the National American Woman Suffrage Association (forerunner to the League of Women Voters), put its considerable resources at the disposal of Pres. Woodrow Wilson (1913–1921). In 1918 Wilson reversed his earlier position and publicly supported a constitutional amendment to give women the vote, even taking the unusual step of appearing on the floor of the Senate to make a speech on behalf of the cause. The hard-fought victory was finally won in 1920 when the 19th Amendment to the Constitution was ratified by the states.

CONCLUSION

Progressive women enjoyed other victories as well. The 18th Amendment, which banned the sale and distribution of liquor in interstate commerce, reflected decades of work in the temperance cause. (In 1933 the amendment was repealed.) But perhaps newly enfranchised women reformers' greatest political victory came with the passage of the Sheppard–Towner Act by Congress in 1921. This act provided federal funds on a state-matching basis for the establishment of programs to improve maternal and child health. From 1921 until 1928 the act supported a variety of activities from training African American midwives in the South to taking public health nurses to remote mountain areas in Kentucky under the auspices of the Frontier Nursing Service, founded in 1925 by Mary Breckinridge. A widow who had also lost both her children before they reached the age of five, Breckinridge had gone to France during World War I to care for orphaned children.

Although the distinctive dynamic activity identified with Progressivism had largely receded by the 1920s, many women remained active in social reform, providing an important continuity between the close of the Progressive Era and the beginning of Pres. Franklin Roosevelt's New Deal.

Both inside and outside of formal political arenas, women were in American public life to stay.

—Lynne Curry

FURTHER READING

Addams, Jane. *Twenty Years at Hull House.* 1910. Reprint, New York: Viking Penguin, 1998.

Blair, Karen J. *The Clubwoman as Feminist: True Womanhood Redefined, 1868–1914.* New York: Holmes and Meier, 1980.

Carson, Mina. *Settlement Folk: Social Thought and the American Settlement Movement, 1885–1930.* Chicago: University of Chicago Press, 1990.

Davis, Allen. *Spearheads for Reform: The Social Settlements and the Progressive Movement, 1890–1914.* New York: Oxford University Press, 1967.

Fitzpatrick, Ellen. *Endless Crusade: Women Social Scientists and Progressive Reform.* New York: Oxford University Press, 1990.

Higginbotham, Evelyn Brooks. *Righteous Discontent: The Women's Movement in the Black Baptist Church, 1880–1920.* Cambridge, Mass.: Harvard University Press, 1993.

Ladd-Taylor, Molly. *Mother-Work: Child Welfare and the State, 1890–1930.* Urbana: University of Illinois Press, 1994.

Lasch-Quinn, Elizabeth. *Black Neighbors: Race and the Limits of Reform in the American Settlement House Movement, 1890–1940.* Chapel Hill: University of North Carolina Press, 1993.

Lindenmeyer, Kriste. *"A Right to Childhood:" The U. S. Children's Bureau and Child Welfare, 1912–1946.* Urbana: University of Illinois Press, 1997.

Muncy, Robin. *Creating a Female Dominion in American Reform, 1890–1935.* New York: Oxford University Press, 1991.

Polachek, Hilda Satt. *I Came a Stranger: The Story of a Hull House Girl.* Urbana: University of Illinois Press, 1989.

Terrell, Mary Church. *A Colored Woman in a White World.* Washington, D.C.: Ransdell, 1940.

Wiebe, Robert H. *The Search for Order, 1877–1920.* New York: Hill and Wang, 1967.

WOMEN IN THE WORLD WAR II AND POSTWAR ERAS

When the United States entered World War II on December 7, 1941, the nation was far from ready to fight and win a multifront war. The armed services needed millions of men to engage enemy forces around the globe; to fight successfully, those servicemen would need weapons and ammunition, military vehicles, ships and aircraft, and food and medicine. The United States was also bound by the terms of the Lend Lease Agreement, which promised to supply U.S. allies with military equipment. The nation soon realized that the number of men was insufficient to both serve in the armed forces and to produce all the necessary supplies. Women would be needed too.

Early in the war the federal government asked women to leave their homes and enter the workforce; in mid-1942 the government proposed that young women enlist in the armed forces for home-front duty. On factory floors and military posts and in offices and laboratories, American women proved themselves capable of successfully performing a wide variety of jobs that they would never have had the chance to attempt before the war. They riveted aircraft parts together and welded ships, learned to drive and repair 2.5 ton trucks, and manufactured bullets and bombs. They repaired radios and turret guns, drew maps, and decoded top-secret military messages. They trained as air-traffic controllers and taught soldiers and sailors how to aim at a moving target from a moving aircraft or vessel. Women across the country pitched in and did what was necessary to help win the war. In the process, they proved that women were fully capable of handling industrial jobs that required mechanical aptitude and physical strength as well as professional jobs that required management

skills. But American women held these jobs only temporarily. Once the war was won, women workers were replaced by returning male veterans. Although many Americans expected women to return to the home, a surprising number of women opted to remain in the labor force, albeit at lower-paying and more restricted jobs.

"ROSIE THE RIVETER": WOMEN IN INDUSTRY DURING THE WAR

A woman who stepped into a man's place on the assembly line was called "Rosie the Riveter," a name taken from a popular song. Millions of Rosies worked in factories building aircraft and ships for the military. Because the aircraft industry was relatively new, its managers seemed to have fewer preconceptions of women's abilities and within two years of the Japanese attack on Pearl Harbor, on December 7, 1941, more than 475,000 women worked in aircraft factories, riveting wings onto planes and assembling engines. Shipyards also employed large numbers of women. Shipyard Rosies told newspaper reporters that welding was similar to "sewing a fine seam," and that making sand-core molds for aluminum casings was similar to "mixing up a cake recipe." By the end of the war, more than 225,000 women were employed at shipyards around the country.

Although every industrial job was hazardous, women who worked in munitions plants held the most dangerous jobs of all. Munitions workers loaded cartridge shells with explosive powder, inserted fuses into hand grenades, sticks of dynamite, and bombs, and mixed chemical weapons, including mustard gas, phosgene, and gel-type incendiaries. Although these production line jobs were repetitive and boring, they required exact measurements and the utmost patience. The wrong mixture could lead to an explosion, and the possible harm from potential accidents was addressed by building munitions plants in remote areas. Women workers could not wear jewelry because metals and precious stones could spark an explosion. They were required to wear rubber-soled shoes, flameproof uniforms, and protective hair caps. "Goop," a gel-type incendiary chemical, was more likely to ignite on rainy days; production, however, could not wait out the weather. "Goop" saved lives—marines and soldiers fighting in the South Pacific used these incendiaries against enemy soldiers hiding in caves on the islands of Saipan and Okinawa.

WOMEN GOVERNMENT WORKERS

Although many male government workers went into the armed forces when the war started, the government needed to expand during the war, and women workers filled the personnel shortage. In every federal office where women had formerly worked as secretaries and file clerks, they learned new skills and became budget analysts, archivists, researchers, statisticians, personnel managers, photographers, laboratory technicians, artists, and writers.

The shortage of men impelled some agencies to employ women as security guards. The Tennessee Valley Authority (TVA) recruited and trained women to guard reservoirs, hydroelectric dams, and electric power plants, all of which were used to generate electricity vital to the war effort. The production of aluminum, for example, which was used to make aircraft, demanded a high level of electrical output. Top-secret installations that were involved in the atomic bomb project also needed security. The women guards were trained in self-defense, marksmanship, judo, and riot control. They worked in uniform and patrolled their assigned perimeters day and night, carrying 0.38-caliber pistols and accompanied by guard dogs.

The TVA also hired and trained women as mapmakers. The women worked with old maps and aerial photographs to design maps of the European coastline used in the planning for D-Day (June 6, 1944), the invasion of enemy-controlled northern France. Later, they created maps of Europe to help commanders plan troop movements for the invasion of Germany, which began in October of 1944. Women mapmakers responsible for producing maps of tiny islands in the Southwest Pacific faced particular difficulties because so little information about the geography of these islands was available.

MILITARY WOMEN

One of the most important ways women contributed to the war effort was as army and navy nurses. Military nurses served everywhere U.S. troops were stationed. Almost half of the army's 60,000 nurses served overseas. Although most military nurses worked in hospitals miles away from the front lines, some received assignments that placed them in field and evacuation hospitals close to the action. For example 89 army and navy nurses assigned to military hospitals in Guam and the Philippines when the war started were captured by Japanese troops when those islands fell to the enemy in late 1941. They were held as prisoners of war for almost three years before being freed by American forces in early 1945.

Sixty army nurses were part of the first contingent of troops to invade North Africa in November of 1943. They landed on the beach under fire and established their hospital in a bombed-out shelter with no water or electricity. African American nurses were sent to Burma to nurse black soldiers building the Burma Road, a highway the American military constructed to funnel critical supplies and equipment to China, an ally during the war. When U.S. forces invaded Italy in 1943 and France in 1944, army nurses followed the troops within days of the invasion to set up hospitals and care for the wounded. Sixteen military nurses were killed by enemy fire during the war.

The army established the Women's Army Auxiliary Corps (WAAC) in 1942 because commanders realized that many essential desk jobs needed to be done at home. The army trained WAACs to work as budget and payroll clerks; manage supply requisitions and personnel records; operate telephone switchboards and telegraph transmitters and receivers; repair radios, trucks, tanks, and aircraft; analyze aerial photographs; and perform myriad other necessary jobs. By 1943 the army realized that it could also use women overseas. Because WAACs were auxiliaries rather than official members of the army, however, the army was uncertain whether they would be protected under the Geneva Convention if they were captured by the enemy. So in mid-1943, the army abolished the WAAC and established the Women's Army Corps (WAC), making women official army personnel. The army then sent WACs to Great Britain, North Africa, Italy, the Southwest Pacific, India, and China. As American troops moved into France and Germany in 1944, WACs followed them. One unit of African American WACs was sent to Europe to perform the vital mission of straightening out the army's postal system—prompt receipt of mail from home was critical to the morale of the American troops.

More than 80,000 WAVES (Women Accepted for Volunteer Emergency Service) served in the U.S. Navy during the war. The navy assigned WAVES to top-secret jobs in message code rooms as cryptographers and trained them as air tower control managers, weather forecasters, hospital corpsmen, laboratory technicians, aircraft mechanics, statisticians, file clerks, and parachute packers.

The U.S. Coast Guard created the Coast Guard Women's Reserve in November 1942. Looking for a catchy name for its women to help with recruiting, the coast guard came up with the acronym SPAR, using the initials of the its motto: Semper Paratus—Always Ready! Recruiting brochures advised women: "Don't be a Spare—Be a SPAR!" Coast guard women worked as storekeepers, pharmacist's mates, radar technicians, legal secretaries, file clerks, photographers, radio technicians, weather forecasters, parachute riggers, and in many other assignments.

The U.S. Marine Corps was the last service to accept the idea of women enlisting in its ranks. By early 1943, however, it was apparent that the corps needed women to fill desk jobs so as many marines as possible could be sent into combat. One woman joked "the Marines would have preferred to enlist dogs, ducks or monkeys, but women are smarter!" The Marine Corps Women's Reserve was established in February of 1943. Women marines never received a catchy nickname or acronym like the women of other services (WACs, WAVES, and SPARs) because the corps wanted its women to understand that they were marines so that they would live up to corps traditions of honor and service. This decision disappointed the American public, which bombarded the corps with suggestions like Marinettes, Femarines, Glamarines, and Dainty Devil Dogs. The proud traditions of the corps appealed to many women volunteers, and the marines never had a problem recruiting.

Women recruits trained at Camp Lejeune, North Carolina, and learned marine corps ways. After boot camp, women marines received assignments as clerk typists, file clerks, telephone operators, IBM tabulating machine operators, payroll clerks, draftsmen, motor transport drivers, librarians, radio operators, mechanics, weather observers, and control tower operators. They served on marine corps bases and air stations in Virginia, North Carolina, and California.

UNIFORMED CIVILIAN SERVICE ORGANIZATIONS

Women did not have to join the military to serve their country in uniform. Some opted to volunteer with one of several civilian organizations that worked closely with the military. Women who served with the merchant marines, Red Cross, and the United Service Organizations (USO) made significant contributions to the war effort. When the United States entered the war in December 1941, women were serving aboard U.S. merchant marine vessels as cooks, messmates, and waitresses. German and Japanese submarines attacked all the ships they encountered. Dolores Martinez, a fireman and water tender working on the unarmed SS *Prusa*, died in an explosion when the ship was torpedoed by the Japanese on December 19, 1941, about 150 miles south of Hawaii.

Women Air Force Service Pilots (WASPs) were civilian women pilots trained by the U.S. Army Air Forces to fly domestic missions, thus freeing male pilots to be sent overseas for combat duty. WASPs lived and worked on military bases and were subject to military orders and discipline just like WACs and WAVES, however they were not official members of the military. The 1,102 WASPs, including two Chinese Americans (Maggie Gee and Hazel Ah Ying Lee) and one Native American (Ola Mildred Rexroat), flew military aircraft from the factories where they were built to the military bases where they were needed. Unfortunately, weather forecasting was less sophisticated than it is today, and many times WASPs flew into unexpected blizzards and thunderstorms. Thirty-eight WASPs, including Lee, died in the line of duty during the war.

Women pilots who wanted to contribute to the war effort but could only work part-time often served in the Civil Air Patrol, where they performed many flying jobs necessary for the nation's security. They patrolled the coastlines and land borders looking for groups attempting unauthorized entry, monitored national forests during fire seasons, carried cargo destined for war plants, and flew search and rescue missions. Several women pilots died in weather-related accidents. Women also performed necessary ground jobs: typing flight reports, manning plotting boards, and handling radio communications.

Red Cross nurses served on every major military base in every theater of war alongside army and navy nurses. However not all Red Cross women stationed overseas were nurses. Many were recreation workers, assigned to Red Cross Clubs or canteens, places where soldiers on leave could visit to get "home cooked" meals, showers, freshly laundered uniforms, and help communicating with their families back home. Some Red Cross women ran Clubmobiles (converted army 2.5 ton trucks) that were able to reach soldiers in the field near the front lines and provide them with freshly made doughnuts and coffee.

On the home front women who were unable to work full-time outside the home could still volunteer with the Red Cross. Red Cross volunteers passed out sandwiches, coffee and cakes to soldiers traveling cross-country by train to coastal ports for deployment overseas. Women volunteers wrapped bandages, assembled food and medicine packets for American and Allied POWs, and staffed canteens, recreational buildings near isolated military posts. Red Cross volunteers also collected more than 13 million pints of blood for American troops overseas.

In 1943, in an attempt to alleviate the shortage of nurses, Congress passed the Bolton Act, establishing the Cadet Nurse Corps. Young women who aspired to be nurses could join the Cadet Nurse Corps, and the government would pay their tuition and room and board at nursing school. In exchange Cadet Nurses promised that when they graduated, they would work at a military hospital or veteran's hospital for the duration of the war. More than 124,000 nurses graduated from the Cadet Nurse Corps before the program ended.

The American Women's Volunteer Service (AWVS) trained volunteers to drive ambulances and perform first aid in case of enemy attack or domestic emergencies and established centers to care for children of women who worked in war plants. These volunteers also conducted successful war bond drives, collected canned goods for military and emergency civilian use, and ran classes on home and automobile repair for wives whose husbands were in the service.

The Postwar Era

Throughout World War II the American people told themselves that when the war was over and the men came home, women would quietly leave their wartime occupations and return to the kitchen. Everyone assumed that the war-fueled economic boom would end, and returning soldiers would need their jobs back. As soon as the war ended, women workers began receiving termination notices.

To the surprise of many, however, the economy did not slow when the war ended, and women who liked earning a paycheck realized that they had a variety of options. The idea of women working outside the home was now more accepted, and although many women were forced out of high-paying factory and professional positions in favor of men, many lower-paying jobs remained available to them.

Young women usually wanted to work only for a couple of years until they got married. Marriage and a family were what every woman was supposed to want after World War II; the average age of a woman at marriage dropped from 21.5 in 1940 to 20.5 in 1947 and 20.3 in 1950. Where two children had been their mothers' goal, young women of this era wanted three or four. The average age of a woman at the birth of her first child dropped significantly, and birth rates leaped from 20.4 per 1,000 to 24.1 per 1,000 during the five years between 1945 and 1950.

Many women chose not to attend college, and women's educational levels declined dramatically. Few women wanted to stay in the workforce long enough to develop careers. Instead they opted for jobs that required minimal training and investment; they worked as secretaries, sales clerks, bookkeepers, and waitresses. Fewer women became managers, accountants, lawyers, doctors, professors, or architects. Men even began edging into professional jobs that had been the traditional preserve of women, becoming librarians, social workers, and elementary school teachers.

Older women whose children were already grown often wanted to work part-time to help pay for their children's education, a second car, or some other family luxury that a single-income family found difficult to afford. They were happy with low-level jobs that required little training and could be picked up or dropped according to the needs of the family. The number of married women in the workforce in 1950 was higher than it had been in 1945.

Most Americans of the postwar era agreed that women should not aspire to professional careers. The prevalent attitude was that women's true fulfillment lay in marriage and children, so career women could never be truly happy, and often had psychological problems. Furthermore, warned women's magazines, women who had high-powered careers often rendered themselves unfeminine and unappealing to men. Women appeared to heed the media's warnings. They had been 50% of all professionals in 1930 (before the Great Depression pushed many women out of the workforce), but by 1950 they represented only 35% of professional workers.

American women, who had worked and sacrificed during World War II to help defend America and democracy, built their lives around their families and communities during the early postwar years. Women told themselves that they were not interested in pursuing individual goals, seeking higher education, or having a career. Instead they sought to create and maintain idealized nuclear families. Many women wanted a safe home in the suburbs, happy children, and two cars in the garage. Before the 1950s were over, however, American women began to sense that something was missing from the American Dream.

—Judith Bellafaire

BIBLIOGRAPHY

Chafe, William. *The Unfinished Journey: America Since World War II*. New York: Oxford University Press, 1991.

Coleman, Penny. *Rosie the Riveter: Women Working on the Homefront in World War II*. New York: Crown Publishers, 1995.

Coontz, Stephanie. *The Way We Never Were: American Families and the Nostalgia Trap*. New York: Basic Books, 1992.

Hartman, Susan. *The Homefront and Beyond: American Women in the 1940s*. Boston: Twayne Publishers, 1982.

Holm, Jeanne, ed. *In Defense of a Nation: Servicewomen in World War II*. Arlington, Va.: Military Women's Press, 1998.

Weatherford, Doris. *American Women and World War II*. New York: Facts On File, 1990.

HISTORY OF AMERICAN FEMINISM

Feminism is a global movement for social change that is as much a part of the modern era as nationalism, socialism, and liberalism. Like these other movements feminism draws its power from the value that we now place on individual self-determination and society-wide development. Despite differences in how feminists mobilize and what they demand, the common beliefs that define feminism are as follows: existing social arrangements are systematically disadvantageous to women; these arrangements (the gender order) are not mere reflections of unchangeable biological differences between men and women but socially produced by the concerted activity of human beings; and the gender order is therefore subject to change by the collective action of people who can imagine less disadvantageous alternatives and organize to bring them about.

American feminism, unlike that of many other countries, is most closely identified with classical political liberalism, that is, the idea that the abstract individual citizen is endowed with inalienable political rights, economically self-determining, and independent (free of obligations to others beyond those contractually chosen). The universalism of the liberal ideal has appealed to many feminists, who use it to criticize how actual social arrangements fail to include real women equally, limiting their freedom and citizenship. Other feminists have challenged the covert masculinity of the liberal idealization of independence, which makes no allowance for being a child or having children.

American feminist history is usually thought of as coming in "waves" of social transformation. Periods of lesser mobilization and perhaps even of reactionary politics alternate with periods of renewed vitality and the emergence of new issues, though demarcation of these alternating periods is neither completely agreed upon nor sharp.

First-wave feminism is usually seen as running from the beginning of the 19th century to the early 20th century. However, some historians see two waves in this period, considering the active period before the Civil War, which gradually subsided into inactivity by the 1890s, as separate from the wave of activity that began to take shape in the new century and ultimately won women's national suffrage in 1920. Eleanor Flexner and Ellen Fitzpatrick's classic *Century of Struggle* (1959) covers this entire era, from early in the 19th century to 1920. Flexner and Fitzpatrick focus on the passing of the torch between the first generation—epitomized by Elizabeth Cady Stanton and Susan B. Anthony, who led the fight for married women's property rights, child custody, and right to employment, and initiated the then-unrealistic demand for the right to vote—and the next generation, symbolized by Stanton's daughter, Harriot Stanton Blatch, who, with Carrie Chapman Catt, focused on actually winning women's suffrage. Flexner and Fitzpatrick see this extended wave of activism as subsiding after suffrage was won.

Nancy Cott, Alice Rossi, and other scholars, however, interpret the women's organizations and politics of the 1920s and 1930s as continuing and diversifying the turn-of-the-century mobilization, which had focused only on winning the right to vote. Historians agree that the "doldrums" period of the 1940s and 1950s (during and after World War II), by contrast, shows little mobilization on the subject of gender issues.

Second-wave feminism is usually defined as the mobilization that emerged in the period of social ferment of the 1960s and that continued, despite increasing opposition, into the 21st century. Again, however, some historians would divide this wave into two smaller, distinct mobilizations. They present the groups and issues of the 1960s and 1970s as a "second wave" separate from a "third wave" of a new generation of activists in the 1990s and 2000s, following a period of heightened reaction against feminism associated with Ronald Reagan's presidency (1981–1989). Because a married woman's right to hold a job and to safety from assault by her husband, and the right of all women to education and to professional advancement were established in the 1990s in a way they were not in the 1960s, the focus of concerns for young women of the early 21st century is also not what it was in the 1960s. As in the earlier passing of the torch, some of the veterans, such as Alice Walker, the distinguished African American writer, are literally the mothers of the next generation of feminists. Walker's daughter Rebecca is one of many who proudly claim the title "third wave."

The wave metaphor is useful for pointing out the fluctuations in the extent of feminist mobilization and showing that even when feminism seems to be in retreat, its energy is likely to return in full force. When the wave metaphor is applied to the shorter periods, it also can highlight the change of generations in a movement with such a long and rich history. The language of waves is less useful for demarcating the distinctive qualities of specific historical periods (numbers are nondescriptive names and the boundaries are vague enough that, as described above, two, three, or even four "waves" can be discerned). Because the wave metaphor tends to make each period seem homogeneous and different from what came before or after, it is of no help in analyzing specific legacies of theory or practice that connect the periods but that also typify the divisions among activists within these eras. For example feminists in all periods have struggled to define women's citizenship along the competing axes of equality and difference, trying simultaneously to emphasize the claim to equal rights with men based on their similar humanity and to legitimate differences of treatment that recognize the needs of mothers.

Remembering that the commonly used wave metaphor may still sometimes be useful, this essay leaves it aside to speak instead of four chronologically distinct periods of feminist activism in the United States: the Civil War era, the suffrage era, the Sixties era, and the end of the millennium. Each period produced concrete gains for women but also set an agenda for future mobilization around the problems it left unaddressed. Each of the following four sections therefore not only describes some of the key actors and issues characteristic of the period but also discusses the divisions among feminists as harbingers of future problems.

THE CIVIL WAR ERA (1848–1880)

Although women who violated gender conventions and raised claims on behalf of women can be found in colonial, revolutionary, and early-19th-century America, the collective organization of feminists into a recognizable social movement dates from 1848 when the "Declaration of Sentiments" was adopted at Seneca Falls. Modeled on the Declaration of Independence, this manifesto was written by a group of women (and a few men) in this small town in upstate New York, many of whom—Lucretia Mott and Elizabeth Cady Stanton, among them—had recently returned from participation in the World Anti-Slavery Convention in London. Both the connection between abolitionism and women's rights and the international context of discussion that spurred the writing of the "Declaration of Sentiments" are characteristic of this first period of organized resistance to institutionalized gender subordination.

The exclusion of both African Americans and women from the promises of freedom and self-determination of the American Revolution led both women and men to see race and gender as parallel problems facing the republic. Middle-class women were also travelers who increasingly built voluntary ties of friendship with other women and who, like Harriet Martineau, wrote, compared, and spoke about the differences of social conditions between countries and classes. Access to higher education also became important as invention and discovery joined travel as spurs to social imagination. Utopian communities resisting conventional ideas of marriage blossomed. The idea that husbands owned women's bodies rankled women, and women demanded control over what they produced, whether children (who were then still automatically given into fathers' custody) or earnings and property (including what they brought into the marriage, which husbands took). Protestant sects, from Unitarians to Shakers, stressed individual revelation and thus empowered women to form their own judgments of right and wrong. The beginnings of industrialization brought farmers' daughters into mills and factories to work for wages before marrying. Both the promises and the problems emerging in this period led women to question their loss of identity, status, and self-determination when they married. Men's claim that the subordination of women was done for their protection and care was famously challenged by former slave Sojourner Truth. Her speech, "Ain't I a Woman?", delivered at the 1851 women's rights convention in Akron, Ohio, made clear black women's exclusion from any kind of social protection.

Feminist activism in this period was typified by many women's rights conventions that proposed women also be treated as citizens who could own property, earn wages, have custody of their children, travel freely, attend school, and, ultimately, vote. Married women's property acts were passed in some states throughout the 1840s and 1850s, and institutions of higher education for women, for example, Vassar College in 1861, were founded. The status of women was a visible and contentious issue, and social experimentation flourished: Lucy Stone championed a married woman's right to keep her own name as a symbol of her continued legal existence, and Amelia Bloomer advocated dress reform. During the Civil War, women's mobilization abated, and as freedom and citizenship for African Americans was won, deference to their pressing needs in "the Negro's hour" of liberation allowed many feminists to accept that despite their efforts, the right to vote would be extended only to African American men. But those unhappy with black men enjoying rights that white women lacked brought racist appeals into the campaign for suffrage, and the movement became more conservative and narrower in later decades.

By the 1880s the period of Reconstruction after the Civil War had come to an end, and in the 1890s the South intensified its disenfranchisement of black male voters, instituting the wide-ranging social segregation of African Americans known as Jim Crow. The 1880s and 1890s were a more conservative political era, marked by economic depressions and political reactions not only against African Americans but also against the working class, which was composed increasingly of new immigrants.

THE SUFFRAGE ERA (1890–1920s)

At the end of the 19th and beginning of the 20th century, industrialization and urbanization provided new problems and opportunities for feminist mobilization. New waves of immigrants transformed American cities. Economic development brought both extremes of economic exploitation and new opportunities for independence to both women and men. Socialism, an appeal to workers to organize and claim control over the profits generated by their labor, was becoming a mass movement of resistance to capitalist efforts to keep wages low. The American Federation of Labor was formed in 1881, but fear of socialists and anarchists also grew. Socialist theories offered an analysis of the status of women that paradoxically valued their waged work as an aspect of their emergence as worthy, socially productive individuals yet also demanded that married women not compete with men for jobs lest this lower men's wages below the minimum needed to support a family. Few working-class men enjoyed such a "family wage," and both wives and children labored for even less. Socialists demanded the right to vote for every adult and organized politically to achieve this goal.

Middle-class women also mobilized to demand the right to vote, both to use the vote to ameliorate such visible social problems of the cities as poverty, desertion, drunkenness, child abuse, and child labor and to use their votes to counter those of working-class men. Social reform, temperance, nonpartisan "good government" rather than urban parties and political machines, and international arbitration as a substitute for war were all social goods that moral reformers argued would result if women had the right to vote. Western feminists and Christian missionaries combined in international campaigns against foot binding in China; suttee (widow burning) in India; and polygamy, prostitution, and sexual trafficking (also known as "white slavery") globally. Moral reform competed with socialism as a template for social change, culminating in what is called the Progressive movement at the turn of the century.

Competing suffrage groups merged in 1890 under the leadership of Carrie Chapman Catt in the National American Woman Suffrage Association (NAWSA), which led the fight for the vote, combining state-level mobilization for partial, local suffrage with a demand for the right to

vote in national elections. Campaigns, rallies, speeches, and referenda were commonplace, but women's civic involvement in organizations devoted to political and moral reform outside of the electoral process also blossomed. Among the most notable were the Women's Trade Union League (WTUL), formed in 1902 as an alliance of working- and middle-class women dedicated to improving the situation of working women, and the Women's Christian Temperance Union, a largely middle-class organization founded in 1874 and growing in strength at the turn of the century as it campaigned against alcohol. Both actively supported women's right to vote.

Inspired by British suffragists, some U.S. campaigners, including Harriet Stanton Blatch and her Women's Political Union, began using confrontational tactics. The most radical activists, spearheaded by the Congressional Union for Woman Suffrage, founded in 1913 under the leadership of Alice Paul, repeatedly chained themselves to the White House fence and went on hunger strikes in prison whenever they were arrested. When the 19th Amendment securing women's suffrage was finally ratified in 1920, this group renamed itself the National Woman's Party and introduced the Equal Rights Amendment (ERA) in 1923. NAWSA renamed itself the League of Women Voters and adopted a policy of nonpartisanship, while other suffrage activists entered party politics for the first time. One activist, Chase Going Woodhouse, a Connecticut legislator, gave voice to the sentiment of the age when she said she wanted her tombstone to read "Born a woman, died a person."

National acceptance of overt racial subordination by Jim Crow laws in the South kept suffrage in practice restricted to white women after 1920. African American women maintained their struggle for rights throughout the 1940s and 1950s, a period of growing political quiescence for white women. In the 1930s and 1940s, some feminists, among them members of the WTUL and the newly formed (1920) Women's Bureau of the Department of Labor, fought against the ERA, seeing its constitutional guarantee of equal treatment of women and men as a threat to the minimum wage and maximum hours laws that had been accepted as constitutional, explicitly to protect women, only in 1907. Other feminists, such as Alice Paul and members of the National Woman's Party, emphasized that by restricting the work women—but not men—could do, these laws were being used to define women as unqualified for the jobs, usually better paid, where they might compete with men.

Mass mobilization was replaced by individual emancipation efforts after suffrage. In the 1920s younger women found new opportunities in emerging office work and in the growing professions of teaching and nursing. Cities offered escape from parental supervision and cheap amusements for working-class women, and the so-called "flappers"—middle-class young women who cut (bobbed) their hair short, raised their hemlines, and abandoned their corsets—also made the most of their new earnings and personal freedoms. Feminism appeared to be "irrelevant" or "old-fashioned" when race seemed the issue for black women and when white women's emancipation seemed not only a political fact but also a goal for which individuals could strive in their private lives.

THE SIXTIES ERA (1960–1982)

As the children of the postwar baby boom began to come of age, they encountered a new movement for racial equality that went from seeking the enforcement of the Supreme Court's 1954 school desegregation order to demanding civil rights and the end of Jim Crow. The civil rights movement encouraged questioning of other inequalities and power relations, giving rise to the revival of socialist politics (in student-driven community organizing referred to as the New Left) and challenging

American involvement in the conflict in Vietnam. The women's liberation movement also grew from these roots in the 1960s, when women began to question gender inequality both inside the civil rights, New Left, and antiwar movements in which they participated as well as in the wider society these movements critiqued.

Another strand of feminism reemerged from the old debates about the ERA, equal pay, and nondiscrimination in employment. Pres. John F. Kennedy's Commission on the Status of Women (CSW) issued a report in 1963 that identified continuing inequalities in the labor market. Explicit discrimination against women in hiring or job assignment was made illegal by Title VII of the Civil Rights Act of 1964, which also set up an Equal Employment Opportunities Commission (EEOC) to help enforce the law. Women in various state CSWs and public figures like Betty Friedan (1921–), the author of the 1963 bestseller *The Feminine Mystique*, then formed the National Organization for Women (NOW) in 1964 to be a "NAACP for women," lobbying the EEOC to take women's discrimination complaints seriously (50,000 complaints had been lodged by 1969). NOW's first successful campaign in 1966 was to eliminate gender segregation from classified ads. The 1974 Equal Credit Opportunity Act (ensuring access to loans for married and divorced women) and the 1972 Title IX promising equality in education (but primarily used to begin to equalize resources for women's sports) were also passed. In 1972 the ERA was passed by Congress and sent to the states for ratification.

The women's liberation movement focused less on equal employment issues than on cultural change and on the elimination of violence against women. Reclaiming both socialist and moral reform traditions, feminist writers like Kate Millet, Robin Morgan, and Mary Daly critiqued the lack of attention and resources devoted to stopping domestic assaults on women, rape, pornography, and prostitution. They coined new words to raise consciousness about old problems; the terms *sexual harassment, date rape*, and *wife battering* challenged the legitimacy of male power in the "private" lives of women. Women's groups founded hotlines that became rape crisis centers and shelters for women fleeing abusive husbands (the first of these in 1975). These organizations evolved from self-help groups to service-providing institutions that increasingly received state funding (for example, from marriage license fees), and also won changes in the law that would facilitate prosecution of violent men and withdraw the marital rape exemption. In the classic text *This Bridge Called My Back* (1981), women of color ended their invisibility within the movement; discussions of race, class, and gender began to focus on the personally meaningful, positive, racial and ethnic, and sexual identities that women claimed as well as the structures of oppression they faced.

In January 1973 the Supreme Court ruled in *Roe v. Wade* that a woman's individual right to citizenship and control over her own body extended to privacy in making a decision about abortion with her doctor in the first trimester of pregnancy. The Right to Life (for the fetus) movement (often called the New Right) that developed to overturn this decision increasingly mobilized conservatives, especially fundamentalist Protestants, opposed to women's rights in general. Ronald Reagan, as a candidate for president in 1980, supported a constitutional amendment to ban abortion and withdrew the Republican party's long-standing endorsement of the ERA. Conservative Republican Phyllis Schlafly, a John Birch Society activist and writer for presidential candidate Barry Goldwater, led a Stop-ERA movement that used images of co-ed bathrooms, women in military service being put into battle, and abortion rights to encourage state legislators to refuse to ratify the ERA. Despite widespread support for this constitutional amendment expressed in public opinion polls, it failed to achieve ratification by a sufficient

number of states by the extended deadline of 1982. The strong forward momentum of feminists in ensuring legal rights and social services was stopped, and the battles that were fought became increasingly defensive.

THE TURN OF THE MILLENNIUM (1990–PRESENT)

American feminism in the 1990s began to take cognizance of a more global movement for women's rights. Also revitalized from its roots in the suffrage era, transnational feminism began to emerge in 1975 when the United Nations Decade for Women was begun with a conference in Mexico City. Subsequent conferences in Copenhagen (1980), Nairobi (1985), and Beijing (1995) increasingly became venues not only for governments to engage in assessing their relative progress in securing women's rights but also for the mobilization of nongovernmental organizations (NGOs) from around the world on specific issues of gender—from reproductive rights and the survival of girl children to violence against women and mainstreaming women's concerns in government policy. In this global movement, often defined by the phrase "women's rights as human rights," American feminists were relative latecomers. Although they shared the classic liberal commitment to women's political and social rights, many American feminist groups joined in critiquing neoliberal economic policies. These economic measures, imposed on debtor countries by the International Monetary Fund and the World Bank, emphasized opening markets to international competition while slashing social services to balance the government's budget. Feminists saw them as increasing the double day of work for poor women, who often were drawn into export-oriented manufacturing jobs, small-scale entrepreneurship, or even the sex trade to earn money for their families while managing the unpaid work at home with less income and less help from social services.

Active in such global economic politics as the antisweatshop movement, feminists in this era drew new meaning from slogans like "the personal is political," coined in the 1960s; they showed how consumer choices of clothing, food (with or without hormones, antibiotics, and genetic modification), and energy use (the car-dependent lifestyle they grew up with) were both domestic (feminine, local) and macro-political (masculine, global). They challenged other dichotomies based on gender, too, such as the expectation that men but not women will be actively sexual, engaged in sports, and ambitious for personal success. The loosening of these gender double standards allowed more women to be treated as free and equal individuals in the sense of classic liberalism discussed earlier. Feminist politics and gay rights politics also converged in challenging conventional definitions of appropriate sexuality.

Since 1980 resistance to changes in gender norms have become defined as part of a general "culture war" of values that newly divided the Democratic and Republican parties, making gender politics highly visible even when women's movements were not protesting on the street. Homosexuality, abortion, divorce, and single motherhood in this period became lightning rods for anxieties over gender relations on the one side (the New Right), while feminist mobilizations stressed free choice in these matters on the other. The New Right mobilized to overturn *Roe v. Wade,* seeing the second Bush presidency (2001–) as an opportunity to secure both legislation and judicial appointments that would advance its "family values" agenda.

Nevertheless in this end-of-the-millennium era feminists were able to build on significant past gains. For example feminist success in gaining access to the military was greater than that of gay rights groups (homosexuality remained grounds for expulsion from the service, but women's share of positions grew from 2% in 1970 to 16% of the army and 19% of the air force in 2000, including jobs in combat such as missile technician or fighter pilot that had been previously closed). White women's gains through affirmative action programs in education also outstripped those of men and women of color, with women making up half of all students in law, medical, and business schools by the mid-1990s. Both in the military and in affirmative action programs, less political backlash was encountered by white women than by gays and persons of color, as women's gains came to be taken as the new institutional norm.

Feminist organizations from rape crisis centers to women's studies programs became well institutionalized, too, despite their opponents' claims that they were "unnecessary" drains on the budget and presented a vision of women as victims that was "old-fashioned." Feminist mobilizations at the end of the millennium were defensive, trying to prevent rollbacks of these opportunities, but they were also able to build on an increased acceptance of women as free agents, individual citizens entitled to equal rights. For example antifeminist mobilization took aim at Title IX and sought to eliminate its affirmative action for women's sports claiming it was unfair to men, while the success of American women's sports teams indicated to many people how effective implementation of government policy opened the doors for individual women to achieve. However, women who were not achievers in the accepted sense, for example, indigent mothers who depended on government aid to help balance their care of children with their need to earn a living, found ever fewer supports available.

The limits of what classical liberalism could offer American feminists remained unclear. On the one hand the norm of women's citizenship seemed finally to have been affirmed. After the terrorist attacks on the World Trade Center and the Pentagon in 2001, support for women's rights came to be seen as one of the characteristics dividing the world, with the expanded version of liberal individualism for which 19th-century feminists fought considered to be a critical feature of what makes American society good. On the other hand the classic liberal emphasis on the freedom of individuals—"blind" to color or gender and unencumbered by family ties—made the contention that women and mothers share important political interest difficult to support. The U.S. focus on individuals as such leaves American women lagging behind those in nearly all industrialized countries both in political representation in higher office and in government support for young children and the work of raising them. At the end of the millennium, ending the gender gap in political representation and seeking government support for caregiving work in and outside of conventional families defined two frontiers of expanding the concept of citizenship, a central concern for American feminists ever since Seneca Falls.

—Myra Marx Ferree

FURTHER READING

Baxandall, Rosalyn, and Linda Gordon. *Dear Sisters: Dispatches from the Women's Liberation Movement*. New York: Basic Books, 2000.

Cott, Nancy F. *The Grounding of Modern Feminism*. New Haven, Conn.: Yale University Press, 1987.

Ferree, Myra Marx, and Beth B. Hess. *Controversy and Coalition: The New Feminist Movement across Three Decades of Change*. 3rd ed. New York: Routledge, 2000.

Flexner, Eleanor, and Ellen Fitzpatrick. *Century of Struggle: The Woman's Rights Movement in the United States*. 1959. Reprint, Cambridge, Mass.: Belknap Press of Harvard University Press, 1996.

Friedan, Betty. *The Feminine Mystique*. 1963. Reprint, with a new introduction, New York : W. W. Norton, 1997.

Moraga, Cherríe L., and Gloria E. Anzaldúa. *This Bridge Called My Back: Writings by Radical Women of Color*. Expanded and rev. 3rd ed. Berkeley, Calif.: Third Woman Press, 2002.

Naples, Nancy. *Community Activism and Feminist Politics: Organizing across Race, Class, and Gender*. New York: Routledge, 1998.

Rosen, Ruth. *The World Split Open: How the Modern Women's Movement Changed America*. New York: Viking, 2000.

Rossi, Alice. *The Feminist Papers: From Adams to de Beauvoir*. 1973. Reprint, with additional editing, introductory essays, and new preface. Boston: Northeastern University Press, 1988.

Rupp, Leila J., and Verta Taylor. *Survival in the Doldrums: The American Women's Rights Movement, 1945 to the 1960s*. New York: Oxford University Press, 1987.

POLITICAL PARTICIPATION AND SOCIAL ACTIVISM

On August 26, 1920, the 19th Amendment, which enfranchised the women of the United States, was finally ratified. Only then were women fully recognized as independent political participants in one of the world's largest and most powerful democracies. Only if the definition of *political* is very narrow, however, can the granting of suffrage be considered the beginning of women's public and civic participation. If politics is understood as acting in a public arena to sustain or change social and power relationships, women had been political actors since the nation's beginnings.

COLONIAL ERA THROUGH THE AMERICAN REVOLUTION

Native American women of various tribes, confederacies, and nations held a number of important positions within their communities. Kinship management and agricultural responsibilities, for example, fell under their jurisdiction, giving them a voice within community affairs. Colonial migrant women also exercised power in various ways: the simple act of leaving England and other nations to find religious asylum in the new world was a political act, as was writing about the meaning and experience of their captivity by indigenous peoples, as Mary Jemison and Mary Rowlandson did in their captivity narratives.

In general, however, colonial women, in particular those in New England communities, were denied access to power and thus politics. The 17th and 18th century concept of women saw them as licentious, requiring careful management by society of their lustful urges (this understanding would change dramatically by the 19th century). A woman's fate in a Puritan settlement was decided largely through her role and standing in the church community. Cultural and legal practices and social conventions—for example, women were not allowed to testify in court on their own behalf—tended to suppress, yet never fully cut off, any efforts a woman might have made to effect social change.

In 1637 Anne Hutchinson was exiled from the Puritan colony of Massachusetts Bay for having gathered groups of women and men (separately) in her home to discuss her interpretations of the Bible and the local sermons. Her charisma, forcefulness, and religious authority—thought to be unbecoming to a woman—prompted church officials to consider her a threat to the community and to their power. The ostensible witches of Salem are another case. Women were blamed for a society's ills (both by men and by other women) and summarily hung or drowned for the degree to which they sought or were perceived to have sought to undermine the traditional patriarchal hierarchy. Both Hutchinson and the women of Salem tried to marshal religious rhetoric to support moves beyond traditional roles, but were ultimately unable to transcend their cultures' restraints on women.

During the American Revolution women participated in the political work of the nation in a number of ways. Although there were few known women soldiers (Deborah Sampson was one), women organized on both sides of the battle lines. In the early days of the struggle women used their power as consumers to express their political views; they refused to drink tea (a British import from India), wove their own cloth (rather than buying cloth from Britain), and occasionally wrote opinion pieces in colonial newspapers.

Women acted politically in other ways. One of the most well known, Abigail Adams, took over the management of a farm, managed investments, and reared children while her husband, John Adams, later president of the United States, was in Philadelphia helping to draft the Declaration of Independence. She wrote to her husband, reminding him to "remember the ladies" in allocating political rights, as well as serving as his political confidante. Abigail Adams was especially concerned with the *femme covert*, a term referring to the fact that, in marriage, women lost control over their affairs, such as their dowry and property, wages they earned, and custody of their children if widowed (or, in rare cases, divorced). Much to Adams's dismay, the British laws of coverture remained in place in the young republic.

The exclusion of women as political subjects—despite Abigail Adams's eloquent arguments—helped to give rise to what historians now call "republican motherhood." Although women were not recognized as political subjects in their own right, women were now understood to be crucial to the teaching of the nascent republic's citizenry. Because women had demonstrated their ability to participate in politics through their efforts in the Revolutionary War, they could no longer be considered to be lacking in virtue. Although the vote and property rights were not extended to them, women were no longer thought to be immoral by virtue of their sex. They were of particular significance to the political health of the nation and, hence, needed to be further educated. This logic formalized basic education for girls, prompting the founding of secondary schools like the seminary opened by Emma Willard in Troy, New York, where young women were schooled in teaching. Women's educational opportunities expanded throughout the 19th century, as some seminaries developed into colleges, such as Mary Lyon's Mount Holyoke, in Massachusetts, and as men's schools opened their doors to women, including Oberlin in Ohio.

ABOLITIONISM AND SUFFRAGE IN THE 19TH CENTURY

The 19th century was characterized by ongoing and increasingly successful political struggles and social activism of many different kinds. Antislavery activism had begun in the 18th century—among the early public voices on the subject was that of poet Phillis Wheatley, an African American woman—however, the movement grew in strength and numbers only in the 19th century. From the beginnings of the antislavery movement, women were significantly involved in its development.

African American women resisted slavery in myriad ways, from outright flight and physical resistance, to sass and secrecy when dealing with their masters, to writing and speaking out on the immorality of slavery. The first full-length slave narrative published by a woman, Harriet Wilson's *Our Nig* (1859), was written about slavery in the North. It was followed by Harriet Jacob's powerful indictment of slavery and the sexual double standard, *Incidents in the Life of a Slave Girl* (1861), which was initially published under the pen name of Linda Brent. Sojourner Truth and Frances Ellen Watkins Harper set precedents as mid-19th-century speakers on slavery and its abolition.

White women joined the abolition movement in great numbers. Southerners Sarah and Angelina Grimké defied their culture's bounds of respectable femininity and hit the lecture circuit to testify firsthand about the corruption that slavery breeds. Other women conveyed this message by writing poetry, prose, and novels. The second best-selling book in the 19th century was Harriet Beecher Stowe's *Uncle Tom's Cabin* (1852), a political work cloaked in the garb of fiction.

Women organized, also, against the excesses of capitalism. As women were drawn into the factories in greater numbers after 1830s, they made common cause with each other in auxiliary unions and then unions of their own. One of the earliest strikes occurred in 1828 in a Dover, New

Hampshire, textile mill, where women workers successfully demanded that penalties for lateness and talking on the job be dropped. The Lowell Female Labor Reform Association (LFLRA), in Lowell, Massachusetts, grew to be one of the biggest and most politically active shops within the New England Workingman's Association, addressing issues from the ten-hour day to raising relief funds for Ireland to combating the potato famine. The Knights of Labor, the most visible and progressive union of the 19th century, officially admitted women to its ranks in 1882, prompted by the efforts of shoemakers in Philadelphia.

The religious revival of the early 19th century—called the Second Great Awakening—was part of the fuel that sustained this movement of women into more public roles. The leaders of the religious revival urged their audiences to act on behalf of their newly invigorated beliefs about the perfectability of society. These exhortations to action appealed more to women than to men— and to slave women as well as free women; women began to rediscover their own religious and moral authority. This new sense of power propelled them into—and validated their presence in—a moral reform effort on many fronts: from combating prostitution to abolition work, from the reform of prisons to public education, and from the elimination of alcohol to the establishment of and participation in utopian communities. Although women were forced to engage in these efforts outside of the official realm of politics, their efforts were political in intent.

However, women's work on behalf of women's rights and the right to vote—more overtly political aspirations—were what shaped the possibilities of the 20th century—and the 21st. The suffrage movement was launched officially in the 1848 meeting in Seneca Falls, New York, where a group of 240 women (as well as some men)—led by Elizabeth Cady Stanton and Lucretia Mott—drafted the Declaration of Sentiments, in which they addressed the omission of women in the Declaration of Independence.

The women's rights movement that arose from this meeting was multifaceted; it included efforts to dismantle the law of coverture, to further efforts to abolish slavery (particularly because of the acute vulnerability of enslaved women), and to expand women's opportunities in education and, later, in employment. As with many social movements, it fractured along lines of race, class, political strategy, and region. The movement to expand women's rights and win suffrage emerged in the Northeast and was marked by the concerns of the abolitionist community. After the Civil War, however, the goals narrowed to one primary aim: women's suffrage. In 1869 women's rights activists divided over political strategy. Stanton and Susan B. Anthony focused on the vote for women with the National Woman Suffrage Association (NWSA) replacing the American Equal Rights Association, which the pair had founded in 1866 to work for the voting rights of both white and black women. The American Woman Suffrage Association (AWSA)—which included Lucy Stone, her husband, Henry Blackwell, and black abolitionist Frederick Douglass, a longtime supporter of women's rights—placed more primacy on securing the vote for newly freed African American men. The wrangling between the two groups over both the 14th Amendment, which introduced the word "male" into the Constitution, and the 15th Amendment, which granted voting rights to all men (and only men), solidified this split, a division that would only begin to heal in the 1890s, when the two groups reunited in the National American Woman Suffrage Association (NAWSA).

The rise of industrialism naturalized women's seclusion in the domestic sphere, alongside men's work in public spaces. This 19th-century concept of separate spheres argued that women "naturally" inhabited the more private space of the home, while men tended to be and act in the outside world. This social ordering encouraged the exclusion of women from participation in men's activities and cultivated the rise of equivalent female spaces. Cateogries of race, class, and gender became more and more constricting as the population of the young republic expanded.

Single-sex organizations, in which women met to discuss their particular concerns and to strategize about securing a different future, arose. These groups included women's suffrage associations and moral reform organizations, for example, the Women's Christian Temperance Union (WCTU), a powerful political group founded in 1874. Literary clubs provided a space for women to satisfy their intellects—efforts generally unacceptable elsewhere.

Black middle-class women, often excluded from the spaces and agendas of white women's clubs, created their own organizations. The year 1896 marked the inauguration of a national black women's club movement with the unification of two young organizations—the Colored Women's League and the National Federation of Afro-American Women—into the powerful National Association of Colored Women (NACW), which was dedicated to the needs of African American women. Mary Church Terrell, charter member and first president of the NACW, gathered a powerful group of women to lead the organization. Terrell worked with Ida B. Wells-Barnett, the leader of a vocal antilynching campaign in England and the United States, to address the increasingly grim conditions within their communities. Another associate, Maggie Lena Walker, formed mutual benefit societies, including her Independent Order of Saint Luke, which invested in the Richmond, Virginia, African American community by funding a bank and trust company. Other women acted independently by moving with their families, as an expression of their discontent, in an 1877 exodus to Kansas. Then, in increasing numbers during World War I, African Americans moved to northern industrial cities in what historians have deemed "The Great Migration."

The club movement cut across many different groups of women; however, it rarely connected them. The General Federation of Women's Clubs (GFWC), for example, largely excluded black women. Frances Willard, the powerful leader of the WCTU from 1879 to her death in 1898, refused to support the antilynching work of Wells-Barnett, presumably out of Willard's desire not to offend the white supremacist sympathies of the southern members of the WCTU.

The suffrage movement was still marked by racial discord during the 1890s, as various southern suffrage organizations began adopting a "southern strategy" for achieving the vote. This was accomplished with white men's efforts to disenfranchise African Americans for the benefit of white women. Because many suffrage organizations were run as state or regional groups, some women promoted the idea that their votes would offset the African American vote, thus securing white supremacy. Disfranchisement techniques gave way to other, more nationally based strategies for women's suffrage by the 1910s, even when underlying tension over the issue of race did not subside.

Harriet Stanton Blatch continued the suffrage work begun by her mother, Elizabeth Cady Stanton, and bridged the gap between the radical actions of Alice Paul's National Woman's Party and the more conservative position held by Susan B. Anthony's successor, Carrie Chapman Catt, president of NAWSA from 1900 to 1904. The unwieldy and disparate mass of women working for suffrage gradually came into harmony for enough time to push the 19th Amendment through to ratification in 1920.

SOCIAL AND POLITICAL ACTIVISM OF THE 20TH CENTURY

While women had been working within their communities in informal networks of support since the earliest days in America, those energies took on new forms at the turn of the century—commonly considered the beginning of the Progressive Era—with a movement by white women on behalf of new immigrant populations in urban areas. The settlement house movement was started by Jane Addams in Chicago with the opening of Hull House in 1889; this new concept in aid to newcomers and the less fortunate also engendered the modern profession of social work. These efforts were fueled by a genuine desire to help poor and struggling immigrant families, coupled with a desire for new forms of work for women outside the home and for a voice in the direction the nation would take; the reformers presumed that they would be able to shape immigrants' understanding of America. Another example of women's reform efforts was that of Russian immigrant and radical activist Emma Goldman, who was known for her political orations on anarchy, contraception, labor reform, and women's rights. Although she received approval from the Progressives, her views and actions were considered incendiary, and she was deported in 1919.

Many Progressive Era efforts would be related to activism on behalf of the welfare and health of women and children, a trend that continued to grow throughout the 20th century. Women such as Margaret Sanger were persecuted for disseminating information about reproduction; Sanger was imprisoned for opening a birth control clinic in 1916. The issue of the female body would be revisited by women's movement activists in the 1960s as they lobbied to legalize abortion and worked to raise women's awareness about their own health and pleasure; the 1969 book, *Our Bodies, Ourselves*, published by the Boston Women's Health Collective, was enormously popular and widely read. Feminists of this era also opened battered women's shelters to protect victims of domestic abuse and worked to safeguard women's jobs when maternal roles conflicted with professional roles.

In the 1960s, in the second wave of feminism (the first wave was the 19th-century suffrage movement), women united and expressed their anger about sex discrimination. The triggers of this movement were many and varied, but among them were Simone de Beauvoir's provocative *The Second Sex*, published in France in 1949, and Betty Friedan's angry *The Feminine Mystique*, published in the United States in 1963. The report issued in 1963 by the Presidential Commission on the Status of Women, which had been chaired by Eleanor Roosevelt, found and discussed discrimination against women in virtually every aspect of American life. Civil rights legislation passed in 1964 to combat racism and sexism prompted the formation of the Equal Employment Opportunity Commission (EEOC); subsequently, talking about women's rights was no longer treated as a joke. Encouraged by these successes, other women began speaking out and formed the National Organization of Women (NOW) in 1966 with Friedan at the helm.

Women also formed the core of political movements addressing other social inequities, and they labored hard to achieve reforms in post–World War II America. Johnnie Tillmon and Etta Horm fought for welfare reform; Ella Baker, Septima Clark, and Fannie Lou Hamer played pivotal roles in the struggle for civil rights; and working women in the labor movement in San Francisco formed the Union Women's Alliance to Gain Equality (Union WAGE). Women were active within the individual groups agitating for the rights of youth, gays and lesbians, Native Americans, and within the antiwar and peace movements. Not limited to leftist reforms, women of the early right-to-life movement founded Feminists for Life in 1972 after being drummed out of NOW.

However, women's work was not always acknowledged, even by progressive organizations. In response to their experiences within some social movements, women began to challenge the gender status quo in a number of more radical ways. For example, the New York Radical Women (NYRW) garnered media attention by protesting the Miss America Pageant in Atlantic City, New Jersey, in 1968 by crowning a sheep as the winner. The Furies, a lesbian feminist collective, lived as separatists and accused their heterosexual counterparts of threatening the women's rights agenda. By 1971 *Ms.* magazine, the first publication of its kind since the first wave of feminism, began publication with Gloria Steinem atop the masthead. *Ms.* found an audience of 300,000 in its first year.

WOMEN IN POLITICAL OFFICE

The trajectory of progress women have followed in the more traditional form of political participation—that of holding political office—began early in the 19th century. In 1884 Belva Lockwood, the candidate of the National Equal Rights Party, became the first woman to receive votes in a presidential election (approximately 4,000 in six states). In 1917 Jeannette Rankin of Montana was the first woman to be elected to the U.S. Congress. She was followed by a number of firsts: Nellie Taylor Ross became governor of Wyoming in 1924; Hattie Wyatt Caraway was elected to the Senate from Arkansas; Francis Perkins became the first Cabinet member as secretary of labor for Pres. Franklin Delano Roosevelt. The majority of women politicians were white; this began to change as the 20th century wore on. In 1964 Patsy Mink, an Asian American, was elected to the U.S. Congress from Hawaii, followed in 1968 by African American Shirley Chisholm from New York. By 1985 Wilma Mankiller had become the first woman installed as principal chief of a major Native American nation, the Cherokee in Oklahoma.

Dubbed the "Year of the Woman," in 1992 a record number of women ran for office—and won. Twenty-four women were newly elected to the House, among them the first Mexican American,

Lucille Roybal-Allard, from California, and the first Puerto Rican woman, Nydia Velazquez, from New York; six were elected to the Senate, including Carol Mosley Braun, the first African American woman, from Illinois, and both of the senators from California, Dianne Feinstein and Barbara Boxer. Although the numbers of women running for office have not, as of this writing, reached this level since, women are no longer as likely to be silenced, ignored, or forgotten.

—Lyde Cullen Sizer and Marguerite B. Avery

FURTHER READING

Cott, Nancy. *The Grounding of Modern Feminism.* New Haven, Conn.: Yale University Press, 1987.

Echols, Alice. *Daring to Be Bad: Radical Feminism in America, 1967–75.* Minneapolis: University of Minnesota Press, 1989.

Evans, Sara. *Born for Liberty.* New York: Free Press Paperbacks, 1997.

Giddings, Paula. *When and Where I Enter: The Impact of Black Women on Race and Sex in America.* New York: W. Morrow, 1996.

Ginzberg, Lori. *Women and the Work of Benevolence: Morality, Politics, and Class in the Nineteenth Century United States.* New Haven, Conn.: Yale University Press, 1990.

Jones, Jacqueline. *Labor of Love, Labor of Sorrow: Black Women, Work, and the Family from Slavery to the Present.* New York: Vintage Books, 1995.

Kierner, Cynthia. *Beyond the Household: Women's Place in the Early South, 1700–1835.* Ithaca, N.Y.: Cornell University Press, 1998.

Norton, Mary Beth. *Founding Mothers and Fathers: Gendered Power and the Forming of American Society.* New York: Alfred A. Knopf, 1996.

Perdue, Theda. *Cherokee Women: Gender and Culture Change, 1700–1935.* Lincoln: University of Nebraska Press, 1999.

Rosen, Ruth. *The World Split Open: How the Modern Women's Movement Changed America.* New York: Penguin, 2001.

Ryan, Mary. *Women in Public: Between Banners and Ballots, 1825-1880.* Baltimore, Md.: Johns Hopkins University Press, 1992.

RACE AND ETHNICITY IN AMERICAN WOMEN'S HISTORY

Prior to western colonial expansion, groups identified themselves according to religion, with outsiders marked as "ethnic peoples" in late-15th-century English parlance. Not until the influx of eastern and southern Europeans into the United States at the turn of the 20th century did the term *ethnicity* emerge to formally distinguish among Europeans by national origins and culture. In this sense, an ethnic group was defined as a European entity that was "socially distinguished or set apart, by others or by itself, primarily on the basis of cultural or national-origin characteristics." (Feagin and Feagin 1996, 11) The Protestant English-speaking peoples, both those already established and those recently immigrated, were in the great majority and considered their culture and faith, based on Judeo-Christian principles, to be superior to other cultures and faiths. Although the word *ethnicity* specifies cultural difference and can be used to imply the superiority of one culture, it lacks the nefarious implications of inherent and unalterable biological difference and skin color that racial distinctions inevitably make.

From the point of their colonial beginnings, Europeans in what is now the United States wrestled to shape an identity that would render them superior to and distinct from African and Native American peoples. The notion of racial identity began in the 17th century and entered into the academic world, emerging as a theoretical and social construct in the 18th and 19th centuries. Racial classification relegated peoples of African and Native American ancestry to the status of outsiders—making legitimate the robbing of their labor and land based on alleged insurmountable and innate biological and cultural inferiority. Race and racial classifications were based on the pseudoscience of biological difference, resulting in the assumption that Europeans were inherently culturally superior to black-skinned Africans and brown-skinned Native Americans. Because of their black color, national and cultural origins, and condition of enslavement, Africans were classified as the most uncivilized and heathen, whereas the peoples of the white race were alleged to be civilized and Christian and were to be emulated. African descendants were unique as a people marked for racial distinction.

As groups of immigrants arrived in the United States in the 19th and 20th centuries from eastern and southern Europe, Latin America, Asia, and Pacific Rim nations, they petitioned for white designation, which eventually was granted only to immigrants from Europe. Seeking to avoid various degrees of sociopolitical discrimination and economic exploitation, non-European immigrants were accorded ethnic designations (that is, Hispanic or Latin American; Chinese, Japanese, and other Asian American; Hawaiian and Polynesian) according to their national origins and cultural heritages. Although the ethnicity and nationality of non-African immigrant groups were recognized and sometimes honored, the varied groups and cultures of African peoples were conflated into a construct of race.

The status of the first Africans brought into 17th-century North America as free, indentured, or enslaved was uncertain. In the first decades of settlement, the colonists recognized that African peoples originated from many nations with diverse cultures. They distinguished among Africans based on skills that the Europeans needed to become successful farmers, planters, traders, and artisans. Virginians, for example, often requested Igbo, Efik, and Ibibio peoples of the Calabar region of west-central Africa with skills and stamina to cultivate and harvest tobacco. Individual enslavers also noticed and remarked on cultural differences when advertising runaways among the enslaved, commenting on facial scarification, filed teeth, and other cultural markings. As dependence on Africans as cheap labor for agriculture and other industries increased, slave labor skills became uniform enough to eliminate the demand for pairing skills and culture. African ethnicities were reduced to the single racial designation of black.

Racial distinction also determined relationships between white and black women in the United States. Differences in the social status of black and white women were established early in the colonial history of the United States. Tithing (tax) laws that distinguished black women from other female servants and free white women effectively developed a racialized caste. The first tithing act was passed one decade after the first African women arrived in the Virginia colony. This act intended to distinguish between English women and African women, whose identity was bound to agricultural work. The act stated that "all those that work in the ground of what qualitie or condition soever, shall pay tithes." English women servants, who were the predominant European ethnic group at the time, were more likely to be engaged in domestic chores rather than in the arduous agricultural tasks of "working in the ground."

Subsequent tithing acts further clarified and solidified the distinction between black and white women. Following complaints that the tax was burdensome for Englishmen with white women servants who worked sporadically at agricultural tasks, the Act of 1642–1643 specified that males and all "Negro" women were tithable at the age of 16. The response to petitions from black men that black women in free families be exempted from the hardship of the tax was the passage of another act in 1668. Acknowledging that the tax presented a financial hardship for free black women, this act stipulated that black women should not enjoy "exemptions and impunities" of Englishwomen. Free black women were not exempted from the tithe until 1705.

The Virginia Act of 1662 marked another point of distinction between white and black women, for the English departed from the tradition of determining the social status of a child by its paternity when the mother was black. This act specified that children would inherit the social condition of the mother, even when the father was white. Turning these racial distinctions into matters of law helped further the economic, political, and religious aims of slaveholders at a time when blacks and Native Americans captured in sporadic wars were enslaved. The intended racial distinction was emphasized in 1670, when an act limited the terms of service for Native American girls, boys, men, and women, leaving blacks the only peoples that were perpetually enslaved. Court documents and other records from the slavery era show that white women often were enslavers of black women and children.

Denied access to legal marriages and tainted by slavery, the offspring of enslaved women were perceived to be illegitimate, leaving open to question the morals of even free black women, whose character was routinely disparaged by men. Concurrent with the mass sexual exploitation of black women by white men, the Victorian Era shifted the image of white women from being inherently sinful and sexual, a commonly held belief at the time, to that of being virtuous and naturally concerned only with the home and children.

RACE AND THE WOMEN'S RIGHTS MOVEMENT

While enslaved women languished in bondage, white middle-class women sought to improve their lives in various ways by confronting their confinement to the domestic arena. One avenue that they forged was women's movements, which in the United States is commonly considered to have had two waves. The first wave of women's activism had its roots in the moral reform movement, which began in the early

1800s. In the 1830s organized groups of white women reformers joined black women and men and white men in the struggle to end slavery. Because of their experiences with being barred from the public forum and suffrage, white women wanted to reform society by obliterating social injustices, including slavery and women's disenfranchisement and culturally enforced public silence.

Interaction with their male compatriots during the abolitionist movement heightened white women's sensitivity to their lower social status. Early white feminists such as Sarah and Angelina Grimké, Lucy Stone, Elizabeth Cady Stanton, Lucretia Mott, and Susan B. Anthony argued that all individuals were equally human and should be able to decide their own destinies and develop their abilities. They also reasoned that if women themselves did not enjoy equal rights and status with men, they could offer little or no help in securing similar freedoms for others.

Prominent African American female abolitionists joined white women in pressing for female rights. Maria Stewart, Charlotte Forten, and Sojourner Truth were among those campaigning for the freedom and independence of all women of any color. The feminist cause also enjoyed loyal support from black and white male abolitionists including Frederick Douglass, William Lloyd Garrison, and Robert Purvis. As a result women's rights were increasingly associated with the antislavery cause.

Although whites, blacks, women, and men actively participated in both the antislavery and feminist causes, neither movement was ever fully integrated racially or by gender. Furthermore, some of the abolitionists were concerned that they were becoming too closely associated with women's rights and feared that one cause might hurt the other.

The Civil War and Reconstruction resulted in a temporary halt in the movement for women's rights as women concentrated on furthering the abolitionist cause. Feminists expected that equality and the franchise would be granted to both women and emancipated slaves. But women were bitterly disappointed by the wording and passage of the 14th and 15th Amendments.

The 14th Amendment to the Constitution bestowed citizenship on former slaves. It also stipulated that all persons were to be counted equally when apportioning representation in the House of Representatives. The 15th Amendment granted the franchise to former slaves, but restricted the vote to males. Some feminists regarded the amendments as a blatant betrayal of women, many of whom had made significant contributions to the abolitionist cause. White feminists began to reevaluate their relationship with the abolitionist movement. In her book on race and feminism, *Daughters of Jefferson, Daughters of Bootblacks: Racism and American Feminism* (1986), Barbara Hilkert Andolsen commented that a conflict of interest existed that demanded an answer to two questions: Did concern for black people necessitate that white women give their own interests second priority?; Could white women legitimately pursue their own self-interest regardless of the effects of their actions on the political fortunes of black men? Disagreement over how to address these questions created ideological divisions, causing white feminists to play increasingly complicit roles in racial oppression as they pursued their own liberation.

One of the first steps taken by some white feminists after the passage of the 15th Amendment was to distance themselves and their cause from that of African Americans. Two rival organizations, the National Woman Suffrage Association (NWSA) and the American Woman Suffrage Association (AWSA) were formed in 1869; both had their origins within the membership of the American Equal Rights Association. The AWSA was single-minded in pursuit of its goal of securing the vote for women; the NWSA was the more radical organization, supporting a wider range of issues involving women's rights. The radical approach of NWSA to women's suffrage, however, led the organization to oppose ratification of the 15th Amendment because it did not enfranchise women along with black men. White feminist leaders began to distinguish themselves ideologically even more as the century wore on. This split between white and black became more pronounced after 1890 when NWSA and AWSA merged into the National American Woman Suffrage Association (NAWSA) and concurrently a new generation of suffrage leaders, who had no personal connection to or experience with the abolitionist cause, began to assume leadership of the movement. Unlike their predecessors, these new leaders believed that pressing for women's rights would be easier if enfranchisement of African Americans were not part of the fight.

Attempts to garner support for women's suffrage in southern states were met with limited success because white southerners remembered with bitterness the active roles of early feminists in the abolitionist movement. With the Civil War over and emancipation won, suffrage organizers had to decide whether they should cooperate with or condemn southern segregationist Jim Crow practices to obtain white southern support for their cause. This issue and its ramifications were rarely openly debated. However, convention records of NAWSA between 1894 and 1910 provide significant insights.

The NAWSA held its first convention in the South in 1894. Black abolitionist and women's rights supporter Frederick Douglass had attended these annual meetings as an honored guest many times. However, he was asked not to attend the Atlanta, Georgia, conference for fear that his presence would be misconstrued by southern feminists as support for social equality between white women and African Americans. The NAWSA also refused to support a proposal that black women not be forced to ride in railroad smoking cars where they were at great risk of being sexually harassed or attacked. When a newspaper editorial alleged that support for women's suffrage was also support for social equality between the races, the NAWSA responded that the organization had no official position on the question of equality for African Americans. The

statement continued by acknowledging that its members held widely differing opinions with regard to racial equality and that such views often were those that reflected attitudes common to their regions. National NAWSA policy allowed state affiliates to organize chapters in a manner consistent with regional and local positions on race. Thus, southern NAWSA chapters could and did refuse to admit African Americans with the full knowledge of the national officers. These actions and official stances showed that white feminists had clearly decided against challenging racism in the hopes of acquiring southern support for the movement.

In fact, racism was dominant in the majority of white women's reform groups. White women's club members in the South were among the most vehement in their opposition to black women joining their ranks, and many white women in the North supported these racial attitudes. The important issue to be addressed by national NAWSA leaders was whether the women's rights groups would be racially segregated. This issue was settled in Milwaukee, Wisconsin, at the General Federation of Women's Clubs conference when Mary Church Terrell (president of the National Association of Colored Women) and Josephine Ruffin (representing the black women's New Era Club) were denied full participation in the proceedings.

Prior to winning the franchise in 1920, suffragists even presented women's voting rights as an acceptable means of maintaining white Anglo-Saxon dominance. They described immigrants and freemen as ill equipped to vote because of their lack of education, experience, and unfamiliarity with the principles, history, and traditions of the U.S. political system. By comparison, white, native-born suffragists were educated and familiar with American culture and politics. They also intimated that the inherently virtuous nature of (white) women would lead them to be selfless in their voting behavior and that, as moral paragons, women could help restore politics to its former high ethical standards.

Some of the negative attitudes toward black women resulted from lingering racist and sexist stereotypes that dated to slavery; these images portrayed black women as harlots. The white women's movement leaders claimed that their status as ladies would be undermined if they associated with black women. Leaders of the black women's club movement encouraged their members to protest the negative images and to find positive ways to counter the stereotypes.

Knowing that stereotypes were dangerous and the frequent cause of the lynchings of black women and men, Ida B. Wells-Barnett campaigned at home and abroad for federal legislation against lynchings. Throughout the nearly 40 years of her crusade, other black women leaders provided significant support but virtually no white women's organizations endorsed antilynching measures until 1930, when the Association of Southern Women for the Prevention of Lynching was organized. Black women's club leaders continuously encouraged their followers to protest negative images that were perpetuated in newspapers, novels, movies, scientific studies, and lies promoted by individual white racists. At the local and national levels, black women organized sororities and clubs, and created educational and social welfare opportunities and institutions for the positive advancement of themselves and their families. In 1935 Mary McLeod Bethune gave unity to these efforts when she founded the National Council of Negro Women.

Inspired by these organizing successes, black women domestic and day workers—sometimes referring to themselves as "modern slaves"—began to unite against their exploitation by organizing unions in 1937. By 1970 domestic workers' unions, under the very capable leadership of Dorothy Bolden, had expanded into the South, becoming a force in Atlanta, a city of stalwart supporters of Jim Crow. Even at the beginning of the 21st century, the isolated nature of domestic employment made the struggle for unity in demanding equitable pay and decent working conditions difficult.

MODERN FEMINISM

New wave, or modern, feminism shares several similarities with the first wave. First wave activists claimed that all individuals belonged to a common humanity, however, modern feminists emphasize that women are universally linked through their common oppression by men. The origins of first and second wave feminism both trace back to liberation movements for African Americans. First wave activism sprang from the abolitionist movement of the 1830s through the 1860s while modern feminism grew out of the black civil rights movement of the 1950s and 1960s, when individual white women joined the struggle against racism. Despite significant changes in their civil status since the first wave of feminism, women became increasingly aware that a number of inequities and issues, old and new, still needed to be remedied or addressed. As they participated in the various protest movements, which were themselves riddled with discrimination against women, women's less-than-equal status in society was highlighted. Yet criticisms about the first stage feminist movement's inherent racism, narrow focus, and inability to unite women across the divisions of race, ethnicity, and nationality continued to hold true with regard to its contemporary form.

During the civil rights movement of the 1960s and 1970s, many young, college-educated, middle-class black women were caught up in the idealized Victorian concept of women as helpmates to black men. Black women were so focused on the need to eradicate racism that they virtually ignored the feminist movement when it began to resurge in the late 1960s. Many black women believed that if they pursued the goal of social equality with men, they would strike a blow against black liberation. Profeminist black women, including Shirley Chisholm and Pauli Murray, nevertheless expressed black female support of feminism as well as the pursuit of racial justice.

Although some black women joined black feminist groups during the 1980s and 1990s, a number were willing to join forces with white women in the effort to eradicate sexism and racism. Their shared observations are thoughtfully articulated by bell hooks: "White women liberationists," she observed, "saw feminism as 'their' movement and resisted any efforts by non-white women to critique, challenge, or change its direction." (hooks 1981, 190) These attitudes reminded black women that the structure of the movement was founded on a white supremacist ideology that repels black and many other women of color.

The history of black women in the United States has been preoccupied with issues pertaining to race while the diversity of ethnicity among them has been largely ignored. West Indian, Afro-Caribbean, Afro-Latin, and African women from many nations have lived among African American women since the 1790s, when immigrants fled the Haitian Revolution and because the illegal trans-Atlantic slave trade continued until the outbreak of the Civil War. The flow of immigration from the Caribbean and Africa increased noticeably after the 1950s, when U.S. immigration laws were liberalized. Interactions between these immigrant groups and African Americans are not without tensions. Nevertheless, the diverse cultural backgrounds of the immigrants and their observations on racial identity in the United States have enlivened the dialogue on race and ethnicity among women.

—Lillian Ashcraft-Eason and Laurie A. Rodgers

FURTHER READING

Andolsen, Barbara Hilkert. *Daughters of Jefferson, Daughters of Bootblacks: Racism and American Feminism.* Macon, Ga.: Mercer University Press, 1986.

Ashcraft-Eason, Lillian. "Freedom Among African Women Servants and Slaves in the Seventeenth-Century British Colonies." In *Women and Freedom in Early America*, edited by Larry D. Eldridge. New York: New York University Press, 1997.

Baker, Lee D. *From Savage to Negro: Anthropology and the Construction of Race, 1896–1954.* Los Angeles: University of California Press, 1998.

Brown, Kathleen M. *Good Wives, Nasty Wenches, and Anxious Patriarchs: Gender, Race, and Power in Colonial Virginia.* Chapel Hill: University of North Carolina Press, 1996.

Feagin, Joe R., and Clairece Booher Feagin. *Racial and Ethnic Relations.* Upper Saddle River, N.J.: Prentice Hall, 1996.

Hine, Darlene Clark. *HINE SIGHT: Black Women and the Re-Construction of American History.* Bloomington: Indiana University Press, 1994.

hooks, bell. *Ain't I a Woman: Black Women and Feminism.* Boston: South End Press, 1981.

Jones, Jacqueline. *Labor of Love, Labor of Sorrow: Black Women, Work and the Family, from Slavery to the Present.* New York: Vintage Books, 1986.

Kerbo, Harold R. *Social Stratification and Inequality: Class Conflict in Historical, Comparative, and Global Perspective.* 5th ed. New York: McGraw Hill, 2003.

Kesselman, Amy. "A History of Feminist Movements in the U.S." In *Women: Images and Realities. A Multicultural Anthology*, 2nd ed., edited by Amy Kesselman, Lily D. McNair, and Nancy Schniedewind. Mountainview, Calif.: Mayfield Publishing, 1999.

King, Deborah K. "Multiple Jeopardy, Multiple Consciousness: The Context of a Black Feminist Ideology." In *Black Women in America: Social Science Perspectives*, edited by Micheline R. Malson, et al. Chicago: University of Chicago Press, 1988.

Lerner, Gerda, ed. *Black Women in White America: A Documentary History.* New York: Vintage Books, 1973.

Marger, Martin N. *Race and Ethnic Relations: American and Global Perspectives.* 6th ed. Belmont, Calif.: Wadsworth, 2003.

Newman, Louise Michele. *White Women's Rights: The Racial Origins of Feminism in the United States.* New York: Oxford University Press, 1999.

Ramazanoglu, Caroline. *Feminism and the Contradictions of Oppression.* New York: Routledge, 1989.

Vickerman, Milton. *Crosscurrents: West Indian Immigrants and Race.* New York: Oxford University Press, 1998.

Waters, Mary C. *Black Identities: West Indian Immigrant Dreams and American Realities.* Cambridge, Mass.: Harvard University Press, 2000.

CULTURAL REPRESENTATION OF WOMEN

The images of women in the American mass media and popular culture—including newspapers, magazines, television, music, films, magazines, and the like—often promote unrealistic and inaccurate stereotypes and views. Often women are depicted in subordinate, subservient, and male-pleasing roles. Some scholars, Marian Meyers among them, claim that representations of women in popular media and culture work to create and reinforce a particular point of view or ideology that influences our perspectives and beliefs about the world. Popular culture, according to Charles Tatum, often reflects a society's traditions, roots, history, economics, political life, prejudices, values, and attitudes. From the chaste "Indian princess" media portrayals of Native American women to the smart, sophisticated women portrayed by Katharine Hepburn in many of her films, the images of women in the media reveal much about the society that has created them.

Serious analysis of the representation of women in popular culture began during the 1960s and 1970s, with the second wave of the women's movement; these analyses helped to change the political and social climate, and gave birth to feminist critique. At that time research on the representation of women in popular culture showed women as underrepresented in both the producing entities and their products. In 1978 the first book on the topic of representation of women in mass media, *Hearth and Home: Images of Women in Mass Media,* by Gaye Tuchman, Arlene Kaplan Daniels, and James Benét, described the media's representation of women as "symbolic annihilation," that is, the absence, condemnation, and trivialization of women. As a result of the women's movement and other forces,

including MTV (Music Television), marketing targeted at women, and an increase of women in the workforce, significant changes were made in the representation of women in the media. Since the 1970s the imagery of women has become more varied, reflecting the different races, ethnic and class backgrounds, ages, and sexual orientations of our society.

DEFINITIONS AND THEORIES

To better understand the representation of women in popular culture, some knowledge of definitions and theories—varied and conflicting as they often are—can be helpful. Theodor Adorno and Max Horkheimer, German scholars and theorists of mass culture, consider popular culture to be the same as mass culture, or culture produced for consumers by culture industries, for example, television and magazine publishing. Other scholars, Antonio Gramsci and Louis Althusser among them, consider popular culture to be the preponderant ideology used by dominant classes to control groups of people below them. A third view, put forth by "cultural populists," defines popular culture as the ways in which consumers receive messages produced by cultural industries, interpret those messages (not necessarily as the cultural industries intend), and through those interpretations express the interests, experiences, and values of ordinary people. A fourth view—the feminist position—is that popular culture embodies a patriarchal ideology that is largely controlled by men and that often conflicts with the interests of women.

When addressing the representation of women in the media, two primary positions dominate the discussion, according to Michele Ryan in her essay "Representations of Women in the Media." The first position maintains that, within the context of the political economy of a capitalist patriarchy, nearly all representations of women are demeaning, stereotypical, or inaccurate. Many feminists support this position. For instance, some feminists would say that because primarily men control the film and television industries, the masculine perspective is prevalent in those media. The second viewpoint maintains that women are influenced by their own subjectivities and cultural competence when consuming media (that is, when they receive and interpret cultural representations on film and television, and in other media products). Women are not passive consumers of visual and written media; their viewing and reading is a complex interactive activity that enables them to resist dominant representations promoted by the creators of cultural products.

REPRESENTATION OF WHITE WOMEN

The 19th-century feminist, labor, and socialist movements helped to advance political, economic, and sexual emancipation in the United States at the turn of the century. The "emancipated woman" was a well-known term, as white American women made unprecedented gains in white-collar and professional occupations in the 1910s. Images of women maintained traditional feminine archetypes but also represented women joining the workforce as America entered World War I in 1917. The famous recruiting poster, "For Every Fighter a Woman Worker," shows women backing the war effort by going to work. Coexisting with these images were images of women representing freedom, nation, and home. (Higonnet 1994)

In the 1920s the modern advertising industry began; American mass culture also became possible as mass production and marketing techniques joined radio, movies, newspapers, and magazines to advertise and broadcast ideas about the American way of life, including images of the modern American woman. Women were sold, or were used to sell, products and conceptions about life-style rooted in long-standing expectations of women's subordination and domesticity.

During World War II many of the same images of women used in World War I—feminine archetypes that inspired patriotic values about the home front alongside images of women engaged in the industrial workforce—were revived. Posters appeared—such as that featuring Norman Rockwell's painting *Freedom from Want*, which showed a family gathered for Thanksgiving—symbolizing the values of home and nation. (Higonnet 1994)

The economic and cultural pressures of war and the post–World War II recovery reshaped femininity in America. Feminine imagery, skillfully used by the mass media, promoted the American model of womanhood: domestic, maternal, and consumerist. Identifying femininity with products (objects), advertisements encouraged women to view themselves in the ways advertisements portrayed them. General Electric, for example, featured women in advertisements set in the home to sell products; the setting indicated that a woman's happiness depended on products—like washers and dryers—that improved home and family life.

Cinema became an important part of the popular culture in the 20th century, and it strongly influenced and reflected the definition of gender. Higonnet states that, in film, women were represented in a patriarchal order: they were "delivered" to the hero, to a self-sacrificial death, or were punished if they deviated from the female norm. They also were represented as pleasing objects for men—for example, Marilyn Monroe in *Gentlemen Prefer Blondes* (1953)—in a phenomenon labeled the "masculine gaze." In the 1930s and 1940s Hollywood developed and produced "women's films" for female audiences that revolved around female characters and heroines dealing with women's issues and emotions. *Adam's Rib* (1949), for example, tells the story of a happily married couple whose marriage is strained while the husband and wife serve as trial lawyers on opposite sides of a murder case.

Shadowing "women's films" were daytime soap operas, which focused on women in domestic and neighborhood situations, dealing with romance, female emotions and issues, and family tribulations. Soaps provided a fantasy outlet for women in situations similar to those being portrayed on screen. Soaps added a new twist in the 1980s and 1990s by presenting new issues in new ways—women at work and women as assertive. Also, in prime-time soaps like *Dallas*, *Dynasty*, and *Melrose Place*, the imagery of women became more complex, involving issues of class, race, and age.

Women in television advertisements, according to a study by Carolyn Lin published in 1999, were largely depicted in traditional roles that did not reflect their realities. In addition advertisements in magazines from the 1950s to the 1970s reflected the idea that a woman's place was mainly in the home, concerned with household tasks or personal beauty. Even advertisements in *Ms.* magazine in the 1990s often portrayed women as sexual objects despite the magazine's policy of refusing to run advertisements demeaning to women.

Class, race, and gender in the mass media worked to establish dominant and universal feminine values; images of women in the mass media portrayed white, middle-class values with women of color in subordinate roles. The subordinate roles for women of color, however, helped to incorporate variants of the universal feminine ideal into popular culture.

ETHNIC WOMEN AND REPRESENTATION

Women of color have a double stigma—that of ethnicity and gender. Stereotypes about women of color change slowly since most mainstream cultures have little exposure to ethnic communities and traditions. Native American and Mexican American women, or Chicanas, in particular, continue to experience misrepresentations of their heritage and gender.

Transforming stereotypical media images of Native American women has come slowly compared with that of other ethnic women. Even though a high interest in Native American cultures in general exists, Native American women are conspicuously absent from film and television. When they have been depicted in film and television, the imagery that defines them has been locked in the past.

From early contact with Europeans, bifurcated images—the good woman and the bad woman—were created about Native American women, usually in relation to men, by white men based on their own preconceptions of indigenous cultures. These men had little contact with Native American cultures. One image is of the "Indian queen," who symbolized the bounty of the Americas by being full-bodied and surrounded by riches. Eventually the queen became the "Indian princess"—gentle, noble, thin, and lighter skinned. The bifurcate, or opposite, of the princess is the squaw—dark, overworked, and squat.

Pocahontas is the most famous of the princess images. Pocahontas, a Powhatan, supposedly saved the life of John Smith, a white man. As a result of her willingness to sacrifice her life for him—and for the new nation—whites coopted her image. The Indian princess stereotype thrived in the 19th century and continued in the 21st century. The 1995 Disney movie *Pocahontas* reinforced the Indian princess image and spread it throughout mainstream culture with a variety of ancillary products including dolls, costumes, games, and books.

After the Civil War, Native Americans played significant though subordinate roles in the popular arts, through Western adventure literature and movies. Civilization encountering savagery, personified by Native Americans, and white frontier expansion are the themes that appeared in dime novels (1860s) and Wild West shows (1880s), according to Robert Berkhofer, Jr. Westerns, which reached their golden age in film in the 1930s through 1950s, featured Native American male characters, but confined women to minor, one-dimensional roles.

Throughout the history of American film, the princess–squaw dichotomy surfaced at various times. The films *Squaw's Sacrifice* (1909) and *Indian Maid's Sacrifice* (1911) both used the princess image. From the 1920s through the 1940s, the princess image declined but resurfaced in the 1950s and beyond with films like *Broken Arrow* (1950), in which a white man (James Stewart) falls in love with and marries an Apache princess, Sonseeahray, or Morning Star, played by Debra Paget. Sonseeahray dies sacrificing herself for peace. The 1960s saw a decline in the princess and squaw images, and movies with Native American characters in the 1970s had few realistic roles for women. In the movies *A Man Called Horse* (1970) and *Little Big Man* (1971) Native American women who were married to whites died, representing the theme of the woman's self-sacrificial death (Bird 1999).

General interest in Native Americans increased in the last four decades of the 20th century. Nevertheless, during this time, complex and realistic portrayals of Native American women did not keep pace with those of Native American men. Two television series, however, *Northern Exposure* and *Dr. Quinn, Medicine Woman*, which were created and produced by a woman, Beth Sullivan, included Native American women as more authentic and credible characters.

Independent Native American filmmakers currently are producing films with more realistic and complex portrayals of Native American women. For example, *Grand Avenue* (1996), an independent film project picked up by Home Box Office, written by Native American Greg Sarris and starring Native American actors, tells the story of three Native American families, including women, realistically dealing with issues of contemporary life. In mainstream television and film an increase in realistic portrayals of women can also be seen. The 1994 film *Lakota Woman: Siege at Wounded Knee* explores the life of a Lakota woman, and the 1998 film *Naturally Native* tells the story of three Native American sisters selling a line of Naturally Native cosmetics.

Like Native American women and other women of color, Mexican American women, or Chicanas, have two dichotomous images: the señorita (the good woman) and the Mexican prostitute (the bad woman). Señoritas are light-skinned, civilized (Christian), and virginal; they give aid or sacrifice themselves so that the white men can live; sometimes white men marry them. Mexican prostitutes are dark-skinned and uncivilized; white men use them for sexual services but do not marry them. These images continued into the 1950s through cowboy folk music, which often portrayed forbidden love between the Anglo cowboy and the Mexican female, according to Antonia I. Castañeda in her essay "Women of Color and the Rewriting of Western History." In Hollywood at this time Mexican American actresses were cast as hot-blooded women of low repute; for example, Lupe Velez, who starred in the movies *Hot Pepper* (1933) and *Strictly Dynamite* (1934).

In the 1980s and 1990s the late Tex-Mex singer Selena with her *Tejano* music altered the image of Chicanas both in the United States and in Mexico. The first Chicana pop musician to become commercially successful, Selena was popular in Mexican American communities across the United States and emulated by many Mexican American girls. While strong, beautiful, and sexy, her image defied that of the prostitute and she did not abandon her identity as a Chicana. The autobiographical movie *Selena* (1997), made after

Selena's untimely death in 1995, was a hit that helped to change the stereotype of the Mexican American women. Mexican actress Selma Hayek also has helped to change the portrayal of Chicanas in the mainstream media, playing Frida Kahlo, a strong Mexican artist, in the film *Frida* (2002). Nevertheless, stereotypes remain. For instance, Puerto Rican American actress Jennifer Lopez (who played Selena in the movie) portrays a Mexican American maid, another stereotype, in the film *Maid in Manhattan* (2002). The Cinderella-style plot has the rich white prince saving the maid from a life of poverty. As with Native American women, realistic images of Chicanas in popular culture have evolved slowly.

Representations of black women in American culture have suffered from similarly unrealistic stereotyping. First via film and then television, imagery characterizing black women has included the mammy, the maid, and the "big bad mama."

Beginning with D. W. Griffiths's *Birth of A Nation* (1915), black women in film were portrayed as "loyal-to-her-master" mammies, who were typically short on intelligence but long on fealty. So ingrained and beloved in the white American psyche was this image that Hattie McDaniel won the Academy Award for her portrayal of Scarlett O'Hara's mammy in *Gone with the Wind* (1939). During the 1930s and 1940s, a more "enlightened" image of the mammy was the maid. Although smart and sassy, this character type still "knew her place." In the early 1950s Dorothy Dandridge was the first black woman in a lead role in a Hollywood film, with her internationally acclaimed performance in the title role of *Carmen Jones* (1954), a contemporary, predominately-black retelling of Georges Bizet's opera *Carmen*. Dandridge seemed poised to make the transition into more realistic portraits of black women and their lives and experiences, but she was ahead of her time.

The 1970s "blaxploitation" film era—when films about blacks were overwrought with melodrama, grit, and crime—introduced the "big bad mama" character into our cultural imagery. In this period black women had lead roles as tough, violent antiheroes. For instance, Pam Grier performed the title role in *Coffy* (1973); in the story she posed as a prostitute in order to wreak revenge on the black pimp and white drug kingpin who had abused her sister. One-dimensional and cartoonlike, such characters, while strong and tough, were as unreal as the mammy and maids that preceded them.

Television initially offered little change, but gradually more realistic imagery crept in. Louise Beavers starred in her own 1960s show *Beulah*, but she was still a maid. Starting in 1968, Diahann Carroll offered a more complex representation of black women: in the lead role in *Julia*, Carroll portrayed a wife, mother, and nurse, thus incorporating a professional dimension to the character. A major step came with role of Clair Huxtable in *The Cosby Show* (1984 premiere). Played by Phylicia Rashad, Clair was an intelligent, independent attorney who was both an equal of her physician husband and a capable and involved mother to her children.

A contemporary phenomenon that is defining for black women—indeed, for all women in the United States—arose with the success of Oprah Winfrey. Winfrey's achievements as an industry tycoon in a medium that is the prime vehicle for mass culture have transformed the cultural perceptions of black women. Her on-air personality—sympathetic listener and supportive friend—may harken back to the maid and mammy roles of her earliest predecessors in film, but as the head of a huge media empire, the reality of her capabilities and power is beyond question.

Along the same lines, Queen Latifah represents the next generation of successful black women in the Oprah mold. As the first million-CD-selling female rap artist, she moved on to become a television executive in charge of her own syndicated show, an actress twice nominated for an Oscar, and a power broker in Hollywood. This younger version of the Oprah success story adds an additional dimension to the imagery of black women in America: while Oprah seems to be "Everywoman," Queen Latifah offers a more specifically black flavor—with her roots in hip-hop—to mass audiences. Whatever the differences, though, between Oprah and Queen Latifah, it seems clear that the days of the subservient and powerless maids and mammies might be long gone.

CONCLUSION

Over the course of history, cultural representations of women have changed gradually, especially for women of color. Despite imagery of women that often reflects the dominant, patriarchal view of them as subservient to men, the representation of women in the mass media and in popular culture, particularly at the start of the 21st century, is dynamic, representing shifting gender, class, and ethnic identities. As the composition of the culture industries changes and more women actively participate in creating mass media, the evolution toward a more realistic representation of all women in popular culture will continue.

—Mary Jo Tippeconnic Fox and
Tom Terrell

BIBLIOGRAPHY

Berkhofer, Robert E., Jr. *The White Man's Indian*. New York: Vintage Books, 1979.

Bird, S. Elizabeth. "Tales of Difference: Representation of American Indian Women in Popular Film and Television." In *Mediated Women Representations in Popular Culture*, edited by Marian Meyers. Cresskill, N.J.: Hampton Press, 1999.

Castañeda, Antonia I. "Women of Color and the Rewriting of Western History: The Discourse, Politics, and Decolonization of History." *Pacific Historical Review* 61 no. 4 (November 1992): 501–533.

Cott, Nancy. "The Modern Woman of the 1920's, American Style." In *A History of Women, Toward a Cultural Identity in the Twentieth Century*, edited by George Duby and Michelle Perrot. Cambridge, Mass.: The Belknap Press of Harvard University Press, 1994.

Dyer, Gillian. "Women and Television: An Overview." In *Women's Studies, Essential Readings*, edited by Stevi Jackson. New York: New York University Press, 1993.

Higonnet, Anne. "Women, Images, and Representation." In *A History of Women, Toward a Cultural Identity in the Twentieth Century*, edited by George Duby and Michelle Perrot. Cambridge, Mass.: Belknap Press of Harvard University Press, 1994.

Kuhn, Annette. "The Power of Image." In *Women's Studies, Essential Readings*, edited by Stevi Jackson. New York: New York University Press, 1993.

Lin, Carolyn. "The Portrayal of Women in Television Advertising." In *Mediated Women Representations in Popular Culture*, edited by Marian Meyers. Cresskill, N.J.: Hampton Press, 1999.

Meyers, Marian. "Fracturing Women." In *Mediated Women Representations in Popular Culture*, edited by Marian Meyers. Cresskill, N.J.: Hampton Press, 1999.

Pribram, E. Deidre. "Female Spectators." In *Women's Studies Essential Readings*, edited by Stevi Jackson. New York: New York University Press, 1993.

Ryan, Michele. "Representations of Women in the Media: Introduction." In *Women's Studies Essential Readings*, edited by Stevi Jackson. New York: New York University Press, 1993.

Tatum, Charles M. *Chicano Popular Culture*. Tucson: University of Arizona Press, 2001.

Tuchman, Gaye, Arlene Kaplan Daniels, and James Benét, eds. *Hearth and Home: Images of Women in Mass Media*. New York: Oxford University Press, 1978.

STATE
HISTORIES

ALABAMA

Maycomb was an old town, but it was a tired old town when I first knew it.
In rainy weather the streets turned to red slop: grass grew on the sidewalks, the courthouse sagged in the
square. Somehow, it was hotter then: a black dog suffered on a summer's day; bony mules hitched to
Hoover carts flicked flies in the sweltering shade of the live oaks in the square. Men's stiff collars wilted
by nine in the morning. . . . People moved slowly then. They ambled across the square, shuffled in and
out of the stores around it, took their time about everything. A day was twenty-four hours long but
seemed longer. There was no hurry, for there was nowhere to go, nothing to buy and no money to buy
it with, nothing to see outside the boundaries of Maycomb County.
—Harper Lee, *To Kill a Mockingbird*, 1960

During the Civil War Alabama was briefly the capital of the Confederacy, and a century later the civil rights movement was centered there owing to the efforts of ROSA PARKS and other women. In 1967 Alabama was the third state to elect a woman as governor, LURLEEN WALLACE; however, she was a surrogate for her segregationist husband, George Wallace.

> State Population (2000): 4,447,100
> Female Population (2000): 2,300,596
> Women in State Legislature (2003): 10%
> Female College Enrollment (1999): 126,000 (56.5% of total)
> Privately Held Women-owned Businesses (1997): 69,515
> First Year of Full Suffrage: 1920

PREHISTORY TO STATEHOOD
(Prehistory–1819)

Alabama's original native population included the Choctaw, Cherokee, Chickasaw, and Muscogee (or Creek), all of whom practiced nonnomadic agriculture. Because women were the primary farmers in these societies, they had a relatively high status. Like many native cultures, these were matrilineal; women were seen as the heads of families and owned what little property was not communal.

Native Americans lived in towns with permanent housing and large ceremonial mounds, and may have done so for as long as 9,000 years prior to the arrival of whites. A Spanish expedition led by

Alonso Alvarez de Pineda in 1519 counted 40 Indian villages in the first six leagues of an inland river, probably the mouth of Mobile Bay. According to Garcellasso de la Vega, a Portuguese man with the 1538 Hernando de Soto expedition, the capital city of Maubila, "consisted of eighty handsome houses,

61

each capacious enough to contain 1,000 men. They fronted on a large public square." (Pickett 1851, 36) The town was surrounded by high walls, giving Maubila an appearance similar to the walled cities of Europe. It was destroyed by de Soto in October 1540, however. When de Soto's expedition finally sailed away in 1543, it took with it 100 Native American slaves, including women.

For over a century Alabama's native tribes lived without another European presence, until the French established a garrison at Mobile Bay in 1702. A few French women were with the 180 soldiers, and just two years later the settlement began importing brides. But because conditions were primitive, Mobile failed to attract large numbers of women. A 1708 census shows just 28 women among the 157 non–Native American inhabitants of Mobile.

The lack of French women pushed many European men into alliances with Native American women. When the British took over Alabama in 1763, after the French and Indian War, they too established many long-term relationships with Native American women. Moreover, despite the white influence toward patriarchy, matrilineal culture remained strong at the end of the 18th century. Women made the decisions about family life, and if a couple broke up it was the man who went home to his mother.

Although much less was recorded about them, African women added to this cultural mix early in Alabama's history. Less than two decades after the French settlement of Mobile Bay, the *Africaine* arrived with 120 Africans. English-speaking women began arriving in Alabama in significant numbers in the 1770s, when many Tory families escaped there from eastern colonies that fell to the Americans. Some Loyalists left for other parts of the British Empire at the end of the American Revolution, but more stayed, and many additional English-speaking women arrived in a steady stream after this new territory officially opened to Americans after the war. Settlement was briefly slowed by the War of 1812,

but by 1815 the British and their allies were finally vanquished. Settlers then poured west, and Alabama became a state in 1819.

Most of these settlers arrived as families, and a census just prior to statehood showed that the area had already passed through the frontier stage of development when there typically were many more men than women. In 1818 there were 9,974 adult white males and 7,549 adult white females in Alabama. The white total was about twice that of black slaves, who were not enumerated by gender or age. In addition Alabama had 339 "free people of color," most of them in Mobile. The total population would not have been enough to meet the requirements imposed on later territories, but because the U.S. Senate was trying to balance votes from slave and free states, Alabama nonetheless became the nation's 22nd state on December 14, 1819.

STATEHOOD TO THE CIVIL WAR (1819–1860)

Missionaries began their work among Native Americans soon after statehood. They observed that women were more willing than men to adjust to white culture. Catherine Brown, for example, was a Creek who not only adopted an English name, but also ran a school for girls in the early 1820s. Perhaps because women had long been the primary farmers, Cherokee women showed much more willingness to grow cotton and live in a cash economy than did Cherokee men. Far more Native American women than men married whites, and some Native American families without any white members emulated white culture by owning black slaves.

Despite this willingness to accommodate whites, land-hungry Americans kept pressuring the government to force the native population out, and, in 1830, Congress passed the Indian Removal Act. Those Native Americans who had not already moved west were forced to do so. Sometimes in chains, women, children, and men walked under armed guard to Oklahoma, and 4,000 of them died along this "Trail of Tears." As tribes were forced out of the southeastern states, white families poured into Alabama. The diary of Sarah Lide Fountain, a young widow who moved from South Carolina in 1835, reflects the experience of these white settlers. When she crossed the Chatahoochee River from Georgia, she wrote that she:

"entered the Indian nation with gloomy feelings. . . . The roads [are] very rough and hilly, oxen failing. . . . Indians so far more civil than I expected. . . . My oxen give out, and little wagon broke down . . . feel very gloomy here in the midst of the Indians, tho' they seem pretty friendly. . . . Several of the Negroes sick, weather cloudy and gloomy." (Griffith 1972, 138)

By the time she reached Montgomery, she felt better, declaring it "quite a splendid looking town," but as the wagon train went on to more primitive western Alabama, her unhappiness returned. When, after more than five weeks of travel, they finally reached their destination, Fountain did not celebrate, but instead wrote, "Oh! how I would rejoice if I were only back to good old Darlington." (Ibid.) Although a minority of the population, the white families who took up the majority of Alabama's good farmland were cotton planters from Virginia and the Carolinas (where they had exhausted the soil). They brought their slaves along, and female slaves labored at felling trees and creating new cotton fields along with the men. White women of the slave-owning class also worked; they were, in effect, management executives, often responsible for all aspects of life for hundreds of people. At a time when any business or governmental activity could not be conducted without travel, men were frequently gone, and women ran the plantations that supported them.

The majority of white women were not of this planter class, but instead were middle-class farmers or working-class people who subsisted

JUDSON FEMALE INSTITUTE

When Alabama's first higher-education institution for women opened in 1839, it did not presume to call itself a college. Its name, however, did reflect an awareness of women's new roles in the world: the Baptist founders named it for Ann Hasseltine Judson of Massachusetts, one of America's first two female foreign missionaries, who had recently died in Burma.

The trustees of the new school, however, were more concerned with assuring parents that their daughters would be carefully cloistered than with any encouragement of similar overseas adventure. Among the many rules set out were:

LETTERS for the pupils should be directed to the care of the Principal. . . [and are] liable to inspection.

No Books, Magazines, or Newspapers to be received, without permission of the Principal.

Nor shall any Boarder receive, either for herself or for any other Pupils, any Letter or Note, Package, or Parcel; any Bouquet of Flowers, any Memento or Token from any unmarried Gentleman, on penalty of expulsion.

The Boarders never leave the grounds of the Institute, without special permission of the PRINCIPAL.

They attend no public parties, and receive no visitors, except such as are introduced by Parents or Guardians.

Monthly Levies are held [and] are attended by members of the Board of Trustees and other married gentlemen with their ladies. They are designed to FORM THE MANNERS of the young ladies.

They are allowed to spend no more than fifty cents each month.

No young lady will be allowed to have money in her own hands; all sums intended for her benefit must be deposited with the STEWARD.

There were, of course, no similar restrictions on the all-male student body at the University of Alabama, which opened in 1831. An analogous document from that era spoke instead of the $20,000 appropriated for the chemistry department and assured professors, all of them male, that none would be paid less than $2,000 annually. While young men had access to the most progressive education possible, young women had to contend with behavioral restrictions in their quest for education.

—Doris Weatherford

Excerpt from Lucille Blanche Griffith, *History of Alabama, 1540–1900*. Northport, Ala.: Colonial Press, 1962.

on crops grown in the poor soil of the state's northern hills. Most emulated the upper class, however, in their desire to become slaveholders, and they willingly supported the Confederacy when the Civil War came.

Most were also illiterate, for public education did not exist. By the 1850s, however, Alabama had several private boarding schools for upper-class women, including the Judson Female Institute in Marion, the East Alabama Female College in Tuskegee, and the Female Collegiate Institution in Lafayette. Similar schools existed at Moulton and Athens.

CIVIL WAR ERA
(1860–1880)

Most women supported the Confederacy and assumed that the war would end quickly. Instead, they spent the next four years attempting to maintain their homes and support their military.

Unlike northern women, few Alabamans traveled outside their states as nurses. Southern mores still resisted the idea of allowing women to see male bodies, and when KATE CUMMING left Mobile in 1862 to serve as a nurse with the Army of the Tennessee, it was over the objections of her family. She went on to organize dozens of temporary hospitals throughout the South, while Mobile's JULIET OPIE HOPKINS made a great reputation for herself as a Richmond hospital administrator. Robert E. Lee, in fact, wrote to Hopkins, "You have done more for the South than all the women of the Confederacy." (Sterkx 1970, 121)

These women were exceptions, however. The first nurses were not ideological supporters of the war, but Sisters of Charity. They opened hospitals soon after the war began in Mobile and Montgomery, and one historian has said that these nuns—often the object of great prejudice in that time and place—were "the only women in the South possessing a modicum of nursing experience." (Ibid.)

"DON'T FORGET TO PRAY": A CIVIL WAR WOMAN WRITES

Malinda and Grant Taylor, who lived in the hills of northern Alabama, wrote to each other almost weekly from 1862, when Grant entered the Confederate army as a 34-year-old private, to the war's end in 1865. The Taylors were not slave owners and did not support the war politically. Both the North and South drafted soldiers, however, and although the Taylors tried, they could not afford to pay another man to go in Grant's place (a practice that both sides allowed).

A portion of a letter from August 1862 shows how matters both large and small occupied the minds of women left to manage alone. Malinda Taylor had four children; a private's pay was next to nothing; and she had to run their farm—which she nonetheless refers to as his land. It also shows that, although the war was less than a year old, many of their friends and neighbors were dying.

> Grant you have heard of the death of Daddy. Don't grieve after him. I staid all night with Lucreta [a newly widowed sister-in-law] last Monday night. She has given me a heep of troubble.
>
> I saw Mr. Loftin last Saturday. He tolde me a heep about you.
>
> Mary Taylor is staying with me now to dry peaches. I have got 2 bushels and a half dried. They air selling for $5 a bushel in Tus. [Tuscaloosa] I am going to send a bushel up thare Tuesday.
>
> Mem Jacobs is dead. Preacher Roberson is dead. Jim Stags is dead and Narcis Wier and Jim Bensons little girl is dead.
>
> I saw Wick last Sunday. He thinks he wants to come and live on your land. Grant it wont do and I want you to oppose it in your next [letter] to me. His family is on sufferance. You weigh the matter and you will se it wont do. My horses will have his riding to do. The wagon and steers all the hauling to do. Grant it wont do.

At the end of the letter, Malinda tells Grant that she had dreamed of his homecoming the previous night, and she put more emphasis on trying "to bee contented with your lot." Her final words were "don't forget to pray."

—Doris Weatherford

Excerpts from Ann K. Blomquist, and Robert A. Taylor, eds. *This Cruel War: The Civil War Letters of Grant and Malinda Taylor, 1862–1865*. Macon, Ga.: Mercer University Press, 2000.

Similarly Alabamans had little industrial experience, and the munitions and supplies that the state could offer its troops were pitifully poor compared with those of Union soldiers. Some 80 young women worked in munitions manufacture at Selma and Gainesville, and a few hundred were employed in textile production before Union soldiers burned their factories. Most of Alabama women's support for the military came from humble kitchens and sewing rooms.

Almost every town developed a women's organization that sent goods to the front, with the Montgomery's Ladies Aid Association being the largest and most productive. Interestingly both Montgomery and Mobile had a Hebrew Ladies Soldiers' Aid Society. The work these groups did is exemplified by an 1861 letter from the Cahaba Ladies Military Aid Society, which showed that the women sent more than 30 types of goods to soldiers, ranging from underwear to brandy and lobster.

Resistance to Union raiders made some women into local celebrities. Celia and Winne Mae Murphee, for example, became local heroes in 1863 when they served mint juleps laced with a sleep inducement to Union raiders. When the men fell asleep, the sisters took their weapons and turned them over to Confederates. In the same year 15-year-old Emma Samsom helped Gen. Nathan Forrest find a shortcut through the woods that enabled his cavalry to ambush Union troops.

As late as the spring of 1865, however, two-thirds of the state had not been invaded. The important battles were fought elsewhere, and when Union forces finally arrived in great numbers and it became clear that the cause was lost, Alabamans put up little resistance. When Mobile fell on April 10, most of the city's civilians had already fled, and Montgomery—once the proud Confederate capital—surrendered without a fight two days later. The Union victory, of course, brought freedom to Alabama's slaves.

A Young Slave Woman's Experience

Jenny Proctor, age 15 at emancipation, later reflected on her experiences as a slave. She had toiled in the cotton fields since age 10, and before that she had tended younger children. "I's hear tell of them good slave days," she said, "but I ain't never seen no good times then." She bore scars all her life from punishment she endured when she ate a biscuit that she found. Her mistress first hit her with a broom, and then the overseer used a whip; after Jenny fell "to the floor nearly dead, he cut my back all to pieces, then they rubs salt in the cuts for more punishment. . . . "Lord, Lord," she summarized, "it seems impossible that any of us ever lived to see that day of freedom, but thank God we did."

—Doris Weatherford

Excerpts from Federal Writers' Project, *Slave Narratives: Alabama.* Vol. 5. 1937. Reprint, St. Clair Shores, Mich.: Scholarly Press, 1976.

Some slave owners were so bitter about the loss of their human property that a few—like some Loyalists after the American Revolution—left the country. They headed for Central and South America, but because these Catholic nations had already outlawed slavery, there was little to be gained. Most plantation owners, however, had neither the funds nor the desire to do this, and instead they developed a sharecropper system similar to the vassal system of medieval Europe. Although legally free, most former slaves were returned to a slavelike existence through continual debts to the landowning class. Iron mines around Birmingham inspired its development as an industrial city in the 1870s, but much of Alabama remained a nearly feudal society until well into the 20th century.

Suffrage and Progressive Eras (1880–1920)

As late as 1900, 80 percent of Alabamans still lived in rural areas. One result of such isolation was a dearth of organizations for women. Unlike the North, for example, ladies' missionary societies did not begin in Alabama until the 1870s. By the 1880s, however, they were flourishing, as were the beginnings of secular women's clubs. The Alabama Federation of Women's Clubs began in 1895, when nine literary clubs from throughout the state met in Birmingham. As in other states, the clubs' original purpose of self-education soon turned to civic good, and they worked for compulsory education, penal reform, libraries, and other causes.

An Alabama branch of the Women's Christian Temperance Union (WCTU) formed in Tuscaloosa in 1884. When a Birmingham newspaper editor suggested in 1885 that the WCTU could more realistically advance its goals if women had the vote, the indignant women formally responded that they were "not ready to ask for any political favors." The only indication of any support for suffrage in the state was one line in an 1883 report of the National Woman Suffrage Association: "At Huntsville lives Mrs. Priscilla Holmes Drake, whose name has stood as representative [from Alabama] since 1868." (Stanton, Anthony, and Gage 1886, 3:830)

In the next decades JULIA STRUDWICK TUTWILER was Alabama's most visibly progressive woman. Educated in the North and in Europe, she returned home and crusaded for causes ranging from kindergarten to prisons. She lobbied the legislature for years before getting a $2,500 appropriation to create the Alabama Normal College for Girls, a teacher training school, in 1883. "Miss Julia," as she was known all of her life, also developed the state's first vocational school for girls, but neither she nor any other woman was allowed to sit on its board of directors. Tutwiler also found time to be elected president of the elementary education division of the National Education Association in 1891, and she was a force in the 1892 admission of women to "every course, technical, scientific, and agricultural" at the Alabama Polytechnic College in Auburn. (Anthony and Harper 1902, 4:468)

The prestigious University of Alabama, founded in 1831, was a bigger challenge, but Tutwiler wore down the resistance of the all-male trustees. She carefully coached the ten young women who entered, and at the end of their first year these women won two-thirds of the honors awarded in a class of several hundred. Nonetheless, registration for the 1893–1894 year spelled out that female students would be treated differently: "Women of not less than 18 years of age, who are able to stand the necessary examinations, may be admitted to the Sophomore class, or any higher class of the University. Board and lodging can be had by them in the best families. A study room on the campus at the residence of Mrs. A. G. Gorgas has been provided for their use during the day." (Griffith 1962, 419)

These institutions were intended only for whites, but women also played leading roles in the success of schools for African Americans. Tuskegee Institute (now Tuskegee University), founded in 1881 and long led by Booker T. Washington, became Alabama's most famous. Like most such schools, it was coeducational, but the curriculum differed by gender: male students learned agriculture and mechanical skills, while female students worked at sewing and other domestic skills. Female students also had a nationally known leader in their president's wife, MARGARET MURRAY WASHINGTON, who organized the Alabama Federation of Colored Women's Clubs in 1899; three years earlier she had been a founder of the National Association of Colored Women. Finally, Tuskegee owed a great deal of its success to Emily Howland, a white woman of Cayuga County, New York, who endowed it and other schools. Howland visited Tuskegee often.

Tuskegee women had a particularly fine role model in Dr. HALLE DILLON, who in 1891 became Alabama's first woman of either race to pass the state's licensing exam for physicians.

Patty Malone also was a successful African American woman of this era. She was 12 at emancipation, and her Athens owners were so impressed by her natural talent as a contralto that they sent her to music school. Her long singing career included an 1896 European tour with the Jubilee Singers.

In 1892 seven women met in Decatur to organize a suffrage association. They were motivated by a newspaper discussion, and a second group soon began in the town of Verbena. In 1893 the National American Woman Suffrage Association opened an Alabama chapter. Thus there was a nascent organization to welcome Susan B. Anthony and Carrie Chapman Catt when they toured the South in conjunction with the national association's 1895 convention in Atlanta.

Although Alabama's white suffragists viewed the opposition to suffrage as prohibitive, the women made important legislative progress in other areas, including complex changes to laws on the property rights of married women. The most significant change was won in 1897, when the women succeeded in getting the legislature to raise the "age of consent"—the age at which a man could claim that a "woman" had consented to sex—from age 10 to 14.

Other women's organizations began operating in the state at the turn of the 20th century. In 1907 the Women's Christian Temperance Union played a major role in making the state "the driest in the Union." Wearing white ribbons, they marched through the capital singing "Onward Christian Soldiers" on their way to the governor's office, where they furnished the silver pen that he used to outlaw alcoholic beverages anywhere in the state. Women affiliated with the General Federation of Women's Clubs (GFWC) were more affluent and less likely to be prohibitionists, but they became activists in this era as well, especially for improved education and "traveling libraries," an early form of the

ALABAMA LEGAL PROVISION REGARDING WOMEN, 1900

That there were great needs in regard to the legal status of women in 1900 was made clear in Alabama's suffragists' report to the National American Woman Suffrage Association in that year. The state's legal code viewed women as perpetual children, excusing them from some punishments, but also depriving them of basic rights. Among the legal provisions of 1900 detailed in this report were these:

If a woman commits a crime in partnership with her husband (except murder or treason) she can not be punished.

Common law marriage is valid and the legal age for a girl is fourteen years.

The father is the guardian of the minor children, and at his death may appoint a guardian to the exclusion of the mother. If this is not done she becomes the legal guardian of the girls till they are eighteen, of the boys till fourteen.

Alabama is one of the few states that do not by law require the husband to support the family.

The convicted father of an illegitimate child must pay [$500 over ten years] to the Probate Court. Failing to do this, he is sentenced to hard labor for the county for one year.

It is a criminal offense to use foul language to or in the hearing of a woman, or to take a woman of notorious character to any public place for respectable women.

A seducer is sent to the penitentiary if his victim has been chaste.

—Doris Weatherford

Excerpt from Susan B. Anthony, and Ida Husted Harper, *History of Woman Suffrage.* Vol. 4. Indianapolis, Ind.: Hollenbeck Press, 1902.

bookmobile. That women were hungry for such civic involvement is clear from the clubs' explosive growth: the Alabama GFWC grew from nine clubs in 1895 to 53 in 1900.

Although state law banned women from most professions, they were allowed to toil in mills and factories. Textile mills, which had developed early in the nation's history in the Northeast, discovered that they could improve profits by moving south to take advantage of nonunion labor. In the late 19th and early 20th centuries, many mills moved to southern states, where their primary labor force was white women. Most were happy to have the work, which was a more reliable source of family income than subsistence agriculture.

Few African American women got these jobs; their horizons were limited to domestic work in white women's homes. As in other southern states, it was difficult to break out of these employment constraints, for few tax-supported services existed for African Americans. Very often it was African American women who undertook raising the funds to build educational and social service facilities. In Birmingham, for instance, Carrie Tuggle cared for homeless African American children, and in 1903 she finally managed to open an orphanage, though it was limited to boys.

A few African American women in Alabama aligned themselves with the suffrage movement— something that required them to stand up to both white suffragists, who resisted their involvement, and to the majority of black men, who were indifferent and even hostile to this cause. African American ADELLA HUNT LOGAN, a longtime leader at Tuskegee Institute and the founder of its Woman's Club, became a life member of the nearly all-white National American Woman Suffrage Association in 1900, and she also led the suffrage work of the National Association of Colored Women. Although she had met Susan B. Anthony, Julia Ward Howe, and other luminaries, Logan was not acknowledged by Alabama's white suffragists, and her name does not appear in their reports to the national association.

Moreover the first legislative action of Alabama's suffrage league was unlike that of most Americans; instead it resembled the strategies of aristocratic European suffragists, who tied their right to vote directly to their status as property owners. In a 1902 revision of the state constitution, Alabama women with more than $500 worth of property were granted the vote— but only on tax referenda. However, even this small gain had only a 24-hour legislative life before it was repealed. In the end, women were worse off than before: In the pages of the *History of Woman Suffrage*, Birmingham's PATTIE RUFFNER JACOBS lamented that the legislature had "not only refused to grant suffrage to taxpaying women, but it gave to the husbands of tax-payers the right to vote upon their wives' property!" (Harper 1922, 6:1)

"Bitterly disappointed," as Jacobs said, the movement was largely dormant for the next decade. The three-nominee presidential election of 1912, however, energized politicians everywhere, and the Alabama Equal Suffrage Association (AESA) was formally organized on October 9, 1912. They chose six delegates to the national convention the next month in Philadelphia, and they even sent a delegate to the International Woman Suffrage Alliance in Budapest the following year.

Jacobs was president of the AESA during its entire existence, and she organized 81 affiliated suffrage groups between 1912 and 1917. In 1915 the legislature was forced to give women their first formal hearing on a resolution to add a suffrage clause to the state constitution. The measure passed by a 52–43 vote, but this was not enough to meet the constitutional mandate of two-thirds of the legislature. Moreover, because Alabama's legislature met only once every four years, the issue could not be taken up again until 1919.

Far from giving up, suffragists organized in support of a national amendment. They raised more than $10,000, paid a field organizer, sent out regular press releases, held parades, organized a Men's Committee, and maintained a Selma headquarters. They brought in national leaders, including the Rev. Dr. Anna Howard Shaw, and soon had affiliates in 55 of the state's 67 counties.

Despite all of this support for suffrage, however, when the federal amendment finally passed, just 1 of Alabama's 12 congressional representatives voted for it. Undaunted, Jacobs led the Alabama women in a campaign for legislative ratification. The speakers she recruited included the state chairman of the Democratic party and the chief justice of the Alabama Supreme Court.

Meanwhile, the opposition also organized, and the Southern Women's Anti-Ratification League was born in Montgomery in June 1919. These "women of wealth and social standing," as Jacobs called them, included Marie Bankhead Owen, the daughter of a powerful U.S. senator. More than a half-century after the Civil War, these women still saw that conflict as the central issue, and their resolution assured legislators that "we look with confidence to you to protect us from this device of northern Abolitionists." (Ibid., 6:7n)

Suffragists crowded into the capital on July 17, 1919, but by a 13–19 margin the state Senate refused to ratify and the issue was dead. When Alabama women got the vote in August of the next year, Jacobs reminded the conservative women that they could vote now only because this precious right had been won for them by outsiders. Making the point visible, Alabama suffragists hired a brass band and paraded through Birmingham streets with 36 automobiles to honor the 36 states that had made it possible for them to vote.

1920s THROUGH WORLD WAR II ERA (1920–1950)

Although the boom years of the 1920s brought relatively little change to this historically poor state, some women served as models of the era's "new woman." The very personification of the era's "flapper" was Zelda Sayre, whose southern charms attracted her future husband, writer F. Scott Fitzgerald. Tallulah Bankhead, daughter of

THE ROLE OF EUNICE RIVERS-LAURIE IN THE TUSKEGEE SYPHILIS STUDY

Born to poor Georgia sharecroppers in 1899, Eunice Rivers-Laurie graduated from the Tuskegee Institute's nursing school in 1923. Rivers-Laurie is most often remembered for her role as a public health nurse attached to the United States Public Health Service (USPHS) Study of Untreated Syphilis in the Negro Male, commonly known as the Tuskegee Syphilis Study. Now regarded as an example of unethical medical experimentation, the study documented the pathological effects of syphilis by monitoring its progress in 399 infected African American men between 1932 and 1972.

From 1930 to 1965 white USPHS doctors relied on Rivers-Laurie, an African American, as their liaison to the test subjects. A respected caregiver, her work among poor rural blacks helped her establish trusting relationships with the men and their families. Rivers-Laurie monitored the men's whereabouts and assisted doctors in gathering and examining the men each year. She also ensured that the men never received any treatment for their syphilis. As each man died of syphilis, syphilis-related complications, or of other causes, Rivers-Laurie persuaded the man's family to consent to an autopsy.

Why Rivers-Laurie would facilitate an unethical study tainted by race and class prejudice has puzzled many commentators. The professional subordination of nurses to doctors' orders had some effect in shaping Rivers-Laurie's actions, as did being a black woman working under white male doctors in the segregated South. Although the men did not receive treatment for syphilis, Rivers-Laurie believed that the aspirin, iron tonic, and checkups they did receive represented far more medical care than what was available to their neighbors. The net effect of these forces allowed Rivers-Laurie to say in 1977, "I don't think it was a racist experiment." She died in 1986 never having changed her mind.

—Gregory Michael Dorr

Alabama's longtime U.S. senator William Bankhead, was celebrated on international stages in the 1920s, and in the next decade her sultry drawl was a major moneymaker for Hollywood

"I Didn't Let This Coward Me Down": A Black Woman Overcomes

The Federal Writers' Project was a New Deal program that gave employment to writers who could not otherwise sell their work during the Great Depression. One result was that these writers interviewed the descendents of former slaves. Mrs. Rhusses L. Perry of Tuskegee was the only black writer employed by the Alabama office of the Federal Writers' Project—and she was hired late in 1938 only after much pressure from Washington. What follows is the life story of Janey Leonard as told to Mrs. Perry:

I was born right here in this community in 1876. My parents were farmers and always worked hard. My dad was brought here from Georgia a slave. Right here on this spot my dad and mother bought 320 acres which belonged to the white people to whom my parents had been slaves. . . .

I was only fifteen when I married the first time. I married Henry McBride. My life was shocked by a mob who lynched him. A man was found dead and they suspicioned that my husband did it. They had his trial but the jury split on it. So the side that wanted him hung took him and lynched him.

I didn't let this coward me down. I decided to work and try to make a mark in life. Booker T. Washington would go round lecturing to farmers. I took this in and profited by it. When he would send county agents around I always cooperated with them and I always found that they could help us in our farm problems.

I made a sad mistake when I married my second husband. His name was John Leonard. . . . We had only one room and a dirt floor kitchen. But I had seen over to Tuskegee the nice toilets [outhouses] and I wanted one so I tore down an old shed and built a toilet. I was the first in my community.

I kept on trying to make little additions to the home and trying to fix it so it would look attractive and this made my husband mad. He treated me so bad that I just went to court and asked for a divorce. Well, the court gave him everything. . . . I did have forty acres of land my father left for me. But I did not have a mule or nothing to start my farm on the following year. When the deacons asked my husband why we parted, he said, "She's just too damned high-minded. She wants too much."

I had a son [from the McBride marriage] in Cincinnati, Ohio. He decided to come down and help me on the farm. This was in 1918. We made eight bales of cotton. This helped me to pay the debt of $1,011.75 and to buy back the forty acres which the court gave my husband. I did a lots of peddling and working at night. I was so anxious to pay my debts and start fixing up my home that I had one dress for Sunday and one pair of slippers which I bought for fifty cents. I went to church and was not shamed.

Mrs. Laura Daily and Mr. Robert Thurston was demonstrators at this time [federally paid home economists–agriculturists] and they taught me how to do proper terracing and to plant winter cover crops which has improved my land so very much. Mrs. Daily helped me with the plans for this new home which I am in now. I have gladly followed the plans of the government ever since. The government is making it possible for us to enjoy electricity and pump system of running water. God bless the Roosevelts. Theodore Roosevelt gave farmers rural [mail] delivery and then comes F. D. Roosevelt and gives the farmer the joy of bright lights and running water. If I did vote I surely would vote for Roosevelt.

—Doris Weatherford

Excerpt from Federal Writers' Project, *Slave Narratives: Alabama.* Vol. 5. 1937. Reprint, St. Clair Shores, Mich.: Scholarly Press, 1976.

studios. Another Alabama native who became internationally famous in this era was HELEN KELLER. Deaf and blind due to an early childhood fever, she left her Tuscumbia birthplace to be educated in Massachusetts, and by the 1920s she had grown into an independent woman who was an advocate not only for the disabled, but also for other, more controversial, causes.

In 1922 Amelia Worthington Fisk became the first woman on the state Democratic Executive Committee, an important position at that place and time. Much more significant, though, was that Hattie Hooker Wilkins of Selma was elected to the state legislature in 1922, though she served just one term. Another decade would pass before Alabama elected a second woman to its legislature—Sybil Pool of Linden served three terms, beginning in 1936. After she left the House, Alabama would not have any women in its legislature until the 1960s.

Suffrage leader Pattie Ruffner Jacobs also continued to be a model. With the support of her businessman husband, Solon Jacobs, she became the first national secretary of the new League of Women Voters (founded in 1920), and she also received impressive appointments in the traditionally male political world. Jacobs was Alabama's first woman on the National Democratic Committee, an extremely powerful position in what was then a thoroughly Democratic state.

The Great Depression brought such abject poverty that many Alabamans lived in what today would be considered Third World conditions, and famine-associated diseases such as pellagra and beriberi appeared in both blacks and whites. Washington once again called on Pattie Jacobs. She was appointed the state's director of the Woman's Division of the National Recovery Administration (NRA). She was in charge of the thousands of jobs that the NRA created, and was also Alabama's representative on the powerful Tennessee Valley Authority (TVA).

It was in fact the TVA that finally transformed Alabama from a sharecropping economy to a modern one. The TVA's construction of dams on the Tennessee River and its tributaries was especially important, for they not only prevented spring floods that could have washed away good topsoil, but they also made it possible to produce electricity. During the 1930s and 1940s, the TVA brought electricity to millions of southern women who, well into the 20th century, were still scrubbing their laundry on washboards and heating their irons on wood stoves.

African American Sue Berta Coleman never received the prestigious appointments that Jacobs did, but she did similar work among African American women. Educated at Tennessee's Fisk University, she also studied social work in Chicago with the internationally known Jane Addams. Coleman was employed as a home economist and social worker by the U.S. Steel Corporation in its Bessemer community, and during the Great Depression she led federally funded New Deal programs.

The 1930s brought other milestones. Although two other Birmingham women were credentialed physicians when Dr. Louise Branscomb opened her practice there in 1931, she soon became the state's most successful female physician. After graduating from Woman's College of Alabama in Montgomery, she went on to New York City's prestigious Barnard College and then to Baltimore's Johns Hopkins Medical School. After overcoming prejudices to build her practice, Dr. Branscomb courageously risked it by

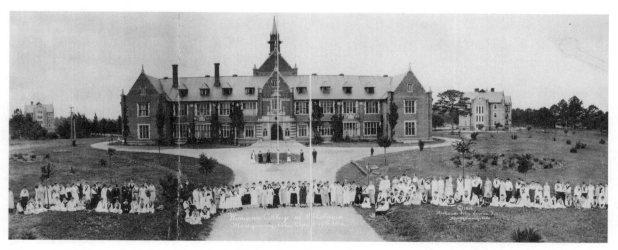

Woman's College of Alabama in 1918. The college boasted many important graduates, including Dr. Louise Branscomb. (Library of Congress)

volunteering at birth-control clinics and treating venereal disease patients of both races.

DIXIE BIBB GRAVES became a U.S. senator in this era, not through her own work but because of her husband's position. The aristocratic Bibb family stretched back to Alabama's colonial days, and her husband (who was also her cousin) was the governor in 1937, when a vacancy occurred in the U.S. Senate. Governor Graves was widely criticized for appointing his wife to the office, and she went on to create more negative national headlines when she spoke against a federal antilynching bill as an invasion of states' rights. Florence Reville Gibbs followed Graves's precedent in 1940–1941, when she served out the last months of her husband's term in the U.S. Senate.

The 1940s and World War II, however, brought other progressive changes. Alabama women met women from other states who were serving at the military bases that the state's powerful congressmen brought to Alabama, and local women also found well-paid jobs there. Munitions plants, in particular, hired women, who were thought to be more careful than men.

The war effort resulted in a critical need for child care. The federal Children's Bureau, for example, reported that one Alabama community with 156 working mothers of 167 preschool children had no such facility. The person to deal with such problems was Alabama's commissioner of public welfare, Loula Dunn. An outstanding sociologist, Dunn was also the first female executive director of the American Public Welfare Association. She went to Europe near the war's end at the specific request of the British government.

Coastal Alabama's shipyards were especially important to the war effort, and federal officials ensured an adequate labor supply by forcing them to hire minorities. Thousands of women got these jobs in Mobile shipyards, especially as riveters.

However, while shipyards and other employers were likely to employ white women and African American men, they rarely took the final step of including African American women.

POSTWAR AND CONTEMPORARY ERAS (1950–present)

During the 1950s and 1960s, Alabama became a center of the civil rights movement. It was there that the symbolic act precipitating the movement took place. On December 1, 1955, Rosa Parks, tired after a long day of work, refused to give up her bus seat to a white man. Police took her from the bus, arrested and jailed her, and Parks's action gave young Martin Luther King, Jr., the catalyst for the Birmingham bus boycott, which began the first massive resistance to segregation.

The very next year another Alabama woman did something equally heroic but much less well known. Prior to any black man, young AUTHERINE

Rosa Parks on her arrival at the Montgomery courthouse for the bus boycott trial in 1956. She is standing with E. D. Nixon, one-time president of Alabama's chapter of the NAACP. (AP/Wide World Photos)

LUCY successfully filed suit in federal court for the right to study library science at the University of Alabama. When she tried to enroll on February 3, 1956, a mob of a thousand assailed her. Male university officials were cowed by the rioters, and their response was to suspend Lucy three days later. She went back to court, and with Thurgood Marshall, future Supreme Court justice, as the lawyer assigned by the NAACP, again won. Soon afterward, though, the university expelled her over a questionable technical violation of school rules. This time, neither Marshall nor the NAACP supported her, and Lucy's case died. Decades later, in the same graduation ceremony as her daughter, she finally received the master's degree that she had long sought.

Throughout the civil rights movement, CORETTA SCOTT KING stood courageously by her husband, Dr. Martin Luther King, Jr., as he fought for equal rights. Following his assassination in 1968 she dedicated her life to continuing the struggle.

In 1960 an Alabama woman awakened the nation's conscience on race, Nelle Harper Lee called herself "HARPER LEE" when her novel *To Kill a Mockingbird* was published. The book won the Pulitzer Prize—the first to go to a woman in 19 years—and was also made into an award-winning movie. The best-seller was based on an actual case in Lee's hometown, Monroeville, and yet its author, who is white, continued to live there almost anonymously after the book's publication.

Racism came to a head on Sunday, September 15, 1963, when dynamite exploded in a Birmingham Sunday school, killing four African American girls. Addie Mae Collins, Cynthia Wesley, and Carole Robertson were 14 years old, and Denise McNair was only 11. White supremacists within the FBI apparently withheld documents that would have convicted their killers, and it was not until 2001 that the white men responsible

TIMELINE

United States Events		Alabama Events
	1500	
		1540 Hernando De Soto expedition, including at least two Spanish women, arrives in Alabama.
	1600	
1620 Settlement of Plymouth Colony		
	1700	
		1702 The French establish a garrison at Mobile Bay that includes several women.
1776 United States declares independence		
	1800	
		1819 Alabama achieves statehood.
		1838 The Cherokee are relocated to Oklahoma along the Trail of Tears.
1861–65 U.S. Civil War		1893 The University of Alabama permits female students to enroll.
1914–18 World War I	1900	
1920 Ratification of the 19th Amendment to the U.S. Constitution		
		1922 Hattie Hooker Wilkins becomes the first female elected to Alabama's legislature. Amelia Worthington Fisk becomes the first woman on the state Democratic Executive Committee.
1929–39 Great Depression		1936 Sybil Pool is the second woman elected to the Alabama state legislature.
		1937 Dixie Bibb Graves is appointed the first female U.S. senator from Alabama, completing Hugo Black's term.
1939–45 World War II		1955 Rosa Parks refuses to give up her seat on a Montgomery bus.
		1956 Autherine Lucy becomes the first African American to enroll at the University of Alabama.
		1966 Lurleen Wallace is the first woman elected governor of Alabama.
1975 Vietnam War ends		1983 Ann Bedsole becomes the first woman elected to the Alabama state Senate.
		1993 Alabama creates the Women's Hall of Fame.
	2000	2003 10% of state legislators are women.

for the crime who were still alive were found guilty of the murders. A similar delay in justice also benefited the white men who killed Viola Gregg Liuzzo. A white, 38-year-old Michigan mother of five, Liuzzo was shot on March 25, 1965, while participating in the civil rights march from Selma to Montgomery.

The year after Liuzzo's killing, Alabama became the third state to choose a woman as governor. Like Sen. Dixie Bibb Graves, however, Lurleen Wallace was her husband's personal surrogate. When popular segregationist George Wallace was unable to run for reelection in 1966 because of term limits, his wife ran in his stead. Elected at age 39, she died of cancer less than three years later.

Alabama's third and fourth women in Congress, like the first two, were appointed by the governor to fill vacancies. Elizabeth Bullock Andrews quietly served out her husband's House term in 1972–1973, but MARYON PITTMAN ALLEN was more active. An established journalist when she married the lieutenant governor in 1964, she continued to write and televise news. When her husband, then a U.S. senator, died in 1978, Gov. George Wallace appointed her to replace him. She intended to go on to election in her own right, but her negative comments about Wallace killed her chances with the Alabama electorate.

As elsewhere the 1970s brought dramatic change for women, reflected in the Alabama legislature. Eight women won seats in that decade—compared with four during the five previous decades—including the first black woman, civil rights leader Louphenia Thomas of Birmingham, and the first Republican woman, Ann Bedsole of Mobile. In 1983 Bedsole went on to become the first woman in the state Senate—more than 60 years after women began voting. After a court-ordered special election that same year, teacher Frances Strong of Demopolis, a Democrat, also joined the Senate.

Election to high office is a particularly objective way of measuring the status of women, and in 2003 Alabama had yet to elect a woman to Congress: all those who served were appointed (except Elizabeth Andrews who served out her husband's term in the House). In 2003 approximately 10% of the state legislators were women. The state began bringing public attention to other noteworthy women in 1993 with the creation of the Alabama Women's Hall of Fame. Located at historic Judson College, some 50 significant Alabama women are commemorated there.

—Doris Weatherford

PROMINENT WOMEN

MARYON PITTMAN ALLEN (1925–)

Interior designer Maryon Pittman Allen of Meridian, Mississippi, is one of three women who have served Alabama in the U.S. Senate. After attending Alabama public schools and graduating from the University of Alabama in 1947, she launched her career as a journalist, editor, fashion and food commentator, and public speaker. She won numerous awards for her essays in the *Birmingham News* and *McCall's*, and in 1974 Pres. Gerald Ford named Allen to chair the Blair House Fine Arts Commission. In 1978 she was appointed to fill the unexpired term of her deceased husband, Sen. James Browning Allen. After a bid for renomination failed that same year, she served as advertising and public relations director for C. G. Sloan & Company Auction House and as a partner in Mountain Lake Farms, the Emerald Valley Corporation, and the J. D. Pittman Tractor Company. She also began writing a syndicated column, "Reflections of a News Hen," for the *Washington Post*.

KATE CUMMING (1835–1909)

Kate Cumming devoted herself to the care of the Army of the Tennessee during the Civil War. After her parents emigrated from Scotland to Mobile, she involved herself with local issues and opposed slavery. Influenced by the example of Florence Nightingale in the Crimean War, Cumming ignored her parents' orders and enlisted as a military nurse in 1862. Despite charges that true ladies did not volunteer for nursing, she superintended a series of mobile medical setups, beginning with a makeshift hospital in the Tishomingo Hotel at a railroad junction in Corinth, Mississippi. Cumming's devotion to the South is evident in an incisive Civil War memoir, *A Journal of Hospital Life in the Confederate Army of Tennessee from the Battle of Shiloh to the End of the War* (1866), which chronicles the gradual decline of supplies and food as the South lost the war. On a mission to Georgia's notoriously overcrowded Andersonville Prison, she observed the filthy, starved, and physically debilitated Union inmates. In pity, she wrote, "May heaven help us all! But war is terrible." She defended the southern staff against charges that it had abused Union prisoners by attesting to the privations of all Georgians. In retirement in Birmingham, she joined the United Daughters of the Confederacy and tended army graves.

HALLE DILLON (1864–1901)

Physician Halle Tanner Dillon Johnson of Pittsburgh, Pennsylvania, was the first woman doctor licensed by the state of Alabama. The daughter of a Methodist minister and a teacher, she wrote for the *Christian Recorder*, which her father edited. Widowed in her mid-20s, she decided to study medicine and became the only African American student at Woman's Medical College of Pennsylvania. When she pursued a medical license in Alabama, the local media exploited her ten-day test with headlines and debate over the issue of whether women should practice medicine.

In 1891 educator Booker T. Washington appointed Dillon as the first campus physician of Tuskegee Institute, a respected black college in Alabama. While attending to student health needs, she supervised the health department, taught hygiene classes, and maintained a dispensary. In addition to treating patients from the surrounding community, she encouraged young women by establishing the institute's nurse training school. She died in childbirth at age 37.

DIXIE BIBB GRAVES (1883–1965)

Alabama's first female U.S. senator, Dixie Bibb Graves was the fourth female in the U.S. Senate. Born on a plantation in Montgomery County, Alabama, she was intelligent and well informed, and she disarmed others through courtesy and southern gentility. Graves learned goal setting and negotiation through membership in the Alabama Historical Society, the United Daughters of the Confederacy, the Daughters of the American Revolution, the American Red Cross, the American Legion Auxiliary, literary and women's clubs, and missionary societies. She represented the National Foundation for Infantile Paralysis and served as a trustee of the Alabama Boys' Industrial School and a director on the board of ultra-conservative Bob Jones University.

Graves crusaded for temperance and literacy, and also presided over the Alabama branch of the League of Women's Voters, a nonpartisan organization established in 1920 by Carrie Chapman Catt to encourage women to inform themselves on issues and participate at all levels of government. Graves's personal campaigns centered on child labor and humanitarian aid to the disadvantaged. Her husband, Gov. David Bibb Graves, appointed her to complete the unexpired term of Sen. Hugo Black, who had been appointed to the U.S. Supreme Court, in 1937. She served in the Senate for three months, but did not seek election to another term.

JULIET OPIE HOPKINS (1818–1890)

One of the many American volunteers who staffed hospitals during and after the Civil War, Juliet Ann Opie Hopkins of Jefferson County, Virginia, earned a reputation for battlefield nursing. In 1837 she married Commodore Alexander Gordon, but was widowed 12 years later. In 1854 she married Judge Arthur Francis Hopkins of Mobile, Alabama, and disposed of their land to raise money for the Confederacy. At the beginning of the Civil War she organized a drive to collect and distribute clothes and medical supplies to casualties. After her ailing husband resigned his post as hospital administrator for Alabama soldiers in Richmond, Virginia, in 1861, she superintended the local hospitals that treated the sick and injured soldiers from her state.

After the state closed the Richmond hospital in 1863, she worked for several months before returning to Mobile to manage the Camp Watts facility and establish the Matron Alabama Hospitals. Hopkins earned the respect of Gen. Robert E. Lee and his soldiers for her bravery and sacrifice at the battle of Seven Pines, Virginia, where she was wounded in 1862. Dubbed the "Florence Nightingale of the South," she impoverished herself and her family by contributing around $500,000 of her own money to wartime medical care. Alabama's Confederate mint printed her likeness on $50 bills and 25-cent coins. After her death she was buried with military honors near her son-in-law, Maj. Gen. Romeyn Beck Ayres, at Arlington National Cemetery.

PATTIE RUFFNER JACOBS (1875–1939)

Reformer Pattie Ruffner Jacobs, a native of West Virginia, was Alabama's leading suffragist. After studying at Ward's Seminary in Nashville, Tennessee, she married Birmingham industrialist Solon Jacobs and relocated to Alabama with him. A stalwart campaigner for justice, she fought for health initiatives to control tuberculosis, for prisoners' rights, for limited overtime for factory workers, ansd for an end to prostitution and child labor. In 1910 she founded and presided over the Alabama Equal Suffrage Association, a grassroots effort to enact women's rights through a constitutional amendment. To spread the message across Alabama, she spearheaded 50 state leagues and, in the last decade of the national fight for the vote, served as an officer of the National American Woman Suffrage Association, for which she lobbied Congress on behalf of disfranchised Alabama women. In 1920 Jacobs returned from Washington, D.C., to organize newly enfranchised women in the League of Women Voters, for which she served as national secretary.

Among the issues Jacobs campaigned for was the eight-hour work day. She was appointed Alabama's delegate to the Democratic National Committee in 1933, a position she maintained during the last six years of her life. Pres. Herbert Hoover named her to the Liberty bond drive, and Pres. Franklin D. Roosevelt chose her to head the Women's Division of the Consumer Advisory Board of the National Recovery Act and as publicity spokeswoman for the Tennessee Valley Authority. Huntsville playwright Bette Yeager commemorated Jacobs's political activism in the drama *Women Great of Heart* (2000).

MAE JEMISON (1956–)

Physician Mae Carol Jemison of Decatur, Alabama, became the nation's first female African American astronaut. She grew up in Chicago and developed an interest in biomedical engineering at Morgan Park High School. On a National Achievement Scholarship, she majored in black studies and chemical engineering at Stanford University. After completing medical training at Cornell in 1981, she worked for the Peace Corps in Liberia and Sierra Leone for two and a half years as a medical officer, teacher, and researcher. She returned to the United States to study engineering in Los Angeles.

After Jemison's selection, out of a field of 2,000, by the National Aeronautics and Space Administration for astronaut training, she joined 15 other candidates in a rigorous fitness program. In 1992 she completed an eight-day flight aboard the space shuttle *Endeavour* as the crew's science-mission specialist. On the journey she performed experiments measuring the effects of weightlessness and motion sickness on crew performance. For her achievements she earned an Essence Science and Technology Award, an Ebony Black Achievement citation, a Montgomery Fellowship from Dartmouth College, and numerous honorary degrees. She went on to teach at Dartmouth.

HELEN KELLER (1880–1968)

Humanitarian Helen Adams Keller, a native of Tuscumbia, set a standard of achievement that fundamentally reshaped thinking about the abilities of the handicapped. Rendered blind and deaf by scarlet fever in 1882, she lived like an untamed animal until, at the recommendation of Alexander Graham Bell, she was sent to teacher Anne Sullivan to learn finger spelling. In 1889 Keller entered the Perkins Institute in Boston, and then went on to learn speech and braille at the Horace Mann School for the Deaf in Massachusetts and composition at the Wright-Humason Oral School in New York City. She began her writing career with *Light in My Darkness* (1894) and studied at the Cambridge School for Young Ladies before publishing *The Story of My Life* (1902). While at Radcliffe College, she completed *Optimism* (1903), followed by *The World I Live In* (1908) and *Out of the Dark* (1913).

Thanks to a stipend from Andrew Carnegie in 1906, Keller was able to focus on political activism. She championed the handicapped, women's rights, socialism, blinded veterans of World War I, and world peace. From her home in Westport, Connecticut, she advocated educating the blind and deaf, a crusade she pursued through the San Francisco Exposition, the American Civil Liberties Union, and the American Foundation for the Blind, which she cofounded. The French awarded her the Legion of Honor, and Eleanor Roosevelt proclaimed her "America's Goodwill Ambassador."

CORETTA SCOTT KING (1927–)

Civil rights leader Coretta Scott King of Marion, Alabama, contributed to the struggles for nonviolent social change and for social justice for African Americans. She grew up in a middle-class home and studied music at Antioch College, Ohio, where she joined the National Association for the Advancement of Colored People. After graduating in 1951 she completed two music degrees from the New England Conservatory in Boston, where she met Martin Luther King, Jr.

After marriage in 1953 Coretta Scott King settled into her husband's Baptist church in Montgomery, Alabama. Two years later he led the city's bus boycott as a first step toward civil rights for black citizens. She assisted in fund-raising and in organizing marches and demonstrations. In the years before her husband's assassination in Memphis on April 4, 1968, she reared four children and taught voice at Morris Brown College. Simultaneously she wrote and delivered speeches for peace at home, joined a disarmament conference in Geneva, Switzerland, and appeared on church and public platforms with civil rights leaders to sing spirituals and promote her husband's vision of nonviolent protest. When he served a jail term in the spring of 1963, she fulfilled his speaking commitments.

In widowhood Coretta Scott King completed the Memphis protest and addressed the Poor People's March on Washington, D.C. She coordinated efforts to establish the Martin Luther King, Jr., Center for Nonviolent Social Change (the King Center), which opened in Atlanta in 1968. Into the 1970s she promoted new laws to assure fair housing and employment standards for women and blacks and worked to further the establishment of a national holiday honoring her martyred husband. In April 2000 she announced the winner of a competition to design a King memorial for the National Mall in Washington, D.C. At age 75 she advised Americans to celebrate the Martin Luther King national holiday through cooperation, nonviolence, humanitarianism, and grassroots activism, and to give back to the community in an effort to secure a more just and prosperous future.

HARPER LEE (1926–)

The author of *To Kill a Mockingbird* (1960), Nelle Harper Lee of Monroeville earned a respected position in American literature with the publication of only one novel. The daughter of a newspaper publisher, Lee developed a childhood friendship with author Truman Capote, who became her confidant. While attending public schools, she read English, French, and American literature. She attended Huntingdon College in Montgomery from 1944 to 1945 and studied law at the University of Alabama from 1945 to 1949. After spending a year at Oxford University she moved to New York City to write professionally.

After the success of *To Kill a Mockingbird*, she continued submitting essays to *Vogue* and *McCall's*, but published no other long works. Lee's blockbuster novel expresses her knowledge of law and deductive logic, as well as her intuitive sense of the conversations of children. The work won awards from the Alabama Library Association and the Literary Guild, as well as a Pulitzer Prize and the Brotherhood Award from the National Conference of Christians and Jews. During the filming of Horton Foote's screen adaptation, Lee became close friends with the film's star, Gregory Peck, who played the lead character, Atticus Finch. In 1966 Pres. Lyndon Johnson appointed Lee to the National Council of the Arts. She has lived in her native Monroeville for decades.

ADELLA HUNT LOGAN (1863–1915)

A proponent of human rights and women's suffrage, Adella Hunt Logan of Sparta, Georgia, promoted the health and education of children and full citizenship for women. Born to a Confederate war veteran and a free black mother, she studied at Bass Academy and began teaching school in 1879. That same year, on a scholarship to Atlanta University, she became the first African American from Hancock County to graduate from college. She taught at a missionary school in Albany, Georgia, and joined the faculty of Tuskegee Institute as teacher, librarian, and principal. After marrying Warren Logan, a fellow teacher at Tuskegee, in 1888, Adella had nine children; six were reared to adulthood at Tuskegee. Logan extended her classroom experience by supporting community literacy and hygiene programs, establishing Tuskegee's model school for teacher training, and becoming a charter member of the National Association of Colored Women's Clubs. In her efforts to encourage blacks to campaign for women's suffrage, she attended a conference of the National American Woman Suffrage Association (without identifying her race) to gather details of campaign strategy. After an emotional breakdown in 1915, she entered the Battle Creek Sanitarium in Michigan, but returned to Tuskegee during the terminal illness of her mentor, Booker T. Washington. In despair at his loss, she leaped to her death from a campus building.

AUTHERINE LUCY (1929–)

Civil rights activist Autherine Juanita Lucy of Shiloh, Alabama, was the first African American graduate student enrolled at the University of Alabama. Born on a cotton farm to a large family, she completed high school at Linden Academy. In 1952 she earned a B.A. in English from Miles College and chose to study for an advanced degree in library science from the University of Alabama. Entering the all-white graduate program required over three years of court suits pressed by the NAACP on her behalf. During this period, while attorney Thurgood Marshall represented her, she worked as a secretary. On June 29, 1955, a court order allowed her to enroll.

In February 1956 Lucy enrolled as the first African American student at the University of Alabama. She attended for only three days, during which police escorted her to classes through chanting, egg-throwing mobs. On February 5, 1956, the college expelled her, claiming that it could not guarantee her safety. She declined scholarships from European colleges, moved to Texas, and taught school. At the age of 59, with the aid of two supportive professors at the University of Alabama, she returned to the graduate school to complete an M.Ed. in elementary education. Three years later she received her diploma at the same time that her daughter Grazia earned a B.A. in corporate finance.

ROSA PARKS (1913–)

Rosa Louise Lee McCauley Parks of Tuskegee became known as the "Mother of the Civil Rights Movement." After her parents' separation, she grew up among strong women in Pine Level, Alabama, and worked in the fields while nursing her grandparents. While attending the Montgomery Industrial School for Girls, she cleaned classrooms to earn tuition. Her education at Booker T. Washington High School ended when her mother required daily care (she went back to receive her high school diploma in 1934). Despite limited opportunity she read, sewed, and took an active part in an African Methodist Episcopal church. After marrying Raymond Parks in 1932, she worked as a maid, seamstress, and office clerk.

Parks joined the civil rights movement after World War II. As secretary of Montgomery's chapter of the National Association for the Advancement of Colored People, she set an example for youth by registering to vote. On December 1, 1955, after refusing to give up her bus seat to a white male, she was arrested and pressed her case as an example of majority injustice against blacks. While supporting a year-long bus boycott, she and her husband were fired from their jobs and found low-paying work only with difficulty. When his health failed in 1957, the couple moved to Detroit. In 1965, U.S. congressman John Conyers hired her as a staff assistant. Her numerous awards include the Spingarn Medal, the Nonviolent Peace Prize, an honorarium from *Ebony* magazine, the Eleanor Roosevelt Women of Courage Award, and the Congressional Gold Medal.

JULIA STRUDWICK TUTWILER (1841–1916)

Educator and social activist Julia Strudwick Tutwiler of Greene Springs made equal opportunity for women her life's goal. Encouraged by a strong father, she studied at Vassar College and at Washington and Lee University in Virginia before joining the faculty of Tuscaloosa Female Seminary in 1868. After postgraduate work in France and Germany, she brought European kindergarten strategies to her father's school in Greene Springs. As a principal of Livingston Female Academy, she secured state monies for women's industrial training (the impetus to the establishment of Alabama Normal College) and published a monograph, *The Technical Education of Women* (1882). With Tutwiler's aid, the Alabama Girls Industrial School opened in 1896 and the University of Alabama began a cooperative program with the women of Alabama Normal College.

Because of her work for the prison committee of the Women's Christian Temperance Union, she was called "Angel of the Prisons." She also canvassed for prison night schools, a juvenile reform school, inspection of cells, and the abolition of convict leasing, a system that allowed the state to hire prisoners out to work in logging, farming, and road repair. Her poem "Alabama" became the state song. Her name survives in the Julia Tutwiler College of Education at the University of West Alabama.

LURLEEN WALLACE (1926–1968)

Lurleen Burns Wallace of Tuscaloosa rose from a laboring-class background to the governorship of Alabama. Educated in public schools she completed training at Tuscaloosa Business College at age 16. Married the following year to George Corley Wallace, she reared four children and followed her husband's political advance to state legislator. She was content with needlework, piloting light aircraft, and teaching in a Methodist Sunday school until her husband became governor in 1963.

When her husband determined to circumvent the state-mandated limit on terms of office by launching his wife's campaign for governor, she agreed to support his segregationist policies and programs, which were his platform for a run for the presidency. The third woman elected as a state governor in the United States, she took office in 1967 and fought the forced desegregation of public schools, while also initiating her own campaign for better health care for the mentally ill. Her brief career in public office ended with the onset of a virulent cancer that killed her at age 42.

MARGARET MURRAY WASHINGTON (ca. 1865–1925)

One of the founding faculty members of Tuskegee Institute, Margaret James Murray Washington of Macon, Georgia, promoted the science of home economics. The daughter of a laundress, she was reared by Quakers, who encouraged her to teach school. She studied at Fisk University, where she met educator Booker T. Washington, whom she married in 1891. At his urging she became principal of Tuskegee Institute and managed student work in the kitchen garden, orchard, dairy, barn, and henyard. To uplift the self-esteem of female students, she instilled racial pride, character, wellness, and respect for the home and family.

Washington's methods called for the preparation of African American householders and leaders. She set an example of order and cleanliness and carried classroom lessons into rural Alabama through health clubs, the National Federation of Afro-American Women, Mothers' Meetings, and the Alabama State Federation. At an old firehouse she established Saturday home-care tutorials for women. In 1898 she taught African Americans at the Russell Plantation school the basics of cooking and housecleaning. Until her death at age 70, she supported women's self-fulfillment through the National Association of Colored Women (which she helped found in 1896) and the Southern Federation of Colored Women's Clubs.

—Mary Ellen Snodgrass

PROMINENT SITES

Alabama Women's Hall of Fame
Judson College
A. Howard Bean Hall
Marion, AL 36756
Telephone: (334) 683 5243
Web: http://home.judson.edu/extra/fame/fame.html
This project was established in 1970 to honor the women of Alabama's past. Inductees include Helen Keller and Tallulah Bankhead, as well as lesser-known women who led extraordinary lives. The women's accomplishments are explored through biographies, portraits, letters, and bronze plaques.

City Hall/Emma Sansom Monument
90 Broad Street
Gadsden, AL 35901
Telephone: (256) 549 4500
Web: http://www.ohwy.com/al/e/emsanmon.htm
The Emma Sansom monument, located across the street from Gadsden's City Hall, commemorates the bravery of 15-year-old Emma Sansom. In May of 1863 she led Confederate general Nathan Forrest to a spot in Black Creek, near Gadsden, where he could ford the creek and escape Union gunfire. After returning the girl to her home, Forrest ordered his troops directly into battle. The next day he overtook the Union soldiers and wrote a short note to Emma expressing his thanks.

Civil Rights Memorial
Southern Poverty Law Center
400 Washington Avenue
Montgomery, AL 36104
Telephone: (334) 956 8200
Web: http://www.splcenter.org
In 1988 the Southern Poverty Law Center decided to build a memorial in honor of the victims of the civil rights movement. The artist Maya Lin, who had designed the Vietnam Memorial in Washington, D.C., created a monument that was influenced by a phrase in Martin Luther King, Jr.'s "I Have a Dream" speech: "until justice rolls down like waters and righteousness like a mighty stream." She created a sculpture made of black granite engraved with the names of 40 people who gave their lives during the struggle. Water runs over the names, which visitors are encouraged to touch.

Coretta Scott King's Childhood Home
Perry County Road 29 North
Perry County Chamber of Commerce
1200 Washington Street
Marion, AL 36756
Telephone: (334) 683 9622
Coretta Scott King was born in Perry County in 1927. She was the valedictorian of her class at Lincoln High School and went on to attend Ohio's Antioch College. She moved to Boston to attend the New England Conservatory of Music, and there she met and married Martin Luther King, Jr. After his death she continued his crusade for equal rights in America. Her childhood home is not open to the public, but visitors who want to drive to the home may contact the Perry County Chamber of Commerce for directions to the site.

Elmwood Cemetery
600 Martin Luther King Drive
Birmingham, AL 35211
Telephone: (205) 251 3114
Elmwood Cemetery is the final resting place for Pattie Ruffner Jacobs (1875–1939), a leading suffragist in Alabama. Jacobs founded the Birmingham Equal Suffrage Association in 1910, as well as the Alabama Equal Suffrage Association the following year. She held office in the National Equal Suffrage Association and in the League of Women Voters. The first National Democratic Committeewoman from the state of Alabama, Jacobs served on the National Committee from 1933 until her death.

Ivy Green/Birthplace of Hellen Keller
300 West North Commons
Tuscumbia, AL 35674
Telephone: (256) 383 4066
Web: http://www.alabamatravel.org/north/ig.html
The birthplace and childhood home of Helen Keller has been transformed into a museum dedicated to Helen's extraordinary life.

Lake Lurleen State Park
13226 Lake Lurleen Road
Coker, AL 35452
Telephone: (205) 339 1558

Lurleen B. Wallace is the only female to date who has served as governor of Alabama. She was elected in 1966 and held office until May of 1968, when she died of cancer. Her husband, George Wallace, was governor before her and was unable to run again due to term limits. He encouraged her to run for his office, and, although she was diagnosed with cancer before the gubernatorial race, she won in a landslide victory. The state park was named in her honor because she was from the Tuscaloosa area and was very fond of the native landscape.

Rosa L. Parks Library and Museum
251 Montgomery Street
Montgomery, AL 36104
Telephone: (334) 241 8615
Web: http://www.tsum.edu/museum
Constructed on the site of the Old Empire Theatre, where Rosa Parks inadvertently ignited the civil rights movement by refusing to give up her seat on a city bus, the museum explores the bus boycott that followed Ms. Parks's act of civil disobedience.

Sixteenth Street Baptist Church
1530 6th Avenue North
Birmingham, AL 35203
Telephone: (205) 251 9402
On September 15, 1963, four girls were in the basement of the Sixteenth Street Baptist Church when a bomb planted by white supremacist Robert Edward Chambliss detonated. All four girls were killed and 20 other people were injured. The church was a center of the civil rights movement, and the bombing took place on the annual Youth Sunday, sparking continuing violence in the city. Tours are available at the church on Tuesdays to Fridays and on Saturdays by appointment.

RESOURCES

FURTHER READING

HISTORY

Anthony, Susan B., and Ida Husted Harper. *History of Woman Suffrage.* Vol. 4. Indianapolis, Ind.: Hollenbeck Press, 1902.

Beidler, Philip D. *First Books: The Printed Word and Cultural Formation in Early Alabama.* Tuscaloosa: University of Alabama Press, 1999.

Bernhard, Virginia. *Southern Women: Histories and Identities.* Columbia: University of Missouri Press, 1992.

Bernhard, Virginia, ed. *Hidden Histories of Women in the New South.* Columbia: University of Missouri Press, 1994.

Blomquist, Ann K., and Robert A. Taylor, eds. *This Cruel War: The Civil War Letters of Grant and Malinda Taylor, 1862–1865.* Macon, Ga.: Mercer University Press, 2000.

Brewer, Willis. *Alabama, Her History, Resources, War Record, and Public Men: From 1540 to 1872.* Montgomery, Ala.: Barrett & Brown, 1872.

Brown, James Seay, Jr., ed. *Up Before Daylight: Life Histories from the Alabama Writers' Project, 1938–1939.* University: University of Alabama Press, 1982.

Brown, Virginia Pounds. *Alabama Heritage.* Huntsville, Ala.: Strode, 1967.

Caffey, Francis G. *Suffrage Limitations at the South.* Boston: Ginn & Company, 1905.

Cott, Nancy F., ed. *Root of Bitterness: Documents of the Social History of American Women.* 2nd ed. Boston: Northeastern University Press, 1996.

Crittenden, Judith Sullivan. *The Legal Status of Homemakers in Alabama.* Washington, D.C.: USGPO, 1977.

Davidson, Cathy N., and Linda Wagner-Martin, eds. *The Oxford Companion to Women's Writing in the United States.* New York: Oxford University Press, 1995.

Federal Writers' Project. *Slave Narratives: Alabama.* Vol. 5. 1937. Reprint, St. Clair Shores, Mich.: Scholarly Press, 1976.

Feldman, Lynne B. *A Sense of Place: Birmingham's Black Middle-Class Community, 1890–1930.* Tuscaloosa: University of Alabama Press, 1999.

Gaston, Paul M. *Women of Fair Hope.* Athens: University of Georgia Press, 1984.

Griffith, Lucille. *History of Alabama, 1540–1900, As Recorded in Diaries, Letters, and Other Papers of the Times.* Northport, Ala.: Colonial Press, 1962.

Griffith, Lucille. *Alabama: A Documentary History to 1900.* Tuscaloosa: University of Alabama Press, 1972.

Hamilton, Virginia Van der Veer. *Alabama: A Bicentennial History.* New York: Norton, 1977.

Harper, Ida Husted. *History of Woman Suffrage.* Vol. 6. New York: J. J. Little & Ives, 1922.

Hughes Wright, Roberta. *The Birth of the Montgomery Bus Boycott.* Southfield, Mich.: Charro Press, 1991.

Jones, James. *Bad Blood: The Tuskegee Syphilis Experiment.* Expanded ed. New York: Free Press, 1993.

Jones, Katharine M. *Heroines of Dixie.* Indianapolis, Ind.: Bobbs-Merrill, 1955.

Jordan, Weymouth T. *Ante-bellum Alabama: Town and Country.* University: University of Alabama Press, 1987.

Lofton, J. Mack, Jr. *Voices from Alabama: A Twentieth-Century Mosaic.* Tuscaloosa: University of Alabama Press, 1993.

Mabunda, L. Mpho, ed. *The African American Almanac.* 7th ed. Detroit, Mich.: Gale, 1997.

Moore, Albert Burton. *History of Alabama.* Tuscaloosa: Alabama Book Store, 1951.

Morton, Patricia, ed. *Discovering the Women in Slavery: Emancipating Perspectives on the American Past.* Athens: University of Georgia Press, 1996.

Owen, Thomas McAdory. *History of Alabama and Dictionary of Alabama Biography.* 1921. Reprint, Spartanburg, S.C.: Reprint Co., 1978.

Pickett, Albert James. *History of Alabama.* 1851. Reprint, Birmingham, Ala.: Birmingham Book and Magazine Company, 1962.

Rogers, William Warren. *Alabama: The History of a Deep South State.* Tuscaloosa: University of Alabama Press, 1994.

Schroeder-Lein, Glenna R. *Confederate Hospitals on the Move.* Columbia: University of South Carolina Press, 1994.

Scott, Anne Firor, ed. *Southern Women and Their Families in the 19th Century, Papers and Diaries.*

Bethesda, Md.: University Publications of America, 2000.

Smith, Susan L. *Sick and Tired of Being Sick and Tired: Black Women's Health Activism in America, 1890–1950.* Philadelphia: University of Pennsylvania Press, 1995.

Snodgrass, Mary Ellen. *Encyclopedia of Southern Literature.* Santa Barbara, Calif.: ABC-CLIO, 1997.

Snodgrass, Mary Ellen. *Historical Encyclopedia of Nursing.* Santa Barbara, Calif.: ABC-CLIO, 1999.

Snodgrass, Mary Ellen. *Encyclopedia of Kitchen History.* London: Fitzroy-Dearborn, 2002.

Stanton, Elizabeth Cady, Susan B. Anthony, and Matilda Joslyn Gage. *History of Woman Suffrage.* Vol. 3. Rochester, N.Y.: Charles Mann Printing, 1886.

Steckel, Minnie Louise. *Alabama Women and Their Employers, 1938–1939.* Montevallo: Alabama Federation of Business and Professional Women's Clubs, in collaboration with Alabama College, 1939.

Sterkx, H. E. *Partners in Rebellion: Alabama Women in the Civil War.* Rutherford, N.J.: Fairleigh Dickinson University Press, 1970.

Thomas, Mary Martha. *Riveting and Rationing in Dixie: Alabama Women and the Second World War.* Tuscaloosa: University of Alabama Press, 1987.

Thomas, Mary Martha. *The New Woman in Alabama: Social Reforms, and Suffrage, 1890–1920.* Tuscaloosa: University of Alabama Press, 1992.

Thomas, Mary Martha, ed. *Stepping Out of the Shadows: Alabama Women, 1819–1990.* Tuscaloosa: University of Alabama Press, 1995.

Thrasher, Max Bennett. *Tuskegee: Its Story and Its Work.* 1900. Reprint, New York: Negro Universities Press, 1969.

United States Commission on Civil Rights, Alabama Advisory Committee. *Where Are Women and Blacks? Patterns of Employment in Alabama Government: A Report.* Washington, D.C.: USGPO, 1979.

Weatherford, Doris. *American Women's History.* New York: Prentice Hall General Reference, 1994.

Wiggins, Sarah Woolfolk. *From Civil War to Civil Rights: Alabama, 1860–1960.* Tuscaloosa: University of Alabama Press, 1987.

BIOGRAPHIES AND AUTOBIOGRAPHIES

Brinkley, Douglas. *Rosa Parks.* New York: Viking, 2000.

Brooks, Sara. *You May Plow Here: The Narrative of Sara Brooks.* Edited by Thordis Simonsen. New York: Simon & Schuster, 1987.

Coleman, Juliet Bestor. *Connecticut Yankee in Early Alabama: Juliet Bestor Coleman, 1833–1850.* Edited by Mary Morgan Ward Glass. Mobile: Historical Activities Committee, National Society of Colonial Dames of America in the State of Alabama, 1980.

Hague, Parthenia Antoinette. *A Blockaded Family: Life in Southern Alabama during the Civil War.* 1888. Reprint, Lincoln: University of Nebraska Press, 1991.

Herrmann, Dorothy. *Helen Keller: A Life.* Chicago: University of Chicago Press, 1999.

Hine, Darlene Clark, ed. *Black Women in America.* New York: Carlson Publishing, 1993.

Keller, Helen. *The Story of My Life.* 1902. Reprint, Mahwah, N.J.: Watermill, 1980.

Keller, Helen. *Light in My Darkness.* 1920. Reprint, West Chester, Penn.: Chrysalis, 2000.

Krapp, Kristine, ed. *Notable Black American Scientists.* Detroit, Mich.: Gale, 1999.

Kudlinski, Kathleen V. *Helen Keller: A Light for the Blind.* New York: Viking, 1989.

McDowell, Deborah E. *Leaving Pipe Shop: Memories of Kin.* New York: Scribner, 1996.

Melton, J. Gordon. *Religious Leaders of America.* 2nd ed. Detroit, Mich.: Gale, 1999.

Parks, Rosa, and Gregory J. Reed. *Quiet Strength: The Faith, the Hope, and the Heart of a Woman who Changed a Nation.* Grand Rapids, Mich.: Zondervan, 1994.

Robinson, Jo Ann Gibson. *The Montgomery Bus Boycott and the Women Who Started It: The Memoir of Jo Ann Gibson Robinson.* Knoxville: University of Tennessee Press, 1987.

Sicherman, Barbara, and Carol Hurd Green, eds. *Notable American Women.* Cambridge, Mass.: Belknap Press, 1980.

Smith, Jessie Carney. *Notable Black American Women.* Detroit, Mich.: Gale, 1992.

Smith, Margaret Charles, and Linda Janet Holmes. *Listen to Me Good: The Life Story of an Alabama Midwife.* Columbus: Ohio State University Press, 1996.

Stanton, Mary. *From Selma to Sorrow: The Life and Death of Viola Liuzzo*. Athens: University of Georgia Press, 1998.

Tarry, Ellen. *The Third Door: The Autobiography of an American Negro Woman*. Tuscaloosa: University of Alabama Press, 1992.

Windham, Kathryn Tucker. *Odd-Egg Editor*. Jackson: University Press of Mississippi, 1990.

USEFUL WEB SITES

"Alabama Moments in American History"
http://www.alabamamoments.state.al.us/Contents.html
Alabama Women's Hall of Fame
http://www.awhf.org
Tuskegee Institute
http://www.nps.gov/bowa/tuskin.html

SELECTED ORGANIZATIONS AND INSTITUTIONS

Alabama Department of Archives and History
624 Washington Avenue
Montgomery, AL 36130
Telephone: (334) 242 4435
Web: http://www.archives.state.al.us/index.html
Founded in 1901 the department works to preserve the records of Alabama's past and to serve researchers' information needs. Includes an online listing of Alabama women's history research sources.

Alabama Women's Hall of Fame
A. Howard Bean Hall
Judson College
Marion, AL 36756
Telephone: (334) 683 5243
Web: http://home.judson.edu/extra/fame/fame.html
Provides a permanent place of honor for Alabama's most outstanding women, and a place for people to visit and learn about the significant contributions of these women.

Auburn University Women's Studies
6010 Haley Center
Auburn, AL 36849
Telephone: (334) 844 6363
Web: http://www.auburn.edu/academic/other/womens_studies

Dedicated to the promotion of research and scholarship about women and gender across the disciplines.

Birmingham Public Library
2100 Park Place
Birmingham, AL 35203–2974
Telephone: (205) 226 3610
Web: http://www.bplonline.org
Includes an online listing of collections relating to women's history.

Julia Tutwiler Library
The University of West Alabama
UWA Station 12
Livingston, AL 35470
Telephone: (205) 652 3613
Web: http://library.uwa.edu
Julia Tutwiler was a leader in the fight for coeducation in Alabama's colleges and universities. Those interested in research can visit the Alabama Room Archives and Special Collections at the library.

University of Alabama in Huntsville Women's Studies Program
344 Morton Hall
Huntsville, AL 35899
Telephone: (256) 824 6210
Web: http://www.uah.edu/colleges/liberal/womensstudies
Focuses on the contributions, perspectives, and experiences of women in all areas of human endeavor.

University of Alabama Women's Studies
Box 870272
Tuscaloosa, AL 35487–0272
Telephone: (205) 348 5782
Web: http://www.as.ua.edu/ws
Offers a master of arts in women's studies, as well as an undergraduate minor.

Women's Historical Collections
Auburn University Archives and Manuscript Department
231 Mell Street
Auburn University, AL 36849–5606
Telephone: (334) 844 1732
Web: http://www.lib.auburn.edu/archive/find-aid/women.htm
Includes an online directory to the collection, including published and unpublished material.

ALASKA

Everything seemed exaggerated. Edges sharper. Skies bluer. Mountains higher, snow deeper, temperature lower, daylight longer, sunlight briefer, depending on the season. The very air sometimes seemed more utterly still than anywhere else in the world, yet it pulsed almost palpably with life. . . .
Cross the winter night sky swept the northern lights, eerie dazzling curtains of swaying green and blue and orange. Then, miraculously, June came, it was summer, it was daylight round the clock. . . . Up, up far north in Barrow on the shore of the frozen Arctic Ocean the United States flag whipped aloft in the wind for eighty days and eighty nights, for there was during that period no sunset hour in which to lower it.
—Edna Ferber, *Ice Palace*, 1958

Alaskan contact with the outside world was initiated by Anna Ivanovna, Russia's monarch during the 1730s, when she sent Danish mariner Vitus Bering on his second voyage to the sea that is now named for him. Anna died in 1740, but some of Bering's men landed on the North American mainland in 1741. Another female Russian monarch, Catherine the Great, also sent expeditions to the area, in addition to authorizing the first Christian missions, which arrived in the 1790s.

Americans came to this icy frontier in the second half of the next century, at the same time that they were settling the American West. Men almost unanimously encouraged women to come to this unsettled territory, for they viewed women as essential to a full life and civilization in the vast frontier.

PREHISTORY TO AMERICAN SETTLEMENT (Prehistory–1867)

It is assumed that Alaska's original peoples came from Asia via the land bridge of islands that once linked North America to Asia near the Arctic Circle. Except for childbearing, the most important contribution of women to their society was the manufacture of garments, which were of paramount importance in this frozen world.

Experienced modern travelers still testify that no clothing is as suitable for the area's harsh

State Population (2000): 626,932

Female Population (2000): 302,820

Women in State Legislature (2003): 20%

Female College Enrollment (1999): 16,000 (59.3% of total)

Privately Held Women-owned Businesses (1997): 16,633

First Year of Full Suffrage: 1913

environment as that made by the Eskimo women in Alaska's far north. Mukluks, boots made of reindeer or seal skin, enable dogsled drivers to mush 40 miles a day without frostbite or blisters. Women made these mukluks—as well as other garments and articles, including fish nets—by chewing animal hides and sinews to make them malleable.

The parka was also the invention of Eskimo women. Using needles made of walrus tusks, they sewed knee-length parkas of reindeer or caribou skin (or even muskrat); the hood was usually lined with wolverine fur. Mary Lee Davis, who in the 1920s lived in northern Alaska with Eskimos that still adhered to the skills inherited from their ancestors, said that she soon "realized what matchless needle-workers these Eskimo women are, their stitching so perfect, their seams absolutely waterproof without greasing." (Davis 1931, 168)

Despite the imperative for practicality in this unforgiving climate, women nonetheless made distinct styles of garments for men and women. White observers noted this more than a century before Davis commented that "no perfect Eskimo lady would be seen wearing a striped mukluk, just as . . . men's parkas must have a straight edge. These are very serious matters, and to offend such ancient customs would brand you as ignorant, or revolutionary and radical." (Ibid.)

The Eskimos were relatively gentle and family-oriented. They were described by early travelers as contented and so fond of singing that songs pervaded every aspect of life. Anthropologists observed that families were small and parents avoided corporal punishment in the discipline of their children. Because the Eskimo diet was almost exclusively raw meat and seafood, women nursed their children until they reached the age of four or five, when their teeth were strong enough to chew meat.

While northern Alaskan family structure was quite egalitarian, farther south, and especially among coastal tribes, native cultures were more patriarchal and less democratic. Polygamy was common, and female infanticide was not unknown. Girls went through a rite of passage at puberty that called for months of isolation and hunger. Belief in witchcraft was genuine, and women were much more likely than men to be victims of witch-hunts. Slavery among Alaska Natives actually lasted longer in southern Alaska than it did in the American South—some cases were found even in the 20th century.

The Aleuts, who lived on the Aleutian Islands and the easternmost part of the Alaskan Peninsula, were suspicious of the first whites they saw, and when Russians first arrived in the mid-18th century, hostile Aleuts drove them out. Death from combat with the native population, as well as from scurvy and other diseases, delayed the first permanent white settlements until the 1790s. Spanish ships came north from California, just as Russians went south to San Francisco, but the Spanish never guessed that the gold for which they lusted was hidden deep beneath Alaskan snow. English ships sailed north from Canada, and people from other nations, including the United States, hunted whales in Alaskan waters. Only the Russians, however, with their greater acclimation to cold weather, hung on. They hunted sea otters almost to extinction, and they enslaved Alaska Natives to cut ancient trees and mine for copper. Given the history of Russian and Spanish explorers in other areas that they conquered, historians consider it likely that they also raped Alaskan women.

Early travelers discovered, however, that some Alaska Natives saw sexual comfort as a natural part of hospitality—husbands were not jealous if their wives chose to sleep with a stranger who sought shelter in their home. Standards of beauty were also very different than those of the European newcomers. Some women tattooed their faces, and "split-lip" women achieved that effect by forcing increasingly larger bits of wood through their lips until they appeared to have two mouths.

Despite reports of such different customs, Catherine the Great did not see Christianization as a high priority. She authorized an expedition to search for fossilized ivory in 1771, for example, more than 20 years before she sent priests. When priests did come to the Aleutians and the big coastal island of Kodiak in 1793, close to the end of Catherine's reign, they treated the native people with contempt.

The beautiful Byzantine art that ornamented the new Russian churches attracted some Alaska Natives, but little else in the new religion did, and any conversions that the Russian priests presided over largely resulted from gifts to the Alaska Natives, which sometimes included vodka. Nevertheless, Russian priests opened schools at New Archangel and elsewhere, though the students were almost exclusively the sons of native women and Russian men (despite powerful czarinas, Russia at that time did not generally educate girls). The fathers of these children were usually fur traders. These men traveled almost constantly, and their families were expected to manage alone.

Russian priests were allowed to marry, and some wives accompanied their men to the frontier. That white women were scarce, though, is clear in a saying still used by the Aleutians: "As precious as a bishop's wife." The few women who lived in these remote settlements faced not only nature's perils, but also the constant threat of attack. The Tlingits, a major coastal tribe, killed all the residents of an agricultural community called Glory of Russia in 1805, and the previous year they wiped out the pioneers at Sitka.

American employees of the Hudson's Bay Company also attempted settlement in the early 19th century, and, like the Pilgrims at Plymouth, some were saved by helpful Alaska Natives. One Hudson's Bay worker praised the help given to him and his crew in 1839 by the female chief of the Nahany tribe—his expedition would likely have come to a disastrous conclusion without her intervention and assistance.

In the following decades, the dedication of LADY JANE FRANKLIN to her husband, Arctic explorer Sir John Franklin, became something of

an Alaskan legend. She lived in the area while sending repeated expeditions to search for his ships, which were last seen in 1845; not until 1859 did she find that he had died in 1847.

The highest priority of most white men in Alaska during this period was the fur trade, which soon declined due to overhunting. Many settlers had abandoned Alaska by midcentury, and the white population dropped from a high of about 700 to some 400 in 1867. The cost of administration from Moscow, half a world away, was clearly not worthwhile, and in 1867 the Russian government was glad to accept an American offer of $7.2 million for the claim to Alaska.

Many Americans, especially impoverished southerners recovering from the just-ended Civil War, dubbed the new land "Seward's Folly," but Secretary of State William Seward, who had negotiated the purchase, would eventually prove prescient. On March 30, 1867, Russia formally transferred the land and, along with it, the native peoples who lived there to the United States.

FROM AMERICAN SETTLEMENT TO TERRITORIAL STATUS (1867–1912)

Lizzie Fall Kinkead, whose husband had just been appointed as Alaska's first postmaster, arrived in Sitka, the territory's first capital city, in 1867, and she immediately set about improving life there. Her priority was a school, which opened in the fall of 1868 after she persuaded the overwhelmingly male population to build it because it could double as a Masonic lodge. Addie Messer of Illinois agreed to come north as the first teacher, but she stayed just a year, during which the salary fell from an initial $75 per month to $50. Catherine Murphy, an Irish widow with four children to support, accepted the lower salary in 1870. She was replaced in 1872 by two male teachers, who were paid even less.

These low salaries were an indication that Sitka's new economy was in decline almost before it began. A gold strike was disappointing, the populace was moving on, and education was clearly not the frontier's highest priority. Lizzie Kinkead found even less interest in her desire for a temperance society, although alcoholism (and its resulting violence) was a daily fact of life in the region. An 1869 Christmas Eve celebration at Sitka, for instance, got so out of hand that a drunken native Alaskan bit off the finger of a military wife who was trying to stop him from beating his wife.

Another fact of life for white women was a hugely imbalanced gender ratio. While this phenomenon increased respect for women because of their scarcity, life in Alaska could be terribly lonely. Long months of almost total darkness and blinding blizzards made travel impossible, particularly for women with infants, and the isolation and boredom could be literally maddening.

Wives of military officers, however, had virtually no choice about where they would live. Emily McCorkle Fitzgerald, who was married to the army surgeon assigned to Sitka in 1874, was typical in her mixed reaction to this difficult post. She felt that the natural scene was beautiful beyond any previous experience, but that everything

humans touched, including the town itself, was a disappointment to her. She also complained that the Alaska Natives were untrustworthy—a feeling so common that curfews were placed on their presence in town.

In addition to complaints about Alaska Natives—especially their personal hygiene—American women also were shocked by the different moral code of Russian women, some of whom remained in Sitka after it was no longer a Russian colony. The transition to a new order was hard on the Russians. Unemployment and death rates were high, and the *Alaska Times*, a new newspaper in 1869, wrote of "the impoverished condition of many Russian families . . . they are willing to work, but there is no labor to offer remuneration or reward." The result was that "a shocking number" of wives of Russian men had "given themselves up openly to prostitution." (Hinckley 1972, 56)

Presbyterian AMANDA MCFARLAND arrived in 1877 determined to change this scene. One of Alaska's first missionaries, she would prove a more constant presence than her boss, Sheldon Jackson, who arrived with her. Although historians give Jackson more visibility, he actually spent

Tlingit women weaving baskets ca. late 1800s. (Denver Public Library, Western History Collection, B. C. Towne, X–32126)

much of his time on fund-raising tours in the United States. McFarland was older than Jackson, and her long career working in western missions is well documented by Presbyterian mission records. After her husband died while they were working with the Nez Percé in Idaho, she came north to serve the Tlingits.

McFarland opened a school in Wrangell, which soon had 80 students, and she then added a home to shelter girls. The need for this was made clear when a white man bought one of McFarland's students from her father for 20 blankets. McFarland successfully saved the 13-year-old girl, but she worried that another offer would be coming and she might not be successful again.

McFarland was also astute enough to see that her work could be counterproductive: the more that she taught her girls about hygiene and manners, the more attractive they became to white men who would exploit them. Nor was it only fathers who saw such human commerce as the natural destiny for girls, for McFarland also wrestled with mothers who sold unwilling daughters.

From the beginning, McFarland was helped by SARAH DICKINSON, a Tlingit woman married to a white fur trader. Dickinson could reach out to the community in a way that McFarland could not. Other female missionaries soon joined them, and other schools were opened, including one north of Juneau that Sarah Dickinson operated alone. According to an Alaskan historian, this "was Chilkat country and still dangerous," but women there "came to see the Indian woman who spoke and dressed like a white woman." (Hinckley 1972, 136)

Moravians headquartered in the Pennsylvania Dutch country began a mission they called Bethel in the Kuskokwim Valley in the early 1880s. One of these women, Edith Kilbuck, mused in her diary about the negative influence of white men on this work: "The natives say, 'nearly all the

---

WITCHCRAFT AND WITCH-HUNTS

A year after McFarland's arrival in Alaska, whites were shocked by a resurgence of belief in witchcraft. According to the records of German anthropologists:

> In 1878 two girls were accused of witchcraft in Wrangell and submitted to the most gruesome tortures. They were dragged by the hair to the beach where they were held under water until they were nearly drowned and then laid, naked, on hot ashes. Through the efforts of the missionary one girl was saved from death but on the following night the other one was hanged.
>
> In the summer of 1882 two Chilkar women . . . were accused of witchcraft. To persuade them to confess their guilt, of which they themselves seemed to be convinced, they were bound . . . [and] beaten. . . . The unfortunate ones succeeded in escaping to the missionary who hid them until they could go south on a steamer. . . . In the instances [of witch hunts] brought to our attention the accused were always women.

—Doris Weatherford

Excerpt from David H. Kraus, trans., and James W. Vanstone, ed. *V.S. Khromchenko's Coastal Explorations in Southwestern Alaska, 1822.* Chicago: Field Museum of Natural History, 1973.

---

white men we see are rough and carry revolvers as though we were wild animals to be afraid of. Why don't you Christianize those of your own kind?'" (Ibid., 154) Despite such skepticism, the mission carried on until the late 1890s, when Bethel suffered a series of severe epidemics. By 1901, according to one writer, half of the adults and all of the babies in the town had died.

Baptists, Methodists, Quakers, and other Protestants also built schools, and in the late 1880s Catholics arrived, including three Sisters of St. Ann assigned to Holy Cross on the Yukon River. Their vegetable garden especially impressed the Alaska Natives, as Sister Mary Joseph Calasanctius wrote: "They would pull up a turnip—they had never seen this vegetable before—they examine it carefully—and just as carefully return it to the soil." (Cantwell 1992, 123)

Far beyond the Arctic Circle, a Presbyterian school opened in 1890 for the northernmost Eskimos at Point Barrow. It was endowed by a wealthy woman, New York's Margaret Vanderbilt Shepard, who had also supported the pioneer Presbyterian school at Sitka (writer Septima Collins called it "the Shepard School" during her 1890 tour). Collins was extremely impressed by this school, which taught gender-differentiated vocational skills. Some 150 Native Alaskan students boarded there at that time, ranging from three-year-old children to a married couple in their twenties. The teachers were both married and unmarried women who came from midwestern and eastern states.

Like the schools that white women ran for blacks in the Deep South at the end of the Civil War, Alaska's schools were strictly segregated. When, in 1888, a teacher tried to integrate the few students she had in a small town near Juneau, her Presbyterian supervisor overruled her decision. She coped by teaching her native students in the morning and the whites in the afternoon, but white parents nonetheless complained that

---

A GLOBAL TRAVELER AT MUIR GLACIER

Many Americans were fascinated by the natural wonders of Alaska, especially the glaciers, and some of the many travel writers who visited Alaska were women. One of these women, Septima Collins, was inspired to see Muir Glacier by Kate Field, a popular columnist for the *New York Tribune*. Field had told her readers that seeing a glacier in Europe could not begin to compare with seeing those in Alaska. "In Switzerland," Field wrote, "a glacier is a vast bed of dirty air-holed ice that has fastened itself, like a cold porous plaster, to the side of an Alp. . . . In Alaska, a glacier is a wonderful torrent that seems to have been suddenly frozen when about to plunge into the sea. . . . Think of Niagara Falls frozen stiff, add thirty-six feet to its height, and you have a slight idea of the terminus of Muir Glacier."

Septima Collins was the widow of a Civil War general and lived in a fashionable home on Fifth Avenue in New York. It was a Union war hero, William Sherman, who wrote the introduction to her book, *A Woman's Trip to Alaska* (1890). When she went to see the Muir Glacier, the yacht on which she sailed was making its maiden voyage in these waters, and although it was June, the sea was ice-bound. Collins wrote of the glacier's grandeur:

> Once, and only once, we came to a dead stop; the surface of the water could be nowhere seen; the narrow channel was itself a glacier. . . . We women did not at the moment comprehend that . . . one of these bergs might render the ship entirely helpless in a place beyond the reach of succor. . . .
> The glacier [is] over five thousand feet wide, and at least eight hundred feet high. . . .

Hereafter the Swiss *mer de glace* will have to be printed in very small type. . . .

> When I speak of ice, I mean the veritable, pure, clear, crystal ice of the ice pitcher. A wall a hundred yards high . . . sharp and edged like flint, aqua-marine in color . . . with a froth of snow. If I did not know that it was ice, I should believe that it was glass. . . .
> We are too close for our own safety. . . . While we are moving [away], a sharp detonation rings out like the firing of a rifle, and one of the beautiful spires. . . is shivered into atoms, and its fragments fall with a splash four hundred feet. Later, there is a report like a cannon . . . this we are told is the parting of the sea somewhere far back in its mountain home. . . .
> Next . . . is the climb to the top of the glacier. . . . The ascent is exceedingly difficult; what looks like a mountain of rock over which you must wend your way . . . is really a mountain of ice covered by a layer of slimy mud. . . . I wore india-rubber high boots when I started, and I needed crutches before I finished. . . . [It is] infinitely more laborious than the ascent of Vesuvius on foot through lava, or any work to be done on the trails of the Yosemite. . . . A slip into one of those crevasses, which is covered by a thin layer of ice, means to be precipitated in an instant to a depth where no human aid can reach you.

When Collins saw Muir Glacier, only 11 years had passed since famed explorer John Muir became the first white known to have seen it. A decade later an earthquake destroyed it.

—Doris Weatherford

Excerpt from Septima Collins, *A Woman's Trip to Alaska*. New York: Cassell, 1890.

their children had to sit at desks occupied by Alaska Natives an hour earlier. Many native mothers chose not to subject their children to such hostility, and the majority of Native Alaskans remained illiterate.

In 1886 the U.S. secretary of the interior sent pioneer ethnologist Alice Cunningham Fletcher to investigate the educational needs of Alaska Natives in coastal Alaska and the Aleutians. An affiliate of the prestigious Peabody Museum in Massachusetts, Fletcher had a long history with the Omaha tribe of Nebraska, and her reports were highly influential in the 1887 passage of the Dawes Act, which governed federal Indian policy for decades.

Although Alaska still was not officially organized as a territory, it was included in the 1890 census. One woman who worked on the census, Eliza Scidmore, was assigned to southeast Alaska, where, due to the warmer climate around Sitka and Juneau, most Americans lived. Widely respected in and out of Alaska, Scidmore was the first woman elected to the board of the National Geographic Society, and a glacier was named for her.

She kept detailed records containing more information than those of typical census takers, and one of Scidmore's prescient observations concerned the transformation of the native economy in regard to fishing. By the end of the 1890s, salmon canneries dotted the coast of her census area. About a million cases of salmon were packed during each spring rush, and, like U.S. factories in that era, these employed large numbers of women and children, as well as men. By the era of World War I, the Bureau of Fisheries reported that as many as a third of Alaska's coastal native peoples—including even Eskimos and Aleuts—worked at canning salmon.

These canneries, of course, ran the risk of depleting the salmon supply, which was also the case with other animals in the 1890s. Eskimos were so damaged economically by the excessive whale hunting that they faced starvation. In an effort to supply a substitute food source, government officials created a program to import reindeer from Siberia. A young Eskimo woman played a major role in this importation. Sinrock Mary, or Mary Antisarlook, was known thereafter as "Mary the Reindeer Queen." Better at domesticating reindeer than most of her peers, she eventually ranched some 85,000 reindeer.

Other Alaskan women had even longer records of entrepreneurship, for travelers arriving in the 1860s found that women already had developed systems to meet ships and sell their handmade goods, such as goat-horn spoons, moccasins, and totems. These women took pride in their heritage and understood that outsiders also would be interested in it. Decades later travelers would still be buying these craft items.

Nor did they have any false modesty about the worth of their work. Travelogues of whites are unanimous in believing that the prices native women charged, especially for handmade baskets, were exorbitant, and yet they not only bought them, but also many buyers profitably resold their purchases. Ella Higginson, for example, wrote in 1908 of three women whose basketwork was so esteemed that people traveled to their obscure villages for their wares. A person could get a "little twined bowl," she wrote, "that was so soft and flexible that he could fold it up and carry it in his pocket . . . [and] it would be worth fifty dollars by the time he reached Seattle, and at least a hundred in New York." (Higginson 1908, 94) For many Alaska Native families, money from such sales might well be all the cash they had.

Other native women earned a living in less wholesome ways. The Gambells, a missionary couple on St. Lawrence Island in the Bering Sea, felt that their isolated community's tranquility was permanently destroyed when an Inupiat woman named Hoonakia introduced alcohol in 1897. Within three weeks of her arrival, children fearful of drunken parents sought shelter at the Gambells, and violence spread throughout the community. Native hunters exchanged their weapons for liquor, and famine was the ultimate result.

In addition to alcoholism, both whites and Alaska Natives suffered from syphilis, which had been introduced to the area by white whalers. A physician stationed at Point Barrow in 1889 said that nothing else took so much of his time and medications: "The unfortunate of both sexes . . . came to the station to ask for medical assistance. . . . The blight bids fair to depopulate the coast, nearly every infant bearing marked indications" of the mother's infection. (Mitchell 2001, 140)

This pattern of cultural collision repeated every few years, as rumors of gold brought thousands of white men (and a handful of women) to the newest boomtown. Circle City, for example, no longer a viable town today, had a population of over 1,000 men and 40 women in 1896. Some historians credit the beginning of the great Klondike gold strike, which reached its height in 1899, to an indigenous woman, KATE CARMACK. She found yellow stones in a stream near Dawson in the Yukon Territory.

Alaska Natives who had lived around this gold for centuries could not comprehend the white man's mania for this particular bit of their land, but gold and rumors of gold would be the key to

WOMEN SEARCH FOR KLONDIKE GOLD

In the summer of 1898, the nation's attention turned from the Spanish-American War to the discovery of gold in the Klondike. Thousands of men and a few women headed north to this region where Alaska meets the Yukon Territory of Canada. Among the prospectors were two unlikely women: Mary E. Hitchcock, the widow of a U.S. Navy commander, and Edith Van Buren, the grandniece of former U.S. president Martin Van Buren. They did some actual mining, but they also investigated, and then invested in, the claims of other miners. Hitchcock kept detailed notes and spent the next year writing *Two Women in the Klondike* (1899). She writes of life in Circle City:

> Midnight. Such excitement! The *Bella* came in from Dawson. . . [Some miners] were so burdened by a bag on the back that it needed no X-rays to tell us of the gold within. . . . "They're just carrying it that way for effect," whispered one of the women. . . . "They'd oughter have it stolen to teach 'em not to put on so many airs. . . . " We were much interested in a Mrs. C___, from Dawson, who modestly showed us the nuggets from her several bags. They were of all sizes and she had panned them herself. . . . One alone was worth two hundred and fifty dollars. . . .
>
> We were greatly astonished at the size of Circle City. . . . M___, who has been thirty-five years in Alaska, and has a handsome Indian wife . . . informed us that, although Dawson has a population of from ten to forty thousand, Circle City contains more houses, and is much healthier, as the former

is in a frightful sanitary condition. We peeped into the dance-hall. . . .

The boomtown soon became a ghost town, however, as most of the transient people who lived there—including the women at the dance halls—moved on with the next rumor of gold elsewhere. Yet Hitchcock saw the unwritten rules that governed such motley societies, as is clear in her comments on Dawson:

> We were first escorted to the dance-hall of the place, and slipped through a private entrance into a box that was curtained, so that we were free from observation while able to see all that took place. Nothing could have been more highly proper than the dancing, which consisted of waltzes, polkas, [etc.]. . . . The "girls," as they were called, seemed to be between twenty-five and thirty years of age. A lot of Dawson "society" men were dancing with them. . . . According to the rules of the house, drinks at one dollar each must be ordered after every dance. In case the "girl" does not care to drink, her partner gives her a check which she is allowed to "cash in" later, receiving twenty-five cents from the proprietor of the dance-hall. She is also paid twenty-five dollars a week. . . .

After the Klondike camps began to close down for the winter, the two women traveled around Alaska, often under unpleasant conditions, gathering more stories for Hitchcock's memoir.

—Doris Weatherford

Excerpts from Mary E. Hitchcock, *Two Women in the Klondike*. New York: G. P. Putnam's Sons, 1899.

Alaska's Americanization. By the turn of the century, the era of whalers and fur traders was largely over. It would be replaced by the miner, the saloon, and the dance hall.

The outpost of Nome boomed into a city overnight during the summer of 1900, when 20,000 people camped on its beaches—bringing with them diseases to which the native population had no immunity. Frances Kittredge, whose husband was a Nome physician, mentioned in her writings an epidemic that seemed to be devastating the Eskimo population. One image of the time was of a young Alaska Native who had to protect the corpse of his mother, a victim of the epidemic, from scavenging animals.

The Alaska Native Brotherhood (ANB) and the parallel Alaska Native Sisterhood (about which much less has been written) were formed at the turn of the century. Organized to overcome racism, the ANB consciously modeled itself on a white male lodge, the Arctic Brotherhood. No women served on the ANB board. Nevertheless, women worked behind the scenes with the men. Both the short-lived sisterhood and the ANB itself owed much to the family of TILLIE PAUL. Tillie, her three sons, and Frances Lackey Paul, the wife of her son William (who was one of the primary leaders of the ANB), all worked for the furtherance of ANB goals.

FROM TERRITORY TO STATEHOOD (1912–1959)

Although the native rights movement was just beginning when Alaska achieved territorial status in 1912, recognition of women's rights there—particularly white women's rights—was far ahead of the rest of the nation. According to records of the National American Woman Suffrage Association:

Woman suffrage in Alaska possesses the unique record of being granted without any solicitation whatever from the residents. It is not known that a suffrage club ever existed in the Territory; it is quite certain that prior to the convening of the first Territorial Legislature in Juneau in 1913 no suffrage campaigning whatever had been carried on, yet two members, coming from towns not less than 1,500 miles apart, brought drafts for an equal suffrage bill . . . The [House] vote was unanimous, [and] Senator Elwood Brunner of Nome, the only member who had expressed him[self] as unfavorable, had the good sense or caution to absent himself during the roll call. This was also the first bill to be approved by [new territorial] Governor J.F.A. Strong, on March 21, 1913. (Harper 1922, 713)

Women already had some voting experience, for the legal code that governed the area prior to territorial status gave them the right to vote in school elections. This first territorial legislature also made school attendance compulsory for white children and created four regional Boards of Children's Guardians—and the governor appointed a woman to each board. The only important right that women lacked was that of jury service. Unlike Wyoming, Alaska's men succumbed to fears that women would not be tough enough for jury duty in a territory known to attract men who were running from the law.

Women generally considered themselves much greater advocates of law and order than men, and this was particularly true of attitudes toward alcohol abuse. Energized by their new voting rights, women began a prohibition campaign in 1916 and, to the amazement of almost everyone, won a plebiscite on the issue by a two-to-one margin. It was Congress, not the territorial legislature, that followed up on this expression of voter opinion. On February 14, 1917, Congress enacted what was termed a "Bone Dry Prohibition Law" for the Alaska Territory. Congress was far away, however, and life in Alaska did not change dramatically as a result.

A few weeks after this prohibition law was enacted, the United States entered World War I, and

Alaska women did what they could for the soldiers in European battlefields halfway around the globe. The Red Cross developed 30 units of women in Alaska, some in isolated mining towns with just two or three members. Fairbanks women raised $8,000 to buy wool, and about 600 Alaskan women signed up to knit for the Red Cross.

These small numbers reflect the reason that statehood was still a dream, and why achieving territorial status had taken from 1867 to 1912. Alaska's white population remained small, and there were very few white women. When it became a territory, Alaska had approximately 30,000 whites, of whom no more than 6,000 were women. This sparse population was especially striking in the context of the territory's vast land mass. These 30,000 white people lived in an area of 586,400 square miles, with approximately one white woman in every 100 square miles.

If the number of white women was small, the number of native women voters was infinitesimal; and these women were often subjected to discrimination. Native Alaskan women—as well as men—had to submit to technical ethnic litmus tests in order to determine their eligibility for voting. Suffragists estimated in 1922 that not even 500 Alaska Native women could vote.

One of them was Tillie Paul, who remained known by that name despite her 1905 marriage to William Tamaree. By 1923 she had decades of activism behind her, but Alaska Natives of both genders still found it difficult to vote. Outraged that her uncle, a highly respected Tlingit man, had been denied a ballot, Paul took him back to the polls, pointed out the law to white officials, and succeeded in seeing him vote. A few months later, however, a Ketchikan grand jury indicted her for wrongly encouraging a Native Alaskan to vote. The trial turned on the man's literacy and citizenship, and when he was acquitted the charges against her were dropped.

Paul's daughter-in-law, Frances Lackey Paul, was less visible, but nonetheless important to the native rights cause in this era. Her parents had been missionaries, and she met William Paul when both attended a Presbyterian college in Tacoma, Washington. Her white family helped him establish his career, and, as one of their children later said, "when mother realized he was spending ninety percent of his time in political matters, she went back to teaching school" to ensure some livelihood. (Mitchell 2001, 224) Frances Paul also stood by her controversial husband when he was disbarred in 1937; she testified on his behalf at the bar hearing, which he refused to attend. She was also a friend of Mary Lee Davis, whose books in the 1930s helped interpret Alaska for Americans farther south.

In the next decade it was Ruth Muskrat Bronson who was the important female leader for native rights. An Oklahoma native, Bronson looked white, though she was part Cherokee. She lived in the fashionable Georgetown section of Washington, D.C., but she did more for Alaska Natives than nearly anyone else in this era. Bronson accepted the unpaid position of executive director of the National Congress of American Indians in 1946, and until Alaska achieved statehood at the end of the next decade, she learned the details of every bit of congressional legislation affecting Alaska. Washington-based attorney Frances Lopinsky also monitored legislation. In a 1949 memorandum to the attorney for Alaskan tribes, for example, she pointed out that the economic opportunities created by a bill introduced by the chairman of the House Committee on Public Lands seemed reserved almost exclusively for whites.

Statehood, ultimately achieved in 1959, was a result of the military's strategic need for bases in the Pacific following World War II. Thousands of Americans, including women, were assigned to these remote locales during the war. The first

HONORING PERATROVICH

The civil rights activist Elizabeth Wanamaker Peratrovich, whose audacious, improvised speech to the Alaska legislature from the legislative hall's public gallery prodded lawmakers into passing a key 1945 civil rights bill, is honored in the gallery from which she spoke. The plaque outside the Peratrovich Gallery reads:

> The Peratrovich Gallery is dedicated to Elizabeth Wanamaker Peratrovich (1911–1958), who championed the cause of civil rights in Alaska. She spoke before the Territorial Legislature on February 8, 1945, when a bill prohibiting racial discrimination in Alaska was being debated. According to the legislative custom of the time an opportunity was offered to anyone present who wished to speak on the bill. Elizabeth Peratrovich was the final speaker on that day and represented her people as the Grand President of the Alaska Native Sisterhood. "I would not have expected" she said, "that I, who am barely out of savagery, would have to remind gentlemen with five thousand years of recorded civilization behind them of our Bill of Rights." Following her speech, there was a wild burst of applause from the gallery and the Alaska Civil Rights Act passed by a vote of 11–4. In naming this Gallery for Ms. Peratrovich, we honor her for her vision, her wisdom, and her courage in speaking out for what she believed right. She symbolizes the role the gallery plays in the legislature and the importance of public opinion in the legislative process. She reminds us that a single person speaking from the heart can affect the future of all Alaskans.

members of the Women's Army Corps arrived at Kodiak Island early in 1943, and by war's end the U.S. Navy had sent some of its female WAVES there as well. ANFESIA SHAPSNIKOFF, an Aleut born in 1901 and educated at the last Russian school in Alaska, is credited with preserving priceless Russian art during the war. Perhaps the best-known woman to serve in Alaska during the war years, however, was Dr. Ruth Gruber, whose Interior Department appointment was hotly debated in the U.S. House of Representatives because some congressmen saw Gruber as being too liberal.

Postwar Alaska fitted the "liberal" stereotype in many ways. As longtime Alaskan Sally Carrighar pointed out, when Alaska became the 49th state in 1959 it was spending 51% of its budget on education; salaries for its teachers (a largely female occupation) were the highest in the nation; and, Carrighar averred, "no racial discrimination has been allowed in Alaska for fifteen years." She also added that native women, especially Eskimos, "are truly emancipated. . . . More of them vote than white women do. . . [and] they think for themselves." (Carrighar 1958, viii)

These changed racial attitudes owed a great deal to ELIZABETH PERATROVICH, who, with her husband Roy, was active in both the movement for statehood and the native rights movement. The couple took on the challenge of integrating their Juneau neighborhood, and Elizabeth served as president of the Alaska Native Sisterhood. During a 1945 legislative debate, Peratrovich was so outraged by a senator's disparagement of the native population that she stood in the gallery and asked to be heard. Her effect on legislators was electric, and a civil rights bill passed with only 5 of 16 senators voting against it.

FROM STATEHOOD TO CONTEMPORARY ERA (1959–present)

In 1960, the year after statehood was achieved, SADIE BROWER NEAKOK became the state's first female magistrate. Her judicial work revolved around reconciling the U.S. legal system with the system of tribal law that was integral to many communities in Alaska.

Two women composed the state song that was adopted with statehood: Elinor Dusenberry wrote the music, and Marie Drake the lyrics, for "Alaska's Flag." Drake had worked as an educational administrator in Alaska since the 1920s, routinely traveling hundreds of miles between schools. Dusenberry actually composed the music in Nebraska, where she was homesick for Alaska.

THE WOMEN OF THE IDITAROD

In 1974 Mary Shields and Lolly Medley became the first women to compete in and finish the Iditarod dogsled race. While they were preparing for the race, the two women drew much attention from male mushers, many believing it was impossible for a woman to complete this demanding event. However, Shields and Medley proved the skeptics wrong, with Shields finishing a respectable 23rd, and Medley finishing just 26 minutes later. Both Shields and Medley were welcomed to the finish line by a group of women carrying a banner proclaiming, "You've Come a Long Way, Baby."

In 1985 Libby Riddles became the first woman to win the Iditarod—she finished some two hours ahead of her closest competitor. After finishing the race in 1980 and 1981, racing borrowed dogs both times, Riddles decided that in order to win the Iditarod she would have to train her dogs herself. After teaming up with Joe Garnie to breed and train sled dogs, Libby entered the race again in 1985 and was victorious. Her victory would pave the way for Susan Butcher, who would come to dominate the Iditarod like few others.

Butcher moved to Alaska when she was 20 years old, and she immediately became interested in dogsled racing. Working odd jobs in the summer in order to train in the winter, Butcher won an unprecedented three consecutive Iditarod races from 1986 to 1988. She also won in 1990, and she was leading in 1991 before an unexpected blizzard derailed her hopes for a fifth title. During the period of her Iditarod dominance, Butcher was considered the premier long-distance musher in the world. Rick Swenson, a competing musher at the time of Butcher's victories, once admitted "The rest of us are just in a different class."

More recently DeeDee Jonrowe has found success as an Iditarod competitor. Born in Germany, Jonrowe fell in love with dogsled racing while studying and playing basketball at the University of Alaska–Fairbanks. After competing in smaller races for years, Jonrowe concentrated her efforts on the Iditarod and placed second in 1993. In October 1996 Jonrowe was severely injured in an automobile accident and spent weeks in the hospital. But in a testament to her competitive nature, she rehabilitated in time to finish fourth in 1997. Jonrowe has since authored a book entitled *Iditarod Dreams* (1995), chronicling her experiences preparing for the Iditarod.

—David C. Francis

Ruth Bronson served as a model for Janie Leask, who was president of the Alaska Federation of Natives in the 1980s. Leask flew between her home and Washington, where she explained to indifferent lawmakers the ramifications of their policies on her people. Leask also played a role in honoring Elizabeth Peratrovich, who died the year before statehood was achieved. In 1989, the 30th anniversary of statehood, the capitol gallery in which Peratrovich demanded to speak against discrimination was named for her.

Alaska women still maintain traditions of adventurism. In 1914, for example, mountain climber Dora Keen led the first expedition to a range north of Anchorage (the range is now named for her), and such traditions provide role models for modern adventurers such as Libby Riddles and Susan Butcher. In 1985 Riddles became the first woman to win the challenging Iditarod dogsled race; Butcher, who won the race a total of four times, went on to become the first person to win it three consecutive years, starting with her victory the year after Riddles won.

Alaska's population remains so small, however, that it still elects just one member (who serves at large) to the U.S. House of Representatives. That, plus the continuing imbalance of women and men in the population, is a factor in Alaska's status as one of the seven states that, as of this writing, have never had a woman in Congress. In 1994, however, FRAN ULMER took office as lieutenant governor, making her the first woman to be elected to a statewide office in Alaska. The mayor of Juneau from 1983 to 1985, Ulmer served as a state representative from 1987 to 1994. A Democrat,

Lt. Gov. Fran Ulmer in 2002 campaigning for Alaska's governorship, an election she lost. (AP/Wide World Photos)

she lost her 2002 bid for governor to Republican Frank Murkowski.

Alaska set a major precedent in 1994 when women led both legislative chambers. Republican majorities elected Speaker of the House Gail Phillips and Senate President Pro Tempore Drue Pearce.

Republican Lisa Murkowski assumed the U.S. Senate seat of her father, who appointed her to that office when he vacated it upon his 2002 election to Alaska's governorship. A seasoned politician in her own right, Lisa Murkowski was a three-term state representative and Alaska House majority leader.

—Doris Weatherford

TIMELINE

United States Events	Alaska Events
1620 Settlement of Plymouth Colony	**1600**
	1700
	1741 Russians first land in Alaska.
1776 United States declares independence	
	1790s First permanent white settlements established.
	1800
1861–65 U.S. Civil War	
	1867 United States buys Alaska from Russia for $7.2 million.
	1877 Amanda McFarland arrives as first female missionary and establishes Mrs. McFarland's Home and School for Girls in Wrangell.
	1886 Ethnologist Alice Cunningham Fletcher investigates the educational needs of Alaska Natives for Department of Interior.
	1899 Alaska gold strike reaches its peak.
	1900
	1912 Alaska established as a territory, women granted school suffrage as part of the legal code.
	1913 Women given full suffrage.
1914–18 World War I	
1920 Ratification of the 19th Amendment	
1929–39 Great Depression	
1939–45 World War II	
	1959 Alaska achieves statehood.
	1960 Sadie Brower Neakok becomes the state's first female magistrate.
1975 Vietnam War ends	
	1980s Janie Leask named president of the Alaska Federation of Natives.
	1989 Gallery in state capitol dedicated to Elizabeth W. Peratrovich.
	1994 Fran Ulmer becomes first woman elected to statewide office when she wins as lieutenant governor.
	2000
	2002 Ulmer loses governor's race to Republican Frank Murkowski, who appoints his daughter Lisa Murkowski to his U.S. Senate seat.

PROMINENT WOMEN

KATE CARMACK (1857–1920)

Known as the "First Lady of the Klondike," Kate Carmack of Caribou Crossing on the Chilkoot Trail aided the party that precipitated the gold rush of 1896. Born Shaaw Tlaa, she was a member of the Stick tribe in central Alaska. She married prospector George Carmack, who named her Kate, and in 1893 she gave birth to a daughter, Graphie Grace. The Carmacks joined Kate's brother, Skookum Jim, and his son, Tagish Charlie, in a search for gold near their cabin at Rabbit Creek on August 16, 1896. To support the company, she took in laundry.

Some credit Carmack with finding the first gold in the Klondike, one of the world's largest strikes. She gave up hard labor, lived in a comfortable home in Dawson City, and traveled to California in 1898 to visit her sister Rose, who reared Graphie. The Carmacks's marriage dissolved, however, soon after their arrival in California.

After George left Kate to marry a white woman, Kate and Graphie settled at a cabin in Caribou Crossing (now Carcross). Kate lost her share of the Klondike wealth to George because the government did not recognize their tribal marriage. She lived on a government pension and handouts from Skookum Jim until her death from influenza.

SARAH DICKINSON (dates unknown)

Sarah Dickinson, born a Tlingit and married to a white fur trader, was one of Alaska's first public school teachers. She was employed in 1880 at a rudimentary classroom in the Northwest Trading Company building, which was near Haines House, a mission built in 1879 to serve the Tlingit Indians of Chilkat and Chilkoot Valleys. The elementary school, operated by the Bureau of Indian Affairs, taught the basics, such as reading and arithmetic, as well as woodworking, art, crafts, and music. The retention of native languages was also encouraged.

Dispatched to Alaska by S. Hall Young, a Presbyterian missionary at Fort Wrangell, Dickinson was useful for her knowledge of both native and white cultures and languages. She interpreted worship services led by evangelist Philip McKay to native congregations. Her ability to step across cultural frontiers was invaluable in the region, especially in territory thinly populated by whites, and paved the way for white missionaries to accompany and follow her. Caroline and Eugene Willard joined Dickinson at the Chilkat school in 1881. Dickinson interpreted for the Willards, and their American connections encouraged the local chief to free his slaves, an idea he had ridiculed when Dickinson, herself an Native Alaskan, had urged it.

LADY JANE FRANKLIN (1791–1875)

A Victorian lady and newcomer to the North American Northwest, Lady Jane Griffin Franklin gathered useful geographic and navigational information about the Arctic while combing the Alaskan wild for her lost husband. A British intellectual known for an interest in science, she was no less adept at travel, mountain climbing, and adventure. In 1837, while her husband, naval explorer and scientist Sir John Franklin, was lieutenant governor of Van Diemen's Land (now Tasmania), she helped support the construction of a botanical garden, museum, and library, as well as an agricultural settlement on Tasmania's Huon River. Locals admired her for being the first woman to climb Mount Wellington, and they esteemed her social activism in transforming Tasmania from a penal colony to a thriving society.

After the disappearance in 1847 of the *Erebus* and *Terror,* expeditionary ships that Sir John led to Canada's Baffin Bay, Lady Jane spent her inheritance looking for him throughout the frozen expanse stretching west to Alaska. She engaged Cap. Leopold McClintock to head a search party and equipped her yacht, *Fox,* for iceberg-choked waters. After ten years and 50 attempts to locate Franklin, McClintock solved the mystery of the lost men, who had been disoriented by lead-tainted tinned food and eventually froze to death in Inuit territory. Because the combined search efforts aided the search for the fabled Northwest Passage, in 1860 Franklin became the first woman to earn the Founder's Medal from the Royal Geographic Society, and she was also honored by the society's Lady Franklin Bay Expedition of 1881–1884. Her devotion to her husband survives in a two-act stage play by Stella Kent and in a ballad, "Lady Franklin's Lament."

MARGARET KEENAN HARRAIS (dates unknown)
Educator and judge Margaret Keenan Harrais of Valdez, Alaska, displayed respect for justice and attempted to strengthen the circuit court system by making internal changes to the system. In the 1920s she lived in a two-room cabin in an isolated portion of the Upper Chitina Valley on the south side of the Wrangell Range, where she cultivated berries and raised vegetables and fodder for her horses.

In 1941, while serving as a U.S. commissioner in the territorial judicial system in Valdez, Harrais challenged a fee system that prevented working-class people from serving on the circuit court. She argued that the fees paid to circuit judges were so small that they dissuaded individuals without independent means from taking on the court positions. In 1947 she compiled a statement of mining claims for the Alaska Territorial Department of Mines. In this statement she called attention to a wealth of copper, lead, zinc, and silver that lay untapped on her property, which she had surveyed in 1926 and 1927.

AMANDA MCFARLAND (1832–1912)
The first female missionary to Alaska, Amanda Reed McFarland of Fairmont, West Virginia, earned a reputation for courage. The wife of the Rev. David McFarland, with whom she had worked as a missionary to Illinois, she was a veteran of Presbyterian outreaches in Santa Fe, New Mexico, and among the Nez Percé of Idaho. After she was widowed, she reshaped her career at the summons of Rev. Dr. Sheldon Jackson, who told her of the great educational and spiritual need among Alaska Natives. On arrival by steamer, she discovered herself to be the only white female in a gold-rush settlement.

McFarland's contribution to social betterment included education, spiritual leadership, and a home and school for girls (known as Mrs. McFarland's) that she founded in Fort Wrangell and operated without pay. After turning down a counteroffer from the Sitka school district, she remained among poor Alaska Natives to fight slavery, prostitution, and witchcraft. Her school became so famous for rescuing girls that applications exceeded the available space. In 1880 she built a larger structure, which she supervised until it burned in February 1883. McFarland took some of her students to a dormitory in Sitka, and in 1886 she moved on to an industrial boarding school among the Haida at Howkan. At her retirement at age 65 she was known as the "Mother of Protestant Missions in Alaska."

MARGARET MURIE (1902–)
Author Margaret Elizabeth "Mardy" Murie of Seattle, Washington, excited readers with her description of the northern wild. The daughter of a sea captain, she grew up in Fairbanks, Alaska, was educated at Reed College and Simmons

College, and in 1924 she became the first woman to graduate from the University of Alaska at Fairbanks. When she met her future husband, biologist Olaus J. Murie, he was studying caribou for the government wildlife service. At age 22 she took the job of secretary to the expedition's Alaska station. In 1927, after Olaus was posted to Jackson Hole, Wyoming, to study a decline in migratory elk herds, she again worked as his secretary. The couple made their Wyoming home a base from which they launched scientific expeditions. She described her home life in Wyoming in *Wapiti Wilderness* (1966).

In 1946 Murie joined Olaus in serving the Wilderness Society, and a decade later their efforts stopped a dam project on the Colorado River. Working jointly until 1962, they promoted the conservation of natural resources through the society's western headquarters in Jackson Hole. Many of their adventures took them back to Alaska, which she described in the best-selling *Two in the Far North* (1962). In 1949 the Muries studied Wyoming elk that had been transported to New Zealand's Fiordlands, while she continued lecturing on rescuing the environment and preserving water, green spaces, wildlife, and solitude. At the request of the University of Alaska, she wrote *Island Between* (1977), which summarized archaeological studies of St. Lawrence Island and the Eskimos of the Bering Sea.

In 1979, 14 years after Olaus's death from cancer, Margaret Murie compiled his life work in *The Alaskan Bird Sketches of Olaus Murie.* Her honoraria include the governor's award from Washington, citations from the National Audubon Society and the Sierra Club, and a degree from the University of Alaska. In 1998 Pres. Bill Clinton awarded her the Presidential Medal of Freedom. The Wilderness Society's Olaus and Margaret Murie Award recognizes young environmentalists who take risks to promote conservation.

SADIE BROWER NEAKOK (1916–)

Judge, mediator, and activist Sadie Brower Neakok of Barrow, Alaska, was the state's first female Native Alaskan to become a magistrate. The daughter of an esteemed whaler, she was educated at the Barrow Bureau of Indian Affairs Day School and at Willard High School in San Francisco. After two years at Stanford University, she returned to her home state, graduating from the University of Alaska in 1938. She was employed as a dietitian at the U.S. Public Health Service Hospital and as a teacher at the Barrow Day School. She also served as a social worker and organized a mother's club that addressed the hygiene and behavioral needs of schoolchildren.

Neakok hosted a 24-part radio series entitled *Our Inupiat Values,* which presented the native view of kinship, cooperation, respect, and spirituality. As a U.S. territorial commissioner representing Alaska Natives, she denounced the U.S. government, which had built a navy base in the area and enacted a policy of strict segregation from local citizens. Although she lacked a law degree, she voluntarily advised natives of their rights and, after 1959, explained how the legal system of the new state of Alaska varied from tribal traditions.

Neakok entered a new phase of mediating between the Eskimo and the white world in 1960, when state troopers took over the governing of Barrow. As a magistrate she condoned incidents of whole villages engaged in acts of civil disobedience against federal game laws that limited the hunting of waterfowl to the summer months and restricted the shooting of caribou, an animal on which the Inuit depend for food and hides. To force a change in state wildlife regulations, she organized a village protest that involved more defiance than a game warden could handle and produced more lawbreakers than the jails could accommodate. In 1977 Neakok retired from her judicial post. A biography of her, entitled *Sadie*

Brower Neakok, an Inupiaq Woman (1989), was written by Margaret Blackman.

ELIZABETH PERATROVICH (1911–1958)

A Tlingit freedom fighter and humanitarian, Elizabeth Wanamaker Peratrovich of Petersburg demanded equal civil rights for Alaska Natives two decades before the civil rights movement liberated African Americans from segregation. Adopted by Presbyterian missionaries Andrew and Mary Wanamaker, she attended high school in Ketchikan and college at Sheldon Jackson College in Sitka. She continued her college studies at Western College of Education in Bellingham, Washington, where she met Roy Peratrovich, whom she married in 1931. As president of the Alaska Native Sisterhood, she joined her husband in lobbying for legislation to halt racial segregation in restaurants, public buildings, housing, and hospitals. On February 16, 1945, the state legislature passed an antidiscrimination law after Elizabeth Peratrovich lectured the all-male state Senate on the American Bill of Rights. In celebration of her successful lobbying, the Peratroviches went dancing at Juneau's Baranof Hotel, a facility formerly closed to Alaska Natives.

Peratrovich's stunning off-the-cuff speech earned the regard of editors at the *Daily Alaska Empire*. In her honor, the state celebrates Elizabeth Peratrovich Day each February 16. An award for humanitarianism, a bronze bust in the Alaskan state capitol, an exhibit at the National Museum of the American Indian at the Smithsonian Institution, and a play by Diane E. Benson, *When My Spirit Raised Its Hands: The Story of Elizabeth Peratrovich and Alaska Civil Rights*, all commemorate Peratrovich's contributions to equal rights.

IRENE RYAN (1909–1997)

Mineral and petroleum engineer and bush pilot Irene Ryan of Boston, Massachusetts, was the first female graduate from the New Mexico School of Mines. While living in oil country in Oklahoma and Texas, she earned money by graphing log entries for drilling companies and looking for fossils in core samples. At age 22 she traveled to Lake Spenard, Alaska, on her father's floatplane. While working as a waitress and bank teller in Anchorage, she learned to fly, and in 1932 she became the first Alaska woman to fly solo.

Ryan challenged restrictions on women's aspirations by majoring in geological engineering at the New Mexico School of Mines. In 1940 she earned a B.S. degree, and she returned to Anchorage at the beginning of World War II. As an employee of the Civil Aeronautics Administration, she designed housing developments, the Fairbanks-to-Skagway military pipeline, and 17 major airfields—most notably, the Anchorage International Airport. After the war she worked as a mineral prospector and oil scout for Shell Oil Company, established the Oil Well Service Company, and drew up geologic surveys and charts for Anchorage Gas & Oil Development, Inc.

In 1955 Ryan was elected to the Alaska Territorial House of Representatives, where she worked to further Alaska's goal of statehood. After successfully lobbying for its admission to the Union, she served in the Alaska State Senate. In 1970, as commissioner of the Department of Economic Development, she became the state's first female Cabinet member. In 1985 Alaska Pacific University proclaimed her "Alaskan of the Year."

ANFESIA SHAPSNIKOFF (1901–1973)

Russian–Aleut basket weaver Anfesia Tutiakoff Shapsnikoff contributed to Alaska's native crafts and promoted respect for Aleutian history. Born in Unalaska on the Aleutian Island of Atka, she studied weaving with a maternal aunt, Mary Prokopiuff LaVigne, and learned to read and write in Aleut, English, and Russian. After becoming a devout member of the Russian

Orthodox Church, she secured church artifacts in an underground vault to protect them in the event of an invasion during World War II.

Shapsnikoff was also active in the community. Affectionately known as "Little Grandma," she was appointed to the Unalaska City Council, the board of health, and the board of the Kodiak and Aleutian Islands Historical Society, which was formed in 1954. In 1967, she traveled to Seward to address the Resurrection Bay Historical Society. At age 70 she initiated a lawsuit that halted the government sale of historic property at Dutch Harbor. Shortly after her death, the University of Alaska published her posthumous article "Aleut Basketry." Ray Hudson and Tricia Brown wrote of her expertise and willingness to teach others in *Moments Rightly Placed: An Aleutian Memoir* (1998).

TILLIE PAUL TAMAREE (1863–1955?)

Peacemaker and civil rights leader Matilda Kinnon Paul Tamaree of Victoria, British Columbia, crusaded for a ban on alcohol and full citizenship for the Tlingit of Alaska. After her mother's death, she was reared by an aunt and uncle and defied tribal traditions by refusing an arranged marriage to an elderly man. Educated at Mrs. McFarland's Home and School for Girls in Wrangell (run by Amanda McFarland), she married Louis Francis Paul at age 16 and taught religion at Klukwan and Sitka. In addition to interpreting for missionaries, she translated hymns into Tlingit, played the church organ, and pastored a Chilkat congregation. The temperance society Paul organized developed into the three main native-rights groups: New Covenant Legion, Alaska Native Brotherhood, and Alaska Native Sisterhood.

She further aided native people by developing a Tlingit alphabet and coauthoring a native dictionary. She pressed for suffrage for native peoples in class-action suits, and in 1923 she was arrested for helping her uncle, Charles Jones, to register to vote. Her son, attorney William Paul, successfully defended them in court. By 1924 Alaska had passed the Indian Citizen Act, which gave voting rights to Native Americans. After almost two decades of widowhood, she married William Tamaree. Tamaree became the first female elder ordained in the Alaska–Northwest Presbyterian Synod in 1931.

FRAN ULMER (1947–)

Alaska lieutenant governor Fran Ulmer, originally from Madison, Wisconsin, was the first woman elected to an Alaskan state office. She majored in economics and political science at the University of Wisconsin and obtained a law degree from the Wisconsin School of Law. Upon settling in Alaska in 1973, she became a key policy adviser to former governor Jay Hammond. She also devoted herself to volunteerism, particularly with Big Brothers and Big Sisters, the Salvation Army, and the March of Dimes.

After chairing the Juneau Planning Commission, Ulmer became the mayor of Juneau in 1983, serving also as president of the U.S. Conference of Women Mayors. During four terms in the Alaska House of Representatives, where she served as minority leader, she supported improvements to education and child care, insurance coverage of mammograms, and prevention of child abuse and neglect. In 1994 she won a race for lieutenant governor, and in 1997 she represented Gov. Tony Knowles at the President's Summit on Volunteerism in Philadelphia. She easily won a second term as lieutenant governor in 1998.

In addition to being designated legislator of the year by the Alaska Cancer Society, she was twice named Kids Champion of the Year and Child Advocate of the Year by the National Association for the Education of Young Children. Ulmer ran a strong campaign for governor in 2002, but lost the election to Republican Frank Murkowski.

ESTHER WUNNICKE (1922–)

Author, attorney, and activist Esther C. Wunnicke of Anchorage, Alaska, earned a reputation for including local voices in discussions of land use and for setting standards for the creation of state parks, controlling pollution, and the laying of gas pipelines. Of unknown native heritage, she grew up in New Mexico and attended George Washington University, where she wrote for the campus law review. She was admitted to the Alaska state bar in 1950. After marrying and settling in Anchorage, she supported the League of Women Voters and became active in the native rights movement. In 1967 she served on the Federal Field Committee for Development Planning in Alaska and influenced the compilation of a published survey, "Alaska Natives and the Land." She gave voice to the Alaska Native perspective on land occupancy and stewardship issues, as well as on federal hiring policies that favored whites over Indians.

In February 1983 Wunnicke was appointed as a commissioner of the Alaska Department of Natural Resources. During a period of contention over Native American rights to reservation lands, she promoted education for public administrators and state fish-and-game management that allowed rural Alaskans to follow traditional methods of subsistence. She helped to shape public policy for Alaska Common Ground, a citizens' pressure group that she founded in 1991. For her commitment to public lands she received a National Public Service award in 1986. In 1994 she was elected vice president of the board of the Pacific Northwest Pollution Prevention Research Center. Among her writings are *Biological Management and Its Contribution to the Socio-Economic Failure of Alaska's Commercial Fisheries* (1969), *Where Alaskan Native People Live* (reprinted in 1990), and *Alaskan Geography* (also reprinted in 1990).

—Mary Ellen Snodgrass

PROMINENT SITES

Alutiiq Museum and Archaeological Repository
215 Mission Road
Suite #101
Kodiak, AK 99615
Telephone: (907) 486 7004, ext. 8
Web: http://www.alutiiqmuseum.com
This museum features women artists who are residents of Kodiak and help keep native craftwork alive. Among these artists are Susan Malutin, who is known for her beautiful work in sewing skins; Arlene Slanner, who helped revitalize the art of Alutiiq grass basket weaving; and painter Helen Simeonoff.

Canyon Creek Cameos—Polly Renner and Nellie Frost
Mile 56.7 of the Seward Highway
Canyon Creek Bridge Turnout
There were about a dozen women in the Canyon Creek area of Alaska during the Turnagain Arm Gold Rush of 1896–1898. This highway marker tells the story of Nellie Frost, who lived on a claim with her husband, and Polly Renner, who founded the Polly Mining Company with her husband and other partners.

Carrie M. McLain Memorial Museum
200 East Front Street
Box 53
Nome, AK 99762
Telephone: (907) 443 6630
This is the only museum in Nome, Alaska, and it is dedicated to Carrie M. McLain, a pioneer who moved to the town in 1905. She was considered to be the most knowledgeable historian of the town, and upon her death in 1973 the town voted unanimously to name the building that housed the town museum in her honor.

Colony House and Palmer Historical Society
316 East Elmwood Avenue
Mailing address: PO Box 1925
Palmer, AK 99645
Telephone: (907) 745 1935
Web: http://www.customcpu.com/ait/david/psociety.htm
Irene and Oscar Beylund were the first occupants of this house (in 1936). They were one of the 203 families who moved to the Matanuska Colony farming community from Wisconsin as part of a New Deal resettlement project. The house has been restored by the Palmer Historical Society as a representation of the homes in the settlement.

Dorothy Page Museum and Visitor Center
323 Main Street
Wasilla, AK 99654
Telephone: (907) 373 9071
Dorothy Page developed the idea of the Iditarod in 1964 and was a cofounder of the first race in 1967. The museum deals with the history of the Wasilla area. There are seven historic buildings behind the museum, including the first school in the town and two types of log cabins.

First Presbyterian Church in Wrangell
PO Box 439
Wrangell, AK 99929
Telephone: (907) 874 3534
In 1877 Dr. Sheldon Jackson invited Amanda McFarland, who lived in Oregon, to come to Wrangell as a missionary. McFarland was the first female missionary in Alaska. The First Presbyterian Church, the site of the ministry, is now the oldest standing Presbyterian church in Alaska. The church was constructed in 1879 and reconstructed on the same site in the 1950s.

First Presbyterian Church of Haines
114 First Avenue South
Haines, AK 99827
Telephone: (907) 776 2377
Web: http://www.wytbear.com/hpc
The First Presbyterian Church of Haines was established in 1881 by Dr. Sheldon Jackson and Mrs. Caroline Willard at a mission to the Chilkat tribes. Caroline Willard was one of the first female missionaries in Alaska. The church bell that is used today by Haines Presbyterian is the same one that was shipped to the Chilkat mission in 1881. It was the first Protestant church bell heard in Alaska.

Glacier Bay National Park and Preserve
PO Box 140
Gustavus, AK 99826
Telephone: (907) 697 2230
Eliza Scidmore was a travel writer and photographer who traveled to Alaska in the 1880s and wrote *Alaska: Its Southern Coast and the Sitkan Archipelago* (1885).

The celebrated book is still used as a travel guide today. The Scidmore Glacier, located within the national park, was named for her.

Gold Rush Women Highway Marker

Mile 197.6 of the Richardson Highway
South side of Isabelle Pass
The highway marker pays tribute to women who participated in the Alaska Gold Rush, with photos and biographies of Ethel Berry, Nellie Cashman, and Margaret Mayo. Nearby Isabelle Pass was named for Isabelle Barnette, who crossed the pass with her husband, E. T. Barnette, in 1902. The couple founded Fairbanks, Alaska.

Iditarod Museum at Iditarod Headquarters

Mile 2.2 Knik Road
Wasilla, AK 99654
Telephone: (907) 376 5155
Web: http://www.iditarod.com/index.shtml
The Iditarod is the most famous and prestigious dogsled race in the world, and it has a rich history where women are concerned. The museum explores the race's past and includes information about Dorothy Page, who had the idea for the race in 1964, and other important women in Iditarod history, including Libby Riddles, the first woman to win the race, and Susan Butcher, who was the first competitor to win three consecutive Iditarods.

Isabel Miller Museum

330 Harbor Drive
PO Box 6181
Sitka, AK 99835
Telephone: (907) 747 6455

Home of the New Archangel Dancers, an all-female troupe that performs traditional Russian dance throughout the summer months. The museum celebrates Eskimo, Russian, and American heritage and history, including the Tlingit women and their work with spruce root baskets.

Peratrovich Gallery

State Capitol
Juneau, AK 99801
Telephone: (907) 465 4648
Web: http://www.legis.state.ak.us/home/capitol.htm
The Peratrovich Gallery provides seating for visitors who would like to watch the Alaska House of Representatives. The gallery honors the actions of Elizabeth Wanamaker Peratrovich, whose impassioned speech from the gallery spurred passage of a key 1945 civil rights bill.

Wrangell–Saint Elias National Park and Preserve

107 Richardson Highway
PO Box 439
Copper Center, AK 99573
Telephone: (907) 822 5234
Web: http://www.wrangell.st.elias.national-park.com
This is the largest national park in America—it is six times the size of Yellowstone. Its highest peak is Mount Blackburn, which rises 16, 930 feet. In 1912 Dora Keen and G. W. Handy were the first people to reach its summit. The trek took them 33 days. Dora Keen was one of the only women in the world to be the first ascender of a major mountain.

RESOURCES

FURTHER READING

HISTORY

Alaska Northwest Publishing. *Interior Alaska.* Anchorage, 1988.

Cantwell, Margaret. *North to Share: The Sisters of Saint Ann in Alaska and the Yukon Territory.* Victoria, British Columbia: Sisters of St. Ann, 1992.

Carrighar, Sally. *Moonlight at Midday.* New York: Knopf, 1958.

Collins, Septima M. *A Woman's Trip to Alaska.* New York: Cassell, 1890.

Davis, Mary Lee. *Uncle Sam's Attic: The Intimate Story of Alaska.* Boston: W. A. Wilde, 1930.

Davis, Mary Lee. *We Are Alaskans.* Boston: W. A. Wilde, 1931.

Driscoll, Joseph. *War Discovers Alaska.* Philadelphia: J. B. Lippincott, 1943.

Graham, Roberta L. *A Sense of History: A Reference Guide to Alaska's Women, 1896–1985.* Anchorage: Alaska Women's Commission, 1985.

Harper, Ida Husted. *History of Woman Suffrage.* Vol. 6. New York: J. J. Little & Ives, 1922.

Harper-Haines, Jan. *Cold River Spirits: The Legacy of an Athabascan-Irish Family from Alaska's Yukon River.* Kenmore, Wash.: Epicenter Press, 2000.

Harvey, Lola. *Derevnia's Daughters: Saga of an Alaskan Village.* Manhattan, Kan.: Sunflower University Press, 1991.

Haycox, Stephen, and Mary Childers Mangusso. *An Alaska Anthology: Interpreting the Past.* Seattle: University of Washington Press, 1996.

Higginson, Ella. *Alaska: The Great Country.* New York: MacMillan, 1908.

Hinckley, Ted C. *The Americanization of Alaska, 1867–1897.* Palo Alto, Calif.: Pacific Books, 1972.

Hitchcock, Mary E. *Two Women in the Klondike: The Story of a Journey to the Gold-Fields of Alaska.* New York: G. P. Putnam's Sons, 1899.

Jochelson, Waldemar. *History, Ethnology, and Anthropology of the Aleut.* Salt Lake City: University of Utah Press, 2002.

Keddell, Georgina Matheson Murray. *Peace Lovin' Folk: Stories of Alaska Highway Pioneers.* Merritt, British Columbia: M. Graham Publishers, 1992.

Khromchenko, V. S. *V. S. Khromchenko's Coastal Explorations in Southwestern Alaska, 1822.* Translated by David H. Kraus and edited by James W. VanStone. Chicago: Field Museum of Natural History, 1973.

Krause, Aurel. *The Tlingit Indians: Results of a Trip to the Northwest Coast of America and the Bering Straits.* Translated by Erna Gunther. Seattle: University of Washington Press, 1956.

Krause, Aurel. *To the Chukchi Peninsula and to the Tlingit Indians, 1881/1882: Journals and Letters by Aurel and Arthur Krause.* Translated by Margot Krause McCaffrey. Fairbanks: University of Alaska Press, 1993.

Lord, Nancy. *Fishcamp: Life on an Alaskan Shore.* Washington, D.C.: Island Press, 1997.

Mergler, Wayne, ed. *The Last New Land: Stories of Alaska, Past and Present.* Anchorage: Alaska Northwest Books, 1996.

Mitchell, Donald. *Sold American: A Story of Alaska Natives and Their Land, 1867–1959.* Hanover, N.H.: University Press of New England, 1997.

Mitchell, Donald. *Take My Land, Take My Life: The Story of Congress's Historic Settlement of Alaska Native Land Claims, 1960–1971.* Fairbanks: University of Alaska Press, 2001.

Morgan, Lael. *Good Time Girls of the Alaska-Yukon Gold Rush.* Fairbanks, Alaska: Epicenter Press, 1998.

Murie, Margaret E. *Two in the Far North.* 5th ed. Anchorage: Alaska Northwest Books, 1997.

Murphy, Claire Rudolf, and Jane G. Haigh. *Gold Rush Women.* Anchorage: Alaska Northwest Books, 1997.

Naske, Claus-M., and Herman E. Slotnick. *Alaska, a History of the 49th State.* 2nd ed. Norman: University of Oklahoma Press, 1987.

Paul, Fred. *Then Fight for It: Behind the Scenes of the Alaska Settlement Act of 1971 and the Creation of the North Slope Borough.* Victoria, British Columbia: Trafford, 2001.

Ritter, Harry. *Alaska's History: The People, Land, and Events of the North Country.* Anchorage: Alaska Northwest Books, 1993.

Ross, Ken. *Environmental Conflict in Alaska.* Boulder: University Press of Colorado, 2000.

Tower, Elizabeth A. *Anchorage: From Its Humble Origins as a Railroad Construction Camp.* Fairbanks, Alaska: Epicenter Press, 1999.

Webb, Melody. *Yukon: The Last Frontier.* Albuquerque: University of New Mexico Press, 1985.

Wold, Jo Anne. *The Way It Was: Of People, Places, and Things in Pioneer Interior Alaska.* Anchorage: Alaska Northwest Publishing, 1988.

BIOGRAPHY AND AUTOBIOGRAPHY

Backhouse, Frances. *Women of the Klondike.* Vancouver, British Columbia: Whitecap Books, 1995.

Beaman, Libby. *Libby: The Sketches, Letters and Journal of Libby Beaman, Recorded in the Pribilof Islands, 1879–1880.* Tulsa, Okla.: Council Oak Books, 1998.

Belsford, Ginna. *Profiles in Change: Names, Notes, and Quotes for Alaskan Women.* Anchorage: Alaska Commission on the Status of Women, 1983.

Blackman, Margaret B. *Sadie Brower Neakok, an Inupiaq Woman.* Seattle: University of Washington Press, 1992.

Brebner, Phyllis Lee. *The Alaska Highway: A Personal & Historical Account of the Building of the Alaska Highway.* Erin, Ontario: Boston Mills Press, 1985.

Breece, Hannah. *A Schoolteacher in Old Alaska: The Story of Hannah Breece.* New York: Random House, 1995.

Brown, Emily Ivanoff, ed. *The Roots of Ticasuk: An Eskimo Woman's Family Story.* Anchorage: Alaska Northwest Publishing, 1981.

Bryant, Jennifer, and Antonio Castro. *Margaret Murie: A Wilderness Life.* New York: 21st Century Books, 1993.

Calder, James Erskine. *Recollections of Sir John & Lady Franklin in Tasmania.* Adelaide, Australia: Sullivan's Cove Press, 1984.

Cookman, Scott. *Ice Blink: The Tragic Fate of Sir John Franklin's Lost Polar Expedition.* New York: John Wiley & Sons, 2000.

Degnan, Frances Ann. *Under the Arctic Sun: The Life and Times of Frank and Ada Degnan.* Unalakleet, Alaska: Cottonwood Bark, 1999.

"DOI Celebrates 150 Years of Service." *Alaska Frontiers* 72 (April 1999).

Ferrell, Nancy Warren. *Barrett Willoughby: Alaska's Forgotten Lady.* Fairbanks: University of Alaska Press, 1994.

FitzGerald, Emily McCorkle. *An Army Doctor's Wife on the Frontier: The Letters of Emily McCorkle FitzGerald from Alaska and the Far West, 1874–1878.* Edited by Abe Laufe. Lincoln: University of Nebraska Press, 1986.

Hudson, Ray. "Education at Unalaska." *Unalaska City School District Newsletter* (1991).

Hudson, Ray. *Moments Rightly Placed: An Aleutian Memoir.* Kenmore, Wash.: Epicenter Press, 1998.

Hunt, Bill. "Margaret Keenan Harrais." *Alaska* (November 1990):58–61.

Jameson, Elizabeth. "Women of the Klondike." *Canadian Historical Review* (June 1999).

Kendler, Mathilde. *Kendlers': The Story of a Pioneer Alaska Juneau Dairy.* Anchorage: Alaska Northwest Publishing, 1983.

Klouda, Warren. "Lady Jane's Quest." *Alaska* (September 1993):28–31.

Kocour, Ruth Anne. *Facing the Extreme: One Woman's Story of True Courage, Death-Defying Survival, and Her Quest for the Summit.* New York: St. Martin's Press, 1998.

LaRocca, Joe. "Royalty Oil & Gas Advisory Board Gutted by Two Governors." *Petroleum News*, 30 September 2001.

Lombardo, Tom. "Margaret Murie, a Life for Nature." *Sierra*, 1 January 1998, 110.

Milhesuah, Devon A. "Commonality of Difference: American Indian Women and History." *American Indian Quarterly* (Winter 1996):15–27.

Neatby, Leslie H. *Search for Franklin: The Story of One of the Great Dramas of Polar Exploration.* Edmonton, Alberta: Hurtig, 1970.

A Recollection of Civil Rights Leader Elizabeth Peratrovich, 1911–1958. Central Council of Tlingit and Haida Indian Tribes of Alaska, 1991.

Riddles, Libby, and Tim Jones. *Race Across Alaska: First Woman to Win the Iditarod Tells Her Story.* Harrisburg, Penn.: Stackpole Books, 1988.

Story, Norah. *The Oxford Companion to Canadian History and Literature.* Toronto: Oxford University Press, 1973.

Szasz, Margaret Connell, ed. *Between Indian and White Worlds: The Cultural Broker.* Norman: University of Oklahoma Press, 1994.

Thomas, Howard. "ASCE Honors Its Life and Charter Members." *Alaska Designs* 24, no. 9 (October 2001):7.

USEFUL WEB SITES

"Amanda McFarland, Mother of Protestant
  Mission in Alaska"
  http://www.yukonpresbytery.com/YukonPresbytery/
  Interviews/amanda.htm
"Honoring Our People: Elizabeth Wanamaker
  Peratrovich," Alaska Federation of Natives
  http://www.nativefederation.org/history/people/
  ePeratrovich.html
"Interview with Esther Wunnicke," LitSite Alaska
  http://litsite.alaska.edu/uaa/aktraditions/ancsa/
  interviews/wunnicke.html
"Irene Ryan," New Mexico Institute of Mining and
  Technology
  http://www.nmt.edu/mainpage/alumni/goldpan/obit/
  ryan.html
"Lieutenant Governor Fran Ulmer"
  http://www.gov.state.ak.us/ltgov/bio.html
"McCarthy Quadrangle," Department of Natural
  Resources http://www.dggs.dnr.state.ak.us/Quads/
  Mccarthy.html
"Sadie Neakok," Alaskool.org
  http://www.alaskool.org/projects/women/profiles/
  acsw1983/S_Neakok.htm
"Voices of Orthodox Women: Matilda Kinnon
  Paul Tamaree."
  http://www.vow.org/tamaree.html

SELECTED ORGANIZATIONS AND INSTITUTIONS

Alaska Women's Network
1119 G Street
Anchorage, AK 99501
Web: http://www.alaskawomensnetwork.org
Connects Alaskan women with each other, and with the rest of the country and the world.

Alaska Women's Resource Center
813 D Street
Anchorage, AK 99501
Telephone: (907) 276 0528
Web: http://www.awrconline.org
Source of information and referral for Alaskan women.

Alaska Historical Society
PO Box 100299
Anchorage, AK 99510
Web: http://www.alaskahistoricalsociety.org
A nonprofit, volunteer-based organization dedicated to the promotion of Alaska history.

Consortium Library
University of Alaska–Anchorage
3211 Providence Drive
Anchorage, AK 99508
Telephone: (907) 786 1848
Web: http://www.lib.uaa.alaska.edu
Online gateway to the Alaska Pacific University and University of Alaska–Anchorage Joint Library Catalog.

University of Alaska–Anchorage Women's Studies Program
3211 Providence Drive
Anchorage, AK 99508
Telephone: (907) 786 1800
Web: http://www.uaa.alaska.edu/womens
Interdisiciplinary minor fosters open, vigorous inquiry about women and gender.

University of Alaska–Fairbanks Women's Center
University of Alaska–Fairbanks
Eielson Building, Room 112
PO Box 757520
Fairbanks, AK 99775
Telephone: (907) 474 6360
Strives to ensure that the university fulfills its mission and goals as they relate to the education of women. Facilities include a small library.

ARIZONA

If one is inclined to wonder at first how so many dwellers came to be in the loneliest land that ever came out of God's hands, what they do there and why stay, one does not wonder so much after having lived there. None other than this long brown land lays such a hold on the affections. The rainbow hills, the tender bluish mists, the luminous radiance of the spring, have the lotus charm. They trick the sense of time, so that once inhabiting there you always mean to go away without quite realizing that you have not done it.
—Mary Austin, *The Land of Little Rain*, 1903

Contemporary Arizona has had more women in top offices than any other state government. Since 1997 the offices of governor, secretary of state, treasurer, attorney general, and superintendent of public instruction have been held by women. Arizonans also have set a number of other precedents for women, including electing the nation's second state senator, first state Senate majority leader, and first state auditor. It is one of the few states that has twice elected a woman as governor, and it is the home of the nation's first woman on the U.S. Supreme Court, SANDRA DAY O'CONNOR.

PREHISTORY TO TERRITORIAL STATUS
(Prehistory–1863)

Thousands of years ago, prehistoric peoples built homes on the cliffs of Arizona's canyons, carving their pueblos—tremendous apartment-style habitations—into the sides of mountains. These dwellings have been found in remote canyons throughout the state, as well as in Colorado and New Mexico. Archaeologists believe prehistoric women made the pottery, some of it highly decorated, used by these peoples; these women also knew the art of weaving. Unlike some contemporaneous societies, no evidence exists that these peoples practiced human sacrifice. Historians believe that women owned their property and that marriage was a relationship between consenting adults that could be easily dissolved.

When the Spanish arrived (perhaps as early as 1528), Arizona's indigenous peoples were of three linguistic groups: the Yuma, including the Mojave and Havasupai, who lived in the western part of the modern state; the Pima, Hopi, and Papago tribes, which were concentrated in the Southwest; and the Navajo and Apache, who were by far the most numerous and lived primarily in what is now northern Arizona and New

State Population (2000): 5,130,632

Female Population (2000): 2,569,575

Women in State Legislature (2003): 27.8%

Female College Enrollment (1999): 180,000 (55.2% of total)

Privately Held Women-owned Businesses (1997): 88,780

First Year of Full Suffrage: 1912

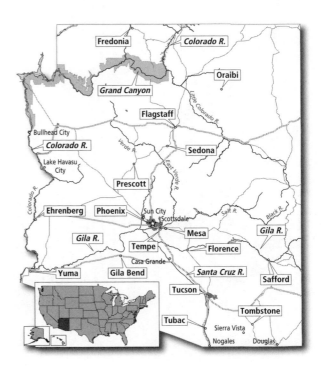

111

Mexico. The Apache were the most feared Native Americans in America, and they were among the last to be subdued by whites.

Yuma women most closely resembled the prehistoric pueblo women in their social organization. They farmed at the bottom of canyons near water; during hunting and gathering seasons, they moved to higher ground. Other non-Apache women also were agriculturists, and early observers especially praised Hopi (literally "peaceful") women for the skill with which they ground the corn they grew. Hopi women were known for their pottery; their tribe was the only one in North America in which weaving was considered to be a man's job.

Navajo women were both highly skilled weavers and accomplished horsewomen who herded animals. More than most Native Americans, Navajo families did not live in villages; instead, they placed their homes—rounded structures of

Apache woman with characteristic dress in Arizona. (© Hulton-Deutsch Collection/Corbis)

adobe called hogans—apart from each other. This maximized the available grass and water in an arid land, but also resulted in women being more isolated and cut off from each other than in most western tribes, where women commonly lived and worked communally.

Apache ("enemy" in other Native American languages) lived very differently from the other Arizona tribes. Like Native Americans of the Great Plains farther north, they did not practice settled agriculture; instead, women joined men in a highly nomadic life dependent on hunting and the spoils of war. The status of women is believed to have been lower than that of women in farming tribes; polygamy was common, with a man allowed to have as many wives as he could afford to buy. Apache women tanned hides, built tepees, and, like their men, were known as fierce fighters who could treat captives brutally.

The Spanish arrived in Arizona much earlier than other areas that were later to be part of the United States. Some of the survivors of conquistador Panfilo de Narváez's 1528 invasion of Florida may have wandered as far as Arizona before reaching Mexico, but the first major expedition was that of Francisco Vázquez de Coronado in 1540. His men did not find the gold they sought, however, and did not stay; records indicate that Coronado cut the planned expedition short because he wanted to return to his new bride, Beatrice de Estrada, in Mexico. Spanish men did not form the long-term relationships with indigenous women the way French men did in the states that border Canada, and Spanish priests were not accompanied by nuns. Although the Spanish did create dozens of missions in the 1600s, most were temporary, and more than two centuries passed before true Spanish settlement began.

The first Spanish settlement was a military presidio, or fort, at Tubac, barely north of the Mexican province of Sonora, in 1752. Two decades later, the government of New Spain developed a major expansion plan, and in October 1775, 29 women set out with a group of men on a march from Tubac to California. Eight of these 29 women bore babies on the trek, with one dying in childbirth. That some were pregnant was not unusual, for women young enough to make such an arduous journey were likely to be pregnant or nursing during most of their childbearing years.

The Tubac presidio moved up the Santa Cruz River to the site of modern Tucson in 1776—the United States and what became the state of Arizona had their beginnings in the same year. More women began to arrive from Mexico and other parts of the Spanish Empire, and colonists settled near the Colorado River in Yuma country. When horses belonging to the colonists ate the mesquite beans that were the staff of Yuma life, however, Yuma men retaliated by killing at least 46 white men, including priests, in 1781. The women were captured and held for ransom, and the next year Spanish troops killed or captured more than 200 Native Americans. This pattern of death avenging death would continue for the next century.

The status of early Hispanic women who settled in the Southwest was mixed. Most women were illiterate; even in upper-class families, for girls to receive no education whatsoever was not unusual. However, the property rights of Hispanic women in the Southwest were stronger than those of contemporaneous women in other areas of North America, and some Hispanic women owned large tracts of land. In the Tucson area, for example, Rita Sosa, Ursula Solares, and Guadalupe Santa Cruz held major land grants in the early 19th century. Societal mores among the Spanish settlers were much less restrictive than for Anglo women: Hispanic women could drink, smoke, dance, and gamble—even adultery was not considered to be particularly shocking.

After Mexico won its independence from Spain in 1821, the Mexican government created the territories of Texas, California, and Nuevo

MEXICAN WOMEN AND AMERICAN MEN

Charles Poston was *alcalde*, or mayor, of Tubac in the 1850s, when American men began drifting into Arizona in search of minerals. At the same time, the male population of Sonora, the Mexican province south of Arizona, had been depleted by war, resulting in a population of women who saw no chance for marriage or who had been abandoned by their soldier husbands. With surprising assertiveness, some of these women—"señoritas and grass widows"—in Poston's words, went north and "sought the American camp on the Santa Cruz River."

The Mexican señoritas really had a refining influence on the frontier population. Many of them had been educated at convents, and all of them were good Catholics. . . . They are exceedingly dainty . . . wear the finest linen they can afford; and spent half their lives over the washing machine. The men of Northern Mexico are far inferior to the women in every respect.

This accretion of female population added very much to the charms of frontier society. The Mexican women . . . could keep house, cook some dainty dishes, sew, dance, and sing. Moreover, they were expert at cards, and divested many a miner of his week's wages over a game of monte.

As the legally appointed *alcalde* under the territorial government of New Mexico (of which Arizona was still a part), Poston was authorized to perform marriages and even to baptize children. A number of the latter had been named Carlos or Carlotta in his honor, and Poston had dutifully recorded the marriages and births at "the Pueblo of Tucson in Pima County."

However, a priest arrived, told the community that these ceremonies were not valid, and banned Poston from performing any more. Poston writes:

I knew there would be a riot on the Santa Cruz if this ban could not be lifted. The women were sulky, and the men commenced cursing. . . . At last I arranged with Father Mashboef to give the sanctity of the church to the marriages and legitimatize the little Carloses and Carlottas with holy water. . . . It cost the company about $700 to rectify the matrimonial situation.

—Doris Weatherford

Excerpts from Charles Poston, *Building a State in Apache Land: The Story of Arizona's Founding*. Tempe, Ariz.: Aztec Press, 1963.

Mexico, which included both modern New Mexico and Arizona. The vast majority of Arizona remained under control of its indigenous peoples; continual warfare between Apache and other tribes and Mexicans resulted in most outsiders avoiding this inhospitable land. In the 1840s, however, increasing numbers of Americans began to pass through Arizona.

Women were part of the first major expedition, known as the Mormon Battalion, during the winter of 1846–1847. Ostensibly part of the U.S. Army, these were, in fact, Mormon men, some accompanied by their wives, who wished to go from Illinois—where Mormons were persecuted—to California. It suited both them and the army to do this under military protection because Arizona was untested country. Top U.S. Army leaders led the way from Santa Fe, New Mexico, to San Bernardino, California. Famed general Stephen Kearney viewed the six-month expedition as so difficult that after a few weeks he sent more than 50 male recruits back to Santa Fe because either they were ill or had proved themselves to be a liability—but the women soldiered on. At least one of them, a Mrs. Hunter, was pregnant; she died soon after arriving in San Diego (in what would become the state of California).

Other U.S. Army troops were engaged in war with Mexico because the United States had annexed Texas; in the 1848 treaty that ended the war, most of Arizona was acquired by the United States. The next year, Americans went west in record numbers when gold was discovered in California. Some followed their golden dreams along river routes; on a Gila River flatboat in November 1849, "perhaps the first child of American parents born in Arizona" was delivered. Famed historian H. H. Bancroft reported that the baby boy was named Gila, but his mother's name is not recorded. (Bancroft 1888, 487)

Arizona's rivers are not readily accessible, though, and most travel was on land; travelers from southern states were the most likely to use a route through Arizona. An 1849 wagon train from Little Rock, Arkansas, included women. Successful trades with local women seem to have made the journey more pleasant: A Mrs. Harris, part of an 1849 Texas train, bartered with Native American women for fresh vegetables, eggs, and chickens, "which we are enjoying with an Epicurean taste." (Officer 1987, 235)

The acquisition of Arizona by the United States arguably improved the status of young white and Hispanic women, who long were favored by Native Americans as ideal captives because of their resale value. The 1850 case of Inez Gonzalez drew particular attention. A 15-year-old resident of the northern Mexico province of Sonora, Gonzalez was traveling to a festival with her affluent relatives when Pinal men attacked, and she was captured. She was sold to Hispanic men—who planned to sell her to the highest bidder. An American surveyor in the area, John Russell Bartlett, wrote:

> A party of New Mexicans came in for the purpose of procuring provisions, having with them a young female. . . By what dropped from them in the course of conversation, it was ascertained that the female . . . had been obtained from the Indians, and that they were taking the girl to some part of New Mexico to sell or make such disposition of her as would realize the most money . . . I deemed it my duty, as the nearest and highest representative of the government of the United States, to interfere. (Bartlett 1854, 2:269)

He did, restoring Inez to her mother. After a year's absence, her joy in seeing the daughter that she had given up for dead was so overwhelming that she "could scarcely believe what she saw." Although that case worked out well, Inez knew of at least 12 other female captives who had disappeared permanently.

The most famous American case of capture on the Arizona overland trail also occurred in 1850, with what became known as the Oatman Massacre. Impatient to get to Yuma, Royce Oatman abandoned the wagon train and took his family alone into the desert. He, his wife, and three of their six children were killed; a son pretended to be dead, while his daughters Mary Ann and Olive Oatman were captured by Apaches, who sold them to Mojaves. Mary Ann starved to death (along with many Mojaves) in an 1852 drought, but Olive eventually was ransomed and reunited with her brother. Olive Oatman wrote a book, *Captivity of the Oatman Girls . . . Among the Apache and Mohave Indians* (1859), about her experiences. It sold widely—perhaps as a result, thousands of people avoided Arizona's overland trails.

The 1850s also saw a rare attempt by women of a western tribe to formally make peace with whites. A group of Apache women went as peace emissaries to Tucson in 1854; they sought a treaty with Mexicans, whom they preferred to the Americans then encroaching on southern Arizona. Unfortunately for the Apache women, Mexico had just sold this land to the United States as part of the 1853 Gadsden Purchase, which transferred some 30,000 square miles in exchange for $10 million.

The purchase established the southern boundary of the United States. Once all of Arizona belonged to the United States, Americans began heeding the call of gold. Gila City, for instance, a settlement near Yuma, had about 1,000 people in 1859, including some women and Germans. A few years later, after the gold rush was over, it became Arizona's first ghost town.

FROM TERRITORY TO STATEHOOD (1863–1912)

Arizona's relatively few Americans hailed mostly from southern states, and, as a result, Arizona became a part of the Confederate States of America in 1862, before it was even officially a territory. The only fighting between Confederate and Union supporters in Arizona, however, resulted in just three deaths. Almost no opposition was voiced when the U.S. Congress authorized the Arizona Territory on February 24, 1863; this action officially separated Arizona from New Mexico.

Pres. Abraham Lincoln appointed territorial officials, and, with their families, they met in Nebraska and formed a train of 28 wagons pulled by 280 oxen. Women were vastly outnumbered by the cavalry company that traveled with them from October to late January, when they stopped at the wilderness where the town of Prescott now stands to build a capital. (The capital would move to Tucson and back to Prescott before settling in Phoenix in 1889.)

Mormon women came to Arizona in the 1860s, moving from Utah into Fredonia and other parts of northern Arizona. One of them, Mrs. David King Udall, would operate Arizona's first telegraph after its installation in 1871. Only after the end of the Civil War in 1865, however, did many Americans seek to settle in this far southwestern corner of their country.

The first territorial legislature met in 1864, and among its first acts was the granting of three divorces; in one, it was the wife who brought the case—uncommon at the time. Territorial governor John Goodwin's first speech highlighted education, an issue traditionally of great concern to women: "The common school, the high school, and the university," he said, "should all be established." (Adams 1930, 1:302) Seven years later, though, the territory still did not have a single public school—but the Sisters of St. Joseph were running a Roman Catholic school in Tucson that attracted more than 100 female students; the 1873 legislature appropriated $300 for the sisters' school.

The 1871 legislature passed with almost no debate a bill assuring married women the right to control their property, and, a decade later, a provision was added to spell out that "the earnings of the wife shall not be liable for the debts of her husband." (Anthony and Harper 1902, 4:473) The 1873 legislature rewrote divorce law, making a divorce easier to obtain in the state than almost anywhere else at that time. Divorce reform legislation may have been passed as a personal favor to Gov. A. P. K. Safford; the same legislature also passed a bill granting his request to be divorced from Jennie L. T. Safford. Safford also recruited the territory's first public school teachers; two California women opened a school in Tucson in 1873, and a man taught in Prescott.

Conflict with Native Americans, however, was the legislators' first priority. With the Civil War over, the army redeployed troops to the West, and by the 1870s the Apache understood that this would be their last stand. Ironically, a century or so after eastern Native American populations had been wiped out or exiled, many easterners were beginning to question the nation's genocidal policy toward its indigenous peoples. When in 1871 the army killed about 100 Apache, most of them women and children, the incident became known as the Camp Grant Massacre.

When Martha Summerhayes moved to Arizona with her husband's army regiment in 1874, Arizona had just four settlements that could be described as towns—and the non–Native American population of all four combined was just over 5,000. Tucson was the largest; its residents were mostly Hispanic; whites were a small minority, and white women were truly rare. Prescott, the capital, was the second-largest town and had a larger Anglo population. Yuma was a town of transients; its location on the Colorado River made it the entry point for most newcomers, who traveled upstream from Mexico's Gulf of California. Phoenix, which is now by far the largest city, was then the smallest, with just 500 residents.

Martha Summerhayes, however, would not live in any of these towns, but instead went with the Eighth Army to several of the ten lonely forts that were intended to keep Native Americans away from these towns. When her husband was posted at Ehrenberg, for instance, she was the only white woman within 100 miles. The isolation, plus probable postpartum depression, became so literally maddening that at one point she left her husband and returned to Massachusetts to restore her equilibrium. Summerhayes returned to him and to Arizona, though, and in time found herself transformed. Instead of her former condemnation of the Hispanic lifestyle, she gradually came to adjust to and even appreciate it. "Life as we Americans live it was difficult in Ehrenberg. I often said: 'Oh, if we could live as the Mexicans live, how easy it would be! . . . The women were scrupulously clean and modest and always wore . . . a low-necked and short-sleeved camisa. . . . I often cried, 'Oh, if I could only dress as the Mexicans do.'" (Summerhayes 1908, 138)

Countless American women in the Southwest went through the same adjustment process and went even further than Summerhayes in adopting clothing that fit their new environment. The Mexican hacienda was different from the housing to which American women were accustomed, but it had real advantages. Adobe walls often were several feet thick, keeping the home cool in summer and warm in winter. Most were organized with connecting rooms arranged around a central patio, which offered easy outdoor socializing—the disadvantage being, as Arizona pioneer Marguerite Kennedy noted decades later, "I soon found that racing its circuit thirty or forty times a day could wear one down to a whisper." (Kennedy 1951, 85) She also found the adobe interior gloomy unless painted white.

Some newcomers had an even bigger adjustment to make, for many women came to the West directly from Europe. Mormon missionaries, for instance, recruited women from Scandinavia and

MARTHA DUNHAM SUMMERHAYES: ARIZONA ARRIVAL, 1874

Martha Dunham was born in 1846 on the Massachusetts island of Nantucket. Dunham, a sophisticated woman, had had an excellent education by the standards of her day and had lived in Europe prior to her 1874 marriage to career army officer John (Jack) Summerhayes. Their first military assignment was in Wyoming, but they were stationed there only briefly before the regiment that Jack commanded was ordered to Arizona to enforce an uneasy truce with the Apache.

With the regiment, they traveled by train from Cheyenne, Wyoming, to San Francisco; from there, they sailed to the Gulf of California and steamed up the Colorado River. Even before they reached the last stretch—across the Mojave Desert in August—Arizona's heat proved to be a killer. As Summerhayes remembered:

> The wind was like a breath from a furnace; it seemed as though the days would never end, and the wind never stop blowing . . .
> He was the third soldier to succumb. It seemed to me their fate was a hard one. To die, down in that wretched place, to be rolled in a blanket and buried on those desert shores, with nothing but a heap of stone to mark their graves! . . . Somewhere there must be a mother or sister, or some one who cares for these poor men, and it's all so sad . . .

By October the regiment had reached Fort Apache, in central Arizona nearly at the New Mexico border. The Summerhayes family moved often within Arizona during the next decade, however, and Martha had to adapt throughout. When she asked her Mexican housemaid "what on earth they did about bathing," for instance,

> She told me the women bathed in the river at daybreak, and asked me [if] I would like to go with them. I was only too glad to avail myself of her invitation, and so . . . I went every morning to the river bank . . . A clump of low mesquite trees at the top of the bank afforded sufficient protection at that hour; we rubbed dry, slipped on a loose gown, and wended our way home . . .

Later, all of Summerhayes's clothing was lost in a steamboat fire; Martha, unskilled as a seamstress, was forced to adopt the loose clothing of Mexican women—and never returned to the American style, despite pressure from her husband's fellow officers. She adopted a more relaxed lifestyle in other ways, too, and even after becoming the mother of two, she lived less and less according to American norms.

When she finally met with family in San Francisco after years at Fort McDowell, north of Phoenix, Summerhayes was set in her unconventional ways:

> I could not break away from my Arizona habits. I wore only white dresses . . . [and] had become imbued with a profound indifference to dress.
> "They'll think you're a Mexican," said my New England aunt (who regarded all foreigners with contempt). "Let them," said I. "I almost wish I were . . . They are the only people who understand the philosophy of living. Look at the tired faces of the women in your streets," I added, "one never sees that sort of expression down below, and I have made up my mind not to be caught by the whirlpool of advanced civilization again."
> Added to the white dresses, I smoked cigarettes, and slept all afternoon . . . I had lapsed back into a state of what my aunt called semi-barbarism.

—Doris Weatherford

Excerpts from Martha Summerhayes, *Vanished Arizona: Recollections of My Army Life.* Philadelphia: J. P. Lippincott, 1908.

continental Europe, and, after marriage to an elder in Salt Lake City, these multiwife families often moved en masse to settle new areas. Both Mesa and Tempe, now large suburbs of Phoenix, were originally settled by Mormons—with high percentages of women in their ranks—in the early 1880s. Because the church insisted on tithes that substituted for taxes, Mesa and Tempe had schools and other benefits of traditional towns in the East sooner than did the Catholic Hispanic women of southern Arizona and, indeed, sooner than the minority of white Protestant families that were officially in charge of the local government. Arizona's first college, Gila, was a Mormon institution.

Perhaps the most famous of the territorial governors was in office as the 1870s turned to the 1880s. John Charles Frémont was near the end of a long career in national military and government affairs. For three decades his wife, Jessie Benton

Frémont, was exceptionally active politically, especially in the antislavery movement. When he had been the Republican party's first nominee for president in 1856, she was the first potential first lady to have her picture on campaign materials. She could not adjust to the high altitude at Prescott, though, and returned to their New York home while he served out the last two years of his term. Their daughter, ELIZABETH (LILY) FRÉMONT, functioned as first lady of Arizona and left interesting memoirs, *Recollections of Elizabeth Benton Frémont,* of pioneer life.

Like other governors of Arizona, Frémont valued education, and the territory finally established a normal school (now Arizona State University) to train teachers—mostly young women—in Tempe in 1885. A second school was added in Flagstaff in 1899. The 1887 legislature also raised the age of consent—the age at which a male may claim in court that a female consented to sex and he therefore might not be convicted of rape—from 10 to 14. Such legislation was more progressive than that of many other states; in 1895 the legislature raised the age to 18.

The 1880s also were the era of two colorful women in Arizona history, NELLIE CASHMAN and Pauline Cushman. Cashman, who was born in Ireland, was a successful miner who had found gold throughout the West, including Alaska. Known as the "Angel of Tombstone," she was especially unusual

---

FROM TEACHER TO RANCH WIFE

Normal schools, the 19th century's teacher-training institutions, credentialed young women interested in earning money by teaching. Teachers were almost invariably single women. The pay, although more than most women could earn in the few other jobs open to them, was not so good as to tempt many women to stay unmarried, and teacher turnover in almost all communities was very high.

The experience of Marguerite Wallace Kennedy is typical. After graduating from a Denver normal school in 1913, she taught just a year before marrying a rancher near Willcox, in southeastern Arizona:

> My one-room desert schoolhouse looked like a tiny cube of sugar upon that vast valley floor. . . . I was not without conveniences, for close to the back door was a well and a hand pump. . . . After no end of pumping and priming, the primer usually gave out just as one heard the gurgling sound of water. . . . Such failure always ended in my sending a big boy a mile or more to fetch another pail of primer.
>
> To this simple edifice of learning came twenty-two pupils, all grades. . . . These homestead children rode to school on donkeys. . . . Little Elaine, who was in the first grade, rode the biggest and meanest burro in the bunch and was bucked off at regular intervals from September right up to the last day of school . . .
>
> *The Course of Study*, that Bible of reference, was nowhere to be found, until late in November when I discovered it hanging from a loop of bailing wire in the girls' privy. . . . The pages in this valuable guide, up to thirty-four were missing, as were the outlines and requirements for more than half the classroom subjects . . . I skipped science altogether that year and did not discover until after Christmas that the seventh grade was studying the wrong history book . . .

After she married the next summer, the new Mrs. Kennedy described her first view of the ranch:

> There was plenty of landscape for me to study while the men talked. . . . Miles and miles of it, too big to grasp, a land someone aptly described as having more rivers and less water, more cows and less butter, and where you could see farther and see less, than any other place in the world. . . . And there were prairie dogs. Hundreds, thousands, millions it seemed. Plump, dun-colored creatures all shrilling a happy serenade as we passed.

The Kennedy ranch supported a large household of male ranch hands, the Mexican foreman's family, and Kennedy's invalid mother-in-law and her nurse. Far in the wilds though they were, their ranch house had a steady stream of visitors. Kennedy's grocery orders routinely featured 800 pounds of beans and a half a ton of flour. At one point Kennedy resorted to putting up a sign on the fence that said "smallpox" to get a break from cooking for strangers.

—Doris Weatherford

Excerpts from Marguerite Wallace Kennedy, *My Home on the Range.* Boston: Little, Brown, 1951.

in befriending the town's prostitutes. Prostitution was a fact of Tombstone life, and the city council voted to lift restrictions on it in 1882. Both famed sheriff Wyatt Earp and the sheriff he replaced openly patronized prostitutes; they even were rivals for one, Josephine Marcus.

Pauline Cushman, who grew up in Michigan, had been a genuine Civil War hero when she spied for the Union in Tennessee. Although her morphine addiction would kill her in California a few years later, she still was called the Major when she ran a hotel in Florence, a community midway between Phoenix and Tucson.

Florence was also the site of PEARL HART's imprisonment for robbing a stagecoach. The last of the West's female desperadoes, her trial in the final year of the 19th century drew a national audience. She beguiled reporters who flocked to her jail cell, and they dutifully telegraphed her message to the world: a woman should not be indicted and tried by a jury of men who were not her peers, nor should she be convicted and sentenced under laws that she had no part in writing. Hart's popularity made her too troublesome a prisoner, and after the sheriff transferred her to Yuma, the governor pardoned her in 1902 on the grounds that the state lacked accommodations for women prisoners.

Hart's message reflected the growth of feminism in Arizona during the 1890s. When the long-delayed University of Arizona finally opened in 1891, from the beginning no voice was raised in opposition to women's attendance. The first agitation for the vote also began in 1891. With statehood in sight, a constitutional convention met that year, and Kansas suffragist Laura M. Johns made a trip to lobby for the inclusion of women's suffrage in the state constitution.

Johns arrived in Tucson, where she was welcomed by Josephine Hughes, who published a newspaper there with her husband, Louis C. Hughes, a future governor. The two women went on to Phoenix, where the relevant committee was supportive of their cause and recommended suffrage to the full body. The proposal lost by just three votes.

As in several other states, these signs of a seemingly easy victory proved false, and more than two decades would pass before Arizona women had full suffrage—although they did get the right to vote in school elections in 1887. Hughes became president of the Territorial Woman Suffrage Association, and in 1895—soon after Carrie Chapman Catt led the winning campaign for suffrage for Colorado women—Hughes invited Catt to their annual convention in Phoenix. Catt also held meetings in Tucson, Tempe, and elsewhere.

Hughes was by then Arizona's most influential woman, for she and her husband had sold their Tucson newspaper and he had been appointed territorial governor. He shared her emancipated views and appointed the first women to hold office in Arizona; a woman served on the board of the State Normal School and another as assistant superintendent of the State Insane Asylum. Hughes was one of just two Democratic governors during Arizona's long territorial history, and when his term ended in 1896, no other followed his example. His wife, however, traveled to the national suffrage convention in Washington, D.C., that year, and, as a result, the national suffrage association funded Laura Johns to organize Arizona women during the next two winters. In 1899 Catt returned to again try to persuade the legislature to grant women the vote.

Although Catt did not mention him by name until he was out of office, the primary impediment to women's suffrage was Morris Goldwater, the president of the Council (as upper chambers of territorial legislatures were called). Catt reported a few months after the 1899 campaign:

> Our bill went through the House by an unprecedented majority . . . and then, as in Oklahoma, the remonstrants concentrated their

opposition upon the Council. Here, as there, the opponents were the saloon-keepers, with the difference that in Arizona they are often the proprietors of a gambling den and house of prostitution in connection with the saloons . . .

I have never found anywhere, however, so many strong, determined, able men, anxious to espouse our cause as in Arizona. The general sentiment is overwhelmingly in our favor. . . . Governor N. O. Murphy . . . did all that was possible. . . The press is favorable, the intelligent and moral citizens are eager for it, but the vicious elements . . . are opposed. (Anthony and Harper 1902, 4:472–473)

Suffragists carried on under the leadership of FRANCES W. MUNDS of Prescott. The national association sent another Kansas woman, Dr. Frances Woods, and both chambers of the 1902 legislature passed suffrage; this time, however, Gov. Alexander Brodie, an appointee of Republican president Theodore Roosevelt, vetoed the bill. The next governor was even more strongly opposed, and Arizona's suffragists retreated. At her own expense, Lida P. Robinson published and distributed a newspaper to keep the spirit alive, but the organization fell into political dormancy.

The last territorial legislature met in 1909, the same year that SHARLOT HALL was elected as territorial historian—a position that was soon abolished. Hall nonetheless became an especially popular figure in Arizona history. A published poet at age 22, she also led the campaign to preserve buildings from the territorial period at Prescott, and the museum she founded there in 1927 is still in operation.

Because state governments were, in general, more conservative than territorial governments, national suffragists feared that the 1909 legislative session might be their last opportunity and pushed hard. Fieldworkers Laura Clay from Kentucky and Laura Gregg from Kansas arrived to organize some 3,000 dues-paying members of the state's suffrage association—a comparatively large number given Arizona's small population. Again, however, the effort failed. Although Arizona's new constitution included several Populist party provisions that were considered radical, granting women the vote seemed even more radical than it had been two decades earlier. Arizona became a state on February 14, 1912, with its women disenfranchised.

FROM STATEHOOD THROUGH WORLD WAR II ERA (1912–1950)

The new state constitution had established a relatively easy process of bypassing the legislature and going straight to the voters with an issue, which is just what Arizona suffragists did. Just months after statehood they took advantage of the presidential election of November 1912 and organized to put suffrage on the ballot. Women in every county collected the required number of petition signatures from men. In the fall they began a major campaign to convince the male electorate to grant women the right to vote.

Frances Munds rented headquarters space at the Adams Hotel in Phoenix; the national association sent experienced Laura Gregg, and Alice Park went at her own expense to offer the benefit of the experience gained in California's successful suffrage campaign of the previous year. National suffrage president Rev. Dr. Anna Howard Shaw delivered speeches in several cities, and almost all of the newspapers supported the campaign. Catt's political judgment of two decades earlier proved correct; once the issue went to ordinary men instead of officials, the frontier's democratic sentiment proved to be strong. Women won by 13,442 to 6,202, carrying every county in the state.

Suffragists immediately formed the Arizona League of Women Voters, with Mrs. M. T. Phelps of Phoenix as president. Moreover—unlike in most other states—women ran for office. In 1913 C. Louise Boehringer became the first female elected official in Arizona. A graduate of the prestigious Teachers College of New York's Columbia University, she won election as school superintendent of Yuma County.

When the first legislative elections were held after women got the vote, longtime state suffrage association president Frances Munds was elected as the state senator from Prescott. She was the second female state senator in the nation, following Utah's Dr. Martha Hughes Cannon, who had been elected in 1896. The 18 years between Cannon's 1896 election and the 1914 election of Munds indicated the depth of the movement's quiescence; Arizonans helped to get suffrage moving again— and the next year Montana would elect the first women to serve in Congress.

In addition to Senator Munds, Rachel Berry of St. Johns won election to the Arizona House of Representatives in 1914; in 1916 three women won state offices: Rosa McKay of Globe, Theodora Marsh of Nogales, and Pauline O'Neill of Phoenix. In 1928 Lena Marks, a Jewish woman who had emigrated with her family from Russia in 1887, was the Republican nominee for speaker of the Arizona House of Representatives.

Arizona women had been enfranchised for eight years when the 19th Amendment came to the state for ratification in 1920. Governor Campbell called a special session of the legislature, and Arizonans saw the amendment introduced by four female legislators. It passed without dissent, and legislators listened "with good-natured amusement" while protests were read from the Iowa and Virginia Associations Opposed to Woman Suffrage. (Harper 1922, 6:15)

The 1920 legislature also passed an uncommonly progressive law that essentially negated the idea of illegitimacy. The act made "every child, whether born in or out of wedlock, a legitimate child, thus forever removing that stigma from innocent children." Every such child was "entitled to support and education to the same extent as if it had been born in lawful wedlock," and the code specified that "this shall apply to cases where the natural father . . . is married to one other than the mother of said child, as well as where he is single."

The year 1920 included one more milestone: Elsie Toles became the first woman to win a statewide election when she won the post of state superintendent of public instruction. Six years later Ana Frohmiller set another important precedent by winning her race for state auditor—a field not typically associated with women. The first woman in the nation to hold this position, Frohmiller had previously been county treasurer for Coconino County, which was the largest county in terms of area in the United States.

Women also made progress in other fields. Alice Mabeth Birdsall built a successful law practice in Phoenix after graduating from law school in Washington, D.C., in 1912. In 1921 Lillian Jaye Marney established Marney Commercial School in Tucson, which taught office skills to perhaps thousands of women over the next decades. Both Birdsall and Marney were active in the Federation of Business and Professional Women after Yuma County school superintendent Louise Boehringer founded the Arizona chapter; Boehringer helped cofound the national body in 1919. In 1923 Carrie Yett was appointed postmaster of Safford, and Edith Robertson Macia became Tombstone's postmaster in 1928. German-born Miriam Stedman Grau, a graduate of Stanford University, was elected Maricopa County school superintendent in 1927, and Gertrude Bryan Leeper became editor of the *Arizona Woman* in 1929.

In Arizona, as elsewhere in the nation, much of the progress made in the early 20th century was wiped out by the Great Depression. The situation of teachers—a largely female profession—illustrates the economic impact. In 1930 Arizona public schools employed 3,273 teachers; four years later the number was down to 2,834, and those who kept their jobs averaged a more than 20%

reduction in salary. In the elections of 1932, nationwide discontent with the economy caused voters to oust incumbent senators and representatives, electing fresh, mostly Democratic, faces to Congress. Democratic presidential candidate Franklin D. Roosevelt was elected in that year with the promise of a New Deal for the American people. Arizona also elected its first female representative to Congress in 1932.

Democrat ISABELLA SELMES GREENWAY campaigned on a platform of helping her old friend Roosevelt push his New Deal policies, designed to end the Depression, through Congress. Greenway had gone to finishing school with Eleanor Roosevelt, the president's wife, and had met her first husband, Robert M. Ferguson, while serving as a bridesmaid at the Roosevelts' wedding. The Fergusons had moved to the Southwest for Robert's health in 1909; after his death in 1922, Isabella married John Greenway—all the while maintaining businesses ranging from a Los Angeles airline to a furniture factory that employed disabled veterans.

Although male Arizonans apparently elected her to the National Democratic Committee in 1928 as a tribute to John Greenway, Isabella Greenway used her new position to establish her own identity and campaigned throughout the state. When Roosevelt ran for president four years later, Greenway not only won her own race overwhelmingly, but also had the honor of seconding Roosevelt's nomination at the national convention. She served on congressional committees of great importance to Arizona, including Indian Affairs, Irrigation and Reclamation, and Public Lands, while her close connections to the White House brought New Deal public works programs and veterans' facilities to Arizona. Reelected easily in 1934, she retired in 1936 and split from Roosevelt when he sought a third term in 1940. She married Harry King in 1939 and lived in Tucson until her death in 1953.

In the same era two Arizona women were establishing outstanding reputations as architects. MARY ELIZABETH JANE COLTER (sometimes Russell-Colter) had a 50-year career building works that have been seen by millions of people, especially at the Grand Canyon. She designed six structures that fit into the natural landscape of the Grand Canyon and is especially known for the colorful, kiva-like Watch Tower. Similarly, Marguerite Staude's Chapel of the Holy Cross fits superbly into the red rocks of Sedona, creating the focal point that helped make the area into the artists' colony it later became. Other women in the arts during this era include writers Nora Laing (*Desert Ships*, 1936), Mary Kidder Rak (*A Cowman's Wife*, 1934), Hilda Faunce (*Desert Wife*, 1934), and Laura Adams Armer, who won the Newbury Medal in children's literature for *Waterless Mountain* (1931).

World War II transformed Arizona, bringing thousands of soldiers to its deserts to train for battle in North Africa. The Army Nurse Corps sent its women to Camp Young, where they carried 30-pound backpacks on 20-mile hikes. Like men, the women had to pass an infiltration test in which they crawled a 75-yard course filled with barbed wire, while live ammunition exploded around them; a nurse held the speed record. Some found that they liked Arizona enough to return when the war was over. The pattern is clear in the decade's population increase: From 1930 to 1940, population rose from 435,573 to only 499,261; between 1940 and 1950, population jumped to 749,587. The next decades would be a boom era for Arizona.

POSTWAR AND CONTEMPORARY ERAS (1950–present)

Neither gold nor the world war ultimately made Arizona the state that it is today. Air conditioning was the key to its growth and development. As home cooling became common in the 1950s and

1960s, millions who had found the desert day simply too hot now considered it tolerable, and the population grew. Many of those who came were venturesome sorts who approved of breaking old patterns and helped establish new roles for women.

In 1950 Arizona almost elected a woman as governor. After a 30-year career in public finance, State Auditor Ana Frohmiller easily won the Democratic party primary. Her record during her 12 terms as auditor was spotless, and the margin by which she won reelection was never less than 70%. Her campaign for governor was very nearly successful; she lost to a Republican man by fewer than 3,000 votes, a fraction of 1% of the electorate.

Arizona also continued its pattern of electing more women to its legislature than did other states. In Florida, for example, which experienced similar postwar growth, only six women served in the state House of Representatives from 1950 to 1970, while Arizona had 27 women in its House during that time. One of them, POLLY ROSENBAUM, served for 40 years.

Arizona set another precedent when LORNA LOCKWOOD was elected to its supreme court in 1960. A 1925 graduate of the University of Arizona College of Law, she was elected to the legislature in 1938 and went on to chair the Judiciary Committee. She spent the 1950s as a Maricopa County superior court judge and moved from there to the supreme court. Although Ohio had much earlier set the precedent for electing women to state supreme courts, Lockwood was the first woman in the nation to serve as a chief justice.

Lockwood retired in 1974, the same year that Sandra Day O'Connor left the Arizona Senate. During her meteoric rise in the state legislative body, O'Connor set still another Arizona precedent in 1972, when her fellow Republicans elected her as the first female majority leader of any state senate. After her senate career, O'Connor won an

TIMELINE

United States Events		Arizona Events
	1500	
		1540 Coronado Expedition.
	1600	
1620 Settlement of Plymouth Colony		
	1700	
		1752 First Spanish settlement is a fort at Tubac.
1776 United States declares independence		1776 Tucson founded.
	1800	
		1821 Mexico wins independence from Spain, creating territories of Texas, California, and Nuevo Mexico, which included both modern New Mexico and Arizona.
		1848 United States acquires most of Arizona territory.
1861–65 U.S. Civil War		1863 U.S. Congress authorizes Arizona Territory.
		1871 Arizona legislature passes bill assuring married women the right to control their property.
	1900	
		1912 Arizona becomes state. Women win the right to vote.
		1913 C. Louise Boehringer becomes the first female elected official in Arizona; voters elected her school superintendent of Yuma County.
1914–18 World War I		1914 Frances W. Munds is elected to the state Senate from Prescott; Rachel Berry is elected to the state House of Representatives from St. Johns.
1920 Ratification of the 19th Amendment		
1929–39 Great Depression		
		1932 Isabella Selmes Greenway elected first U.S. congresswoman from Arizona.
1939–45 World War II		1960 Lorna Lockwood elected to Arizona supreme court.
1975 Vietnam War ends		1981 Sandra Day O'Connor appointed to the U.S. Supreme Court.
		1998 Jane Dee Hull first woman elected governor of Arizona; voters elect women to all the top spots in the state government.
	2000	
		2002 Janet Napolitano is elected governor and Jan Brewer is elected secretary of state.

Women elected to the top five state offices waiting to be sworn in on January 4, 1999. From left: Jane Dee Hull (governor), Betsey Bayless (secretary of state), Janet Napolitano (attorney general), Carol Springer (treasurer), and Lisa Graham Keegan (superintendent of public schools). (AP/Wide World Photos)

elected judgeship and was appointed to the state court of appeals in 1979. Two years later, Pres. Ronald Reagan appointed her as the first woman on the U.S. Supreme Court.

Although other women had stronger credentials, the moderate Republicanism of Arizona made O'Connor acceptable to all sides. With the national feminist movement demanding that women be included on the nation's highest court, when the vacancy occurred soon after Reagan's inauguration, the U.S. Senate confirmed O'Connor by 99–0. At 51 she was young by the standards of the Court—but old enough to remember that when she graduated near the top of her Stanford University law class, she was offered only jobs as a legal secretary.

In 1977 Democrat ROSE MOFFORD was appointed secretary of state and was subsequently

reelected; because Arizona has no lieutenant governor, the secretary of state is next in line of succession. Mofford's tenure overlapped that of Democratic governor Bruce Babbitt, a feminist who appointed a number of women, including Republicans, to high posts in his administration, thus launching careers that later allowed women to win top positions.

When Babbitt left the governor's office in 1986, Carolyn Warner was the Democratic nominee to replace him. Her race echoed Ana Frohmiller's 1950 campaign, in that Warner came very close, but Republican nominee Evan Mecham narrowly defeated her. Mecham's tenure was brief and tumultuous; he soon made history by becoming the nation's only governor to simultaneously face impeachment, a recall election, and criminal prosecution. When the legislature impeached Mecham early in 1988, Secretary of State Rose Mofford replaced him as governor, serving the nearly three years that remained of his term.

Arizona elected its second congresswoman in November 1992. Karan English won the sixth congressional district, a large area that includes Flagstaff, affluent Phoenix suburbs, and disadvantaged Native American reservations. She served just one term, losing in the Republican tide of 1994.

Like Mofford, JANE DEE HULL became governor while she was secretary of state. Hull's career had begun with election to the legislature in 1978, and she went on to serve two terms as speaker of the House—another precedent for Arizona women. When she was elected secretary of state in 1993, Hull became the first Republican to hold that position since 1931. History repeated itself in the governor's office, though, and in September 1997, Republican governor Fife Symington was forced to resign in the national savings and loan scandal. Secretary Hull, also a Republican, replaced

him as governor. Voters elected her to the office in November 1998. After two near-wins and one governor who served but was not elected, a woman had been elected governor of Arizona.

When election of 1998 was over, women held all the top offices. Two Republicans took the top two spots: Jane Dee Hull was governor, and Betsey Bayless, who had replaced Hull as secretary of state, was elected to that position. Arizonans also elected Democrat Janet Napolitano as attorney general. Carol Springer, a Republican who previously chaired the state Senate's Appropriation Committee, became treasurer, and Lisa Graham Keegan continued the tradition begun in 1920 of women as state superintendents of schools. In the 2002 elections, women took the top two spots. Voters elected Napolitano as governor, whose vacancy as attorney general went to a man, Terry Goddard, and Republican Jan Brewer as secretary of state.

—Doris Weatherford

PROMINENT WOMEN

NELLIE CASHMAN (ca. 1844–1925)

The petite "Miner's Angel," philanthropist Ellen "Nellie" Cashman, a native of Queenstown, County Cork, Ireland, supported herself and numerous charities in the goldfields of North America for 53 years. She came to the United States with her parents at age 16, settling in Boston. After her father's death in 1869, she journeyed to San Francisco in search of wealth. Cashman worked in a boot factory, then as a cook in Virginia City, Nevada, and an innkeeper in nearby Pioche.

In 1877 Cashman joined the gold rush at Dease Lake in southwestern Canada, as the lone woman among a group of men, yet made more money operating a boardinghouse than prospecting for gold. On a buying trip to Victoria, she donated $500 to the Sisters of St. Anne for the establishment of a hospital, then returned to Cassiar, British Columbia, with lime juice and a ton of potatoes to treat 85 miners suffering from scurvy (a vitamin C deficiency). After the British Columbia gold strike petered out, she traveled south to the big silver strike in Tucson, Arizona, where she prospered, buying, working, and selling mining claims, boardinghouses, restaurants, and shops. In 1879 she left Tucson to open a restaurant and shoe store in Tombstone, where she helped build the town's first Roman Catholic church. Angered by the glorification of public hangings, she tore down scaffolding to protest turning executions into a spectacle. When her business in the area failed, she supported herself and her sister's five orphaned children at inns she ran in New Mexico, Idaho, the Klondike, and Alaska. In 1994 the U.S. Postal Service honored Cashman with a stamp in the Legends of the West series.

MARY JANE COLTER (1869–1958)

A painter and pioneering folk architect, Mary Elizabeth Jane Colter of Pittsburgh, Pennsylvania, designed six outdoor projects in the Grand Canyon, four of which have been designated National Historic Landmarks. Colter graduated from high school in 1883 at the age of 14. At age 17, following the death of her father, she studied at the California School of Design in San Francisco and apprenticed in architecture. After teaching art in St. Paul, Minnesota, she joined the Fred Harvey Company in 1902, a restaurant, hotel, and lunchroom chain associated with the Santa Fe Railway, to plan depots, hotels, and public buildings throughout the American West. She designed the Harvey House restaurant in Holbrook, Arizona, and a rancho with stone cabins for hikers in Winslow.

At the Grand Canyon, Colter applied her knowledge of Native American arts and crafts to the design of Hopi House, a red sandstone worship center furnished with an authentic Hopi altar. For Hopi handicrafters, in 1905 she created a pueblo with sand paintings and artists' lofts that recreated the look of the sacred site of the Hopi creation myth. For the canyon's south rim, in 1914 she planned Lookout Studio for photographers and Hermit's Rest, a primitive log-and-boulder shelter and refreshment stand that directs visitors' gaze over Yuma Point to the Colorado River. To make her structures look lived in, she equipped them with furniture, rugs, smoky fireplaces, even spiderwebs. The sites became national landmarks after the creation of Grand Canyon National Park in 1919. Her last projects, Bright Angel Lodge and an Anasazi watchtower and kiva decked with genuine petroglyphs, completed in 1935, welcomed travelers with a massive rock hearth and lounge. Colter retired in 1948 at the age of 79. She died ten years later.

LILY FRÉMONT (1842–1917)

Educated traveler and journalist Elizabeth "Lily" Frémont of Washington, D.C., recorded for posterity daily life in frontier Prescott. The daughter and unofficial secretary of Civil War general John Charles Frémont, she followed his career and absorbed the drama of his political climb to power. By age nine she had twice crossed the Isthmus of Panama by mule and had sailed to Europe. During her residence in England, France, and Germany, she learned German and china painting, and received private tutoring in the humanities, dance, and horseback riding. On October 6, 1878, she and her mother, writer Jessie Benton Frémont; her brother Frank; the maid; the Chinese cook, Ah Chung, and the dog, Thor, traveled for four weeks to the frontier capital at the insistence of Lily's father, then territorial governor, who wanted to introduce his shy, refined daughter to Arizona.

Frémont kept a two-year journal of events through 1880, which the Arizona Historical Society's Living Arizona History has cited for its perceptive observations. Central to her journal were the political entanglements between federal officers and local lawmakers and between settlers and the indigenous Pima tribe. Her interests ranged from official visits to the governor's mansion to scandal, fire hazards, racism, burial customs, and mistreatment of the poor. Fond commentary about her married friend, Judge Charles Silent, led historians to believe she harbored an unrequited love. In 1912, seven years before her death in Los Angeles, she published a memoir, *Recollections*.

ISABELLA SELMES GREENWAY (1886–1953)

Isabella Selmes Greenway, a U.S. congresswoman from Arizona, also known as "Arizona's sweetheart," used her talents to better her state politically and economically. Born on a family farm in Boone County, Kentucky, she completed her education at Miss Chapin's School in New York City. While a bridesmaid at the wedding of Franklin and Eleanor Roosevelt, she met Robert Ferguson; she married him in 1905. They moved to Silver City, New Mexico. In addition to serving in the Women's Land Army of New Mexico during World War I, she built a plaza in the Ajo community, home of her second husband, John C. Greenway. While living in Tucson, Arizona, she operated a cattle ranch. In addition she owned an airline and opened a resort hotel, the Arizona Inn, in 1929. The Arizona Inn was a hotel resort and a home furnishings factory that employed disabled veterans.

Supported by her close friends the Roosevelts, Greenway entered politics, canvassed Arizona, and became a Democratic national committeewoman. After completing the term of Lewis Douglas in the 73rd Congress, she won election in 1935 and contributed to the debate on the establishment of social security and to the commissions on Indian Affairs, Public Lands, Irrigation and Reclamation, and the Mount Rushmore National Memorial. For her home state, she secured public works projects and, on behalf of the Yavapai Apache Nation, proposed transferring lands from the Veterans' Administration to the Interior Department. During World War II, she chaired the American Women's Volunteer Service and sponsored international cultural exchange programs.

SHARLOT HALL (1870–1943)

The cultural life of Prescott, Arizona, owes much to poet and philanthropist Sharlot Mabridth Hall, a former member of the electoral college and the first Arizona woman to hold public office. A pioneering feminist and frontierswoman, she traveled west from Kansas to Arizona Territory by covered wagon at age 12. She began publishing original verse in 1901 in *Out West* magazine, which also featured works by Mary Hunter Austin, Jack London, and John Muir. Earning a reputation for courage by addressing Congress on the issue of separate statehood for Arizona, she was named territorial historian in 1909. Two years later, she completed a diary of her travels in northern Arizona. In 1924 she represented the state at the electoral college.

Hall's establishment of a cultural, educational, and historical museum in Prescott provided the area with a learning center and tourist attraction. For its initial holdings, she organized and maintained memorabilia of settlers in an abandoned log cabin. The largest museum in the area, the three-acre campus opened in 1927 and offers outdoor drama, festivals, exhibits, publications, and research facilities; it also features tours of the former governor's mansion and artifacts from Hall's past. In 1982 Margaret F. Maxwell summarized Hall's life and achievements in a biography, *A Passion for Freedom: The Life of Sharlot Hall.*

PEARL HART (1878–1925)

Pearl Hart, a native of Lindsay, Canada, became famous by robbing a stagecoach. After attending a girls' school in Toronto, at age 15 she married gambler Frederick Hart and worked at odd jobs in Chicago at the 1893 Columbian Exposition. Intrigued by Wild West shows, she mastered horseback riding and shooting before abandoning her husband and relocating to Trinidad, Colorado, where she joined a hotel cleaning crew. After giving birth to a son, whom she left with her mother, she moved to Phoenix, Arizona, to cook and take in laundry.

In 1895 the Harts reunited in Phoenix. After the birth of their daughter in 1898, Frederick went to Cuba to fight in the Spanish-American War. Pearl, who gave up her second child as well, cooked in a series of mining camps, where she met Joe Boot, an English brigand. On May 29, 1899, with Boot's assistance, she robbed $400 from the passengers of the Globe Stage at Cane Spring in the Dripping Springs Mountains. The crime earned her the dubious distinction of committing the last stagecoach robbery in the United States. Arrested one mile away three days later, she gained instant celebrity from onlookers at the jail. A jury absolved her of charges in the belief that she stole at the direction of her husband. For brandishing a weapon, she served 18 months of a five-year sentence at Yuma Territorial Prison. On December 19, 1902, Hart was pardoned of her crime. Details of her release and later years are sketchy. After appearing in Buffalo Bill's Wild West Show, she was arrested a second time in Kansas City, Missouri.

JANE DEE HULL (1935–)

Jane Dee Bowersock Hull of Kansas City, Missouri, worked her way from precinct volunteer to governor of Arizona. The daughter of an editor for the *Kansas City Star*, at age 19 she married Dr. Terry Ward Hull. While rearing their two sons and two daughters, she completed a bachelor's degree in education at the University of Kansas in 1957. Five years later, the family moved to Chinle, Arizona, where she worked as a middle-grade English teacher. When the family resettled in Phoenix, she served the Republican party as precinct committeewoman and deputy registrar.

Hull's rise in politics followed a gradual advance from campaigner to candidate for the state House of Representatives. By 1989 she was House speaker and chair of the Ethics Committee. She made a successful run for secretary of state in 1995 and was made governor of Arizona in 1997 when the scandal-plagued Fife Symington resigned. The following year, when five female candidates swept the state's top elective offices, "Iron Lady" Hull became Arizona's first woman to be elected governor and one of 15 U.S. women to hold a governorship. A fiscal conservative and consensus builder, she was honored with the National Legislator of the

Year Award, an economic development honorarium, and a Quality of Life Award.

LORNA LOCKWOOD (1903–1977)

Lorna E. Lockwood, of Douglas, Arizona, the first female chief justice of Arizona's supreme court (1961), was the first U.S. woman to hold that post. The daughter of Judge Alfred C. Lockwood, she attended public school in Tombstone, completed law school at the University of Arizona, and practiced law privately for 13 years. In 1939 she began the first of three terms in the Arizona House of Representatives, where she presided, and chaired the House Judiciary Committee. After a year as assistant state attorney general, she spent 11 years as the Maricopa County superior court judge.

In 1960 Judge Lockwood advanced to the state supreme court, where she served as vice chief and chief justice until her retirement in 1975. To encourage other aspiring female attorneys, she met weekly with young women for lunch at the Arizona Club; this group evolved into the Arizona Women Lawyers Association. She was honored by the Arizona Women's Hall of Fame, the Chi Omega fraternity, and the University of Arizona. After her death the family endowed the Lorna E. Lockwood Scholarship at her alma mater. In 2000, she was named to the *Arizona Daily Star*'s Tucson's Top 100, a slate of the city's female achievers.

ROSE MOFFORD (1922–)

Rose Perica Mofford of Globe, Arizona, successfully advanced through state politics to the post of governor. She graduated from Globe High School in 1939 as valedictorian and with the highest grade point average ever achieved at the school. At age 19 she worked as the secretary to Joe Hunt, the state treasurer. She met her husband, T. R. Mofford, founder of the Phoenix police department, while working for Hunt. In 1954, following 11 years as a homemaker, she returned to the state treasury to manage the office of Wesley Bolin.

Mofford entered politics in 1955 and worked in the field for two decades. She was appointed secretary of state by Gov. Wesley Bolin in 1977 and was elected to that position in 1978, 1982, and 1986. Mofford became Arizona's governor when, following the impeachment of Gov. Evan Mecham in 1987, she was sworn in to replace him. She worked to stabilize state government in the wake of a turbulent investigation of Mecham's mismanagement. One of her first acts was to approve the Martin Luther King, Jr., national holiday. In 1990 she chose not to run for reelection. A Phoenix sports complex bears her name.

FRANCES MUNDS (1866–?)

Suffragist Frances Willard Munds set the example for Arizona women eager to enter public office. During the last decade of a concerted push to pass the 19th Amendment to the U.S. Constitution, she learned the rudiments of campaigning as an officer of the state's Suffrage Association. In 1912 she engineered an unusual strategy—tagging onto the ballot for statehood a referendum for women's right to vote in state elections. Her method proved successful, securing voting rights for women in Arizona eight years before women obtained national suffrage.

In 1914 Munds ran successfully for the office of state senator from Yavapai County. The win made her the nation's second female state senator. Central to her concerns were full citizenship for women, increased funding of public education, and tax exemptions for widows. She served on the Land Committee and chaired the Committee on Education and Public Institutions. In 1918 she was defeated in a campaign for secretary of state.

NAMPEYO (ca. 1859–1942)

One of the nation's greatest native potters, Nampeyo, a Hopi–Tewa clay worker from First

Mesa, Arizona, learned crackle glazing from family members. During her girlhood she mastered her grandmother's methods of firing pots, bowls, and water containers. She refined her knowledge by examining potsherds at the ancient ruin at Sityatki. After blending native clay with powdered stone and ceramic fragments, polishing shapes with a stone, and incising Zuni bird designs, she fired the squat, broad-shouldered pieces over flaming animal dung in the manner of 16th-century Native American artisans.

Nampeyo's pioneering efforts, the start of the Sityatki Revival, were so successful that collectors proclaimed them ancient relics rather than 20th-century interpretations. In 1905, after she demonstrated her craft at Hopi House in the Grand Canyon, the Smithsonian Institution proclaimed her a true artist. She continued working after her sight failed, and she taught ceramic techniques to her four daughters, granddaughter, and great-granddaughter. Her work is displayed at the National Museum in Washington, D.C., and the California Academy of the Sciences in San Francisco.

SANDRA DAY O'CONNOR (1930–)

Sandra Day O'Connor of El Paso, Texas, the first female Supreme Court justice in the United States, advanced the hope of women for full representation in all phases of government. Reared on an Arizona ranch established by her pioneer grandfather, she commuted to Radford School for Girls and graduated from Austin [Texas] High School at age 16. She completed a law degree from Stanford Law School in 1952 and soon thereafter married John O'Connor. Although she had done extremely well in school, she had difficulty finding a position in the era's all-male law firms but worked in the law office of San Mateo County, California. While her husband served in the military in Frankfurt, Germany, she practiced contract law with the Army Quartermaster Corps.

Settled in Phoenix to rear three sons, O'Connor served on the Maricopa County Board of Adjustments and Appeals and the Governor's Committee on Marriage and Family and as administrator for the Arizona State Hospital. She began serving as an Arizona assistant attorney general in 1965. Four years later she completed an unexpired term in the Arizona Senate and held the seat for two elected terms, setting a record as the first U.S. woman to be majority leader of a state senate. After displaying conservative values as a superior court judge and on the court of appeals, in 1981 she was nominated by Pres. Ronald Reagan to the Supreme Court, where, amid pressures from conservatives and liberals, she has displayed cool logic and handed down centrist opinions.

POLLY ROSENBAUM (1899–)

Former teacher Edwynne "Polly" Cutler Rosenbaum of Ollie, Iowa, held a seat in the Arizona House of Representatives from 1949 to 1995. She completed a bachelor's degree in history and political science from the University of Colorado and earned a master's of education at the University of Southern California before taking jobs as a dental receptionist, stenographer, and teacher in Colorado and Wyoming. After her husband's death in 1949, she added politician to her list of achievements by filling his seat in state government and returning to the state House of Representatives through successive reelections.

During Rosenbaum's 46 years in state government she campaigned for more public school classrooms, a community college system to equalize educational opportunities, and libraries for rural residents. In the state legislature, she served on committees governing appropriations, rules, human resources, and aging. At age 95 she ended her political career with the intent to write about state history, speak to women's clubs and historical groups, and champion historic preservation.

—Mary Ellen Snodgrass

PROMINENT SITES

American Museum of Nursing
7025 North 58th Avenue
Glendale, AZ 85301
Telephone: (623) 843 4631
Web: http://www.historic-
glendale.net/nursing_museum.htm
One of the few museums in the United States dedicated to the American nurse. The museum offers exhibits about the history of nurses and their current work.

Arizona Historical Society
949 East 2nd Street
Tucson, AZ 85719
Telephone: (520) 617 1150
Web: http://info-center.ccit.arizona.edu/~azhist/general.htm
Originally the Society of Arizona Pioneers, the Arizona Historical Society was founded in Tucson in 1884. Still headquartered in Tucson, it now has branches throughout the state. The society's collection is divided into various subjects including American Women's Clothing and Accessories, 1850–1970; in addition the collections are open to researchers.

Arizona Inn
2200 East Elm Street
Tucson, AZ 85719
Telephone: (800) 933 1093
Web: http://www.arizonainn.com
The first resort hotel in Tucson was designed by Meriit Starkewather and inn owner Isabella Greenway in 1930. Greenway, who welcomed many famous guests to her inn, including Eleanor Roosevelt, in 1933 became the first women to be elected to Congress from Arizona, serving until 1937. The lobbies and dining rooms of the inn are open to the public.

Arizona Women's Hall of Fame
Hall of Fame Museum
1101 West Washington
Phoenix, AZ 85007
Telephone: (602) 255 2110
Web: http://www.dlapr.lib.az.us/museum/womenhof.htm
This permanent exhibit established in 1979 is a memorial to the women who settled the Arizona frontier. The museum includes photographs and biographies of all inductees.

Birdcage Theatre
On the corner of 6th and Allan Streets
PO Box 248
Tombstone, AZ 85638
Telephone: (520) 457 3421
Web: http://www.tombstoneaz.net
The Birdcage Theatre was not a theater, but a saloon, gambling hall, and brothel that serviced Tombstone for nine years, 24 hours a day, starting in 1881. It opened under the name Elite Opera House, but when Lillian Russell launched her career by singing "She's Only a Bird in a Gilded Cage," written about the club, the owner changed the name the next day. The theatre's back rooms are filled with artifacts of the women who worked there, and bullet holes can be found all over the building.

Chapel of the Holy Cross
780 Chapel Road
Sedona, AZ 86336
Telephone: (929) 282 4069
Web: http://www.diocesephoenix.org/parish/
st_john_vianney_sed/chapel.htm
Marguerite Staude, a sculptor, conceived this piece of architectural art in 1932. She was not able to build the towering cross that rises from the cliff face until 1956. It is now one of the biggest attractions of the area, for both spiritual reasons and its beauty.

Fort Apache
Fort Apache Historic Park
PO Box 628
Fort Apache, AZ 85926
Telephone: (928) 338 1392
Web: http://www.wmonline.com/attract/ftapache.htm
The Fort Apache army post was established in 1870 to enforce a peace treaty with the White Mountain Apaches. A self-guided walking tour is available for the buildings. Martha Summerhayes was one of the few army wives who accompanied her husband out West. She lived at Fort Apache and recorded her time there in her memoirs.

Historic Sahuaro Ranch
9802 North 59th Avenue
Glendale, AZ 85302

Telephone: (623) 939 5782

Web: http://tour.glendaleaz.org/heritage_history_
culture.html

This ranch is on the National Register of Historic Places. Tours include information about the families that lived at the ranch. One of the women who lived in the home was Charlotte Sands Smith. In 1933 she visited the Chicago World's Fair and brought home peacocks. The animals' descendants roam the grounds today.

Inn at Jerome

309 Main Street

Jerome, AZ 86331

Telephone: (800) 634 5094

Web: http://www.innatjerome.com

This bed and breakfast was the former home of Jennie Banters, one of the most powerful and wealthiest madams in Arizona. This former center of the red light district in the early boom days of Jerome has been restyled by the current owners from an Old West building to a Victorian one.

Mary Elizabeth Jane Colter Buildings

The Hopi House, Hermit's Rest, The Lookout Studio, The Desert View

Grand Canyon National Park

PO Box 129

Grand Canyon, AZ 86023

Telephone: (928) 638 7888

Web: http://www.nps.gov/grca/grandcanyon

Mary Elizabeth Jane Colter was one of America's premier architects. She was among the first architects to be strongly influenced by Native American forms. The Hopi House was built to contain the first gift shop in the park and was placed on the National Register of Historic Places in 1987. The National Park Service Web site observes "Colter's ability to draw attention away from the works of man and to emphasize the natural beauty of the park is highlighted in the architectural legacy of the Grand Canyon."

Museum of Northern Arizona

Three miles north of Flagstaff on U.S. Highway 180

Mailing address: 3101 North Fort Valley Road

Flagstaff, AZ 86001

Telephone: (928) 774 5213

Web: http://www.musnaz.org

Dr. Harold S. Colton, a zoologist, and his wife Mary Colton, an artist, founded this museum in 1928. It was originally established to house natural history specimens and Native American artifacts from the area.

Nellie Cashman Restaurant

117 South 5th Street

Tombstone, AZ 85638

Telephone: (520) 457 2212

Nellie Cashman was known as the "Angel of Tombstone." She was a civic leader and helped organize many charitable endeavors, including a hospital, a school, Tombstone's first Catholic church, and individual help for miners in need. The restaurant is decorated with pictures from the late 19th century and stands where Nellie's boardinghouse and restaurant were located.

Pioneer Arizona Living History Museum

3901 West Pioneer Road

Phoenix, AZ 85086

Telephone: (623) 465 1052

Web: http://www.pioneer-arizona.com/index.htm

Costumed interpreters who work in the dress shop, bakery, school, and old southern house populate this Old West re-creation.

Sacred Heart Church

516 East Safford

Tombstone, AZ 85638

Telephone: (520) 457 3364

Web: http://www.tombstone1880.com/sh

Nellie Cashman helped complete the original church structure by securing donations from parishioners and by driving a wagon to the Chiricahua Mountains to haul logs that were milled for construction. The building was used for services until 1947 when a new church was completed. It is now used as the parish hall.

Sharlot Hall Museum–Territorial Women's Memorial Rose Garden

415 West Gurley Street

Prescott, AZ 86301

Telephone: (928) 445 3122

Web: http://www.sharlot.org

The Memorial Rose Garden is "dedicated to those women of Arizona who paved the way for others." The 375 women honored represent the spectrum of Arizona women. The *Rose Garden* exhibit in the museum displays the biographies of these women.

Strawberry Schoolhouse–Pine Strawberry Museum
Fossil Creek Road, 1–3/4 miles west of Arizona
Highway 87
PO Box 464
Pine, AZ 85544
Telephone: (928) 476 3547
A one-room log structure built in 1884, this is the oldest standing schoolhouse in Arizona. It originally also served the community as a meetinghouse and a church.

The accompanying Pine Strawberry Museum documents the history of the area.

Yuma Territorial Prison Historic Park
1 Prison Hill Road
Yuma, AZ 85364
Telephone: (928) 783 4771
Web: http://www.pr.state.az.us/parkhtml/yuma.html
This prison was open from 1876 to 1909 and housed 3,069 during those years, including 29 women. The Prison Museum tells the stories of the inmates, including a detailed section on the women inmates.

RESOURCES

FURTHER READING

HISTORY

Adams, Ward R. *History of Arizona*. 4 vols. Edited by Richard E. Sloan. Phoenix, Ariz.: Record Publishing, 1930.

Anthony, Susan B., and Ida Husted Harper. *History of Woman Suffrage*. Vol. 4. Indianapolis, Ind.: Hollenbeck Press, 1902.

Arizona Women's Town Hall. *Women and the Arizona Political Process*. Edited by Rita Mae Kelly. Lanham, Md.: University Press of America, 1988.

Bancroft, Hubert Howe. *History of Arizona and New Mexico: 1530–1888*. 1888. Reprint, New York: Arno Press, 1967.

Bartlett, John Russell. *Personal Narrative*. Two volumes. New York: D. Appleton and Company, 1854.

Crowe, Rosalie, and Diane Tod. *Arizona Women's Hall of Fame*. 3rd ed. Phoenix: Arizona Historical Society, Central Arizona Division, 1987.

Faulk, Odie B. *Arizona: A Short History*. Norman: University of Oklahoma Press, 1970.

Federal Writers' Project. *Arizona: The Grand Canyon State*. New York: Hastings House, 1956.

Goff, John S. *Arizona Biographical Dictionary*. Cave Creek, Ariz.: Black Mountain Press, 1983.

Harper, Ida Husted. *History of Woman Suffrage*. Vols. 5–6. New York: J. J. Little & Ives, 1922.

Indian Education Unit of the Arizona Department of Education. *A Varied People, Arizona's Indians: A Sourcebook of References, Materials, and Teaching Tools on American Indian Women, Cultures, and Tribal Governments, Highlighting Arizona and the Southwest*. Phoenix: Arizona Department of Education, 1986.

The Journal of Arizona History. Tucson: Arizona Pioneers' Historical Society, 1965– .

Kingsolver, Barbara. *Holding the Line: Women in the Great Arizona Mine Strike of 1983*. New York: ILR Press, 1996.

Officer, James E. *Hispanic Arizona, 1536–1856*. Tucson: University of Arizona Press, 1987.

Powell, Lawrence Clark. *Arizona: A Bicentennial History*. New York: W. W. Norton, 1976.

Rothschild, Mary Aickin, and Pamela Claire Hronek. *Doing What the Day Brought: An Oral History of Arizona Women*. Tucson: University of Arizona Press, 1992.

Trimble, Marshall. *Arizona: A Panoramic History of a Frontier State*. New York: Doubleday, 1977.

Wagoner, Jay J. *Arizona Territory, A Political History*. Tucson: University of Arizona Press, 1970.

Who's Who in Arizona. Scottsdale, Ariz.: Success, 1984–1985.

Who's Who in Arizona in Business, Professions and the Arts: Authentic Biographies of Distinguished Men and Women of Arizona. Phoenix: Arizona Survey, 1938–1940.

BIOGRAPHY AND AUTOBIOGRAPHY

Faunce, Hilda. *Desert Wife*. 1934. Reprint, Lincoln: University of Nebraska Press, 1981.

Fischer, Ron W. *Nellie Cashman: Frontier Angel*. Honolulu, Hawaii: Talei Publishers, 2000.

Frémont, Elizabeth Benton. *Recollections of Elizabeth Benton Frémont, Daughter of the Pathfinder General John C. Frémont and Jessie Benton Frémont, His Wife*. New York: Frederick H. Hitchcock, 1912.

Frémont, Lily. *The Arizona Diary of Lily Frémont, 1878–1881*. Edited by Mary Lee Spence. Tucson: University of Arizona Press, 1997.

Grattan, Virginia L. *Mary Colter, Builder Upon the Red Earth*. Flagstaff, Ariz.: Northland Press, 1980.

Hall, Sharlot M. *Sharlot Hall on the Arizona Strip: A Diary of a Journey through Northern Arizona in 1911*. Edited by C. Gregory Crampton. Prescott, Ariz.: Sharlot Hall Museum Press, 1999.

Kennedy, Marguerite Wallace. *My Home on the Range*. Boston: Little, Brown, 1951.

Ledbetter, Suzann. *Nellie Cashman, Prospector and Trailblazer*. El Paso: Texas Western Press, University of Texas at El Paso, 1993.

Maxwell, Margaret F. *A Passion for Freedom: The Life of Sharlot Hall*. Tucson: University of Arizona Press, 1982.

Oatman, Lorenzo D., and Olive A. Oatman. *Captivity of the Oatman Girls Among the Apache and Mohave Indians*. New York: Dover Publications, 1994. Originally published as *Life Among the*

Indians, 1857. Second (1857) and later printings are titled *The Captivity of the Oatman Girls.*

O'Connor, Sandra Day. *Lazy B: Growing Up on a Cattle Ranch in the American Southwest.* New York: Random House, 2002.

Rak, Mary Kidder. *A Cowman's Wife.* 1934. Reprint, Austin: Texas State Historical Association, 1993.

Rau, Margaret. *The Ordeal of Olive Oatman: A True Story of the American West.* Greensboro, N.C.: Morgan Reynolds, 1997.

Summerhayes, Martha. *Vanished Arizona: Recollections of My Army Life.* 1908. Reprint, Philadelphia: Lippincott, 1963.

Van Sickel, Robert W. *Not a Particularly Different Voice: The Jurisprudence of Sandra Day O'Connor.* New York: P. Lang, 1998.

USEFUL WEB SITES

Arizona Women's News
  http://www.azwomensnews.com
Today's Arizona Woman
  http://www.taw.com/magazine

SELECTED ORGANIZATIONS AND INSTITUTIONS

Arizona Historical Society

949 East Second Street
Tucson, AZ 85719
Telephone: (520) 628 5774
Web: http://w3.arizona.edu/~azhist
A nonprofit state agency that collects, preserves, interprets, and disseminates the history of Arizona, the Southwest, and northern Mexico as it pertains to Arizona.

Arizona History and Archives Division

Arizona State Library, Archives, and Public Records
State Capitol
Suite 342
1700 West Washington
Phoenix, AZ 85007
Telephone: (602) 542 4159
Web: http://www.lib.az.us/archives
An organization dedicated to collecting and preserving historical manuscripts, government records, books, and photographs of Arizona and its peoples.

Arizona Library Association

14449 North 73rd Street
Scottsdale, AZ 85260–3133
Telephone: (480) 998 1954
Web: http://www.azla.org/azinfo/libraries.html
A complete listing of all libraries statewide and links to all electronic resources associated with these libraries.

Arizona State Library, Archives and Public Records

State Capitol
Suite 200
1700 West Washington Street
Phoenix, AZ 85007
Telephone: (602) 542 4035
Web: http://www.lib.az.us/index.html
A state agency that provides access to the archives of historical records, access to all library branches, access to all state, government, and history museums, and fosters an inter-library connection for Arizonans.

Arizona State University Libraries

Box 871006
Tempe AZ 85287–1006
Telephone: (480) 965 6164
Web: http://www.asu.edu/lib
A complete list of all electronic library resources, including catalogs, collections, electronic journals, subject guides, and library departments for the Arizona State University library.

Arizona State University West Women's Studies Program

4701 West Thunderbird Road
Phoenix, AZ 85069–7100
Telephone: (602) 543 3300
Web: http://www.west.asu.edu/wsteam
An interdisciplinary program that focuses on women's experience and the social construction of gender from cross-cultural and historical perspectives. Offers both major and minor programs.

Arizona State University Women's Studies Program

PO Box 873404
Arizona State University
Tempe, AZ 85287–3404
Telephone: (480) 965 2358
Web: http://www.asu.edu/clas/womens_studies
An academic program geared toward exploring the roles and status of women, the effect of political and social systems on women, and cultural assumptions about women, all with an interdisciplinary approach. Offers major, minor, and certificate programs.

Arizona University Department of Women's Studies
PO Box 5695
Flagstaff, AZ 86011
Telephone: (928) 523 3300
Web: http://www.nau.edu/~wst
An interdisciplinary program dedicated to promoting women's studies scholarship and feminist scholars, to improving the academic climate for women, and to transforming society at large. Offers major and minor programs.

Southwest Institute for Research on Women (SIROW)
Department of Women Studies
Communication Building 108
The University of Arizona
PO Box 210025
Tucson, AZ 85721–0025
Telephone: (520) 621 7338
Web: http://w3.arizona.edu/~ws/newweb/sirow.html
A regional research facility that studies women's education, employment, health, history, literature, and culture, and develops community outreach programs.

University of Arizona Library
Main Library
PO Box 210055
1510 East University Boulevard
Tucson, AZ 85721–0055
Telephone: (520) 621 6441
Web: http://www.library.arizona.edu
An online gateway to electronic catalogs, article indexes, subject guides, archived collections, and Web searches for the University of Arizona library system.

University of Arizona Women's Studies Department
Communication Building 108
The University of Arizona
PO Box 210025
Tucson, AZ 85721–0025
Telephone: (520) 621 7338
Web: http://info-center.ccit.arizona.edu/~ws
An interdisciplinary academic program offering students the opportunity to develop their understanding and analyses of feminist thought and movements and to discuss the current status of women around the world.

ARKANSAS

The Freezer Fresh was the only place to hang out, . . . except for the Deep South on Route 66 and the Town Café on Main Street, where the farmers went to drink coffee. . . . But no kids would be caught dead at the Town . . . and everybody, not just kids, went to the Deep South. But the Freezer Fresh was ours. . . . Everybody had a Coke and a burger, and then piled into each others' cars. . . . You'd either go out to the lake (to watch the submarine races, of course) or up on the mountain, to the bluffs under the red airplane-warning lights (to look for UFOs).
—Norris Church Mailer, *Windchill Summer*, 2000

Arkansas was the first state to have two women in the U.S. House of Representatives simultaneously, and also the first to elect a woman to the U.S. Senate. When Blanche Lambert Lincoln was elected in 1998, Arkansas became one of just four states that have had two female U.S. senators. Its congressional delegation was the only one from the South that voted unanimously for the 19th Amendment, which granted the vote to all women.

PREHISTORY

(Prehistory–1541)

Within the state of Arkansas, archaeologists have found well-preserved artifacts of the Toltec people, who lived more than a millennium ago in the delta on what is now the eastern side of the state. The Toltec mounds, which were used as fortifications, temples, and burial sites, were preserved because they were high enough to avoid the frequent floods in the area. The Caddo, who inhabited southwestern Arkansas, made pottery and lived in villages that stretched for miles along the region's rivers. Like women in faraway Montana, high-ranking Caddo women flattened the heads of their infants to denote status.

The Quapaw probably came down the Ohio and Mississippi Rivers and settled in the delta that the Mound Builders had mysteriously vacated. Communal Quapaw homes were built in the shape of a beehive; each family had its separate quarters and shared only the central fire. The delta abounded with fish, waterfowl, and other bounty, so Quapaw women did not have to spend a great deal of time in search of food; turtles and mussels also were dietary staples.

Arkansas's other pre-Columbian tribe was the Osage, who, although they were based in Missouri, roamed the hill country of northern Arkansas. More nomadic than the Caddo or Quapaw, the Osage were hunters and predators, and the status of

State Population (2000): 2,673,400
Female Population (2000): 1,368,707
Women in State Legislature (2003): 16.3%
Female College Enrollment (1999): 67,000 (58.3% of total)
Privately Held Women-owned Businesses (1997): 42,581
First Year of Full Suffrage: 1920

137

QUAPAW WOMEN

During the era of French exploration and colonization, the Quapaw were the most important cultural group in Arkansas. Quapaw is linguistically associated with Dheghian Sioux and the Quapaw are related to the Omaha, Osage, Kaw, and Ponca tribes. The Quapaw controlled all of Arkansas—except the northwest, which was Osage territory, and the southwest, which was the home of the Caddo. They were allies of the handful of French soldiers and traders stationed in Arkansas and acted as intermediaries between the Europeans and native tribes, and as guardians against the British and enemy tribes.

The French commented on the beauty, industry, and cheerfulness of Quapaw women. French explorer Henri Joutel noted the handsomeness of the women, and Jean-Bernard Bossu, another French explorer, observed the pleasure—in singing and smiling—they displayed while working. Quapaw women did not interact indiscriminately with the French, though by the end of the colonial period some Quapaw women had married French men, and there were mixed-blood families within the tribe.

At the beginning of the 18th century, Quapaw women wore clothing made of deer or elk buckskin and cloth woven from buffalo hair. The French commented on their unique hair style—unmarried women wore their hair in braids, which were tied in such a way that each formed a figure eight, while married women kept their hair long and loose and parted in the middle. All females painted their hair parts red to represent the path of the sun.

Quapaw women were in charge of the household and, as among other Plains tribes, probably owned the house and all domestic goods. They not only bore and cared for the children, but they also cultivated and prepared the food. They were the farmers, using hand tools to grow maize, squash, beans, pumpkins, watermelons, and sunflowers. Quapaw men hunted the large land animals of the area (bison, deer, and elk), but once the prey was butchered it was the women who transported it to the village, where they cooked the meat and processed other portions of the animals into raw materials for the manufacture of goods, such as clothing and other essentials. After a buffalo hunt, the women rendered the suet (the fat found in animals' internal body cavities) in copper kettles and traded it, along with their surplus corn, to French or English traders for European domestic goods. From the buffalo hides, women made winter clothing, bedding, and moccasins, and they spun the buffalo hair into yarn and wove it into cloth and bags.

The Quapaw were removed from their native territory in the 19th century. Their cultural legacy, however, lives on in Arkansas, for much of their manners and customs were preserved and passed on by the women of the tribe.

—Gloria A. Young and Carrie V. Wilson

women in these societies was invariably lower than it was in more settled ones.

WHITE EXPLORATION TO STATEHOOD (1541–1836)

Hernando De Soto's Spanish expedition stayed in Arkansas longer than in any other area, from approximately June 1541 to the following spring. They entered in the northeast and departed from the southwest, where they encountered the Caddo, calling them the best fighters they had seen since their arrival in Florida.

More than a century passed before the next Europeans appeared. In 1673 seven Frenchmen canoed down the Mississippi, led by Jesuit missionary Jacques Marquette and his fur-trader companion, Louis Jolliet. When they reached the Arkansas River, the Quapaw warned them that it was still a long way to the end of the Mississippi, and they returned to Michigan.

The French expedition led by René-Robert Cavelier LaSalle landed at the same point in 1682, and Native American women were part of this 54-member expedition. Some of the Frenchmen formed relationships with Quapaw women, and the resulting settlement at the confluence of the Arkansas and Mississippi Rivers became known as the Arkansas Post. This community, which still exists, dates its beginning to 1686 and remains the oldest town in the Midsouth. Arkansas Post grew exponentially in

1719, when Scottish developer John Law (who lived in France) sent some 500 black slaves to the town. The following year, 800 Europeans, mostly German speakers, followed. They lacked the skills to live in this wilderness, however, and Law's French investors lost faith in him. Europeans withdrew their financing and left the colonists to starve. Many fled to the small settlement of New Orleans, and by 1722 Arkansas Post had a mere 47 residents. Although settlers died from mosquito-borne diseases, and Quapaw died from European smallpox, Arkansas Post endured, with some new female settlers arriving in 1727 via Louisiana.

By the 1740s scattered settlements had appeared in northeastern Arkansas. Joseph and Marie Amie Francoeur lived along the White River, where Marie gave birth to at least nine children. Some of her sons married Native American women, and the Francoeur family soon became a sizable community. Meanwhile Antoine and Angelique Janis and their numerous children flourished on the Black River during the 1780s. Arkansas's second still-extant community began in 1797, when Sylvanus Phillips developed the Mississippi River town of Helena. His daughters populated the town under their married names of Patterson, Mooney, and Lewis. In 1799 a Spanish official said that the area's nonnative population totaled 368.

International disputes over much of this land ended with the 1803 Louisiana Purchase. The U.S. government established an Indian agency at Arkansas Post in 1805, and Congress authorized several expeditions to explore the new territory. Other Americans followed, and the 1810 census showed 1,062 residents in the future Arkansas.

A few eastern Native Americans had gone to Arkansas as early as the 1780s, but in 1808 there was a massive migration of Cherokee, who occupied former Osage land. Fort Smith was established in 1817 to maintain peace between the two tribes—and to keep whites out of western Arkansas, which was designated as Indian Territory.

However, some whites, including women, settled in the civilian area around the fort, which was called Belle Point. In 1813, even before the fort opened, Maj. William Lewis Lovely was assigned as the area's Indian agent. He and his wife, Persis Brown Lovely, built a home in what is now the Russellville area, and when he died in 1817 she stayed on. The Cherokee were so fond of her that she was the only one permitted to remain when the other whites were evicted from the area.

By 1820 white families had plantations on both sides of the Red River; the 1820 census showed a nonnative population of 14,273. Arkansas was organized as a territory not because of resident demand, however, but because Missouri was ready for statehood and wanted to detach its

SALLY GOOD'N

In the early 19th century some Native Americans who lived in southeastern states were slave owners, and they took these slaves with them when they moved to the Indian Territory of Oklahoma. Although this was not a common practice, Taylor Polk, an affluent white man of Hot Spring County, Arkansas, bought a slave named Sally Good'n, who was part Choctaw or Cherokee, in the Indian Territory. He is said to have kept her as a concubine in Fort Smith, where he regularly went for jury duty after 1821.

In 1821 Polk married a white woman, Prudence Anderson. She bore a daughter, Eleanor, in 1823, while Sally's first child, Peter, was born in 1827. Taylor Polk did not hide the fact that he was Peter's father, and by 1833 he had built a cabin for Sally next to his plantation home, called "The Wilds," in Caddo Township. Despite Prudence Polk's unhappiness, Taylor Polk now had three sons with Sally.

When Sally bore a daughter in 1838, however, the baby, Eliza, was much darker than her brothers. Convinced that Sally had slept with a black man, Polk sold the mother of his sons "down the river to New Orleans." Prudence Polk, who was described as kind—and who bore more of Taylor's children during this era—then raised Sally's children as well as her own.

—Doris Weatherford

Arkansas district. With Arkansas's western border still undefined, Pres. James Monroe signed the bill creating the Arkansas Territory on March 2, 1819.

Even though Arkansas arguably had less warfare with native tribes than any other state in the nation, its tribes were forcibly moved to Oklahoma after Congress passed the 1830 Indian Removal Act. The Caddo numbered a mere 176 when they departed from Pine Bluff in 1834; the Quapaw were down to 126 in 1826, and they were further decimated by a cholera epidemic in 1833. Meanwhile, the Cherokee and Choctaw, who had moved to southwestern Arkansas, numbered in the tens of thousands, and the forced migrations during this period brought additional tribes from the East. In the midst of this tragedy, on June 15, 1836, Arkansas became the nation's 25th state.

STATEHOOD TO THE CIVIL WAR (1836–1861)

Fort Smith and nearby Van Buren attracted large numbers of transients, including many criminals and prostitutes, and especially Fort Smith developed a reputation as a wild town. Even in notorious towns, however, some women exerted a civilizing influence. Amanda Buchanan ran a Van Buren boarding school that attracted Cherokee girls from nearby Tallequah, Oklahoma, and other Cherokee attended the Cane Hill Female Seminary in Evansville, north of Fort Smith. Cane Hill opened in 1834, and its first principal, Laura Graham, was a graduate of Mount Holyoke Female Seminary in Massachusetts.

The vast majority of Arkansas settlers came from southeastern states in family groups. There were about three men to every two women, a more even ratio than in territories farther west on the frontier. Large caravans of covered wagons traveled to Arkansas from the Carolinas in 1851, 1852, and 1857. The 1851 caravan was led by the families of two sisters, Rosa Falls Ferguson and Frances Falls Oates. According to Pope County tax records, Eliza

Oates and Margaret Bigham became successful farmers, with 13 slaves. Oates was the county's second-largest slaveholder.

Large-scale slave ownership was rare outside the delta, but many middle-class families had a few slaves. Skilled slaves built Potts Inn, which served stagecoach passengers near the old Cherokee headquarters of Galla Rock. The mansion-like inn, which still exists at the beginning of the 21st century, was managed by Pamelia Logan Potts, whose husband, Kirkbride Potts, led cattle drives to the West Coast. Many male neighbors assisted on the cattle drives, leaving Pottsville women alone quite often.

As settlers moved into Arkansas in the 1850s, others who had been there a decade or two were ready to move still farther west. The most notable of these was a 150-member wagon train that gathered at Caravan Springs in Boone County. The settlers were headed to California, but most would die in Utah in 1857, in the still unexplained tragedy known as the Mountain Meadows Massacre. Except for 17 children, the entire wagon train was slaughtered by a Paiute war party that historians suspect had been employed by the Mormons. Some historians believe that the attack was an act of revenge for the arrest of Eleanor McComb McLean, whose husband, Hector McLean, killed her lover, Mormon missionary Parley Pratt, after she had taken the McLean children to Arkansas.

The 1860 census showed that one in four Arkansans was an African slave, but that ratio did not reflect a true picture of the entire state. Just 6 of 75 counties had a black majority, and slave owners were less than 4% of the state's population. These demographics would have tremendous significance when the Civil War began in 1861. Arkansas, in fact, had its own internal civil war, for the northwestern mountains and the southeastern delta were two almost entirely separate realms, with different economies and conflicting goals.

CIVIL WAR AND RECONSTRUCTION ERAS (1861–1880)

Unlike most Confederates, male Arkansans rejected secession in a referendum held in early 1861. However, the vote was a mere test of opinion and had no legal effect. The legislature was controlled by the wealthy and was disproportionately represented by slave owners. Thus, on May 6, 1861, with only one dissenting vote from a Huntsville man, the legislature took Arkansas out of the Union.

For women the war meant genuine hardship. They not only had to run farms and businesses, but they also suffered when soldiers from both sides destroyed their crops and confiscated their livestock. Some communities lost a fourth of their male population during the war. Law enforcement was virtually nonexistent, and the state government degenerated into anarchy. Molly Sinclair Falls, who lived with her sister on the main road running through the Arkansas River Valley, later wrote, "No one can fully appreciate just what we went through. . . . Night riders were frequent visitors. . . . We were robbed seven times." (Ragsdale 1997, 86–87)

Abraham Lincoln appointed an occupation governor, Republican Isaac Murphy, in 1864, and a constitutional convention met near the end of his turbulent administration. To be readmitted to the Union, defeated states had to adopt new constitutions that recognized the rights of former slaves; in this context, Arkansas held its first debate on the vote for women. No state or territory in the nation had yet adopted women's suffrage, and the Arkansas attempt failed, despite an effort by Miles Langley to have women's voting rights written into the constitution. He reported to Susan B. Anthony:

> I made a motion to insert . . . "All citizens twenty-one years of age, who can read and write the English language, shall be eligible to the elective franchise, and be entitled to equal political

THE FOUNDING OF ST. SCHOLASTICA CONVENT

The western frontier of Arkansas was made a little more hospitable to a nascent German colony with the founding of the St. Scholastica convent near Fort Smith in 1879. The Little Rock and Fort Smith Railroad Company offered, at low prices, much of its state land grants to German immigrants. Hoping to entice these farmers to settle, clear the land, and form communities that would eventually make the railroad profitable, the company also donated tracts of land for educational and religious purposes. German Catholics placed a high priority on education and desired an opportunity to practice their religion, even in predominantly Protestant Arkansas. As a result 640 acres were dedicated to a Benedictine monastery and school, while another 100-acre tract was set aside as a convent. It was to this tract of land on Shoal Creek that Sisters Xaveria and Bonaventura moved from a convent in Ferdinand, Indiana, opening St. Scholastica on January 23, 1879.

The sisters promptly founded a school for the settlers, while two others began a school at the monastery's location. Because most of the school's pupils were children of poor farmers who could not afford to pay tuition, the convent had to provide for itself from the land. Neighbors pitched in whenever they could, but the primary responsibility for preparing and planting the rocky soil fell to the four nuns. Just as the neighboring frontier settlers struggled to turn their plots of land into sustaining farms, so the sisters worked the land, raised crops and livestock, and also ran the school.

St. Scholastica, one small piece of civilization on the frontier, struggled for many years. Slowly the number of sisters grew, and the convent eventually became independent from its sponsoring convent in Indiana. The sisters of St. Scholastica aided the settlement of German immigrants, educated generations of Catholic and Protestant children, and founded an organization that remains an important community center.

—Angela Boswell

and legal rights and privileges." The motion was seconded and I had the floor, but the House became so clamorous that . . . the meeting adjourned with the understanding that I was to occupy the floor the next morning. But . . . some of the members tried to "bully" me . . .

I replied that I had been robbed, shot, and imprisoned for advocating the rights of the slaves, and that I would then and there speak in favor of the rights of women! . . . I was met with ridicule, sarcasm, and insult. (Stanton, Anthony, and Gage 1886, 3:805–806)

The *Arkansas Ladies' Journal* offered editorial encouragement: "They tell us that women are not fit for politics. This may be true; and as it is next to impossible to change the nature of a woman, why wouldn't it be a good idea to change politics so that it shall be fit for women?" (Ibid.)

In 1871 Arkansas's judiciary became the nation's second to admit a woman, Missouri's Phoebe Couzins, to the practice of law. The federal Reconstruction government also provided the first public higher education available to Arkansans. African American women arguably benefited more than white women. The University of Arkansas, which opened in 1871 in the Ozark mountain town of Fayetteville, was intended primarily for sons of elite white families, but the coeducational Arkansas Agricultural and Mechanical College featured a curriculum designed for African American women.

SUFFRAGE AND PROGRESSIVE ERAS (1880–1920)

Arkansas's first suffrage society began in 1885 in the mountain resort of Eureka Springs. The town was home to pioneer attorney Lizzie Fyler, who began the society when Missouri attorney Phoebe Couzins visited. Fyler already had taken the initiative of attending the 1884 convention of the National Woman Suffrage Association in Washington, D.C., where she made a presentation about women in Arkansas.

Susan B. Anthony spoke in a number of Arkansas towns in 1889, including Helena, Fort Smith, and Little Rock, where Gov. James B. Eagle

introduced her. The tour was arranged by the Women's Christian Temperance Union (WCTU), which had begun nationally in the previous decade and was still considered radical. Suffrage was even more controversial than temperance, but, according to Catherine Campbell Cunningham of Little Rock, Anthony's "large audience . . . manifested every evidence of approval." (Anthony and Harper 1902, 4:475)

Suffragists worked through the WCTU, holding separate meetings at the end of WCTU gatherings. Clara McDiarmid attended national suffrage conventions, and Dr. Ida J. Brooks, Fannie L. Chunn, and a woman named Bernie Babcock were also important suffragists in the state. In 1888 Mary Burt Brooks, principal of Forest Grove School, joined with Haryot Holt Cahoon and Catherine Campbell Cunningham to establish the *Woman's Chronicle*, a weekly paper that they published for five years. During legislative sessions they put the current issue on every lawmaker's desk.

Although Arkansas had admitted Phoebe Couzins to its bar in 1871, by the end of the century the state legislature had ruled that women could not practice law. However, the university's law school remained open to women, as did its medical school, and presumably a woman could study law in Arkansas and practice in another state, though it does not appear that any did. Elsewhere in the nation it was easier for women to practice medicine than law, but few Arkansas women became physicians during this period, either.

Property laws for Arkansas women also reflected ambivalence. Women in Arkansas were allowed to sell their own property without their husbands' consent, and a woman could have the profits of a business "free from the interference of her husband." If, however, a woman was merely working for pay, her husband could sue her for her wages.

By the late 19th century many states allowed women to vote in school elections, but this was not

THE RECOLLECTIONS OF HARRIET BULLOCK DANIEL

Harriet Bullock (later Harriet Bullock Daniel) was born in Dallas County, in south-central Arkansas, in 1849. Her affluent parents were recent arrivals from Tennessee, and, with the labor of numerous slaves, they soon built an impressive plantation. Harriet's mother, Sara Jane Shepard Bullock, died soon after the birth of her eleventh child when Harriet, the ninth of ten living children, was three.

Although her father remarried and Harriet called her stepmother "Ma," her "Sister Nannie," who never married, assumed much of the maternal responsibility. She was helped by some of the black women, especially a woman named Moriah, who was called Aunt 'Riah. When she was 80, Harriet Bullock Daniel recalled:

Soon after we moved . . . a little Lucy came, and left us when but a few weeks old. Hers was the first grave in the plum orchard back of the garden. In time another little sister was born. . . . We called her "Lute."

Aunt 'Riah told me that when Lute was about two months old, Mother rode horseback . . . to see a sick child. . . . Soon after that Mother herself was taken sick, . . . and all the children away at [boarding] school were called home. After a few days of intense suffering, God took her and her body was laid by that of her little babe in the plum orchard.

I cannot remember my mother and we did not have a picture of her. The neighbors said she was pretty. . . . Pa's grief was terrible. Aunt 'Riah said that after the funeral was over and all the folks gone, Pa went off alone. . . . Uncle Billy finally went out and sat down by him. . . . Just after sundown Pa came into the house, leaning on Uncle Billy's shoulder. Aunt 'Riah said Uncle Billy had had trouble and knew what trouble "Marster" was in, and it almost broke his heart to see him that way.

Aunt 'Riah and other slaves were authority figures to Harriet, and when she got in trouble—as she frequently did—she had to negotiate her way out with them:

In Aunt Rachel's yard was a nice seedling apple tree which bore sweet apples. On our plantation apple trees were rare. . . . No one was in sight and I concluded to climb to the branches and sample the ripening fruit.

As I bit the first apple, Aunt Rachel turned the corner of the house, "Never mind," she screamed, "I am sho gwine ter tell Miss Mary and yer pappy is gwine ter whip yer."

Quickly I slid down the tree; I knew Aunt Rachel like to make quilts, so I said, "If you don't tell on me, I'll give you lots of nice bed-quilt pieces."

We made the bargain and she gave me several apples. I was afraid to ask for the scraps, but when Ma was out calling and the coast was clear, I got her scrap bag, selected a good roll, regardless of value or color, and paid my debt.

—Doris Weatherford

Excerpts from Margaret Jones Bolsterli, ed., *A Remembrance of Eden: Harriet Bailey Bullock Daniel's Memories of a Frontier Plantation in Arkansas, 1849–1872.* Fayetteville: University of Arkansas Press, 1993.

---

the case in Arkansas. However, Arkansas did have an unusual form of suffrage, in which a petition signature counted as a vote. Under the "Three Mile Law," the first version of which passed in 1875, women (and men) signed petitions that could impose a ban on alcohol sales within three miles of a church or school. The law did not apply to incorporated cities, but in rural areas WCTU women went door-to-door obtaining signatures.

Arkansas women participated in the commemoration of the 400th anniversary of the Columbus expedition in Chicago, Illinois, where millions of people attended a yearlong fair that began in October 1892. Little Rock's Jean Loughborough (later Douglass) won the bid to design Arkansas's exhibit space; she also worked on the Woman's Building and spoke at the World's Congress of Representative Women.

By 1900 Arkansas's suffrage movement was so dispersed that the only advocate known to national leaders was Mrs. Chester Jennings, a Little Rock woman who published articles on the topic. A 1911 meeting of the WCTU and the College Women's Club to revitalized suffrage: the new leaders included women with such influential Arkansas names as Cotnam, Pratho, Rose, and Terry. They met twice a month at a library, and, unlike most suffragists, consciously held half of their meetings in the afternoon, for the convenience of women with children in school, and half in the evenings, to allow women and men who worked to attend. When the legislature met in 1913, the women testified on behalf of a women's suffrage measure before the House Judiciary Committee. Although the committee recommended passage, the measure lost in the full House, 35 to 55.

Suffrage societies expanded to Pine Bluff and Hot Springs, and Arkansas suffragists became affiliated with the National American Woman Suffrage Association in 1913. The state suffrage association president was Mrs. O. F. Ellington of Little Rock, who led a May Day event with speeches from the steps of the Old State House. In October, suffragists held the first state convention at Little Rock's Marion Hotel, with new groups from Augusta, Hardy, Malvern, and Fayetteville attending. By the time of the 1915 annual meeting, 11 counties were represented.

In the biannual legislative session that year, a joint resolution proposing a suffrage amendment to the state constitution was introduced in the House, and it passed with 51 in favor, 18 against, and 31 absent. The large number of absentees turned out to be ominous, for a hidden agenda was in play. The next morning, when the proposed amendment should have been routinely filed with the secretary of state for placement on the ballot at the next election, suffragists discovered that three amendments, the maximum number allowed, had already been filed. Suffragists felt it more than possible that the last amendment was filed in response to legislators who wanted to defeat the suffragists, but who did not dare to vote against these prominent women in a public forum.

National suffrage leader Carrie Chapman Catt spoke to a large Little Rock crowd in 1916. Catt helped Arkansas suffragists plan the strategy that would win a limited right to vote the next year. Instead of continuing to work at the much more difficult task of amending the state constitution, their strategy was to change the rules of the Democratic party and win the right to vote in Democratic primaries only. In Arkansas, as in the rest of the South at that time, winning the Democratic primary was tantamount to winning the general election. For decades after Reconstruction, virtually no white people joined the Republican party, which was seen as the party of abolition and postwar martial law. Because antisuffragists invariably raised fears of empowered African American women as an argument for not granting the vote to any women, the strategy of winning the vote solely for Democratic primaries was arguably racist; while African American women also would have a right to vote, the assumption was that they were Republicans who would lack viable candidates. The effect was to exclude them.

Beyond this political crassness, however, was the reality that while the legislature could grant the vote for party primaries, full enfranchisement required a constitutional amendment, meaning it had to pass both the legislature and the male electorate. Suffragists opted to forgo the November general election, knowing that the important decisions were made in the Democratic primaries.

Suffragists went back to the legislature in 1917 with that goal, and John A. Riggs of Hot Springs introduced their bill. Although they had been slower to organize than other states, Arkansas suffragists quickly learned the complexities of politics. They worked deliberately and quietly to obtain enough pledges to win before Riggs brought the bill to the floor, and it passed the House by a vote of 78 to 16. The state Senate then passed it, 27 to 17.

In May 1918 Arkansas women voted in the spring primaries, and in July at least 50 were delegates to the state Democratic convention. Indeed many counties sent more women than men as delegates, and women controlled several committees. Stella Brizzolara of Fort Smith was elected to the powerful State Central Committee, and newspapers commented on the intelligence of these new political participants.

With the support of the full Arkansas delegation, Congress gave final passage to the 19th Amendment that fully enfranchised all American women. Arkansas was among the first states to ratify, with many lawmakers offering to forgo payment for the necessary special session. On July 28, 1919, the Arkansas Senate ratified the amendment by a vote of 29 to 2, while the House vote was 74 to 15. Women from all over the state filled the capitol for this historic event.

1920s THROUGH WORLD WAR II ERA (1920–1950)

Democrats Frances Hunt (a married woman) and Earle Chambers (an unmarried woman) won seats in the Arkansas legislature in 1922. Although the 1920s are remembered as "roaring," for most Arkansans this was a hard decade. Not only did the farm economy decline long before the stock market collapsed at decade's end, but the state also suffered the worst floods in its history in 1927. Thousands of poor sharecroppers lost what little they had, and landlords evicted others. The drought that occurred in the next decade meant continued suffering, and tens of thousands of "Arkies" were forced to leave the state.

In contrast Hot Springs flourished in the 1920s, as wealthy vacationers from Chicago and other cities began using it as a winter resort. Law enforcement turned a blind eye to illegal alcohol, as well as to gambling and prostitution. In addition Arkansas and Nevada had the most relaxed divorce laws in the nation, and many lawyers sought to profit from these laws. Arkansas would continue to have an exceptionally high divorce rate throughout the 20th century.

Northeastern Arkansas elected Pearl Peden Oldfield to the congressional seat that her late husband had held, making her one of the first half-dozen women in the U.S. House of Representatives. Sworn in on January 11, 1929, she quickly filed bills to help constituents still suffering from the 1927 floods. Conditions had grown so bad in eastern Arkansas that nutritional deficiency diseases such as pellagra and beri-beri were becoming common. Oldfield asked for $15 million in food aid in January 1931. The Republican leadership neither supported her bill nor assigned her to significant committees, however, and Oldfield did not run for a second term.

While she was in the House, however, Arkansas became the first state to have two women in Congress simultaneously: Effiegene Locke Wingo took office on December 1, 1930. The recent widow of the representative from southwestern Arkansas, Wingo was elected without opposition. Although she received better committee assignments than Oldfield did, including a position on the prestigious Foreign Affairs Committee, she too retired. Her strongest legacy was the creation of the Ouachita National Forest.

In 1932 Arkansas became the first state to elect a woman to the U.S. Senate when HATTIE WYATT CARAWAY of Jonesboro won a special election to complete the term of her late husband Thaddeus. Meanwhile Mount Ida put women in all of its elected offices, including mayor. All of these women won reelection against men in 1932, as did Caraway. These were exceptions to the rule during the Great Depression, however. In general, the economic collapse proved to be a setback to American women, and even small-town political jobs usually were seen as rightfully belonging to men.

Likewise New Deal programs were largely for, and administered by, men. Arkansas, however, again proved to be an exception. Maxine East was the director of the Federal Emergency Relief Administration in the poorest part of the state, the delta of eastern Arkansas, and women held other significant positions. Arkansas was the first southern state to employ women in Works Progress Administration (WPA) programs, with most assigned to 123 sewing shops throughout the

Hattie Wyatt Caraway. (© Bettmann/Corbis)

state. Even though such "women's jobs" paid less than those for men, it was more money than most women had ever made.

WPA communal canneries offered women whose homes lacked electricity and running water the opportunity to preserve their garden produce with modern equipment. Arkansas was home to many WPA gymnasiums, where girls' basketball games attracted as many fans as boys' games. The National Youth Administration opened a camp named for Florida's Mary McLeod Bethune at Pine Bluff. Supervised by Hattie Rutherford Watson, the camp offered young African American women a chance to learn a range of vocational and leadership skills.

Even educated professionals suffered during the Depression, but the WPA's Federal Writers' Project (FWP) in Arkansas proved especially remarkable. Most southern states used this program to hire writers to collect oral histories from former slaves. Former suffragist Bernie Babcock was the state director of the FWP, and under her leadership Arkansas collected far more slave narratives than any other state, accounting for 689 of the 2,194 narratives collected. This is a notable achievement, given that 17 states participated in the project and Arkansas had had fewer slaves than most southern states. No state, however, hired many African American writers, and only one of the 16 women on the Arkansas project, Pernella M. Anderson of El Dorado, was African American. Likewise only one of the three male writers was African American.

Louise Loughborough used WPA funds to restore the territorial capitol and other significant buildings, while Charlie May Simon built a Perry County retreat for writers and artists. One of Simon's books, *Sharecropper* (1937), was inspired by the Southern Tenant Farmers Union, an unusual agrarian union comprised of farmers of both races. Jennie Lee, a Labour member of Britain's Parliament, led a 1935 protest march in the town of Marked Tree, and African American women took leadership positions in the union. Some trace the civil rights movement of the 1960s to this delta country action.

Aviator Louise McPhetridge Thaden of Bentonville defeated Amelia Earhart in the first Women's Air Derby, and her memoir, *High, Wide, and Frightened*, was published in 1938. Because Thaden had two children, she was not permitted to join the small number of women allowed to fly for the military when the United States entered World War II. She volunteered in the ways open to her, however, and reached the rank of lieutenant colonel in the Civil Air Patrol.

The Civil Air Patrol was home based, but many women were assigned to the major army posts of Camp Robinson (near Little Rock) and Camp Chaffee (near Fort Smith). Arkansas State Teachers College at Conway became one of seven regional basic-training centers for the Women's Army Corps (WAC). Members of this group were called WACs, and many went to war in North Africa and in Europe.

Many more women worked in defense industries. Women had proven more careful than men at handling ammunition during World War I, and they were hired again in large numbers. Arkansas women, many of them African American, held three-quarters of the approximately 13,000 dangerous jobs at several ordnance plants. The Pine Bluff Arsenal exploded twice in 1943, and an African American woman, Anne Marie Young, received the highest civilian award that the War Department gave for her courage in rescuing others.

For many, however, better jobs were available elsewhere, and Arkansas was one of five states whose population declined during the 1940s. Tens of thousands went to southern California, where they worked in shipyards and aircraft factories, and to Detroit, where automobile plants had been converted to tank manufacture and other war needs. For years many Arkansans drifted between the two locales, unhappy with urban life away from home but frustrated at the lack of economic opportunity when they returned.

POSTWAR AND CONTEMPORARY ERAS
(1950–present)

Many Arkansas women left the labor force when the war ended, but they returned sooner than most have recognized. By 1950 the number of working women in Arkansas was back up to the same level that it had been six years earlier, at the height of the war. Most worked in manufacturing, including in shoe factories, which had moved from the North to take advantage of nonunion labor in the South, and food preservation, especially chicken.

As in other states many teachers had left the field of education for better-paid defense jobs during the war, and African American teachers took advantage of this shortage to equalize their pay with that of whites. African American women in several southern states filed suit, and the lead plaintiff in Arkansas was Sue Cowan Morris. She was a well-qualified University of Chicago graduate, but

her supervisor told her the best African American teacher would never be equal to any white. After long court battles, including legal work by future U.S. Supreme Court justice Thurgood Marshall, Morris finally won her case for equal pay.

Her activism was little noted, but that of DAISY BATES had a tremendous impact in 1957, when she advised the nine African American students—the Little Rock Nine—in their efforts to enroll in Little Rock's all-white Central High School. When President Eisenhower sent federal troops to enforce integration in the state, women led both the segregationist Mothers League of Central High and the integrationist Women's Emergency Committee to Open Our Schools. Vivion Brown, a Smith College graduate and attorney, and Adolphine Terry, sister of Pulitzer Prize winner John Gould Fletcher, led the progressives.

In the same era Rosa Zagnoni Marinoni, a Bologna, Italy, native who had moved to Arkansas as a child, was the state poet laureate from 1953

Daisy Bates, who advised the Little Rock Nine, and Clarence Laws, her colleague at the National Association for the Advancement of Colored People. (©Bettmann/Corbis)

to 1970. Lily Peter replaced her in 1971 and held the post for the next 20 years.

Although women had won seats in the state House of Representatives at the first opportunity, none joined the Arkansas Senate until 1964, when Dorothy Allen of Brinkley was elected. Catherine Norrell briefly served in the U.S. House from 1961 to 1963, but unlike Nancy Johnson Hall, Norrell did not develop a career in politics. Hall was appointed secretary of state in 1961, and she served as state treasurer from 1963 to 1980. Arkansas elects its judges, and in 1975 Elsijane T. Roy became the first woman on the Arkansas Supreme Court. The next year Sarah Caldwell became the first woman to conduct the New York Philharmonic Orchestra, as well as the first to direct at the Metropolitan Opera.

Betty Bumpers, the wife of U.S. Sen. Dale Bumpers, drew national attention for her opposition to the Vietnam War, while Hillary Rodham retained her maiden name when her husband, Bill Clinton, was elected governor in 1978. She led educational reform programs and an innovative lending program for businesswomen, including those in agribusiness. Rodham later changed her name to Hillary Rodham Clinton, and she was a powerful, if controversial, first lady from 1993 to 2001, after which she ran a successful

THE WOMEN'S EMERGENCY COMMITTEE TO OPEN OUR SCHOOLS (1958–1963)

In September 1958 a group of white middle-class women met in Little Rock in response to a community conflict over public school integration. A year earlier Arkansas Gov. Orval Faubus had placed Arkansas National Guard troops around Central High School in Little Rock in order to prevent the entry of nine African American students. In response to the unrest, Pres. Dwight D. Eisenhower sent federal troops to Little Rock to restore order and allow the desegregation to begin. By the fall of 1958 Faubus had closed the public high schools of Little Rock under a new state law designed to stop integration. Even this action, however, did not prompt Little Rock's business and civic leaders to offer public opposition to Faubus and his racist policies.

Although the women who met in Little Rock intended to discuss race relations, they were more concerned with the fact that their children had lost two weeks of school, and that the schools remained closed. Thus, the Women's Emergency Committee to Open Our Schools (WEC) was born. In order to direct its message to "the moderates . . . the segregationists who yet realized the importance of public education," the WEC excluded African Americans from membership. At the same time, its leaders supported the formation of interracial advisory boards to give African Americans a public voice, and they attempted to educate fellow members about their racial prejudices and the harm caused by discriminatory practices, including segregation. That they did so in a segregated organization demonstrates not only their own contradictions and internal divisions, but also their pessimistic (and accurate) reading of the political context within which they operated.

The leaders of the new organization brought to it a respectability derived from their connections to prominent Little Rock families and their impeccable credentials as southern "ladies" who had contributed much to their communities. They mobilized more than 1,700 women to work on the political education of their community and on getting out the vote for their candidates and issues. They organized media events; they sought allies, particularly in women's organizations; and they worked to shift the terms of the discourse about school desegregation.

From the beginning the WEC defined itself as an antidote to men's default on their civic responsibilities. And as time passed the WEC's impatience with the timidity, business values, and racial conservatism of Little Rock's power structure intensified. Ironically the organization's success in getting male moderates elected, especially to positions on the school board, enabled the male elite to retain its monopoly on formal power. The WEC broke the back of massive resistance in Little Rock and in Arkansas by redirecting the political debate from integration to the maintenance of the public schools and the necessity for economic development.

—Karen Anderson

campaign to become one of New York's two Democratic senators.

During the century's last two decades, Fayetteville's Ellen Gilchrist published more than a dozen books, including an American Book Award winner, *Victory Over Japan: A Book of Stories* (1984). Joan Hess, a fifth-generation Fayetteville resident, wrote witty mysteries; her book *A Diet to Die For* won the 1989 American Mystery Award.

Two women won statewide office in 1980: Jimmie Lou Fisher replaced longtime state treasurer Nancy Hall, and Julia Hughes Jones became state auditor. Like every woman elected to office in Arkansas, they were Democrats, but Jones switched to the Republican party in 1993—and she then lost her bid for reelection in 1994. Governor Clinton appointed Mary Stallcup as attorney general in 1991, but she held the office only briefly.

At his first presidential inauguration President Clinton showcased poet MAYA ANGELOU, who was born in Missouri but grew up in Arkansas. Clinton also appointed JOYCELYN ELDERS, who had been director of the Arkansas Department of Health since 1987, as U.S. surgeon general in 1993. Elders proved to be controversial, however, and she stepped down in 1994.

In the same 1992 election that moved the Clintons to the White House, Democrat Blanche Lambert Lincoln won the northeastern congressional district. Just 31 years old at the time, she retired briefly in 1996 while pregnant with twins, and then returned in 1998 to win the U.S. Senate seat that Dale Bumpers vacated. With that election Arkansas became one of just four states to have twice elected women to the U.S. Senate. In 2003 three women held statewide elective offices: Lincoln as U.S. senator, Fisher as treasurer, and Secretary of State Sharon Priest, who also served as president of the National Association of Secretaries of State in 2001.

—Doris Weatherford

TIMELINE

United States Events

1620 Settlement of Plymouth Colony
1776 United States declares independence
1861–65 U.S. Civil War
1914–18 World War I
1920 Ratification of the 19th Amendment
1929–39 Great Depression
1939–45 World War II
1975 Vietnam War ends

Arkansas Events

1540 Hernando De Soto expedition arrives in Arkansas and encounters the Caddo.
1682 LaSalle expedition, including Native American women, arrives in Arkansas.
1817 Fort Smith is established; women are among its first settlers.
1836 Arkansas achieves statehood.
1871 Arkansas's judiciary becomes the second in the country to admit a woman—Phoebe Couzins—to the bar.
1885 Arkansas's first suffrage society, led by Lizzie Fyler, is established.
1917 Arkansas women win the right to vote in primaries.
1919 Arkansas ratifies the 19th Amendment.
1929–1930 Pearl Peden Oldfield and Effiegene Locke Wingo win seats in the U.S. Congress, making Arkansas the first state to have two women in Congress simultaneously.
1932 Arkansas is the first state to elect a woman, Hattie Wyatt Caraway, to the U.S. Senate.
1936 Aviator Louise McPhetridge Thaden is first woman to win Bendix Trophy.
1964 Dorothy Allen becomes the first woman elected to Arkansas Senate.
1980 Two women win statewide office: Jimmie Lou Fisher as state treasurer and Julia Hughes Jones as state auditor.
2003 Three women hold statewide offices: Blanche Lincoln as U.S. senator, Sharon Priest as secretary of state, and Fisher as treasurer.

PROMINENT WOMEN

SUSAN ALAMO (ca. 1930–1982)

Charismatic evangelist Susan Alamo turned an insightful religious experience into a lucrative business. Believing that supernatural powers had cured her of tuberculosis, she felt called to preach and prepare others for the second coming of Christ. In the 1960s she married Bernie Lazar Hoffman, a former entertainer and recording promoter; after his conversion to Christian fundamentalism he changed his name to Tony Alamo.

In 1969 the couple formed the Alamo Christian Foundation, an evangelical organization that proselytized the downtrodden of Hollywood, California. After seven years they moved their headquarters to Alama, Arkansas, from which they launched religious campaigns in Arizona, Florida, New York, Oklahoma, and Tennessee. Susan Alamo's work targeted drug addicts, and to keep former addicts clean she employed them in the ministry's businesses (including hog farming, a restaurant and grocery store, a service station, a trucking line, and a clothing factory) in exchange for their upkeep, vocational education, and health insurance.

In 1976 the U.S. Labor Department investigated the foundation's setup, charging that the Alamos unfairly compensated their workers. The ministry's tax-exempt status was revoked, retroactive to 1977. When Susan Alamo died of cancer, ministry followers ringed her body and prayed for several days for her restoration to life. The foundation then faced increasing legal difficulties stemming from allegations of child abuse, embezzlement, and theft.

MAYA ANGELOU (1928–)

A major figure in American literature, Maya Angelou made a name for herself in cinema and television, public speaking, and as an author of verse, screenplays, and several autobiographies. Born Marguerite Johnson in St. Louis, Missouri, Angelou lived with her mother after her parents' divorce and educated herself through reading the Bible and world classics. Raised primarily by her grandmother in Stamps, Arkansas, she graduated with the eighth grade class from Lafayette County Training School in 1940. She would later record her memories of the South in *I Know Why the Caged Bird Sings* (1970), her most beloved work.

During World War II Angelou reunited with her mother in Los Angeles and spent her teenage years in San Francisco, where she trained at the California Labor School and worked as the city's first female streetcar conductor. In *Gather Together in My Name* (1974), she describes how she danced on stage and in nightclubs and, at age 22, married, divorced, and performed in a road show of *Porgy and Bess* in Africa and Europe. While living in Harlem she performed at the Apollo Theatre and off Broadway. She also lived in Cairo during a marriage to a South African politician. In 1961 she was associate editor for the *Arab Observer*, and she worked as a college administrator at the School of Music and Drama in Accra, Ghana, from 1963 through 1966.

In 1973 Angelou settled in Sonoma, California, and began a career writing music, novels, plays, poetry, and autobiographies. In 1987 she issued *Now Sheba Sings the Song,* a poetic tribute to strong African American females. In 1993 Angelou wrote and read a poem, *On the Pulse of the Morning*, for the inauguration of Pres. Bill Clinton. Her many honors include a 1976 *Ladies' Home Journal* Woman of the Year, nominations for a Pulitzer Prize, a Candace Award, a National Book Award, and induction into the National Women's Hall of Fame.

DAISY BATES (ca. 1914–1999)

Civil rights pioneer and publisher Daisy Lee Gatson Bates of Huttig, Arkansas, exposed herself to virulent hatred for attempting to end segregation. Bates was adopted at a very young age after her mother was murdered by three white men. In 1941 she married journalist L. C. Bates and joined him working on the *Arkansas State Press*, a civil rights publication. Augmenting her understanding of the publishing industry, she took business courses at Shorter College and Philander Smith College.

In 1952 Bates was chosen to lead the Arkansas chapter of the National Association for the Advancement of Colored People (NAACP). During the struggle to integrate Arkansas schools in 1957, Bates counseled and supported the nine African American students, who came to be known as the Little Rock Nine, in their attempt to enroll at the all-white Central High School in Little Rock. In the 1960s Bates worked for the Democratic National Committee in Washington, D.C., and supported the antipoverty initiatives of Pres. Lyndon Johnson's Great Society.

Bates accrued significant honors for her courage. In 1986 a second edition of her autobiography, *The Long Shadow of Little Rock* (originally published in 1962) won an American Book Award. The following year an elementary school in Little Rock was named for her. A year after her death, Pres. Bill Clinton honored her at a memorial service attended by the governor of Arkansas, the mayor of Little Rock, and the nine people she coached to end the state's system of segregated and unequal schools.

HATTIE OPHELIA WYATT CARAWAY (1878–1950)

Depression-era populist Hattie Ophelia Wyatt Caraway, originally of Bakersville, Tennessee, was the first female politician to campaign for and win a full term in the U.S. Senate, the first to chair a Senate committee, and the first elected as Senate president pro tem.

Caraway grew up on a farm and clerked in a dry-goods store. At age 14 she entered Dickson Normal College, and then went on to teach school before marrying Thaddeus Caraway and moving to Jonesboro, Arkansas. When her husband was elected to Congress the family resettled in Washington, D.C.

After her husband's death, in 1931, Caraway took his place in the U.S. Senate. On a platform of tax reform and government assistance for poor farmers, she ran for the seat in 1932. She won the first of two full Senate terms in this election, which was a landslide for Democrats. She served her state through membership on the Agriculture and Forestry Commission, and in 1943 she became the first woman in Congress to cosponsor the Equal Rights Amendment. During her second term she endorsed flood control, supported requirements that planes carry parachutes for each passenger, obtained free gardening tools and communal kitchens for poor women, and aided families of soldiers killed during World War II. In 1944 Caraway lost a reelection bid, but was quickly appointed by Pres. Franklin Delano Roosevelt to the Employees Compensation Commission.

JOYCELYN ELDERS (1933–)

Minnie Joycelyn Elders is best known for her controversial tenure as Pres. Bill Clinton's surgeon general. Born and reared in rural Schaal, Arkansas, Elders was the daughter of sharecroppers. In 1948 she entered Philander Smith College on a Methodist scholarship and decided to become a doctor. She went on to train in physical therapy with the U.S. Army, and she was the only woman to earn a medical degree from the University of Arkansas in 1960. In 1963 she became chief of pediatrics at the Arkansas Medical Center. Four years later she completed postgraduate work in biochemistry at the University of Arkansas, and in 1976 she was named a full professor and earned her certification as a pediatric endocrinologist.

In 1987 Governor Clinton appointed Elders to direct the state's public health program. As supervisor of 2,600 workers, she increased HIV testing and extended immunization outreach to small children, which reduced infant mortality in the state. Dr. Elders became an outspoken champion of contraception and sex education to prevent venereal disease and teen pregnancy.

After Clinton was elected president in 1992, he named Elders as the first African American U.S. surgeon general. She promoted the medical use of marijuana, spoke openly about reducing the stigma of masturbation, and increased taxation of alcohol and tobacco. She became so controversial that conservative politicians forced her to resign a year later. She returned to the staff of the University of Arkansas and in 1996 served on the national board of the American Civil Liberties Union.

MARY LEWIS (1897–1941)

Singer and Ziegfeld chorus girl Mary Sybil Lewis of Hot Springs, Arkansas, flourished in saloons, on stage, and in film. Stories of Lewis's childhood as an abused orphan endeared her to fans, who considered her a Cinderella of the entertainment world. After being rescued from the streets of Dallas, Texas, she received singing, violin, piano, and organ lessons from her foster parents, the Rev. William and Anne Lecky Fitch. A versatile performer, Lewis mastered jazz and popular music, Broadway show tunes, spirituals, art songs, and opera.

At the height of her popularity in the 1920s, Lewis performed on radio and in both silent and talking pictures. Her photo appeared often in newspapers alongside headlines announcing recitals and musing over rumored romances. After

marrying an oil baron, she thrived in operatic productions in London, Paris, Monte Carlo, Berlin, Vienna, and New York (at Carnegie Hall). She enjoyed only four years of singing stardom, however, before dying at age 44 of complications resulting from alcoholism.

ROBERTA MARTIN (1907–1969)

Gospel composer and star contralto Roberta Winston Martin of Helena, Arkansas, helped establish evangelical religious music as a popular genre by issuing it in print through her own music publishing house.

Reared in Illinois, Martin attended public school in Chicago. With early childhood training in piano and choral music, she planned to become a concert pianist. Experience as an active Christian at Ebenezer Baptist Church in Chicago altered her focus from secular to religious music.

In 1931 Martin accompanied a gospel choir led by Thomas A. Dorsey and Theodore R. Frye. She developed into a soloist, director, composer, and arranger of gospel music drawn from African hymns and Negro spirituals. The gospel movement grew into a global phenomenon of church anthems and spirituals both in print and on recordings. She formed a men's group, the Frye–Martin Quartet, which eventually became a mixed ensemble called the Roberta Singers. The group released six gold records on the Apollo label. Their performances of such favorites as "Didn't It Rain" and "Amazing Grace," as well as Martin's compositions "I'm Just Waiting on the Lord" (1953) and "God Is Still on the Throne" (1959), fueled enthusiasm for a 1963 tour of Europe, where Martin performed at Gian-Carlo Menotti's Spoleto Festival. In 1998 the U.S. Postal Service honored her by putting her portrait on a postage stamp.

MARTHA MITCHELL (1918–1976)

Martha Elizabeth Beall Mitchell of Pine Bluff, Arkansas, is remembered as a populist hero who demanded honesty and accountability in government. Mitchell attended private schools until her father lost his cotton business in the stock market crash of 1929. She attended Stephens College in Columbia, Missouri, the University of Arkansas, and the University of Miami in Florida, where she earned a degree in history. During World War II, she gave up teaching to work at the Pine Bluff Arsenal and as a Red Cross volunteer.

Mitchell settled in Washington, D.C., working as a receptionist for a military office and as a research analyst in the Chemical Warfare Service. During her first marriage she worked as a buyer for women's clothing in New York City. After a divorce she married attorney John Newton Mitchell, who served as campaign manager (in 1968) and attorney general (1969–1972) for Pres. Richard M. Nixon. Martha Mitchell volunteered with the Salvation Army while the couple lived at the Watergate Hotel in Washington, D.C.

She joined her husband in criticizing Vietnam War protesters, but undermined him with late-night phone calls to the media, particularly to UPI (United Press International) reporter Helen Thomas. Mitchell leaked information that increased outrage at the Republican burglary of the 1972 Watergate Hotel Democratic headquarters and subsequent presidential cover-up. Critics dismissed Mitchell as a self-ennobling crank, and embarrassed Republican politicians implied to the press that she was a mentally unbalanced alcoholic. In 1973 John Mitchell abandoned her for publicly linking him to the criminal behaviors of Nixon and his staff. After Martha Mitchell's death at age 57, John Mitchell, who chaired the 1972 election for Nixon, went to prison for his role in the scandals.

FLORENCE B. PRICE (1888–1953)

America's first-known African American female composer, Florence Beatrice Smith Price of Little Rock, Arkansas, wrote a sizable canon of African American piano works and art songs. Price studied composition and theory at the New England Conservatory of Music, where she performed on piano and organ and produced an original symphony and string quartet. She then taught at Arkadelphia Academy and Shorter College, while still writing art songs.

After postgraduate training at Chicago Musical College, the American Conservatory, the University of Chicago, Chicago Teachers College, and Lewis Institute, Price taught organ and piano privately. In 1928 she published a piano piece, "At the Cotton Gin," and a tone poem, "Songs to a Dark Virgin," through the prestigious G. Schirmer music house. In 1931 she won a Wanamaker Prize for her Symphony in E Minor. The Chicago Symphony performed her original Concerto in F Minor at the Chicago World's Fair in 1934. Because of her creativity, she was called the "Chicago Renaissance Woman."

ALMEDA RIDDLE (1898–1986)

Folk balladeer Almeda "Granny" Riddle of Heber Springs, Arkansas, performed Ozark Mountain songs, children's rhymes, hymns, and bleak tunes of lost love. Riddle learned traditional tunes as a child from her father, a fiddler and group teacher of Sacred Harp vocals (a style of religious music dating back to the 18th century). Riddle flourished in this rich background of individualized hymns, spirituals, and folk melodies, and she acquired a following with her banjo strumming and vocal renditions of familiar folk music.

At the urging of Prof. John Quincy Wolfe of Arkansas College, musicologist and ethnographer Alan Lomax collected her songs for the Library of Congress. He introduced her to scholars and a new generation of listeners, and he arranged concerts at Harvard and the Newport Folk Festival. Among the works she recorded for Rounder and Vanguard Records were "Lonesome Dove," "Bury Me Beneath the Willow," "Merry Golden Tree," "The Blind Child," "Alan Bain," outlaw songs like "Hangman, Hangman" and "Jesse James," and "The Titanic," a dramatic commemoration of the sunken ocean liner. After her son's enlistment in the military during World War II, she added a verse to the song "Worldwide Peace" expressing hope for an end to global violence. Tapes of more than 100 of her songs survive at the Regional Studies Center at Lyon College in Batesville, Arkansas.

SISTER ROSETTA THARPE (1915–1973)

Guitarist and singer Rosetta Nubin "Little Sister" Tharpe of Cotton Plant, Arkansas, was the nation's first American artist to perform southern gospel music in Europe. The daughter of traveling evangelist Katie Bell Nubin, who sang and accompanied herself on the mandolin, Tharpe learned music in the Holiness Church tradition of shouting and testifying. She grew up in Chicago and joined a tent revival tour at age six, performing in the southern blues-gospel tradition.

After Tharpe added secular performances and glittery costumes, she became an acclaimed gospel performer and the first to record this style of music. In addition to making records on the Decca label, she sang jazz and boogie-woogie on radio and in clubs, appearing with Cab Calloway at Harlem's Cotton Club. She also appeared at the Blue Angel in New York City and, at age 23, at Carnegie Hall. Beloved in Europe and at jazz festivals in Antibes and Paris, France, she played both acoustic and electric guitar and developed a broad repertoire that included "Rock Me," "This Train," "Down by the Riverside," "Up Above My Head," and "Precious Lord, Take My Hand." Severely criticized for making the shift from gospel to jazz and blues, she cut ties with the Holiness Church. Although she suffered a leg amputation at age 55, she continued touring in the last 16 months of her life. In 1996 she was inducted into the Arkansas Jazz Hall of Fame.

—Mary Ellen Snodgrass

PROMINENT SITES

Central High Museum and Visitor Center
2125 West 14th Street
Little Rock, AR 72202
Telephone: (501) 374 1957
Web: http://home.swbell.net/chmuseum/index.html
The museum houses an interactive exhibit that depicts the history of the 1957 desegregation of Central High School. Women played a very active roll on both sides of the events surrounding desegregation in Little Rock. Of the Little Rock Nine, the group of students who ultimately desegregated Central High, six were female: Minnijean Brown, Gloria Ray, Elizabeth Eckford, Thelma Mothershed Wair, Melba Pattillo Beals, and Carlotta Walls. Daisy L. Bates was the president of the State Conference of Branches of the NAACP and a copublisher of the *Arkansas State Press*, a liberal weekly paper. She became the students' mentor during the 1957–1958 school year.

The Empress of Little Rock
2120 South Louisiana Street
Quapaw Quarter Historic District
Little Rock, AR 72206
Telephone: (501) 374 7966
Web: http://www.TheEmpress.com
The Hornibrook Mansion, completed in 1888, is an important example of Gothic Queen Anne style architecture. The first owner of the home, James H. Hornibrook, died shortly after the completion of the house, and his wife Margaret died a few years later. The Hornibrook Mansion became the home of Arkansas Women's College (the state's first women's college).

Fort Smith Visitor Center/"Miss Laura's"
2 North B Street
Fort Smith, AR 72901
Telephone: (800) 637 1477
Web: http://www.fortsmith.org/attractions/misslaurasvc.asp
Reportedly the only former bordello that is on the National Register of Historic Places, Miss Laura's currently serves as the visitor center for the town of Fort Smith. (Prostitution was legal in Arkansas until 1924.) Artifacts from its days as a bordello are on display.

Historic Arkansas Museum
200 East Third Street
Little Rock, AR 72201
Telephone: (501) 324 9351
Web: http://www.arkansashistory.com

In 1939 Louise Loughborough began a one-woman campaign to save a block of derelict but historically significant buildings. The restoration project was named the Arkansas Territorial Restoration, and it opened to the public in 1941. Eventually the project outgrew the historic buildings, and a museum center was added. The museum features information on various women in Arkansas and hosts special programs for Women's History Month.

Nevada County Depot Museum
400 West First Street South
PO Box 592
Prescott, AR 71857
Telephone: (870) 887 5821
Web: http://www.pcfa.org/depot_museum
The museum focuses on the history of Nevada County, Arkansas, and is home to a large collection of artifacts. There are records and yearbooks from area schools, including the McRae School, an all-black elementary school and high school built on land donated by Gov. Thomas McRae in 1908. There is also information about Nevada County native Virginia Dell Cassidy, mother of Pres. Bill Clinton.

Old State House Museum of Arkansas
300 West Markham
Little Rock, AR 72201
Telephone: (501) 324 9685
Web: http://www.oldstatehouse.com/general_info
The museum has two collections specific to women's history: the Black Quilts collection, comprising approximately 75 quilts made by African Americans in Arkansas, and the First Ladies Gowns collection. The oldest gown in this collection dates from 1889 and belonged to Mary Kavanaugh Oldham Eagle, who wore it to her husband's inauguration ball.

Shiloh Museum of Ozark History
118 West Johnson Avenue
Springdale, AR 72764
Telephone: (501) 750 8165
Web: http://www.springdaleark.org/shiloh
Established in 1968 to educate visitors on the history of the Arkansas Ozarks, this museum contains more than 50 paintings by primitive artist and Ozark native Essie Ward, known as the "Grandma Moses of the Ozarks."

RESOURCES

FURTHER READING

HISTORY

Anthony, Susan B., and Ida Husted Harper. *History of Woman Suffrage*. Vol. 4. Indianapolis, Ind.: Hollenbeck Press, 1902.

Arkansas Governor's Commission on the Status of Women. *The Status of Women in Arkansas, 1973: Changing Rapidly, Improving Slowly*. Little Rock: The Commission, 1973.

Arnold, Morris S. *Colonial Arkansas, 1686–1804: A Social and Cultural History*. Fayetteville: University of Arkansas Press, 1991.

Arnold, Morris S. *The Rumble of a Distant Drum: The Quapaws and Old World Newcomers, 1673–1804*. Fayetteville: University of Arkansas Press, 2000.

Arsenault, Raymond. *The Wild Ass of the Ozarks: Jeff Davis and the Social Bases of Southern Politics*. Philadelphia: Temple University Press, 1984.

Ashmore, Harry. *Arkansas: A Bicentennial History*. New York: W. W. Norton, 1978.

Assenmacher, Hugh. *A Place Called Subiaco: A History of the Benedictine Monks in Arkansas*. Little Rock, Ark.: Rose Publishing, 1977.

Bernhard, Virginia, ed. *Southern Women: Histories and Identities*. Columbia: University of Missouri Press, 1992.

Blair, Bertha. *Women in Arkansas Industries*. Washington, D.C.: USGPO, 1935.

Bolton, S. Charles. *Territorial Ambition: Land and Society in Arkansas*. Fayetteville: University of Arkansas Press, 1993.

Christ, Mark K, ed. *Rugged and Sublime: The Civil War in Arkansas*. Fayetteville: University of Arkansas Press, 1994.

Delta Kappa Gamma Society. *Pioneer Women Teachers of Arkansas*. Imboden, Ark.: Stovall Printing Company, 1955.

Dougan, Michael B. *Arkansas Odyssey: The Saga of Arkansas from Prehistoric Times to Present*. Little Rock, Ark.: Rose Publishing, 1994.

Earngey, Bill. *Arkansas Roadsides: A Guidebook for the State*. Little Rock, Ark.: August House, 1987.

Federal Writers' Project. *Arkansas: A Guide to the State*. New York: Hastings House, 1941.

Federal Writers' Project. *Slave Narratives: Arkansas*. Vols. 7–9. St. Clair Shores, Mich.: Scholarly Press, 1976.

Ferguson, John Lewis. *Arkansas and the Civil War*. Little Rock, Ark.: Pioneer Press, 1965.

Finley, Randy. *From Slavery to Uncertain Freedom: The Freedmen's Bureau in Arkansas, 1865–1869*. Fayetteville: University of Arkansas Press, 1996.

Fletcher, John Gould. *Arkansas*. Fayetteville: University of Arkansas Press, 1989.

Gerstacker, Friedrich. *In the Arkansas Backwoods: Tales and Sketches*. Translated and edited by James William Miller. Columbia: University of Missouri Press, 1991.

Harper, Ida Husted. *History of Woman Suffrage*. Vol. 6. New York: Little & Ives, 1922.

Huckaby, Elizabeth Paisley, and Ethel C. Simpson, eds. *Tulip Evermore: Emma Butler and William Paisley, Their Lives in Letters, 1857–1887*. Fayetteville: University of Arkansas Press, 1985.

Jacoway, Elizabeth, ed. *Behold, Our Works Were Good: A Handbook of Arkansas Women's History*. Little Rock, Ark.: Arkansas Women's History Institute/August House, 1988.

Johnson, Ben F., III. *Arkansas in Modern America: 1930–1999*. Fayetteville: University of Arkansas Press, 2000.

Kierner, Cynthia A. *Beyond the Household: Women's Place in the Early South, 1700–1835*. Ithaca, N.Y.: Cornell University Press, 1998.

Malone, David. *Hattie and Huey: An Arkansas Tour*. Fayetteville: University of Arkansas Press, 1989.

McRaven, Florence. *Wage Earning Women*. Little Rock: Arkansas Bureau of Labor and Statistics, 1924.

Moneyhon, Carl H. *The Impact of the Civil War and Reconstruction on Arkansas: Persistence in the Midst of Ruin*. Baton Rouge: Louisiana State University Press, 1994.

Murphy, Sara Alderman. *Breaking the Silence: Little Rock's Women's Emergency Committee to Open Our Schools, 1958–1963*. Fayetteville: University of Arkansas Press, 1997.

Nuttall, Thomas. *A Journal of Travels into the Arkansas Territory*. Philadelphia: T. H. Palmer, 1821.

Ragsdale, William Oates. *They Sought a Land: A Settlement in the Arkansas River Valley, 1840–1870*. Fayetteville: University of Arkansas Press, 1997.

Shinn, Josiah H. *Pioneers and Makers of Arkansas.* 1908. Reprint, Baltimore, Md.: Genealogical Publishing, 1967.

Smith, John I. *Forward from Rebellion: Reconstruction and Revolution in Arkansas, 1868–1874.* Little Rock, Ark.: Rose Publishing, 1983.

Smith, Richard M. *The Atlas of Arkansas.* Fayetteville: University of Arkansas Press, 1989.

Stanton, Elizabeth Cady, Susan B. Anthony, and Matilda Joslyn Gage. *History of Woman Suffrage.* Vol. 3. Rochester, N.Y.: Charles Mann, 1886.

Taylor, A. Elizabeth. "The Woman Suffrage Movement in Arkansas," *Arkansas Historical Quarterly* (Spring 1956).

Tucker, David M. *Arkansas: A People and Their Reputation.* Memphis, Tenn.: Memphis State University Press, 1985.

Walker, Pamela D. *The Legal Status of Homemakers in Arkansas.* Washington, D.C.: Homemakers Committee, National Commission on the Observance of International Women's Year, 1977.

Whayne, Jeannie M., ed. *Cultural Encounters in the Early South: Indians and Europeans in Arkansas.* Fayetteville: University of Arkansas Press, 1995.

Whayne, Jeannie, ed. *A New Plantation South: Land, Labor, and Federal Favor in Twentieth Century Arkansas.* Charlottesville: University Press of Virginia, 1996.

Whayne, Jeannie M., ed. *Arkansas: a Narrative History.* Fayetteville: University of Arkansas Press, 2002.

Woods, James M. *Rebellion and Realignment: Arkansas' Road to Secession.* Fayetteville: University of Arkansas Press, 1987.

BIOGRAPHY AND AUTOBIOGRAPHY

Abbott, Shirley. *The Bookmaker's Daughter: A Memory Unbound.* New York: Ticknor & Fields, 1991.

Bates, Daisy. *The Long Shadow of Little Rock: A Memoir.* Fayetteville: University of Arkansas Press, 1987.

Bolsterli, Margaret Jones, ed. *A Remembrance of Eden: Harriet Bailey Bullock Daniel's Memories of a Frontier Plantation in Arkansas, 1849–1872.* Fayetteville: University of Arkansas Press, 1993.

Caraway, Hattie Wyatt. *Silent Hattie Speaks: The Personal Journal of Senator Hattie Caraway.* Edited by Diane D. Kincaid. Westport, Conn.: Greenwood Press, 1979.

Chu, Rosemary. *Rosemary: A Journey from East to West.* Arkadelphia, Ark.: Pete Parks Center for Regional Studies, Ouachita Baptist University, 1999.

Elders, M. Joycelyn, and David Chanoff. *Joycelyn Elders, M.D.: From Sharecropper's Daughter to Surgeon General of the United States of America.* New York: Morrow, 1996.

Fersh, George L., and Mildred Fersh. *Bessie Moore: A Biography.* Little Rock, Ark.: August House, 1986.

Jaggers, Annie Laura M. *A Nude Singularity: Lily Peter of Arkansas: A Biography.* Conway: University of Central Arkansas Press, 1993.

Kite, L. Patricia. *Maya Angelou.* New York: Lerner, 1999.

Lyons, Gene. *Widow's Web: The True Story of a Little Rock Beauty Whose Deadly Wiles Led to Two Murders and Scandalized the Entire State of Arkansas.* New York: Simon & Schuster, 1993.

McMath, Anne. *First Ladies of Arkansas: Women of Their Times.* Little Rock, Ark.: August House, 1989.

Patterson, Ruth Polk. *The Seed of Sally Good'n: A Black Family of Arkansas, 1833–1953.* Lexington: University Press of Kentucky, 1985.

Simon, Charlie May Hogue. *Johnswood.* New York: Dutton, 1953.

Stuck, Dorothy D., and Nan Snow. *Roberta, a Most Remarkable Fulbright.* Fayetteville: University of Arkansas Press, 1997.

Terry, Adolphine Fletcher. *Charlotte Stephens: Little Rock's First Black Teacher.* Little Rock: Academic Press of Arkansas, 1973.

Zeman, Alice Fitch. *Mary Lewis: The Golden Haired Beauty with the Golden Voice.* Little Rock, Ark.: Rose Publishing, 2001.

USEFUL WEB SITES

"Catherine Dorris Norrell," Women in Congress http://bioguide.congress.gov/congresswomen/index.asp

"National Womens History Project," Performers–Arkansas
http://www.nwhp.org/tlp/performers/
arkansas-performers.html

"Pearl Peden Oldfield," Women in Congress
http://bioguide.congress.gov/congresswomen/index.asp

SELECTED ORGANIZATIONS AND INSTITUTIONS

Arkansas Historical Association
416 Old Main, University of Arkansas
Fayetteville, AR 72701
Telephone: (479) 575 5884
Web: http://www.uark.edu/depts/arkhist/home
Works to promote Arkansas history by publishing the *Arkansas Historical Quarterly* and holding annual conferences and other events.

Arkansas History Commission
One Capitol Mall
Little Rock, AR 72201
Web: http://www.ark-ives.com
The commission keeps and cares for Arkansas's state archives, and also collects historical materials about the state.

University of Arkansas Libraries
365 North Ozark Avenue
Fayetteville, AR 72701–4002
Telephone: (479) 575 4101
Web: http://www.uark.edu
Online gateway to the library catalog and special collections, including the women's studies manuscript collection, at: http://www.uark.edu/specialcollections/manuscripts/womensstudies.asp

CALIFORNIA

Mrs. Yorba was so ill when her daughter came that the child struggled miserably into existence, and failing to cry, was put away as dead, and forgotten for a time. It was discovered to be breathing by Mrs. Polk, who coaxed it through several months of puny existence with all a native Californian woman's resource . . . The child's health mended, although as Magdalena progressed in years, she still spoke but seldom. . . . Only once did she lose her temper—when Helena Belmont hung up all her dolls in a row and slit them that she might have the pleasure of seeing the sawdust pour out. . . . Helena probably was the only person who ever understood the reticent, unhappy and incongruous mixture of Spanish and New England traits; and Magdalena was Helena's most enthusiastic admirer.
—Gertrude Atherton, *The Californians*, 1908

Like Florida and New Mexico, California has a Spanish history appreciably longer than its English history. Its 1911 suffrage victory was a campaign model for other states, and California set an important precedent in 1992 when it was the first state to elect women to both seats in the U.S. Senate.

As with most Native American groups, women worked with each other communally and quite separately from men.

State Population (2000): 33,871,648

Female Population (2000): 16,996,756

Women in State Legislature (2003): 30%

Female College Enrollment (1999): 1,129,000 (56% of total)

Privately Held Women-owned Businesses (1997): 700,513

First Year of Full Suffrage: 1911

PREHISTORY
(Prehistory–1535)

California is so vast and disparate that generalizing about its indigenous peoples is difficult. Women in the south, such as the Serrano and Yuma, appear to have led lives similar to those of the agriculturalists of Arizona and New Mexico. They planted corn, squash, and melons, while also harvesting desert resources like cacti. They were noted for their basket making, and for beautiful inlaid work using mother-of-pearl.

The hot climate required only simple housing and clothing. During chilly nights, indigenous peoples took shelter in caves or lived in round homes built of palm fronds and willow. Yuma males, for example, rarely wore clothing but used elaborate body ornamentation; women wore a short skirt from infancy and had less body ornamentation.

Like most Native Americans, the peoples of southern California were matrilineal, tracing descent through their mothers. Unmarried women and men had almost complete sexual freedom, and women had sexual relations with male visitors as a customary part of hospitality. Polygamy, too, was common among chiefs throughout California, although not among people of lesser status; chiefs used plural marriages as a way to solidify relationships with other tribes.

In the north women of the Patwin, Wintun, Maidu, and other tribes spent winters in wicki-ups—thatched huts framed by bent saplings. Nomadic in summer, the women gathered wild produce such as juniper berries, elderberries, and several kinds of tubers. Men assisted only in the fall, when they climbed trees to knock down pinecones. Women then harvested pine nuts from the cones and dried these for winter. Coastal women spent much of their time digging for clams and oysters.

Northern women made clothing of deerskin, furs, and goose down for both sexes, and they may have adorned themselves more than men. At age five, Yurok girls were tattooed with a black stripe extending from both corners of the mouth to below the chin. An additional parallel line was added every five years.

These northern groups, unlike most Native Americans, were patrilineal, with descent traced through the father. Both women and men were shamans, or healers, and in some tribes, such as the warlike Yuki, women could be chiefs. Yuki women participated in war dances, and when the tribe won a victory against another tribe they spared neither male nor female of the defeated. Northern peoples were unusual in their ceremonial burial of the placenta after a child was born. The mother chose a place associated with a characteristic that she wanted the child to exhibit.

WHITE EXPLORATION TO MEXICAN ACQUISITION
(1535–1822)

The Spanish began to explore the California coastline in 1535, but the area held little allure for settlers because it was believed to contain no precious metals. In addition, it was remote from the government of New Spain in Mexico City, and could be reached only by crossing a harsh desert. Not until 1769 did Spain, alarmed by the growing presence of Russians in the north and the expansion of the British Empire to the east, move to establish a permanent colony in California.

Spanish settlement was shaped by the sword and the cross. In 1769 Spain established a military outpost, or presidio, in San Diego and another at Monterey. Accompanying the soldiers were Roman Catholic priests who, between 1769 and 1823, built a chain of 21 missions from San Diego north to San Francisco. These missions were intended to convert Native American tribes to Catholicism and to imbue them with Spanish culture. Native Americans were forced to live in mission communities in virtual slavery and to assimilate; when they resisted, the missionaries requested military protection and presidios formed nearby. Often civilian settlements developed near the presidios to supply the fort's needs.

The military and religious character of Spanish settlement had a significant effect on Native American women. Religious leaders forced them to abandon their tribal identities and exploited them economically. Native Americans who survived became known as Mission

Indians—slaves tending vineyards, looking after livestock, and serving in the homes of Europeans. Within a generation they numbered 20,000.

While religious leaders and settlers exploited Native Americans, the military frequently abused them. Spanish soldiers, who considered tribal women inferior, had a long and horrific history of raping and killing women in the lands they conquered, and California was no exception. Even when Native American women at San Luis Obispo were friendly to the newcomers, that friendliness was used as justification for exploitation of unwilling women. For example, soon after San Gabriel was founded, Franciscan friar Junipero Serra wrote that soldiers were killing indigenous men to take their wives. Similar situations occurred elsewhere, and sexual abuse was so grave and widespread at Mission San Diego that the mission was moved upriver, away from the presidio.

Spanish authorities took no action until 1773, when three soldiers gang-raped two very young Native American girls in a canyon near San Diego, attacking them so ferociously that one died. More than a year later the men were put on trial; after brief imprisonment, however, they were allowed to settle elsewhere. The brutality of Spanish rule took its toll on the population of Native Americans. Within 50 years their numbers were reduced by two-thirds, to little more than 50,000.

Although both the missionaries and the military were ambivalent about introducing Hispanic women into this harsh frontier society, some began coming from New Spain in 1774. Seven were on board the *Santiago*, but only one settled permanently. While these women were coming by the sea route, another expedition was making the first overland journey from the province of Sonora in Mexico; the journey took almost six months of hard travel over mountains and across deserts. Expedition members included the wives and families of soldiers as well as new colonists. A number of the women were pregnant and the expedition had to stop several times for childbirths and miscarriages. These women gave birth under very primitive conditions; at least one died and others feared for their lives.

Hispanic women transported their culture, with mores that were very different from those of the British colonies. Unlike English colonial women, California women could smoke, drink, and gamble without loss of respectability. They could divorce more easily and were more likely to retain their maiden names and to own property. Their less restrictive clothing would be the envy of countless female diarists. On the other hand, Hispanic women had less educational opportunity and, in fact, were so discouraged from learning that even affluent families in which women had leisure sometimes did not allow their women to learn to read.

Many older women were powerful within their families because of their dowries: the property that a young woman brought to a marriage often was the foundation of family success, and the institution of the dowry made a woman's financial contribution measurable. California's first noblewoman was Doña Eulalia de Callis, a native of Spain's Catalonia, who came to Monterey in 1783 with her husband, Gov. Pedro Fages. He had received his semiroyal position largely through her family. When she caught him with an Native American servant girl, she threatened divorce. He had to beg friends to intercede.

The newcomers were ethnically diverse: the Spanish had been in Mexico long enough to intermarry with both Native Americans and with Africans. Los Angeles, for instance, began with 12 families who arrived on September 4, 1781. They included couples who were listed as "Spaniard/Indian," mestizo/mulattress," "Indian/mulatress," "Indian/Indian," "mulatto/mulattress," and "negro/mulatress." Only two men were listed as Spaniards, and no original mother of the City of Angels was white.

The end of the 18th century brought "foreigners," as the Spanish labeled other nationalities. Some of these men, including Russian fur trappers from Alaska's Sitka, came to trade. Others deserted their ships because sailors of this era worked in conditions that resembled slavery; some sailors were abandoned when their ships sailed without them—and all were apt to leave any offspring behind.

The Spanish government did not welcome these settlers, particularly if they were Protestants. It did not allow foreigners to own land and, on occasion, imprisoned foreign men not married to California women. Nevertheless, many men converted to Catholicism and acquired property by marrying Hispanic women. Joseph Chapman is an example: Pirates abandoned him in 1818, and in 1821 he married Guadalupe Ortega. He was penniless, but her dowry and her citizenship enabled the purchase of land in Los Angeles and later in Santa Barbara.

In 1812 Russians established Fort Ross (or Russo) about 100 miles north of San Francisco. It was not a military establishment, but rather a trading post. Few Russian women came, and in the 1840s Russia abandoned this outpost. But while they were there, Russian men married or lived with local women, and a generation later newcomers were surprised to see blue-eyed, fair-skinned young people on some islands. It probably was a child of one of these relationships who became known as the "Lone Woman of San Nicholas Island," or Juana Maria as she was later called. After swimming away from a ship during an 1836 storm and presumed to be drowned, she lived alone on this island for 18 years. When she was finally rescued, no one understood the language she spoke.

Although wary of the Russians, the Spanish government did not trouble itself to displace them—in part because the empire was busy dealing with rebellions elsewhere. After more than three centuries of rule from Spain, in 1810 Mexicans followed the example of the British colonists and began to revolt. Californians joined the rebellion in 1821, and on March 25, 1825, California formally became a territory of Mexico.

FROM MEXICAN ACQUISITION TO STATEHOOD (1822–1850)

American whalers and clippers had put into California ports since the end of the 18th century, but only during the 1820s did American settlers begin making the long, arduous journey overland to the West Coast. The first to come were fur trappers who arrived at San Gabriel from northern Utah in 1826. Next came missionaries, including women, with the first arriving in Idaho in 1836. Once these groups had demonstrated that wagons could pass over the Rocky Mountains, organized groups of settlers began moving west.

Women and their families piled their possessions in canvas-covered wagons that were lightweight but sturdy enough to make a trip over the mountains. Following wagons loaded with food, water, and household goods, many walked the 2,000 miles to California. The wagon trains departed from Missouri in May and, if all went well, arrived in California before the winter. The first American woman to make the journey overland may have been Nancy Kelsey, the only woman in an 1841 expedition. She came with her husband and infant daughter, Ann, and nearly died in the unmapped Nevada desert.

Most historians credit Kelsey as being the first white woman in California, but historian Hubert Howe Bancroft wrote that married women with the names Burrows and Walker arrived in the Sacramento Valley in 1841, just a few weeks before Kelsey's group. Further details on Mrs. Burrows were not given, but Bancroft described Mary Young Walker as "the first white woman to arrive in California by land." (Bancroft 1890, 5:762)

An 1843 group included three women and three girls, and the next year, eight women were in the expedition that was the first to take wagons over the dangerous High Sierra. With that proved possible, dozens of women crossed in 1845, using the trail that entered California near modern Truckee and Emigrant Gap.

The Donner party left Illinois too late in the spring of 1846 and chose an untested route to California. In early November, the group became snowbound in the Sierras with little food or shelter. Forty-one of the 87 died of exposure and starvation; some lived only because they resorted to cannibalism. Tamsen Donner, whose husband led the group, stayed with him as he died, knowing that would mean her own death. Five women joined ten men in a desperate search for help; eight of these men died during that horrific experience, but the five women survived. Two-thirds of the survivors of the tragedy were women.

The Americans moving to California made no attempt to assume Mexican citizenship or assimilate into Mexican society, and a fearful Mexican government banned further emigration from "the Americas" in 1845. The measure had little effect and served only to strain relations between Mexico and the United States. In March 1846 the two nations went to war. At the end of the conflict in 1848, California became a U.S. territory.

Just one year later the Gold Rush transformed California almost overnight. The story of the discovery of gold at Sutter's Mill in January 1848 is well known. What few have noted is the woman associated with its discovery: Elizabeth Bays Wimmer, called Jennie, went west in 1846 with her husband, Peter, and their seven children. Peter found work with prospector John Sutter on his property on the American River. Jennie Wimmer cooked and washed clothes for miners, and when they were debating the nature of a piece of ore, she offered to test it in the lye kettle she used to make soap. The cleaned sample revealed gold.

As word leaked out about gold, the territory's population exploded from about 15,000 whites in 1848 to 92,597 in 1850. When San Francisco's first newspaper began publishing in the summer of 1847, its publisher said the town's population was 459; of them, 138 were female, including eight Native American women, one Hawaiian, and one black. The population grew to perhaps 1,000 in 1848 and, at the end of 1849, jumped to some 20,000. Most were men who lived in tents that ran up from San Francisco Bay.

Although some women prospected for gold, more realized that they could make more money by feeding and housing the dream-seekers. Jane Caulfield, for example, bought wheat and milled flour; the store she ran was vastly more profitable than her husband's mining. Other women came with less independence, and several contemporary Californians cited cases of sexual exploitation. Some women were imported as saloon dancers, others presided at gambling tables, still others came as mail-order brides, and many became prostitutes.

Men, desperate for decent food and other forms of domesticity, left many records testifying that they were lonely not only for female companionship but also for things associated with women. A Norwegian, for instance, wrote home that on Sunday miners made their way to the grocery store with bouquets of wildflowers. If a woman were present, she would judge the best; the prize for the finest bouquet was whiskey.

Almost a century after Catholic missions began, Sister Mary Frances led the Sisters of Charity to San Francisco in the dramatic year of 1849; she would devote herself to establishing schools until her death in 1881. A convent of French nuns followed in 1851, while the Sisters of the Third Order of Saint Dominic began work at Monterey.

As a result of the Gold Rush, California's population boomed, and the military government in the territory could not contain the lawlessness that came with so many transient men eager to get rich quick. Because they needed better law enforcement, most women joined men in clamoring for statehood. The military governor called a constitutional convention in September 1849, and one month later delegates adopted a constitution as if California were already a state. California's action precipitated a congressional debate over whether it should be admitted as a free or slave state. Since the Missouri Compromise of 1820, Congress had been careful to balance the admission of any new free state with admission of a slave state. But no territorial expansion of slavery seemed likely in 1850, and California's admission as a free state would upset this balance.

Most Californians, however, did not advocate slavery, including an appreciable number of white southerners who said they had left home because slavery devalued their labor. Elizabeth Benton Frémont wrote that her mother, southerner JESSIE BENTON FRÉMONT, worked as hard to make California a free state as her northern father, future presidential candidate John C. Frémont. The relatively few southerners who had brought slaves also were more willing to cooperate in emancipation plans than would have been allowed in the South. One slave, for example, earned the price of her own freedom and that of her husband, daughter, and three grandchildren by working at night.

The Compromise of 1850 traded California's admission as a free state for northern acceptance of the federal Fugitive Slave Law, and although

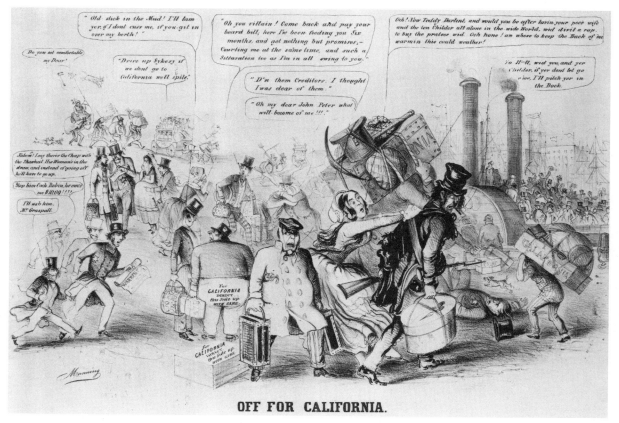

OFF FOR CALIFORNIA.

This lithograph mocks the many men who left their wives and children behind as they sought their fortunes in the California Gold Rush of 1849. (© Bettmann/Corbis)

THE SHIRLEY LETTERS: A WOMAN'S NARRATIVE OF LIFE IN THE GOLD RUSH

In January 1848 a settler scooped gold nuggets from a California river. The discovery excited imaginations worldwide and touched off an international treasure hunt that gradually gave rise to a mining industry. For Americans, the Gold Rush became a defining national experience. The promise of easy riches sent thousands of young American men and a number of women (and even children) scrambling to California seeking fortunes seemingly unearthed by the turbulent rivers of the rugged Sierra.

Many miners kept journals or wrote letters describing life in "the mines," which at first were the riverbeds or pits dug in the riverbanks. Some of their letters appeared in hometown newspapers, and many accounts were published as books. Remarkably, with a ratio of ten men to every woman in the mines, the finest of these accounts was the work of a woman, Louise Clappe.

In 1850 Clappe and her husband arrived in San Francisco from New York. By the autumn of 1851 Mr. Clappe began practicing medicine in the northern mines. Mrs. Clappe, at age 32, was settled in a cabin on Indian Bar, a gold camp beside the Feather River in what is now Plumas County. For 15 months Clappe observed and wrote. Calling herself Dame Shirley, in her lively and eloquent voice she captured the world of the raucous young mining community.

> . . . Since I last wrote you, . . . I have become a mineress; that is, if the having washed a pan of dirt with my own hands, and procured therefrom three dollars and twenty-five cents in gold dust . . .will entitle me to the name. I can truly say . . . that "I am sorry I learned the trade"; for I wet my feet, tore my dress, spoilt a pair of new gloves, nearly froze my fingers, got an awful headache, took cold, and lost a valuable breastpin in this my labor of love.
> Dame Shirley
> November 25, 1851

Compassionate, detailed, and witty, Clappe's 23 "letters" to her sister have become a literary classic. Published as *The Shirley Letters from the California Mines, 1851–1852*, they endure as a critical and insightful narrative of American history.

—Marlene Smith-Baranzini

Excerpt from Louise A. K. S. Clappe, *The Shirley Letters from the California Mines, 1851–1852*, edited by Marlene Smith-Baranzini. Berkeley, Calif.: Heyday Books, 2000.

some considered this "an unholy bargain," California became the nation's 31st state on September 9, 1850. California, bordering the Pacific Ocean, was thus a state earlier than most territories in the Midwest; most of the country between it and the rest of the Union remained inhabited only by indigenous peoples.

STATEHOOD TO PROGRESSIVE ERA (1850–1890)

The constitution that the new state adopted was far in advance of those of most states in this era: decades before married women in the East had the right even to keep their own wages, California wives were financially empowered. The law not only assured them of their separate property, but also exempted "the homestead and other property" from forced sale in a bankruptcy. The legal system was so unusually accessible to women that, in 1857, Rose O'Neal Greenhow—who later ran a Confederate spy network from her Washington, D.C., home—went to San Francisco and obtained $10,000 by suing the city for her husband's accidental death there.

Black women, however, still faced danger and discrimination. Although California had entered the Union as a free state, some slaves were still held illegally, and escaped slaves from the South were subject to return under the Fugitive Slave Act. In 1852, for instance, the *San Francisco Herald* reported that a mulatto woman was arrested and sent back to slavery. When she learned of a similar case, Mary Ann Israel-Ash, a black woman from Sonoma County, mortgaged her home and used the $1,100 to buy the freedom of a family being forced back to the South.

Black women, like black men, had fewer civil rights than whites. They could not testify in court, for example, and could be denied passage on the city's new streetcars. This changed as a result of campaigns by MARY ELLEN PLEASANT, a black philanthropist and early activist. She was involved in two lawsuits in the mid-1860s that desegregated the streetcars and earned blacks the right to have their testimony heard.

Despite second-class status, several black women became successful businesswomen. Pleasant owned a series of laundries and boardinghouses and lent money to miners and businessmen. Ellen Huddleston was termed a "financier and investor" in San Francisco, while Ellen "Biddy" Mason made a similar fortune in Los Angeles, where she became known as a "great financier."

The Chinese may have experienced more brutal racism in this era than did blacks in California. Chinese immigrants first came to California during the Gold Rush, not only to find gold but also to escape the corrupt and oppressive rule of the Manchu dynasty. When the gold fever died they stayed on as agricultural and garment workers; during the 1860s they helped build railroads. Between 1850 and 1882, when legislation curtailed entry of Chinese, more than 250,000 Chinese entered the country through the Golden Mountain, as they called San Francisco. Most of these newcomers were men. Many were married but only a few hundred were able to bring their wives and families. By the time immigration was halted in 1882, Chinese men outnumbered Chinese women by 21 to 1. Many of the women who did come were prostitutes, brought to California by force and treated as slaves. Some managed to escape and others finally earned their freedom. Congress barred the importation of prostitutes in 1870, but Chinese women continued to be exploited.

Women were among California's earliest journalists and publishers. Oakland's Mrs. S. M. Clark began publishing the weekly *Contra Costa* in 1855, and in 1858 San Franciscans Hermione Day and Mrs. A. M. Schultz began a semimonthly magazine, *The Hesperian*; Elizabeth T. Schenck later took over the publication of the magazine.

BIDDY MASON

A former slave, Bridget "Biddy" Mason sued for her freedom and later became a well-known philanthropist and one of the wealthiest women in California.

Mason was born a slave in Georgia in the early 1800s. At age 18 she was given as a wedding gift to a Mississippi couple, Robert Mays Smith and Rebecca Dorn Smith. The Smiths converted to Mormonism and moved from Mississippi to Salt Lake City, Utah, in the 1840s. During the seven-month journey, Mason walked behind the 300-wagon caravan tending cattle.

After several years in Salt Lake City, the Smiths, along with Mason and fellow slave Hannah Embers, moved to a Mormon settlement in San Bernardino, California, in search of gold. California's constitution, adopted in 1849, made slavery illegal, declaring, "Neither slavery nor involuntary servitude unless for the punishment of crimes shall ever be tolerated in this state." The law stated that any slave brought into the state would automatically become free.

After Rebecca Smith died, Robert Smith decided to move to Texas, which was a slave state. He tried to bring Mason and Embers, but the women sued for their freedom. Judge Benjamin Hayes declared Mason and Embers and their children "free forever" in an 1856 Los Angeles trial. In its February 2, 1856, issue, the *Los Angeles Star* published the full text of Hayes's opinion in the trial, with the headline "Suit for Freedom."

A free woman, Mason moved to Los Angeles and worked as a nurse and midwife. She saved enough money to buy a house downtown, at 331 Spring Street, becoming one of the first African American women to own land in the city.

Mason later bought and sold large amounts of real estate and was able to amass a fortune of about $300,000. She became known for her philanthropy, giving to charities and visiting jail inmates.

In 1872 Mason and her son-in-law, Charles Owens, founded the First African Methodist Episcopal Church, the oldest black church in Los Angeles. Mason died in 1891. Her grave was unmarked until 1988, when Los Angeles mayor Tom Bradley erected a tombstone.

—Erica Pearson

The state's major female publishers were Emily Pitts Stevens and Laura deForce Gordon.

CHINESE AMERICANS SUE CALIFORNIA TO ENROLL THEIR DAUGHTERS IN PUBLIC SCHOOL

In the late 19th century, Chinese Americans Joseph and Mary Tape fought to get their daughter Mamie enrolled in public school. They had to sue the San Francisco Board of Education.

Mary Tape was brought up in a Shanghai orphanage, immigrating to San Francisco, California, with missionaries when she was 11. Mary, who spoke English and wore typical American clothes, later married Joseph Tape, who worked for the Chinese consulate. The two had four children.

In 1884 the San Francisco Board of Education denied their daughter Mamie Tape entry into Spring Valley Elementary, because "the association of Chinese and white children would be very demoralizing mentally and morally to the latter." Mary and Joseph Tape sued the board for barring Mamie. A lower court ruled in their case (*Tape v. Hurley*) that all children, regardless of race, had the right to a public school education.

The decision was upheld in state and federal courts, but the Board of Education avoided complying by creating a separate school for Chinese children in Chinatown. Furious, Mary Tape wrote a letter of protest:

> To the Board of Education—dear sirs: I see that you are going to make all sorts of excuses to keep my child out off the Public schools. Dear sirs, Will you please to tell me! Is it a disgrace to be Born a Chinese?

Didn't God make us all!!! What right have you to bar my children out of the school because she is a chinese Decend. They is no other worldly reason that you could keep her out, except that. . . .You have seen my husband and child. You told him it wasn't Mamie Tape you object to. If it were not Mamie Tape you object to, then why didn't you let her attend the school nearest her home! Instead of first making one pretense Then another pretense of some kind to keep her out? . . . I will let the world see Sir What justice there is When it is govern by the Race prejudice men! just because she is of the Chinese decend, not because she don't dress like you because she does. just because she is decended of Chinese parents I guess she is more of a American then a good many of you that is going to prevent her being Educated Mrs. M. Tape.

Despite Mary Tape's efforts to integrate San Francisco schools, her children, including Mamie Tape, all went to the separate Chinatown school. San Francisco's schools were integrated in the 1920s, decades before the Supreme Court ordered school desegregation in *Brown v. Board of Education* (1954). Today more than half the students at Spring Valley Elementary are of Chinese descent.

—Erica Pearson

Excerpt from Organization of American Historians. "Mary Tape, An Outspoken Woman." http://www.oah.org/pubs/magazine/deseg/source1.html (April 11, 2003).

Stevens began her career as one of the owners of the *San Francisco Mercury*; by 1869 she was its sole proprietor and changed the weekly's name to the *San Francisco Pioneer*. Both she and Gordon were active feminists, and when Gordon began the *Stockton Daily Leader* in 1873, it was believed to be the only daily newspaper in the world edited and published by a woman. Stevens moved to Oakland in 1878 and began the *Daily Democrat*, while her sister Gertie de Force Cluff founded the *Valley Review* in Lodi in 1879; both women were active in the Pacific Coast Press Association. Amanda Slocum Reed joined her husband in publishing the radical *Common Sense*; in 1878 she began *Roll Call,* with her young daughter Clara Reed as its typesetter.

Still other women were active in printing. A woman named Lyle Lester began a San Francisco printing business in 1860 and soon was so successful that she employed a large number of girls and women as compositors. Delia Murphy Dearing also was a well-known San Francisco printer, and a third firm, the Woman's Cooperative Printing Company, eventually evolved into Mrs. Richmond & Son.

Early in California's history a number of women had become known as writers and publishers. Among the many women who wrote of the early statehood era were Mrs. D. B. Bates, *Incidents on Land and Water, or Four Years on the Pacific Coast* (1857); Mary Rockwood Powers, *A Woman's Overland Journey to California* (1858);

and Mary E. Anderson, *Scenes in the Hawaiian Islands and California* (1865). Eliza Woodson Farnham published *California: In-doors and Out* (1856) and also was one of the strongest suffragists.

The foundation was laid for women's higher education in California shortly after statehood. Mary Atkins had begun Benicia Female Seminary—as private schools for women were then called—in San Francisco in 1854. Riding a mule, Atkins recruited students from the area, ultimately achieving a student body that included the daughters of miners as well as those of wealthy merchants and bankers. In 1865 Cyrus and Susan Tolman Mills, who had been missionaries in Hawaii, bought the school; 20 years later the school received its charter as a college. The goal was to "give girls a serious education, not to be a finishing school." Nevertheless, the founders saw higher education as bettering women within the confines of traditional roles. Mills was to educate future "wives, mothers, and teachers and hence shape the destiny of individuals and nations." The college, the oldest West Coast women's college, still flourishes at the beginning of the 21st century.

California's suffrage movement began in 1868 with a speech by Laura Gordon in San Francisco; she also spoke to the state legislature in Sacramento. The Woman Suffrage Association of San Francisco, the first in the West, was established on July 27, 1869, at the home of Nellie Hutchinson. More than 40 women were founders, including two physicians, Mrs. S. J. Corbett and Mrs. E. P. Meade. Well-known journalists Elizabeth Schenk and Emily Pitts Stevens served as president and vice president, respectively.

Just six months later, on January 26, 1870, the suffragists held a convention in San Francisco to form a statewide association; they already had more than 100 delegates who represented a wide geographic range. In addition to San Francisco, suffrage groups had been established in Alameda,

Los Angeles, Mayfield, Oakland, Petaluma, Sacramento, San Diego, Santa Clara, Santa Cruz, Solano, and Sonoma.

After some debate the delegates voted to remain independent of the national suffrage bodies and concentrate on their own state. Gordon made more than 100 speeches in 1870 alone and toured Oregon and Washington in 1871. She was in Seattle when she received a telegram informing her that the Independent party of San Joaquin County had nominated her to run for state senator. She hurried back to Stockton, where she met vehement opposition, particularly from Republicans. Nevertheless, she spoke every night, using the platform to educate male voters on suffrage. She garnered some 200 votes, as well as a similar number that were rejected because of technical irregularities.

Emily Pitts Stevens led other women in speaking to the legislature in 1871; suffragists won their first victory in 1873, when the law was modified to allow men to elect women to education-related offices. By the turn of the century, women served on school boards or as school superintendents throughout the state. The liberal 1873 legislature also passed an act requiring equal pay for teachers doing equal work.

Using the gender-neutral language of the 1870 15th Amendment to the U.S. Constitution that enfranchised black men, women attempted to vote in several states. San Jose's Sarah Knox Goodrich was one. She paid her taxes under protest and attempted to vote in important elections, but was rejected. When Ellen Rand Valkenberg of Santa Cruz was not permitted to register, she sued officials under the equal protection clause of the 14th Amendment (1868) and paid the costs of taking the case to the California Supreme Court, which ruled against her.

The last decades of the 19th century opened greater opportunities for women in business and the professions, but only with struggle. Nettie C.

Tator applied for admission to the state bar in 1872. Tator passed her examination and was unanimously recommended by her local committee, but masculine pronouns in the legal code were presumed to mandate the exclusion of women. The issue languished until 1877, when Clara Foltz drafted a bill to solve the problem. State senators passed it by a wide margin, but the state House of Representatives held several heated debates before passing it by two votes on the last day of the session in 1878. When California next revised its constitution, Laura Gordon successfully led an effort to amend it to read "no person shall, on account of sex, be disqualified from entering upon . . . any lawful business, vocation or profession." Foltz and Gordon also sued to gain entry to Hastings College of Law of the University of California, which had been established in 1877. The courts ruled in their favor in 1879.

California women made strides in other occupations during the last decades of the 19th century. Elise Wiehe Hittel began the Ladies' Silk Culture Society of California in 1880, and three years later the state legislature not only appropriated $7,500 for this new industry, but also created a State Board of Silk Culture—with a mandate that five of its nine members be women. Other women developed industries that proved more important than silk: raisin making and the preservation of other fruit, especially dates, among them. Ellen McConnell Wilson was one of the largest agriculturalists in Sacramento County, with more than 6,000 sheep in the 1880s. Rosa Smith (later Eigenmann) discovered a new species of fish in San Diego waters in 1880 and became the first woman recognized as an ichthyologist.

By 1886 the state had 73 licensed female physicians and two women recently graduated from dental school. Medical schools and societies opened to women without the long fight that eastern women had to wage. Political parties also saw the growing importance of women, and

Gordon and Foltz were hired as speakers for the Democratic party in the 1888 presidential campaign; the Republicans countered with suffragist Addie Ballou.

Dr. Milicent Washburn Shinn was the most prominent literary woman on the coast in the mid-1880s; Shinn, an honors graduate and the first woman Ph.D. recipient from the University of California, was editor of the *Overland Monthly Magazine*. Other women who published books on the state in this era include Mary Cone, *Two Years in California* (1876); Caroline Nichols Churchill, *Over the Purple Hills* (1877); Sue A. Sanders, *A Journey to, on, and from the "Golden Shore"* (1887); and Mary H. Wills, *A Winter in California* (1889).

PROGRESSIVE ERA
(1890–1920)

The 1893 enfranchisement of Colorado women inspired the Golden State's 1896 campaign to amend its constitution to enfranchise women. The campaign was the first in so large and diverse a state, and the National American Woman Suffrage Association poured more resources into the campaign than they had into any previous effort. Under the leadership of the politically savvy Ellen Clark Sargent—whose husband, U.S. senator A. A. Sargent, was the chief suffrage supporter in Washington, D.C.—women raised about $19,000 for the effort. Journalist Ida Husted Harper provided a steady stream of information to the state's newspapers, while suffrage leader Flora M. Kimball used the name "Betty Snow, an Antisuffragist," to send letters to newspapers making such ridiculous arguments against the vote that she converted many to the cause.

Southern California women ran a model campaign, organizing Los Angeles as well as San Bernardino, Kern, Santa Barbara, and other surrounding counties. Their goal was to reach every voter regardless of his race or station in life. They enlisted the wives of workers and immigrants, who held noontime meetings in workshops, factories, and railroad stations, while the men ate their lunch. African American women also became involved, and black leaders like Dr. Mary T. Longley, president of the Colored Woman's Club, converted many black men, who then became active in the cause.

Women also lobbied for the support of the many minor political parties that were active in this period. They went to both the Populist convention in Sacramento and the Socialist Labor convention in Stockton, where male delegates endorsed suffrage. Most of the state's more than 250 newspapers also supported them. However, 2 of the 27 that did not, the *Los Angeles Times* and the *San Francisco Chronicle*, were highly influential.

Women won every county in southern California—and would have won the state but for San Francisco and Oakland. The statewide totals were 110,355 in favor of suffrage and 137,099 opposed, with the vast number of negative votes coming from those two cities.

California did not allow a second campaign on constitutional amendments, and women turned to the courts and the state legislature to continue their struggle. In 1900 Sargent sued San Francisco for a tax refund because she could not vote. Her son, an attorney, based his case on "no taxation without representation," but the court rejected the argument. Suffragists submitted bills during every legislative session after their 1896 loss, but although all were debated, none was passed.

Women, however, continued to raise awareness of suffrage. In 1901 Indiana's May Wright Sewall, president of the International Council of Women, toured the state; Vida Goldstein of Australia, where women had recently won most voting rights, followed the next year. Supporters in King's River Canyon also held a campout with the Sierra Club, where pioneer environmentalist John Muir endorsed suffrage.

Attorney Gail Laughlin, who had political experience in western states, was hired as state organizer, and 52 clubs united into the California Equal Suffrage Association in 1904. Susan B. Anthony added to the effort with a tour of the state in 1905, a year before she died. Katherine Reed Balentine began a monthly feminist magazine, *The Yellow Ribbon,* and Maud Wood Park organized chapters of her College Equal Suffrage League at Berkeley and Stanford in 1908. After the death of her husband, Leland Stanford, Jane Lathrop Stanford became one of the state's greatest philanthropists and endorsed suffrage.

San Francisco also had a Votes for Women Business Club, and a statewide Men's League began with John Hyde Braley, who recruited 100 prominent men in Los Angeles and Pasadena. On the other end of the economic spectrum, Maude Younger organized waitresses and other blue-collar women into the Wage Earners Suffrage Club. Oakland held one of the nation's first parades by women in 1908, when 300 women marched behind a yellow silk suffrage banner.

Reform-minded men, however, made the difference in returning suffrage to the ballot. In the 1910 election they threw out the conservative Republican machine and replaced it with liberal Republicans aligned to the progressive wing of the party. The 1911 California Senate passed the suffrage amendment 35–5; the state House of Representatives voted 66–12; and suffrage again was placed on the November ballot.

Women then began an eight-month fight for ratification. Republican governor Hiram Johnson had campaigned on a promise to support suffrage; when he did not include suffrage in his priorities, women considered themselves betrayed. Five minor political parties and the labor federation kept faith with suffrage, however. Women passed out millions of leaflets in English, Italian, German, and French, and organized lectures in support of suffrage. Among other speakers they brought in

Montana's Jeannette Rankin, soon to be the nation's first congresswoman; Margaret Haley of Illinois, cofounder of the American Federation of Teachers; and Alma Lefferty, a member of the Colorado legislature. More than 1,000 people bought tickets to hear England's Sylvia Pankhurst.

Newspapers printed more than 10,000 columns from material provided by suffragists. They placed billboards over miles of country, paid for huge electric and other signs, spent long weeks of automobile campaigning in the country and villages, and even subjected themselves to hecklers at vaudeville shows. International opera star Lillian Nordica sang in San Francisco's Union Square to crowds who then heard suffrage speakers address them from automobiles.

Antisuffragists countered with New York's Minnie Bronson, the nation's most visible female opponent but, although California's antisuffragists had a long list of prominent supporters, they appeared to have few activists, and they were not an important factor in the campaign.

Gail Laughlin did not allow optimism to overtake strategy, however, and from the office of the new Woman Suffrage party in San Francisco's Lick Building she ran a tightly controlled effort to ensure that the city's political machine could not steal the election. When the polls opened, 1,066 trained observers were watching. Most volunteers went on duty before daylight and stayed until after midnight. In addition, suffragists paid Pinkerton detectives to guard ballots for the next two days while results trickled in from rural areas.

The final tally showed that of 246,487 ballots, suffrage won by 3,587—one vote per precinct throughout the state. Days later, Los Angeles's Caroline Severance, who founded the feminist New England Woman's Club in 1868, had the honor of being the first California woman to register to vote.

Californians elected four women to the legislature in 1918; despite their presence, two men—

Robert Madison of Santa Rosa and C. W. Greene of Paso Robles—voted against ratification of the 19th Amendment to the U.S. Constitution, which extended the vote to all American women. State senators unanimously ratified the amendment on November 1, 1919, and the next August Tennessee became the last state necessary to amend the Constitution.

Although still facing discrimination, African American women began making strides in the professions in the early years of the 20th century. Among them were Dr. Ruth J. Temple, who became the first female African American physician, while Dr. Vada Somerville was the first female dentist. Others formed women's clubs for self-improvement and to address civic issues. Kate Bradley-Stovall founded the Southern California Alumni Association, which provided a means of social and business contacts for college educated blacks. Hettie B. Tilghman was the longtime president of the California Federated Colored Women's Clubs, an affiliate of the Washington, D.C.–based National Association of Colored Women. Los Angeles's Sojourner Truth Club benefited from the international experience of Josephine Leavell-Allensworth; she had traveled with her husband, an army colonel, before they retired to California.

The University of California–Berkeley had its first female graduation speaker in 1900: Lillian Moller (later Gilbreth), the author of the groundbreaking *Psychology of Management* (1914). She and her husband, Frank Gilbreth, used new film techniques to study time-motion processes and became known as the first efficiency experts—while she also bore 12 children in 17 years. The family was the basis for the 1948 book and later movie *Cheaper by the Dozen*.

San Francisco's Kathleen Thompson Norris was a popular novelist of this era; her book *Mother, A Story* (1911) was especially popular. In 1911 Lois Weber and her husband, Wendell Phillips Smalley, experimented with matching sound to film; after they divorced, Weber went on to become Hollywood's most prominent female director for three decades. Louise Miller Boyer became one of the era's most successful screenwriters, while an adventurous female protagonist brought millions to see the silent film *The Perils of Pauline* (1914).

1920S THROUGH WORLD WAR II ERA (1920–1950)

California's movie industry spread the image of the "New Woman" of the 1920s. These women, known as flappers, shortened their skirts, danced to jazz, drove cars, and were more sexually liberated than women of earlier times. One of those who promoted the flapper image was Anita Loos. Best known for her novel *Gentlemen Prefer Blondes* (1925), Loos also wrote more than 200 movie scripts, as well as books on film production. Actress Clara Bow's short hair inspired millions of women to cut the long hair they had piled on their heads for centuries, while Mae West not only acted in but also wrote the risqué play *Sex* (1926). She reached the height of her celebrity after age 40; also an astute businesswoman, West was the first actress to earn more than $1 million.

The women of the 1920s also entered careers once considered the domain of men. Many earned a good living from the new phenomenon of radio, which needed female voices for comedies and soap operas, many of which were aimed at women. Evangelist AIMEE SEMPLE MCPHERSON engendered major headlines during the decade, while Florence "Pancho" Barnes—who changed her name from Florence Leontine Lowe—became a daring aviator. She not only was a stuntwoman for the daringly titled *Hell's Angels* (1929), but also set the women's air speed record of almost 200 miles per hour.

Rosalind W. Alcott began her Wall Street career by disguising her voice on the telephone so that others thought she was a man. She sold her stock a month prior to the crash of 1929, moved to Los Angeles, and after 50 years of retirement there, was still a millionaire when she died in 1990 at 104. Ellen Browning Scripps multiplied her inheritance from the Scripps newspaper chain more than 40-fold, and in 1925 she endowed Scripps College, a liberal arts institution for women in the college town of Claremont.

Women continued to make inroads into political and government offices. In 1920 Frances H. Wilson became the first female assistant state attorney and in 1921 Mabel Walker Willebrandt replaced ANNETTE ABBOTT ADAMS as a federal assistant attorney general. Seven years later Willebrandt became the first woman to chair a committee at a Republican party convention.

The most significant precedent of the decade, however, was the 1923 election of California's first, and the nation's fourth, congresswoman, Mae Ella Nolan. She was the first woman to chair a congressional committee, the Committee on Expenditures in the Post Office Department. Just two years later, San Francisco elected FLORENCE KAHN, who also was the nation's first Jewish congresswoman, making California the first state to send two women to Congress concurrently. Nevertheless, the state's voters failed to elect women to statewide executive offices; half a century would pass before it did so.

The Great Depression of the 1930s hit California extremely hard. Hundreds of thousands of retired people lost their savings, and tourism, one of the state's major industries, vanished. The Depression especially hurt women, who were just beginning to make career gains. Agricultural laborers, including women, suffered the most economic hardship. Mexicans and Filipinos were all but banished from the state during the 1930s, replaced by whites from the Dust Bowl states, particularly Oklahoma, who came to California in search of work. Only the movies kept rolling along relatively unscathed because, more than ever, people needed the temporary

LUISA MORENO AND THE FOUNDING OF UNITED CANNERY, AGRICULTURAL, PACKING, AND ALLIED WORKERS OF AMERICA

During the 1930s Guatemalan American activist Luisa Moreno and a group of union organizers worked to unionize farm and canning plant laborers in an attempt to improve working conditions, compensation, and benefits.

In November 1936 the American Federation of Labor (AFL) held its 46th annual conference in Tampa, Florida. A group of the delegates, including Moreno, an AFL professional who organized workers in Florida cigar factories, had traveled to the conference determined to convince labor leaders that they should create a union for underrepresented food-processing and agricultural workers.

The delegates made speeches at the convention, describing the awful working conditions for farm-and food-processing workers, and explained the great difficulty migrant laborers had paying monthly union dues. AFL leaders, however, were not receptive to Moreno and others' concerns.

Frustrated, the group of delegates decided to form an independent international union, called the United Cannery, Agricultural, Packing, and Allied Workers of America (UCAPAWA). Seven months later the union became a reality, and various local branches assembled in Denver, Colorado. The new organization consisted of delegates from various regions and backgrounds, including Mexican, Filipino, and Japanese agricultural workers from California; black sharecroppers from the South; Florida turpentine workers; and New York mushroom canners.

Union officers made a practice of hiring black, Latino, Asian, and female labor organizers to carry out campaigns in these groups and communities. Women and minorities also held important positions within the UCAPAWA. Moreno, who led many important campaigns for UCAPAWA among California cannery workers, was the union's international vice president from 1941 to 1947.

The union dissolved in 1950, amid accusations of involvement with the Communist party. During the 13 years of the union's existence, women made up one-half of UCAPAWA's total membership. Women union members organized for better wages, maternity leave, and equal pay for equal work.

As part of a UCAPAWA drive to increase wages from $16 to $22 per week, a woman walnut packer in Los Angeles wrote this song, to the tune of "Yankee Doodle.":

The walnut girls aren't satisfied
They're asking for more money
They're getting sixteen bucks a week
And think it isn't funny
Union shop and twenty-two!
Twenty-two is jake!
Union shop and twenty-two!
To get the girls some steak!

—Erica Pearson

Excerpt from Vicki Ruiz, *Cannery Women, Cannery Lives: Mexican Women, Unionization, and the California Food Processing Industry, 1930–1950.* Albuquerque: University of New Mexico Press, 1987.

escape from their worries and problems that motion pictures offered.

As it had in the Gold Rush almost a century earlier, California transformed with World War II. America's Pacific fleet was destroyed by the 1941 bombing of Pearl Harbor in Hawaii, and millions of workers, both civilian and military, moved to California to manufacture the equipment to fight the war against Japan. The need for ships, planes, munitions, and more was so great that the federal government insisted that contractors hire women, and hundreds of thousands of California women got the best-paid jobs of their lives. The state's per capita income tripled during the war years; much of that increase was the result of women having the opportunity to join the workforce.

Women did everything from the most delicate to the heaviest work. *Business Week* praised women in a California mine who could "wield an 8-pound sledge in the best of manlike tradition," while at one of the state's many aircraft factories, women made delicate instruments. At a Lockheed plant, two black women with just one year of experience set a speed record for riveting. A plant manager at Consolidated Aircraft found that women were able to work monotonous assembly lines for longer hours than men.

Women at the Douglass Aircraft Company in Long Beach working on the tail fuselage of a B-17F bomber. (Library of Congress)

Perhaps more than anywhere else in the nation, in California women forced changes in worker benefits. Because women there often lacked extended families, government and industry had to address the need for child care. A 1944 Los Angeles report, for example, said that aircraft factories employed 101,000 women who had 19,000 children without dependable care—and the resultant absenteeism caused ten fewer bombers to be built each month. One community that responded was Vallejo, which developed a program that cared for 1,000 children during 13-hour workdays. Douglass Aircraft—the nation's largest private employer of women during the war years—developed one of the first child-care centers at its Santa Monica plant, but the Oregon and northern California shipyards run by Henry J. Kaiser set the futuristic model. They provided not only 24-hour child care, but also cafeterias with take-home meals, an important innovation.

Desperate to see their men for what might be the last time, hundreds of thousands of women also came to the West Coast, especially San Diego and San Francisco. They came in overcrowded railroad cars with no place to stay; hotels put them up in lobbies or on cots in halls.

Military women, too, poured into the state. The Navy Nurse Corps worked at a giant San Diego hospital, while the both the Army Nurse Corps and the Women's Army Corps departed from California to assignments in the Pacific. During the early days of the war, when coastal residents lived in realistic fear of bombing, the Women's Ambulance and Defense Corps of America quickly organized dozens of state chapters. It trained volunteers to function as air raid wardens and to handle other emergency needs; the corps' motto was "The Hell We Can't."

The state's Japanese Americans suffered greatly during the war, when most families lost their property when they were forced into internment camps in Nevada, Wyoming, and elsewhere. Many of these Japanese Americans had been born in the United States, but they were not considered citizens. Men could get out of the confinement of the camps by volunteering for the military, but most women spent the war years imprisoned.

As the war ended, Californians elected their third and most controversial congresswoman, HELEN GAHAGAN DOUGLAS. A liberal with Hollywood connections, she became a victim of the anticommunist witch-hunts of the postwar period. She lost a bitter 1950 campaign for the U.S. Senate when her opponent, Richard Nixon, painted her as a communist sympathizer. It would be decades before another California woman ran for the Senate.

POSTWAR AND CONTEMPORARY ERAS (1950–present)

The state's population soared from 6.9 million in the 1940 census to 10.6 million in 1950, bringing with it a great demand for nurses, teachers, and social workers to handle the needs and problems of newcomers and the postwar baby boom. Exponential growth would characterize California for the rest of the century.

The decade of the 1950s was a conservative era, when many families returned to the traditional model of husband as breadwinner and wife as homemaker. Women made little progress until the dramatic social reforms of the 1960s transformed American society. California women joined the effort to help migrant workers, and DOLORES HUERTA cofounded the United Farm Workers in 1962. Los Angeles advertising executive Helen Gurley Brown wrote about the liberated woman in her bestseller *Sex and the Single Girl* published the same year. Diahann Carroll became the first African American woman to star in a television series with the 1968 *Julia*.

DAUGHTERS OF BILITIS

In 1955 San Francisco lesbian couple Del Martin and Phyllis Lyon and six other women founded the Daughters of Bilitis, the first lesbian-rights organization in the United States.

The group's name came from the 1920s book of poems *The Songs of Bilitis*, written by Pierre Louys; the book included poems about love between women. At first the Daughters of Bilitis remained in the closet. "If anyone asked what Bilitis stood for, we would say, 'oh, we enjoy reading Greek poetry,'" Martin told the *San Francisco Chronicle* in 2000.

The Daughters of Bilitis soon opened a dozen chapters across the country and in Melbourne, Australia; each chapter was dedicated to fostering the awareness and acceptance of homosexuality. The group held conventions every two years, starting with a conference in San Francisco in 1960. The next conference, in Los Angeles, was covered on television. Even though the *New York Times* had a policy banning the use of the word *homosexual*, the 1964 conference garnered a mention in the newspaper's pages.

The organization published a monthly magazine, *The Ladder; A Lesbian Review*. A May 1966 issue included reviews of lesbian literature and a short article instructing readers how to conceal their sexual orientation by choosing the "most heterosexual answers possible" on personality tests given by prospective employers.

In 1972 Martin and Lyon wrote the book *Lesbian/Woman*, the first widely circulated book that describes lesbian life from a lesbian perspective. It became an underground classic, and the two women began giving lectures at colleges around the country.

In 1976 San Francisco mayor George Moscone appointed Martin to the City Commission on the Status of Women. In 1989 and 2000, Martin and Lyon were honored as community grand marshals in San Francisco's annual Gay Pride Parade.

Today, Martin and Lyon focus their activism on raising awareness about aging in the gay community, working with groups like Old Lesbians Organizing for Change. "We've made incredible progress," Lyon told the *San Francisco Chronicle* in 2000. "Things have happened that we've never dreamed would come up in the early days. It is certainly rather amazing."

—Erica Pearson

As wartime and baby boom children entered young adulthood, California led major cultural change in the 1960s. San Francisco hippies especially mystified their elders with avant-garde music, poetry, and clothing—and in the last years of the decade, Berkeley students conducted the first major protests against the Vietnam War. Actor Jane Fonda would be arrested during this era, as would radical activist ANGELA DAVIS. In the next decade female students at Berkeley led the way in defining sexual harassment when they exposed the behavior of some male professors.

California also led the nation in adopting the concept of no-fault divorce. Its 1969 law was revolutionary: the marital contract could be terminated by simple mutual consent, rather than the expensive and often humiliating experience of going to court to prove fault on a limited number of permissible grounds. Such change was especially helpful to women, who often lacked the money or power to win an adversarial case.

Women also made political progress during the decade. In 1961 Democratic governor Edmund "Pat" Brown appointed Shirley Mount Hufstedler to the superior court of Los Angeles County; Pres. Lyndon Johnson promoted her to the federal appellate level in 1968. Voters finally elected their first woman to statewide office in 1966, when Republican party activist Ivy Baker Priest became state treasurer; she had held the ceremonial position of U.S. treasurer under Pres. Dwight Eisenhower.

The 1970s continued to see dramatic advances. California elected an African American woman, YVONNE BRAITHWAITE BURKE, to Congress in 1972; March Fong Eu became the nation's first Asian American woman to be elected to a statewide office when she won a race for secretary of state in 1974. Gov. Jerry Brown appointed Rose Bird as the first female member of the California supreme court in 1977, and feminists throughout

the world cheered San Francisco's 1979 election of its first female mayor, DIANNE FEINSTEIN. She initially filled out the term of Mayor George Moscone after his 1978 assassination.

March of 1980 saw the establishment of the National Women's History Project (NWHP). In March of that year, Pres. Jimmy Carter issued the first proclamation for women's history, and the NWHP soon expanded nationally, bringing attention to women's history every March. Also in 1980 Candy Lightner began the highly effective Mothers Against Drunk Driving (MADD) in California.

California led the nation in developing the concept of comparable worth. When an independent study showed that assistant mechanics for the city of San Jose averaged an annual salary that was $9,000 more than that of graduate nurses, women went on a nine-day strike. They won $1.5 million to begin salary adjustments.

The 1980s were generally a regressive decade for women. This was especially evident when conservatives managed to remove Rose Bird from the California supreme court following a scurrilous 1986 campaign. Yet California women continued to make some strides. Poland-born Sula Galante Burton, a San Francisco Democrat, won a special 1982 election to replace her husband in Congress. BARBARA BOXER won her congressional seat in 1982, while NANCY PELOSI gained hers in a special 1987 race.

Two 1988 court cases were victories for feminists. Courts upheld a state law requiring employers to provide women with job security during maternity leave, as well as affirmative action plans that encouraged promotion of female employees. The next year, however, San Francisco's Judge Marilyn Hall Patel threw out a comparable worth case that would have benefited state employees.

The 1990s brought great progress compared with the 1980s. Kathleen Brown, daughter of Gov. Pat Brown and sister of Gov. Jerry Brown, won election as state treasurer in 1990, but lost her 1994 bid for the Democratic gubernatorial nomination. Susan Golding became mayor of San Diego in 1992; she won 1996 reelection with a resounding 78% of the vote. Superintendent of Public Instruction Delaine Eastin became the first woman in that nonpartisan position in 1994; in the same year, Democrat Kathleen Connell was elected to the post of state controller. The most significant milestone, however, was passed in 1992, when California elected Feinstein and Boxer to the U.S. Senate, thus becoming the first state with women in both U.S. Senate seats.

California sent far more women to the U.S. House of Representatives in the 1990s than any state ever. In chronological order of election, they were: Lynn Schenck of San Diego, who won in 1992, but lost in the 1994 Republican backlash; Andrea Seastrand of Santa Barbara, a Republican who won in 1994, but lost in 1996; MAXINE WATERS of south-central Los Angeles; Lynn Woolsey of Sonoma County, who went from welfare to a high-tech position and became a model for the National Women's History Project based in her district; Lucille Roybal-Allard of downtown Los Angeles, who was the nation's first Mexican American congresswoman; Anna Eschoo of the Palo Alta area, the only member of Congress of Syrian heritage; Zoe Lofgren of San Jose, an attorney who campaigned with an ironing board as her traveling desk; and Juanita Millender-McDonald of Carson, an educator whose career focused on girls. All but Seastrand were Democrats.

The trend continued with the 1996 election, when Loretta Sanchez astonished the nation by defeating a powerful conservative Orange County incumbent. Ellen Tauscher won the district centered in Contra Costa County that year, and Barbara Lee of Oakland joined them in 1998. Mary Bono of Palm Springs, widow of entertainer Sonny Bono, won his vacant seat later in 1998; she was the only Republican

TIMELINE

United States Events		California Events
	1600	
1620 Settlement of Plymouth Colony		
	1700	
		1769 Spain establishes its first permanent colony in California at San Diego.
		1774 Hispanic women begin coming to California.
1776 United States declares independence		1781 Women help found Los Angeles.
	1800	1825 California becomes a territory of Mexico.
		1841 The first American women arrive in California.
		1848 California becomes a U.S. territory.
		1849 California Gold Rush.
		1850 California becomes a state.
1861–65 U.S. Civil War		1869 Forty women found the Woman Suffrage Association of San Francisco, the first in the West.
	1900	1911 California women gain the vote.
1914–18 World War I		1918 Four women are elected to the state legislature.
1920 Ratification of the 19th Amendment		1923 California elects its first U.S. congresswoman, Mae Ella Nolan.
1929–39 Great Depression		
1939–45 World War II		1969 California adopts no-fault divorce.
1975 Vietnam War ends		1978–79 Dianne Feinstein is appointed San Francisco's first female mayor in 1978 and is elected in her own right the next year.
		1980 The National Women's History Project is established.
		1992 California becomes the first state to elect two female U.S. senators, Dianne Feinstein and Barbara Boxer.
	2000	2002 Democrats elect Rep. Nancy Pelosi as their House leader, making her the highest-ranking woman ever in Congress.
		2003 California has the highest percentage of women in the U.S. Congress.

House Minority leader Nancy Pelosi of California passes the gavel to the speaker of the House, Republican Dennis Hastert of Illinois, on January 7, 2003, at the convening of the 108th Congress. With this act, Pelosi became the highest-ranking woman in the history of the U.S. Congress. (© Reuters NewMedia Inc./Corbis)

California congresswoman serving at the beginning of the 21st century. Lois Capps of Santa Barbara also won a special election that year, while largely Latino voters in eastern Los Angeles chose Grace Napolitano in the general election.

In the first elections of the new century, every California woman elected to Congress was a Democrat. They were Diane Watson of Los Angeles, who had served as ambassador to Micronesia during the Clinton administration; Hilda Solis, whose east Los Angeles district was 90% Hispanic and Asian; Jane Harman, a Harvard-educated attorney whose district centered in Redondo Beach; and Susan Davis, who defeated an incumbent Republican in San Diego.

The 2002 elections achieved great gains for women in the U.S. Congress. International media focused on the victory of Linda Sanchez in a northern Orange County district adjacent to that of her sister: Loretta and Linda Sanchez were the first sisters to serve in Congress. And, in a major achievement, Rep. Nancy Pelosi was elected as the House Democratic leader, thereby making her the first woman to lead a major political party and the highest-ranking woman in the history of Congress.

Women held 18 of California's 53 House seats (34%) in the 108th Congress (2003–2004). This percentage was the best in the nation and slightly better than that in its own legislature, where women held 30% of the seats. California, however, was also one of relatively few states with no women in a statewide elected executive office as of 2003.

—Doris Weatherford

PROMINENT WOMEN

ANNETTE ADAMS (1877–1956)

Judge Annette Abbott Adams of Prattville blazed the trail for the female politicians and jurists. An 1897 graduate of California State Normal School in Chico and a 1904 graduate of the University of California at Berkeley School of Law, she taught school before becoming one of the state's first female high school principals in Alturas. After completing an advanced law degree at her alma mater in 1912, she formed an all-woman law firm in San Francisco and was president of the California Democratic Women's Club.

Democratic president Woodrow Wilson appointed Adams assistant U.S. attorney for the Northern District in 1914; four years later she was promoted to U.S. attorney for the district. She was the first woman in the nation to hold these posts. In 1920 she became the first woman to serve as a U.S. assistant attorney general. Replaced at the end of the Wilson administration, she returned to private practice in 1921, and during the 1920s argued a number of natural resource suits, including complicated cases involving water rights. After Democrats retook the White House, she served as special assistant counsel to the U.S. attorney general from 1935 to 1941, litigating oil cases. In 1942 she was named presiding judge of the California court of appeals. She was the first woman to hold that position.

ELSIE ALLEN (1899–1990)

Pomo activist and basket maker Elsie Comanche Allen of Santa Rosa helped preserve her tribe's ancient crafts. Reared in Cloverdale by her grandmother Nellie Burke, Allen mastered the weaving of fish traps, storage baskets and trays, baby carriers, and burden frames. After a brief attendance at a Native American boarding school in Covelo, she found work as a farm laborer and hospital domestic. At the request of her dying mother, she revived Pomo weaving traditions, but could not devote much time to her craft until she was in her sixties.

Allen taught art at the Mendocino Art Center and sold baskets through a Pomo women's club to raise money for scholarships and to finance lawsuits on behalf of civil rights for Native Americans. In 1972 she published *Pomo Basketmaking: A Supreme Art for the Weaver* and demonstrated technique at the Smithsonian Folklore Festival in Washington, D.C. From 1979 to 1981 she worked with the Native American Advisory Council on a cultural record of the Pomo and was instrumental in the relocation of endangered plants threatened by a dam over the Russian River. In her later years she became known as the Pomo Sage. Five years after her death in 1990, a high school in Santa Rosa was named for her.

DOROTHY ARZNER (1897–1979)

San Francisco native Dorothy Arzner thrived in the male-dominated world of film production. Born to emigrants from Germany and Scotland and educated at Westlake School for Girls and the University of Southern California, she enlisted in the Los Angeles Emergency Ambulance Corps at the outbreak of World War I. She returned to California to seek acting jobs with William de Mille at Famous Players-Lasky Studio, but found work only as a script typist. After studying script supervision and silent film, in 1921 she edited scenes for Realart Studios.

Arzner's first major success was *Fashions for Women* (1927), which established her name among professionals. For Paramount she directed *The Wild Party* (1929), Clara Bow's first talkie. Arzner devised the first boom microphone by wiring it to a fishing pole. By 1930 she was selecting her own material, writing scripts, and directing stars Claudette Colbert, Katharine Hepburn, Fredric March, Ginger Rogers, Merle Oberon, Rosalind Russell, and Sylvia Sidney. Three years later Arzner launched a film career independent of any studio. She completed *Dance, Girl, Dance* in 1940 and made training films for the Women's Army Corps during World War II. While in retirement from the screen, she directed plays at the Pasadena Playhouse and TV commercials for Pepsi-Cola. She earned honors from the First International Festival of Women's Films in 1972 for championing the female perspective. The Director's Guild of America staged a tribute to her in 1975.

SHIRLEY TEMPLE BLACK (1928–)

An actress and ambassador, Shirley Temple Black won viewers' hearts during the Great Depression as a curly-topped, tap-dancing child screen star. She grew up in Santa Monica and made her first film appearance when she was four. After debuting in *Stand Up and Cheer* (1934), she developed into a public phenomenon, the subject of photos, movie magazine covers, look-alike dolls, and child beauty contests. After 40 films and 50 TV productions, her career ended in her late teens with marriage to actor John Agar, a divorce, and disappearance from the screen.

Remarried to Charles A. Black in 1950, Shirley Temple Black took an interest in the National Multiple Sclerosis Society and the National Wildlife Federation. A Republican, Temple ran unsuccessfully for Congress in 1967, and Pres. Richard Nixon appointed her as a U.S. representative to the United Nations in 1969. While battling breast cancer in 1972, she supported other mastectomy patients. President Nixon appointed her ambassador to Ghana in 1974, and Pres. Gerald Ford made her chief of protocol during 1976, the last year of his administration. She served as ambassador to Czechoslovakia during the administration of George H. W. Bush. She has written autobiographies including *My Young Life* (1945) and *Child Star* (1988).

BARBARA BOXER (1940–)

An advocate for families, consumers, and the environment, Barbara Levy Boxer of Brooklyn, New York, was one of six female U. S. senators elected in 1992—the first from California. Before graduating with economics and political science degrees from Brooklyn College in 1962, she married classmate Stewart Boxer. Shortly afterward she was rejected from a stockbroker training program because of her sex. On her own, she earned a stockbroker's license and reared a family in Marin County, California. The 1968 assassination of Robert Kennedy precipitated her involvement in social initiatives.

Supported by her neighborhood, Boxer cofounded a training corps for high school dropouts, a women's support group, and a childcare center. She also took part in antiwar protests and was involved in the environmental movement. In 1971 she entered politics with an unsuccessful run for county supervisor. After joining the editorial staff of the *Pacific Sun* in 1972, she won a term as a Marin County supervisor, during which she crusaded for the closure of California's nuclear power plants and chaired the Bay Area Air Quality Management Board. Elected to the U.S. House of Representatives in 1982, Boxer presided over the Democratic New Members Caucus. During ten years in the House, she established a liberal record, championing family and medical leaves and calling for reductions in defense spending. One of her most visible initiatives was publicizing egregious military waste. In 1992 Boxer was elected to the U.S. Senate, where she supported initiatives against sexual harassment and for gay rights, breast cancer research, and the protection of wetlands.

YVONNE BRAITHWAITE BURKE (1932–)

Attorney Yvonne Braithwaite Burke used her success as leverage for her support of minorities, women, and the poor. Born in Los Angeles, she attended the University of California at Berkeley on scholarship. She earned tuition for the University of Southern California Law School by modeling and working in clothing factories and libraries. Following her graduation in 1956, she went into private practice. Ten years later Burke made a name for herself by defending the Watts rioters, and the governor appointed her attorney to the McCone Commission, which was formed to investigate the causes of the riots. As California's first black assemblywoman, elected in 1966, she supported job opportunities and child care for women, prison reform, and fair allotment of state construction contracts.

Burke won a seat in the U.S. House of Representatives in 1972 and became the first congresswoman to give birth while in office. She returned for a second term, but resigned to make a run, unsuccessful, for the post of California state attorney general. She served on the powerful Los Angeles County Board of Supervisors from 1979 to 1980, after which she returned to the practice of law.

ANGELA DAVIS (1944–)

Orator, writer, and activist Angela Yvonne Davis of Birmingham, Alabama, was a major figure in the black power movement of the 1960s. The daughter of teachers, she grew up in a segregated neighborhood and took part in civil rights demonstrations during the mid-1950s. She embraced Marxism while studying at Elizabeth Irwin High School in New York and worked toward a degree in French literature from Brandeis. During her junior year abroad at the Sorbonne in Paris, she committed herself to action against oppression following the Ku Klux Klan bombing of a Birmingham church in 1963. After graduation, she studied philosophy in Frankfurt, Germany, and upon her return to the United States joined the Student Non-violent Coordinating Committee and the Communist party, and, in 1969, earned a master's degree from the University of California at San Diego. She began work on a doctoral degree, but never completed it.

In 1969, because of her radical politics, Davis lost her teaching post in the philosophy department of the University of California at Los Angeles. After receiving threats to her life, Davis purchased several guns that were used in a 1970 courtroom shootout that left several people dead. Davis did not take part in the incident, but because she owned the guns, she was indicted for murder. She went underground, and the FBI placed her on its Ten Most Wanted list. Arrested in New York, she was transported to California and jailed. From her cell, she compiled "Reflections on the Black Woman's Role in the Community of Slaves," an essay concerning the unique contributions of black women to American history, and wrote an autobiography, *If They Come in the Morning* (1971). Her case became an international cause celebre, with supporters demonstrating around the world. A jury acquitted her in 1972.

While writing, giving interviews, and agitating worldwide, she taught at San Francisco State and the University of California at Santa Cruz. In 1980 and 1984 she ran for president on the Communist party ticket. In 1986 she served on the board of the National Black Women's Health Project, and taught throughout the 1980s and 1990s at various universities.

LENA FRANK DICK (ca. 1889–1965)

Famed Washoe basket maker Lena Frank Dick of Coleville established Native American crafts as an art. She learned basketry from her mother in childhood and refined her weaving and shaping techniques under the teaching and example of Paiute artist Louisa Keyser, known as Dat So La Lee. Dick's steady output ended at age 46, when her vision dimmed, forcing her to spend the last years of her life performing menial domestic work.

Dick's work was overshadowed by that of the more famous Keyser and was frequently mislabeled as that of the Paiute weaver. Her basketry gained renown a decade after her death, when craft articles issued pictures of prize baskets under her own name. Art historians have isolated unique stylistic details in the 28 baskets that survive. Dick is best known for chevrons and angular patterns in black and red. The state of California exhibits 13 of her known projects.

HELEN GAHAGAN DOUGLAS (1900–1980)

Actress and politician Helen Gahagan Douglas became a victim of the vicious anticommunist crusade of the post–World War II years. Born in Boonton, New Jersey, she knew in childhood that she wanted to appear on the stage but attended Barnard College in New York at the insistence of her parents. Against their wishes, she appeared in summer stock in New York City and got her first Broadway role in *Manhattan* (1922). Lauded by critic Heywood Hale Broun, she quit college, took numerous stage parts, and studied opera in Europe. After marrying actor Melvyn Douglas in 1931, she continued to find roles in plays, operas, and cinema while rearing their three children.

Douglas gave up entertainment for politics in the latter half of her life. She actively opposed racism and the Nazi party and supported Franklin Roosevelt's social policies, migrant workers, organized labor, and the environment. In 1940 she served as a delegate to the Democratic National Committee, and the following year she was chosen vice chairman of the Democratic State Central Committee. In 1944 she won election to the U.S. House, where she supported New and Fair Deal legislation. Douglas had anticommunist lendings, but opposed the domestic anticommunist crusade of the postwar period. In 1950 she waged a bitter campaign for the U.S. Senate against Richard Nixon, following a primary in which her conservative opponent accused her of procommunist sympathies. Nixon picked up the theme, calling her the "Pink Lady," and eventually won the election by an overwhelming margin. Thereafter, Douglas returned to the theater and pursued a career as a writer and lecturer.

DIANNE FEINSTEIN (1933–)

San Franciscan Dianne Feinstein shares with Barbara Boxer the title of first female Californian elected to the U.S. Senate. Reared in a Catholic–Jewish family, she graduated from Sacred Heart High School and from Stanford University, where she received a degree in history and political science in 1955. After graduation, she joined the staff of California's Industrial Welfare Commission and served on the Women's Board of Parole and a city crime commission. In 1969 she was elected to the San Francisco board of supervisors and would become the board's first female president.

Though she ran for the position unsuccessfully in 1971 and 1975, in 1979 Feinstein became San Francisco's first female mayor by serving out the term of George Moscone, who had been murdered by a disgruntled supervisor. She astutely handled public upheaval following Moscone's assassination as well as police, budget, and AIDS crises, and was elected to the U.S. Senate in 1992. She served on the Senate Appropriations Committee and became the first woman to serve on the Senate Judiciary Committee. Among the issues she was involved with were the environment, gay rights, cancer research, and abortion and reproductive rights.

DIAN FOSSEY (1932–1985)

San Franciscan Dian Fossey was the foremost authority on the mountain gorilla of Africa. Fossey grew up with a love of animals and began her college education at the University of California at Davis in the preveterinary medicine program. After two years she transferred to San Jose State University and switched her major to occupational therapy. Following her graduation in 1954, she moved to Kentucky to be near the horses she loved, and worked at the Kosair Crippled Children's Hospital in Louisville.

In 1963 she traveled to Africa and met anthropologist Louis Leakey, who encouraged her to study primatology. In 1967 Fossey set up the Karisoka Research Centre on the slopes of the Virunga Mountains of Rwanda; she remained its director from 1967 to 1980. During those years she studied the gorillas while attempting to protect them from poachers. To publicize their plight she wrote about them for *National Geographic* and published *Gorillas in the Mist* in 1983, which would be made into a film in 1988. Her plea for environmental sanctuary generated sympathy for the gorillas and their endangered habitat among members of the African Wildlife Foundation, the World Wildlife Fund, and the Rwandan government. Fossey was forced to leave Africa because of ill health in 1980. By the time she returned three years later her funding had run out, and she had to abandon her research. She was brutally murdered there in December 1985; the circumstances of her murder remain unknown.

JESSIE BENTON FRÉMONT (1824–1902)

Born to Virginia gentry and reared in Washington, D.C., and St. Louis, Missouri, Jessie Anne Benton Frémont was a major political figure of the mid-19th century and especially its westward movement. The daughter of Missouri's U.S. senator Thomas Hart Benton, she married army explorer John Charles Frémont at age 17. She coauthored her husband's vivid reports on expeditions, as well as *The Story of the Guard* (1863), a chronicle of the early years of the Civil War.

The Frémonts moved to California in 1849 and led the fight for its admission as a free state. She helped support the family by writing for the *New York Ledger, Atlantic Monthly*, and *Harper's*. She is best known for *A Year of American Travel* (1878) and *Far West Sketches* (1890), in which she described their Bear Valley ranch and offered her observations of miners and the growing town of San Francisco. Her writings encouraged many pioneers to move to the West.

MAGGIE SMITH HATHAWAY (ca. 1910–2001)

Actress, doo-wop singer, and civil rights activist Maggie Smith Hathaway of Louisiana helped to open California golf courses to nonwhite players. The daughter of a farmer, she learned from her parents the importance of education. After arriving in Los Angeles in her twenties, she worked in film as an exotic player and as a stand-in for Lena Horne. Following an argument with a director who wanted her to play a stereotypical black role, Hathaway quit Hollywood. In the 1950s she recorded rhythm-and-blues numbers with the Robins Trio; she also played a bit part in the film, *The Manchurian Candidate* (1962).

During the 1950s heavyweight prizefighter Joe Louis encouraged her to play golf, and Hathaway become a top-ranked player at a time when many courses banned blacks. She campaigned against segregation as a writer for the *California Eagle*, earning for herself the nickname First Lady of Minority Golf. She and Sammy Davis, Jr., founded a branch of the NAACP in Hollywood and created the group's Image Awards. For her civil rights activism, she received the NAACP Sterling Award in 1993. A former segregated golf course at Jesse Owens Park was named for her in 1997.

DOLORES HUERTA (1930–)

Chicana labor leader Dolores Fernandez Huerta of Dawson, New Mexico, cofounded the United Farm Workers Union. Reared by her grandfather, she grew up in a multicultural neighborhood in Stockton, California, during the Great Depression; her mother worked two jobs at a cannery and cafe to feed her family. The meager income stretched to include dance, violin, and piano lessons as well as membership in the Girl Scouts. From her estranged father, a miner who became a New Mexico state legislator, she learned the necessity for organized labor. She completed her education with an associate degree from Stockton College and became an elementary schoolteacher.

After seeing her pupils come to school hungry and without decent clothes, Huerta decided to devote her life to fighting poverty. In 1955 she helped found the Stockton Community Services Organization, which fought to implement social and economic change for Hispanics, and five years later she helped found the Agricultural Workers Association to aid migrant workers. She joined labor leader Cesar Chavez in founding the National Farm Workers Association in 1962. While he was the association's charismatic visionary and spokesman, she handled the work of organizing laborers into unions and negotiating agreements with commercial growers. When the United Farm Workers Union was formed in 1965, Huerta became a vice president, serving until 1999. During her long tenure in the organization, she was not only an advocate for the poor but also a symbol of women's achievement in an area traditionally dominated by men.

FLORENCE PRAG KAHN (1866–1948)

U.S. representative Florence Prag Kahn of Salt Lake City, Utah, was an aggressive advocate of her district at a time when many still doubted that women could be successful politicians. Born into a Jewish family that had emigrated from Poland, she grew up in San Francisco and attended Girls' High School and the University of California at Berkeley from which she graduated in 1887. At age 21, she began teaching high school English and history. In 1899 she wed Julius Kahn, a Republican representative from San Francisco, and developed an interest in political issues and legislative action.

After her husband's death in 1924, Florence Kahn completed his congressional term and went on to win the seat for five consecutive terms. During her 12 years in Congress, she supported a strong national defense and favored military preparedness and benefits for military nurses and veterans. She also denounced Prohibition and film censorship and promoted a federal highway system and airport and harbor development. She was so outspoken in her support for national policing that she was known as the Mother of the FBI. Kahn was largely responsible for bringing a number of projects to her city, including military bases and hospitals, improved port facilities, and funding for the San Francisco Bay Bridge. After retirement in 1937, she remained active in Republican politics as well as in Jewish and women's organizations.

LAURA KEENE (1826–1873)

Actress Laura Keene was America's first female theatrical producer. Little is known of her early life; she was born in London, England, as Mary Moss and frequented the studio of painter J. M. W. Turner as a child. At age 26 she came to the United States with a theatrical troupe and managed the Charles Street Theatre in Baltimore. In 1854 she traveled to San Francisco to perform at the Metropolitan Theater, then toured Australia with actor Edwin Booth. On return to San Francisco, she managed the Union and American theaters, where she produced comedies and extravaganzas.

In 1855 a venture known as Laura Keene's Varieties brought her fame as the first female theatrical producer in New York City. At Laura Keene's Theatre, built especially for her, she served as manager and starred in comedies for seven years. She was on stage in the social comedy *Our American Cousin* at Ford's Theatre in Washington, D.C., on April 14, 1865, when John Wilkes Booth assassinated Pres. Abraham Lincoln. Later in her career, she traveled the West, wrote plays, and, in 1872, founded and edited *Fine Arts* magazine.

BILLIE JEAN KING (1943–)

Winner of 20 Wimbledon tennis championships, Billie Jean Moffitt King of Long Beach used her court career to demand equality and respect for women and homosexuals. In girlhood she preferred baseball, but chose tennis as a sport that encouraged female players. She trained with coaches Alice Marble and Frank Brennan in the 1950s and debuted in competitive play in 1957. In 1961 she won a doubles title at Wimbledon. After marrying Larry King in 1965, she won her first Wimbledon singles tournament in 1966.

In her efforts to gain equality for women in sports, she formed the Women's Tennis Association in 1973 and founded the Women's Sports Foundation the following year. In 1973, two years after becoming the first female athlete to earn $100,000, King dramatized her campaign for equality with a match against Bobby Riggs, a self-proclaimed "male chauvinist pig," whom she soundly beat before a huge television audience. She has been awarded numerous honors, including *Sports Illustrated*'s Sportswoman of the Year, *Sport* magazine's Tennis Player of the Year, *Time*'s 1976 Woman of the Year; and in addition, has been inducted into the Women's Hall of Fame.

MAXINE HONG KINGSTON (1940–)

Chinese American author Maxine Hong Kingston from Stockton produced a feminist classic, the autobiographical novel *The Woman Warrior* (1976). Born to immigrant laborers, she grew up in San Francisco's Chinatown and studied at the Chung Wah Chinese School to learn to read and write her family's native language. On scholarship to the University of California, she graduated in 1962 with a degree in American literature; that same year she married actor Earll Kingston. She began teaching high school mathematics and English in California and later Hawaii.

While teaching creative writing at Mid-Pacific Institute, Kingston completed her bestseller, which brought the offer of a visiting professorship at the University of Hawaii. She continued her exploration of Chinese upbringing, writing the male-centered novels *China Men* (1980) and *Tripmaster Monkey: His Fake Book* (1989) as well as numerous articles for journals and newspapers.

AIMEE SEMPLE MCPHERSON (1890–1944)

Aimee Kennedy Semple McPherson, founder of the International Church of the Foursquare Gospel, was one of the few women in the male-dominated field of Christian evangelism. Born in Ingersoll, Canada, and reared as a member of the Salvation Army, she became a Pentecostal when she was 18. Shortly thereafter, she married her minister, Robert James Semple, was ordained, and traveled to China as a missionary. The couple preached in that country until her husband's death in 1910. The following year, she married Harold McPherson, though their marriage ended. From 1915 to 1923 Sister Aimee toured the United States and Canada as a platform minister and healer, and published *Bridal Call*, a monthly magazine that contained transcripts of her sermons.

Establishing herself in Los Angeles in the 1920s, Sister Aimee McPherson built the Angelus Temple in 1923, founded a Bible college, the Lighthouse of International Evangelism, and in

1927 formed an independent holiness church, the International Church of the Foursquare Gospel. She was one of the first evangelists to recognize the potential of radio, and she was the first to offer telephone counseling to the lonely and fearful. Her mental health deteriorated following an alleged kidnapping in 1926, and she suffered a nervous breakdown in 1930. McPherson died of an accidental overdose of barbiturates in 1944.

JULIA MORGAN (1872–1957)

Julia Morgan, California's first licensed female architect, built a reputation for sophisticated building projects. A native of San Francisco, she earned an engineering degree in 1894 from the University of California before becoming the first female to enter L'Ecole des Beaux-Arts in Paris. In 1902 she returned to San Francisco where she entered the architectural field. Practicing with John Galen Howard, director of construction for the University of California, she became sufficiently well known to open her own business in San Francisco in 1904. Morgan designed elegant, eclectic, yet practical structures, and her career would span 40 years of success.

For publishing magnate William Randolph Hearst's family, Morgan spent two decades building San Simeon, a 127-room hilltop castle formed of cast concrete and native material. Structurally simple and appealingly upbeat, her works blended artistic technique and expression with economy and function as illustrated in the Berkeley Women's City Club and Asilomar, a Pacific Grove conference complex. Her unique projects, which range from churches and private homes to YMCAs on California's Pacific coast and in Honolulu, display a preference for the use of indigenous materials and a concern for fitting the building into its topographic setting. In 1921 Morgan was admitted to the American Institute of Architects.

ELLEN OCHOA (1958–)

Astronaut Dr. Ellen Ochoa of Los Angeles set an example of high achievement for Latinas with her first space flight in July 1990. Born in La Mesa, she was valedictorian at Grossmont High School and at San Diego State University, where she majored in physics in 1980. Awarded a scholarship to Stanford University, she earned a masters in 1981 and a doctorate in 1985 in electrical engineering. After earning a pilot's license, she joined the research staff at Sandia National Laboratories and completed astronaut training in Houston in 1991. Supervising 40 scientists, she headed Intelligent Systems Technology Branch of NASA's Ames Research Division in Mountain View, California, and managed instruments and robotics on NASA space flights. For three expeditions totaling 719 hours in space, she earned two technology awards and medals for service and leadership.

Ochoa's contributions to science include three patents in the field of optical processing. With regular speaking engagements, she carried a message of encouragement and challenge to youth. In 1989 she was awarded the Hispanic Engineer National Achievement Award for most promising engineer in government, the pride award from the National Hispanic Quincentennial Commission in Washington, D.C., and the Albert Baez Award for Outstanding Technical Contribution to Humanity.

NANCY PELOSI (1940–)

Nancy D'Alesandro Pelosi of Baltimore, Maryland, became the first woman to serve as minority leader in the U.S. House of Representatives. The daughter of Baltimore's mayor, she learned political negotiation in childhood and earned a bachelor's degree from Trinity College in Washington, D.C., in 1962. She married Paul Pelosi and settled in San Francisco. While rearing her five children, she did volunteer work for the Democratic party, serving as chair of the state Democratic party. From 1976 to 1996, she was a Democratic national committeewoman from California.

In 1987 Pelosi won a seat in the U.S. House of Representatives, where she established a liberal record, focusing on education, minimum wage, ergonomics and workplace safety, AIDS and breast cancer research, family planning, and prescription drug coverage. In 2001 she was named House Democratic whip, becoming responsible for the party's legislative strategy and keeping members informed of upcoming issues and votes. In November 2002 House Democrats elected her minority leader by an overwhelming majority. She became the first woman to lead the congressional delegation of a major national political party and the highest-ranking female in congressional history.

MARY ELLEN PLEASANT (1814–1904)

Activist and philanthropist Mary Ellen "Mammy" Pleasant (or Plaissance) of Philadelphia championed the downtrodden and homeless and promoted civil rights for California blacks. According to her autobiography, as a child she lived with a Quaker family in Nantucket, Massachusetts, who forced her to clerk at their store rather than go to school. She married a well-to-do Cuban tobacco planter and moved to Boston, where she became involved in the abolition movement. Her husband's death in 1848 left her financially comfortable, and she resettled in San Francisco during the 1849 Gold Rush. She worked as a cook and domestic for several merchants while investing in stocks and lending money to miners and businessmen at high rates of interest. She also procured mistresses for wealthy men from whom she may have received financial advice.

Pleasant spent her wealth on aiding freed blacks and on rescuing young girls from sexual exploitation. She also helped abandoned babies.

She was involved in two court cases that advanced civil rights for black Californians: in 1863 she won the right for blacks to testify in court and three years later sued for damages when she was denied passage on a streetcar. For her efforts she earned the title of Mother of Civil Rights in California.

HARRIET QUIMBY (1875?–1912)

Aviator Harriet Quimby was the first American woman licensed as a pilot and the second in the world. Though little is known about Quimby's early life, she was born in Coldwater, Michigan, and spent her teens in Arroyo Grande, California, where her parents operated a grocery store. The family later relocated to San Francisco, where she became a journalist, writing for the *San Francisco Dramatic Review* and reporting for the *Call-Bulletin* and *Chronicle*. She moved to New York City in 1903. As a photojournalist and editor for *Leslie's Illustrated Weekly,* she wrote theater reviews as well as articles on subjects as varied as political scandal and household tips.

In 1911 Quimby took flying lessons and obtained her pilot license. While still working for *Leslie's,* she earned high fees at air meets. In 1912 she flew a monoplane over the English Channel. That same year she crashed into Boston Harbor, when her male passenger shifted his weight; neither wore seatbelts, and they fell from the open plane.

JEAN STAFFORD (1915–1979)

Fiction writer Jean Stafford of Covina wrote of the struggle for female identity against societal limitations. When her family lost their money in the 1929 stock market crash, they moved to Boulder, Colorado, where her father wrote pulp fiction and her mother ran a boardinghouse. Jean attended the University of Colorado, earning bachelor's and master's degrees in 1936, and studied philosophy for a year at Heidelberg, Germany.

She married poet Robert Lowell in 1940; they were divorced in 1948.

Stafford published her first novel, *Boston Adventure*, in 1944. A satiric view of Boston society, it became a best-seller. She published her second novel, *The Mountain Lion*, three years later. It told the story of the coming-of-age of a brother and sister in the Colorado high country. Although highly acclaimed, it was a commercial failure. A third novel, *The Catherine Wheel*, appeared in 1952.

During the 1950s Stafford submitted short fiction to *The New Yorker, Vogue, Harper's Bazaar*, and other journals and in 1965 conducted an interview with the mother of Lee Harvey Oswald, the alleged assassin of Pres. John F. Kennedy. Stafford won a Pulitzer Prize for *The Collected Stories of Jean Stafford* (1969). Her works reflected her own experience: a woman's isolation set against the grandeur of the West. Her last years, marred by alcoholism and solitude, ended in death from stroke.

AMY TAN (1952–)

A skilled storyteller, Amy Tan of Oakland became a best-selling novelist during the rise of multicultural and feminist literature. She grew up in San Francisco and attended high school in Montreux, Switzerland. On scholarship at Linfield College, she earned part of her tuition working at a pizzeria. With a degree in English, she pursued a doctorate in linguistics at the University of California at Berkeley and taught handicapped children while writing and publishing her own journal, *Emergency Room Reports*.

In 1983 Tan used information about her mother's emigration from China to complete an assignment for a composition workshop at the Squaw Valley Community of Writers. In 1989 she crafted the family story into a woman-centered best-seller, *The Joy Luck Club*, the subject of a popular 1993 movie, and wrote a sequel, *The Kitchen God's Wife* in 1991. She has also written a children's book, historical fiction, and essays and sketches for magazines and anthologies. Her skillful plots garnered her a Commonwealth Club award, Bay Area Book Reviewers prize, and American Library Association's best book for young adults award.

MAXINE WATERS (1938–)

U.S. representative Maxine Moore Carr Waters, born in St. Louis, Missouri, has founded programs to empower minority women. Reared in a housing project, she knew firsthand the hardships her single mother faced in trying to support a family on limited wages. In her teens she bussed tables in a restaurant and worked in a factory. She married at age 18 and settled in Los Angeles in the early 1960s. She took low-paying jobs in sweatshops and as a telephone operator before getting a federal job in 1966 as assistant teacher and supervisor of volunteers for the city's Head Start program.

At age 30 Waters returned to school, earning a bachelor's degree in sociology from California State University in 1972. She involved herself in city issues as deputy and campaign manager for a city councilman and developed a reputation for shrewd strategy as manager of campaigns for Mayor Tom Bradley and Sen. Alan Cranston.

While serving from 1976 to 1990 in the California State Assembly, she lobbied for women's and citizens' rights, affirmative action, child abuse prevention, and controls on police strip searches. She rose to become the state's first female and first African American majority whip. In 1978 she cofounded the Black Women's Forum, a movement to involve more women in government. Six years later she cofounded the National Political Congress of Black Women, which sought empowerment for nonwhite females. Late in the 1980s she opened the Maxine Waters Employment Preparation Center as a means of employing the jobless. In 1990 Waters won a seat in the U.S. House of Representatives, where she continued to champion women, children, minorities, veterans, the unemployed, and the poor.

HELEN WILLS (1905–1998)

Tennis star Helen Newington Wills of Centreville battled gender stereotypes to make athletics a viable career choice for women. She grew up in a well-to-do family and practiced tennis at the Berkeley Tennis Club. From 1923 to 1931, she netted seven singles and four doubles titles, including two gold medals at the 1924 Olympics in Paris.

Wills made headlines in 1927 by abandoning the third set of a match against Helen Jacobs because Wills could no longer conceal a severe spinal injury. After a two-year retirement, she returned to defeat Jacobs at Wimbledon and over the next six years won 180 straight matches. The Associated Press named her Athlete of the Year in 1935. Nicknamed Queen Helen, she remained a media favorite and a supporter of competitive women's athletics. At the height of her career, she issued an autobiography, *15–30: The Story of a Tennis Player* (1937). In 1969 she was inducted into the Tennis Hall of Fame.

—Mary Ellen Snodgrass

PROMINENT SITES

California State Military Museum
1119 2nd Street
Sacramento, CA 95814
Telephone: (916) 442 2883
Web: http://www.militarymuseum.org
The official military museum and historical research center for the state of California, the museum hosts a number of permanent exhibits, including ones on women in the armed forces and on contributions of Asian Americans during World War II.

Chinese Historical Society Museum and Learning Center
650 Commercial Street
San Francisco, CA 94111
Telephone: (415) 391 1188
Web: http://www.chsa.org/about.htm
The first organization of its kind in North America, the Chinese Historical Society was incorporated in 1963. Its museum focuses on the Chinese experience in the United States, including the experiences of women from the Gold Rush to the present day.

Exotic World Burlesque Museum
29053 Wild Road
Helendale, CA 92342
Telephone: (760) 243 5261
Web: http://www.exoticworldusa.org
The museum features photos, costumes, jewelry, and shoes from burlesque stars of America's past, including Betty Page and Sally Rand. Some photos and costumes date from the 18th century.

Grace Hudson Museum/Sun House
431 South Main Street
Ukiah, CA 95482
Telephone: (707) 467 2836
Web: http://www.gracehudsonmuseum.org
The museum focuses on the life works of Grace Hudson (1865–1937) and her husband, Dr. John W. Hudson (1865–1936). An artist, Grace Hudson's body of work was primarily oil portraits of members of the local Native American community. The museum holds the largest collection of her work in the world.

Mary Aaron Memorial Museum
704 D Street
Marysville, CA 95901
Telephone: (530) 743 1004
Web: http://www.syix.com/yubacity/msvlplaces.html
The museum is housed in one of the first brick structures built in Marysville. It is filled with artifacts chronicling the lives of Marysville residents, particularly those of the early Chinese community.

Rosie the Riveter Monument: Honoring American Women's Labor During WWII
Marina Bay Park
Mailing: Rosie the Riveter Trust
PO Box 70415
Richmond, CA 94807
Telephone: (510) 236 2024
Web: http://www.rosietheriveter.org
The memorial is located in Marina Bay Park, the former site of ship construction by women during World War II. Designed by Susan Schwartzenberg and Cheryl Barton, it evokes the process of constructing ships. A walkway in the memorial has a carved timeline of the war with facts about the home front and quotes from women workers. Porcelain enamel panels reproduce memorabilia and letters.

San Jose Museum of Quilts and Textiles
110 Paseo de San Antonio
San Jose, CA 95112–3639
Telephone: (408) 971 0323
Web: http://www.sjquiltmuseum.org/index.htm
The mission of this museum is to promote the art, craft, and history of quilts and textiles and to provide an understanding of their role in the lives of their makers, in cultural traditions, and as historical documents. The museum features regularly changing exhibitions of contemporary and historical quilts and textiles from around the world as well as exhibits related to California and the West.

Sarah A. Mooney Museum
542 West D Street
Lemoore, CA 93245
Telephone: (559) 925 0321
Web: http://www.lemoore.com/sammm.htm
The Mooney family came to Lemoore in 1875 and built their Victorian home in 1893. In 1925 Sarah left the home to her granddaughter, Marie Blakely. In 1973 Marie donated the home to the Lemoore District Chamber of Commerce as a memorial museum dedicated to Sarah. It is decorated with Victorian furnishings from Lemoore families.

RESOURCES

FURTHER READING

HISTORY

Anthony, Susan B., and Ida Husted Harper. *History of Woman Suffrage.* Vol. 4. Indianapolis, Ind.: Hollenbeck Press, 1902.

Atherton, Gertrude Franklin Horn. *California, An Intimate History.* 1914. Reprint, Irvine, Calif.: Reprint Services, 1993.

Bancroft, Hubert Howe. *History of California.* 7 vols. 1886–1890. Reprint, San Rafael, Calif.: Bancroft Press, 1990.

Beasley, Delilah. *The Negro Trail Blazers of California* 1919. Reprint, New York: G. K. Hall, 1997.

Bjork, Kenneth O. *West of the Great Divide: Norwegian Migration to the Pacific Coast.* Northfield, Minn.: Norwegian-American Historical Association, 1958.

Blegen, Theodore C. *Land of Their Choice: The Immigrants Write Home.* Minneapolis: University of Minnesota Press, 1955.

Boessenecker, John. *Badge and Buckshot: Lawlessness in Old California.* Norman: University of Oklahoma Press, 1988.

Bouvier, Virginia Marie. *Women and the Conquest of California, 1542–1840: Codes of Silence.* Tucson: University of Arizona Press, 2001.

Butruille, Susan G. *Women's Voices from the Mother Lode: Tales from the California Gold Rush.* Boise, Idaho: Tamarack Books, 1998.

Clavigero, Francesco Saverio. *The History of Lower California.* Translated and edited by Sara E. Lake and A. A. Gray. Riverside, Calif.: Manessier Publishing, 1971.

Cleland, Robert Glass. *California in Our Time (1900–1940).* New York: A. A. Knopf, 1947.

Cott, Nancy F., ed. *Root of Bitterness: Documents of the Social History of American Women.* 2nd ed. Boston: Northeastern University Press, 1996.

Ellison, Joseph W. *California and the Nation, 1850–1869; a Study of the Relations of a Frontier Community with the Federal Government.* Millwood, N.Y.: Kraus, 1974.

Englander, Susan. *Class Conflict and Coalition in the California Woman Suffrage Movement, 1907–1912: the San Francisco Wage Earners' Suffrage League.* San Francisco: Mellen Research University Press, 1992.

Francke, Lizzie. *Script Girls: Women Screenwriters in Hollywood.* London: British Film Institute, 1994.

Gibbs, Jewelle Taylor, and Teiassha Bankhead. *Preserving Privilege: California Politics, Propositions, and People of Color.* Westport, Conn.: Praeger, 2001.

Gullett, Gayle Ann. *Becoming Citizens: The Emergence and Development of the California Women's Movement, 1880–1911.* Urbana: University of Illinois Press, 2000.

Harper, Ida Husted. *History of Woman Suffrage.* Vol. 6. New York: J. J. Little & Ives, 1922.

Heizer, R. F., and M. A. Whipple. *The California Indians.* Berkeley: California Indian Library Collections, 1992.

Holliday, J. S. *The World Rushed In: The California Gold Rush Experience.* Norman: University of Oklahoma Press, 2002.

Jensen, Joan M., and Gloria Ricci Lothrop. *California Women: A History.* San Francisco: Boyd & Fraser Publishing, 1987.

Johnson, Susan Lee. *Roaring Camp: The Social World of the California Gold Rush.* New York: W. W. Norton, 2000.

Kanellos, Nicolás. *Hispanic Firsts: 500 Years of Extraordinary Achievement.* Detroit, Mich.: Gale, 1997.

Lamar, Howard R., ed. *The Readers Encyclopedia of the American West.* New York: Crowell, 1977.

Lavender, David. *California: A Bicentennial History.* New York: W. W. Norton, 1976.

Lemke-Santangelo, Gretchen. *Abiding Courage: African American Migrant Women and the East Bay Community.* Chapel Hill: University of North Carolina Press, 1996.

Levinson, Robert E. *The Jews in the California Gold Rush.* Berkeley, Calif.: Commission for the Preservation of Pioneer Jewish Cemeteries and Landmark of the Judah L. Magnes Museum, 1994.

Levy, Jo Ann. *They Saw the Elephant: Women in the California Gold Rush.* Norman: University of Oklahoma Press, 1990.

Lick, Sue Fagalde. *Stories Grandma Never Told: Portuguese Women in California.* Berkeley, Calif.: Heyday Books, 1998.

Maffly-Kipp, Laurie F. *Religion and Society in Frontier California.* New Haven, Conn.: Yale University Press, 1994.

McCarthy, Helen, et al. *Ethnography and Prehistory of the North Coast Range, California.* Davis: University of California Press, 1985.

Moratto, Michael J. *California Archaeology.* New York: Academic Press, 1984.

Moynihan, Ruth B., Susan Armitage, and Christiane Fischer, eds. *So Much to Be Done: Women Settlers on the Mining and Ranching Frontier.* 2nd ed. Lincoln: University of Nebraska Press, 1998.

Nunis, Doyce B., ed. *Women in the Life of Southern California: An Anthology Compiled from the* Southern California Quarterly. Los Angeles: Historical Society of Southern California, 1996.

Ono, Kent A. *Shifting Borders: Rhetoric, Immigration, and California's Proposition 187.* Philadelphia: Temple University Press, 2002.

Paul, Rodman W. *California Gold: The Beginning of Mining in the Far West.* Lincoln: University of Nebraska Press, 1965.

Peffer, George Anthony. *If They Don't Bring Their Women Here: Chinese Female Immigration Before Exclusion.* Urbana: University of Illinois Press, 1999.

Rawls, James J., and Walton Bean. *California: An Interpretive History.* 7th ed. New York: McGraw-Hill, 1998.

Rhoades, Elizabeth R. *Foreigners in Southern California During the Mexican Period.* 1924. Reprint, San Francisco: R and E Research, 1971.

Rohrbough, Malcolm J. *Days of Gold: The California Gold Rush and the American Nation.* Berkeley: University of California Press, 1997.

Rose, Cynthia. *American Decades.* Farmington Hills, Mich.: Gale Group, 2002.

Ruiz, Vicki. *Cannery Women, Cannery Lives: Mexican Women, Unionization, and the California Food Processing Industry, 1930–1950.* Albuquerque: University of New Mexico Press, 1987.

Solomons, Selina. *How We Won the Vote in California, A True Story of the Campaign of 1911.* San Francisco: New Woman Publishing, 1912.

Stanton, Elizabeth Cady, and Susan B. Anthony, and Matilda Joslyn Gage. *History of Woman Suffrage.* Vols. 1–3. Rochester, N.Y.: Charles Mann Printing, 1886.

Starr, Kevin. *Endangered Dreams: The Great Depression in California.* New York: Oxford University Press, 1996.

Starr, Kevin. *Embattled Dreams: California in War and Peace, 1940–1950.* New York: Oxford University Press, 2002.

Tong, Benson. *Unsubmissive Women: Chinese Prostitutes in Nineteenth-century San Francisco.* Norman: University of Oklahoma Press, 1994.

Trafzer, Clifford E., and Joel R. Hyer, eds. *Exterminate Them! Written Accounts of the Murder, Rape, and Enslavement of Native Americans during the California Gold Rush.* East Lansing: Michigan State University Press, 1999.

Weatherford, Doris. *American Women and World War II.* New York: Facts On File, 1990.

Weiler, Kathleen. *Country Schoolwomen: Teaching in Rural California, 1850–1950.* Stanford, Calif.: Stanford University Press, 1998.

Young, Stanley, and Melba Levick. *The Missions of California.* San Francisco: Chronicle Books, 1998.

Yung, Judy. *Unbound Feet: A Social History of Chinese Women in San Francisco.* Berkeley: University of California Press, 1995.

Yung, Judy. *Unbound Voices: A Documentary History of Chinese Women in San Francisco.* Berkeley: University of California Press, 1999.

BIOGRAPHY AND AUTOBIOGRAPHY

Bass, Charlotta A. *Forty Years: Memoirs from the Pages of a Newspaper.* 1960. Reprint, Los Angeles: C. A. Bass, 1979.

Beauchamp, Cari. *Without Lying Down: Frances Marion and the Powerful Women of Early Hollywood.* New York: Scribner, 1997.

Black, Shirley Temple. *Child Star.* New York: McGraw-Hill, 1988.

Blumhofer, Edith Waldvogel. *Aimee Semple McPherson: Everybody's Sister.* Grand Rapids, Mich.: W. B. Eerdmans, 1993.

Boxer, Barbara. *Strangers in the Senate: Politics and the New Revolution of Women in America.* Washington, D.C.: National Press Books, 1994.

Bryan, Vernanne. *Laura Keene: A British Actress on the American Stage, 1826–1873.* Jefferson, N.C.: McFarland, 1997.

Chin, Soo-Young. *Doing What Had to Be Done: The Life Narrative of Dora Yum Kim*. Philadelphia: Temple University Press, 1999.

Clappe, Louise A. K. S. *The Shirley Letters from the California Mines, 1851–1852*. Edited by Marlene Smith-Baranzini. Berkeley, Calif.: Heyday Books, 2000.

Directors. Vol. 2 of *International Dictionary of Films and Filmmakers*. Detroit, Mich.: St. James Press, 1996.

Frémont, Elizabeth Benton. *Recollections*. New York: Frederick H. Hitchcock, 1912.

Gale Research. *Notable Native Americans*. Detroit, Mich., 1995.

Hammontree, Patsy Guy. *Shirley Temple Black: A Bio-bibliography*. Westport, Conn.: Greenwood Press, 1998.

Karasick, Norman M. *The Oilman's Daughter: A Biography of Aline Barnsdall*. Encino, Calif.: Carleston Publishing, 1993.

King, Billie Jean. *Billie Jean*. New York: Viking Press, 1982.

Mayne, Judith. *Directed by Dorothy Arzner*. Bloomington: Indiana University Press, 1994.

Mowat, Farley. *Woman in the Mists: The Story of Dian Fossey and the Mountain Gorillas of Africa*. New York: Warner Books, 1988.

Parry, Melanie, ed. *Larousse Dictionary of Women*. New York: Larousse, 1996.

Roberts, Jerry. *Dianne Feinstein: Never Let Them See You Cry*. San Francisco: HarperCollinsWest, 1994.

Royce, Sarah. *A Frontier Lady: Recollections of the Gold Rush and Early California*. 1932. Reprint, Lincoln: University of Nebraska Press, 1977.

USEFUL WEB SITES

"Nancy Pelosi," House Web Site
http://www.house.gov/pelosi/bio_pel.htm
"NASA Biographical Data: Ellen Ochoa"
http://www.jsc.nasa.gov/Bios/htmlbios/ochoa.html

SELECTED ORGANIZATIONS AND INSTITUTIONS

California Digital Library
Office of the President
University of California
415 20th Street, 4th Floor
Oakland, CA 94612–2901
Telephone: (510) 987 0555

Web: http://www.dbs.cdlib.org
Online gateway to a catalog of holdings in the libraries of the nine University of California campuses, the California State Library, California Academy of Sciences, California Historical Society, Center for Research Libraries, and the Graduate Theological Union.

California Historical Society
678 Mission Street
San Francisco, CA 94105
Telephone: (415) 357 1848
Web: http://www.californiahistoricalsociety.org
Works to engage the public's interest in the history of California. California women played an important role in printing and publishing in the state, and the society houses the Kemble Collection on Western Printing and Publishing. It also houses diaries and other manuscripts of early settlers and business and political materials. Its official publication, *California History*, has frequent articles on all aspects of women's experience in the state.

California State Archives
1020 O Street
Sacramento, CA 95814
Telephone: (916) 653 7715
Web: http://www.ss.ca.gov/archives/archives.htm
Maintains the historical records of state government and some local governments. The archive also has an oral history program containing interviews of state government officials.

National Women's History Project
3343 Industrial Drive, Suite #4
Santa Rosa, CA 95403
Telephone: (707) 636 2888
Web: http://www.nwhp.org/index.html
An educational organization aiming to honor the history of women in all its diversity through a wide range of educational programs and informational materials, such as an online biographical resource and a list of women's history performers.

Pomona College Women's Studies
333 North College Way
Claremont, CA 91711
Telephone: (909) 621 8000
Web: http://www.pomona.edu/academics/departments/socialsciences/women.shtml

The program offers an interdisciplinary major that focuses on the "ranging impact of feminist research on critical inquiry into these multiple forms of difference."

Stanford University Program in Feminist Studies
Serra House, 556 Salvatierra Walk
Stanford, CA 94305–8640
Telephone: (650) 723 2412
Web: http://www.stanford.edu/dept/femstudies
The interdisciplinary undergraduate program investigates the significance of gender in all aspects of life and focuses on how gender differences and gender inequality are created and perpetuated.

University of California–Berkeley Beatrice Bain Research Group
3415 Dwinelle Hall, #2050
University of California
Berkeley, CA 94720–2050
Telephone: (510) 643 7172
Web: http://socrates.berkeley.edu:7013/index.html
Works to foster and coordinate scholarship and research about women and gender across disciplines.

University of California–Berkeley Women's Studies Department
3326 Dwinelle Hall #1070
Berkeley, CA 94720
Telephone: (510) 642 8513
Web: http://womensstudies.berkeley.edu
One of the nation's earliest women's studies programs, it was founded in 1976 to introduce the subject of women as a serious academic discipline. It considers the position of women throughout history, across the world and in different economic, ethnic, and racial groups and examines sexual inequality and conflict created by gender roles. Students can receive an interdisciplinary major or minor.

University of California–Davis Women's Studies Program
Hart Hall
Davis, CA 95616
Telephone: (530) 752 4686
Web: http://cougar.ucdavis.edu/wms
The interdisciplinary programs integrates women's issues and perspectives—in all their social, ethnic, and national diversity—into existing curricula and focuses on the relationship of gender to society.

University of California, Irvine Women's Studies Program
352 Murray Krieger Hall
Irvine, CA 92697–2655
Telephone: (949) 824 4234
Web: http://www.hnet.uci.edu/WomensStudies
Offers both an undergraduate program, with faculty from the fields of humanities, social sciences, and the arts, and a graduate program emphasizing feminist studies.

University of California–Los Angeles Center for the Study of Women
288 Kinsey Hall
PO Box 951504
Los Angeles, CA 90095–1504
Telephone: (310) 825 0590
Web: http://women.ucla.edu/csw/index.html
A nationally recognized center for research on women and gender that sponsors conferences and seminars and administers grants that enable feminist scholars to exchange ideas and secure funding.

University of California–Los Angeles Women's Studies Programs
240 Kinsey Hall
PO Box 951504
Los Angeles, CA 90095–1504
Telephone: (310) 206 8101
Web: http://women.ucla.edu
Drawing on the humanities, social sciences, life/physical sciences and other areas, the program views women from their own perspectives rather than from the male points of view. The university offers both undergraduate and graduate degrees in the subject.

University of California–Riverside Women's Studies
900 University Avenue
Riverside, CA 92521
Telephone: (909) 787 6427
Web: http://WomensStudies.ucr.edu
The program combines theory with informed action, and focuses on understanding the varieties of feminism in the contemporary world.

University of California–San Diego Critical Gender Studies
2073 Humanities and Social Sciences, Muir College
University of California–San Diego

9500 Gilman Drive
La Jolla, CA 92093
Telephone: (858) 534 3589
Web: http://www-muir.ucsd.edu/instructional/
    critical-gender/index.html
The critical gender studies program offers students the opportunity "to study gender, race, class, sexuality, and nationalism as intersecting categories of analysis and experience."

University of California–Santa Barbara Women's Studies Program
4706 South Hall
Santa Barbara, CA 93106
Telephone: (805) 893 4330
Web: http://www.womst.ucsb.edu/index.html
Offers students "the opportunity to discover the variety and richness of women's historical, cultural, and social contributions, as well as to obtain a clear understanding of the dynamics of gender, race, and class inequality as it has been experienced and struggled against by the world's women."

University of California–Santa Cruz Women's Studies
Department of Women's Studies
UC Santa Cruz
1156 High Street
Santa Cruz, CA 95064–1077
Telephone: (831) 459 4324
Web: http://humwww.ucsc.edu:16080/wst

An interdisciplinary program that offers both undergraduate and graduate studies. The program "examines and develops feminist scholarship in the humanities, social sciences, natural sciences, and arts" and "helps students develop theoretical, empirical, and methodological perspectives for studying the status and experiences of women."

University of Southern California Center for Feminist Research
Taper Hall of Humanities 331-C
Los Angeles, CA 90089–4352
Telephone: (213) 740 1739
Web: http://www.usc.edu/dept/cfr/html/home.htm
The Center for Feminist Research provides University of Southern California's feminist community with a variety of seminars, workshops, conferences, and informal gatherings that bring together a network of people who share interests and concerns.

University of Southern California Gender Studies Program
Taper Hall of Humanities, Room 331-C
Los Angeles, CA 90089–4352
Telephone: (213) 740-8286
Web: http://www.usc.edu/dept/LAS/gsp/htm/home.htm
The program offers a bachelor's degree, a minor, or a graduate certificate and is home to the Center for Feminist Research (see above).

COLORADO

*The children in the primary grades were sometimes required to make relief maps
of Moonstone [Colorado] in sand. Had they used colored sand . . . they easily could have
indicated the social classifications of Moonstone, since these conformed to certain
topographical boundaries and every child understood them perfectly.
The main business street ran, of course, though the centre of town. To the west . . .
lived all of the people "in society." . . . In the part of Moonstone that lay east of Main Street,
toward the deep ravine . . . [was] Mexican Town. . . . Here the old women washed in the back
yard, and the men sat in the front doorway and smoked their pipes.*
—Willa Cather, *The Song of the Lark*, 1915

Colorado was the third state to grant women full voting rights, and the first to elect women to its state legislature. Unlike other western states that were more liberal to women in the 19th century than in the 20th, Colorado—especially Denver—was relatively consistent in extending equality to women throughout its history.

PREHISTORY

(Prehistory–1541)

Colorado's earliest inhabitants lived condominium-style in cliffs and caves above their fields, grew cotton and processed its fibers into yarn for weaving, crafted pottery, and even built towers of adobe blocks. However, by the time the Spanish arrived in this area in the 1500s, nothing remained but the well-preserved homes of these early indigenous peoples.

The peoples who later inhabited the region were related to—or at least indirectly influenced by—Native Americans of the Great Plains, especially in that settled agriculture was not part of their economy. Women gathered roots, berries, and other wild produce; men hunted available game, roaming in small bands in search of food. The Ute lived in the western portion of what became the modern state; they were one of the first western tribes to acquire horses. The Comanche, who lived in eastern Colorado, obtained horses around 1680 and

soon became superior riders. They pushed their traditional enemy, the Apache, south, but as the Arapaho, Cheyenne, and Kiowa were pushed from their plains' homes, these tribes came to Colorado.

They became nomadic hunters, especially of the American bison, creating an economy in which the status of women was low. Women spent their days butchering buffalo and other animals, cutting the meat into thin slices, drying it, and pounding it into the

State Population (2000): 4,301,261

Female Population (2000): 2,135,278

Women in State Legislature (2003): 33%

Female College Enrollment (1999): 143,000 (54.6% of total)

Privately Held Women-owned Businesses (1997): 114,807

First Year of Full Suffrage: 1893

pemmican that was the staple of their diet. Nomadic women stored food in rawhide bags and used buffalo brains for tanning acid that turned hides into usable material for sewing; they used needles made from bone and thread made of animal sinew.

Both men and women enjoyed jewelry, especially earrings. Both sexes often braided their hair and removed any visible body hair by pulling it out. Although both men and women painted their bodies for special occasions, men were likely to depict actual scenes, while women were more apt to draw abstract and geometric patterns.

Like other Native Americans of the Plains, these tribes lived in movable homes, including tepees made of buffalo skins, which women carried and erected. They sometimes constructed rough buildings for other purposes, including two-level

Arapaho woman, ca. 1880. This photograph shows a style of dress influenced by American women who began settling Colorado in the late 1850s. (Denver Public Library, Western History Collection, X–32340)

shade houses of poles and brush that allowed an occupant to sit up high and view activities below; these were useful, too, in keeping drying meat from dogs. Women also erected wickiups, temporary shelters made of poles covered with brush, sometimes supported on one side by a tree.

Polygamy was fairly common in these tribes. Rarely did more than two or three women share a man, though, and although first wives had higher social standing than later wives, often the women were sisters. Some tribes, especially the Arapaho, had formal women's organizations; most of these groups were by invitation only and were limited to mature women of high status in the community. They held feasts, led ceremonies, and passed on tribal traditions to younger women.

Ute women sometimes participated in combat; they routinely looted battlefields and dead bodies, and they joined in prewar and postwar victory dances, including the "scalp dance." Ute women also found time for sports, especially a game similar to field hockey; bets were common on this and other games, and women, like men, engaged in gambling on athletic competitions and games of chance. Like other nomads, these women often traveled and lived independently from men, developing strong bonds.

WHITE EXPLORATION TO TERRITORIAL STATUS (1541–1861)

Spanish men reached the edge of modern Colorado as early as 1541, and during the next two centuries, Spanish colonists made occasional military incursions into the region, their northernmost frontier. No women went north from New Mexico, however, and no permanent Hispanic settlements were created. In these early encounters, Native Americans acquired horses from the Spanish and the Spanish, in return, sometimes acquired indigenous women.

However, for most of three centuries that followed these early encounters, white people largely ignored Colorado. Change began slowly when

France sold the vast area known as Louisiana to the United States in 1803. The government sent several exploratory parties west, including the Lewis and Clark Expedition that ventured into the Northwest and an expedition led by Zebulon Pike in 1806–1807, which explored the southwestern reaches of the Louisiana Purchase. Pike's exploration party did not include white women, though, and again no permanent settlements resulted.

The first American settlement began in 1826, when the four Bent brothers of Missouri built a fur trading post on the Arkansas River, near modern La Junta. Bent's Fort soon became one of the West's most important centers of early commerce. A locally famous woman associated with the fort was an African American slave, Charlotte Green, whose culinary skill was known for hundreds of miles. Native American women were a regular part of Bent's Fort.

Upstream from Bent's Fort, on the Arkansas River near present-day Pueblo, a small settlement began in the 1830s with men who had given up fur trapping to settle with Mexican women. They attempted to compete with the Bent brothers, who complained about the new trading post in an 1842 letter to the superintendent of Indian affairs. Other trading posts, such as Fort Misery, west of the Continental Divide, and Hardscrabble, on the Arkansas River upstream from Pueblo, also included Mexican women.

These remote posts were sometimes raided by the Ute, and the traders also invited conflict by crossing into Mexican territory. Indeed, Spain held claim to Colorado despite incursions by American men; after Mexico declared independence from Spain in 1821, Mexico made large land grants to its pioneers. In the next decades, Spanish-speaking women accompanied men to develop communities scattered throughout southern Colorado. They lived in whitewashed adobe homes, cultivated and ground corn for tortillas, and raised sheep and dyed wool.

In 1846, while the Mormon vanguard moved toward Utah from Iowa, a parallel group of 43 Mormons from Mississippi arrived at Pueblo in August. Welcomed by about a dozen families of Native American men and Mexican women, they decided to spend the winter. Men of the Mormon battalion that had participated in the Mexican War soon joined them, and by spring, 275 Mormons were living in Pueblo. Winter brought nine deaths, but seven births and one marriage.

Even after Texas became an independent republic and the United States won its war against Mexico in 1848, Colorado remained largely unaffected. Its development was slowed partly because cartographers were confused by its five major river systems and upland valleys; for decades, no accurate maps existed. Those who did travel through the area used the Old Spanish Trail, which actually was an old Ute trail, through terrain so rough that only pack animals, not wagons, could pass successfully.

The federal government built Colorado's first military fort (as opposed to forts that actually were trading posts) in the San Luis Valley in 1852. The fort's garrison was to protect Americans on the Old Spanish Trail; despite the trail's difficulties, it had enough travelers that an estimate of attacks during the summer of 1846 counted 47 Americans dead, 330 wagons destroyed, and 6,500 cattle stolen.

As in Montana, Nevada, and other western states, gold finally lured large numbers of whites to Colorado. Although silver ultimately became its most important underground resource, Colorado sprang into being almost overnight when gold was found in Cherry Creek in the summer of 1858. At the time the only street in what became Denver was "Indian Row," inhabited by white men and their Native American wives; the first white woman to join them was Mrs. S. M. Rooker, who arrived from Salt Lake City on August 30, 1858.

Others soon followed, including Henri and Katrina Murat, who were descendants of Napoleon

CLARA BROWN

Clara Brown arrived in Denver by wagon train from Kansas in 1859, after being freed from slavery by her master just two years earlier. She walked most of the 600-mile journey, working as a cook for the other prospectors to pay her passage. She came not in search of gold, but to find her long-lost daughter, Eliza Jane, who had been separated from her at the auction block in 1835.

Brown was born into slavery in Virginia. At age three she was sold, with her mother, to a tobacco farmer named Ambrose Smith, of Spotsylvania County, Virginia. In 1809 the Smiths moved to Kentucky, then considered the "far West." There, Brown married another of Smith's slaves, Richard, and bore four children: Richard, Margaret, and twins, Paulina Ann and Eliza Jane.

After Smith's death in 1835, Brown and her family were sold at auction to separate owners. She was purchased by George Brown, a friend of the Smiths, whom she served until his death in 1857. Freed by George Brown's heirs, she traveled farther west to Leavenworth, Kansas, as cook to Jacob Brunner's family. When the Brunners moved to California in 1858, Brown chose to remain in Kansas until she could locate her only remaining daughter, Eliza Jane.

Rumors suggested Eliza Jane had also headed west, so when the opportunity arose to join a wagon train bound for Colorado, Brown took it. After a short stay in Denver, where the devout Brown helped found the Union Sunday School, she established herself in the nearby mining camp of Central City, doing laundry in her home, which also served as a makeshift hospital, hotel, and restaurant, as well as the camp's first Sunday school.

Industrious, generous, and, though functionally illiterate, fiscally savvy, by 1866 Brown had amassed nearly $10,000 from investments in mining claims, real estate, and savings. She used her money to bring 16 freed slaves from Kentucky to Colorado, and to support Central City's first Methodist Church.

After nearly 50 years of searching, Brown, age 82, reunited with Eliza Jane and Eliza's daughter in Council Bluffs, Iowa, in 1882. Three years later, Brown died in Denver. Her spirit and deeds have been commemorated by the St. James Methodist Church of Central City, the Colorado Pioneers Association, and the Colorado Women's Hall of Fame.

—Laura J. Lambert

and part of the Florida Murat family. Katrina Murat, one of the first four white women in Denver, later was dubbed "the Mother of Colorado."

Colorado's story was recorded from the beginning in the pages of the *Rocky Mountain News*, an enterprise born of a decision by Elizabeth Sumner Byers. Her husband, a member of the Nebraska territorial legislature, was wounded in gunfire on the streets of Omaha; the man responsible had no cash and offered a printing press instead. William Byers rejected the press, but his wife convinced him to take it and move to the gold rush area. They left Nebraska in March 1859 and traveled through a severe snowstorm. "I was the eighth white woman in Denver," she later wrote. "When I climbed out of the little buckboard with my two babies I felt I was in the advance guard of civilization." (Ellis 1959, 47)

Tens of thousands of such "fifty-niners" came to Colorado. Although thousands soon left disappointed, those who stayed successfully petitioned Congress for territorial status. On February 28, 1861—just prior to the inauguration of Abraham Lincoln—Congress ensured the loyalty of this area to the Union by making it a territory.

TERRITORIAL STATUS TO STATEHOOD (1861–1876)

The new territory's white population was between 30,000 and 40,000; by far the majority had lived there less than two years and men outnumbered women about five to one. The shortage of women was clear in one of Denver's first stores: proprietor Salomon Schulein had taken seriously a newspaper prediction that women were on their way, but he soon was forced to advertise reduced prices for the wedding outfits he had stocked.

Most of the women who came at this time were already married. But some were unmarried women who went because they could earn an excellent living providing miners with services ranging from hotels to brothels. Some women were also teachers. Indeed, Denver's first schools were private ones opened in 1860 by two unmarried women, Lydia Maria King and Indiana Sopria.

Prices were high on frontiers, where both goods and labor were scarce. One woman who took advantage of the need for manufactured items was Mrs. L. E. Miller. She moved to Colorado from Wisconsin in 1860 and then traveled the state selling sewing machines for $160 each. Sewing machines—important laborsaving devices for women—were new at the time and Mrs. Miller was the first in the West to sell them.

The Civil War barely slowed development, and Colorado women nearly unanimously supported the Union. Journalist Elizabeth Byers organized 15 women who met regularly at the Broadwell House, where the hotelier gave them free use of his largest room for their work. They made underwear, bedding, and bandages for Colorado soldiers.

Even before the war ended, a new kind of nonmining settler began to arrive, as people took advantage of the Homestead Act. The 1862 federal program offered 160 acres of free land to anyone—male or female—who lived on it for five years. Approximately 12% of Colorado homestead claims in this era were filed by unmarried women; 42% of claims filed by women were "proved up" (completed) during the required period, compared with 37% of male claims.

That the success rate for both women and men was less than half is attributable to the hardships encountered in homesteading life, which were harder in Colorado than in other regions. The soil was not nearly as good as that of the Midwest; winters were long and severe; and most important, the area was arid. Most homesteaders had additional jobs; unmarried women often taught during the winter and farmed in the summer.

The Homestead Act also attracted millions of Europeans to America. The town of Colfax began in 1869 as a communal settlement of the Chicago-based German Colonization Company, which urged working-class German families to take advantage of the Homestead Act. Such groups came into being for almost all nationalities, and, like native-born Americans, noncitizens were eligible for free land.

The new railroads built in the 1870s brought more immigrants, and by 1880 one in every four Colorado residents would be foreign-born. In addition to homesteaders, immigrant men were miners, especially coal miners. Mining corporations recruited men from Italy to China; they lived in crowded coal camp boardinghouses and rarely had the opportunity to immigrate with their women.

Political party bosses encouraged immigrant men—many of whom could not read in any language—to vote, which they could do after taking out the "first papers" that certified six months residency. Many men never completed the process of citizenship, but nonetheless continued voting for a lifetime. This situation rankled American suffragists, whose records in state after state criticized immigrant men for voting against women's suffrage.

Colorado also attracted many newcomers from the East whose grandparents and great-grandparents had been born in the United States, and who read, wrote, owned taxable property, and understood American government. Two such women, sisters Mary G. Campbell and Katherine G. Patterson, moved to Colorado in this period. They commented on the lack of women in the territory, noting that by 1858 only three white women were residents of Denver. Similar scarcity boded well for women on other frontiers, where men eager to attract them granted greater equality. In fact, a man was the first to raise the question of women's rights in Colorado.

The territorial governor brought up the issue of women's suffrage. In most territories, the governor—who was appointed by the president—was more conservative than the frontiersmen he governed. Gov. Edward McCook, however, saw the example of Wyoming, which granted women the vote in 1869, and said to the legislature in 1870:

> It has been said that no great reform was ever made without passing through three stages—ridicule, argument, and adoption. It rests with you to say whether Colorado will accept this reform in its first stage, as our sister territory of Wyoming has done, or in the last; whether she will be a leader or a follower; for the logic of a progressive civilization leads to the inevitable result of a universal suffrage. (Stanton, Anthony, and Gage 1886, 3:713)

The issue was debated off and on for weeks. One of the strongest negative arguments was made along racial lines: if "our intelligent women" were allowed to vote, that "right might be claimed . . . [by] the poor, degraded Chinese women who might reach our shores . . . and what then would become of our proud Caucasian civilization?" (Ibid., 715) Ultimately both houses of the legislature voted against the governor's recommendation.

As the nation approached the centennial of the Declaration of Independence, Colorado leaders moved to make it the "Centennial State" by attaining statehood in 1876. By then, enough interest in women's suffrage had been aroused that an organizing meeting in Denver drew attendees from all over the territory. Rev. Mrs. Wilkes of Colorado Springs pointed out that although women owned one-third of the property in Colorado, they could not vote in an election in which men rejected a public water system, even though health authorities declared the city's water unsafe.

The territorial suffrage society elected Alida C. Avery, a Denver physician, as president, and a committee spoke to the men who were drafting the proposed constitution for the new state. Polite silence greeted the women after their speeches.

When the delegates took a vote on the issue weeks later, it failed 24 to 8. On August 1, 1876, Colorado became the 38th state without its women fully enfranchised.

STATEHOOD THROUGH THE PROGRESSIVE ERA (1876–1920)

The constitutional convention did allow suffrage to be submitted to male voters after statehood had been achieved, though, and suffragists worked hard in the 1877 statewide election. Male supporters came from Wyoming, and eastern suffrage leaders, including Susan B. Anthony and Lucy Stone, attracted crowds at rallies. Local opposition was strong, however, especially from clergymen. The Roman Catholic bishop of Denver reasoned:

> The class of women wanting suffrage are battalions of old maids disappointed in love—women separated from their husbands or divorced by men from their sacred obligations—women who, though married, wish to hold the reins of the family government, for there never was a woman happy in her home who wished for female suffrage. . . . Who will take charge of those young children (if they consent to have any) while mothers as surgeons are operating indiscriminately upon the victims of a terrible railway disaster? (Ibid., 719–721)

Although many women worked the polls throughout election day, the measure lost. Some 10,000 men voted for it, but twice that many voted against it. Women, however, did make gains in education. The fall of 1876 saw the opening of the University of Colorado, which, like those of most western states, admitted women from the beginning. In fact, at a time when northeastern states had no women at all in public universities, the first Colorado class was composed of 39 men and 27 women.

At the same time Colorado fought its last war against Native Americans. A band of Ute rebelled against federal agent Nathan Meeker, killing him and ten other men at the White River Indian Agency on September 29, 1879. They captured Arvilla Meeker and her adult daughter Josephine, as well as Flora Ellen Price and her two young children. Susan, the sister of Chief Ouray and a leader in her own right, prevented their deaths; she herself had been rescued by white soldiers at Fort Collins when Plains Native Americans were going to kill her in 1863. Her presence helped maintain peace when federal troops rescued the white women, but the conflict known as the Meeker Massacre would result in the end of what remained of Ute power.

Price and the Meekers identified 12 Ute men as the murderers, but Chief Ouray insisted that the testimony of women could not be used to convict men. After protracted negotiations Ouray and his wife, CHIPETA, went to Washington, D.C., along with other Ute men, where they signed the following agreement on March 6, 1880:

> The chiefs and headmen of the confederate bands of Utes now present . . . hereby promise and agree to procure the surrender, to the United States . . . those members of their Nation . . . who were implicated in the murder of the . . . employees in the White River Agency . . .
>
> The Southern Utes agree to remove to and settle upon the unoccupied agricultural lands on the La Plata River. . . . The White River Utes agree to . . . settle on the Uintah Reservation in Utah. (Simmons 2000, 191)

A year later all of the Utes had been moved out of their homeland, something that caused a number of writers to take pen in hand. One was HELEN HUNT JACKSON, whose *Century of Dishonor* (1881) was written from Colorado Springs.

As the frontier faded Colorado was developing a literature based on the frontier, much of it written by women. Rose Kingsley penned *South by West*; or *Winter in the Rocky Mountains and Spring in Mexico*, which was published in London in 1874. Isabella Bird (later Bishop), whose travelogue on Japan sold well, wrote *A Lady's Life in Colorado* (1879). This restless traveler stayed in Colorado longer than she did in most lands, pioneering preservation and tourism in Estes Park.

Alice Polk Hill issued *Tales of the Colorado Pioneers* in 1884. Emma Homan Thayer, who moved to Denver in 1882, wrote and illustrated beautiful books on wildflowers, but also wrote fiction, some of it set in Colorado. Patience Tucker Stapleton wrote editorials and other articles for her husband's *Rocky Mountain News* as well as magazine articles, poems, and four novels before she died at age 32. Harriet Louisa Wason of Del Norte published several volumes of poetry, beginning with *Letters from Colorado* in 1887.

Journalism was the vocation of Caroline Nichols Churchill, who began a newspaper, *The Colorado Antelope*, in 1879, the year that she moved from Canada to Denver. In 1882 she changed its name to the *Queen Bee*. A self-described eccentric, Churchill was involved in every aspect of publishing the paper. Until her 1926 death she wrote articles that supported a range of women's issues, set the type, ran the printing press, sold and distributed the copies.

The Boston-based *Atlantic* magazine ran an 1879 article about Leadville by Helen Hunt, who did not use her recently acquired surname, Jackson. The 1880 census would show Leadville to be Colorado's second-largest town, with a population of 15,000, but it still was a rough frontier. According to Hunt:

> The middle of the street was always filled with groups of men talking. Wagons were driven up and down as fast as if the street were clear. . . . Everybody was talking, nearly everybody was jesticulating [sic]. All faces looked restless, eager, fierce. It was a Monaco

gambling room emptied into a Colorado spruce clearing. (Henderson 1927, 81)

The talkative men that Hunt referred to were mostly foreign-born. Most came without women, and had to wait until they saved enough to return home or send for their wives or fiancees. Almost none married American women. For the immigrant woman, Colorado life was lonely, far from family and friends, and locked in a language understood by few of her neighbors.

Helen Hunt Jackson had only a few more years to live (she died in 1885) when she married a Denver banker and moved to Colorado in 1875; she would not be alive when Colorado suffragists reorganized in 1891. Denver women unsuccessfully tried to elect Mrs. Scott Saxon to the school board that year, prompting new discussion of the suffrage issue. Early in 1893 suffragists got a bill introduced to the legislature to put the issue on that fall's ballot. It passed the state House of Representatives 34–27 and the Senate 20–10.

In May of that year, tens of thousands of women went to the World's Fair in Chicago, Illinois, which provided an opportunity for women across the country to meet on women's issues. Denver's Ellis Meredith, who worked for *The Rocky Mountain News* while also editing the *Western Clubwoman*, was among those who attended the weeklong conference of women, and she asked the national suffrage leadership for assistance with Colorado's fall suffrage campaign. The response was not encouraging. Susan B. Anthony pointed out that the 1877 election had been disproportionately lost in the Spanish-speaking areas of the state; she replied to Meredith's request by inquiring, "Are all those Mexicans dead?" The eastern women who led the National American Woman Suffrage Association, however, reluctantly sent young Carrie Chapman Catt to help. Catt had grown up in frontier Iowa and would prove to be especially adept at winning votes from frontier men.

CLIMBING TO THE HEIGHTS

Katherine Lee Bates, a Massachusetts schoolteacher, reached the summit of Pikes Peak near Colorado Springs in 1893. Bates's ascent was part of an early tradition of adventurous women who would accomplish extraordinary feats in the West. Julia Archibald Holmes, the first woman known to have scaled Pikes Peak, had moved with her family from Massachusetts to Kansas in the late 1840s, intent on making it a free state. Her home was a stop on the Underground Railroad, and she grew up among liberals who promoted female equality. She married abolitionist James Holmes in 1857, and they passed through Colorado on their way to New Mexico.

Wearing the era's bloomers, moccasins, and a hat, she climbed the mountains in the summer of 1858 with her husband and two other men. It took them six days to reach the summit, and even though it was August, they endured several snowstorms.

I feel amply repaid for all my toil and fatigue. . . . Nearly everyone tried to discourage me . . . and now, here I am the first woman who has ever . . . gazed upon this wondrous scene.

Other women adventurers would follow in the Colorado mountaineering tradition. Addie Alexander in 1871 reached the summit of Longs Mountain, a more difficult ascent than Pikes Peak according to many observers, including William Byers, the mountain-climbing editor of *Rocky Mountain News*. Byers had reached the Longs summit three years earlier. Bates, who in 1893 climbed Pikes Peak two decades after Alexander's feat on Longs, was so moved by the view from the top that she composed the lyrics to the now popular patriotic hymn "America the Beautiful."

—Doris Weatherford

Excerpt from Janet Robertson, *The Magnificent Mountain Women: Adventures in the Colorado Rockies*. Lincoln: University of Nebraska Press, 1990.

Aside from Catt, native-born Colorado women staffed the fall campaign, a fact that worked in the women's favor. Although inexperienced, Colorado women organized well. They chose a name that deliberately omitted any reference to gender and appealed to democratic ideals by calling themselves the Equal Suffrage Association (ESA). With Martha Pease as president, they made a point of bringing working-class women into the organization, even paying "moderate salaries" to some who could not afford to donate their time. They formed a Young Woman's League and, in a prominent building where the space was donated by ELIZABETH TABOR, they filled a Denver headquarters with volunteers. Ellis Meredith and a journalist colleague, Patience Mapleton of the *Republican*, wrote campaign literature, and hundreds of women delivered 150,000 copies in house-to-house canvasses.

The few out-of-state women who did come were the kind with whom Colorado men could identify, including Wyoming's Theresa Jenkins and Leonora Barry Lake of the Knights of Labor, an association of unions supported by many miners. Catt obtained an early endorsement from the Populist party, forcing competing parties to do the same or risk alienating possible future voters. On November 3, 1893, by a vote of 35,798 to 29,451, Colorado became the third state to grant women full suffrage.

Colorado women achieved electoral success immediately following their enfranchisement. Colorado had as many as 15 functioning political parties in the 1890s, and people tended not to vote for an individual, but for an entire party slate of candidates. In addition, all parties had organized female auxiliaries; even Democrats, a minority in the state, formed 12 Democratic Women's Clubs under the leadership of suffragist Mary C. C. Bradford. Democrats nominated her for state superintendent of public instruction, but because Republicans won the election of 1894, Antoinette J. Peavy became superintendent of public instruction. Bradford, however, went on to be elected by peers as president of the National Education Association.

That was just two years after North Dakota was the first to elect a woman to statewide office. More astonishing, three Republican women— Pueblo's Carrie Clyde Holly, Denver's Clara Clessingham, and Frances S. Klock—won seats in the state legislature. They were the first female lawmakers in the nation.

Colorado women's successful strategy continued. They maintained their loyalty to each other and kept their party associations fluid. When Colorado's Republican party split in 1896 and the "main" party dissolved its women's clubs, those women moved to the "Silver Republicans" and joined a Fusion party ticket that elected Democrat Grace Espy Patton as state superintendent of public instruction. The Fusion candidates—Olive C. Butler of the National Silver party, Evangeline Heartz of the Populists, and Martha A. B. Conine, nonpartisan—won, thus displacing the Republican women in the legislature. The pattern continued in 1898, when Helen Grenfell, a Silver Republican, won the top education job and three more women joined the Colorado House of Representatives: Democrat Frances S. Lee, Populist Harriet G. R. Wright, and Dr. Mary F. Barry, a Silver Republican.

These early women in the Colorado legislature passed a number of major bills during their first six years in the legislature. The new laws included an equal guardianship act, raising the "age of consent" (the age at which a man can legally argue that a female consented to sex) from 16 to 18, and establishing a State Industrial School for Girls. Populist Evangeline Heartz was the lead sponsor of a law requiring school boards to conduct their meetings in public view, something of great importance to educators, most of whom were women. Heartz also took the lead on a workers' compensation law for railroad employees; the grateful beneficiaries rewarded her with a huge box of candy and a note saying, "The thanks of 5,000 railroad men."

By 1900 women held many positions throughout the state, including the elective office of school superintendent in 29 counties; 508 Colorado women were members of school boards, far more than in any other state. Women had been elected to the offices of county clerk, county treasurer, tax assessor, and others. Two female physicians were county coroners.

When the century turned, Colorado women had another reason to celebrate. Without any significant opposition, their right to vote, which had been merely law, became part of the state constitution in a referendum that ended the common practice of allowing male noncitizens to vote. The Equal Suffrage Association did not fold its tents after that victory, however, but continued meeting and organizing. Among the most active of these behind-the-scenes strategists were former Colorado first lady Eliza Routt and Katherine Patterson, whose husband was a U.S. senator. ESA leaders reported in 1920 that during all the years since women began voting in 1894, no bill that the ESA opposed had been enacted and all bills that it supported had passed.

The ESA also remained active to respond to falsehoods about Colorado's experience with female voters. Members sponsored testimony by male supporters, hiring them to speak in other states about Colorado's positive experience with women voting. One of these, Omar E. Garwood, was a founder of the National Men's League for Woman Suffrage.

In 1913 the Colorado Senate became the second in the nation to have a female senator, HELEN RING ROBINSON; Utah had been the first in 1910. Robinson garnered much in the suffrage movement, and during the next decade, made speeches as far away as New Hampshire and Georgia. In 1920 she represented American women at the Eighth Conference of the International Woman Suffrage Alliance in Geneva, Switzerland.

Colorado women continued to set precedents in government. They were appointed to the Civil Service Commission in this era, and a woman held the appointed office of registrar of U.S. land. Colorado's attorney general appointed

Mary Wolfe Dargin as an assistant attorney general in 1917. From 1894 to 1920 women consistently held the position of state superintendent of schools. By then women had been elected to offices in 75 cities and towns, including Denver, and a woman had been elected to a judgeship in Eagle County. Several women had been delegates to national party conventions and five had served as presidential electors, in charge of casting a state's official ballot for president in the electoral college. No other state in the nation could point to similar opportunities for and achievements of its women.

When Congress passed the 19th Amendment, granting women nationwide the right to vote, and sent it to the states for ratification, Colorado ratified it in a special session on December 8, 1919. Sen. Agnes Riddle introduced the amendment in the state Senate, while in the House its sponsors were Dr. May T. Bigelow and Miss Mable Ruth Baker. The speaker of the House called on Representative Bigelow to preside while the House, like the Senate, ratified unanimously.

1920s THROUGH WORLD WAR II ERA (1920–1950)

Colorado may have been the first state to insist that local school boards pay adequate salaries to teachers. A 1921 bill established a minimum salary of $75 a month for any teacher in the state, with steps rising to a minimum $1,200 annual salary for teachers with four-year college degrees. This was a particularly great gain for female teachers.

Women also achieved as authors. Jean Milne Gower memorialized Colorado's earliest people with her 1923 volume of poetry, *Echoes from the Cliff Dwellings*. The next year Vera Campbell published a bibliography on the subject, *Myths and Legends of Colorado* (1924). Margaret Clyde Robertson won an international prize for her 1925 ballad, "The Woman in the Wagon." A

Boston publisher issued *Colorado, the Queen Jewel of the Rockies* (1918) by Mae Lucy Baggs, while Boston's Little, Brown & Company published Courtney Ryley Cooper's *High Country* (1926). Doubleday, another prestigious publisher, issued Clarice E. Richards's memoir of "dry farming" on the plains of eastern Colorado, *A Tenderfoot Bride* (1924). During much of this era, the state's poet laureate was Nellie Burget Miller; she published her collection of regional poetry, *In Earthen Bowls*, in 1924.

The 1930s ushered in the Dust Bowl, which wiped out farm families in neighboring Kansas and Oklahoma, and also affected eastern Colorado, where wheat fields were abandoned as the wind blew topsoil away. Many Colorado families headed for the Pacific Coast region with other midwesterners. Colorado wheat sales dropped by two-thirds between 1929 and 1932, while hogs lost three-fourths of their value. In the urban economy, department store sales fell by one-third. One in every three banks in the state failed. Lifetime savings evaporated and many widows and retired women found themselves suddenly without an income or any hope of one.

As in many states Colorado voters adopted the programs of Pres. Franklin Roosevelt's New Deal as soon as they were available. The New Deal, however, assumed that men were the breadwinners and few programs existed for women. Nowhere was this more clear than in the Civilian Conservation Corps, which helped to preserve Colorado's natural resources while opening more parks and forests to users, but which was limited to young men. The Works Progress Administration alone spent $111 million in Colorado, most of it on transportation and construction of public buildings, jobs that rarely went to women.

Colorado developed one idea to cope with the Great Depression that others copied. The state was the first to employ people, many of them women, to write local history. In 1933 and 1934 the State Historical Society of Colorado proposed and managed an oral history project in which writers were paid to interview pioneers. Archivists were able to preserve not only personal histories, but also many photographs and other artifacts.

World War II finally gave women a chance to earn an independent income. Although Colorado is landlocked and its mountains make flying hazardous, its congressional delegation was powerful enough that the federal government built a half-dozen major military bases in the state. Lowry Field near Denver was established in 1937 and expanded rapidly. Within a year after the 1942 formation of the Women's Army Corps (WAC), some 400 women had graduated from the photography school at Lowry. The largest base was Camp Carson; construction began in 1942 and the first WACs arrived in May of 1943. Jobs for women ranged from teaching male cadets on aircraft simulators to rigging parachutes to launching weather balloons and more.

Even though Colorado is far from any ocean, the state's boosters got naval contracts, too. Civilian women worked on parts of ships that were completed in coastal states, and they worked in the Continental Airlines Modification Center, which refitted civilian planes for military use. Members of the Navy Nurse Corps treated wounded sailors at the Hotel Colorado in Glenwood Springs, a luxury resort turned into a wartime hospital. About 100 U.S. Navy WAVES learned Japanese at the University of Colorado; these women then worked as military interpreters. The munitions industry also hired women. The Denver Ordnance Plant that opened in 1941, for example, contracted with Remington Arms, and by 1943, 19,500 people, most of them women, worked there.

The Women's Land Army played a significant role in harvesting crops for farmers whose usual labor supply had gone to war. Other Colorado women took the lead in efforts aimed at maintaining the morale of soldiers, as Denver's USO (United Services Organization) began before the nation's did, almost a full year before the United States officially entered the war. Led by Helen R. O'Donnell, the Civilian/Military Hospitality Association, opened a recreation center in Denver early in 1941 to provide wholesome entertainment for soldiers. It became a model for the USO, and Denver soon had clubs scattered around the city, including two that were intended for women—military women, war workers, and the wives of transient men.

The American Women's Volunteer Services (AWVS) was especially popular in Colorado. Denver's AWVS was one of the nation's first, beginning months prior to U.S. involvement in the war and offering services that ranged from teaching rehabilitation classes for wounded soldiers to organizing Victory Gardens and distributing ration books, which limited purchases of scarce goods to keep prices down. The AWVS also stressed conservation and recycling of needed materials. In June 1943 alone, for example, Colorado women saved and donated 87,835 pounds of household cooking fats and oils, which could be used for explosives, as well as 30,743 pounds of nylon and silk stockings that could be used to make parachutes.

MORE PIONEER WOMEN OF COLORADO

In 1948 former Colorado state senator Eudocia Bell Smith wrote a chapter on women for a four-volume history of the state. She talked with many old timers, some of whom were children when Colorado was first settled. Many of the early settlers still relished the story of Mrs. Joseph Wolff, who was the young mother of an infant in 1859 when she came to Auraria, the larger of the two settlements that would later combine into Denver. At the time, according to Smith:

> Indians of the Cheyenne and Arapaho tribes were seen in numbers on the streets almost every day. They peered through windows and entered . . . if doors were unlocked. . . .
>
> A famous chief . . . picked out Mrs. Wolff and handing her a pumpkin, ordered her to take it to his tepee and cook it. She showed her true pioneer spirit by promptly boxing his ears, an act that made her extremely unpopular with her associates who were afraid the Indians would retaliate. Great was the relief of everybody when [a Native American woman] came calling and, in high good humor, asked to be shown the "squaw" who had the nerve to defy Spotty. She then invited Mrs. Wolff and her husband to a grand pow-wow the following day.

Smith quoted a reminiscing Mrs. Eli Ashley, who arrived in 1861, about society in those days:

> Nearly every coach from the East at this period brought wife or sweetheart who on arrival became wife, and social entertainments for them were always planned. If the entertainment was to be larger than a dinner, the hostess invited her most intimate friends to help her in the preparation of salads, cakes and ices, for few private houses in Denver knew the luxury of hired help. . . .
>
> When quarilles were danced they were mostly formed by two women and six men [who hoped] to at least touch the hands of women and, if possible, secure one as partner for a later dances [sic]. All women were belles.

Out of town, life could be lonely and frightening. Elizabeth Lewis Entriken lived alone in a log cabin in the Platte canyon at a time when the area was filled with desperados, many of them with criminal pasts and bounties on their heads. She conquered fear, according to Smith, "by putting a lighted lamp in her window and leaving her door unbolted at night."

> Regardless of the hour when some one entered, she prepared a hot meal; in the attic upstairs were two rooms with clean beds and plenty of blankets. Furtive and filthy men crept to that beacon of friendliness in the night; rough and insolent men burst in to become gentle, abashed before the cheery welcome of a motherly little woman.

Colorado's pioneer women showed courage, independence, and ingenuity in overcoming the hardships of the frontier and in developing the modern landscape of their state.

—Doris Weatherford

Excerpts from Le Roy Reuben Hafen, *Colorado: A Story of the State and Iits People.* Denver, Colo.: Old West Publishing, 1943.

Colorado also was home during the war to many Japanese American women who were interned. From Washington to California, people of Japanese ancestry—some of them from families that had lived in the United States for generations—were forced to leave the Pacific Coast for interior prison camps. Colorado's Re-Location Center was located in the Arkansas River Valley near the town of Granada. During the four years of the war, 10,324 people of Japanese ancestry were processed in the center. Most of those who stayed the entire time were women; men could gain release by joining the military.

POSTWAR AND CONTEMPORARY ERAS (1950–present)

The 1950 census revealed that the frontier's gender imbalance finally was gone, and men no longer significantly outnumbered women. Only men, however, would be the first students at the new Air Force Academy that opened in Colorado Springs in 1955. Although the air force was the most liberal of any military service in its treatment of women, the prestigious academy would be all-male until 1976, when Congress opened all of the federal government's military academies to women.

In the postwar years, Colorado women continued, though, to achieve milestones. FLORENCE SABIN was born in Central City in 1871; she went on to teach at the prestigious medical school of Johns Hopkins University in Maryland and was the first woman elected to the National Academy of Sciences. In 1959 Colorado honored Dr. Sabin with one of the two statues that each state is allowed in the U.S. Capitol. One of a few to be sculpted by a woman, it was carved by Denver sculptor Joy Buba.

Euterpe Taylor became the first female member of the Southern Ute Tribal Council in 1948, and Sunshine Smith soon followed. Martha Evenson challenged tribal use of funds in 1961 and did not back down when the male chief, Sun

TIMELINE

United States Events		Colorado Events
	1500	1541 First Spanish settlers reach edge of modern Colorado.
1620 Settlement of Plymouth Colony	1600	
1776 United States declares independence	1700	
	1800	
		1858 First sightings of gold in Cherry Creek and first white female settler arrives from Salt Lake City.
1861–65 U.S. Civil War		1862 Women begin to take out land claims under the Homestead Act.
		1873 Ute Chief Ouray and wife Chipeta make the last of their missions to Washington, D.C.
		1876 Colorado earns statehood.
		1877 University of Colorado opens; women enroll.
		1893 Colorado becomes third state to grant women full voting rights.
		1894 Antoinette Peavy elected as first female state superintendent of public instruction. Three women elected to state legislature.
	1900	1912 Colorado Senate becomes second in nation to have a female senator.
1914–18 World War I		
1920 Ratification of the 19th Amendment		
1929–39 Great Depression		
1939–45 World War II		
		1966 Virginia Blue elected state treasurer.
		1972 Patricia Schroeder elected as Colorado's first female U.S. representative.
1975 Vietnam War ends		1979 Judy Pinnecoose becomes first female elected as Ute Tribal Council chairman.
		1994 Secretary of State Vikki Buckley becomes the nation's first black Republican woman in a statewide office.
	2000	2002 Republican Marilyn Musgrave is elected U.S. representative; Democrat Diana DeGette is reelected to her fourth term in the U.S. House.

Dance, opposed her. The Tribal Council elected Judy Pinnecoose (later Knight-Frank), a 32-year-old single mother, as chairman. A decade later, the *Denver Post* ran headlines when the entire tribe chose her as chief.

Colorado women had won the elective position of superintendent of public instruction since the 1890s, but not until 1966 did a woman win another statewide office. Republican Virginia Blue would serve as state treasurer until 1970. In 1972 Mary Estill Buchanan, also a Republican, became secretary of state; she was appointed to fill a vacancy, but was elected in her own right and served for ten years.

One of the most important results of the 1972 election was Colorado's first congresswoman. Denver sent PATRICIA SCHROEDER to Washington that year and voters continued to reelect her until her retirement in 1996. Schroeder became one of the nation's most important feminist leaders of the last quarter of the 20th century. She served on the powerful House Armed Services Committee, where she helped to transform the situation of women in the U.S. military.

The highest state office yet achieved came in 1978, when Democrat Nancy Dick was elected lieutenant governor. She served two four-year terms, and in 1994 another Democrat, Gail Schoettler, was elected to that position. Republican GALE A. NORTON was elected the state's first female attorney general in 1990; her two terms ended with the 1998 election, but in 2001, Pres. George W. Bush appointed her as secretary of the interior.

In 1994 Colorado became the nation's first state to elect a black Republican woman to a statewide office. Vikki Buckley served as secretary of state until her 1999 death, when Donetta Davidson, also a Republican, was appointed to the office. Democratic attorney DIANA DEGETTE replaced Patricia Schroeder when Schroeder

Pat Schroeder at a news conference in 1993. (© Wally McNamee/Corbis)

retired in 1996. DeGette had served in the Colorado legislature, where she rewrote domestic violence laws and sponsored a bill to protect abortion clinic users from harassment. In 2002 voters sent another woman—Republican Marilyn Musgrave—to the U.S. House of Representatives and reelected DeGette to her fourth term.

Colorado women reached their greatest numbers in the state legislature with the 1998 election, when women won 35 percent of the seats. By 2003 the number had slipped slightly, but still was higher than that of most states. A national Status of Women Commission report in 2000 listed Colorado as the nation's fourth-best place for women to work. The only category in which Colorado women fell below average was in reproductive services, a reflection of a large rural population that lacked ready access to clinics.

—Doris Weatherford

PROMINENT WOMEN

MARY COYLE CHASE (1907–1981)

Journalist and playwright Mary Coyle Chase of Denver won a Pulitzer Prize for her whimsical comedy *Harvey* (1944), one of Broadway's most loved and long-running successes. The daughter of frontier prospectors, she attended public schools and the University of Denver before graduating from the University of Colorado. After seven years on the staff of the *Rocky Mountain News,* she worked as a lobbyist and radio scriptwriter; she also wrote two children's books for the Works Progress Administration, vignettes for *Ladies' Home Journal,* and 14 plays. The first of her successful Broadway plays was *Now You've Done It* (1937), directed by Antoinette Perry for whom theater's Tony Award is named.

Chase wrote *Harvey* during the tense days of World War II; the Broadway production ran for 1,775 performances. The fantasy presented a casting problem until the producer proposed making the title character a hallucination. Chase adapted *Harvey* to the screen in 1950 starring Jimmy Stewart as Elwood P. Dowd, a congenial drunk. The film became a popular classic, earning Oscars for the male and female leads, and returned to popularity in 1972 on the Hallmark Hall of Fame. Chase also succeeded with the plays *Sorority House* (1939), *Bernardine* (1952), and *Mrs. McThing* (1952), which starred Helen Hayes in its first production. Chase's manuscripts are in the archives of the Denver Public Library.

CHIPETA (1843–1924)

Chipeta was a peacemaker during the removal of the indigenous peoples of the Plains from the Midwest to Utah. A Kiowa Apache orphan, she was named Chipeta, meaning White Singing Bird, by the Ute and grew up among them at Conejos, Colorado. After she married Ouray, a compassionate negotiator and chief of the Uncompahgre Ute tribe; in 1859 she joined him in attempting to maintain peace between Native Americans and whites who had flooded into Colorado after the 1858 discovery of gold.

Chipeta accompanied Ouray on various diplomatic missions aimed at defining land claims for the Ute as white settlers encroached on their territory. Between 1862 and 1873 she journeyed to Washington, D.C., several times with Ouray and other Ute ambassadors to help negotiate treaties that were to end conflicts between the Ute and white settlers and to define Ute territorial claims to the land west of the Continental Divide. During these trips, the U.S. diplomats referred to Chipeta as the "Queen of the Utes." The final mission, in 1873, gave over claim to further lands in exchange for peace and resettlement with the U.S. Indian agencies.

Conflict continued, though, and in September 1879, belligerent braves massacred federal Indian agent Nathan C. Meeker, took his family hostage, and burned Meeker's White River Indian Agency. Chipeta organized relief for the white captives and also swam the Gunnison River to warn white pioneers of a planned attack. Chipeta journeyed west into exile with her husband, who refused to be resettled at the Uintah Reservation at Bitter Creek, Utah; she continued settlement work with the Ute. Ouray died of kidney failure in 1880 while the couple were on a peacekeeping mission to the Southern Ute Agency at Ignacio, Colorado. Chipeta promised Ouray to keep secret his burial place.

At age 40 Chipeta remarried, adopted three children, and then lived for more than 40 years in poverty. She survived the attack of a white posse in 1887, when vigilantes stole her sheep and goats, shot a Native American boy, and burned her lodge. In her last days, she divulged the location of Ouray's remains so the couple could be reunited in death. In 1956 the Ute Museum in Montrose was built near her grave.

SARAH PLATT DECKER (dates unknown)

Before and after women won the vote, Sarah Platt Decker supported the evolving role of women in politics. Well educated and traveled, she founded the Denver Woman's Club in 1894 and was national president of the General Federation of Women's Clubs from 1904 to 1908. Although she had no direct experience with working-class problems, in 1905 she joined representatives from the Women's Trade Union League and the Association of Social Settlements in demanding an investigation into workplace conditions for women in U.S. factories.

In 1913 Platt published a broadside for the National American Woman Suffrage Association answering questions about women's rights and the voting record of Colorado women. She also served on the Colorado State Board of Charities and Corrections and compiled stories of settlers in Durango, Silverton, Ouray, and Telluride in the four-volume *Pioneers of the San Juan Country,* which was published in 1961. A city park, a branch of the Denver Public Library, a chapter of the Daughters of the American Revolution, and a scholarship for needy undergraduates at the University of Colorado bear her name.

DIANA DEGETTE (1957–)

Within six years, attorney Diana DeGette Lipinsky advanced from freshman member of the U.S. House of Representatives to at-large whip. Born in Tachikawa, Japan, she attended Denver public schools and earned a bachelor's degree from Colorado College in 1979. After graduating from the law school of New York University in 1982, she specialized in cases of employment and

civil rights. She worked as deputy public defender and served two terms in the Colorado House of Representatives. Denver voters elected her in 1996 to the congressional seat formerly held by Patricia Schroeder.

DeGette involved herself in diverse projects, including delayed medals for a World War II hero, action against the tobacco industry, investigation of the collapse of the company Enron, improvements to race relations and to children's health programs, and an increase in loans for first-time minority homeowners. In 2000 she earned plaudits from the Juvenile Diabetes Research Foundation for sponsoring legislation to boost funding for medical research by over 60% on juvenile diabetes. In 2002 DeGette was elected to her fourth term in the House.

LAURA GILPIN (1891–1979)

Photographer Laura Gilpin of Colorado Springs earned renown for documenting in black-and-white pictures the indigenous culture and desert landscape of Mesa Verde. Educated at the Baldwin School, Rosemary Hall School, and Clarence White School in New York, she developed a professional interest in photography in 1915. At age 27, she began postgraduate study of photogravure, which imparted a classical elegance, grace, and compassion to her style of portraiture.

Gilpin began a 60-year career making artistic autochrome and platinum prints of people and ancient ruins. Her institutional clients included the Denver Opera House and Boeing Aircraft. During the Great Depression, while she earned a living operating a turkey farm and producing postcards and lantern slides, Gilpin shifted to analysis of Navaho and Pueblo society and environment through the camera's eye. In 1930 she featured Canyon de Chelly during an 11-year study of the Santa Fe tribe. Her candid shots detailed disappearing lifestyles and 20th-century alterations to the land. She compiled notable picture collections, including *Rio Grande Country* (1950) and *The Enduring Navaho* (1968). Her precise images earned an International Salon medal, a Photographic Society of America citation, Western Heritage and Southwest Library Association awards, a Guggenheim Fellowship, and commendation from the United States Department of the Interior.

EDITH BANFIELD JACKSON (1895–1977)
Pediatrician Edith Banfield Jackson blended clinical skill with compassion for the welfare of parent and child. Her mother, a wealthy, educated mother of six, committed suicide when Edith was four years old. After graduating from Vassar in 1916 and Johns Hopkins School of Medicine in 1921, Edith began a six-year training analysis with Viennese neurologist Sigmund Freud in 1930 and also studied child psychiatry with Anna Freud.

At age 41, Jackson joined the departments of pediatrics and psychiatry at Yale, where she taught preventive pediatrics for 23 years. She developed a specialty in the emotional needs of young parents. In the 1940s she directed the Department of Pediatrics at Yale New Haven Hospital. Because of her holistic treatment of family health, she helped to establish the importance of pediatrics in the lives of young children. She wrote articles on achievements in child psychiatry for the *Psychoanalytic Quarterly* and in 1947 joined the editorial staff of *The Psychoanalytic Study of the Child.* For her contributions to family-oriented maternity and neonatal care and to rooming-in and bonding of mother and infant, she won awards from the American Academy of Pediatrics and the American Psychiatric Association. Her papers are in the archives of the John Hay Whitney Medical Library at Yale University. The Edith B. Jackson Child Care Program in New Haven, Connecticut, preserves her name and influence.

HELEN HUNT JACKSON (1830–1885)
Author Helen Maria Fiske Hunt Jackson was a native of Amherst, Massachusetts, and a close friend of poet Emily Dickinson. She married army officer Edward Hunt when she was 20, but lost her entire family—her husband and two children—by the time she was 35. Financially and emotionally drained, she began writing in an attempt to retain her sanity.

Encouraged by critic Thomas Higginson, Hunt soon was writing for respected magazines; Ralph Waldo Emerson proclaimed her poetry the best by an American woman. Like other women, she often used pseudonyms, including male ones.

Hunt went to Colorado in 1873 and soon married businessman William Jackson; they settled in Colorado Springs. The region's Native Americans were in desperate condition, and an 1879 tour by Ponca Chief Standing Bear—interpreted by Nebraska's Susette La Flesche—drew Jackson's attention. After careful research based on Americana files in New York's Astor Library, she published *Century of Dishonor* (1881). Its criticism of the Bureau of Indian Affairs earned enough attention and respect in Washington, D.C., that the Interior Department commissioned Jackson to report on California's Native Americans.

She intended her novel, *Ramona* (1884), to be a catalyst for this cause in the same way that Harriet Beecher Stowe's *Uncle Tom's Cabin* (1852) energized the antislavery cause. Although Jackson died the year following its publication, *Ramona* has gone through more than 300 printings and has been the basis of three films. Featuring a Cahuilla Indian in the San Jacinto Mountains, it is performed as an annual outdoor pageant in Hemet, California.

FRANCES JACOBS (1843–1892)
Colorado's "mother of charities," Frances Wisebart Jacobs of Harrodsburg, Kentucky,

founded Colorado's Community Chest and established care for tubercular patients in Denver. The daughter of Jewish emigrants from Bavaria, she settled in Colorado in 1865, joined her husband in operating a clothing store, and cofounded the Denver Hebrew Benevolent Ladies Society to aid the poor. In 1887 she represented Jewish citizens in an ecumenical drive to initiate the Charity Organization Society, a forerunner of the United Way.

The focus of Jacobs's volunteerism was the rescue of homeless tuberculosis patients, who were sheltered in the city jail because there was no local sanitarium. Allied with Rabbi William Sterne Friedman of Temple Emanu-el, Jacobs helped incorporate Denver's Jewish Hospital Association and began planning a free, nonsectarian center for treatment of tuberculosis. The staff set up a multidisciplinary regimen of counseling, recreation, rehabilitation, and occupational training. Before the hospital was completed, Jacobs died at age 49 from an infection she contracted while making home visits to the sick. Founders named the hospital for her and Colorado developed a reputation for tuberculosis rehabilitation. Commemorating her courage and generosity are a stained-glass portrait window in the state Capitol rotunda, a city park, and the Frances Wisebart Jacobs award for community volunteerism.

GALE A. NORTON (1954–)

Politician Gale Ann Norton of Wichita, Kansas, became the first woman appointed as U.S. secretary of the interior. Reared in Colorado, she hiked in the Rocky Mountains and learned to ski in her youth. In 1975 she graduated from the University of Denver and earned a law degree there in 1978. After beginning legal work as clerk to the Colorado court of appeals, she directed her alma mater's program in transportation law.

Norton earned admiration from conservatives for public stands against liberalism. At age 25, she served the Mountain States Legal Foundation as lead counsel and advocated free-market logging, mining, and exploration for fuel on protected lands. In 1983 she studied relaxed air pollution regulation at the Hoover Institution. Two years later, she began two years' service to the Department of the Interior, supervising 500 million acres of public lands. To the astonishment of the public, she delivered a diatribe against a wheelchair ramp at the state Capitol. In 1990 she was elected to the first of two terms as state attorney general. In 1996, she ran for a U.S. Senate seat, but was defeated in the primaries.

In 2001 Pres. George W. Bush nominated Norton to be the nation's first female secretary of the interior. Although opposed by the Sierra Club and the National Association for the Advancement of Colored People, she won the appointment and pursued an agenda of more state and local control of forests and waterways, including a system that allowed self-auditing in lieu of federal regulation. In 2002 she approved 15 new National Recreation Trails, but halted the grizzly bear recovery program in the Bitterroot wilderness of Idaho and Montana.

HELEN RING ROBINSON (?–1923)

Politician Helen Ring Robinson of Denver was the first woman elected to the Colorado Senate and the second female state senator in the nation. She supported women's suffrage and gained the backing of female activists by familiarizing herself with women's needs. During two consecutive terms in the state Senate, which began in 1912 and ended in 1916, she wrote a minimum wage law for women and proposed the acceptance of women on juries, a bill that failed.

Robinson made an impact locally and nationally. She encouraged and applauded the cooperation between immigrant workers from many nations while they participated in the lethal coal mine strike at Ludlow in 1914. During World War I she lectured for the National Food Administration and served on a naval commission. In 1920 she came into verbal conflict with Molly Brown, a socialite, fellow Denverite, and political rival for Robinson's Senate seat. Brown accused Robinson of mishandling charitable donations—accusations that caused a stir but proved to be unfounded.

JOSEPHINE ROCHE (1886–1976)

A progressive and a humanitarian, Josephine "Josie" Aspinwall Roche of Neligh, Nebraska, promoted fairness and decent work conditions for those working in the coal-mining industry. After she graduated from Vassar College and Columbia University with a master's degree in sociology, she worked in settlement houses in New York City. In 1910 she moved to Denver and became the nation's first female officer to walk a police beat. During World War I, she accepted appointment by Pres. Woodrow Wilson to direct the Foreign Language Education Service and to serve as a federal publicist on the Committee on Public Information.

Roche gave up a subsequent job as spokesperson for juveniles in Denver courts to preside over the Rocky Mountain Fuel Company, which she inherited in 1927 from her father, John J. Roche. As a manager, Josephine Roche irked fellow mine owners by facilitating the organization of her workers in the United Mine Workers of America. Her employees reciprocated by accepting half-pay during an economic downturn when coal profits fell.

Roche, who became an outspoken champion of laborers, chastised John D. Rockefeller for inhumane labor practices and publicized her pro-labor, antiexploitation philosophy during an unsuccessful run for the governor's office in 1934. She contributed to the National Bituminous Coal Code and served on the Bituminous Coal Authority. In 1932 contented miners carried signs in a Labor Day procession urging "Buy Josie's Coal." Two years later, Pres. Franklin D. Roosevelt appointed her to the U.S. Treasury Department as assistant secretary and named her the director of the U.S. Health Service and a member of the National Youth Administration. She also chaired the Coordinated Health and Welfare Activities Board and the National Consumers' League and promoted the concept of social security. After age 60, she reported on European coal mining for the *New York Herald Tribune*.

FLORENCE SABIN (1871–1953)

A scholarly leader in the study of anatomy and public welfare, Dr. Florence Rena Sabin of Central City, Colorado, investigated the origin of the lymphatic system and the behavior of the immune system; she also worked to improve her state's public health and welfare. After completing a degree from Massachusetts's Smith College in 1893, she became the first female graduate of Johns Hopkins Medical School, where she interned and compiled *An Atlas of the Medulla and Midbrain* (1901). At age 31, she joined the school's staff as a teacher of anatomy and was the first woman to become full professor at the medical school there.

Dr. Sabin published *The Origin and Development of the Lymphatic System* (1916) and advanced in 1917 to professor of histology, the study of microscopic elements of tissues. In 1924 she became the first woman to preside over the American Association of Anatomists in 1925, and she became the first female lifetime member of the National Academy of Sciences.

In 1925, at the Rockefeller Institute for Medical Research, Sabin supervised the department of cellular studies, where, for the National Tuberculosis Association, she explored the connections between infection and the development of the brain and lymphatic and circulatory systems. After retirement in 1938, she began caring for her ailing sister Mary. In 1944 Dr. Florence Sabin chaired a Colorado gubernatorial health commission, which upgraded public health statutes. Sabin's name survives in the Sabin Arthritis Award given annually to a woman dedicated to health issues. A bronze monument in the Capitol's National Statuary Hall in Washington, D.C., recognizes Dr. Sabin as the "first lady of American science."

PATRICIA SCHROEDER (1940–)

A respected congresswoman and feminist, Patricia Scott Schroeder of Portland, Oregon, was the first Colorado female to serve in Congress. She was a 1961 Phi Beta Kappa graduate of the University of Minnesota and a 1964 graduate of Harvard Law School, where she met and married her husband, James Schroeder. She moved with her husband to Denver after earning her law degree and practiced law for the National Labor Relations Board. In the late 1960s, she shifted to teaching law courses in Colorado, providing legal counsel to Planned Parenthood, and serving as a hearing officer for the Colorado Department of Personnel.

At age 33, Schroeder began a 24-year political career promoting environmental, family, women's, and children's issues, and challenging the Vietnam War and waste in the Pentagon. In 1972 state voters elected her as Colorado's first woman member of the U.S. House of Representatives. While serving on the Armed Services Committee, she alarmed entrenched interests by disclosing mismanagement of funds and the dissemination of misinformation to the public. She supported greater opportunity for women in the military, federal funding of abortions for poor women, child-abuse centers, and Head Start programs and championed gender equity in worker pay and social security. Among her triumphs were

additional screening for breast and cervical cancer, stronger laws against rapists and abusers of women, and the establishment of a national database of pedophiles. In 1987, after an initial campaign, she chose not to run for the presidency. She remained in Congress until her retirement in 1996, having enjoyed one of the longest careers of any woman in the U.S. Congress. She became president of the Association of American Publishers in 1997.

ELIZABETH (BABY DOE) TABOR (1854–1935)

The Silver Queen of the West, Elizabeth Bonduel McCourt Doe Tabor of Oshkosh, Wisconsin, earned widespread disapproval as the second and much younger wife of a millionaire. After divorcing her first husband, Harvey Doe, in 1880, she began an affair with a divorced silver magnate, Horace A. W. Tabor, owner of the Matchless Mine, mayor of Leadville, Colorado, and lieutenant governor of the state. After several years of vitriolic legal battles between Tabor and his first wife, in March 1883 he married Elizabeth. Wed in Washington, D.C., at an elegant ceremony celebrated at the Willard Hotel, Elizabeth was admired for her blue eyes and blond sausage curls, which complemented designer clothes and diamonds. Among the guests at the reception was Pres. Chester A. Arthur.

After Horace Tabor lost his wealth in the panic of 1893, he survived as a day laborer and Denver's postmaster until 1899. On her husband's advice, Elizabeth retained ownership of the mine for 36 years and lived in a cabin on the mining company's land. While trying to work the mine, she lived on credit and died a penniless hermit. Local people discovered her frozen remains in her cabin amid stacks of old newspapers. In 1956 librettist Douglas Moore produced an opera on the Tabor romance, *The Ballad of Baby Doe* (1956). Her wedding gown survives in Denver at the State Historical Society.

MILDRED PITTS WALTER (1922–)

Denver-based children's author and activist Mildred Pitts Walter of Sweetville, Louisiana, entertained and stimulated young readers with characters who were not afraid of growth and change. She became the first in her family to attend college, working her way through school to compete a bachelor's degree in education from Southern University in Baton Rouge in 1944. She taught elementary school for 18 years in the Los Angeles system. During the 1970s she worked for civil rights for the Congress of Racial Equality.

After reviewing lackluster children's books for the *Los Angeles Times* and noting the paucity of children's books with African American themes and characters, Pitts decided to write for youngsters. To add realism to her writing, she revisited the 1957 racial clash at Little Rock's Central High School in *The Girl on the Outside* (1982). Pitts was awarded an Irma Simonton Black second place award for *Ty's One-Man Bank* (1980) and Parents' Choice and Coretta Scott King awards for *Because We Are* (1984).

In her later years, Pitts moved to Denver where she established with two colleagues, Shirley Sims and Hazel Whitsett, Denver's Northeast Women's Center, an organization that supports women's social, political, and economic advancement. Her numerous honors include a Christopher Award, Carter G. Woodson award, and Virginia Library Association Jefferson Cup. She has donated her collected papers to the University of Minnesota.

—Mary Ellen Snodgrass

PROMINENT SITES

Aurora History Museum
15001 East Alameda Drive
Aurora, CO 80012
Telephone: (303) 739 6660
Web: http://www.ci.aurora.co.us/index.cfm
This museum's collection focuses on local artifacts, which are displayed in the permanent *Portrait of Aurora* exhibit. The artifacts include aprons, "girls and boys" toys dating from the 1920s, quilts, and women's clothing. An archive contains papers on women who have lived in Aurora. An annual program in March, "Aurora Women; Sculptors of Our Community," is coproduced with Aurora Women's Organization.

Cady Building Walking Tour of Salida
Web: http://www.peaksnewsnet.com/walking
This walking tour has been developed to teach visitors about Salida's origins and history. Egbert and Lena Wheeler erected the building at 139-141 F Street in 1888 as Gambles Hardware. When Egbert died, Lena continued to run the hardware store in the 1890s. Although the building has had about five owners over the years, it is still and has always been a hardware store. A walking tour booklet is available online.

Colorado History Museum and Colorado Historical Society
1300 Broadway
Denver, CO 80203
Telephone: (303) 866 3682
Web: http://www.coloradohistory.org/default.htm
The Historical Society has several exhibits pertaining to women. A trunk on display belonged to Irma Dantels, who died in 1901 at the age of 12. It came to the museum unopened and offers a glimpse into a girl's life in the late 19th century. Women represented in the Colorado timeline include Florence Sabin, Josephine Roche, Molly Brown, and Baby Doe Tabor, as well as innovative educator Emily Griffith.

Dr. Justine Ford House/Black American West Museum and Heritage Center
3091 California Street
Denver, CO 80205
Telephone: (303) 292 2566
Web: http://www.theblackmarket.com/ProfilesInBlack/BAWMH.htm
This house was both home and office to the first African American woman doctor in the state of Colorado. Dr. Justine Ford (1871–1952) specialized in gynecology, obstetrics, and pediatrics.

Molly Brown House Museum
1340 Pennsylvania Street
Denver, CO 80203
Telephone: (303) 832 4092
Web: http://www.mollybrown.org
Margaret "Maggie" Tobin Brown is remembered as the Unsinkable Molly Brown because she survived the sinking of the *Titanic*. She was a member of society, not just in Denver but all over the world, and wild stories about her past and rise to wealth circulated—unchecked by her. She and her husband were the second owners of this home that was built in 1890, and she kept it until her death in 1932.

Littleton Historical Museum
6028 South Galley Street
Littleton, CO 80120
Telephone: (303) 795 3950
Web: http://www.littletongov.org/museum
The museum complex features a 1860s living history farm, an 1890s turn-of-the-century living history farm, and Littleton's first schoolhouse. Interpreters are located at all the sites to show visitors what life was like for women and other members of the community in Littleton's past.

Ute Indian Museum
17253 Chipeta Drive
Montrose, CO 81401
Telephone: (970) 249 3098
Web: http://www.coloradohistory.org/hist_sites/UteIndian/Ute_indian.htm
The museum is located on what was Chief Ouray and his wife Chipeta's homestead. Visitors can see Chipeta's crypt and a large collection of Ute artifacts. The museum teaches visitors about the daily lives of the Ute.

Walking Tour of Buena Vista, Colorado
Web: http://www.peaksnewsnet.com/bvwalking/author.html

The walking tour features several places related to women's history. Number 15, the Palace Manor, was the home of Elizabeth "Cockeyed Liz" Sturgeon. She was a madam who gave up her brothel to marry "Foozie" Enderline. Number 3, the Wedge Building, or Flatiron, is said to have been the first building built as a business in Buena Vista. In the 1890s it was Anna Calder's Milliners Shop. A walking tour booklet is available online.

Wings Over the Rockies Air and Space Museum
7711 Academy Boulevard
New Lowry Community Hanger #1
Denver, CO 80230
Telephone: (303) 360 5360
One of the permanent exhibits is *Dresses for Duty*, which displays female military uniforms from the Civil War to Desert Storm.

RESOURCES

FURTHER READING

HISTORY

Bakken, Gordon Morris, and Brenda Farrington. *The Gendered West*. New York: Garland, 2001.

Bradford, Mary C. *Equal Suffrage in Colorado from 1893 to 1908*. Denver: Colorado Equal Suffrage Association, 1912.

Butler, Anne M. *Daughters of Joy, Sisters of Mercy: Prostitutes in the American West, 1865–90*. Urbana: University of Illinois Press, 1985.

Clyne, Rick J. *Coal People: Life in Southern Colorado Company Towns, 1890–1930*. Denver: Colorado Historical Society, 1999.

Deutsch, Sarah. *No Separate Refuge: Culture, Class and Gender on an Anglo-Hispanic Frontier in the American Southwest*. New York: Oxford University Press, 1987.

Ellis, Amanda M. *The Strange, Uncertain Years: An Informal Account of Life in Six Colorado Communities*. Hamden, Conn.: Shoe String Press, 1959.

Fetter, Rosemary, and Marcia Goldstein. *Colorado Suffrage Centennial: Celebrating 100 Years of Colorado Women Making History*. Denver: Colorado Committee for Women's History, 1993.

Hafen, LeRoy Reuben. *Colorado and Its People*. 4 vols. New York: Lewis Historical Publishing, 1948.

Henderson, Junius, ed. *Colorado: Short Studies of Its Past and Present*. 1927. Reprint, St. Clair Shores, Mich.: Scholarly Press, 1971.

Jameson, Elizabeth. *All That Glitters: Class, Conflict, and Community in Cripple Creek*. Urbana: University of Illinois Press, 1998.

Jones-Eddy, Julie. *Homesteading Women: An Oral History of Colorado, 1890–1950*. New York: Twayne Publishers, 1992.

Paul, Rodman Wilson. *Mining Frontiers of the Far West, 1848–1880*. Rev. ed. Albuquerque: University of New Mexico Press, 2001.

Robertson, Janet. *The Magnificent Mountain Women: Adventures in the Colorado Rockies*. Lincoln: University of Nebraska Press, 1990.

Simmons, Virginia McConnell. *The Ute Indians of Utah, Colorado and New Mexico*. Niwot: University Press of Colorado, 2000.

Stanton, Elizabeth Cady, Susan B. Anthony, and Matilda Joslyn Gage. *History of Woman Suffrage*. Vols. 2–3. Rochester, N.Y.: Charles Mann Printing, 1886.

Uchill, Ida Libert. *Pioneers, Peddlers, and Tsadikim: The Story of Jews in Colorado*. Denver, Colo.: Sage Books, 1957.

Wyckoff, William. *Creating Colorado: The Making of a Western American Landscape, 1860–1940*. New Haven, Conn.: Yale University Press, 1999.

Young, Richard K. *The Ute Indians of Colorado in the Twentieth Century*. Norman: University of Oklahoma Press, 1997.

BIOGRAPHY AND AUTOBIOGRAPHY

Alderson, Nannie, and Helena Huntington Smith. *A Bride Goes West*. Lincoln: University of Nebraska Press, 1969.

Babb, Sanora. *An Owl on Every Post*. Albuquerque: University of New Mexico Press, 1994.

Backus, Harriet Fish. *Tomboy Bride*. Boulder: Pruett Publishing, 1969.

Bluemel, Elinor. *Florence Sabin; Colorado Woman of the Century*. Boulder: University of Colorado Press, 1959.

Bluemel, Elinor. *Opportunity School and Emily Griffith, Its Founder*. Denver, Colo.: Green Mountain Press, 1970.

Brown, Margaret Duncan. *Shepherdess of Elk River Valley*. Denver, Colo.: Golden Bell Press, 1967.

Bruÿn, Kathleen. *"Aunt" Clara Brown: Story of a Black Pioneer*. Boulder, Colo.: Pruett Publishing, 1970.

Burke, John. *The Legend of Baby Doe: The Life and Times of the Silver Queen of the West*. Lincoln: University of Nebraska Press, 1989.

Collins, Catharine Wever. *An Army Wife Comes West: Letters of Catharine Wever Collins, 1863–1864*. Denver: State Historical Society of Colorado, 1954.

Cornell, Virginia. *Doc Susie: The True Story of a Country Physician in the Colorado Rockies*. Carpinteria, Calif.: Manifest Publications, 1991.

Ellis, Anne. *The Life of an Ordinary Woman*. 1929. Reprint, Boston: Houghton Mifflin, 1999.

Goldberg, Jonathan. "Photographic Relations: Laura Gilpin, Willa Cather." *American Literature* 70 (March 1998):63–95.

Halaas, David Fridtjof. "Baby Doe Tabor." *Colorado History NOW*, October 1999.

Houston, Tracy. "The Remarkable Ms. Roche." *Denver Business Journal,* 12 November, 1999, 26.

Jones, Rebecca. "100 Women of Influence." *Rocky Mountain News,* 8 November 1993.

Mathes, Valerie Sherer. *Helen Hunt Jackson and Her Indian Reform Legacy.* Norman: University of Oklahoma Press, 1997.

Schroeder, Pat. *24 Years of House Work . . . And the Place Is Still a Mess: My Life in Politics.* Kansas City, Mo.: Andrews McMeel Publishing, 1998.

Whitaker, Rosemary. *Helen Hunt Jackson.* Boise, Idaho: Boise State University, 1987.

Wolf, Mark. "Women of Consequence: The Colorado Women's Hall of Fame." *Rocky Mountain News,* 3 November 1999.

USEFUL WEB SITES

Colorado Women's Agenda
  http://www.womensagenda.org
Colorado Women's Hall of Fame
  http://www.cogreatwomen.org
"Statement of Miss Josephine Roche, Assistant Secretary of the Treasury, on the Economic Security Act"
  http://www.ssa.gov/history/pdf/s35roche.pdf

SELECTED ORGANIZATIONS AND INSTITUTIONS

Colorado Women's Agenda
1420 Ogden Street
Denver, CO 80218
Telephone: (303) 863 7336
Web: http://www.womensagenda.org
A network promoting a broad range of issues for women, including economic security, social justice, and political power.

Center for Women's Studies
University of Colorado–Colorado Springs
1420 Austin Bluffs Parkway, Box 7150
Colorado Springs, CO 80918–3733
Telephone: (719) 262 4139
Web: http://web.uccs.edu/wmst
An interdisciplinary program that encourages the study of women and gender across the curriculum.

Colorado College Women's Studies Program
14E Cache La Poudre, Room 132
Armstrong Hall
Colorado Springs, CO 80903
Telephone: (719) 389 6976
Web: http://www2.coloradocollege.edu/dept/WS/Welcome.html
This program examines theories about and attitudes toward women and gender, working to understand ways in which a more equitable society can be achieved.

Colorado State Archives
1313 Sherman Street, Room 1B-20
Denver, CO 80203
Telephone: (303) 866 2358
Web: http://www.archives.state.co.us
A legal repository for selected historical and contemporary records and information from statewide resources and local governments in Colorado.

Metropolitan State College of Denver Institute for Women's Studies and Services
Campus Box 36
PO Box 173362
Denver, CO 80217–3362
Telephone: (303) 556 8441
Web: http://www.mscd.edu/~women
The institute combines a multidisciplinary major and minor academic program in women's studies with a variety of services for women, including direct support and community outreach.

University of Colorado–Boulder
Women's Studies Program
Campus Box 246
Boulder, CO 80309–0246
Telephone: (303) 492 8923
Web: http://www.colorado.edu/UCB/AcademicAffairs/ArtsSciences/WomenStudies
An interdisciplinary program in women's studies that examines women's lives in both U.S. and international contexts. Its theoretical foundations are rooted in a full range of fields such as anthropology, history, literature, sociology, and psychology.

Women's Studies Program
University of Denver
2000 East Asbury
Sturm Hall North, Room 419
Denver, CO 80208
Telephone: (303) 871 4419
Web: http://www.du.edu/wstu
An undergraduate program offering courses in a variety of disciplines that evaluate perceptions of women's lives in light of the most recent feminist scholarship.

CONNECTICUT

When I asked her once what she missed most about Italy, she said,
"Nothing! The streets smelled like mule poop."
. . .When I put the same question to Babbo, he thought a minute before he said, "Sunlight."
We lived in New Haven, where the murky green harbor smelled like raw mussels,
and the sky, above the giant oil tanks that squatted onshore, seemed perpetually gray.
—Rita Ciresi, *Sometimes I Dream in Italian*, 2000

Connecticut was one of the few states whose legislature never passed a major suffrage bill. It ratified the federal amendment that allowed women to vote only after other states had made that moot. The state's recent history, however, has been more progressive in terms of women's rights. Connecticut has had far more women in high offices than most states of its size and was the first state to elect a female governor whose husband had not preceded her in the office.

PREHISTORY
(Prehistory–1614)

Archaeologists in western Connecticut have found many prehistoric items nearly 3,500 years old, as well as some flint chips believed to date to more than 12,000 years ago. The presence of flint indicates fire-building ability, and Native Americans also left stone tools, including sharpened knives and scrapers. It seems likely that women used these items, but it is impossible to say much about their lives.

Population estimates when whites arrived in the early 1600s range from a low of 6,000 to a high of 20,000. The best-known tribes were the Tunxis in the west; the Podunks in the Connecticut River Valley; and in the southeast, the Pequot. A large number of smaller, scattered tribes, which were called the Connecticut by most whites, lived in the area. All lived in terror of the New York Mohawk and the Rhode Island Narragansett.

Whites learned to look on native Connecticut peoples as weak. Historian Alexander Johnston

wrote, "[T]he Indian rule, that all work is to be done by the women, was enforced in its full rigor; but the correlative virtue of prowess in war was not so prominent in the men, who were rather prone to shout at a distance than to expose their lives to the hazards of battle."

State Population (2000): 3,405,565
Female Population (2000): 1,756,246
Women in State Legislature (2003): 29.4%
Female College Enrollment (1999): 89,000 (56.7% of total)
Privately Held Women-owned Businesses (1997): 72,393
First Year of Full Suffrage: 1920

(Johnston 1887, 27) This disinclination toward warfare proved their downfall, because the Puritans who settled Connecticut were not pacifists.

WHITE EXPLORATION TO THE AMERICAN REVOLUTION
(1614–1776)

The first European in Connecticut probably was Dutchman Adriaen Blok (or Adrian Block), who

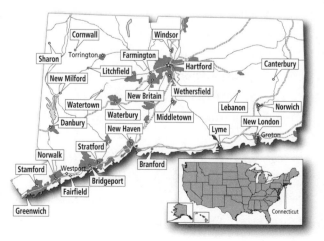

explored the north shore of Long Island Sound in 1614. By 1618 Dutch traders had settled in New Jersey, and two years after that, the Pilgrims landed at Plymouth. The Bay Colony was a theocracy uninterested in international trade, but the Dutch, in contrast, were eager businesspeople. By 1633 they had a trading post at what would later become Windsor, Connecticut, which the Dutch would manage to hold until 1654, shortly before their New Netherland colony fell to the English and became New York. This handful of Hollanders usually is forgotten in the history of Connecticut, which commonly begins with English families from Massachusetts.

The Massachusetts general court heard requests from Watertown residents to be allowed to move to Connecticut in 1634, but permission was denied. According to George L. Clark's *History of Connecticut*, ten "householders and planters" ignored that ruling and went down the Connecticut River to settle in Wethersfield, probably in the autumn of 1634. (Clark 1914, 11) The next year, in October, about 60 other Massachusetts residents, including women, went overland to Hartford.

Like settlers from Plymouth to Cincinnati, these people led their families into a wilderness at the beginning of winter. Cargo boats were trapped in ice when the Connecticut River froze in mid-November, and some would-be settlers "struggled through the snow and ice" to get back to Boston. Others hung on, surviving on "ground nuts and acorns dug from under the snow." (Johnston 1887, 24) In the warmth of the next June, dissident clergyman Thomas Hooker led most of his congregation to Hartford. Many histories date Connecticut from Hooker's 1636 arrival, and he often is considered the state's founder, even though he arrived later than others.

By 1637 approximately 800 whites resided in the area; almost all were families from Dorchester, Watertown, and Newtown (later Cambridge), Massachusetts. The Pequots, angry about this land-taking, began attacking isolated families that spring. Old histories offer various numbers of white fatalities, but all say there were fewer than a dozen, including from one to three women. The Pequots also captured two girls (whose names were not recorded by historians) and held them for ransom—a customary practice both in intertribal warfare and with colonists from Florida to New Mexico.

Tensions between whites and the Pequots came to a head in 1636, with the murder of a trader, John Oldham. The following spring, the first act of the colony's legislative body was to declare the "Pequot War." On May 28, 1637, Puritans attacked the major Pequot stronghold at Mystic. Only about 80 Pequot women survived; they were dispersed around the colonies—some sold as slaves in Massachusetts, some "given" to other tribes.

The second act of the Connecticut colony's leadership was to write a constitution. On January 14, 1639, men from Hartford, Wethersfield, and Windsor adopted what is often termed the world's first constitution. Nonetheless, the colony remained much more a theocracy than a democracy as, for example, church attendance was mandatory. In addition, 11 of 12 capital crimes enumerated in the 1642 legal code were based on specific biblical commands, and citizens could be executed for idolatry and blasphemy.

Other capital crimes included adultery and witchcraft. Alse Young of Windsor was indicted as a witch in 1647; she was hanged the following year. The town of Windsor also executed both John and Joane Carrington in 1651. The 1650s also saw the hanging of "Goody" Bassett in Stratford and Goodwife Knapp in Fairfield, among others. Historian Mary Jeanne Anderson Jones writes of Windsor's Lydea Gilburt, who "was found guilty . . . of conspiring with the devil to cause the death of Henry Stiles, whom Thomas

Allyn had accidentally shot." (Jones 1968, 105) Between 1647 and 1738, Connecticut executed 37 so-called witches, mostly women.

Women in 17th-century Connecticut were voiceless in both church and state, and divorce was nearly impossible. For example, despite being a member of the powerful Winthrop family, Elizabeth Feake could not sever her marriage, even though her husband had been declared legally insane. When she and William Hallet attempted to marry without court permission in 1647, they were charged with the capital crime of adultery. A decade later, however, Saybrook's Robert Wade was allowed to divorce Joan Wade because "she had refused to live with him either in Connecticut or in England for almost fifteen years." (Ibid., 118)

Colonial women did have more property rights than women would have in later years. Susannah Hooker, for instance, was the executor of her husband's estate when he died in 1647. After suing to stop slanders against herself and her late husband, she married William Goodwin, one of the 1635 settlers. Margaret Lake received a major land grant in the New London area. She came from England as a widow in 1635, but stayed in the more-populated Massachusetts; her daughter, Hannah Lake Gallup, took over the land in 1643. A third notable pioneer was Lady Alice Boteler of Old Saybrook, who continued to use that name even after marrying Col. George Fenwick. She died after bearing a daughter in 1645.

Religious conservatism increased as the century continued, and Connecticut's Puritans had no tolerance even for other forms of Protestantism. For example, they did not allow Massachusetts dissident Ann Hutchinson to stay when Puritans banished her there in 1642; she moved on to New York and would later die there. Part of the clergy's objection to Hutchinson was her popularity with men as well as women, and some of her followers had refused to participate in the Pequot War.

When the first adherents of the new Society of Friends, commonly called Quakers, appeared in the 1650s, they were not welcomed by Connecticut Puritans. New Haven banned them with such zeal that Quaker preacher Mary Dyer found no sanctuary in Connecticut. She returned to Boston, where she was executed.

One salient difference between the Quakers and the Puritans was their attitude toward Native Americans. Puritans generally believed that Native Americans were akin to animals without souls, and Connecticut's first attempt to Christianize them did not begin until 1657. King Philip's War of 1675 disrupted what little effort had been made, and at its end surviving Native Americans finally settled on the Housatonic River. Called Schaghticoke, they would remain there into the 21st century.

In the 1680s Sir Andros Edmonds attempted to revoke the royal charter. Although the story may be apocryphal, Connecticut residents long praised Hartford's Ruth Haynes Wyllys as the protector of the precious document. Both a daughter and a wife of former colonial governors, she allegedly conspired with a young lieutenant to hide the charter in an oak tree. It disappeared during the 1687 crisis and reappeared after England deposed Edmonds's commander, King James II, in 1688.

King James was replaced by his daughter Mary II, along with her husband William, and the college that became Yale University was established during their reign, in 1701. It moved permanently to New Haven in 1717, just after Mary's sister, Queen Anne, reigned in her own right. Despite these powerful role models, no college on either side of the Atlantic would accept female students for more than a century.

Like Harvard, Yale's chief purpose was to educate clergymen. Most Native Americans continued to reject Christianity, but when the legislature established an Indian school at Farmington in

1733, about 15 Tunxis saw the advantages of learning English. Unlike schools for whites, those for minorities commonly were coeducational. Of the approximately 20 Native Americans who attended the Moor Indian Charity School in Lebanon in 1762, at least four were female—but they were only "taught sewing and housework." (Johnston 1887, 51) The most anglicized Connecticut Native American woman at this point may have been Eunice Mossack, who was admitted to the Farmington church in 1765.

By then, blacks had replaced Native Americans as household slaves. The first was a boy brought from Dutch Guiana to Hartford in 1639; by 1756, Connecticut had 3,632 slaves, or one to every 35 whites. Lawmakers were less concerned with slavery than with the possibility that emancipated slaves could become a public burden. In 1711 a law outlined the obligations of masters if they freed "negro, malatto [sic], or Spanish Indian . . . servants." (Ibid., 157) Wealthy families in New Haven and New London were especially likely to own slave ships.

When the slave census was taken in 1756, Britain and its North American colonies were well into the French and Indian War. It was not unusual for women to accompany men to battle during that time, and indeed, one Connecticut militia commander requested that "men's wives" stay in the camp so that they could "wash and mend." The welcome to women, however, was limited to "while they behave decently"; Harold E. Selesky writes that a 1757 "general review of the women" probably was aimed at expelling prostitutes. (Selesky 1990, 183n)

The French and Indian War was a major factor in the American Revolution of the next decade. Many military men, including George Washington, got their training in the British army during the 1760s and used those skills to defeat their former colleagues in the 1770s. Maj. Gen. Israel Putnam was one such colleague; he

married Deborah Lothrop Avery Gardner, a twice-widowed and independently wealthy Norwich woman, just before the Revolution began. She accompanied him to Massachusetts in 1775 but died two years later, while traveling with his troops.

AMERICAN REVOLUTION TO THE CIVIL WAR (1776–1861)

Connecticut's location between the main rebel centers of Boston and Philadelphia meant that the colony was overrun by soldiers of both sides. Connecticut's best-known Revolutionary War woman probably is SYBIL LUDINGTON, who rode her horse through the night to alert the rebels of oncoming British troops. The British raided Danbury in 1777 and burned Fairfield and Norwalk in 1779, but according to Fairfield's Rev. Andrew Eliot, it mattered little which troops controlled the town. Both American and British troops—as well as men from the German province of Hesse hired by the British—attacked civilians.

Mary Fish Noyes Silliman unequivocally supported independence as a widow; she married Gold Seleck Silliman in 1775, and she continued to support independence for more than a year while he was a prisoner of war. Both had children from earlier marriages, and at age 43 and pregnant, she had to move the family from Fairfield.

In the midst of war, the Sharon Literary Club was founded in January 1779—a century prior to the national "club movement"—in Sharon, in northwestern Connecticut. The group also was unusual in consisting of mixed gender: the chairman was Rev. Cotton M. Smith, but the key leader was his daughter. Although young Juliana Smith had learned to read on her own, she soon edited the club's magazine, *Clio*. Most of its material came from her brother's friends at Yale, one of whom was Noah Webster. Nonetheless, neither she nor other female club members routinely

THE RIDE OF DEBORAH CHAMPION

Like Sybil Ludington, Deborah Champion (later Gilbert) of New London made a much longer and more dangerous ride than that of Paul Revere. In her own words:

Father laid his hand on my shoulder (a most unusual caress with him) and said solemnly: "Deborah. . . hast thou the heart and the courage to go out in the dark . . . and ride . . . to Boston town?"

. . . It was finally settled that I should start early in the early morning and Aristarchus [a slave] should go with me. He has been devoted to me since I made a huge cake to grace his wedding with Glory. . . . He has his fair share of wits, also. . . .

We met few people on the road, almost all the men being with the army and only the very old men and the women at work in the villages and farms. Dear heart, but war is a cruel thing! . . . I heard that it would be almost impossible to avoid the British, . . . so I plucked up what courage I could and secreting my papers in my saddlebags under all the eatables mother had filled them with, I rode on, determined to ride all night. . . .

A soldier in a red coat proceeded to take me to headquarters, but I told him it was too early to wake the captain, and to please let me pass for I had been sent in urgent haste to see a friend in need, which was true if ambiguous. . . .

When I arrived in Boston, I was very fortunate to find . . . General Washington and I gave him the papers, which proved to be of utmost importance. . . . [He] compliment[ed] me most highly.

—Doris Weatherford

Excerpt from Harry Clinton Green and Mary Wolcott Green, *The Pioneer Mothers of America*. Vol. 2. New York: G. P. Putnam's Sons, 1912.

spoke at meetings. Instead, 1779 records say that "all of the women and such of the men as were not engaged in speaking or reading [were] expected to knit stockings or do some other work to help our brave and suffering soldiers in their desperate struggle to gain the Liberty of our Native Land." (Smith 1900, 275)

In 1781 the British burned New London, destroying 65 homes and a number of other buildings and ships. More than 40 women were widowed, among them Sarah Stedman, who had

"seven children under thirteen years and no estate," as well as "Elizabeth Lebarry, with five minor children . . . , their house burned, and nothing left but the clothing on their backs." (Van Dusen 1961, 169)

It was one of the last battles of the revolution, which officially ended in 1783. The following year, Connecticut abolished slavery. At that time, it had a black population of 6,464, or 3.2% of its entire population. For at least the next four decades, however, the *Hartford Courant*, the nation's oldest newspaper, continued to run ads from people trying to recapture runaway slaves. (At the end of the 20th century, both the *Courant* and Aetna, a Hartford-based insurance company, would apologize for their roles in promoting and insuring the slave trade.)

On January 9, 1788, Connecticut became the fifth state when it ratified the Constitution of the new United States. War widows and needy women had a chance for new employment in 1788, when the nation's first woolen mill began in Hartford. There, as elsewhere, textile mills were the first major industry to hire women.

Schoolmasters were much more common than schoolmarms when Litchfield's Sarah Pierce founded a school in her home in 1792. Incorporated as the Litchfield Female Academy in 1827, it attracted young women from all over North America. Pierce also wrote innovative history textbooks, and among her nearly 2,000 students were CATHARINE BEECHER and HARRIET BEECHER STOWE.

Lydia Huntley Sigourney probably was Connecticut's best-known woman at the time. One of America's first women to pursue a writing career, she published her first book as an unmarried Norwich teacher in 1815 and then moved to Hartford when she married in 1819. Her book, *Traits of the Aborigines of America* (1822), was based on Henry Schoolcraft's explorations in Arkansas and Missouri.

THE FIELDINGS: NOTED PRESERVERS OF MOHEGAN–PEQUOT LANGUAGE AND CULTURE

Fidelia Hoscott Fielding, a member of the Mohegan tribe in Connecticut, was the last fluent speaker of the Eastern Algonquin language used by both the Mohegan and Pequot tribes. The diary Fidelia kept in her native tongue is largely credited with saving the Mohegan–Pequot language. Fidelia and fellow-Mohegan Emma Fielding Baker played important roles in preserving their culture's language and customs, passing on Mohegan historical records and oral traditions to great-niece and anthropologist Gladys Tantaquidgeon.

Another woman, Emma Fielding Baker, born in 1828, is known for organizing the Mohegan Green Corn Festival in 1861 to revitalize and unify the tribe during the year that their reservation was disbanded. She was later involved in representing the tribe in land disputes over Native American burial grounds.

Born in 1827, Fidelia was raised by her maternal grandmother, who spoke only Mohegan Pequot. In the latter half of the 19th century, Fidelia, who called herself Dji'ts Bud dnaca, or Flying Bird, recorded her life in her diary. Around 1900 anthropologist Frank Speck sought out Fidelia to learn about and preserve the Mohegan–Pequot language. Four of her diaries were found and published by Speck after she died. It turned out that Fidelia had recorded enough so that the tribe could restore the language nearly a century later. "A language is the lifeblood of a people, and the document that saved ours is to us a national treasure," Melissa Fawcett Sayett, the tribe's historian and a descendant of Fidelia, has said.

While staying with Fidelia and her family, Speck met Fidelia's young great-niece Gladys Tantaquidgeon. Gladys grew up to study under Speck at the University of Pennsylvania, and joined the Bureau of Indian Affairs in the 1930s. Gladys Tantaquidgeon later left her career in 1947 to became a curator of the Tantaquidgeon Indian Museum. She also served on the Mohegan Tribal Council.

All three women—Gladys, Fidelia, and Emma—are members of the Connecticut Women's Hall of Fame.

—Erica Pearson

Sigourney acceded to her husband and published it anonymously. As her husband's fortunes declined, however, she continued to write. Eventually the author of dozens of books such as *Letters to Young Ladies* (1833), Sigourney would charge $500 for the use of her name in the 1840s.

In the same era PRUDENCE CRANDALL's school for black girls in Canterbury, Connecticut, was ended by a violent mob in 1834. Also the fury of Cornwall residents forced the closing of a seminary for Cherokee men, when two local white women married students.

Litchfield's famed Sarah Pierce retired in 1833, and her school closed a decade later—but Sarah Porter began a Farmington school in 1843. Miss Porter's School ultimately became perhaps the nation's most elite finishing school for its wealthiest daughters; among its famous graduates was first lady Jacqueline Kennedy Onassis.

Despite such models—including Frances M. Caulkins, who published an 1845 history of Norwich and an 1852 New London one—in many ways, Connecticut women were less visible than women in other states. Harriet Beecher Stowe did not live there when *Uncle Tom's Cabin* made her a celebrity in 1852; and Maria Stewart, a black lecturer born in Hartford, left the city for more receptive places such as Boston and New York. Elizabeth Cady Stanton noted in the *History of Woman Suffrage* that, except for Canterbury's Prudence Crandall two decades earlier, records showed that no women from the state supported the antislavery cause.

Nor did any Connecticut women join New York, Massachusetts, and Ohio at women's rights conventions. Indeed, liberalism was so unusual that ISABELLA BEECHER HOOKER was pleasantly surprised when an 1861 Hartford audience did not attack Pennsylvania abolitionist and feminist Anna Dickinson.

CIVIL WAR TO THE PROGRESSIVE ERA (1861–1890)

Connecticut history has a claim to Sarah Emma Edmonds (later Seelye), a Canadian who worked in Hartford before joining a Michigan regiment disguised as a man named "Frank Thompson." Not only was Edmonds's gender not discovered, but she even used it to her advantage by spying dressed as a woman. In 1865 a Hartford publisher issued her bestseller, *Nurse and Spy in the Union Army*. Edmonds lived in Connecticut only briefly, though, and few of the state's women emulated her, nor did they teach in "freedman's schools" to the extent that other northern women did.

Connecticut women's volunteer work was largely limited to their own state. According to John Niven's *Connecticut for the Union* (1965), when a hospital for wounded soldiers opened in New Haven in 1862, Sarah Woolsey wrote to Georgeanna Woolsey that 240 men had arrived from Virginia "all dreadfully neglected and needing attention of every kind. . . . Only one surgeon [was] on board to care for them, no nurses and hardly any provisions; the wounds of many had not been dressed for nearly a week." (Niven 1965, 323)

Yet even though they were daughters of powerful families, the Woolseys, Harriet Terry, and Rebecca Bacon had to fight for permission to nurse: "Authorities would not permit any of the young New Haven girls to enter the hospital for several days because of the 'sights and sounds.'" Among the sounds, according to Sarah Woolsey, was "an awful boy with no arms, who swears so frightfully (all the time he isn't screeching for currant pie, or fried meat, or some other indigestible) that he turns you blue." (Ibid., 323)

Some Connecticut women did go South on personal, if not organizational, missions. Isabella Hooker's 1864 trip to nurse a wounded soldier proved pivotal to Connecticut feminism.

Although Anna Dickinson had introduced Hooker to feminist ideas, it was meeting Caroline Severance in South Carolina that expanded her network. Severance later hosted Hooker in Massachusetts, as did Paulina Wright Davis in Rhode Island.

Frances Ellen Burr had been introduced to women's rights when she lived in Ohio in the 1850s. By the postwar era, she and her niece, Ella Burr McManus, were writing for the family-owned *Hartford Times*, and Burr drew up a petition for the vote that was presented to the 1867 legislature. According to Elizabeth Cady Stanton, Burr did "more to popularize the question of woman suffrage throughout the State than any other person." (Stanton, Anthony, and Gage 1886, 3:319)

Lucy Stone and her husband, Henry Blackwell, came from New Jersey to address the relevant state House of Representatives committee about suffrage. Two of its three members sent a long, favorable report to the House, which rejected suffrage with 93 in favor and 111 against. Comparatively speaking, this was not a bad margin of loss for a first attempt, and in December 1867, Stanton and Susan B. Anthony spoke at Hartford's Allyn Hall.

Although almost two years passed before the Connecticut Woman Suffrage Association began in autumn 1869, its founding meeting was superb. Many supporters came from other states, including Minnesota singers, the Hutchinsons, who moved the writer for the usually conservative *Hartford Courant* to comment: "There stood the family of singers, with the same cheerful, hopeful courage in their uplifted faces with which for twenty years they have sung of the good time almost here." The paper praised the event and its leader, concluding with "this convention has been inspired and managed by one person—Mrs. Hooker of this city."(Ibid., 322–323)

Gov. Marshall Jewell hosted Julia Ward Howe, Susan B. Anthony, and other luminaries at the governor's mansion. He also issued a long paper in which he deplored "the low wages of female teachers, and the injustice of excluding girls from the scientific schools and polytechnic institutions of the State." On the other hand, Jewell tried to restore obsolete divorce laws. Connecticut had made divorce easier than most states in 1849, and he felt that the number of divorces in 1868—478, compared with 4,734 marriages—was excessive. Stanton, however, did not support the governor in this matter. When he told Stanton that the majority of divorce seekers were women, she hoped that there would be no change at least until women could vote. Comparing Connecticut to Canada, where slaves escaped prior to 1865, she asked that "fugitive wives . . . [may] keep that little State, like an oasis in the desert, sacred to sad wives." (Ibid., 323–324)

In 1870 the state legislature appointed as chaplain New Haven's Rev. Phebe Hanaford, a Unitarian minister also active in New Jersey. In Stanton's words, "Mrs. Hanaford acted as chaplain both in the Senate and House of Representatives, and received a check for her services which she valued chiefly as a recognition of women's equality." (Ibid., 3:327) In another milestone two years later, Middletown's Wesleyan University, a Methodist institution founded in 1831, became the state's first college to admit women in 1872.

National attention came to Connecticut suffragists the next year. Abby Smith and her sister Julia of Glastonbury had run the family farm alone for 40 years. After Abby Smith attended the 1873 Woman's Congress in New York, the sisters decided they would no longer pay their property taxes if they were not allowed to vote. Many cartoonists mocked the case of the "Glastonbury cows," but it was a serious issue.

Four times Glastonbury officials confiscated the sisters' cattle for nonpayment of taxes, but they carried on with their protest, winning admiration from some unexpected sources. Amos Lawrence of the textile mill–owning family in Lawrence, Massachusetts, wrote the Smiths in January 1874, after their first action:

You deserve . . . great honor, not only because you have suffered in a good cause, but because you have set an example. . . .

Your case has its parallel in every township of New England. In the town where this is written a widow pays into the treasury $7,830 a year, while 600 men, a number equal to half . . . the voters, pay $1,200 in all. Another lady pays $5,042. Yet neither has a single vote. . . . Each one of the 600 men who have no property, . . . many of whom cannot read or write, has the power of voting away the property of the town, while the female owners have no power at all. (Ibid., 330)

Glastonbury did not relent, though, and four years later, the sisters petitioned the legislature, saying that they also had "seen eleven acres of our meadow-land sold to an ugly neighbor for a tax of fifty dollars—land worth more than $2,000. And a threat is given out that our house shall be ransacked and despoiled of articles most dear to us." There is no evidence, however, that the legislature heard their January 1878 appeal. (Ibid., 3:336)

Abby Smith died in July, and Julia went on to achieve success in another area. She had taught herself Latin, Greek, and Hebrew, and translated the Bible five times in those languages before she was satisfied that her translation was superior to that of the King James version. At age 87, she married a retired judge who admired her work and moved to Hartford, where she addressed the state suffrage association at age 91.

Although the legislature did not respond to unmarried women such as the Smiths, it had passed reforms of married women's property rights in 1877. Again it was a governor, Richard Hubbard, who encouraged and supported the reform. The current state laws, he said, were a "scandal of jurisprudence" that allowed a man to "strip his wife, by . . . disposition to strangers, of all claim on his estate . . . and thus add beggary to widowhood." (Ibid., 325)

The state's first woman admitted to the practice of law was Mary Hall, when the Connecticut supreme court ruled in her favor in 1882. A successful Hartford attorney thereafter, Hall also was an officer of the local Equal Rights Club organized by Frances Burr in 1885. Its president was Emily P. Collins, who had pioneered the movement in New York 40 years earlier.

From 1884 onward suffragists introduced bills in every legislative session and saw them defeated in one or both houses. The sole victory came in 1887, when women won the right to serve as school trustees. Other states also undertook this measure, largely because rural townships often lacked enough literate men willing to serve. Although these women could not vote for themselves, by 1900 men had elected about 45 of them.

PROGRESSIVE ERA
(1890–1920)

A number of Connecticut's surviving Native Americans lived near New Milford in the late 19th century, with a female chief called Vinie, the queen of the Schaghticokes. She was then about age 75 and had inherited this position as the great-granddaughter of Mawwehu, the Pequot chief. However, as the community had no more than 50 residents, fewer than a half-dozen of whom claimed only Native American ancestors, she had little to reign over. Like others, the queen supported herself by making baskets and cultivating a few acres of land.

In 1889 the Hartford Theological Seminary began admitting women, and Yale opened its first graduate departments to women in 1892. The 1893 legislature mandated that the State Agricultural School at Storrs, Connecticut, admit women, but still no publicly funded liberal arts college accepted them. Meanwhile, Wesleyan University continued to admit women but, as of 1900, limited them to a quota of 20% of its student body.

In 1893 the state legislature granted women the right to vote in school elections. In the next election 4,471 women voted. However, they were disillusioned by the fact that the number of nominees and the available positions appeared to have been made in male caucuses since their numbers were an exact match to each other.

In some towns, however, women organized politically. Led by Ella L. Bennett, Willimantic women not only ousted a corrupt superintendent of schools, but also consolidated rural schools. For that election, in October 1895, suffragists registered 1,129 women. Suffragists also filed a bill for presidential suffrage in 1895—something that would not be adopted until 1913 in Illinois—but both that and municipal rights consistently were voted down. Part of the problem was the failure of Hartford women to reach out to most of the rest of the state: for example, nearly all state suffrage conventions were held in Hartford. By the turn of the century, the association had so few members that its 1903 "convention" was held in Isabella Hooker's home.

Instead of political leaders, many of Connecticut's notable women of this era were authors and artists (see sidebar on p. 232). For example, poet Anna Hempsted Branch, author of "The Dance of All Dead Bones," published books in 1905 and 1910. Mary Wilkins Freeman had additional influence with regional tales, such as *A New England Nun and Other Stories* (1891).

When the suffrage movement revived in 1909, it was largely owing to women from the southwestern part of the state, especially Greenwich's

THE ARTIST'S COLONY AT LYME

In 1899 Florence Griswold, a descendant of one of New England's first families, opened her home in Old Lyme, Connecticut, to a group of artists, who later became know as the Lyme Art Colony, and established the first summer impressionist art colony in America.

Born to prosperous sea captain Robert Harper Griswold and Helen Powers Griswold, Florence and her three siblings were raised in a privileged environment. With the decline in Florence's father's investments, however, the family's financial situation deteriorated and in 1878 her mother decided to open the family home as a finishing school for young ladies. In 1899, at the age of 49, Florence Griswold inherited the family home and transformed it into a boarding-house. For the next decade, at $7 per week per room, Griswold offered hospitality to a group of artists who would gain national attention for their work. Not only did she provide basic room and board, she also created a salon in her home to promote the artists' work, and later donated one acre of land to the Lyme Art Association for a gallery.

The Griswold residence housed an average of 15 artists who came to Old Lyme for the summer to paint outside, or *en plein air*. Regular boarders included artists at various stages of their careers such as William Henry Howe when he was just beginning, Matilda Browne when she became well known, and Childe Hassam when he was quite famous. Female artists such as sculptor Bessie Potter Vonnoh, first lady Ellen Axson Wilson, and sisters Breta and Lydia Longacre came to Lyme and stayed at the Griswold house. A full-fledged art colony soon developed that would play a pivotal role in the rise of American Impressionism and would lead to Old Lyme being coined the "Giverny of America," after the area in France made famous by impressionist painter Claude Monet.

In 1937 Griswold died at the age of 87 in the home in which she was born. An obituary in the *New York Times* proclaimed, "In her delicate and high-bred way Miss Florence had her part in fostering an authentic American art. The memory of this gracious spirit survives, and not in the Griswold House alone, but as part of no inconsiderable chapter in the history of our native art." In 1947 the Florence Griswold Association opened a museum in her honor in the Griswold house. The art galleries that line the main street of Old Lyme, the Lyme Academy College of Fine Art, and the Lyme Art Association are all testaments to the creative environment fostered by Griswold. Old Lyme, now part of the Connecticut Impressionist Art Trail and the Connecticut Women's Heritage Trail, is considered a cultural tourism destination for the state of Connecticut.

—Laurie Bradt

KATHARINE HOUGHTON HEPBURN and Caroline Ruutz-Rees. They brought England's Emmeline Pankhurst to Hartford, and an explosion of energy followed: From just nine women at the 1906 suffrage convention, membership would soar to 32,366 in 1916. Conventions were held in unprecedented places, including Greenwich (1910), Bridgeport (1911), and New Haven (1912). With young Emily Pierson as field organizer, they held a 1911 automobile parade for suffrage—one of the first in the nation—and in 1913, the energetic new leadership collected more than 18,000 petition signatures. In 1914 the state Democratic party endorsed suffrage. By 1916 the state suffrage association had 81 affiliates, including a men's league.

Republicans controlled state government, however, and according to Annie G. Porritt, press secretary for the suffrage association, women's petitions failed owing to the virulent opposition of the Republican power bloc. Many lawmakers were strongly influenced by liquor lobbyists, who opposed suffragists in most states. These lobbyists also funded the State Association Opposed to Woman Suffrage, which began in 1910 with Mrs. Daniel Markham as president.

As elsewhere, most Connecticut women supported World War I, which began in 1914; the United States entered that war in 1917. Ruutz-Rees headed the Woman's Division of the State Council of Defense, while Katherine Ludington of Old Lyme took over the suffrage association presidency. After three bills for variants of suffrage failed that year, activists gave up on their state and worked instead for an amendment to the U.S. Constitution.

They met failure, however, with Connecticut's delegation to Congress, especially with the state's Republican senators. Porritt considered Sen. Frank Brandegee an especially obdurate adversary. But on June 4, 1919, the senator's colleagues from other states provided the necessary two-thirds majority to send the 19th Amendment, which granted all voting rights to all American women, to the states for ratification. Just days later, the Connecticut Woman Suffrage Association held its jubilee convention, celebrating the 50 years since it began in 1869.

The next year would bring the final victory, but without help from Connecticut. Senator Brandegee and others determinedly postponed the vote on ratification until early summer of 1919, knowing that most state legislatures would have adjourned by then. The national suffrage association nonetheless ran a highly successful campaign to persuade governors to call special sessions of state legislatures to ratify the amendment. By March 1920, when West Virginia ratified, 35 of the necessary 36 states had done so.

With Connecticut's image as an enlightened state at risk, suffragists collected more than 100,000 petitions and held mass meetings in 40 municipalities during the first week of May. This had, in Porritt's words, "not the slightest effect," as Gov. Marcus A. Holcomb "remained obdurate." (Harper 1922, 6:77–76) As the 1920 election neared, Ludington urged women to pressure him and his Republican colleagues:

> One of the most important presidential elections in years is to be held. . . . No women can vote in this election . . . until the 36th State has ratified. It is curious how slow the public—women as well as men—have been to realize this. They talk of our being "almost" voters. They do not seem to understand that . . . women will not vote until the 36th state ratifies. (Ibid., 77–78)

Instead of Connecticut, Tennessee made the 19th Amendment a reality. It was added to the Constitution on August 26—and in September, Holcomb called a special session to help his party out of its dilemma with a belated ratification. Even then, the process was so inefficient that the legislature ended up taking three votes on the moot point, with 11 House members voting negatively to the end.

1920S THROUGH WORLD WAR II ERA (1920–1950)

One factor in Connecticut's refusal to deal with female enfranchisement was its immigrants. Most came from culturally conservative areas of Europe, and because they were accustomed to alcohol use, they were sympathetic to the blandishments of the liquor industry. The 1920 census showed Connecticut to have 908,420 residents, of whom 238,210 were foreign born. Many immigrant women toiled in the factories of such cities as Waterbury, Danbury, and Bridgeport. Already by 1890, for instance, 47% of employees in Connecticut rubber plants were women.

World War I cut off immigration for a time, and when it swelled again, Congress passed quotas in 1924 that virtually ended the flow, especially from the southeastern European countries. For women, this often led to heart-rending decisions about leaving family in Europe or returning there. Indeed, the 1930s would be the only decade when more people left America than entered.

Most of the era's immigrants were Catholic, and they turned out in unprecedented numbers to vote for Democrat Al Smith, the first Catholic presidential nominee. Although he lost, this 1928 election is sometimes termed "the Al Smith Revolution" because it led many previously indifferent voters, especially new female voters, into the Democratic party.

Nevertheless, in 1928, Connecticut elected its fourth Republican governor of the decade; but the following year, after the national economy collapsed, the state joined the rest of the nation in voting Democratic during the 1930s. In part to break this trend, Republicans nominated the first woman to statewide office in 1938. Sara B. Crawford would serve just two years as secretary of state, however, as Democrat CHASE GOING WOODHOUSE won the position in 1940. With minor exceptions, the office evolved into an unofficial "woman's job," because women of both parties (five Republicans, nine Democrats) have held it ever since. Connecticut is the only state with this record.

Clare Boothe Luce, Connecticut's first U.S. congresswoman, greeting Gen. George S. Patton on a trip to the western European front in 1944 during World War II. (AP/Wide World Photos)

The United States entered World War II late in 1941, although the war had begun in 1939. In the 1942 election CLARE BOOTHE LUCE became Connecticut's first congresswoman. By 1944 so many men were overseas and unlikely to cast ballots that "both parties took particular pains to appeal to women." (Jefferies 1979, 22)

More important to most women, though, was the growth that war brought, as Connecticut's population rose to over 2 million for the first time. Among the newcomers were the SPARs, the Coast Guard's female unit (acronym derived from the Coast Guard motto Semper Paratus, Always Ready). Alone among the military services, SPARs had a coeducational experience. LaVerne Bradley reported for *National Geographic* in 1943 the following:

> Officer candidates for the SPARS train along with Coast Guard cadets at the U.S. Coast Guard Academy, New London, Connecticut. . . . The SPARS have their own lectures and their own drills, but their life is cadet life. . . . SPARS go down to the sea in ships. (Weatherford 1990, 54)

Civilian women who could not get jobs in the 1930s were begged to take them in the 1940s, often changing labor practices. Groton shipyards, for example, looked to the wives of naval submarine men for motivated workers in claustrophobic submarine construction. The legal ban on night work for women was lifted in response to the state's arms manufacturers, including Colt, Remington, and Winchester.

New Britain used an especially thoughtful recruiting method. According to a labor expert, some two dozen experienced factory women were hired to talk personally with "the five thousand women who had not replied to the recruiting letters. Each . . . told the housewife . . . about war work as only a woman could do. The result was an average of sixty housewives . . . were recruited by each." (Ibid., 118)

Josephine Von Miklos wrote in *I Took a War Job* (1943) about her experiences in Connecticut armament plants and shipyards—where she learned that she was more successful if she hid her mechanical aptitude until hired. In time the war would help change attitudes about both women and minorities. Over a million people bought Ann Lane Petry's story of urban black women, *The Street* (1946), and an African American woman chaired the Red Cross Canteen Committee, which welcomed soldiers in Branford, a town near New Haven. A postwar study of Branford, however, showed that equality was far from reality. The town had three women's clubs during this time, and a member of two of them told a sociologist that "no Negro could get in even if Hell froze over." (Lee 1961, 64) Margaret Taylor Hancock meanwhile was quietly chronicling her life among Branford's blacks. With her daughter, Shirlee Taylor Haizlip, as the writer, she published the bestseller, *The Sweeter the Juice* (1994), when Hancock was in her eighties.

POSTWAR AND CONTEMPORARY ERAS (1950–present)

In the 20th century a number of successful women who started their own businesses resided in Connecticut. Margaret Rudkin set this example in 1937, when she started baking Pepperidge Farms bread; two decades later, her reputation and her achievement were becoming nationally known. LILLIAN VERNON began her mail-order business from her home in 1951; by the century's end, half the households in the nation were on its mailing list. Beatrice Fox Auerbach implemented toll-free ordering from Hartford's G. Fox department store, and when she retired in 1965, had multiplied her business tenfold.

Ellen Ash Peters was the top graduate in her 1954 law school class at Yale, but could not find a job as a lawyer. Initially settling for teaching, three decades later she would become chief justice

THE MOST FAMOUS "ANCIENT": MISS PORTER'S DAY AND BOARDING SCHOOL

In 1843 the 30-year-old Sarah Porter founded a day and boarding school for young women in Farmington, Connecticut. Daughters of the nation's elite have attended Miss Porter's School ever since.

A minister's daughter, Porter received her own education in after-hours classes with Yale professors who were willing to teach female students. She believed that young women should be able to get the same preparation for college as young men. The original class at Miss Porter's included 25 girls, nine of whom were boarding students. Porter said of her students, "They came as girls; they left as women." By the 1850s Miss Porter's girls studied trigonometry and chemistry as well as music, history, and Latin. Required activities included Bible study on Sundays and lectures by prominent speakers.

By 1885 the school's reputation and the number of its students had grown, and to accommodate boarders, Porter bought the schoolhouse and surrounding property, as well as the Union Hotel on Farmington's Main Street.

Miss Porter's most famous alumna, or "ancient" as they are called in school lore, is Jacqueline Kennedy Onassis. When Onassis (then Jacqueline Bouvier) graduated from Miss Porter's School in 1947, according to the boarding school's yearbook, her ambition was "never to be a housewife." Onassis was on the staff of the school's newspaper, *The Salgamundo*, both writing and drawing cartoons. In *The Salgamundo*'s June 10, 1947, edition, Onassis wrote about the sadness she felt at leaving the school and its traditions:

> We shall never live here again, to sing Hymns on Sunday evenings and walk down to Swan Pond under the great bending trees. There will be no more Tap Days, Field Days, Mountain Days for us, no more rushing to the store for Hershey bars on Wednesday afternoons or sitting nervously outside Mr. Johnson's office waiting for our marks.

—Erica Pearson

Excerpt from Rita Niro, "Miss Porter's Recalls Its Most Famous Grad." *The Hartford Courant*, 27 May 1994.

of the Connecticut supreme court in 1984. *A Wrinkle in Time* (1962) made Madeleine L'Engle

TIMELINE

United States Events	Connecticut Events
	1600
	1614 Dutchman Adriaen Blok explores Connecticut.
1620 Settlement of Plymouth Colony	
	1636 Thomas Hooker founds Connecticut.
	1637 Puritans attack Pequots at Mystic.
	1639 Connecticut constitution is drafted.
	1675 King Philip's War.
	1700
	1701 College that would become Yale University established.
1776 United States declares independence	1776–1783 Revolutionary War rages in Connecticut.
	1784 Connecticut abolishes slavery.
	1788 Connecticut ratifies the U.S. Constitution.
	1800
1861–65 U.S. Civil War	
	1870 State legislature appoints Phebe Hanaford as chaplain.
	1882 First woman, Mary Hall, practices law in Connecticut.
	1893 Women given the right to vote in school elections.
	1900
1914–18 World War I	
1920 Ratification of the 19th Amendment	
1929–39 Great Depression	
	1938 Republicans nominate first woman to statewide office.
1939–45 World War II	
	1942 Clare Boothe Luce becomes Connecticut's first congresswoman.
	1974 Connecticut elects Democrat Ella Tambussi Grasso as governor.
1975 Vietnam War ends	1984 Ellen Ash Peters becomes state supreme court justice.
	1990 Rosa L. DeLauro becomes the state's sixth congresswoman.
	1999 Denise Nappier elected state treasurer.
	2000
	2003 Moira K. Lyons becomes speaker of the House.

famous; she published dozens of imaginative stories and served as president of the Authors Guild in the 1980s.

Another influential woman, ESTELLE GRISWOLD, was arrested when she opened her birth control clinic, but in *Griswold v. Connecticut* (1965), the U.S. Supreme Court ruled that states could not ban the sale of contraceptives to married couples. Later the abolition of the ban was expanded to unmarried people following a Massachusetts case. Soon after Griswold's momentous case—and 267 years after its founding—Yale University finally admitted female students to its undergraduate college in 1968.

Another achievement of these tumultuous counterculture years was Pres. Lyndon Johnson's appointment of New Haven native Constance Baker Motley as the first black woman on the federal judiciary. A Manhattan district court judge in 1966, Motley was widely expected to eventually become the first black woman on the U.S. Supreme Court—a precedent that has yet to be set.

Much more attention went to Connecticut in 1974, when it elected Democrat ELLA TAMBUSSI GRASSO as governor. It was the first state to elect a female governor who did not have a previously elected husband. Indeed, her husband, educator Thomas Grasso, maintained such a low profile that, when he died in 1999, many were surprised that Governor Grasso had been married.

Grasso had been elected to Congress in 1970, and almost a decade passed before Connecticut had another congresswoman. BARBARA KENNELLY, a Democrat, won a special election in 1982, and NANCY JOHNSON, a Republican, followed in that year's general election. ROSA L. DELAURO became the state's sixth congresswoman in 1990.

Both Grasso and Kennelly served in the position of secretary of state in the 1960s and 1970s, and Connecticut began electing women to state offices other than that in 1988. After an initial appointment as attorney general,

Denise Nappier, Connecticut's state treasurer since 1999, speaking to the state legislature on April 4, 2002. (AP/Wide World Photos)

Democrat Clarine Nardie Riddle won that powerful position. Eunice Groark, the candidate of a minority party, was elected lieutenant governor in 1990, and Republican M. Jodi Rell followed at the next election and was reelected in 2002. In 1995 Nancy Wyman became comptroller, an office she continued to hold in 2002, and Denise Nappier has been the state treasurer since 1999; both are Democrats.

Not only does this give Connecticut a much better record than most states in electing women to powerful offices, but also, as of the 2002 elections, Connecticut's state legislature was 29.4% female, higher than average. In 2003 Democrat Moira K. Lyons was the speaker of the House, a position that women have yet to achieve in many states.

—Doris Weatherford

PROMINENT WOMEN

MARIAN ANDERSON (1902–1993)

The first black female to perform with the Metropolitan Opera Company, contralto Marian Anderson earned the supreme compliment from Arturo Toscanini, who considered her voice a phenomenon that comes but once a century. Born to black laborers in Philadelphia, she sang at the Union Baptist Church, where members paid for her education at a music school. She studied free under Giuseppe Boghetti and, in her late teens, sang with the Philadelphia Choral Society. In 1925 she established herself in professional music by outsinging 300 competitors with her rendition of "O Mio Fernando," which won her an outdoor recital with the New York Philharmonic Orchestra.

Anderson challenged barriers to black performers while touring black college campuses in the South. At age 28, she traveled to Europe to debut in Berlin and returned over the next five years for more European tours. She thrilled audiences in Denmark, England, Germany, Holland, Norway, Russia, and Sweden before singing for Finnish composer Jean Sibelius and finally appearing in New York in 1935. She flourished in South America, Japan, Africa, and Europe, but could not rent concert space at Constitution Hall in Washington, D.C., because of the bigotry of the Daughters of the American Revolution. To atone for the slight, first lady Eleanor Roosevelt arranged for Anderson to sing an Easter program at the Lincoln Memorial. She later sold a half-million copies of her recording of "Ave Maria" and earned a standing ovation for performing with the Metropolitan Opera in Giuseppe Verdi's *Un Ballo in Maschera* (The Masked Ball).

In an era of limited opportunity for African Americans, Anderson reflected on her phenomenal

career with the autobiography, *My Lord, What a Morning* (1956). Four years later she retired but returned to Washington, D.C., to accept one of the first Kennedy Center awards. Her broad range and tone won her a Spingarn Medal, the Bok Award, the Presidential Medal of Freedom, and appointment as a U.N. delegate and U.S. goodwill ambassador as well as honorary degrees from 50 colleges and universities. In 1977, on her 75th birthday, she received the Handel Medallion at Carnegie Hall. Subsequent honoraria include a New York City Human Rights Award, a Grammy for lifetime achievement, and the National Medal of Arts. A longtime resident of Danbury, Anderson was elected to the Connecticut Women's Hall of Fame. The Marian Anderson Scholarship at the Charles Ives Center in Danbury honors her name.

CATHARINE BEECHER (1800–1878)

Consummate educator and reformer Catharine Esther Beecher of East Hampton, New York, proposed methods of elevating housework from mindless drudgery to a domestic science. Born to a Congregationalist minister, her family moved to Litchfield, Connecticut, in 1810. She studied literature, math, and science at Sarah Pierce's Litchfield school and learned needlework and piano at home. After her fiance drowned in 1822, she chose to remain single and to devote her life educating women and promoting domestic science.

At age 23, Beecher opened the Hartford Female Seminary, which offered courses in astronomy, laboratory science, and physical education at a time when girls were usually encouraged to concentrate on needlework. In 1831 Beecher began focusing on training teachers; two years later she established the Western

Female Institute in Cincinnati, Ohio. She managed the large household of her father, Rev. Lyman Beecher, and was a maternal figure for her half-sister, Harriet Beecher Stowe.

After returning to the East, she lectured on home maintenance, diet, and health. In 1841 she published *A Treatise on Domestic Economy for the Use of Young Ladies at Home and at School,* a touchstone of the home economics movement. In 1852 she established the American Woman's Educational Association and continued writing texts on methods of improving society through a disciplined home life and child care. Her work, *The American Woman's Home: Or, Principles of Domestic Science* (1869), was the era's most-read book on homemaking. At age 73, she published *The New Housekeeper's Manual* (1873). Although she opposed the suffrage movement led by another half-sister, Isabella Beecher Hooker, she earned the respect of the nation for contributions to classroom operation, staff development, and domestic science.

PRUDENCE CRANDALL (1803–1890)

Reformer, abolitionist, and teacher Prudence Crandall of Hopkinton, Rhode Island, was a champion of education for African American students. Brought up in the Quaker tradition, she attended the New England Friends' Boarding School and taught in Plainfield, Connecticut. At age 28, she opened a girl's academy in Canterbury, Connecticut. Two years later she courted censure by admitting Sarah Harris, a black student, who wanted to certify in teaching.

Abolitionist William Lloyd Garrison advised Crandall to open a separate school for black children. With that aim, she set up a teacher-training institute at a boardinghouse and recruited black students. Her neighbors were so outraged that they ousted her from the Congregational church and refused her trade at local stores. Two months later local agitators

successfully lobbied the state assembly to outlaw the founding of such schools.

Crandall was tried, convicted, and jailed for violating this "Black Law." She encountered vandalism, rock throwing, and the polluting of her well. When a violent mob assembled at her school on September 9, 1834, she closed the academy and retreated to Illinois, where she taught in her home. At age 71, she married Calvin Philleo, a Baptist clergyman, and retired to Elk Falls, Kansas, where she actively supported temperance and suffrage. The Connecticut assembly offered her a pension in 1886.

ROSA L. DELAURO (1943–)

Rosa L. DeLauro of New Haven, Connecticut, is a six-term U.S. congresswoman representing her home state. Born to a politically active family, DeLauro was described by Tom Oliphant as a "hero for working families." An honor graduate of Marymount College, she holds advanced degrees in international politics from Columbia University and the London School of Economics.

DeLauro's political career began with her direction of EMILY's List, an acronym for Early Money Is Like Yeast, which was part of a nationwide push to increase the number of women in elected office. From 1981 to 1987 she headed the staff of U.S. senator Christopher Dodd, earning the praise of a wide variety of constituencies in Connecticut, including the state nursing association, New England school superintendents, U.S. Marines, the National Breast Cancer Coalition, National Organization of Italian American Women, Society of Gynecologic Oncologists, and the United Way.

In 1990, during her candidacy for Connecticut's open seat in the U.S. House of Representatives, DeLauro pledged to oppose new taxes. She won the seat and took office in 1991. Among other legislative successes, DeLauro was part of the political network that passed the Brady Bill (an assault weapons ban). DeLauro supports minimum wage increases, affordable child care, job fairs for the unemployed, an anticrime youth council, and "Kick Butts Connecticut," an antitobacco initiative for public schools. In April 2001 DeLauro joined House Minority Leader Dick Gephardt in convening a series of weekly strategy meetings with such groups as the AFL-CIO, environmental agencies, and women's and civil rights groups. The purposes of these closed sessions were to design policy on education, health care and prescription drugs, the environment, retirement and aging, and other key topics.

CHARLOTTE PERKINS GILMAN (1860–1935)

A renowned socialist speaker, writer, and feminist, Charlotte Anna Perkins Gilman of Hartford, Connecticut, was ahead of her time in seeking equal personal and economic rights for women. A member of the prestigious Beecher clan, she educated herself through reading. After two years at the Rhode Island School of Design in Providence, she began a career in commercial art and teaching.

Wed to artist Charles Walter Stetson in 1884, Gilman gave birth to a daughter but became desperately unhappy with her domestic routine; she suffered a nervous breakdown in 1885. While recovering, she toured the American West and issued verse and essays in *Pacific Monthly* and *Pacific Rural Press*. She earned fame for describing a woman's mental breakdown in the feminist classic, "The Yellow Wallpaper" (1892), which she published in *New England Magazine*. Shortly after she and Stetson divorced in 1894, she sent her daughter to live with her father and his new wife. Freed from domestic responsibilities, Gilman edited *Impress* magazine and championed women's suffrage.

At the Women's Congress at the World's Columbian Exposition of 1893, Gilman co-formed the Chicago Household Economic Society and demonstrated neighborhood cooperatives to simplify housework. She wrote idealistic living plans for the *American Fabian* and *Forerunner*, and published a best-seller, *Women and Economics: A Study of the Economic Relation between Men and Women as a Factor in Social Evolution* (1898), a protest against women's economic dependence on men. She continued fighting patriarchy with radical treatises on child care, women's work, and on the creation of communal kitchens and urban women's hotels, which she described in a dozen leading magazines and journals.

Gilman advocated full economic independence for women and promoted time-saving appliances. She envisioned home economics as a blend of art, science, handicraft, and business. She added to world utopian literature in 1915 with a woman's version, *Herland*, and that same year she cofounded the Women's Peace party with Jane Addams. Upon her diagnosis of terminal breast cancer, she killed herself with chloroform. Her autobiography, *The Living of Charlotte Perkins Gilman*, was published posthumously in 1935.

ELLA GRASSO (1919–1981)

Without losing an election, Ella Tambussi Grasso of Windsor Locks, Connecticut, became the nation's first female governor to obtain the office on her own political strength and name. The daughter of Italian immigrants, she grew up in a working-class atmosphere and attended the Chaffee School, a private college preparatory institution, on scholarship. She was a Phi Beta Kappa, magna cum laude graduate of Massachusetts's Mount Holyoke College, earning a B.A. in 1940 and an M.A. in 1942 in sociology and economics. A research assistant for the Federal War Manpower Commission, at age 24, she joined the League of Women Voters.

In 1952, after election to the Connecticut legislature, Grasso rose to assistant floor leader and chair of the Democratic party's platform committee. In 1958 she advanced to chief legislative strategist for the Connecticut general assembly and served the first of three terms as Connecticut's secretary of state. In 1971 she won election to the U.S. House of Representatives, where she supported economic growth.

In 1974 Grasso became governor of Connecticut, setting a precedent as the first woman to win the governorship without following her husband into office. She advocated open public records, and aid to the needy. Reelected in 1978, her peers chose her to chair the 1979 Democratic Governors' Conference. Governor Grasso resigned her office just weeks prior to her death from ovarian cancer. Straightforward and unglamorous, she is best remembered for making herself available to the public and for demanding accountability in spending the taxpayers' money.

ESTELLE GRISWOLD (1900–1981)

Estelle Griswold of Hartford was a reproductive rights advocate who helped end outmoded birth control laws. Educated at the Hartt College of Music and in Paris, she married and became a medical technologist in Washington, D.C. During World War II, she aided the U.N. Relief and Rehabilitation Association and church organizations in relocating displaced persons and in battling poverty in Rio de Janeiro, Algiers, and Puerto Rico. During these eyewitness experiences with the poor, she began to crusade for population control as a method of curbing human misery.

As a service to Connecticut women, Griswold and Dr. Charles Lee Buxton, chairman of the Yale School of Medicine Department of Obstetrics and Gynecology, operated a shuttle to surrounding states offering legal abortions. In 1965 Griswold came to prominence in the court case *Griswold v. Connecticut*, which challenged a state ban on birth control. Four years earlier, she opposed the law by opening a state branch of the Planned Parenthood League in New Haven, where she and Buxton examined married women and dispensed birth control information and prescriptions for contraceptives. After police closed the busy center, Griswold received backing from the American Civil Liberties Union in pressing an appeal before the Supreme Court. On June 5, 1965, a Court ruling established a constitutional right to marital privacy.

KATHARINE HOUGHTON HEPBURN (1878–1951)

Katharine Houghton Hepburn of Corning, New York, was a suffragist and birth control advocate. The daughter of the industrialist who established the Corning Glass Works, she absorbed scholarship and feminism from her mother, who believed that girls deserved advanced education. Orphaned at age 14, Hepburn lived with her Uncle Amory, who supported her at Pennsylvania's Bryn Mawr College. She completed two degrees in chemistry and physics by 1900 and received an M.A. in art history from Boston's Radcliffe College. She taught in the Baltimore public schools, married a surgeon, Tom Hepburn, and moved to Hartford, Connecticut, to rear their six children. One daughter, her namesake, became a major stage and film actor.

At age 32, Hepburn began lobbying for women's rights and birth control. In 1913 she helped to revive the Connecticut Woman Suffrage Association and founded the Connecticut Birth Control Movement, for which she picketed. Her activism took on a militant tone under the influence of U.K. suffragist Emmeline Pankhurst. Hepburn supported Margaret Sanger's birth control initiative and pressured a legislative committee to legitimize the dispersal of family planning information to the poor and uneducated.

ISABELLA BEECHER HOOKER (1822–1907)

Feminist advocate Isabella Beecher Hooker of Litchfield, Connecticut, was a dedicated worker for full citizens' rights for women. Born to Harriet Porter and the Rev. Lyman Beecher, a prominent liberal clergyman, she attended Hartford Female Seminary, which her sister Catharine Beecher founded. After marrying John Hooker in 1841, she settled near Farmington, Connecticut, and hosted the outstanding personalities of her day, including her sister, Harriet Beecher Stowe, and Mark Twain.

Initially opposed to crusading suffragists, Hooker eventually involved herself in the struggle for legal rights for married women and for women's right to vote. In 1869 she arranged a women's rights convention, at which Susan B. Anthony delivered an address. Hooker also published prosuffrage letters in *Putnam's Magazine* and organized the Connecticut Woman Suffrage Association. She pressed state legislators to accord women property rights, became an officer of the National Woman Suffrage Association, and composed the Declaration and Pledge of Women of the United States, which she presented to Congress along with 80,000 signatures. She issued *Womanhood: Its Sanctities and Fidelities* (1874) and lectured across Connecticut on gender discrimination. In 1888 she co-organized the first International Convention of Women in Washington, D.C.

NANCY JOHNSON (1935–)

U.S. congresswoman Nancy Lee Johnson of Chicago was the first Republican woman to be a member of the Committee on Ways and Means and chair its subcommittee on health. An activist in New Britain, Connecticut, she was educated at the University of London, Radcliffe College, and the University of Chicago before marrying and establishing a family. In 1976 she entered politics as a successful candidate for the Connecticut state Senate. After three terms in office, she advanced to a career in federal politics.

Upon election to the first of ten terms in the U.S. House of Representatives in 1982, Johnson gained a reputation for efficiency. She advocated greater Medicare funding for prescription drugs, coverage for the uninsured, upgrades to public education, environmental protection, and affordable housing. She nurtured passage of the Taxpayer Bill of Rights II and supported pension reform, an increase to the child care tax credit, and eliminating the earnings limit on working retirees. Her most important position was in 1996, when she chaired the House Ethics Committee's investigation of Speaker Newt Gingrich. In 2002 she worked on legislation that would provide displaced workers with $1 million in reemployment services, and she proposed the Child Sex Crimes Wiretapping Act, a federal initiative against child sex predators.

BARBARA KENNELLY (1936–)

Politician Barbara Bailey Kennelly of Hartford, Connecticut, has thrived in public and private reform efforts. She received a B.A. from Trinity College in Washington, D.C., and an M.A. in government from Trinity College in Hartford. She served on the Hartford Court of Common Council from 1975 to 1979 and, over the next four years, as secretary of the state of Connecticut. In 1982 she won a special election to fill a vacancy in the U.S. House of Representatives, beginning the first of seven terms. Kennelly's moderate activism moved her into other positions of responsibility. After rising to vice chair of the House Democratic Caucus and chair of the House Appropriations Committee, she became the first female to chair the House Intelligence Committee. At age 62,

Kennelly retired from Congress in order to make an unsuccessful run for state governor. In 1999 Pres. Bill Clinton appointed her counselor to the administrator of the Social Security Administration. During her tenure, the bureau tackled streamlining the claims process and benefits, insuring retirees, and providing more disability and survivors insurance.

CLARE BOOTHE LUCE (1903–1987)

Dancer, editor, and playwright Ann Clare Boothe Luce of New York City made numerous contributions to politics and literature. A 1919 graduate of an Episcopal school on Long Island and the Castle School in Tarrytown, New York, she studied dance at the Denishawn School. Following a divorce from her first husband, she took up drama, satire, and editing for *Vogue* and *Vanity Fair* magazines. After marrying prominent magazine publisher Henry R. Luce in 1935, she wrote *Abide with Me* (1935), a play that ran two years on Broadway. She followed with *The Women* (1936) and screenplays *Kiss the Boys Goodbye* (1938) and *Margin for Error* (1939). As a war correspondent for *Life* magazine, she traveled in Europe and the Philippines before representing Connecticut in the U.S. House from 1943 to 1947.

Grieved by the accidental death of her daughter Ann in 1944, Luce returned to writing with a column, "The Real Reason," in *McCall's* magazine. As a supporter of Pres. Dwight D. Eisenhower, she was appointed ambassador to Italy in 1953. She obtained minor government board appointments under presidents Richard Nixon and Gerald Ford. For her multiple contributions to the arts and government, she earned the Laetare Medal for outstanding Catholic volunteerism and honorary doctorates from Fordham and Temple universities.

After her husband died in 1967, Luce moved to Honolulu, Hawaii, and lived there alone for many years. At age 80, she received the Presidential Medal of Freedom.

SYBIL LUDINGTON (1761–1839)

Sybil Ludington Ogden (also Sibbell or Luddington) of Fredericksburg, New York, earned national fame in her teens as a war heroine. The first of 12 children born to Abigail and Col. Henry Ludington, leader of the 7th Regiment of the Dutchess County Militia and an aide to Gen. George Washington, she was keenly aware of the patriots' hardships during the American Revolution. On April 26, 1777, the family received word that Gov. William Tryon's 2,000-strong force had attacked and torched Danbury, Connecticut, 25 miles from the Ludingtons' home and gristmill.

Ludington realized the danger to the militia's depot of munitions, beef and pork, and shoes, and volunteered to replace the wearied messenger. She rode her horse 40 miles across Putnam County to spread the alarm and to muster troops. The lengthy gallop took her through Carmel, Mahopac, Kent Cliffs, Farmers Mills, and Stormville, New York, before she completed the circuit at dawn. She carried nothing with her but a stick to goad her horse and to rap on families' gates and shutters to awaken them to danger from the redcoats. Because of her courage, the 400 men of the militia turned the British back to their fleet, anchored in the Long Island Sound, in a skirmish called the battle of Ridgefield.

Ludington earned the thanks of General Washington and the admiration of her neighbors. At age 23, she wed Catskill attorney Edward Ogden, settled in Unadilla, New York, and bore a son named Harry. The town of Fredericksburg was later named Ludingtonville; markers there point the way along her route. In 1961 Anna Huntington sculpted a life-size bronze statue of Sybil riding sidesaddle and waving her stick. The original stands at Gleneida

Lake in Carmel, New York, and there is a copy in Constitution Memorial Hall in Washington, D.C. In 1976, at the nation's bicentennial, the postal service issued a commemorative stamp featuring Ludington. On April 26, 2002, local historians repeated her famous ride.

HARRIET BEECHER STOWE (1811–1896)

Writer Harriet Elizabeth Beecher Stowe of Litchfield, Connecticut, produced an emotional novel that stirred a nation to overthrow slavery. The daughter of influential Congregationalist preacher Lyman Beecher, she grew up in a deeply religious household, and read the contemporary romances of her liberal uncle, Samuel Foote, which inspired her melodramatic writing style. She studied at a boarding school in Hartford led by her sister Catharine Beecher, who had reared Harriet after their mother died in 1815. When Catharine opened a school in Cincinnati, Ohio, Harriet taught classes while absorbing strong abolitionist tenets from her father's Lane Theological Seminary.

After marrying theologian Calvin Ellis Stowe in 1836, Harriet bore seven children. She began writing and opened a school to supplement the family income. While in Louisiana and Kentucky, she witnessed brutality toward black slaves and the disruption of families when owners put parents or children up for sale. When the family settled in Brunswick, Maine, she composed her masterwork, *Uncle Tom's Cabin* or *Life Among the Lowly* (1852), which was serialized in the abolitionist *National Era* and sold 300,000 copies in its first year. Public response was so extraordinary that she published the documentation of her sources in *A Key to Uncle Tom's Cabin* (1853) and toured Europe.

In 1856 Stowe published *Dred: A Tale of the Great Dismal Swamp*, then turned to lighter fiction and verse, sometimes under the pen name Christopher Crowfield. Stowe wintered near Jacksonville, Florida, to improve the health of one of her sons. An active suffragist, her home was in Hartford, next door to author Mark Twain.

LILLIAN VERNON (1927–)

Entrepreneur Lillian Menasche Vernon Katz of Leipzig, Germany, extended her business by exploiting catalog sales; hers was the first company founded by a woman to be listed on the New York Stock Exchange. Born to a Jewish manufacturer, her family immigrated to Holland and then in 1937 to New York City, in flight from Nazi persecution. After marrying a clothier, Samuel Hochberg, in 1951, she used money they received in wedding gifts to organize the Vernon Specialties Company, a mail-order source of monogrammed purses, belts, and accessories. She wrote her own copy and advertised in *Seventeen* magazine, bringing in nearly $11,000 per month in the first quarter. Over time she expanded her stock to include cuff links, buttons, and combs. Within three years, the company expanded from a home business to a rental building and advertised in fashion magazines.

After launching the Lillian Vernon Corporation, she led others in the industry by publishing 189 million copies of color catalogs of her charm bracelets, kitchen organizers, makeup cases, shoe bags, and gift items, netting an average 5 million orders per year. After her second marriage to Robert Katz, she created a sales empire that won her a place in the Direct Marketing Association Hall of Fame, as well as an Ellis Island Medal of Honor and the Big Sisters National Hero citation. In 1987 she began warehousing and shipping from a center in Virginia Beach. By 1994 she moved her business to TV shopping networks and outlet stores, which her sons operate. She remains active as a board member of Lincoln Center, Meals-on-Wheels, and the White House National Business Women's Council. Vernon was a Greenwich, Connecticut, resident and was inducted into the Connecticut Women's Hall of Fame in 1998.

CHASE GOING WOODHOUSE (1890–1984)

Scholar and politician Chase Going Woodhouse served Connecticut as secretary of state from 1940 to 1942. Born in Victoria, British Columbia, she came of age in Indian territory, where her father worked as an engineer. After earning a B.A. in 1912 and an M.A. in 1913, both in political economics at the Science Hill School, McGill University, she attended the University of Berlin. She was named a fellow at the University of Chicago and taught economics at Connecticut College, Smith College, Vassar College, Oregon State, Columbia University, and the universities of Iowa and Texas.

In 1917 she married Prof. Edward Woodhouse. Her club activities included membership in the League of Women Voters and the American Association of University Women and directorships of the Institute of Women's Professional Relations, Connecticut Federation of Democratic Women's Clubs, and the International Association of Altrusa Clubs.

She chaired the Connecticut War Labor Board and defeated a Republican incumbent to win the coastal Connecticut U.S. House district in 1944. After losing the 1946 election, she served in postwar Germany with Gen. Lucius Clay. Woodhouse regained her House seat in 1948, but lost again in 1950 and retired to Sprague.

—Mary Ellen Snodgrass

PROMINENT SITES

Bush-Holley Historic Site
39 Strickland Road
Greenwich, CT 06807
Telephone: (203) 869 6899
Web: http://www.hstg.org/SiteTree/index.cgi/30
In 1884 Edward and Josephine Holley purchased this home with hopes of using it as a boardinghouse for artists. From 1890 to 1920 the home was at the center of the Cos Cob artist colony. Boarders included American impressionist painters like John Henry Twachtman and Theodore Robinson. The house was run by Josephine and later by her daughter Constance.

Connecticut Women's Hall of Fame
Hartford College for Women
University of Hartford
1265 Asylum Avenue
Hartford, CT 06105
Telephone: (860) 768 5643
Web: http://www.cwhf.org
Honorees include Emily Dunning Barringer, the first female physician to receive a surgical residency; Madeline L'Engle, author of novels, poetry, and prose; and Lillian Vernon, entrepreneur whose company was the first founded by a woman to be traded on the New York Stock Exchange. The Hall of Fame has an extensive Web site that includes information on a 14-location Women's Heritage Trail, and there is a picture gallery of inductees along with brief biographies permanently displayed at the site.

Florence Griswold Museum
96 Lyme Street
Old Lyme, CT 06371
Telephone: (860) 434 5542
Web: http://www.flogris.org
The artists' settlement that thrived here at the beginning of the 20th century was considered by some to be the most famous impressionist art colony in America. It could not have happened without Florence Griswold, who opened the home to artists and sold their work from her hallway "gallery." In 1913 she received a letter from President Wilson about the happy times he enjoyed when his first wife, Ellen Axson Wilson, took painting classes at Griswold's home. Today the museum houses many of the impressionist works that were created there.

Harriet Beecher Stowe Center
77 Forest Street
Hartford, CT 06105
Telephone: (860) 522 9258
Web: http://www.harrietbeecherstowecenter.org
Harriet Beecher Stowe, author of *Uncle Tom's Cabin*, lived in this home located in the Nook Farm section of Hartford from 1864 until her death in 1896. The center comprises three buildings. The Visitor Center, housed in a former carriage house, is home to exhibits and visitor information. Tickets can be obtained there for the Stowe House where furnishings and memorabilia of the family are on display. The Katherine Seymour Day House is home to the Stowe Center Library, which is open by appointment and used for special exhibits.

Hill-Stead Museum
35 Mountain Road
Farmington, CT 06032
Telephone: (860) 677 4787
Web: http://www.hillstead.org/index.html
Theodate Pope, one of the first licensed female architects in Connecticut, designed Hill-Stead as a retirement home for her parents. The mansion boasts 36 rooms and 33,000 square feet. It was completed in 1901, and is now a National Historic Landmark. It still contains the Popes' impressionist collection, including work by Mary Cassatt. Landscape architect Beatrix Farrand designed the unusual sunken garden.

Prudence Crandall House
Intersection of Routes 14 and 169
Canterbury, CT 06331
Telephone: (860) 546 9916
Web: http://www.chc.state.ct.us/
    Crandall%20Museum.htm
In 1833 Prudence Crandall established the first academy for African American young women in New England. Crandall was arrested twice and put on trial and, although she was acquitted in 1834, the school was open for only 18 months before an angry mob forced it to permanently close. The museum shares the story of Crandall and the strong young women who came to her school from as far away as Philadelphia and Boston.

Women's Table
Yale University
Sterling Library
120 High Street
New Haven, CT 06511
Yale graduate Maya Lin designed this tribute to the women of Yale University, which is located on the Yale campus, across from the entrance to Sterling Library.

Lin was a 21-year-old undergraduate student when she received national attention after winning a contest to design the Vietnam War Memorial. The sculpture includes a granite table with water flowing from its center and over the edges. The number of women who attended Yale annually from 1707 to 1992 is recorded in a spiral design: zeros mark the years until 1873, when the Yale art school first admitted women.

RESOURCES

FURTHER READING

HISTORY

Allis, Marguerite. *Connecticut River*. New York: G. P. Putnam's Sons, 1939.

Andersen, Jeffrey, et al. *Connecticut and American Impressionism*. Storrs, Conn.: William Benton Museum of Art, 1980.

Anthony, Susan B., and Ida Husted Harper. *History of Woman Suffrage*. Vol. 4. Indianapolis, Ind.: Hollenbeck Press, 1902.

Bacon, Georgeanna Woolsey, ed. *Letters of a Family during the War for the Union, 1861–1865*. 2 Vols. New Haven, Conn.: Tuttle, Morehouse & Taylor, 1899.

Beecher, Catharine E. *The New Housekeeper's Manual*. New York: J. B. Pond & Co., 1873.

Beecher, Catharine E., and Harriet Beecher Stowe. *American Woman's Home*. 1869. Reprint, Hartford, Conn.: Stowe-Day Foundation, 1994.

Bingham, Harold J. *History of Connecticut*. New York: Lewis Historical Publishing, 1962.

Bushman, Richard L. *From Puritan to Yankee: Character and the Social Order in Connecticut, 1690–1765*. New York: Norton, 1970.

Clark, George L. *A History of Connecticut: Its People and Institutions*. New York: G. P. Putnam's Sons, 1914.

Cott, Nancy F., ed. *Root of Bitterness: Documents of the Social History of American Women*. 2nd ed. Boston: Northeastern University Press, 1996.

Cunningham, Janice P. *Back to the Land: Jewish Farms and Resorts in Connecticut, 1890–1954*. Hartford: Connecticut Historical Commission, 1998.

Dayton, Cornelia Hughes. *Women Before the Bar: Gender, Law, and Society in Connecticut, 1639–1789*. Chapel Hill: University of North Carolina Press, 1995.

Fennelly, Catherine. *Connecticut Women in the Revolutionary Era*. Chester, Conn.: Pequot Press, 1975.

Gesualdi, Louis J. *The Italian Immigrants of Connecticut, 1880 to 1940*. New Haven: Connecticut Academy of Arts and Sciences, 1997.

Green, Harry Clinton, and Mary Wolcott Green. *The Pioneer Mothers of America*. 3 Vols. New York: G. P. Putnam's Sons, 1912.

Harper, Ida Husted. *History of Woman Suffrage*. Vol. 6. New York: J. J. Little & Ives, 1922.

Hepburn, Katharine Houghton. *Woman Suffrage and the Social Evil*. New York: National Woman Suffrage Publishing Co., 1914.

Hewes, Amy. *Women as Munition Makers: A Study of Conditions in Bridgeport, Connecticut*. New York: Russell Sage Foundation, 1917.

Hickox, George A. *Legal Disabilities of Married Women in Connecticut*. Hartford, Conn.: Case, Lockwood & Brainard, 1871.

Hill, Ann C. *The Legal Status of Homemakers in Connecticut*. Washington, D.C.: Homemakers Committee, National Commission on the Observance of International Women's Year, USGPO, 1977.

Hollister, G. H. *The History of Connecticut*. 2 Vols. Hartford: L. Stebbins & Co., 1855.

Hooker, Isabella Beecher. *Womanhood: Its Sanctities and Fidelities*. Boston: Lee and Shepard, 1874.

Jeffries, John W. *Testing the Roosevelt Coalition: Connecticut Society and Politics in the Era of World War II*. Knoxville: University of Tennessee Press, 1979.

Johnston, Alexander. *Connecticut: A Study of a Commonwealth-Democracy*. Boston: Houghton, Mifflin and Co., 1887.

Jones, Mary Jeanne Anderson. *Congregational Commonwealth: Connecticut, 1636–1662*. Middleton, Conn.: Wesleyan University Press, 1968.

Klein, Woody. *Westport, Connecticut: The Story of a New England Town's Rise to Prominence*. Westport, Conn.: Greenwood Press, 2000.

Knight, Kate Brannon. *History of the Work of Connecticut Women at the World's Columbian Exposition, Chicago, 1893*. Hartford, Conn.: Hartford Press, 1898.

Lee, Frank F. *Negro and White in Connecticut Town*. New York: Bookman Associates, 1961.

Lever, Janet. *Women at Yale: Liberating a College Campus*. Indianapolis, Ind.: Bobbs-Merrill, 1971.

Mersky, Roy M., and Jill Duffy. *A Documentary History of the Legal Aspects of Abortion in the United States: Griswold v. Connecticut*. Littleton, Colo.: Fred B. Rothman Publications, 2001.

Moeller, Roger W. *A Paleo-Indian Site in Western Connecticut*. Washington, Conn.: American Indian Archeological Institute, 1980.

Morgan, Forrest. *Connecticut as a Colony and as a State: Or, One of the Original Thirteen*. Hartford: Publishing Society of Connecticut, 1904.

Moynihan, Ruth Barnes. *Coming of Age: Four Centuries of Connecticut Women and Their Choices*. Hartford, Conn.: Aetna Life and Casualty, 1991.

Nichols, Carole. *Votes and More for Women: Suffrage and after in Connecticut*. New York: Haworth Press, 1983.

Niven, John. *Connecticut for the Union*. New Haven, Conn.: Yale University Press, 1965.

Pryse, Marjorie, ed. *Selected Stories of Mary E. Wilkins Freeman*. New York: W. W. Norton, 1983.

Root, Mary Philotheta, ed. *Chapter Sketches, Connecticut Daughters of the American Revolution; Patriots' Daughters*. New Haven: Connecticut Chapter, Daughters of the American Revolution, 1904

Roth, David Morris. *Connecticut, a Bicentennial History*. New York: W. W. Norton, 1979.

Selesky, Harold E. *War and Society in Colonial Connecticut*. New Haven, Conn.: Yale University Press, 1990.

Shepard, Odell. *Connecticut Past and Present*. New York: Alfred A. Knopf, 1939.

Smith, Helen Evertson. *Colonial Days and Ways, as Gathered from Family Papers*. New York: Century Co., 1900.

Speth, Linda E. *Women, Family, and Community in Colonial America*. New York: Haworth Press, 1983.

Stanton, Elizabeth Cady, Susan B. Anthony, and Matilda Joslyn Gage. *History of Woman Suffrage*. Vols. 1–3. Rochester, N.Y.: Charles Mann Printing, 1886.

Taylor, John M. *The Witchcraft Delusion in Colonial Connecticut, 1647–1697*. New York: Grafton Press, 1908.

Taylor, Robert Joseph. *Colonial Connecticut: A History*. Millwood, N.Y.: KTO Press, 1979.

Todd, Charles Burr. *In Olde Connecticut*. Detroit, Mich.: Singing Tree Press, 1968

Trumbull, Benjamin. *A Complete History of Connecticut*. 1818. Reprint, New York: Arno Press, 1972.

Van Dusen, Albert E. *Connecticut*. New York: Random House, 1961.

Wawrose, Susan C. *Griswold v. Connecticut*. New York: Franklin Watts, 1996.

Weatherford, Doris. *American Women and World War II*. New York: Facts On File, 1990.

BIOGRAPHY AND AUTOBIOGRAPHY

Anderson, Marian. *My Lord, What a Morning: An Autobiography*. 1956. Reprint, Urbana: University of Illinois Press, 2002.

Buel, Joy Day, and Richard Buel, Jr. *The Way of Duty: A Woman and Her Family in Revolutionary America*. New York: W. W. Norton, 1995.

Fritz, Jean. *Harriet Beecher Stowe and the Beecher Preachers*. New York: G. P. Putnam's Sons, 1994.

Gilman, Charlotte Perkins. *The Living of Charlotte Perkins Gilman: An Autobiography*. 1935. Reprint, Madison: University of Wisconsin Press, 1991.

Hedrick, Joan D. *Harriet Beecher Stowe: A Life*. New York: Oxford University Press, 1994.

Holland, Barbara. *Katharine Hepburn*. New York: Park Lane Press, 1998.

Hooker, Isabella Beecher. *A Mother's Letters to a Daughter on Woman Suffrage*. Hartford, Conn.: Press of Case, Lockwood & Brainard, 1870.

Housley, Kathleen L. *The Letter Kills but the Spirit Gives Life: The Smiths—Abolitionists, Suffragists, Bible Translators*. Glastonbury: Historical Society of Glastonbury, Conn., 1993.

Primus, Rebecca. *Beloved Sisters and Loving Friends: Letters from Rebecca Primus of Royal Oak, Maryland and Addie Brown of Hartford, Connecticut, 1854–1868*. New York: Alfred A. Knopf, 1999.

Rudd, Jill, and Val Gough, eds. *Charlotte Perkins Gilman: Optimist Reformer*. Iowa City: University of Iowa Press, 1999.

Sklar, Kathryn Kish. *Catharine Beecher: A Study in American Domesticity*. New York: W. W. Norton, 1976.

Smith, Julia Evelyn. *Abby Smith and Her Cows: With a Report of the Law Case Decided Contrary to Law*. Hartford, Conn.: American Publishing Co., 1877.

Stowe, Charles Edward, and Lyman Beecher Stowe. *Harriet Beecher Stowe: The Story of Her Life*. Boston: Houghton Mifflin Co., 1911.

Strane, Susan. *A Whole-Souled Woman: Prudence Crandall and the Education of Black Women*. New York: W. W. Norton, 1990.

Vernon, Lillian. *An Eye for Winners: How I Built One of America's Greatest Direct-Mail Businesses.* New York: HarperCollins Publishing, 1996.

Westbrook, Perry D. *Mary Wilkins Freeman.* Rev. ed. Boston: Twayne Publishers, 1988.

USEFUL WEB SITES

On-line Exhibits, Connecticut Historical Society
   http://www.chs.org/exhib/digexhib.htm

Web Reference Sources, Connecticut State Library
   http://www.cslib.org/webref/index.htm

SELECTED ORGANIZATIONS AND INSTITUTIONS

Connecticut Historical Society
One Elizabeth Street at Asylum Avenue
Hartford, CT 06105
Telephone: (860) 236 5621
Web: http://www.chs.org
This is a nonprofit museum, library, and education center that preserves and presents the history of the diverse people of the state. Its collection comprises an extensive costume and textile resource including quilts, coverlets, bed hangings, linens, and samplers and an African American resource that includes textiles, costumes, toys, and dolls.

Connecticut State Library
231 Capitol Avenue
Hartford, CT 06106
Telephone: (860) 757 6500
The official library of the state of Connecticut, this institution is home to the state's public records and archives and is host to the Museum of Connecticut History, which houses, among other historical objects, an exhibition of political signs and buttons and women's suffrage banners, as well as a voting booth from the early 20th century.

Southern Connecticut State University Women's Studies Program
501 Crescent Street
New Haven, CT 06515
Telephone: (203) 392 6133
Web: http://www.southernct.edu/undergrad/schas/WMS
This program offers an undergraduate minor, a graduate certificate, and an M.A. degree in women's studies. Students study in a variety of disciplines and conduct independent research.

University of Connecticut
Women's Studies Program
354 Mansfield Road, Box U-181
425 Beach Hall
Storrs, CT 06269
Telephone: (860) 486 3970
Web: http://www.sp.uconn.edu/~womstu4/home.htm
Interdisciplinary academic program that focuses on the critical analysis of gender and the pursuit of knowledge about women, and offers a major and graduate certificate program.

Wesleyan University
Women's Studies Program
287 High Street
Middletown, CT 06459
Telephone: (860) 685 3296
Web: http://www.wesleyan.edu/wmst
This is an interdisciplinary major that focuses on the social construction of gender.

Women, Gender and Sexuality
Trinity College
300 Summit Street
Hartford, CT 06106
Telephone: (860) 297 5369
Web: http://www.trincoll.edu/depts/wmgs
Students explore gender and sexuality as social constructs and analyze how these issues have impacted traditional disciplines.

DELAWARE

The baby wailed and drooped through the heat of his first summer; but, when Mamma cut long sprays of pungent chrysanthemums for the brass vases that stood on the altar to the glory of God and in memory of Mary Clarissa Campion, when burrs pattered from the chestnut trees, and the frost touched the persimmons with orange and vermillion, he grew stronger, looked about him with interest, and presently was amiably plunging from outstretched hands to outstretched hands.
Other events besides Victor's first steps . . . took place, though none seemed so important. Trains grew on to dresses, and crinolines were full at the bottom instead of the top, so that ladies turned from tulips to morning glories. Pamela bonnets, like saucers with strings, became so fashionable that even Mamma, who prided herself on being conservative, succumbed; although she only wore hers in the carriage . . .
—Anne Parrish, *The Perennial Bachelor*, 1925

Delaware styles itself "the first state" because it was the first to ratify the U.S. Constitution, doing so on December 7, 1787. Delaware also was the only state to have been founded by Swedes; at the time of Delaware's founding, Sweden was ruled by Queen Christina.

Delaware is small in area and is not densely populated. Its low population makes Delaware one of the seven states that are entitled to only one seat in the 435-member U.S. House of Representatives, so it is perhaps understandable that Delaware has never sent a woman to Congress. In 2000, however, Delaware joined similarly low-population Montana as one of the 13 states to have elected women as governors.

PREHISTORY

(Prehistory–1638)

Delaware's indigenous people were the Lenni-Lenape; European settlers called them "the Delaware." The Lenape were a typical eastern woodlands tribe, living in permanent villages along creeks and rivers. Their dwellings, called wigwams, were single-family structures framed with wood and covered with bark. Corn was basic to their diet, and women prepared it in a variety of ways; women also were the primary farmers, growing beans, squash, and other vegetables. Because they were

close to both the Atlantic and to fresh water, the Delaware diet included fish and seafood.

Delaware men also hunted for deer and other large game with bow and arrow; the women needed animal hides to make clothing.

State Population (2000): 783,600
Female Population (2000): 403,059
Women in State Legislature (2003): 29%
Female College Enrollment (1999): 28,000 (59.6% of total)
Privately Held Women-owned Businesses (1997): 13,662
First Year of Full Suffrage: 1920

251

SOCIAL AND POLITICAL STATUS OF WOMEN OF THE LENAPE TRIBE

The Lenni-Lenape, later named the Delaware by Europeans, inhabited the region that is present-day Delaware and parts of New Jersey, Pennsylvania, and New York until the middle of the 19th century. Their society was matrilineal, with kinship ties traced through the female line. Women were influential and respected members of their community, playing a central role in virtually every aspect of Lenape life including planting and harvesting, food preparation, child care, trading, treaty negotiations, and political leadership.

Lenape women held land titles because all land deeds and territorial claims were inherited through the mother. Women often held or owned land in conjunction with their brothers. Both men and women appear on early land transaction documents; however, the female identity of the signatories often was not recognized by historians and anthropologists because the assumption was that tribal societies were similar to European cultures and that all signatories were male.

Lenape government also differed greatly from the European model. Lenape leadership consisted of a number of leaders, each governing a different aspect of tribal life. The community council and community members at large were responsible for making most of the decisions. Sachems, or chiefs, performed ceremonial and executive duties. All leaders were elected based on their kinship relations and abilities, and included both men and women. War leaders, however, were not elected on the basis of lineage and their position was effective only in times of war. Lenape women chose matrons to represent them during peace negotiations and during the selection or replacement of sachems. These matrons were the center of tribal society. They held political power over women and men; men could be appointed as leaders only by the consent of the matrons.

With the arrival of European settlers in the early 17th century, Lenape society was forced to change. Initially the Lenape resisted conforming to European gender roles; however, as warfare increased, the role of tribal men slowly expanded and replaced the influence of women. Ultimately most members of the Lenape tribe were displaced to Oklahoma where they continue to maintain their tribal identity.

—Theresa Hessey

Delaware women were especially adept at using bone needles and sinew thread to craft robes covered with feathers, which were both warm and shed rain. Women and men wore deerskin leggings for warmth in winter and went nearly naked in summer; both sexes also decorated their bodies with paint and tattoos.

Delaware couples married by mutual consent and divorced in the same way, without any particular ceremony or regulation, and white men discovered that both married and unmarried women viewed sex as routine hospitality to visitors. As a baby's father could not necessarily be identified, the Delaware, like other tribes, were matrilineal: children belonged to the clan of the mother, not the father, with descent traced through the mother's lineage.

Traditionally hospitable, the Lenape welcomed whites. Their riverside villages were particularly vulnerable to attack. Lacking guns and any water transport beyond the hollowed-out logs that they used as canoes, they were ill-prepared to defend themselves. As a result they crossed the river named for them when whites began to crowd them and began their decades-long move west in the mid- to late 1600s. Most of the Lenape who survived would settle in the Indian Territory of Oklahoma. A few would settle in Canada.

WHITE EXPLORATION TO STATEHOOD (1638–1776)

Delaware is the only state in the union founded by Scandinavians. Swedish families settled in the area in 1638, during the reign of Queen Christina. A most unusual monarch, Christina was born in 1626 and became queen at age six, when her father was killed in battle. She officially acceded to Sweden's throne at 18, but Queen Christina was an intellectual, not a politician nor a person content to fill her life with ceremonial duties. She brought famed French philosopher René Descartes to Stockholm, and, after abdicating in 1654, she moved to Rome, the cultural center of Europe. The queen never married nor returned to Sweden.

Her subjects in the New World named their first settlement Fort Christina. In the far north of the state, it was very near where the Delaware Memorial Bridge now stands. These colonists, who became known for introducing the log cabin to America, soon were joined by others, including Dutch families who came under Swedish sponsorship from Utrecht in 1640 and Finnish families who sailed with Swedes from Stockholm the next year. They came for the economic opportunities of a new land, not for religious freedom like the Puritans who were settling in New England in the same era. The Delaware River had three settlements along its shores within a decade, but the number of women settlers is difficult to ascertain. Presumably most colonists came as families, but the names of women are obscured in listings of male heads of households. Some women traded with indigenous peoples, who were said to have especially prized the colorful, tasseled caps of the Swedish women. Occasionally widows are named in legal records, but New Sweden's record keepers were less likely to individualize women than those in the Dutch and English colonies.

Unlike Holland and England, the mother country took relatively little interest in Swedish emigres. Dutch and especially British agents of corporations and monarchs attempted to supervise closely their New World colonies, but New Sweden was more independent of investors and monarchic control. For example, when the Lutheran minister at Fort Christina died in 1643 (leaving a widow and children), he was not replaced for several years. No proper church was built until 1667—three decades after the initial settlement—and as late as 1693, a minority of pious Lutherans still were seeking a minister from Sweden.

THE CHURCH AS A SLAVE OWNER

Ministers were slow to commit themselves to New Sweden because Swedish clergymen were very much a part of the upper class. Neither they nor their wives were accustomed to living without a parsonage that included servants, and they knew they would miss the cultural life and other comforts of sophisticated Sweden. Even the more democratic Norwegian women who were married to Lutheran pastors on the later Iowa frontier, for example, would find the adjustment very hard.

As a result of these class differences, conflict between newly arrived clergy and the hardworking pioneers who preceded them in America was not unusual; in 18th-century Delaware, such conflict was frequent. Pastors were expected to keep detailed records, and their congregants did not hesitate to question spending. Because of this practice, a parenthetical but important reference to a woman exists.

In 1729 Pastor Sam Hesselius was formally charged with selling land that belonged to the church at Christina, and a hearing was held before three justices of the peace at Brandywine Ferry. Pastor Hesselius was acquitted:

As regarded the sale of the land, it was found that it was done by the advice of the officers of the congregation generally, and so was the congregation's own act, and not the Pastor's. From the proceeds of the sale, a negress was purchased for the inventory of the parsonage, and so belonged to the congregation.

The fate of this nameless black woman appeared in other brief entries, with few details about her life or condition. By 1733 John Eneberg was the pastor of the Christina church; unlike most, he was unmarried and therefore "lived in the houses of other Swedes," while the parsonage was rented out. "The negress who had been purchased," the record continues, "also was hired out, and as she grew older she also grew worse."

No further attention is given her until the church's 1742 inventory, 13 years after the church became a slave owner. That inventory's sole report is: "The negress, who, some years before, had been bought for the price of fifty acres of land, was old and contrary, and being set up at auction was sold for seven shillings."

—Doris Weatherford

Excerpts from Benjamin Ferris, *A History of the Original Settlements on the Delaware.* 1846. Reprint, Baltimore: Gateway Press, 1987.

When a pastor was finally dispatched to the New World colonists, an anonymous woman deserved some of the credit. A woman of Göteborg, Sweden, who was likely illiterate, urged her local church officials to contact the nearly forgotten Delaware colonists, especially to see if her brother, Peter Gunnarsson Rambo, was still alive. The church officials sent a letter conveying an inquiry about the status and condition of the American colonists.

The Swedes in America responded with, among other things, a list of requests. Specifically, these colonists—some of whom had been in America for six decades—wanted "twelve bibles, forty-two psalm-books, . . . two hundred catechisms, and as many primers, for which, when received, we promise punctual payment. . . .We promise also, a proper maintenance to the ministers that may be sent us." (Acrelius 1966, 187) Subsequently, a series of Lutheran ministers regularly rotated between the mother country and Delaware and neighboring Pennsylvania.

Military and political change occurred when colonial powers came into conflict over the small colony. Because the Dutch who settled New Netherland (later New York) were more powerful than the small Swedish colony, the Swedes offered little resistance when the Dutch took over Delaware in 1655. Dutch control, however, would last less than a decade; in 1664 Britain took control of the colony.

The transfer of Delaware to Dutch control had little effect on women; Dutch and Scandinavian women had many linguistic and cultural traits in

The marriage of Hannah Callowhill to William Penn, who was the proprietor of Pennsylvania, in 1696. Upon Penn's illness and death, Hannah took over many of his responsibilities as the proprietor of Pennsylvania, which then included Delaware. (Hulton Archive/Getty Images)

common, including use of the maiden name. Dutchwomen were somewhat more advanced than Swedes in terms of independent commercial enterprise and prenuptial agreements, but both groups arguably had a higher status than that of British women, who would lack fundamental property rights until the 1800s.

About a thousand Europeans lived in Delaware when the British took over. Swedes had arrived in four separate expeditions, and, during their three decades in America, many intermarried with the Dutch. After Delaware became an English colony in 1664, the pattern of intermarriage would continue, especially with nearby Pennsylvanians. William Penn became proprietor of Pennsylvania, which then included Delaware, in 1682 following a land grant made to Penn by the English monarch Charles II in payment of a debt owed to Penn's father. Penn visited the Delaware area in 1683 and commented on the Swedes there: "The Swedes . . . of the river Delaware are a plain, strong, and industrious people . . . So they have fine children, and almost every house full. It is rare to find one of them without three or four boys, and as many girls; some [have] six, seven, and eight sons." (Ferris 1987, 137)

A decade later 30 Swedes signed a letter addressed to the "Postmaster at Gottenburg," reporting on their status. Dated May 31, 1693, it said:

> We are for the most part husbandmen. We plough, and sow, and till the ground; and as to our meat and drink, we live according to the old Swedish custom. . . . Our wives and daughters employ themselves in spinning wool and flax, and many of them in weaving; so that we have great reason to thank the Almighty. . . . We live also in peace and friendship with one another; and the Indians have not molested us for many years. (Ibid., 151–152)

Those peaceful relationships were a result of the pacifist philosophy of William Penn; when a series

of strokes debilitated him, Penn appointed his wife, Hannah Callowhill Penn, to act as proprietor of Pennsylvania (still including Delaware) in his stead; she served in this capacity from 1712 to her death in 1726.

The incorporation of Wilmington in 1735 truly began Delaware's development—and Wilmington owes its origins to Quaker minister ELIZABETH LEWIS SHIPLEY. Wilmington began its rise to become Delaware's only major city with the construction of a Quaker meetinghouse in 1738 and, two years later, a jail. Wilmington was unusual in that one of its earliest settlers, a British man, was married to a black woman. They had twin daughters, and, decades later, the family's log cabin still stood on Wilmington's Fourth Street. Fifth Street in this era featured a shop for the sale of "Drugs and Medicines, Chemical and Galenical"; the shop's proprietor, Catharine Dean, a Dutchwoman, sold pharmaceuticals and treated patients.

Like other Dutchwomen, Dean was apparently quick to learn English and assimilate. By the 1740s the Swedish churches—which the churchgoing Dutch also joined, having never built churches of their own—were conducting some services in English. The Anglicization was so complete by 1759 that even the Swedish Christmas festival, which includes girls wearing candle-lit wreaths in their hair, had been abandoned.

STATEHOOD THROUGH THE CIVIL WAR (1776–1865)

Most of the Revolution bypassed Delaware's isolated peninsula, as the fighting in the mid-Atlantic region concentrated in the higher-population areas between Philadelphia and New York City. Indeed, Delaware had only one battle, the battle of the Brandywine, near Newark in September 1777.

Delaware's women nonetheless were affected by the war. Most joined in the boycott of British goods, the burden of which was felt keenly by women. Many ran family farms while their men went to war; nearly 4,000 men enlisted from the small state, which established its independence from Pennsylvania at the same time it approved the Declaration of Independence.

Delaware had enough Loyalists, however, to make themselves a force. Mrs. John Dickinson, married to a Revolutionary War leader, had her home attacked by Loyalists. Another Tory betrayed the husband of Hannah Erwin Israel. Mr. Israel was an active rebel who was arrested when he passed through British lines to visit his elderly mother in Philadelphia. The Israels lived near Wilmington; Hannah was 19 years old and pregnant when British troops came to confiscate their cattle. While they shot at her, she drove the herd into the barn.

Delaware's future was influenced by yellow fever more than the Revolution. Philadelphia had major epidemics in the 1790s; Wilmington's population increased as people fled to its higher ground. By 1798 the mosquito-borne disease also reached Wilmington, causing 82 deaths that summer, compared with about 4,000 dead in Philadelphia. Many refugees settled permanently in Delaware, and the Wilmington area especially began to grow.

A second major influence on Delaware's development was the arrival in 1801 of the du Pont family, who had fled the French Revolution to settle in the Wilmington area, where they opened a munitions plant. The factory and its employee housing were planned together, becoming a model for other company towns. The du Pont daughters soon persuaded their

REVOLUTIONARY NEWS: THE CORRESPONDENCE OF GEORGE AND GERTRUDE READ

Letters that George Read, a signer of the Declaration of Independence, wrote to his wife, Gertrude, bear a similarity to the more famous and highly political correspondence between John and Abigail Adams of Massachusetts. Read's letters speak frequently of the new nation's news, as John Adams's letters to his wife Abigail did.

Gertrude Ross Read spent most of the war at their New Castle home, where she cared for five children—the eldest of whom was just nine when the correspondence began. Her brother, George Ross, also signed the Declaration, and her sister-in-law, Katy Thompson, was married to an army general. These family connections weave through her husband's letters, the first of which was written in 1774, during the First Continental Congress:

MY DEAR G_____,

I am still uncertain as to the time of my return home. As I expected it, the New England men declined doing any business on Sunday. . . . I have no prospect of being with you till Thursday evening. Five of the Virginia men are gone. . . . The two objects before us . . . are an address to the king and one to the people of Canada. . . . Your brother came to Congress this afternoon. All your friends are well. No news but the burning of the vessel [the *Peggy Stewart* in Maryland] which I take for granted you will have heard. . .

After the war began in 1775, Read's letters continued to mix family news with the political:

I have this morning wrote [sic] to Katy [his sister who was married to the general] proposing to her to send her oldest son George, to Philadelphia, to the college, where Ned Biddle [another brother-in-law] will provide him with board and lodging, and that she should send her second son to Wilmington, where you will do the like for him. I presume that you will approve of the last.

The Province ship left town yesterday. . . . A ship outfitted by Congress and called the Reprisal is ordered down also. . . . Little else has been talked of. . . . I flatter myself that I shall see you on Saturday next. Last Saturday the Congress sat, and I could not be absent. . . . This day is their [Delaware's] election for additional members of the Assembly. Great strife is expected. . . . My love to our little ones, and compliments to all acquaintances.

—Doris Weatherford

Excerpts from Harry Clinton Green and Mary Wolcott Green, *The Pioneer Mothers of America*. Vol. 3. New York: G.P. Putnam's Sons, 1912.

father to add a school, and the family thus began to influence Delaware as they would for more than two centuries.

The school was significant since Delaware did not have anything close to the tradition of public education of colonial New England. Although the Wilmington Friends School was begun in 1748, soon after the town's chartering in 1739, non-Quaker girls had no schooling comparable to that of boys until 1818, almost two centuries after the first settlement in Delaware. A public school law was finally passed in 1829, but it was far from adequate and specifically excluded black children. Wilmington's free blacks had begun the nation's first church controlled by blacks, the United Church of Africans, in 1813, and they opened a school for their children in 1824, but many decades would pass before the state developed a comprehensive system of public education.

Delaware also gained its first theater during this time, and women were part of it from the beginning. The very first play performed by the Wilmington Theater Company in 1834 was written and produced by a wife and her husband, referred to as "Mr. and Mrs. Barns."

Women were involved in the other arts as well. Delaware's first acknowledged female poet, ELIZABETH CHANDLER, was just 18 years old in 1825, when she won a literary prize for her antislavery poem "The Slave Ship." Mary Parker Welch also wrote on abolition, especially in her memoir, *Memoirs of Mary Parker Welch*, edited by George T. Welch. Her book discussed how different slavery could be even in the same neighborhood. Her parents had inherited slaves—but they treated them well, taught them a trade, and emancipated them when they reached age 28. At the same time, some of Welch's neighbors were cruel to their slaves, and she came to the conclusion that the institution inevitably encouraged brutality. Unlike most female abolitionists, Welch also added an economic element to her

argument, emphasizing that Delaware was too far north and too industrialized to support a slave-based economy.

The most notorious of female slave traders was a Delaware woman, Patty Cannon. She lived in the Chesapeake Bay area on the Maryland border, where she kidnapped both free blacks and slaves and sold them to dealers who transported their human cargo down the Atlantic coast for resale in the Deep South. She allegedly killed slave traders for their cash. Cannon was finally arrested when the body of one such man was dug up in a field. Presumably she died in a Georgetown, Delaware, jail in 1829, although some say that the dead woman identified as Cannon was another of her victims and that Cannon escaped.

Like other northern states, Delaware's legislature debated adoption of a gradual abolition law in the 1830s, but, unlike its neighbors, Delaware neither ended slavery nor allowed women to join the more public part of the debate. When some 300 Wilmington women sent an abolitionist appeal to the legislature in 1839, the legislature chastised them for daring to exercise the right to petition. Instead, the *House Journal* records the legislators' response: Female constituents were told to stop their "unwarranted interference in subjects that more properly should belong to their fathers, husbands, or brothers" and to concentrate on "matters of a domestic nature, and be more solicitous to mend the garments of their husbands and children, than to patch the breaches of the Laws and Constitution." The state's abolitionist societies lacked prominent female leadership, although Philadelphia's Lucretia Coffin Mott preached at the funeral of one of Delaware's most important abolitionists, Thomas Garrett.

Delaware was the northern state most philosophically aligned with the South at the time of the Civil War; although the legislature allowed a representative of Mississippi to address members about joining the Confederacy, secession never was considered seriously. Most understood that their state was both too far from the heart of the Confederacy and too small to survive outside the Union. The effect, however, was to prolong slavery in Delaware: because the state did not secede, Abraham Lincoln's 1863 Emancipation Proclamation did not apply, since it freed slaves only in the states in rebellion against the Union. Delaware even rejected a pilot program proposed by the federal government that would have offered compensation to slave owners for their loss.

CIVIL WAR THROUGH PROGRESSIVE ERA (1865–1920)

Women, like former slaves, found their civil rights lagging those of women in neighboring states; few Delaware women were active in the struggle for women's rights. Delaware's most prominent women's rights pioneer in this era was a man; abolitionist Thomas Garrett contributed articles to the founding issues of *The Revolution*, a journal that Susan B. Anthony and Elizabeth Cady Stanton began publishing in 1868. One prominent woman activist of this time was Mary Sorden Stuart of Greenwood. She was Delaware's only representative at national women's rights conventions. She wrote in 1886:

> My father was the first man in the State Senate to propose the repeal of some of our oppressive laws, and succeeded in having the law giving all real estate to the eldest male heir repealed. . . .
>
> Prior to 1868, bonds, mortgages, stocks, etc., . . . went into the possession of the husband the moment the woman answered, "I will," in the marriage ceremony. I worked hard to get the law passed giving the wife the right to her own separate earnings, and at last was greatly helped by the fact that a woman petitioned for a divorce, stating in her application that she was driven from her home, that she and her two children had worked hard and saved $100 . . . and now her husband claimed the money. It was a case in

point, and helped the members of our legislature to pass the wages bill. . . .

> The law of 1871 gave a married woman the right to make a will, provided her husband gave his written consent, with the names of two respectable witnesses attached . . .
>
> Delaware College, the only institution of the kind in the State, was open to girls for thirteen years [after 1872], but owing to a tragedy committed by the boys in hazing one another . . . the doors were thereafter closed to girls, although they were in no way directly or indirectly implicated in the outrages. When Governor Stockley was appealed to, he simply gave some of the old arguments against coeducation. . . . We have women who are practicing physicians. . . . We have none who practice law or preach in our pulpits, and all the political offices of the State are closed to women. No notaries, bank cashiers, telegraph operators. . . . (Stanton, Anthony, and Gage 1886, 3:817–818)

By comparison, women had held political offices in Wyoming and other western states for more than a decade; they had been admitted to coeducational colleges in Iowa and other states of the Midwest also for more than a decade. Delaware's only achievement for women was in the practice of medicine, which perhaps was influenced by the nearby Women's Medical College of Pennsylvania. The Pennsylvania college was the first medical school for women in the United States, granting its first degrees in 1851.

In 1881 celebrity lawyers Belva Ann Lockwood of Washington, D.C., and Phoebe Couzins of Missouri joined Susan B. Anthony and Elizabeth Cady Stanton in speaking to committees of the Delaware legislature. Although Lockwood used the state's own legal code to demonstrate that women arguably were entitled to vote under its current laws, only two legislators voted for her resolution.

Suffrage activist Mary A. Stuart decided that if reason would not work, perhaps ridicule would. In the 1884 election campaign, Republicans used an image—Ship of State—that featured an eagle; Stuart placed a blue hen in a glass coop atop it. Her emblem for cooped-up women attracted attention through the campaign, but with little positive result. Instead, women's progress was measured by the abolition of a colonial relic; in 1889 the legislature banned the use of the pillory, or whipping post, for women. Men, however, still could be publicly whipped as punishment for crimes into the 20th century.

The state's first suffrage organization—the Delaware Equal Suffrage Association—was finally established in 1895. It formed at the state's only true city, Wilmington, but was led by Pennsylvania's Rachel Foster Avery. In 1896 the National American Woman Suffrage Association sent Rev. Henrietta G. Moore of Ohio and Mary Garrett Hay of New York to prepare for a proposed revision of Delaware's constitution the following year. National leader Carrie Chapman Catt also visited; she then sent field organizers Mary C. C. Bradford of Colorado and Laura Gregg of Kansas to Delaware.

They gathered petition signatures from 1,592 men and 1,228 women, and Carrie Chapman Catt joined three Delaware women—Emalea P. Warner, Margaret W. Houston, and Emma Worell—in speaking to the relevant committee of the constitutional convention. The women's appeal failed in a 17–7 vote. This 1896 attempt and an 1881 attempt organized by outsiders were the only suffrage bills introduced during the 19th century; the first campaign for a constitutional amendment to be truly undertaken by Delaware women would wait until 1913.

The association continued under the leadership of Martha S. Cranston of Newport, however, and women did win some rights at lower levels of government. In the towns of Milford, Newark, Townsend, and Wyoming, women who paid property taxes in their own right were permitted to vote for town commissioners. Throughout the state, female property tax payers could vote for school trustees.

Instead of the vote, women worked on issues like raising the age of consent from age 7 to age 15 in 1895. Five years later, however, feminists reported that "it has been very difficult to secure the conviction of men for this crime, and those convicted have been repeatedly pardoned by the governor." (Anthony and Harper 1902, 4:565)

As late as 1900 the father remained the sole legal guardian of children, and he alone had the authority to appoint a guardian for children should he die. Decades later than other states, Delaware women still were prohibited from becoming lawyers. In January 1900 the Delaware supreme court turned down the application of a woman to practice law; the court's reasoning was that a lawyer was an officer of the state and, as such, must be able to vote.

At the turn of the century, prospects for a woman becoming an attorney or any kind of professional were further limited by lack of education facilities and access to education. The state had just one public high school, in Wilmington, and its one public college, at Newark, excluded women. The creation of a college for women became a higher goal for suffragists than suffrage itself, and they worked for it decade after decade. In 1914 Delaware finally opened the Delaware College for Women; it was the nation's second-to-last state to open a public college for women; three years later, neighboring New Jersey would be the last. Black women in Delaware could go to a public college before white women could; Delaware State College, which was limited to black students, was coeducational from its 1892 opening.

With the 1913 march of women from New York to Washington, D.C., Delaware suffragists turned their full energies to the cause of women's suffrage. An overflow crowd welcomed this "Pilgrim Band" to Wilmington, and several Delaware women joined them on the march south to Washington. MABEL VERNON became the best known. A graduate of Swarthmore, she would prove particularly valuable in the successful campaign for suffrage in Nevada the next year and, in 1917, she would be one of the first women arrested for picketing the White House.

The state suffrage association held its 1914 convention in the deeply conservative capital city of Dover. Not only did Dover lack any suffrage organization, but also the mayor refused his traditional welcome to the conventioneers. Disappointed by this, Martha Cranston, the association's only president since its 1896 beginning, retired in 1915. Her successor, Mary Clare Brassington, led the struggling

society for just two years before moving from Delaware in 1917.

Young women like Vernon were diverging from older suffragists all over the nation during this era, as they evolved from leadership in the Congressional Union, which had been an arm of the National American Woman Suffrage Association (NAWSA), into the much more radical National Woman's Party (NWP), founded in 1916. Delaware's suffragists, too, split into separate affiliates of these rival national bodies.

Competition between the NAWSA and the NWP may have helped encourage the many rallies, parades, and other functions that drew

'TIL THE JONQUILS TURN BROWN: THE LONG FIGHT FOR THE VOTE

By the time Delaware took up the issue of ratification of the 19th Amendment in June 1920, only one more state was needed to grant all women the vote under the U.S. Constitution. National antisuffragists were desperate to stop the momentum, and they made a last stand in Dover. Conservative lobbyists dominated the antisuffrage cause; in Delaware, Pennsylvania Railroad lobbyists were especially visible. The liquor industry had long opposed suffrage, and it now was particularly committed to keep women from voting because it was beginning its drive to repeal Prohibition, which legislators, mostly male, recently had added to the Constitution.

Delaware's other powerful business interest, the du Pont family, supported suffrage; Alfred Irénée du Pont, Thomas Coleman du Pont, and Pierre Samuel du Pont all worked on its behalf, but without effect. Rural men generally opposed it, and as state suffrage leader Mary R. de Vou said, the antisuffragists "rushed every farmer and small politician they could secure" to Dover. Many of the antisuffrage women were from out of state, and virtually all were from wealthy families. These women placed red roses in men's buttonholes, and supporters retaliated with jonquils—an indication that they did not expect the campaign to go on into June, long after yellow jonquils turn brown.

The state House of Representatives soundly defeated suffrage on April Fool's Day. Members were heartened by one of the women, state antisuffragist

president Mary Wilson Thompson, who shouted encouraging advice to her conservative allies on the floor until the Republican floor leader asked her to be quiet.

Despite the loss suffragists continued to work furiously on a new strategy. The legislature had strong Republican majorities, and the Republican state convention was scheduled to meet in Dover. Suffragists greeted the male delegates with hundreds of marching women, a parade of decorated automobiles, and 20,000 petition signatures—a strong showing in such a small state.

The demonstration had its effect, and on May 5, the Delaware state Senate ratified 11–6. Instead of forwarding its resolution to the House as is standard procedure, however, Senate leaders hung on to it. Literally locked away, the resolution waited while the du Ponts, the governor, U.S. senators, the president of the United States, and others tried to change votes in the lower house. House speaker Alexander P. Corbitt was strongly opposed, however, and no members dared defy him. The Delaware House formally delivered its death blow on June 2; the last tally was 24–10.

Delaware, the first state, lost its opportunity to be the last state needed to fully enfranchise half of America's citizens. That honor went to Tennessee.

—Doris Weatherford

Excerpt from Mary R. de Vou's report on Delaware. In *History of Woman Suffrage*, vol. 6, by Ida Husted Harper. New York: J.J. Little & Ives, 1922.

attention to the issue of women's suffrage. Despite attempts in 1913, 1915, and 1917, however, neither group made much headway in meeting the state's constitutional requirement of a two-thirds vote in each house during two consecutive sessions. After 1917 suffragists shifted their focus from state government to federal government. At the direction of national president Carrie Chapman Catt, Delaware women worked to convince men to oppose the incumbent U.S. senator and to replace him with a pro-suffrage man, J. Heisler Ball. Delaware and Massachusetts were the two states in which Catt's strategy was successful in the 1918 election, and those men provided the two votes necessary to achieve the required two-thirds majority for passage of the suffrage amendment out of the U.S. Senate and on to the states for ratification debate in June of 1919. Delaware's ratification campaign was one of the longest in the nation.

1920s THROUGH WORLD WAR II ERA (1920–1950)

One of the women most visible in the antisuffrage movement was Wilmington's EMILY P. BISSELL, who traveled as far as Oregon in 1900 to oppose women's right to vote in that state. Nevertheless, Bissell is also one of Delaware's most famous women. She founded the state's first free kindergarten and was a founder of its Red Cross chapter and Anti-Tuberculosis Society.

Delaware's most innovative program for needy women, Mother's Pensions, was first adopted in 1917 and served as a model for welfare programs elsewhere. These "pensions" provided widows with financial support for children under 16. The program was largely an achievement of the General Federation of Women's Clubs whose first president was Emalea Pusey Warner, the suffragist who spoke to the 1897 Delaware legislature. During her long life, Warner also established sewing rooms to employ poor women, a visiting nurse program, fresh-air vacations for urban women, and more.

The marriage of Alfred du Pont and JESSIE BALL DU PONT in 1921 also affected Delaware's needy. A teacher in her native Virginia and later in California, Jessie du Pont funded a variety of health and education causes—especially for blacks, although she would oppose school integration—after she moved to Delaware. When she died in 1970, Jessie Ball du Pont had given $100 million to charity, much of it in Delaware and in Jacksonville, Florida, the site of her winter home.

In the 1920s CECILE STEELE, an Ocean View, Sussex County, farm woman, created a revolution in the food industry by starting the chicken broiler industry. She laid the foundation for a major segment of the food industry and helped to transform the American diet by making poultry cheaper than beef or pork.

In 1921 Delaware College for Women merged with the all-male Delaware College to become the University of Delaware; although the legislature had resisted female higher education for decades, the women's college had a mere seven-year existence. After women began voting in 1920, the legislature retroactively ratified the 19th Amendment in 1923. The next year saw the election of Delaware's first female legislator, Florence M. Hanby of Brandywine. From 1925 to 1927 Republican Fannie Harrington served as Delaware's first female secretary of state; Harrington was also Delaware's first female statewide official.

A Delaware woman won the prestigious Harper Prize for her 1925 novel, *The Perennial Bachelor*; Anne Parrish used her Claymont neighborhood as the setting for this bestseller. Other female novelists whose settings were in their native Delaware include Katharine Virden (*The Crooked Eye*, 1930), Gertrude Crownfield (*Where Glory Waits,* 1934), and Ella Middleton Tybout (*Poketown People*, 1904). Artist Henryette

Stadelman (who did not use her married name of Whiteside) had paintings, which were acclaimed for their use of color, displayed in New York museums; she also founded the Wilmington Academy of Art in 1928, now closed. Other artists who achieved recognition in this era were Ellen Thompson Pyle and Ethel Pennewell Brown Leach. Wilmington native Kathryn A. Ross made her operatic debut in Italy in 1926; she went on to star as Aida with the Philadelphia Opera Company.

During the Great Depression, Delaware was one of relatively few states in which the Federal Writers' Project—a program that employed writers—was headed by a woman. Jeanette Eckman was its director during its years of operation (1935–1941); Eckman also wrote the revised version of the state guidebook published in 1955. In Delaware, as elsewhere, the Federal Writers' Project was important not only for the employment it provided, but also and especially because these writers often preserved history that otherwise would have been lost.

The 1930s Depression was not as severe in Delaware as elsewhere; the state had no failures of any significant bank. Cecile Steele deserves credit, as the chicken industry grew by almost 700 percent in the decade. The du Pont chemical enterprises also expanded despite the Depression, in part because European nations were preparing for war.

The little state became of prime importance to the nation in World War II, as its munitions and shipbuilding industries were vital to victory. Munitions plants especially liked to hire women because their executives believed that women were better workers: they were less likely than men to take risks with live ammunition and more careful about obeying the many rules to prevent explosions. The industry also employed many black women, giving some their first opportunity for jobs beyond domestic service. Shipbuilders, in

contrast, were the most reluctant of any war industry to hire women. The federal government made clear to managers that the nation could not afford the luxury of discrimination, however, and thousands of women worked on ships on the Delaware River.

Delaware women also joined the military, which opened its doors to women for the first time. Veteran pilot Nancy Harkness Love began the Women's Auxiliary Ferrying Squadron (WAFS) at an army base near Wilmington. The tremendous shortage of nurses was answered, in part, by a Delaware woman, Lucile Petry Leone, who became director of the Cadet Nurse Corps that recruited young women into the profession. Leone went on to become an assistant surgeon general and was a top official with the United States Public Health Service.

POSTWAR AND CONTEMPORARY ERAS (1950–present)

For the first time in the state's long history, Delaware began to grow at a faster rate than the United States generally and women began to have greater opportunities. The need for labor had been so great during the war that the government encouraged labor unions, and thousands of women who worked in Wilmington textile plants and other factories joined unions for the first time. The higher wages lasted after the war, as pent-up consumer demand kept the highly industrialized area humming. By 1950 women numbered 36,223 of the 126,637 in the state's workforce.

World War II gave African Americans their first real opportunity to join the American mainstream, and Delaware played a role. Ethel Belton was 15 years old in 1952 and lived in Claymont, between Wilmington and Philadelphia, but Claymont High School was for white students only. Tired of the long bus ride into Wilmington to go to all-black Howard High School, Belton joined other NAACP plaintiffs in filing suit. Her case was one of several bundled under *Brown v. The Board of Education of Topeka, Kansas*, the historic 1954 case in which the U.S. Supreme Court ruled against segregated schools.

No women in Delaware had been elected to statewide office after Fannie Harrington, who was secretary of state (1925–1927) in the 1920s, until 1957, when a woman became state treasurer—an office that other women would hold for most of the rest of the century. The first was Republican Vera G. Davis, who took the post in 1957; Democrat Annabelle Smith Everett replaced her in 1959 and held the position until 1966. Emily Womach, a Democrat, took it over in 1971, and two Republican women—Mary D. Jornlin and Janet C. Rzewnicki—held it from 1983 to 1999.

Women began to reach the pinnacle of success in 1992, when Democrat RUTH ANN MINNER won election as lieutenant governor. Minner did not adopt the low profile usual for lieutenant governors; she began a comprehensive review of state government designed to make its agencies more citizen-friendly, and—from her personal knowledge of the need—worked to expand the offerings and access to adult education.

Donna Lee Williams was elected as Delaware's first female insurance commissioner in 1992, and has since been reelected twice. During her tenure, Republican Williams strengthened licensing requirements, increased Medicare options, and fought insurance fraud.

In 1995 M. Jane Brady became Delaware's attorney general; she also was the first woman in that position. Brady graduated from law school in 1977 and began a career as a federal prosecutor in her home state. In 1990 she went into private practice and prepared for her successful race for attorney general. A Republican, Brady is married to an officer in the state police and has advocated for victims' rights.

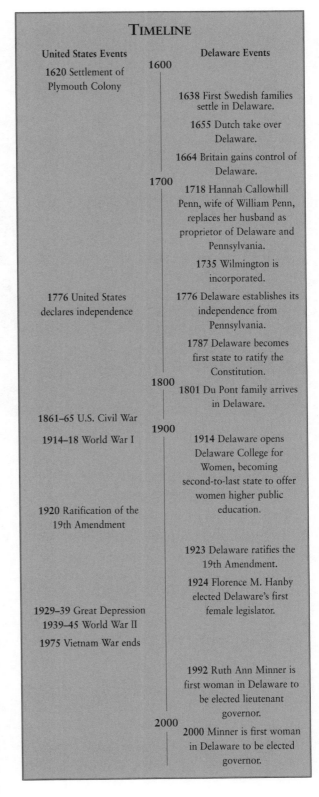

TIMELINE

United States Events		Delaware Events
1620 Settlement of Plymouth Colony	1600	
		1638 First Swedish families settle in Delaware.
		1655 Dutch take over Delaware.
		1664 Britain gains control of Delaware.
	1700	1718 Hannah Callowhill Penn, wife of William Penn, replaces her husband as proprietor of Delaware and Pennsylvania.
		1735 Wilmington is incorporated.
1776 United States declares independence		1776 Delaware establishes its independence from Pennsylvania.
		1787 Delaware becomes first state to ratify the Constitution.
	1800	1801 Du Pont family arrives in Delaware.
1861–65 U.S. Civil War	1900	
1914–18 World War I		1914 Delaware opens Delaware College for Women, becoming second-to-last state to offer women higher public education.
1920 Ratification of the 19th Amendment		
		1923 Delaware ratifies the 19th Amendment.
		1924 Florence M. Hanby elected Delaware's first female legislator.
1929–39 Great Depression		
1939–45 World War II		
1975 Vietnam War ends		
		1992 Ruth Ann Minner is first woman in Delaware to be elected lieutenant governor.
	2000	2000 Minner is first woman in Delaware to be elected governor.

In the 2000 election Ruth Ann Minner was elected governor. She defeated Republican John Burris, the former state House of Representatives majority leader, with 59% of the vote. Governor

Lt. Gov. Ruth Minner during her successful campaign for governor in 2000. (AP/Wide World Photos)

Minner's highest current priority is "Liveable Delaware," an initiative intended to reduce urban sprawl and improve community planning.

Although Delaware is one of six states that has never sent a woman to represent it in Congress, it joins Vermont as the two of those six that have elected a woman as governor. As of 2003 Delaware had three women in statewide offices: Ruth Ann Minner as governor, Jane Brady as attorney general, and Donna Lee Williams as state insurance commissioner.

—Doris Weatherford

PROMINENT WOMEN

EMILY P. BISSELL (1861–1948)

Social worker Emily P. Bissell of Wilmington, Delaware, created Christmas seals, a means of funding "fresh air" hospitals to fight tuberculosis, rampant among poor urban immigrants and on the reservations of Native Americans. She helped organize the state chapter of the Red Cross and was a volunteer worker when her cousin, Dr. Joseph Wales, asked her to raise $300 to maintain the nearby Brandywine Sanatorium. She had read Jacob Riis's magazine article about a Danish fund-raiser who sold postal seals to aid needy children. When she broached the idea to the state Red Cross, officials declined to pay printing costs of $40 for the 1907 Christmas season. On her own, she raised the money and issued 50,000 decorative seals through the Wilmington post office for a penny each. When the first stickers reached the market on December 7, Bissell enlisted women's clubs, churches, schools, retailers, and Leigh Mitchell Hodges, columnist for the *Philadelphia North American*, to urge readers to "Stamp Out Tuberculosis." Concerted efforts brought in $3,000.

To further the campaign, Bissell organized the Delaware Anti-Tuberculosis Society, hired a designer for the 1908 seals, and sold the fund-raising idea to other American newspaper publishers. The seals gained the support of Pres. Theodore Roosevelt as well as the speaker of the House of Representatives and chief justice of the Supreme Court. The American Red Cross took charge of selling the seals and, with help from the National Tuberculosis Association, raised $135,000 the next year. The original sanatorium was expanded into the Emily P. Bissell Hospital, a treatment center for lung disease. As an art form, the seals, with their official double-barred cross of Lorraine, chronicled American design at the same time that they raised funds to improve national health.

Bissell was also a very prominent campaigner against women's suffrage. At the national as well as local level, Bissell was active in a range of anti-suffrage activities.

ANNIE JUMP CANNON (1863–1941)

One of the first female Delaware residents to attend a university, Annie Jump Cannon of Dover used her knowledge to organize scientific findings about stars. The daughter of a state senator, she learned the constellations in childhood from her mother and, by candlelight, studied star placement through an attic window. She advanced her knowledge of the heavens at Wellesley College. Although scarlet fever left her partly deaf, she traveled alone to Italy to view a solar eclipse.

In 1894 Cannon furthered her knowledge of astronomy and physics through graduate courses in spectroscopy. Two years later she joined the staff of the Harvard College Observatory as a teaching assistant and focused and enlarged the school's astronomy program. At age 48, she was named curator of observatory photos and, using prism plates, began classifying variable stars down to the ninth magnitude at the rate of 60,000 stars per year. By 1924 her star identifications filled nine volumes of *The Henry Draper Catalogue*.

For perfecting the Harvard System—a universal recording, classification, and cataloging of stars by temperature, composition, color, and radiation—and for issuing two more volumes of the *Draper Catalogue Extension*, Cannon was awarded six honorary degrees in astrophysics. In 1925 she was elected to membership in the American Philosophical Society, was awarded an honorary doctorate by Oxford University—the first woman to be so honored—and also became the first female to hold office in the American Astronomical Society. At age 68, she was awarded the Draper Gold Medal by the National Academy of Sciences, again the first woman to be so honored. Cannon used the cash honorarium to found the American Astronomical Society's award for distinguished female astronomers. In 1994 she was inducted into the Women's Hall of Fame for identifying a total of 400,000 stars.

ELIZABETH CHANDLER (1807–1834)

Journalist and writer Elizabeth Margaret Chandler of Centre, Delaware, focused on women and minorities. Born into a family with English Quaker roots, she lived in Philadelphia with her maternal grandmother after her mother, Margaret Evans Chandler, died shortly after Elizabeth was born. She was educated in Quaker schools and received rigorous home instruction in religion. Orphaned at age nine, she became shy and introspective. In 1820 she ended formal schooling and began self-directed reading and composition. Her friends published her poetry and sketches anonymously in newspapers.

By 1823 Chandler had become reclusive, limiting her activities to Quaker meetings and to writing voluminously on philanthropy and abolition for the press. For the periodical *Genius of Universal Emancipation*, she wrote "The Recaptured Slave," "The Slave's Appeal," and "The Wife's Lament." The periodical *Casket* awarded her a prize for the antislavery poem "The Slave Ship," which Benjamin Lundy liked well enough to invite the poet to contribute regularly to the *Genius*.

In 1829 Chandler edited the women's page of the *Genius*, which issued her "Appeal to the Ladies of the United States," an essay on abolition. At age 23, she moved to a farm in Michigan territory with her brother and aunt; Chandler continued her work for the *Genius* by mail. She joined a neighbor, Laura Haviland, in establishing the Michigan Female Anti-Slavery Society. Two years later Chandler died of a fever. In 1836 Benjamin Lundy wrote her biography as part of her collected writings that he published in *Poetical Works of Elizabeth Margaret Chandler, with a Memoir of Her Life and Character and Essays, Philanthropic and Moral*.

JESSIE BALL DU PONT (1884–1970)

Philanthropist Jessie Dew Ball du Pont of Ball's Creek, Virginia, promoted cultural and educational projects in Delaware and the nation. A descendant of Mary Ball Washington, mother of George Washington, she learned business from her father, the commonwealth attorney, while driving his buggy around the county to collect his legal fees. After a year's study at Farmville State College, she taught school in Virginia and California before marrying Alfred Irénée du Pont, of Delaware. When his hearing failed, she became his executive assistant and adviser.

Jessie du Pont developed a strategy to use the family's fortune in beneficent causes. Widowed in 1935, she initiated her charitable plans by founding the Alfred I. du Pont Institute for Crippled Children at Nemours and used her wealth to help churches, museums, and colleges and universities. Among her projects was the preservation of the Jacksonville Treaty Live Oak, a historic tree in Jacksonville, Florida. Her will left directions and money to found the Jessie Ball du Pont Religious, Charitable and Educational Fund, which underwrites research at the Virginia Foundation for Independent Colleges. At Stratford Hall Plantation, the home of the Lee family, the Jessie du Pont Library stores books and maps from colonial times and on colonial themes. In 1951 the construction of du Pont Hall at Mary Washington College honored Jessie du Pont as a patron of education and provider of scholarships to needy students.

RUTH ANN MINNER (1935–)

Ruth Ann Coverdale Minner of Milford, governor of Delaware from 2001 to present, entered politics to give voice to the frustrations of other single mothers. Raised on a tenant farm, she dropped out of school at age 16, married Frank Ingram, and raised their three boys. Widowed at age 32, she earned a high school equivalency diploma while holding two jobs—librarian and state agricultural surveyor. In 1969 she married Roger Minner and helped him open a trucking company. Her volunteer work for the state Democratic party and her work as receptionist for Gov. Sherman W. Tribbett led to her interest in helping women through legislation.

In 1974 Minner was elected to the first of four terms as a state representative. From majority whip to state senator, she continued to rise in politics and campaigned for the Delaware Land and Water Conservation Act. In 1993 she began two terms as lieutenant governor, working to expand adult literacy while in that office. Elected governor of Delaware in 2000, Minner continues working to build coalitions, protect the environment, strengthen gun control laws, and promote education and public safety.

MARY ANN SHADD CARY (1823–1893)

Educator and writer Mary Ann Shadd Cary was the first African American woman to enroll in law school and to publish a newspaper. Born in Wilmington, Delaware, Shadd was educated in a Quaker school in West Chester, Pennsylvania, sent there by her parents at the age of ten. Returning to Wilmington six years later, she opened a school for blacks. She also taught in Trenton, New Jersey, and New York City, before she moved north at age 28 to Windsor, in Ontario, Canada, across the river from Detroit. Because the 1850 Fugitive Slave Act endangered free blacks, her family soon followed her.

In 1853 Shadd launched a newspaper—*The Provincial Freeman*—in Windsor. The newspaper helped to keep U.S. blacks informed of the then-favorable conditions for African Americans in this region of Canada. In 1854 Shad was named the editor of the newspaper, the first black woman in such a position in North America. In 1856 she married Thomas F. Cary, a Toronto barber, who died in 1860.

During the Civil War, Mary Cary returned to the United States and worked as an army recruiting officer to enlist black soldiers in Indiana and elsewhere. In 1869 Cary enrolled in law school at Howard University, Washington, D.C., becoming the first African American woman to attend law school. Financing her night classes by teaching during the day, she earned her law degree in 1883.

While studying law at Howard, Cary became active in the women's rights movement, attending meetings of the National Woman Suffrage Association. She helped to establish the Colored Women's Progressive Franchise Association in 1880. Cary was one of two black representatives at the annual meeting of the Association for the Advancement of Women in New York in 1887.

ELIZABETH LEWIS SHIPLEY (?–1777)

A prescient Quaker minister, Elizabeth Lewis Shipley of colonial Wilmington, Delaware, foresaw the development and greatness of Delaware. She was responsive to dreams, which she believed to be (and implemented as) instructions from God. In the 1730s, having left her Ridley, Pennsylvania, home to make a preaching tour through Delaware, Shipley visualized a productive farm plot at Old Brandywine Ford. In 1735 she and her husband, William Shipley, whom she married in 1728, followed her vision and established their home on the nearby hillside.

History records the Shipleys' contributions to the settlement in William's name, Wilmington being a corruption of Willington. In 1736 he joined community settlers in selecting Wednesday and Saturday as official market days; in 1740 he signed a petition requesting that the town of Wilmington be incorporated. Before Elizabeth's death in 1777, she glimpsed a panorama of the American

Revolution—she dreamed of an invasion force and foretold that colonists would repel its advance and establish an independent nation. Her prediction came true after 4,000 Delaware settlers volunteered for the militia to defeat advancing British. The Shipley home at Wilmington became a campus of the Delaware Technical and Community College.

CECILE STEELE (dates unknown)

An innovator in the poultry business, Cecile Steele of Ocean View, Delaware, contributed to the state's economy when she launched a broiler-growing industry that reached a value of $1.6 billion. In spring 1923 a supplier made a mistake after Steele ordered 50 chicks to replace losses to her egg-laying stock. When the hatchery delivered ten times that number, Steele decided to focus her Delmarva farm on poultry as meat. Until that time chicken as meat, which was expensive, had been considered secondary to the main product of eggs. She penned the oversized flock in a piano box while a builder erected a henhouse. By fall Steele was ready to sell 387 of her birds, which brought 62 cents per pound.

The handsome profit encouraged Steele to double her chick order the next year. She and her husband, Coast Guard officer Wilmer Steele, went into the broiler business full-time and began raising 25,000 chickens at a time. Delaware's mild climate and sandy soil encouraged free-range growing methods that produced broad-breasted hens and tender meat. Within four years, the area supported 500 broiler-growers. Her hen farm made Sussex County into the top broiler-producing county in the nation.

MABEL VERNON (1883–1975)

A pacifist and suffrage organizer, Mabel Vernon of Wilmington, Delaware, entered the right-to-vote movement and collected 500,000 signatures demanding full citizenship for women. Educated at Swarthmore College and Columbia University, Vernon left her job teaching German at a high school in Radnor, Pennsylvania, in 1913 to campaign for women's rights. As an on-the-road speaker and activist during the 1914 Nevada drive to gain new members for the suffrage movement, she preceded the coast-to-coast campaign of Dr. Alice Paul, whom the National American Woman Suffrage Association had expelled for raucous, disruptive public behavior.

Vernon, who served as the first national organizer of the radical wing of the women's suffrage movement, set about influencing congressmen and directing the campaign for equal rights. On her own, in protest of the U.S. involvement in World War I, she formed a peace initiative called the People's Movement and was arrested in 1916 for interrupting a prowar speech by Pres. Woodrow Wilson. In June 1917, she and five other militant suffragists were arrested in Washington, D.C., for obstructing traffic. Because they refused to pay a $25 fine, they spent three days in jail. She led a group of women on a train—the Suffrage Special—and, to raise campaign funds, acted as auctioneer at the sale of Paul's headquarters. From 1925 to 1929 she served as secretary of the Women's Party. In later years, she supported the Women's International League for Peace and Freedom and the Equal Rights Amendment.

—Mary Ellen Snodgrass

PROMINENT SITES

Air Mobility Command Museum
1301 Heritage Road
Dover Air Force Base, DE 19902
Telephone: (302) 677 5938
Web: http://www.amcmuseum.org
The Women's Air Service Pilots, or WASP, was a quasi-military unit created by Congress to handle noncombat flying duties for the Army Air Force during World War II. The exhibit *Flying Females: The WASPs of WWII* honors these women and features artifacts donated by two Delaware WASPs.

Anna Hazard Museum
17 Christian Street
Rehoboth Beach, DE 19971
Telephone: (302) 227 6181
A Camp Meeting Era tent houses Rehoboth Beach's first museum of local history. It is named for Anna Hazard, civic leader and one-time owner of the structure.

Biggs Museum of American Art
406 Federal Street
Dover, DE 19903
Telephone: (302) 674 2111
Web: http://www.biggsmuseum.org
The museum is located in the upper two floors of the Delaware State Visitors Center in the Old State House. Many pieces by and about Delaware women are on permanent display, including a sampler stitched in 1825 by southern Delaware's Sarah Ann Hazzard, who was eight years old at the time she completed the needlework, as well as works in oil and watercolor by Dover-born artist Betty Harrington.

Delaware Agricultural Museum and Village
866 North DuPont Highway
Dover, DE 19901
Telephone: (302) 734 1618
Web: http://www.agriculturalmuseum.org
The museum has seasonal exhibits, which regularly feature women and their work. The work of Cecile Steele, the pioneer of the broiler chicken industry, and her chicken house are on display. During Living History events first- and third-person interpreters describe the women's suffrage movement and the Women's Christian Temperance Union.

Delaware History Museum
504 Market Street
Wilmington, DE 19801
Telephone: (302) 656 0637
Web: http://www.hsd.org/dhm.htm
The permanent exhibit *Distinctively Delaware* explores the last 400 years of Delaware's history. Information about Cecile Steele, women's suffrage, and the Lenni-Lenape is on display as well as a history of bathing suits used in the 20th century.

Delaware Toy and Miniature Museum
PO Box 4053
Route 141
Wilmington, DE 19807
Telephone: (302) 427 8697
Web: http://www.thomes.net/toys
The museum collects toys and miniatures from the 18th to 20th centuries. Estate collections of Mrs. Jean Austin du Pont, Miriam Wentworth, and Helena Rubenstein are featured. More than 100 dollhouses and miniature rooms are on display. The miniature rooms from the 18th and 19th centuries provide a glimpse into interior styles of the times.

Hagley Museum and Library
298 Buck Road East
Wilmington, DE 19807
Telephone: (302) 658 2400
Web: http://www.hagley.lib.de.us
Hagley is located on the former du Pont family estate, Eleutherian Mills. On a 230-acre site, the museum includes Blacksmith Hill, which features the social and familial history of the first workers who operated the powder mills. Interpreters in period dress demonstrate daily life throughout the exhibit. Eleutherian Mills is filled with five generations of du Pont memorabilia.

The Historical Society of Delaware Research Library
505 Market Street
Wilmington, DE 19801
Telephone: (302) 655 7161
Web: http://www.hsd.org
Open to the public, this reference library has comprehensive holdings on state history and a women's history collection. The library focuses not only on the Delaware

women who made major contributions to society, it also explores the daily lives of regular women.

Old State House

406 Federal Street
Dover, DE 19903
Telephone: (302) 739 4266
Web: http://www.destatemuseums.org/sh/index.html
The second oldest State House in continuous use in the country. During the suffrage movement in Delaware, it was still in use by state legislators and the women who petitioned them for the vote. Tours focus on a range of historical topics—the Civil War and African Americans, for instance; visitors must call in advance for dates. Research is currently under way to create a women's history tour.

University Gallery

University of Delaware
114 Old College
Newark, DE 19716
Telephone: (302) 831 8242
Web: http://www.museums.udel.edu/art/index.html
One of the highlights of University Gallery's permanent exhibit is a large collection of the work of pioneering photographer Gertrude Kasebier (1852–1934). Rare works by Mary Cassatt are also part of the collection. Works by Elizabeth Carlett and Selma Burke, who created the image of Franklin D. Roosevelt that appears on the dime, are included in the Paul R. Jones Collection, a recent acquisition of the museum.

RESOURCES

FURTHER READING
HISTORY

Acrelius, Israel. *A History of New Sweden.* 1759. Reprint, Ann Arbor, Mich.: University Microfilms, 1966.

Anthony, Susan B., and Ida Husted Harper. *History of Woman Suffrage.* Vol. 4. Indianapolis, Ind.: Hollenbeck Press, 1902.

Chesapeake Bay Girl Scout Council. *Legacy from Delaware Women.* Wilmington, Del.: Chesapeake Bay Girl Scout Council, 1987.

Clay, Jehu Curtis. *Annals of the Swedes on the Delaware.* Chicago: John Ericsson Memorial Committee, 1938.

Conrad, Henry C. *History of the State of Delaware.* 3 vols. Wilmington, Del.: Henry C. Conrad, 1908.

Federal Writers' Project. *Delaware: A Guide to the First State.* Rev. ed. New York: Hastings House, 1955.

Ferris, Benjamin. *A History of the Original Settlements on the Delaware.* 1846. Reprint, Baltimore, Md.: Gateway Press, 1987.

Harper, Ida Husted. *History of Woman Suffrage.* Vol. 6. New York: J. J. Little & Ives, 1902.

Hoffecker, Carol E. *Delaware: A Bicentennial History.* New York: W. W. Norton, 1977.

Hoffecker, Carol E. *Beneath Thy Guiding Hand: A History of Women at the University of Delaware.* Newark: University of Delaware Press, 1994.

Munroe, John A. *History of Delaware.* Newark: University of Delaware Press, 1984.

Pyle, Katharine, and Emily P. Bissell. *Once Upon a Time in Delaware.* Wilmington, Del.: Mercantile Printing, 1911.

Stanton, Elizabeth Cady, Susan B. Anthony, and Matilda Joslyn Gage. *History of Woman Suffrage.* Vols. 1–3. Rochester, N.Y.: Charles Mann Printing, 1886.

Trenkwalder Schönenberger, Regula. *Lenape Women, Matriliny, and the Colonial Encounter Resistance and Erosion of Power (c. 1600–1876): An Excursus in Feminist Anthropology.* Bern: Peter Lang, 1991.

Weslager, C. A. *The Delaware Indians: A History.* New Brunswick, N.J.: Rutgers University Press, 1972.

Plowman, Terry. "Billion-Dollar Poultry Industry Traces Its Roots to 1923 Error." In *Delmarva Millennium.* Vol. 1. Wilmington, Del.: Thomson-Chesapeake, 1999.

BIOGRAPHY AND AUTOBIOGRAPHY

Babbitt, John S. "Emily Bissell and the Christmas Seal Story." *Stamps,* 24 December 1994, 1–2.

Bracher, Katherine. "Death of Annie J. Cannon." *Mercury,* May–June 1991, 86.

Cheek, Mary Tyler Freeman, and Ralph B. Draughon, Jr. *Jesse Ball DuPont.* Stratford, Va.: Robert E. Lee Memorial Association, 1985.

Doyle, Kathleen. "'Stamping' Out Tuberculosis: The Story of Christmas Seals." *American History Illustrated,* November–December 1989, 66–68.

Greenstein, George. "The Ladies of Observatory Hill: Annie Jump Cannon and Cecilia Payne-Gaposchkin." *American Scholar* (Summer 1993): 437–447.

Hewlett, Richard Greening. *Jessie Ball du Pont.* Gainesville: University of Florida Press, 1992.

Jones, Jacqueline. *Creek Walking: Growing Up in Delaware in the 1950s.* Newark: University of Delaware Press, 2001.

Kidwell, Peggy Aldrich. "Three Women of American Astronomy." *American Scientist,* May–June 1990, 244–251.

Low, Betty Bright, and Jacqueline Hinsley. *Sophie du Pont: A Young Lady in America, Sketches, Diaries and Letters.* New York: Harry N. Abrams, 1987.

Rhodes, Jane. *Mary Ann Shadd Cary: The Black Press and Protest in the Nineteenth Century.* Bloomington: Indiana University Press, 1998.

USEFUL WEB SITES

"Chronology of Colonial Swedes on the Delaware, 1638–1713," The Swedish Colonial Society http://www.colonialswedes.org/history/chronology.html

"Governor Ruth Ann Minner: Biography" http://www.state.de.us/governor/biography.htm

Mary Washington College: duPont Hall http://www.mwc.edu/vcenter/tour/dupont.htm

SELECTED ORGANIZATIONS AND INSTITUTIONS

Delaware Public Archives
121 Duke of York Street
Dover, DE 19901
Telephone: (302) 744 5000
Web: http://www.state.de.us/sos/dpa
Operates a research room serving many interests, including genealogy and national and local history.

Historical Society of Delaware
505 Market Street
Wilmington, DE 19801
Telephone: (302) 655 7161
Web: http://www.hsd.org
Encourages a greater understanding and appreciation of Delaware history. Home page includes a section on Delaware women's history.

Historical Society of Delaware Research Library
505 Market Street
Wilmington, DE 19801
Telephone: (302) 655 7161
Web: http://www.hsd.org/library.htm
Library includes a large collection of books, newspapers, maps, manuscripts, and photographs relating to the history of Delaware and its people.

University of Delaware Library
181 South College Avenue
Newark, DE 19717–5267
Telephone: (302) 831 2965
Web: http://www.lib.udel.edu
Online gateway to the library catalog, resources, and other information.

University of Delaware Library
Women's Literary Papers and Manuscripts
Special Collections
181 South College Avenue
Newark, DE 19717–5267
Telephone: (302) 831 2229
Web: http://www.lib.udel.edu/ud/spec/guides/wmnlit.htm
Online guide to the library's collection of women's literary papers and manuscripts.

University of Delaware
Women's Studies Interdisciplinary Program
333 Smith Hall
University of Delaware
Newark, DE 19716
Telephone: (302) 831 8474
Program examining the rich heritage, challenges, and concerns of women.

FLORIDA

They crossed Juniper Creek, then, after two miles of narrow road, picked up the main road to the river and to Volusia. Penny stopped to rest. In the late afternoon they passed Captain McDonald's house and Jody knew they were nearing Fort Butler. Around a bend in the road, the dry growth of pines and scrub oak disappeared. There was a new lushness. Sweet gums and bay were here, and, like sign-posts indicating the river, cypress. Wild azaleas were blooming late in the low places, and the passion flower opened its lavender corollas along the road. They reached the St. John's River. It was dark and aloof. It was a pathway to the world . . .
—Marjorie Kinnan Rawlings, *The Yearling*, 1938

Florida, like California, Arizona, and New Mexico, has a long Spanish history and significant Spanish culture that have been largely ignored—and a similar fate has befallen its women's history.

In terms of women's rights, Florida's record is mixed. Florida was the first southern state to elect a woman to Congress, but it did not ratify the 19th Amendment, which gave women the vote, until 1969, when the legislature formally ratified it in observance of the 50th anniversary of the League of Women Voters. At the beginning of the 21st century, Florida was the fourth most populous state in the nation; however, it has elected but one woman to the U.S. Senate, a record equal to New York, but falling short of Texas and California.

PREHISTORY
(Prehistory–1513)

The first humans probably came to Florida about 8000 B.C. and lived in a world that is known to us only from fossil records. In the "Bone Valley" of west-central Florida, for instance,

there is evidence of bison, giant sloths, rhinoceroses, camels, tapirs, and even saber-toothed tigers. The women who bore and reared their young in this environment lived on a peninsula that has been eroding for thousands of years, and much of their habitat is now under the ocean's waves.

These women likely learned to fashion the tools they needed to carry water and to cook food

State Population (2000):
15,982,378
Female Population (2000): 8,184,663
Women in State Legislature (2003): 24.4%
Female College Enrollment (1999): 389,000 (56.8% of total)
Privately Held Women-owned Businesses (1997): 337,811
First Year of Full Suffrage: 1920

Pensacola
Tallahassee
Apalachicola R.
Jacksonville
St. Johns R.
St. Augustine
Gainesville
Ocala
Daytona Beach
Orlando
Tampa
St. Petersburg
Sarasota
Fort Pierce
Fort Myers
West Palm Beach
Everglades
Fort Lauderdale
Miami
Key West

over fire. By 1500 B.C. women were cooking with clay pottery and stone vessels—some of which were made from Georgia rock, indicating travel and a trading system. In general the Calusa and Tequesta lived in the south; the Tocobagas and Timucua in the central peninsula; and the Apalachee roamed the north.

These societies were matrilineal. Children took the mother's name and belonged to the clan of their mothers. Indeed, matriarchy was so real that the legal code of the 19th-century Seminole tribe specified that a newly married couple must live with the bride's clan; women were the heads of households, and if a couple separated, the man went home to his mother.

Chiefs might have more than one wife, but most marriages were monogamous, and fidelity was expected of both men and women. During pregnancy women separated from their husbands, a practice that may have been based in easing workloads and sexual activity.

Both women and men farmed, growing corn and other vegetables. Warm weather meant little need for clothing or shelter; both genders typically covered only their genitals, and housing usually consisted of no more than a palm-frond roof supported by poles for shelter from the rain.

WHITE EXPLORATION AND SETTLEMENT (1513–1783)

In the first half of the 16th century, several European expeditions landed in the region, including Ponce de León's in 1513 and 1522, and Panfilo de Narvaez's in 1528. De León's expeditions were unsuccessful mainly because the earlier ill-treatment by Columbus of the indigenous peoples of the islands south of Florida gave European explorers a bad reputation. De Narvaez landed at Tampa Bay in 1528 and attacked without provocation a Timucuan chief, Hirrihigua, cutting off his nose. When Hirrihigua's mother objected, the Spaniards set their dogs on her to eat her alive.

ULELA, AN EARLY POCAHONTAS

When Panfilo de Narvaez's 1528 expedition failed to return to Cuba, his anxious wife sent out a search party. As the party sailed into Tampa Bay, the Native Americans living there made clear that they had not forgotten de Narvaez's cruelty. Only two mariners dared to come ashore. One was fortunate enough to be quickly killed; the other, Juan Ortiz, was to be slowly roasted alive.

His screams from the fire, however, moved Ulela, the chief's daughter, who persuaded her father to spare his life. She treated Ortiz's wounds and cared for him, and he lived with her tribe for seven years. Ulela saved his life a second time and helped him escape when her people would have killed him for presumed treason. In 1539, however, Ortiz joined Hernando de Soto's expedition as an interpreter, in effect aiding the European settlers in their attacks on Ulela's tribe and other groups.

Neither Ulela nor the much more famous Pocahontas were unusual. Especially in eastern tribes, the decision on whether captives would live or die often was made by the women.

—Doris Weatherford

De Narvaez advanced north, but his destructive march ended badly. He and all but four of his 400 soldiers died; the survivors wandered for eight years, eventually arriving in Mexico.

At least one woman had sailed with Ponce de León. When Hernando de Soto's 1539 expedition marched through the southeastern portion of the present-day United States it included at least two women. Ana Mendez, an illiterate woman in her thirties, had been a servant of Dona Isabel de Soto; Mendez survived the expedition and testified before a Spanish commission in 1560 about her experience. The other woman, Francisca Hinestrosa, disguised herself as a man to accompany her soldier husband. She died in the battle of Chicaza (fought in present-day Mississippi) in 1541. According to at least one record, she was pregnant at the time.

De Soto and half his expedition would die while "alienating almost every Indian tribe from

Tampa to Memphis." (Mormino and Pizzo 1983, 24) For native women along the route, the invasion brought rape, disfigurement, torture, and murder; they often saw their sons and husbands brutally killed, their homes destroyed, and were themselves enslaved.

In 1549 a Dominican, Father Luis Cancer, set out to undo the damage done to Christianity by these early invaders. He knew that the indigenous peoples were prepared to fight and therefore took the precaution of going from Vera Cruz, Mexico, to Havana, Cuba, where he secured the services of a female guide, Magdalena. A native Floridian, Magdalena had gone to Cuba, converted to Roman Catholicism, and learned Spanish. With two priests and a sailor, Magdalena went ashore in the Tampa Bay area. After several days, she returned to the ship and reported that they had found the Timucua, who were friendly. The ship's crew did not believe her; thus only Father Cancer went ashore—where he was immediately beaten to death. Whether Magdalena engaged in a complex deception or whether she was herself deceived is still a matter for debate. Magdalena was, however, one of many women who guided explorers, predating more famous women like Idaho's Sacagawea by more than two centuries.

The Spanish began a settlement at Pensacola in 1559, but a hurricane and hostile tribes forced them to abandon it in 1561, and Pensacola would wait until 1698 for permanent settlers. The first non-Spanish Europeans to arrive in Florida were French Protestants, called Huguenots, who built Fort Caroline on the St. Johns River near the modern Florida–Georgia border in 1564. Spanish soldiers killed most of them the following year; the few who escaped were protected by Native Americans.

Among the approximately 300 French at Fort Caroline, only four were women. Neither France nor Spain sent many women to the New World in this era. Nuns did not accompany priests from either

Catholic nation; most of the men sent were young, unmarried soldiers who intended to return home.

Nonetheless, when St. Augustine—the oldest city in the United States—was founded in 1565, it soon had some 100 women among its population of 1,300. On September 8, 1565, these settlers held the first celebration of thanksgiving at a permanent North American community peopled by Europeans. Several other thanksgivings were held at temporary sites as early as 1513; all of them predated the famous Thanksgiving of the Massachusetts Pilgrims in 1621.

About the time that St. Augustine was founded, Don Pedro Menendez de Aviles and his party of soldiers and Jesuit priests landed on the west coast of Florida. They were more diplomatic than their predecessors, and in 1567 friendly Calusa handed over to them four women and three men who were termed "Christians," in other words, Europeans. According to the Calusa, these individuals were the sole survivors of as many as 200 Europeans who had been shipwrecked on Florida's coasts during the previous decades. The women, who remained nameless in the records, might also have been the abandoned captives of pirates.

Within the next few decades, however, other European women came to Florida, and Spanish society was firmly established. The best example may be Maria Menendez y Posada, who married Juan Menendez Marquez in 1593 (almost exactly a century after Columbus's first voyage) and established a family dynasty that held power in Florida for five generations. In the European tradition, Maria's dowry included the title of royal treasurer for her husband.

Although women never were allowed such positions, some did inherit tremendous wealth, which they might pass along to their daughters and sons. By 1689, for example, Antonia Basalia de Leon, the daughter of a widow who owned large amounts of land near modern Jacksonville, married Francisco Tomas, a scion of the Menendez family. Together, their families owned tens of thousands of acres in central Florida; some 7,000 head of cattle were raised on La Chua ranch alone.

Compared with women in the English colonies to the north, Spanish women were very free in some ways, but less so in others. They could drink, smoke, dance, and gamble without societal disapproval, and their clothing was less constricting. On the other hand, they were less likely to be educated and to engage in commerce of any sort.

In Florida, however, the Spanish population remained overwhelmingly male, and men routinely forced themselves sexually on Native American women. Evidence exists showing that some priests seemed to make excuses for rape: Friars at Apalachee complained to the Spanish governor in 1567, "Sir, these Indians are very jealous and they are excited beyond measure when someone approaches their wives, daughters, or sisters. And the lieutenant and the soldiers who are there are men and by that fact are weak . . . ." (Henderson and Mormino 1991, 160) At the same time, priests attempted to impose their view of proper family structure on the tribes and clans; violence erupted in northwest Florida in 1675, when a priest tried to separate an elderly Chacato leader from three of his four wives.

Florida's indigenous peoples were disappearing, dying in battle or from European diseases to which they had no immunity. Women and children were the particular targets of night raids on Native American villages in northern Florida; they were sold into slavery in the newly established English colony of Carolina. The Spanish did not try to protect them. By 1708, Florida's governor reported to Spain that some 10,000 had been sold as slaves in the Carolinas. They were probably disproportionately women, for male warriors were likely to have been killed.

In a reversal of the usual situation, African women who ended up in Florida were much more likely to be free. Already in 1687, for example, three black women, eight men, and a child escaped from slavery in British Georgia by sailing to Spanish Florida. When Georgians demanded their return, Governor Quiroga refused to send them, saying that they had converted to Catholicism and their skills made them assets to St. Augustine. A few years later, in 1693, a royal edict made this policy on runaway slaves official: King Charles II of Spain granted freedom to "both men and women." He may have been motivated less by humanitarian reasons than by economics— the loss of slaves weakened the rival British colonies. Whatever his motivation, the effect was clear: During the next decades, many other blacks went south to freedom in Florida, some with help from Native Americans.

Fewer and fewer Native Americans remained, as Florida's tribal population was reduced to perhaps no more than a thousand by the beginning of the 1700s. Most had died from diseases imported by whites, not from combat. In 1708 a British agent candidly summarized that his men "drove the Floridians to the Islands of the Cape, have bought and sold many Hundred of them, and Dayly now continue that trade so that in some few years they'el Reduce these Barbarians to a farr less number." A map in the Colonial Office of London summarized the situation in Tampa Bay: "Tocobagoa Indians, Destroyed 1709." (Mormino and Pizzo 1983, 18)

Florida was ceded to Britain in 1763 as part of a treaty that settled warfare on two continents, and at least one place name reflects this: Charlotte County is named for England's Queen Charlotte. The British had Florida just 20 years, however, before granting it back to Spain in 1783 as a result of the Treaty of Paris that settled the American Revolution. Spain sent no more expeditions, though, knowing that American expansion into the territory was inevitable. As the 1800s began, much of Florida was "a mere geographic expression, except for mapmakers, a handful of Cuban fishermen and occasional pirates." (Ibid., 31)

AMERICAN SETTLEMENT TO THE CIVIL WAR (1783–1860)

Despite Florida's status as a Spanish territory, American families began drifting into the area soon after the Revolution. Ownership finally passed from Spain to the new United States in 1819 with the Adams–Onís Treaty; by then the burgeoning white population to the north was pressing the Seminoles of Georgia and Alabama into the peninsula. The Seminoles were not a traditional tribe, but rather a combination of groups who called themselves by a name meaning in the Creek language "people who choose to live by themselves." By 1800 Florida's Seminole population numbered about 5,000.

Seminole women and men born in the early 1800s would experience disruption and violence all of their lives, as whites continued to press them farther south. Happy to find allies, Seminoles welcomed blacks into their community. Runaway slaves found Seminole life far preferable to that in the American Deep South, and the groups lived together in Florida. Some Seminoles may have owned black slaves, or they may have simply told whites that they did as a way of protecting the blacks among them. Whatever the case, such alliances alarmed southern whites.

The infant U.S. Army responded to these fears and, in July 1816, attacked a fort that the Native American–black alliance had built on the Apalachicola River near Tallahassee. The first cannon shot landed in the gunpowder storage area and instantly killed 342 civilians, including women. This was the beginning of the First Seminole War (1816–1818).

Tallahassee was a planned capital that began in 1824. It was chosen because most Floridians lived in the centuries-old Spanish towns of

FLORIDA'S FIRST FIRST LADIES

When Rachel Jackson became first lady of the newly acquired Florida territory in 1821, she traveled by water to the capital of Pensacola from her home near Nashville, Tennessee, via New Orleans, Louisiana. She saw that the old Spanish city, which had been founded in 1698, was decidedly dilapidated: The "government house" was so unstable that it was propped up with logs, and her husband refused to use it.

Andrew Jackson, soon to be president of the United States, had great respect for his wife, a fact that ambitious men soon discovered. Many began going to her to plead for patronage positions. The Jacksons also took up the case of Mercedes Vidal, a woman of mixed race who had been the common-law wife of a Spanish official. He died in 1806, leaving appreciable property to her and their children—but the male administrators of the estate had dallied for more than a decade in releasing it. When Governor Jackson learned of the situation, he had the administrators imprisoned.

Neither he nor Rachel enjoyed their time in Pensacola; in 1822 the appointed governorship passed to William Duval, who was criticized when he spent much of that year in Kentucky, where his wife lived. In 1834 Andrew Jackson, now president, appointed an old friend, John Eaton, as Florida's third territorial governor. Jackson appointed Eaton in direct response to a situation that centered on the era's strict standards for female behavior. Shortly after Peggy Eaton's sailor husband died in the Mediterranean, she married John Eaton. Rumors began circulating that they had had a prior relationship and that, as secretary of war, Eaton was responsible for the assignment that caused the sailor's death. In addition, many thought that Peggy Eaton's origins were too low class for her to associate with other Cabinet wives. Because the Jacksons had suffered from the same kind of painful gossip, the president appointed Eaton to the territorial governorship, enabling the Eatons to leave Washington, D.C., for isolated Tallahassee.

—Doris Weatherford

St. Augustine and Pensacola, more than 400 miles apart, with St. Augustine on the Atlantic coast and Pensacola on the Gulf coast. Tallahassee lay halfway between them, in a locale that was a traditional Native American camp.

The year 1824 also marked the beginning of confinement for the Seminole and their Miccosukee cousins to a large reservation in

The Seminoles had a long history of conflict with white settlers in Florida. The struggle was marked by three wars, the first one beginning in 1816 and the last one ending in 1858. Seminole women fiercely resisted capture. This woman, known as Mrs. Cypress Charlie, lived in Coconut Grove, Miami, ca. 1880. (Historical Museum of Southern Florida)

south Florida. The army headquarters, Fort Brooke, was at the reservation's northern border and grew into the city of Tampa. During the Second Seminole War (1835–1842), some 40,000 U.S. Army troops would pass through Tampa; one of their chief complaints was the lack of women. The few white women in Florida were almost certainly married and lived in or near the forts that eventually became cities, including Fort Lauderdale, Fort Myers, and Fort Pierce. Some of these women nursed soldiers during the Seminole Wars, including future first lady MARGARET TAYLOR. The wife of commanding general Zachary Taylor, she and her daughter, Ann Wood, helped nurse soldiers through a yellow fever epidemic at Fort Brooke. Guerrilla warfare would continue for years, but the first ship of deportees exiled to the Indian Territory of Oklahoma sailed out of Tampa Bay on April 11, 1836. More than 400 Native Americans left their homeland that morning; 25 of them died before seeing their new, unchosen land.

The federal government had spent upward of $20 million on the largely unsuccessful Second Seminole War; with the military now preparing to fight the Mexican War (1846–1848), Congress turned to civilians to secure its territory in Florida. It passed, specifically for Florida, the 1842 Armed Occupation Act; this became a model for the 1862 Homestead Act that was to be so important to families in midwestern territories and states. The 1842 act gave 160 acres of land to any "head of family" who settled south of Gainesville and lived on the claimed land for four years. During the nine months that the law was in effect, more than 1,300 claims were made, with about one in six filed by a female family head.

Florida became the 27th state in 1845, with a significantly lower population compared to the population required of territories that joined the United States in later years. At the time, this huge area—the distance between Pensacola and Key

West is greater than the distance between New York and Chicago—had slightly more than 50,000 residents, most of whom were located near the border with Georgia and Alabama.

These north Florida residents would long dominate the state's history, but the Third Seminole War (1856–1858) again brought attention to the south. White expansion into southern Florida's Everglades, an area that the Seminoles had been promised, triggered significant resistance. The Seminoles' guerrilla style of warfare forced the federal government to change military tactics. The government recruited volunteers by offering bounties: $500 for a Native American man, between $250 and $500 for a woman, and $100 for each child. On August 2, 1857, for example, one volunteer marched 15 Seminole women and children into Fort Myers and received $1,500.

Despite being hunted, the capture of resourceful and strong Seminole women was rare. In the end the federal government paid only 41 bounties, and Secretary of War John B. Floyd was forced to admit that Native Americans in Florida had outsmarted the army. The federal government concluded that paying Seminoles to go to Oklahoma would be less expensive than killing them, and terms were worked out in a conference at Fort Myers in the spring of 1858. Some 300 Seminoles refused to go and hid deeper in the Everglades. They remained legally fugitives until 1917, when 100,000 acres of swampland was set aside as their reservation.

CIVIL WAR ERA
(1860–1880)

The people who dominated Florida lived in its far north and identified culturally with the Deep South. Accordingly, the young state was quick to secede. Some Florida women, whose roots were in the Carolinas and Virginia, defied the gender norms of their era and participated in the political decision to go to war. On November 24,

1860—shortly after Abraham Lincoln's election as president—26 women joined several dozen men in signing a petition that urged secession. Florida joined the new Confederate States of America on January 10, 1861, before Georgia, Louisiana, and other states more typically associated with the Confederacy.

The resources of the new Confederate government were limited, and like other southerners Florida's women organized to supply the army. In 1861 the Florida legislature made a direct appropriation of $10,000 to the Ladies Military Aid Society for cloth; the women used it for sewing into uniforms. Soldiers facing the "bleak weather" of Virginia in January asked for flannel underwear, and women began collecting shoes and blankets. Women conducted fundraisers for hospitals farther north, and south Florida women sent these hospitals palmetto fans for hot weather and citrus fruit for cold.

Many women, however, found themselves accepting charity. The 1862 legislature appropriated $20,000 for aid to needy families of soldiers, but such funds were erratically distributed and unreliable.

Florida had almost no industry, and its population was by far the smallest of any Confederate state; however, its incomparably long coastline made it invaluable to the Confederacy in its attempts to smuggle essential goods through the Union's naval blockade. A sergeant's wife, whose name does not appear in the records, found herself in a position of trying to protect part of that coastline. With her husband gone from their home at Fort McRee near Pensacola when naval forces from the USS *Supply* landed, she locked the fort, met the invaders, and refused to turn over the keys. The Union men then destroyed the fort.

Pensacola was under siege for months in 1861. It became virtually a ghost town, a fate that Tampa avoided despite two Union invasions. Jacksonville suffered the most, with four invasions that included a disastrous 1863 fire. Some families were confined to a stockade near Tallahassee, Camp Smith, because they were suspected of harboring deserters.

The governor, who committed suicide just days before the South's surrender, sent upward of 14,000 men to the Confederate army from a white population of about 70,000. At least one-third of these soldiers died. Another 2,000 or more Floridians joined Union forces, almost half of them blacks who enlisted in the last two years of the war. Although these thousands of deaths had a profound effect on the women who were left to struggle alone, Florida did not suffer nearly as much as states to the north, some of which lost a quarter of their young men.

Florida was the refuge toward which many Confederate officials fled after the war. Confederate attorney general George Davis, for instance, sought shelter at the isolated Columbia County plantation of his cousin, Mrs. Thomas Hill Lane. Most of these men fled with their wives and children; eventually all were captured, and some were confined at Fort Jefferson on the Dry Tortugas, Florida's far western coastal islands.

Although the federal government had better uses for its army than occupying Florida during the war, martial law was established as soon as troops became available. The purpose of the occupation forces was to dampen any remaining secessionist fires and to enforce the newly acquired rights of black citizens. Most whites strongly resented these victorious Yankees—especially the black soldiers. Reconstruction forced some changes in Florida law, changes that benefited blacks, but the 1865 convention that revised the state constitution retained many vestiges of the past. A black person was flogged, for instance, for offenses for which a white was merely fined. The most positive change may have been the legalization of marriage for blacks. Although couples married informally in slavery, even free black people could not legally marry. In 1866, when marriage became possible for blacks, hundreds of Florida couples rushed to establish themselves publicly as husband and wife.

Reconstruction governments throughout the South promised black families "forty acres and a mule," but little of that promise was kept. Instead, especially in Florida—which never had a strong plantation economy—the limited occupational choices made finding work easier for black women than for men. Women were assumed to be innately suited for cooking, cleaning, and child care, but black men seldom were thought to be similarly essential. They were more likely to be unemployed while their wives worked steadily.

Because prewar law forbade teaching blacks to read, one of their highest priorities became enrolling in the schools that northern women began all over the South during Reconstruction. Many of these women used their own money and resources to support their schools, and they taught both sexes and all ages. Some schools had been established, especially near Jacksonville, long before the end of the war, when federal troops quickly seized and held sea islands off the Florida coast.

Other schools began inland after the war. Anna M. Kidder of Vermont, for instance, who built a school at Ocala, was ostracized and mistreated by local whites. She also found the climate hard to bear, but by 1869 she had settled in enough that she wrote, "I haven't heard any grumbling from the Whites about my school lately." On the other hand, she took local segregation for granted. While discussing signs of an improving economy, Kidder wrote in a letter home, "I know of one colored well and two white ones that have been dug." (Weatherford 1997, 120) Although she was a credentialed physician, Dr. ESTHER HILL HAWKS worked primarily as an administrator for these schools. She had moved with Union troops along the coastal islands from South Carolina and Georgia and ended up in the Jacksonville area at the war's end. Her husband, also a physician, bought land farther south in Indian River County, and, for the rest of her life, Dr. Hawk practiced medicine in Lynn, Massachusetts, during the spring, summer, and fall and spent winters with her husband in Florida.

Harriet Beecher Stowe, whose book *Uncle Tom's Cabin* (1852) fanned the abolitionist flames leading up to the Civil War, also became a part-time Floridian during Reconstruction. She bought an orange grove at Mandarin, on the St. Johns River near Jacksonville, in the hope that working there would rehabilitate her son Frederick, who had become an alcoholic while serving in the Union army. Stowe supported several unmarried daughters and her husband, a retired professor, so despite the fame and money that *Uncle Tom's Cabin* brought her, she worked steadily during her winters in the state. She wrote *Palmetto-Leaves* (1873) as a record of her life in Florida.

Stowe offered a role model for Florida women who desired educational opportunities in this era, but there were few such opportunities in their home state. During the Civil War, Tampa's Emma J. Miller became the first female college graduate from Florida, but she had to go to Georgia for her education. Other exceptional women of the era included Amanda Mann, who was appointed postmaster at Brooksville in 1867, and Clementine Wilkinson and Sarah Fountain, both postmasters in Bartow.

Florida's first Roman Catholic sisterhoods began during Reconstruction. The first was the Sisters of Saint Joseph, a French order, which established a convent in St. Augustine in 1866; the Sisters of the Holy Names of Jesus and Mary subsequently developed convents in Key West and Tampa.

SUFFRAGE AND PROGRESSIVE ERA (1880–1920)

The end of slavery brought about progress for southern women, both black and white. The women's rights movement had been so closely associated with abolitionism, however, that it was difficult to separate women's rights from the states' rights arguments of unreconstructed southerners. The spread of feminism thus lagged about a generation behind in the South compared with the North, and Florida was very much a state of the South.

A few women in Florida were suffrage activists in the postwar era, including Dr. Esther Hill Hawks, who was listed in the 1870 records of the National Woman Suffrage Association as the vice president for Florida. She was, however, only a part-time resident, and consistent suffrage activity did not begin until the 1880s. Even then, most Florida leaders had roots in northern states.

On April 22, 1880, Tampa's Kate Binkley sent a petition to national women's suffrage leader Elizabeth Cady Stanton. Binkley had acquired its 14 signatures "by hard work," and most of the women who signed were related to each other. They were either self-supporting or the wives of working-class men, and they called for the right to vote because they were taxpayers. One of the signers, Julia Sevier, followed up with a letter to Susan B. Anthony in 1885; the letter makes clear not only that she and Anthony had already corresponded, but also that Sevier considered herself to have advocated suffrage for 20 years.

ELEANOR (Ella) McWILLIAMS CHAMBERLAIN emerged in the 1890s as Florida's most prominent suffragist. She had moved to Tampa from Iowa in 1882 and, a decade later, attended a suffrage convention back in Iowa. She organized at least 100 women in Florida and, in 1895, appeared with Anthony on the stage of the national convention held in Atlanta, Georgia—when Anthony told the group that "for several years" Chamberlain had sent her boxes of oranges. (Anthony and Harper 1902, 4:240) Chamberlain also wrote a feminist newspaper column; she resisted the editor's request for more traditional subjects, saying in her *Tampa Morning Tribune* column that "the world is not suffering for another cake recipe." Her leadership was crucial to the nascent group, however, and when she temporarily moved out of state in 1897, Florida's suffrage association died.

This era also saw the beginning of the transformation of southeastern Florida from a few trading posts with Seminoles to the state's most populous area. Ivy Stranahan, who would be president of the state suffrage association in 1917, was a founder of the city of Fort Lauderdale, and JULIA TUTTLE is considered to be "the mother of Miami," which flourished in this era.

A highly astute land developer, Tuttle moved to Florida from Ohio in 1891; she bought a square mile of land at the mouth of the Miami River. Tuttle induced the president of the Florida East Coast Railroad to extend the line to Miami by sending him orange blossoms during a freeze farther north and lived to fulfill "the dream of my life, to see this wilderness turned into a prosperous country." (Parks 1981, 4)

Bertha Honoré Palmer, who organized women's activities during the 1892–1893 World's Fair held in Chicago, Illinois, bought much more land in Florida than had Tuttle; Palmer would bring a number of innovations to southwestern Florida. She planned her home near Sarasota to have its own electrical and water systems, and she fought free-range ranchers to protect her experiments in animal husbandry.

In 1898 Americans focused on Florida during the Spanish-American War. Although fought mostly in Cuba, troops departed from Florida, especially Tampa and Key West. Both towns had been transformed in the earlier decades by emigration from Cuba, when cigar manufacturers moved their businesses away from that island and its tumultuous politics. In both cities Spanish-speaking women worked for wages very nearly equal to those of men; they lived in planned communities centered around cigar factories, where they enjoyed active social and political lives.

Most of these Cubans strongly supported the war, and PAULINA PEDROSO was the most visible female leader. Pedroso, who was black, was born and died in Cuba. During her exile in Tampa, Pedroso was seen as the closest friend of Latin American leader José Martí even though Martí was white. Red Cross founder Clara Barton organized her war activity from Florida, while postmistress Mabel Bean was recruited by the army to spy on the Spanish. For the first time the military contracted with women as paid nurses, some of whom served in hospitals on Florida's east coast.

Susan B. Anthony visited Florida during the last winter of her life, in 1905–1906, staying with future president of the National American Woman Suffrage Association, the Rev. Dr. Anna Howard Shaw. Although Shaw spent many winters near Lakeland, she never was especially visible for suffrage in her vacation home. Florida's suffrage movement revived in 1913, when Jacksonville women went to Washington, D.C., for the suffrage parade in conjunction with the inauguration of Woodrow Wilson. When the state legislature met in April, these women moved on to Tallahassee. Rochelle Cooley, president of the Equal Franchise League of Jacksonville, wrote:

> The House of Representatives decided to hear us . . . at an evening session. . . . The whole House, the whole Senate and the whole town [came]. Seats, aisles, the steps of the Speaker's rostrum were filled, windows had people sitting in them and as far as one could see people were standing on chairs to hear the first call for the rights of women ever uttered in the Capitol of Florida. (Harper 1902, 6:118)

One of those who addressed the state legislators was Jeanette Rankin of Montana, who soon would become the nation's first congresswoman. The women elected Dr. Mary Safford, an Orlando Unitarian minister originally from Iowa, as president of the Equal Franchise League, and at every legislative session between 1913 and 1920, the women introduced at least one suffrage bill. Some passed in one house of the state legislature but never in both; thus women were regularly denied the vote in Florida.

The victories that women did have in this era began with a bill legislators had apparently not fully read before passing. In 1915 the St. Lucie County town of Fellsmere, which was then eight times larger than neighboring Palm Beach, sent its incorporation papers to the legislature, and the city charter, which explicitly gave women the right to vote in municipal elections, was ratified.

When the Fellsmere coup became known, women in other towns also pushed for the vote in local elections, and by 1920, when the federal suffrage amendment became law, women were voting in 23 Florida towns. One town, Moore Haven in DeSoto County, immediately elected Marion Horwitz O'Brien as mayor, and she went on to serve in an executive position in the governor's office. Aurantia in Brevard County also sent in a charter that included the names of its first five city commissioners, all of whom were women.

Florida's legislature was one of the few still in session when Congress passed the 19th Amendment that granted women all voting rights in June 1919. The legislature was scheduled to adjourn the next day, but Gov. Sidney Catts sent a special message to legislators, urging them to first ratify the amendment. Mary Safford was the official president of the suffrage association, but MAY MANN JENNINGS, wife of former governor William Sherman Jennings, was its most politically astute member. A superlative vote counter who feared last-minute maneuvering by the legislators, Jennings refused to endorse the governor's call to extend the session. Florida women thus turned down Catt's offer rather than take the chance that the amendment might lose its first vote. By Florida's next regular session in 1921, the constitutional requirement of ratification by three-fourths of the

states had been met by others, and American women everywhere, including Florida, had already voted in a major presidential election.

1920S THROUGH WORLD WAR II ERA (1920–1945)

Mary Baird Bryan, wife of three-time Democratic presidential nominee William Jennings Bryan, had passed the Nebraska bar in 1888, a time when few women were lawyers, let alone married lawyers with a child. After the Bryans retired to Miami in 1921, Mary used her sharp political mind to both promote women's suffrage and develop campaign strategy for her daughter, RUTH BRYAN OWEN, who in 1928 became the first woman from the South to win a seat in the House of Representatives. Owen, a young widow with four children, campaigned in a district that ran hundreds of miles along Florida's east coast—from the state's northern border to its most southern keys.

Florida's Ruth Bryan Owen, the first woman from the South to win a seat in the U.S. House of Representatives. (© Corbis)

In Congress, Owen worked on issues relating to children and families and introduced legislation to protect the Everglades.

Also in 1928 Orlando voters elected the first woman, Edna Giles Fuller, to the state legislature. Floridians also elected the first woman in a statewide race: Mamie Eaton Greene of Monticello had been appointed to the State Railroad Commission—then an elected office—by the governor in 1927, when her husband died while in that position. She subsequently ran for the position, was elected, and served until 1934.

U.S. representative Owen and state representative Giles both lost their seats in 1932, when Floridians voted out nearly four of every five incumbents. The state and the nation were then deep into the Great Depression and no other women would be elected to major office by Florida voters for more than a decade. The failing economy had a highly regressive effect on Florida women. An exception was Carita Doggett Corse of Jacksonville. Corse headed the New Deal's Federal Writers' Project in her state, and under Corse's direction, in the 1930s Florida writers collected oral histories from former slaves.

The state's most famous writer was MARJORIE KINNAN RAWLINGS, who won the Pulitzer Prize in 1939 for *The Yearling*, a novel based on her life in Cross Creek, near Gainesville. At the same time MARJORY STONEMAN DOUGLAS was writing both fiction and nonfiction for national publications;

A WOMAN'S MEMORIES OF SLAVERY AND FREEDOM

Margrett Nickerson, a slave in Leon County as a young woman, recounted her life as a slave, beginning with her pre–Civil War childhood. Her story was transcribed by a woman with the Federal Writers' Project in 1936, who wrote the words as she heard them.

. . . I was big enough to tote meat an' stuff from de smokehouse to de kitchen and to tote water in and git wood for granny to cook . . . and I carried dinners back to de hands.

On dis plantation dere was 'bout a hunnerd head; cookin' was done in de fireplace in iron pots and de meals was plenty of peas, greens, cornbread, burnt corn for coffee. . . .

Dere wuz rice, cotton, corn, tatter fields to be tended to and cowhides to be tanned, thread to be spinned, and thread wuz made into ropes for plow lines.

. . . We had church wid de white preachers and dey tole us to mind our masters and missus and we would be saved; if not, dey said we wouldn't. Dey never tole us nuthin 'bout Jesus. On Sunday after workin' hard all de week, we would lay down to sleep and be so tired; soon ez yo' git sleep, de overseer would come an' wake you up and make you go to church.

. . . I ain't mad now and I know taint no use to lie, I takin' my time. I done prayed and got all de malice out o' my heart and I ain't gonna tell no lie fer um and I ain't gonna tell no lie on um. . . .

I wanter tell you why I am cripple today. . . . Joe Sanders would hurry us up by beatin' us with strops and sticks and run us all over de tater ridge; he cripple us both [Margrett and her sister]. . . . At night my pa would try to fix me up 'cause I had to go back to work next day. I never walked straight frum dat day to dis and I have to set here in dis [wheel] chair now.

. . . When de big guns fiahed, . . . we wuz in de field, but I 'member dey wuz all very glad . . . Carr read de free papers to us on Sunday. . . . Den he asked dem what would stay wid him to step off on de right and dem dat wuz leavin' to step off on de left.

. . . We went to Abram Bailey's place near Tallahassee. Carr turned us out without nuthin . . . Fust we cut down saplins fur we didn't have no house, and took de tops uv pines and put on de top; den we put dirt on top uv dese saplins. When de rain come, it would wash all de dirt right down in our face and we'd hafter buil' us a house all over ag'in. We didn' had no body to buil' a house fur us, cause pa was gone and ma jes had us gals. . . .

Margrett Nickerson grew up and bore 12 children, but when interviewed in her eighties, she could recall the names of only seven. She remained illiterate all of her life.

—Doris Weatherford

Excerpts from Federal Writers' Project, *Slave Narratives: Florida.* Vol. 3. 1936. Reprint, St. Clair Shores, Mich.: Scholarly Press, 1976.

Marjory Stoneman Douglas receiving the Medal of Freedom from Pres. Bill Clinton on November 30, 1993, for her work as an advocate for the preservation of Florida's Everglades. (AP/Wide World Photos)

her classic *The Everglades: River of Grass* (1947) would make her an environmentalist icon.

One of Florida's most internationally known woman of the era was an African American, MARY MCLEOD BETHUNE. The founder and president of Bethune-Cookman College in Daytona Beach, she had a second home in Washington, D.C., where she spent time during much of the 1930s and 1940s. Bethune was the only woman of color with official status at the founding conference of the United Nations.

Bethune was a friend of another African American educator, Blanche Armwood of Tampa, who established models throughout the South for the federally funded Household Arts Training Schools. Armwood, who had passed the state teachers' examination at age 12, also earned a law degree and was a nationally recognized civil rights leader and an orator for the Republican party.

ZORA NEALE HURSTON of Eatonville—a town near Orlando completely governed by blacks—began her New York writing career as a participant in the Harlem Renaissance; after achieving much success, she died in poverty in Florida's St. Lucie County. The only black artist who exhibited at the 1939 World's Fair was sculptor Augusta Savage of Green Cove Springs; her tremendous creative talent also went almost totally unrecognized in her home state.

The next decade brought World War II, and those four years changed Florida more dramatically than had the preceding four centuries. The war, and the spread of air conditioning technology that followed it, transformed parts of the state from a parochial southern backwater to an international destination with a cosmopolitan culture. Again, women played major roles. JACQUELINE COCHRAN, a native of Florida's Panhandle region near Pensacola and the first woman to break the sound barrier, headed the Women's Air Service Pilots during the war, while Bethune served on the Advisory Committee for the new Women's Army Corps (WAC). Bethune's influence may have brought the nation's second military post for women to Daytona Beach.

Throughout Florida navy bases and army camps appeared overnight; the strategic peninsula featured flat land and warm winters that made it ideal for training purposes. Gasoline rationing ended tourism, but hotels quickly became classrooms, where women often taught male cadets, or hospitals, where women nursed wounded soldiers. Women riveted and welded at shipyards that dotted the coast, especially in Tampa and Jacksonville. Air WACs worked as plane mechanics and ran control towers at several U.S. Army Air Force bases, especially near Pensacola.

The effects of World War II can be personified in Mary Lou Baker of St. Petersburg, the second woman in the state legislature. An attorney, she kept her maiden name and kept secret the fact that

WAC: WOMEN IN A MAN'S ARMY

The Women's Army Corps (WAC) officially came into being in 1943 with the passage of the WAC bill. The announcement that women would be incorporated as auxiliary units into the U.S. military had come only a year earlier with the formation of the Women's Auxiliary Army Corps (WAAC), which later became the WAC.

Despite past prohibitions against women serving in the military, officials realized that the global nature of World War II would require a larger, more diversified army. Estimates were made that women were capable of performing more than 1.3 million military jobs, which would release more men for fighting at the front. These considerations led many to believe that the first legal opportunity for women to participate in large-scale military operations was a result of desperation for victory over the Germans rather than of societal acceptance. However, American women's organizations advocated military service on the grounds that women, like men, should enjoy the right to participate in all responsibilities of citizenship. When the United States entered World War II after the attack on Pearl Harbor, Hawaii, in December of 1941, a large number of American women enlisted. Support for the 1943 WAC bill, which incorporated women directly into the military, then increased.

Modeled after British and Canadian women's units, the WAC had strict enlistment requirements: recruits had to be between 21 and 45 years of age, between 5 and 6 feet tall, and at least 105 pounds in weight. In addition, WAC recruits had to pass both physical and mental examinations comparable to those required of male officers.

Despite popular publicity photos of WACs working in shipyards and airfields, the vast majority of them held clerical or technical jobs similar to those held by civilian women. In fact, while the WACs were subjected to boot camp, they rarely received training in mechanics and none in weapons use and maintenance.

The Roosevelts, both the president and his wife, Eleanor, repeatedly praised the WAC for its efforts, and in 1948 Pres. Harry S. Truman approved the Women's Armed Services Integration Act, which established a 2% population of women in the peacetime military.

—Catherine Griffis

Source from Catherine Griffis, "Effects on Women," *International Social Science Review* (Spring-Summer 2000): 26.

---

she was pregnant when she was reelected during the war. Like many other women, she had to say good-bye to her husband when he served overseas, but the fact that she was a lawyer made her more aware than most of how far behind Florida was in fundamental property rights for women. She sponsored bills that assured married women of family property and granted them power of attorney for absent husbands.

POSTWAR AND CONTEMPORARY ERAS (1945–present)

One seldom-noticed effect of the war was the end of gender-segregated higher education. The nation had millions of young men entitled to education under the GI bill; colleges could not handle swelling enrollments; and states that had single-sex public colleges and universities solved this problem by opening women's colleges to men.

The pattern was especially evident in Florida, which historically had three public institutions. Florida Agricultural & Mechanical College, later University (FAMU), in Tallahassee—like most black colleges—was coeducational when it was opened after the Civil War. Southern states typically segregated white students by gender and Florida State College for Women (FSCW), which also was in Tallahassee, was reserved for white women. White men went to the prestigious University of Florida at Gainesville. In 1947, however, both white institutions became coeducational. While the change to coeducational status had some advantages, many women felt squeezed out of their historic place: When FSCW became Florida State University (FSU), its female students found it difficult to win student government offices and exercise other forms of leadership.

A second seldom-noticed change was in eligibility for jury service; a 1949 law abolished the requirement for all-male juries, which had been a serious handicap for female defendants, witnesses, and lawyers. Nevertheless, a woman was still unlikely to face a jury of her true peers: The law gave women an automatic exemption from jury service; women had to go to the courthouse and indicate their willingness to be called. The U.S. Supreme Court upheld this exemption in 1961, and not until the feminist movement of the 1970s did jury service become truly open to women.

Although the nation's highest court allowed the exclusion of women from jury service to stand, it had mandated racial integration of schools in 1954. Civil rights leaders then worked for integration in other areas of life, and black women all over Florida became activists; young FAMU women especially subjected themselves to repeated arrest in Tallahassee demonstrations. Some were inspired by Harriet Moore, who died with her husband, NAACP field director Harry Moore, when segregationists bombed their home in the rural community of Mims on Christmas night of 1951. The Moores helped pave the way for people like Alabama's Rosa Parks, whose attempt to desegregate Montgomery's public transit system came four years after they died. A decade after the Moore murders, Fort Lauderdale's Eula Johnson earned brief national attention for her innovative integration of beaches with a "swim-in."

FAMU alumna Althea Gibson was the first American black to play tennis at Wimbledon; in 1958 she won the American Tennis Association's women's championship, and the Associated Press named her Woman Athlete of the Year. In the same year Tallahassee's Bernice Gaines Dorn became the state's first female black attorney, exactly 60 years after the first white woman, Louise Pinnell of Jacksonville, was admitted to the bar in 1898. Another highly accomplished female lawyer of this era was Jane Steele Bannon of Tampa, who prosecuted Nazi war criminals in Yugoslavia.

After 1947 the Florida House of Representatives always had at least one woman, but the Senate had none until 1962, when Orlando elected Beth Johnson. By coincidence, the second woman in the state Senate also was named Beth Johnson; she was elected from Cocoa in 1966. Four years later, the House would have its first black woman, Gwen Cherry of Miami. The first black woman in the state Senate was Carrie Meek, also of Miami, elected in 1982; she went on to become the first black Floridian in the U.S. Congress since Reconstruction. The first Cuban American in the legislature, ILEANA ROS-LEHTINEN, was also elected from Miami in 1982; she later went on to the U.S. Congress.

Florida women set records in other areas. Betty Skelton raced both cars and planes. She twice won the World Light Plane Altitude Record; four times won the Feminine World Land Speed Record (at 315 mph); and was the first woman admitted to the NASCAR International Automotive Hall of Fame. Agriculturist Lena Smithers Hughes of Orlando did important experiments with Valencia oranges, bringing longer growing seasons for fresh citrus, while biochemist FLORENCE SEIBERT, who invented the skin test for tuberculosis, continued her cutting-edge medical research for three decades after her St. Petersburg "retirement." Engineer JoAnn Hardin Morgan, a Titusville native, became the first woman to fill an executive position at the Kennedy Space Center.

Florida State University athletic director Barbara Jo Palmer played a major role in the 1972 Education Act's Title IX, which created equity for female students in high school and college athletics and other areas. Increased public attention to women's sports benefited native Floridian and tennis champion Chris Evert. A number of internationally known women followed the precedent that athlete Babe Didrikson Zaharias of Texas set when she moved to Tampa in the 1950s; among them are five-medal Olympic swimmer Bonnie Blair and tennis star Jennifer Capriati.

TIMELINE

United States Events		Florida Events
	1500	
		1513 Don Juan Ponce de León sails up Florida's west coast.
		1549 Magdalena serves as a guide to Father Luis Cancer.
	1600	
1620 Settlement of Plymouth Colony		
	1700	
1776 United States declares independence		
	1800	
		1819 Adams–Onís Treaty cedes Florida from Spain to the United States.
		1845 Florida becomes a state.
1846–48 Mexican War		
1861–65 U.S. Civil War		1867 Amanda Mann appointed postmaster of Brooksville.
	1900	
1914–18 World War I		1915 City of Fellsmere's charter allows women to vote in municipal elections.
1920 Ratification of the 19th Amendment		1920 Marion Horwitz O'Brien elected as mayor of Moore Haven.
		1927 Mamie Eaton Greene becomes first woman to hold statewide office when appointed to the State Railroad Commission.
		1928 Ruth Bryan Owen is the first female from Florida elected to the U.S. Congress; Edna Giles Fuller is the first woman elected to the state House.
1929–39 Great Depression		
1939–45 World War II		1949 Women allowed to serve on juries.
		1962 Beth Johnson is the first woman elected to the state Senate.
		1969 Florida ratifies 19th Amendment.
1975 Vietnam War ends		1980 Paula Hawkins is first woman elected to the U.S. Senate.
		1985 Rosemary Barkett becomes first woman appointed to the state supreme court.
		1992 Janet Reno appointed U.S. attorney general and Carol Browner appointed head of the Environmental Protection Agency.
	2000	
		2003 Women hold 4 of Florida's 25 U.S. House seats.

On the negative side, Florida played a key role in killing the Equal Rights Amendment to the U.S. Constitution. Although female senators unanimously supported it, the 1977 state Senate fell short of ratification by one vote. Florida was the last state that could have made ratification possible before time expired, and thousands of women on both sides of the issue repeatedly marched in Tallahassee.

The 1980s brought many milestones. When she became commissioner of education in 1986, Tampa's Betty Castor also was the first woman elected to Florida's powerful Cabinet. Miami's Rosemary Barkett, who was born in Mexico to Lebanese parents, was the first woman appointed to the state supreme court in 1985, and Gwen Margolis, also of Miami, became the first female president of the Florida Senate in 1990. Other women followed in these positions, but none yet has followed Paula Hawkins of Maitland, who served one term (1980–1986) in the U.S. Senate. At the same time, Tampa became the first major city to elect a woman, Sandy Freedman, as mayor; Glenda Hood followed her in Orlando.

ELLEN T. ZWILICH, a Miami native, won the 1983 Pulitzer Prize for musical composition. Significant women who retired to Florida in this era include Susan B. Anthony II, the niece of her famed namesake and a feminist writer, who lived in Key West. That artist colony also had attracted Elizabeth Bishop, the winner of the 1952 Pulitzer Prize for poetry, while Alene Duerck, the U.S. Navy's first female admiral, retired to the Orlando area.

Pres. Bill Clinton named Miami's JANET RENO as the first woman in American history to serve as attorney general, and he appointed Carol Browner, also of Miami, to head the Environmental Protection Agency. Her fellow attorneys elected Martha Barnett, a native of Pasco County's Dade City, as president of the American Bar Association in 2000.

At the beginning of the 21st century, Florida had five women in its 23-member congressional delegation. In addition to Democrat Meek and Republican Ros-Lehtinen, they included Democrat Karen Thurman, a former teacher who represented a rural district in west-central Florida; Tillie Fowler, a Jacksonville Republican who announced her intention to retire in 2002; and Democrat Corrine Brown, the state's second African American congresswoman, whose district also includes parts of Jacksonville. National attention, most of it negative, focused on Secretary of State Katherine Harris, a Republican who was in charge of the 2000 election. Approximately 500 disputed Florida ballots caused Democrat Al Gore to lose Florida's electoral votes and thus the presidency.

The 2002 congressional election was a nationwide Republican sweep. After a decade in the U.S. House, Karen Thurman lost a close race to Republican state senator Ginny Waite-Brown, and former secretary of state Katherine Harris won an open seat from Sarasota. Although the 2000 census gave Florida two more congressional seats, women held fewer U.S. House seats in 2003, with four in a 25-member delegation.

—Doris Weatherford

PROMINENT WOMEN

BYLLYE AVERY (1937–)

Administrator and lecturer Byllye Yvonne Avery of Waynesville, Georgia, established a national health project to help guard the well-being of black women. She completed a degree in psychology from Talladega College and earned a master's degree in special education in 1969 from the University of Florida. In the early 1970s Avery aided women seeking abortions in traveling from Florida to New York, where laws favored women's right to choose, and she also opened the Gainesville Women's Health Center in 1974 to offer services closer to the citizens of Florida.

Avery was not a one-issue activist. She also founded a birthing center in Gainesville called Birthplace in 1978, supported the Children's Defense Fund, taught retarded and emotionally disturbed children, and in 1981 presided over the beginnings of the National Black Women's Health Project in Atlanta, Georgia. She contributed to the films *It's Up to Us* (1985) and *On Becoming a Woman* (1987), and wrote about her concerns for black women in a handbook, *An Altar of Words: Wisdom, Comfort, and Inspiration* (1999). In 1993, she was named a visiting fellow and lecturer of the Harvard School of Public Health. Her crusade for women's welfare earned her a MacArthur Foundation Fellowship and the Essence award for community service in 1989, a Woman of Achievement citation from the Ms. Foundation, and the Lienhard Award for the Advancement of Health Care as well as four honorary degrees.

MARY JANE MCLEOD BETHUNE (1875–1955)

Educator and religious leader Mary Jane McLeod Bethune of Mayesville, South Carolina, became the nation's first black female to found a college. The daughter of former slaves, she was a child prodigy who completed studies at the Mayesville Presbyterian Mission at age 11 before entering Scotia Seminary for Negro Girls. After a year at the Moody Bible Institute, she failed to obtain a Presbyterian mission to Africa and chose to educate blacks at the Haines Institute and the Kindell Institute.

After marrying and giving birth to a son, Bethune taught in Florida and founded the Daytona Literary and Industrial School for Negro Girls in 1904. From an initial student body of five, the institution developed into Bethune-Cookman Collegiate Institute. During this period, she allied with the Methodist Episcopal Church and contributed to debate about segregated congregations. After World War I, she campaigned to end lynching and Ku Klux Klan terrorism.

Bethune's later years were extremely productive. In 1936 she was appointed to head the Negro Division of the National Youth Administration, an organization whose advisory committee she had joined, as one of only two African Americans, the previous year. In 1935 she also founded the National Council of Negro Women, which she served as president until 1949.

A spokeswoman for equality, Bethune supported the National Association for the Advancement of Colored People and the Southern Conference for Human Welfare and served on the Charter Conference of the United Nations. A symbol of her activism for racial harmony in the South was an honorary doctoral degree in 1949 from Rollins College, a white institution near Orlando.

ELEANOR MCWILLIAMS CHAMBERLAIN (?–1934)

As a means of improving home and family, suffragist author and organizer Eleanor "Ella" C. McWilliams Chamberlain led the fight for the vote for Florida women. After marrying Fielding P. Chamberlain and settling in Tampa, she began to share her husband's interest in securing women's rights. In 1892 she returned from a women's conference in Iowa with the intention of leading Florida women to full citizenship.

After forming the Florida Woman Suffrage Association in January 1893, Chamberlain organized the state's suffrage campaign, paying particular attention to recruitment of both female and male volunteers and coverage by newspapers and magazines. She began writing a suffrage column for the *Tampa Journal*, attended strategy conferences in Atlanta and Washington, D.C., and lectured to women's groups. Within two years she called a state convention in Tampa of 100 activists and voiced her protest that male immigrant noncitizens and black males had more legislative representation than southern females, who shared the status of Indians, criminals, and the mentally impaired.

In 1897, when the Chamberlains moved to the Midwest, the Florida suffrage effort lagged for lack of leadership. Ella Chamberlain's activism shifted in widowhood, when she returned to Tampa. She began visiting prisoners and transporting poor and neglected patients from tenements to a local hospital. In 1913 she addressed Florida legislators about the plight of widows with small children.

JACQUELINE COCHRAN (ca. 1908–1980)

Aviator and business leader Jacqueline "Jackie" Pittman Cochran Odlum of Muscogee, Florida, succeeded in two fields formerly closed to women. *Life* magazine published a disputed story that she had been adopted as a baby by poor sawmill workers. After two years of education at an elementary school, at age nine she began work as a beautician's aide. She later studied nursing and assisted the company doctor at a sawmill. After moving to New York City and working at a prestigious Fifth Avenue salon, she met a millionaire,

Floyd Odlum. Odlum encouraged her to take flight lessons and they married in 1936.

While living on a ranch in Indio, California, Cochran obtained a pilot's license and in 1934 was the first female entrant in the annual Bendix Transcontinental Air Race and in the MacRobertson London–to–Melbourne Race. She started Jacqueline Cochran Cosmetics in 1935 and helped to pioneer the cosmetics industry.

In 1937 she became the first female pilot to make an instrument landing and placed third in the Bendix classic competition, which she followed up a year later with first place. She then began setting records for altitude, distance, and speed. She was the first female to break the sound barrier, which she accomplished in 1953 in an F-86 Sabrejet, and the first to achieve Mach 2, two times the speed of sound.

During World War II, Cochran trained female pilots, supplied combat dispatches to *Liberty* magazine, and ferried Hudson bombers to Europe. She established the Women's Air Force Service Pilots (WASP), a branch of the U.S. Army Air Force. The success of the WASPs earned her promotion to full colonel. In addition to being the first female recipient of a Distinguished Service Medal, Cochran won the Fédération Aéronautique Internationale gold medal, 15 Harmon trophies, and two consecutive Associated Press Woman of the Year in Business citations. In 1950, the U.S. Postal Service honored her with a portrait stamp. She summarized her adventures in *The Stars at Noon* (1954).

MARJORY STONEMAN DOUGLAS (1890–1998)

One of America's most honored ecologists, Marjory Stoneman Douglas was born in Minneapolis, Minnesota. She attended Wellesley College in Massachusetts before settling in Coconut Grove, Florida, in her twenties. In 1915 she joined the *Miami Herald,* which her father owned, as book-page editor and, during World War I, volunteered as a relief worker in

Europe for the Red Cross. At the war's end, she returned to the United States enthusiastic to campaign for women's suffrage.

Douglas sided with environmentalists on the issue of maintaining the Everglades as a water reservoir for south Florida and fought the Army Corps of Engineers over diversion of the Kissimmee River to agricultural use. She researched local data and folk history for *The Everglades: River of Grass* (1947), a lyric treatise supporting restoration of the unique swamplands of south Florida through conservation. Twenty years later, she compiled a wetlands history, *Florida: The Long Frontier* (1967). She also wrote fiction and a stage play, taught English at the University of Miami, and edited for the university press. For decades of dedication to southern Florida, she won a Wellesley College Alumnae Achievement Award and the Barbour Medal for Conservation and received commendations from American Motors Corporation, the Florida Audubon Society, the Florida Historical Association, and the Florida Wildlife Federation. In 1993, when she was 103, Pres. Bill Clinton awarded her the Presidential Medal of Freedom. Six months before her death, Vice Pres. Al Gore named a 1.3-million-acre section of wetlands for Douglas.

ESTHER HILL HAWKS (1833–1906)

Despite 19th-century discrimination against female doctors, New England healer, abolitionist, and educator Esther Hill Hawks treated wounded members of the Union army during the Civil War. After marrying Dr. John Milton Hawks, she studied his medical reference works in private at their home in Manchester, New Hampshire. She ignored his warning about prejudice against female physicians and enrolled in medical school to become one of the nation's first female doctors.

The war years frustrated Esther Hawks. The Union army at first rejected her services as a doctor. Dorothea Dix, head of the U.S. Sanitary Commission, also refused Hawks's offer to volunteer as a nurse on the grounds that she was too young and attractive to work among wounded soldiers. In 1862 Hawks and her husband treated former slaves and black soldiers on a federally occupied site on the Sea Islands of South Carolina. In a journal Hawks recorded impressions of hunger and suffering in the war-damaged region during combat and Reconstruction.

After the war Esther and John Hawks migrated south to aid freed slaves at Mosquito Inlet, a colony in Volusia County, Florida, sponsored by the Florida Land and Lumber Company. The newly liberated settlers operated a sawmill to supply wood for new housing. Hawks ran and taught in the school that served the colony. In letters to the Freedmen's Aid Society, she described racism among white parents and the removal of her school from its original Halifax River location. After enemies burned the school in 1869, Hawks returned to New Hampshire to open a medical practice and later founded a hospital in Boston that remained in use into the 21st century. After Hawks's diary was recovered from a pile of trash in Essex County, Massachusetts, in 1975, editor Gerald Schwartz published *A Woman Doctor's Civil War: Esther Hill Hawks's Diary* (1989). Sandra R. Hansen featured Hawks in a touring play, *Civil War Women*.

ZORA NEALE HURSTON (1891–1960)

Ethnographer and writer Zora Neale Hurston of Eatonville, Florida, built a unique career as a writer. The daughter of a Baptist minister and a former school teacher, she grew up in the nation's first incorporated black town. She joined an itinerant drama troupe and completed her education at the Morgan Academy in Baltimore, Maryland, and at Howard University in Washington, D.C.

In New York City, Hurston lived among Harlem's artists and collaborated with Langston Hughes on the play *Mule Bone* (1930) and the magazine *Fire!* At Barnard College, she researched the *Clothilde*, the last slave ship, and earned a postgraduate degree from Columbia University. During the Great Depression, with the encouragement of anthropologist Franz Boas, Hurston researched and wrote about folklore and customs in rural Florida. She traveled the Caribbean in search of Afrocentric island traditions. While residing in Haiti, she wrote *Their Eyes Were Watching God* (1937), a classic feminist novel.

Hurston's career was seriously damaged by unfounded accusations of molesting a boy. Although she wrote other books as well as short pieces for *American Mercury, Journal of American Folklore, Negro Digest*, and the *Saturday Evening Post*, her income declined. In her last years, she taught drama, supervised the library at Patrick Air Force Base near Orlando, and worked as a domestic in Miami. She died in a home operated by the St. Lucie County welfare agency. In 1973, novelist Alice Walker found Hurston's grave and erected a marker proclaiming Hurston a "genius of the South."

MAY MANN JENNINGS (1872–1963)
Suffragist, prohibitionist, and environmental leader May Austin Elizabeth Mann Jennings earned the title "Mother of Florida Forestry." Daughter of a state senator, she lived in Crystal River, Florida, in early childhood and attended St. Joseph's Convent School in St. Augustine. At age 19, she married attorney William Sherman Jennings, who was elected governor of Florida in 1900.

Through involvement in women's clubs and civic organizations, Jennings accomplished much for Florida. She advocated preservation of natural resources in the Everglades, the creation of a state board of forestry, home economics education, public libraries, and fair treatment of prisoners and reservation Seminoles. In 1914 she presided over the Florida Federation of Women's Clubs, was the leading strategist for the state suffrage

movement, and supported environmental initiatives of the Audubon Society. At her urging, the state funded the 1,800-acre Royal Palm State Park outside Miami. She received an honorary degree from Stetson University, a dormitory at the University of Florida was named for her, and she is listed among the top 50 most important Floridians of the 20th century. In 1947 Jennings shared a podium with Pres. Harry S. Truman at the dedication of Everglades National Park.

RUTH BRYAN OWEN (1885–1954)
Diplomat and politician Ruth Bryan Owen Rohde of Jacksonville, Illinois, was the first female elected from a southern state to the U.S. House of Representatives. The daughter of orator and politician William Jennings Bryan and Mary Elizabeth Baird Bryan, she studied at Monticello Seminary and the University of Nebraska and was her father's secretary and campaign aide during his three campaigns for the presidency. At age 25, after marrying Maj. Reginald Altham Owen, an English engineer, she settled in Jamaica.

During World War I, Owen lived in London and superintended the correspondence and coffers of the American Woman's War Relief Fund. She also worked in Cairo, Egypt, as an operating room nurse. To support the family after her husband's health became impaired, she lectured on pacifism and directed civic organizations while teaching oratory at the University of Miami. In 1931 she produced a popular classroom text, *Elements of Public Speaking*.

Elected to the U.S. Congress in 1928, Owen became the first female member of the House Committee on Foreign Affairs. A Democrat, she proposed the creation of Everglades National Park and the preservation of citizenship for U.S. women after they married noncitizens. Owen supported international disarmament, a state referendum on Prohibition, and advocated the creation of a department of home and child. In

1933 Pres. Franklin D. Roosevelt appointed her as ambassador to Denmark, the first such post granted to a woman. During a two-week stopover on her way home from Denmark, she lived with the indigenous peoples of West Greenland and later published *Leaves from a Greenland Diary* (1935) based on that experience.

When she married Borge Rohde, a Danish national, in 1936 Owen was forced to resign and became a Danish citizen. She supported the creation of the United Nations, for which she chaired the Speakers Research Committee and helped to draft the U.N. Charter. King Frederick IX of Denmark awarded her a Distinguished Service Medal.

PAULINA PEDROSO (1826–1913)

Cuban civic leader Paulina Pedroso, who immigrated to Florida from Cuba in the 1880s, provided disenfranchised Afro-Hispanic Floridians with opportunities for personal advancement as well as social and medical support. While employed in cigar making and as a cook in Tampa, she cofounded Los Libres Pensadores de Martí y Maceo (The Freethinkers of Martí and Maceo) in support of Latin American leader Jose Martí, who boarded at the family inn on his frequent visits to Florida. To support the freeing of Cuba from Spanish rule, she hid him from assassins, treated his wounds, secured medicines, and helped him recuperate. She also rallied Florida women of color to the cause, organized parades and fiestas, and held raffles to raise funds, earning for herself the name "the black mother of Martí."

In 1900 in Ybor City, the cigar-making center of Tampa, Pedroso and her husband Ruperto championed the Martí-Maceo Society, a recreational, social, and educational club that later provided poor Cuban Americans with medical aid and death benefits. Four years later, to extend opportunities for Latinos against whom white Tampans discriminated, the club merged with La Unión, a similar group from West Tampa. After a strike by tobacco workers in 1910, Pedroso left Florida and returned to adulation in her homeland of Cuba, where she spent the remainder of her life. For courage and altruism, Pedrosa was inducted into the Florida Women's Hall of Fame in 1993. The site of her home became the Park of Friends of Martí in Ybor City. A stage play, *¡Cuba Libre!: The Road to Cuban Independence* (1999), by Jorge Acosta and Paul J. Dosal, dramatizes her role in liberating Cuba from Spanish rule.

MARJORIE KINNAN RAWLINGS (1896–1953)

Conservationist, feminist, historian, and author, Marjorie Kinnan Rawlings of Washington, D.C., won the Pulitzer Prize for *The Yearling* in 1939. Showing an early talent for writing, at age 16 she won a *McCall's* magazine writing award. Rawlings graduated Phi Beta Kappa from the University of Wisconsin in 1918. After a decade as the publicist for the Young Men's Christian Association (YMCA) and editor of *Home Sector*, she pursued a career in news reporting and wrote columns for the *Louisville Courier-Journal* and *Rochester Journal-American*.

She came to Cross Creek, in central Florida, with her husband, Charles Rawlings, in 1928, but the marriage soon ended. In solitude, she enjoyed nature and produced regional fiction, beginning with *South Moon Under* (1933) and the fiction anthology *When the Whippoorwill* (1940), and the pastoral idyll *Cross Creek* (1942). Two of her stories were filmed as *The Sun Comes Up* (1949) and *Gal Young 'Un* (1979). In 1938 she published *The Yearling*, a Pulitzer Prize–winning young adult novel, set near her home in Cross Creek. The MGM screen version, released in 1946, won an Oscar nomination for best picture. Into the 1950s she continued writing fiction for *Atlantic, Collier's, Harper's, The New Yorker, The Saturday Evening Post,*

Scribner's, and *Vogue,* and published three more novels—*Jacob's Ladder* (1950), *The Sojourner* (1953), and *The Secret River* (1955). Rawlings left her rural home as a legacy to the University of Florida. Her significance to American literature is attested to and preserved by the Rawlings Society, the *Journal of Florida Literature,* and the *Rawlings Newsletter.*

JANET RENO (1938–)

Lawyer and politician Janet Reno of Miami, Florida, was the first female U.S. attorney general. The daughter of journalists, she grew up on the edge of the Everglades, attended Dade County schools, and earned a degree in chemistry from Cornell University. She earned a law degree from Harvard, and after working in various positions, was appointed as prosecuting attorney for Miami/Dade County in 1978. The first Florida woman to hold this position, she was reelected for 15 years.

Named attorney general by Pres. Bill Clinton in 1993, Reno held the post longer than had any previous attorney general. She concentrated on juvenile delinquency, crime, and child abuse, and won support for her handling of the Oklahoma City bombing. As the U.S. prison population spiraled upward, Reno advocated alternative sentencing of nonviolent criminals. She made political enemies as a result of two major FBI controversies: the deaths of members of the Branch Davidian cult in a disastrous federal siege and at their compound in Waco, Texas; and the violent seizure and return to his father in Cuba of six-year-old Elian Gonzalez, who had been taken in by relatives in Miami following his rescue during an attempt to flee Cuba with his mother, who drowned off the Florida coast. Following incidents of fainting in public and announcing that she had Parkinson's disease, Reno lost Florida's gubernatorial primary in 2002. She is honored at the National Women's Hall of Fame.

ILEANA ROS-LEHTINEN (1952–)

Educator and Republican politician Ileana "Lily" Ros-Lehtinen was the first Latina and the first Cuban-born woman to serve in the U.S. Congress. A native of Havana, at age seven she accompanied her family in flight from the regime of Cuban dictator Fidel Castro. She majored in English at Dade County Community College and earned a master's degree in education at Florida International University. She founded Eastern Academy and in 1982 was working toward a doctorate at the University of Miami when she successfully campaigned for a seat in the Florida House. She modified her name after marrying House colleague Dexter Lehtinen and won a state Senate seat in 1986.

Strongly anti-Castro, she moved to the U.S. House of Representatives in a special election in 1989. In Congress, she supported veterans' benefits and the death penalty for convicted drug lords. In 1991 she denounced a Cuban venue for the Pan-American Games, voted against the North American Free Trade Agreement, and voted for impeachment of Pres. Bill Clinton. Ros-Lehtinen focused on the rights of immigrants and the assimilation of new citizens into the national fabric. In 2001, the Youth Crime Watch of America selected her as its elected official of the year.

FLORENCE SEIBERT (1897–1991)

Biochemical researcher Florence Barbara Seibert of Easton, Pennsylvania, developed a test for tuberculosis and improved intravenous drug therapy. Stricken by polio in early childhood, she overcame confinement to metal braces and became a scholar at Goucher College in Baltimore, Maryland. During World War I she worked as a chemical engineer at Hammersley Paper Mill before attending Yale University on scholarship and completing a doctorate in biochemistry in 1923. Her research into contamination of intravenous fluids resulted in improved purification procedures for the preparation of intravenously delivered medication. After postgraduate study at the University of Chicago, she taught pathology at the Sprague Memorial Institute in Chicago and joined the biochemistry staff at the University of Pennsylvania in 1932. By 1955 she had obtained a full professorship.

With a Guggenheim fellowship, Seibert studied in Uppsala, Sweden, in 1937 and 1938 where, aided by her sister, Mabel Seibert, she purified tuberculin for use in the first tuberculosis skin test. Her protocol met the standards of both the U.S. government and the World Health Organization. After retiring at age 61, she began advising the U.S. Public Health Service and directing the Cancer Research Laboratory at the Veterans' Administration Hospital in St. Petersburg, Florida. Until her last months, she and Mabel continued their volunteer cancer research, which earned Florence the Garvan Medal for distinguished service to chemistry by female scientists and a place in the National Women's Hall of Fame. Florence Seibert's private papers, including correspondence with drug manufacturers Eli Lilly, Merck, Sharpe and Dohme, and Parke-Davis, are housed at the American Philosophical Society in Philadelphia.

MARGARET TAYLOR (1788–1852)

A reluctant first lady, Margaret "Peggy" Mackall Smith Taylor of Calvert County, Maryland, flourished earlier in her marriage as a military wife living on the frontier. Daughter of a major in the American Revolution, Margaret was reared on a plantation and was schooled in the social graces at home. After marrying Lt. Zachary Taylor, an infantry officer and subsequently the hero of the Mexican War, she lived on the Taylor family farm in Louisiana. Zachary Taylor was posted to Indiana, Minnesota, Wisconsin, and Arkansas, where Margaret followed and made homes. She supported her husband's attempts to bring the rule of law to these regions and volunteered as a garrison nurse. While living at Tampa's Fort Brooke during the Second Seminole War, she and her adult daughter, who also was married to an army officer, nursed soldiers through a yellow fever epidemic.

After Taylor's election as the 12th president of the United States in 1848, Margaret Taylor regretted the intrusion of political office on family life and on the rearing of their children. She refused the social role of first lady, which she relegated to Mary Elizabeth "Betty" Taylor Bliss, her youngest daughter, who was married to William Wallace Smith Bliss, Zachary Taylor's secretary and military aide. Taylor's presidency ended after 16 months with his death from enteritis. In widowhood, Margaret Taylor lived her last two years in East Pascagoula, Mississippi, with her only son Richard.

JULIA TUTTLE (1849–1898)

Visionary real estate developer Julia De Forest Sturtevant Tuttle of Cleveland, Ohio, helped shape the expansion of settlements in southern Florida. She first saw the possibilities of the region during a family visit to her retired parents in 1871 and returned for a vacation in 1875. After the death of her husband, industrialist Frederick Tuttle, in 1891, she left Cleveland for the south Florida frontier. Purchasing 640 acres along the northern bank of the Miami River, she sold alternate lots to improve the value of her unsold land.

Tuttle realized the investment potential of Florida's east coast as an international port and commercial center. During the Great Freeze of 1894–1895, she mailed orange blossoms to Henry Morrison Flagler, a North Florida entrepreneur and builder of the Florida East Coast Railroad. This proved there had been no frost in Miami, and to further tempt him, she offered land on which he might extend his railroad to South

Florida. Her gift inspired him to turn the semi-tropical wilderness into the city of Miami, which settlers incorporated in 1896. For her faith in her adopted state, she was dubbed the "Mother of Miami" and inducted into the Florida Women's Hall of Fame. Her family papers and business correspondence are deposited in the archives of the Historical Museum of Southern Florida. A causeway between Miami and Miami Beach, named after her, acknowledges her pioneering role; the annual Julia Tuttle Award of the Greater Miami Chamber of Commerce honors others who share her faith in south Florida.

ELLEN T. ZWILICH (1939–)

Composer Ellen Taaffe Zwilich of Miami, Florida, won a 1983 Pulitzer Prize for writing the lyric symphony, Symphony No. 1 (Three Movements for Orchestra). She begged for piano lessons at age five; by age ten, she wearied of lessons and wrote her own scores—the start of a career that produced a variety of musical works. Earning degrees from Florida State University and Juilliard, Zwilich began private study of composition, theory, and violin and became the first woman to earn a doctorate in composition from Juilliard in New York in 1970. Conductor Leopold Stokowski chose her for the violin section of the American Symphony Orchestra.

Influenced by Bartók, Shostakovich, and Stravinsky, Zwilich became one of the few musicians to earn a living from commissions, grants, and prizes for her string trios and quartets, pieces for harpsichord, vocal art songs, chamber music, piano-voice duets, concerti, and symphonic suites. In 1985 she debuted Symphony No. 2 (Cello Symphony), commissioned by the San Francisco Symphony. Two years later she provided an original overture to open the National Museum for Women in the Arts.

Zwilich identified the key to her success as the ability to think like an instrumentalist. For young pianists who shared her enthusiasm for sprightly melodies, she upgraded piano teaching with Peanuts Gallery, a children's suite based on the Charles Schulz cartoon strip. Her honors included three Marion Freschl prizes, an Elizabeth Sprague Coolidge Chamber Music award, a Viotti Gold Medal in 1975, a Guggenheim fellowship, and grants from the National Endowment for the Arts and the Martha Baird Rockefeller Fund. In 1999 she was named Musical America Composer of the Year.

—Mary Ellen Snodgrass

PROMINENT SITES

AH-THA-THI-KI Seminole Museum
Big Cypress Seminole Reservation
West Boundary Road
HC-61 Box 21-A
Clewiston, FL 33440
Telephone: (863) 902 1113
Web: http://www.seminoletribe.com/museum
This 60-acre site includes exhibits on the history and culture of the Seminole tribe and a Seminole village. The museum displays beadwork, which was traditionally made by the women of the tribe.

Amelia Earhart Park
401 East 65th Street
Hialeah, FL 33013
Telephone: (305) 769 2693
Web: http://www.co.miami-dade.fl.us/parks/
    Parks/amelia_earhart.htm
At the entrance of the park, a sign explains that the 515-acre park and recreation area were named for Earhart, whose last flight, an attempt to circumnavigate the globe at the equator, originated in Miami on June 1, 1936.

Clara White Mission
613 West Ashley Street
Jacksonville, FL 32202
Telephone: (904) 354 4162
Web: http://www.clarawhitemission.org
Founded in 1904 by the activist and successful businesswoman Eartha Mary Magdalene White, the mission is currently a black history museum, as well as a homeless center that provides meals for the local community. In 1928 White renamed the mission in honor of her mother Clara, a former slave. The museum displays some of White's writings as well as much of her former home's furnishings.

Colonial Spanish Quarter
Visitor Center
53 St. George Street
Mailing Address: PO Box 210
St. Augustine, FL 32085
Telephone: (904) 825 6830
Web: http://www.historicstaugustine.com/csq/history.html
Founded in 1565, St. Augustine is the oldest continuously occupied settlement of European origin in the United States. The Quarter is a living history museum, focusing on 1740 and representing the Spanish soldiers and their families that had occupied the area. Women reenact activities such as candle making for visitors.

Florida Women's Hall of Fame
The Capitol
South Adams Street
Tallahassee, FL 32399
Telephone: (850) 488 6167
Web: http://www.fcsw.net/historyhof.htm
The Hall of Fame was established in 1982, but temporarily abandoned in 1986. In 1992 a law was passed reestablishing the Hall. Since 1993 three women have been inducted in the Hall of Fame annually. Plaques that include brief biographies and photos of each inductee hang in the State Capitol.

Florida Women's Heritage Trail
Florida Department of State
Division of Historical Resources
R.A. Gray Building
500 South Bronough Street
Tallahassee, FL 32399
Telephone: (800) 847 7278
Web: http://www.flheritage.com/magazine/wht
This guide is available for purchase and contains entries on locations throughout the state that are significant to women's history. Each entry includes a short synopsis of what visitors will find at the site as well as its address and phone number.

H. B. Plant Museum in the Tampa Bay Hotel
University of Tampa
401 West Kennedy Boulevard
Tampa, FL 33606
Telephone: (813) 254 1891, ext. 23
Web: http://www.plantmuseum.com/index.shtml
A stunning example of Victorian architecture, this huge former hotel stretches a quarter-mile on four floors. One of five Florida hotels owned by Henry and Josephine Plant, it was an army headquarters during the Spanish-American War. A collection, "Ladies and Their Pastimes," shows what women did on their visits to the hotel.

Historical Museum of Southern Florida
101 West Flagler Street
Miami, FL 33130

Telephone: (305) 375 1492
Web: http://www.historical-museum.org/index.htm
The museum explores and preserves the history, cultures, and folkways of southern Florida. Several of the museum's permanent collections—including those on southeast Florida, aviation and maritime history, and Native Americans—include material on women's history.

Historic Pensacola Village
120 East Church Street
Pensacola, FL 32501
Telephone: (850) 595 5985, ext. 100
Web: http://www.historicpensacola.org
This area contains ten historic buildings and museums, including the Julee Cottage, that are open to the public. A former slave bought the home in 1804. It is thought that she also bought other properties in Pensacola, and used her earnings to purchase the freedom of other slaves.

Historic Spanish Point
Gulf Spanish Association
337 North Tamiami Trail
Osprey, FL 34229
Telephone: (941) 966 5214
Web: http://www.historicspanishpoint.org
Operated by the Gulf Spanish Association, this historic area includes four restored gardens that were once located on the property of Chicago real estate tycoon Bertha Palmer. Her winter home is still standing and is now used as an education center, with its interior rooms doing duty as classrooms.

Jewish Museum of Florida
301 Washington Avenue
Miami Beach, FL 33139
Telephone: (305) 672 5044
Web: http://www.jewishmuseum.com/index2.html
This museum is dedicated to communicating the Florida Jewish experience from 1763 to the present to both Jews and non-Jews. Women are represented in the core exhibit; the museum has also mounted temporary exhibits that focus specifically on women.

Jose Marti Park
1303 8th Avenue
Tampa, FL 33605
The park is located on the site of Paulina Pedroso's former home. She was an Afro-Cuban patriot who housed Martí after his exile from Cuba.

Kennedy Space Center Visitor Center
Kennedy Space Center
Titusville, FL 32899
Telephone: (321) 449 4444
Web: http://www.ksc.nasa.gov
Former astronauts, female and male, narrate exhibits in the center. Female astronauts are featured throughout the exhibits, including the Astronaut Memorial that honors the 17 astronauts who died in service.

Key West Lighthouse and Keeper's Quarters Museum
938 Whitehead Street
Key West, FL 33040
Telephone: (305) 294 0012
Web: http://www.kwahs.com/lighthouse.htm
Barbara Mabrity served as the keeper of the Key West Lighthouse for 32 years, longer than any other person. Her husband was the first keeper of the lighthouse and she was the assistant keeper from 1826 until 1832 when he died of yellow fever. She took up full duties after his death.

Kingsley Plantation
Fort George Island State Cultural Site
11676 Palmetto Avenue
Jacksonville, FL 32226
Telephone: (904) 251 3537
Web: http://www.cr.nps.gov/goldcres/sites/kingsley.htm
The oldest surviving antebellum plantation home in Florida, it was named for Zephaniah Kingsley who owned the plantation from 1813 to 1839. Kingsley's wife was former slave Anna Jai. Freed in 1811, Jai went on to be a successful businesswoman and was active in managing the plantation. Alhough a former slave, Jai became a slave owner after she was freed.

Marjorie Kinnan Rawlings Historical Site
18700 South CR 325
Cross Creek, FL 32640
Telephone: (352) 466 3672
Web: http://abfla.com/parks/MarjorieKinnanRawlings/marjoriekinnanrawlings.html
Rawlings was author of the Pulitzer Prize–winning book *The Yearling*. She and her husband Charles moved to Cross Creek in 1928; now their home and surrounding farm and marshland are open for tours. The site shows a way of rural life that has almost disappeared in Florida.

Museum of Florida History
500 South Bronough Street
Tallahassee, FL 32399

Telephone: (850) 245 6400

Web: http://www.dos.state.fl.us/dhr/museum/quilts

Every fall, this museum mounts an exhibit of quilts made by Floridians; it also offers an exhibit on Florida during the Civil War that examines women's everyday lives and important work on the home front during the war. A 1920s Florida farm kitchen demonstrates women's contributions to farm economy.

The Oldest Schoolhouse

14 St. George Street

St. Augustine, FL 32084

Telephone: (888) 653 7245

Web: http://www.oldestschoolhouse.com

Built before 1763 this is said to be the oldest wooden schoolhouse in the United States. It became coeducational in 1788, thus reportedly making it the oldest school in which females were educated with males in the United States.

Stranahan House

335 Southeast 6th Avenue

Fort Lauderdale, FL 33301

Telephone: (954) 524 4736

Web: http://www.stranahanhouse.com

Built in 1901 and originally used as a trading post with the Seminoles, this house is one of the oldest homes in Fort Lauderdale. The pioneer Ivy Stranahan lived here with her husband, Frank. She worked with the Seminoles and was also active in the Florida suffrage movement.

Tallahassee Museum

3945 Museum Drive

Tallahassee, FL 32310

Telephone: (850) 576 1636

Web: http://tallahasseemuseum.org

The museum includes Bellevue, the 1840s plantation home of Princess Catherine Murat, great-grandniece of George Washington, and wife of Prince of Naples Achille Murat. The prince was a nephew of Napoleon Bonaparte.

The Women's Park

10251 West Flagler Street

Miami, FL 33174

Telephone: (305) 480 1716

Web: http://www.co.miami-dade.fl.us/parks/
    Parks/womens_park.htm

This 15-acre lakeside park is dedicated to every woman in Miami-Dade County. The park features a time capsule buried under a rock monument, as well as offering gallery exhibit space for history materials and art shows.

Ybor City State Museum

1818 East 9th Avenue

Tampa, FL 33605

Telephone: (813) 247 6323

Web: http://www.ybormuseum.org

Known for its cigar-making industry, Ybor City, designated a National Historic Landmark District, is Tampa's Latin Quarter. The museum displays a painting of Afro-Cuban patriot Paulina Pedroso.

Zora Neale Hurston Branch Library

3008 Avenue D

Fort Pierce, FL 34947

Telephone: (772) 462 2154

Web: http://www.st-lucie.lib.fl.us/hbl.htm

Located in the town where Hurston lived for the last part of her life, the library recently received funding to produce a heritage trail in honor of Hurston.

Zora Neale Hurston National Museum of Fine Arts

227 East Kennedy Boulevard

Eatonville, FL 32751

Telephone: (407) 647 3307

Web: http://www.zoranealehurston.cc

Located in the oldest surviving incorporated black municipality, which was the setting of many of Hurston's books, this museum features works by artists on the Black Diaspora. The Zora Neale Hurston Festival of Arts and Humanities, held on museum grounds every January, offers speeches, street festivals, and educational presentations in celebration of African American culture.

RESOURCES

FURTHER READING

HISTORY

Anthony, Susan B., and Ida Husted Harper. *History of Women Suffrage.* Vol. 4. Indianapolis, Ind.: Hollenbeck Press, 1902.

Arnade, Charles W. *Florida on Trial, 1593–1602.* Coral Gables, Fla.: University of Miami, 1959.

Brown, Canter. *Women on the Tampa Bay Frontier.* Tampa, Fla.: Tampa Bay History Center, 1997.

Bulmahn, Lynn. "Freedmen Came to Volusia, But Seldom Found Fortune." *NIE World,* 4 February 2001.

Campbell, D'Ann. *A Woman's War Too: U.S. Women in the Military in World War II.* Edited by Paula Poulos. Washington, D.C.: National Archives Trust Board, 1996.

Collins, Gale Forman. *Women's Legal Rights in Florida.* Clearwater, Fla.: Sphinx Publishing, 1993.

Corse, Carita Doggett. *The Key to the Golden Islands.* Chapel Hill: University of North Carolina, 1931.

Davis, Karen. *Public Faces—Private Lives: Women in South Florida, 1870s–1910s.* Miami, Fla.: Pickering Press, 1990.

Denham, James Michael. *A Rogue's Paradise: Antebellum Florida.* Tuscaloosa: University of Alabama Press, 1997.

Federal Writers' Project. *Florida: A Guide to the Southernmost State.* New York: Oxford University Press, 1939.

Gannon, Michael. *Florida: A Short History.* Gainesville: University Press of Florida, 1993.

Greenbaum, Susan D. *More than Black: Afro-Cubans in Tampa.* Gainesville: University Press of Florida, 2002.

Hanna, Kathryn Abbey. *Florida: Land of Change.* Chapel Hill: University of North Carolina Press, 1941.

Harper, Ida Husted. *History of Woman Suffrage.* Vol. 6. New York: J. J. Little & Ives, 1902.

Henderson, Ann, and Gary R. Mormino, eds. *Spanish Pathways in Florida.* Sarasota, Fla.: Pineapple Press, 1991.

Hewitt, Nancy A. *Southern Discomfort: Women's Activism in Tampa, Florida, 1880s–1920s.* Urbana: University of Illinois Press, 2001.

Jahoda, Gloria. *Florida: A Bicentennial History.* New York: W. W. Norton, 1976.

Kennedy, Stetson. *Palmetto Country.* New York: Duell, Sloan & Pearce, 1942.

Landers, Jane. *Black Society in Spanish Florida.* Urbana: University of Illinois Press, 1999.

Leisch, Juanita, "An Army of Women." *Military Images,* 1 May 2000.

Loquasto, Wendy S., ed. *Celebrating Florida's First 150 Lawyers.* Tallahassee: Florida Bar and Florida Association for Women Lawyers, 2000.

Mormino, Gary R., and Anthony P. Pizzo. *Tampa: The Treasure City.* Tulsa, Okla.: Continental Heritage Press, 1983.

Mormino, Gary R. "Tampa's Splendid Little War." *OAH Magazine of History* 12, No. 3 (spring 1998): 1–6.

Morris, Allen. *Women in the Florida Legislature.* Tallahassee, Fla.: House of Representatives, 1995.

O'Flarity, James P. *The Legal Status of Homemakers in Florida.* Washington, D.C.: USPGO, 1977.

Oliver, Kitty. *Multicolored Memories of a Black Southern Girl.* Lexington: University Press of Kentucky, 2001.

Parks, Arva Jeane Moore. *Miami: The Magic City.* Tulsa, Okla.: Continental Heritage Press, 1981.

Quester, George. "The Problem." In *Female Soldiers—Combatants or Noncombatants: Historical and Contemporary Perspectives,* edited by Nancy Goldman. Westport, Conn.: Greenwood Press, 1982.

Rivers, Larry Eugene. *Slavery in Florida: Territorial Days to Emancipation.* Gainesville: University Press of Florida, 2000.

Scott, Anne Firor, ed. *Southern Women and Their Families in the 19th Century, Papers and Diaries.* Bethesda, Md.: University Publications of America, 2000.

Stanton, Elizabeth Cady, Susan B. Anthony, and Matilda Joslyn Gage. *History of Woman Suffrage.* Vols. 1–3. Rochester, N.Y.: Charles Mann Printing, 1886.

Stewart, Jennifer Nichol. "Wacky Times: An Analysis of the WAC in World War II and Its Effects on Women." *International Social Science Review* 75 (spring-summer 2000): 26.

Taylor, A. Elizabeth. "The Woman Suffrage Movement in Florida." *Florida Historical Quarterly* 36 (1957): 42–60.

Tebeau, Charlton W., and Ruby Leigh Carson. *Florida from Indian Trail to Space Age.* 3 vols. Delray Beach, Fla.: Southern Publishing, 1965.

Weatherford, Doris. *Milestones: Chronology of American Women's History.* New York: Facts On File, 1997.

Wright, E. Lynne. *More than Petticoats: Remarkable Florida Women.* Guilford, Conn.: TwoDot, 2001.

BIOGRAPHY AND AUTOBIOGRAPHY

Bethune, Mary McLeod. *Mary McLeod Bethune Papers, 1915–1955.* Edited by Elaine M. Smith, with Randolph H. Boehm. Bethesda, Md.: University Publications of America, 1996.

Bethune, Mary McLeod. *Mary McLeod Bethune: Building a Better World: Essays and Selected Documents.* Edited by Audrey Thomas McCluskey and Elaine M. Smith. Bloomington: Indiana University Press, 1999.

Bigelow, Gordon E. *Frontier Eden: The Literary Career of Marjorie Kinnan Rawlings.* Gainesville: University of Florida Press, 1966.

Douglas, Marjory Stoneman. *Marjory Stoneman Douglas: Voice of the River: An Autobiography.* Englewood, Fla.: Pineapple Press, 1987.

Grace, Lim, and Patrick Rogers, "Lady Everglades." *People Weekly,* 1 June 1998, 109.

Hemenway, Robert. *Zora Neale Hurston: A Literary Biography.* Champaign: University of Illinois Press, 1977.

Keen, George Gillett. *Cracker Times and Pioneer Lives: The Florida Reminiscences of George Gillett Keen and Sarah Pamela Williams.* Columbia: University of South Carolina Press, 2000.

Lipske, Michael. "Marjory Stoneman Douglas." *National Wildlife,* April-May 2000.

Lyons, Mary E. *Sorrow's Kitchen: The Life and Folklore of Zora Neale Hurston.* New York: Macmillan, 1990.

Moseley, Julia Daniels. *Come to My Sunland: Letters of Julia Daniels Moseley from the Florida Frontier, 1882–1886.* Edited by Julia Winifred Moseley and Betty Powers Crislip. Gainesville: University of Florida Press, 1998.

Parker, Idella. *Idella Parker: From Reddick to Cross Creek.* Gainesville: University Press of Florida, 1999.

Phillips, Sarah E. "A Woman Doctor's Civil War." *Perspectives in History* 6, no. 1 (fall 1990).

Pierpont, Claudie Roth. "A Society of One: Zora Neale Hurston, American Contrarian." *New Yorker,* 17 February 1997, 80–91.

Rawlings, Marjorie Kinnan. *Cross Creek.* New York: C. Scribner's Sons, 1942.

Reno, Jane Wood. *The Hell with Politics: The Life and Writings of Jane Wood Reno.* Atlanta, Ga.: Peachtree Publishers, 1994.

Schwartz, Gerald. *A Woman Doctor's Civil War.* Columbia: University of South Carolina Press, 1984.

Simurda, Stephen J. "Byllye Avery: Guardian of Black Women's Health." *American Health* (March 1993).

Tarr, Rodger L. *Marjorie Kinnan Rawlings: A Descriptive Bibliography.* Pittsburgh, Penn.: University of Pittsburgh Press, 1996.

Vance, Linda D. *May Mann Jennings: Florida's Genteel Activist.* Gainesville: University of Florida Press, 1985.

Vance, Linda. "Women in Florida History." In *A Guide to the History of Florida,* edited by Paul S. George. Westport, Conn.: Greenwood Press, 1989.

USEFUL WEB SITES

"Afro-Cubans in Tampa," Florida History Internet Center
http://www.floridahistory.org/events/afro-cubans.htm

"The Byllye Avery Collection,"Black Film Center/Archive
http://www.indiana.edu/~bfca/collection/special/bavery.html

"Byllye Avery," NARAL: Women's Stories
http://www.naral.org/issues/issues_stories11.html

"Historical Timeline of la Sociedad la Unión Martí-Maceo"
http://www.cas.usf.edu/anthropology/Marti-Maceo/HistoryPartOne/timelinepartone.htm

"Historic Clubs," Florida's Latin Quarter
http://www.ybor.org/historicclubs/union.asp

Ileana Ros-Lehtinen, U.S. House of Representatives
http://www.house.gov/ros-lehtinen

"Jacqueline Cochran," Florida International University's Allstar Network
http://www.allstar.fiu.edu/aero/cochran1.htm

"Jacqueline Cochran," Smithsonian National Air and Space Museum, Women in Aviation and Space History
http://www.nasm.si.edu/nasm/aero/women_aviators/jackie_cochran.htm

"Margaret Mackall Smith Taylor," White House Web site
http://www.whitehouse.gov/history/firstladies/mt12.html

"May Mann Jennings," Reclaiming the Everglades
    http://everglades.fiu.edu/reclaim/bios/jenningsmm.html
"Ruth Bryan Owen (Rohde)," Reclaiming the Everglades
    http://everglades.fiu.edu/reclaim/bios/owen.html

SELECTED ORGANIZATIONS AND INSTITUTIONS

Eckerd College Women's and Gender Studies Department
4200 54th Avenue South
St. Petersburg, FL 33711
Telephone: (800) 456 9009
Web: http://www.eckerd.edu
Offers an interdisciplinary major exploring both women's collective undertakings and self-descriptions, and gender itself.

Florida Atlantic University Women's Studies Center
777 Glades Road
Florida Atlantic University
Boca Raton, FL 33431
Telephone: (561) 297 0163 or 3865
Web: http://www.fau.edu/divdept/womenstd/women.htm
Offers an undergraduate and graduate certificate as well as a master of arts in women's studies, preparing students for careers in agencies and institutions that serve women.

Florida Division of Historical Resources
500 South Bronough Street
Tallahassee, FL 32399–0250
Telephone: (850) 245 6300
Web: http://dhr.dos.state.fl.us
Maintains the museum of Florida history and other projects. Publications include the *Florida History and the Arts Magazine* and *Florida Women's Heritage Trail*

Florida Humanities Council
599 Second Street South
St. Petersburg, FL 33701
Telephone: (727) 553 3800
Web: http://www.flahum.org
The Council publishes a quarterly magazine, *The Forum*, and sponsors traveling exhibits, a speaker's bureau, and frequent conferences, called gatherings, throughout the state. It also trains teachers in Florida history, including that of women.

Florida International University Women's Studies Center
University Park DM 212
Miami, FL 33199
Telephone: (305) 348 2408
Web: http://www.fiu.edu/~wstudies
Develops and coordinates academic courses and community programming on women, sexual orientation, and gender.

Florida State Archives
Florida Department of State
Division of Library & Information Services
Bureau of Archives & Records Management
500 South Bronough Street
Tallahassee, FL 32399–0250
Telephone: (850) 245 6700
Web: http://dlis.dos.state.fl.us/barm/fsa.html
The archives has an online catalog and index for researchers interested in the public records series, manuscript collections, and the genealogical collection.
The Florida State Archives: Collections Pertaining to Women's History and Women's Issues.
http://dlis.dos.state.fl.us/barm/fsa/women'sguide.htm

Florida State University Women's Studies Program
214-J William Johnston Building
Tallahassee, FL 32306–2205
Telephone: (850) 644 9514
Web: http://www.fsu.edu/~womenst
Interdisciplinary program that examines the status, accomplishments, perspectives, and development of women in history, culture, and contemporary society.

University of Central Florida Women's Studies Program
Colbourn Hall 207 A
University of Central Florida
4000 Central Florida Boulevard
Orlando, FL 32816
Telephone: (407) 823 6502
Web: http://www.cas.ucf.edu/womensstudies
Academic program offering both graduate and undergraduate certificates and a minor focused on women, women's issues, and gender relations.

University of Florida Gainesville Center for Women's Studies and Gender Research
3324 Turlington Hall
PO Box 117352
Gainesville, FL 32611

Telephone: (352) 392 3365
Web: http://www.wst.ufl.edu/index.html
Interdisciplinary program studying gender, its function in cultures and societies, and its intersection with race and class.

University of Florida George A. Smathers Libraries
PO Box 117001
Gainesville, FL 32611–7001
Telephone: (352) 392 0345
Web: http://web.uflib.ufl.edu
Gateway to online catalog for all University of Florida collections.

University of South Florida Department of Women's Studies
4202 East Fowler Avenue, FAO 153
Tampa, FL 33620–8350
Telephone: (813) 974 3496

Web: http://www.cas.usf.edu/womens_studies/contact.html
One of the oldest of women's studies programs, this department offers both bachelor's and master's degrees.

University of West Florida Libraries
11000 University Parkway
Pensacola, FL 32514
Telephone: (850) 474 2462
Web: http://library.uwf.edu
Online access to university libraries and interlibrary loan.

University of West Florida Women's Studies Program
11000 University Parkway
Pensacola, FL 32514
Telephone: (850) 473 7290
Web: http://www.uwf.edu/womens
Interdisciplinary program offering a minor in women's studies; examines women in historical and contemporary settings.

GEORGIA

Spring had come early that year, with warm quick rains and a sudden frothing of pink peach blossoms and dogwood dappling with white stars. . . . Already the plowing was nearly finished, and the bloody glory of the sunset colored the fresh-cut furrows of red Georgia clay to even redder hues. The moist hungry earth, waiting upturned for the cotton seeds, showed pinkish. . . . The white-washed plantation house seemed an island set in a wild red sea.
—Margaret Mitchell, *Gone with the Wind*, 1936

Although she was appointed, rather than elected, the first female senator was from Georgia. The state also claims the first U.S. college for women and boasts an extraordinary number of acclaimed women authors.

PREHISTORY

(Prehistory–1540)

A thousand or more years ago, Mound Builders lived along rivers in Georgia and in other southeastern states. At Ocmulgee National Monument, near modern Macon, remains of conical and pyramidal mounds contain tens of thousands of sophisticated artifacts. An Etowah Mound, near Cartersville, covered three acres, making it one of the largest aboriginal mounds in the United States. Although the Mound Builders apparently developed extensive trade networks and appreciable knowledge, they left no evidence of why their civilization collapsed at the end of the first millennium A.D.

At the time of European exploration at the end of 15th century, the Cusabo, Yamacraw, Yamasee, and other Native Americans lived in towns along the coast. Because of the warm climate, shelter consisted of wooden poles covered with palmetto. They built larger thatched buildings for communal gatherings. Fish and seafood, supplemented with deer and fowl, were dietary staples.

Native women along the coast were accorded high status. They participated in religious ceremonies, one of which prompted such intensity that women cut each other's arms with sharp shells, drawing blood. More important, however, some women were *cacica*, or rulers. Powerful women lived inland as well. According to records of Hernando de Soto's expedition, which landed in Georgia in 1540:

The *cacica* of Cutifachique, when she came out of her town to cross the river and

State Population (2000): 8,186,453

Female Population (2000): 4,159,340

Women in State Legislature (2003): 21.6%

Female College Enrollment (1999): 178,000 (57.1% of total)

Privately Held Women-owned Businesses (1997): 145,576

First Year of Full Suffrage: 1920

extend . . . the hospitalities of her province, was borne to the water's edge in a chair. There she entered her canoe, over the stern of which was spread an awning. A mat lay extended in the bottom. . . . [Her] shawls were made . . . from the bark of trees and others of feathers, white, gray, vermilion, and yellow, rich and suitable for winter. (Jones 1873, 71)

When whites arrived in the north Georgia mountains, they found the land to be home to members of the Cherokee and Creek (or Muscogee) nations, who were themselves relative newcomers, pushed south from North Carolina and Tennessee. The women of these nations, too, especially the Cherokee, had relatively high status.

WHITE EXPLORATION TO THE AMERICAN REVOLUTION
(1540–1776)

The Spanish began exploring Georgia during the early 16th century and established missions in the area after 1566. Spanish soldiers soon thereafter began marrying local women, especially those of high rank. Although such women adopted Spanish names, they remained independently powerful. Dona Maria Melendez, for instance, ruled a community of some 3,000 people at San Pedro (Cumberland Island), as had Dona Ana before her.

When the Spanish tried to impose their rule, clashes with Native Americans became common. Those who rebelled were killed or sold into slavery. European diseases, especially smallpox, wiped out many more. Still others were killed by Yamasee and Creek warriors allied with the English, who wanted to establish a base in Georgia to buffer their more northern colonies from the Spanish settlements in the South. Their attacks, combined with pirate raids around the turn of the 18th century, had effectively eliminated Spanish influence in Georgia by the time of the first English settlement in 1733.

Georgia was the last of the English colonies along the Atlantic to be settled, so it benefited from the experience of earlier settlements. A London Board of Trustees, and in particular Georgia governor James Oglethorpe, combined liberalism with practicality in governing the colony. Unlike colonies to the north, they prohibited African slavery and recruited a diversity of Europeans to settle there. They looked for skilled people, but did not reject settlers because of their religious beliefs or criminal histories. Most settlers were English, others were Scottish, Swiss, and Welsh, and still others were Moravians or Salzburgers. The women ranged from Elizabeth Stanley, a professional midwife, to an unnamed woman who was publicly whipped for prostitution soon after her arrival.

The *Ann* sailed from Gravesend, England, in November 1732 carrying 41 men, 27 women, and 28 children. Among the Yamacraws who greeted them soon after landing was Mary Musgrove, a native married to English trader John Musgrove. The *Ann's* arrival had been thoughtfully anticipated with stairs enabling the newcomers to easily carry their goods up the 40-foot bluff above the Savannah River, where they pitched tents and settled Savannah. Although there were 28 deaths that summer, probably from mosquito-borne disease, Georgians endured fewer hardships than most early colonists.

When the settlers' chronicler, Peter Gordon, returned to London in November, it was in part to improve the status of women. A disproportionate number of colonists who died were men, and their widows were left without legal claim to the land that they worked, which reverted to the colonial trust. Gordon asked the trustees to allow women to inherit:

This surely would be more agreeable to justice and tend more to the advantage of the Colony thane to have the inheritance intirely cutt of[f]. . . . Daughters would be in the same unhappy circumstances. . . . European, and particularly . . . British women . . . are generally in good esteem and very valuable all owr setlements both in the West Indies and in

America. . . . I think it will naturally follow that if the right of inheritance were in the daughters . . . it would be a means . . . of strengthning the Colony. (Gordon 1963, 55)

The trustees reformed inheritance rules in 1739. Although complex, the new rules recognized the principle of gender equality as seen in one provision proclaiming that "every grantee of lands not exceeding eighty acres, to any one son or any one daughter." (McCall 1811, 96)

In 1749 the trustees lifted their ban on slavery. The black population soared, as white planters imported Africans to do the hard work of cultivating rice in the coastal lowlands. Sixteen years later there were approximately 7,800 black slaves in Georgia, compared with 10,000 free whites.

As Georgia grew, the colony remained a volatile mix of increasingly resentful Native Americans and terrified Africans along with whites who had good reason to fear both. Pirates and other lawless men held the real power, and according to one woman, "before 1776, at the sight of a strange boat on sea or river, women and children ran and hid." (Green and Green 1912, 2:322)

AMERICAN REVOLUTION TO CIVIL WAR ERA (1776–1860)

When the American Revolution began, Georgia had been a colony only slightly more than 40 years; its population was just over more than 30,000 people, with whites barely outnumbering blacks. Thinly scattered along the coast and eastern rivers, Georgians were divided on the rebellion. Many left, abandoning property and leaving crops unplanted for several years. After Savannah fell to the British in December 1778, Col. Elijah Clarke (later a general) led some 400 women and children—but not Hannah Clarke—on a 200-mile trek through the wilderness to the relative safety of the Blue Ridge Mountains. Clarke traveled with

her husband's troops, and once had her horse shot from under her.

Georgia women played an important role in the Revolution. Sarah Williamson, a wealthy widow, used her busy looms and ovens to supply clothing and food to American troops. NANCY MORGAN HART became a spy for the Americans; five redcoats that she captured were hanged. Some black women were also legendary. When revolutionary leader Stephen Heard was captured and taken to Augusta to be executed, Mammy Kate tracked his captors. Pretending to be a washerwoman, she managed to get Heard out to her waiting horse.

Women, however, also suffered emotionally and physically. Dorothy Camber Walton feared that her husband would be executed. One of the youngest signers of the Declaration of Independence, George Walton became a prisoner of war at the fall of Savannah in 1778 and wrote to Dorothy in possible farewell, "Remember that you are the beloved wife of one who has made honour and reputation the ruling motive in every action of his life." (Ibid., 279) He was freed the following year.

As the British moved through Georgia, they burned homes and barns and confiscated food and livestock. They left the economy in ruins and women without resources. Many women thought the most hurtful action by the British was callously destroying treasured items. Several Georgia women singled out the heartbreak of seeing handcrafted featherbeds scattered to the winds.

Independence became official in 1783, and Georgia ratified the U.S. Constitution on January 2, 1788, making it the new nation's fourth state.

The economy of the South fundamentally changed with the 1793 invention of the cotton gin, which made cotton production—and slavery—much more profitable. The invention is credited to Eli Whitney, a young Connecticut man living on the Georgia plantation of Catherine Littlefield Greene. She explained to Whitney the need for a machine that could comb seeds out of cotton. Whitney built it, but it was Greene who conceived the idea and financed the lawsuits when neighbors copied it without recognizing the patent. Had it not been considered improper for a woman to apply for a patent in her own right, Greene might have been recognized as the actual inventor.

As cotton became widely available in the ensuing decades, missionaries introduced Cherokee women to its production and to the manufacture of cotton textiles. Cherokee women, more so than Cherokee men, tried to adapt to economic changes in an effort to stay on their land. Matrilineal heritage—whereby a man moved in with his wife's family, and property was considered to belong to women—encouraged such leadership and a strong attachment to the land. By 1826 Cherokee homes had 762 looms and 2,488 spinning wheels for turning cotton into textiles. Women were earning cash and becoming less dependent on the old hunting economy, but most men, who viewed farming as women's work, remained unwilling to adapt. They did, however, emulate whites in one respect; in 1827 the Cherokee Nation adopted a new constitution giving women fewer leadership roles.

When gold was discovered in Georgia in 1828, the Cherokees' fate was sealed. Congress passed the Indian Removal Act of 1830, and despite 15,000 petition signatures—many from women—the Georgia Cherokee joined other southeastern Native Americans in 1838 on the Trail of Tears, through Alabama, Mississippi, and Arkansas, to the Indian Territory, which later became Oklahoma. A few—perhaps 1,500—managed to hide in the mountains of Tennessee and North Carolina.

As the Native Americans were removed, more blacks were brought in, unwillingly. The United States outlawed the international importation of slaves in 1808, and Georgia dropped its ban on the interstate slave trade in 1824. Many whites

---

CHEROKEE WOMEN ON THE TRAIL OF TEARS

The forced removal of the Cherokee Nation in 1838 from their ancestral homeland to the Oklahoma (or Indian) Territory by the U.S. government is referred to as the Trail of Tears. In December 1835, the signing of the Treaty of New Echota by a small band of Cherokees sealed the fate of the nation, when territory in northwest Georgia was exchanged for land in Oklahoma. Soldiers began deporting the Cherokee in summer 1838, in accordance with the Indian Removal Act of 1830. John G. Burnett, a soldier during the removal, stated:

> Women were dragged from their homes by soldiers whose language they could not understand. Children were often separated from their parents and driven into the stockades with the sky for a blanket and the earth for a pillow.

Eyewitness accounts tell of women being subjected to taunting, physical abuse, and rape by soldiers.

The winter journey through Tennessee, Kentucky, Illinois, Missouri, and Arkansas was made worse by brutal cold and rain. Blankets were wrapped around feeble bodies in futile attempts to find warmth. A lack of wagons forced many women to walk while carrying heavy loads. Mothers carried sick infants, while pregnant women were forced to walk until they collapsed from the pain of childbirth. Dysentery, diarrhea, and colds spread through the camps, leading to reports that 14 or 15 people were buried at each campsite. In all, 4,000 of the 15,000 Cherokees died during their journey from Georgia to Oklahoma.

—D. Lea Stone

Excerpt from Theda Perdue, "Cherokee Women and the Trail of Tears." *Journal of Women's History* (spring 1989):14–30.

---

had long ignored the latter by "renting" South Carolina slaves, and many would ignore the ban as well. As late as 1858—50 years after the importation of slaves supposedly ended—a slave ship arrived in Savannah from Africa.

After the 1820s slavery in Georgia became harsher. Whites were forbidden to teach blacks to read, and it became increasingly difficult to emancipate slaves. Nevertheless, Emily H. Thomas

WESLEYAN AND SPELMAN: PIONEERS IN WOMEN'S HIGHER EDUCATION

Wesleyan College, the first women's university in the United States, and Spelman College, the first African American women's college in the United States, granted the women of Georgia and the South educational opportunities formerly reserved only for privileged men.

Wesleyan College was chartered on December 23, 1836, in Macon, Georgia, founded by a group of Macon citizens and the Georgia Conference of the Methodist Episcopal Church. They set out to establish an institution to provide a liberal arts education to women throughout the South, so Wesleyan opened its doors to 90 women on January 7, 1839. The college was called Wesleyan Female College from 1843 until 1917, when the word "Female" was dropped from the title.

Being the first women's university in the United States is only one of many firsts for Wesleyan. The college established the country's first alumni association in 1859, and the first sororities were founded there. Soong E-ling became the first Chinese American to receive a degree in the United States when she graduated in 1909.

Still a single-sex institution, Wesleyan today offers degrees in subjects ranging from advertising to mathematics. It also fields six varsity athletic teams and is home to 13 academic honor societies and 26 clubs.

Spelman was established by Sophia B. Packard and Harriet E. Giles after they were commissioned in 1879 by the Woman's American Baptist Home in Boston to study living conditions of African Americans in the South. Shocked by the lack of educational opportunities available to black women in the region, they opened Spelman on April 11, 1881, in the basement of an Atlanta church. They had 11 students.

In 1882 Packard and Giles returned to the North, seeking funding to expand the institution. Thanks to a donation from John D. Rockefeller in 1884, the school purchased more suitable accommodations, and its enrollment grew. By 1891 Spelman had 800 pupils and 30 teachers.

Today Spelman offers majors in 26 fields, including courses in prelaw and premed. The college fields teams in basketball, volleyball, cross-country, track and field, and tennis. It also has a chapter of the prestigious Phi Beta Kappa academic society. Like Wesleyan, it remains a women's college.

Wesleyan and Spelman were pioneers in the fields of single-sex education. Both continue to produce graduates that carry on the tradition of academic achievement and liberal thinking established by their founders.

—David C. Francis

(later Emily Tubman) not only freed 48 slaves, she also paid their $50 passage to Liberia.

Fanny Kemble, a popular English actor, was shocked to discover how bad Georgia slavery could be when, in 1834, she moved to a plantation near Altamaha Sound with her new husband, Pierce Butler. She poured her heart out in diaries and finally left Butler in 1846, which also meant leaving her two children. Nowhere in the nation at that time could a woman expect to keep her children if she left the home. Abolitionists would use Kemble's writings in their campaign to end slavery.

Although Georgia was a conservative society, it set a liberal precedent in 1836, when Georgia Female College was chartered in Macon. It was one of the world's first institutions of higher education for women; it was indeed a true college,

requiring advanced mathematics and science, as well as Latin and French. Even more striking, the first degrees it granted, in 1840, were called "bachelor's" degrees, something still being debated even at Ohio's progressive Oberlin College, where a "Ladies Curriculum" was promoted. When the school changed its name to Wesleyan Female College in 1843, it had approximately 200 students, and in 1859, its graduates formed the world's first alumni association. It even kept its doors open as the Civil War swirled around it, closing only for two weeks when Sherman's army marched through central Georgia.

CIVIL WAR ERA TO PROGRESSIVE ERA (1860–1890)

Although most of Georgia's white women supported the Confederacy, several worked to aid the

Union. Cyrena Stone, Emily Farnsworth, Martha Huntington, and a handful of other Atlantans took appreciable risks to aid Union prisoners of war. Mary Summerlin was especially daring as a spy, traveling with a male Union spy on seemingly innocent visits to fortifications and even introducing him to Confederate generals as her out-of-town cousin. Eventually arrested, Summerlin was imprisoned until she became dangerously ill. Mary Hinton, too, was arrested as a Union spy, but she defied the Confederate court:

> I was examined under oath in regard to contributions to those poor half naked, diseased starving Federal prisoners. . . . They wanted to know if other parties gave me money for them. I told them that was information they could not drag from me. (Dyer 1999, 107–108)

Georgia's coastal islands fell quickly to the Union, and in 1863 Union forces entered the northwest corner of Georgia, where at Chickamauga, the two sides sustained 34,000 casualties in two days in September. Sporadic fighting continued through the winter, and in the spring of 1864, Union general Ulysses S. Grant ordered William Tecumseh Sherman to take his army of 99,000 and inflict all the damage they could against the Confederates' resources. The objective was not merely to defeat the Confederate army, but also to destroy the infrastructure that supported it. At Pine Mountain, Stone Mountain, Kennesaw Mountain, and elsewhere, men died by the thousands. General Sherman besieged Atlanta throughout July and August and then burned virtually the entire city. His forces then marched diagonally across the state to Savannah, sacking as they went.

The result was chaos, as Georgians starved through the winter of 1864. A newsman from the North who was following Sherman's army wrote that he had brought a few hundred pounds of supplies. This was "a mere pittance," he said, and he "was obliged to reserve it for those already on the verge of starvation. Women . . . came . . . fifteen miles afoot . . . to get a few mouthsful." (King 1966, 315)

Phoebe Levy Pember is perhaps the most famous of Confederate nurses; a young Georgia widow, she ran hospitals in the capital of Richmond, Virginia. Although Pember is depicted on a U.S. postage stamp, Clara Barton became much more famous when she developed the world's first systems of identifying the missing and dead at Andersonville, a horrific prisoner-of-war camp in southwestern Georgia.

Because most men were away at war, the 1861 Georgia legislature adopted a law giving a married woman the right to deposit money in a bank under her own name rather than under her husband's name. In 1866, when Confederate veterans were barred from politics during Reconstruction, a new law allowed a married woman to own property. To be readmitted to the Union, Georgia and other southern states had to ratify the 13th, 14th, and 15th Amendments to the Constitution, which ended slavery and extended suffrage to male former slaves but ignored suffrage for women.

The abolitionist and women's rights movements had grown up together in the North and those close ties meant that the growth of a rights movement would be slow in Georgia. In 1884, by which time women had been elected to offices in several states, Atlanta's Mary Latimer McLendon was pleased to observe that state representative Martin Calvin

> introduced and carried through the Legislature, under most unfavorable pressure, a bill to render women eligible to employment in the State House. Besides the large number engaged in manual labor . . . many others are employed as stenographers, typewriters and engrossing clerks, the Governor himself having a woman stenographer. (Anthony and Harper 1902, 4:587)

In 1888 the Hon. Augustus DuPont attempted a greater innovation. When he incorporated the town of DuPont, he sought suffrage for all property owners. His attempt, however, failed. At the same time, women worked to establish the State Normal and Industrial College for Girls, a vocational and teacher-training college that began at Milledgeville in 1889.

Decatur Female Seminary, renamed Agnes Scott College for a donor in 1906, was Georgia's first publicly funded institution of higher education for white women. Its 1889 founding followed the establishment of the all-male University of Georgia by almost a century and of coeducational institutions for blacks by more than two decades. As was the case in other southern states, Reconstruction government and northern donors built a number of black institutions. The first in Georgia was Atlanta University, in 1865. Sophia B. Packard and Harriett E. Giles were the primary founders, in 1881, of Spelman College, a women's school that played an important role in making Atlanta the world's foremost locale for black education.

PROGRESSIVE ERA
(1890–1920)

Although the suffrage movement was slow to develop in Georgia, women in the state were an integral part of efforts to help their community and better society during the Progressive Era. In 1891 a group of Athens women founded the Ladies' Garden Club to beautify their community. Their work ultimately became a movement that led to the establishment of similar clubs throughout the United States.

Georgia's suffrage movement was organized in July 1890 by the Howard family of Columbus—Jane Lindsay Howard and her daughters Augusta Howard, Claudia Howard Maxwell, and Miriam Howard Du Bose. The first nonfamily members were Mr. and Mrs. D. M. Allen of

LADIES' GARDEN CLUB OF ATHENS, GEORGIA

In January 1891, the 12 founding members of the Ladies' Garden Club met for the first time in the home of Mrs. E. K. Lumpkin in Athens, Georgia. The organization pioneered a national garden club movement and set the standard for similar clubs that followed. In 1936, the National Council of State Garden Clubs acknowledged the Athens Ladies' Garden Club as the first in the United States.

The original group was drawn together by their love of plants and their community. The nearby University of Georgia and its renowned botanical garden provided a natural wellspring from which gardening could spread throughout the community. The exchange of cuttings and seeds between members resulted in a desire to expand their knowledge of horticulture and to beautify their town. Each member performed experiments with plants, soils, and insect control and shared discoveries with fellow members.

In February 1892, membership was extended to "every lady in Athens who might be interested in growing anything, from a cabbage to a chrysanthemum." That same year they staged a flower and vegetable show, the first ever sponsored by a garden club. As news of the club spread, it received requests for advice on how to organize such a group and to host a flower show. Club member Mrs. Thomas McHatton spoke of the founding members in 1941:

> It was with no thoughts of personal reward that these ladies organized this club. They were thinking only of the benefits to their community, of its greater good and beauty to their state. With the passing of the years, their vision has been justified, their dream realized, for it is largely through the influence of the garden clubs that the basic beauty of the United States is being polished to perfection, and finding its place in the consciousness of a people.

Since the inception of the Ladies' Garden Club, thousands of similar clubs have been established throughout the United States. Thanks to the commitment of the 12 original members to preserve the beauty of their community and to share their knowledge, the garden club movement has flourished and beautified communities, parks, and highways across the nation.

—D. Lea Stone

Excerpt from Mrs. Madison G. Nicholson, *Ladies' Garden Club, Athens, Georgia: America's First Garden Club.* 85th anniversary ed. Athens, Ga.: The Print Shop, 1976.

Douglassville. Atlanta's Mary McLendon joined in 1892 and eventually became Georgia's most prominent suffragist.

The Howard sisters went to the February 1894 convention of the National American Woman Suffrage Association (NAWSA) in Washington, D.C., where they invited NAWSA to hold its next meeting in Atlanta. Pushed by Lucy Stone, the organization accepted. Although NAWSA had been holding conventions since 1848, never had it held one in the South.

Spurred by the organization's acceptance, Mary McLendon and Margaret Chandler quickly organized an Atlanta suffrage society in March 1894. Its 40 members elected Frances Carter Swift president and spent the next months preparing for the meeting. On January 31, 1895, delegates arrived from 28 of the then 44 states. The crowds meeting at De Give's Opera House stood several rows deep. McLendon welcomed them, declaring,

> If Georgia women could vote this National Convention could hold its session in our million dollar capitol. . . . It was built with money paid into our State's treasury by women as well as men, both white and black; but men alone, white and black, have the privilege of meeting . . . to make laws to govern women. (Anthony and Harper 1902, 4:242)

The Howard sisters personally paid most of the convention's expenses but, after Augusta Howard introduced Susan B. Anthony, Howard stepped aside. The convention closed on Saturday night, and on Sunday morning at least five women preached in Atlanta. Tennessee's Lida Meriwether, Maine's Elizabeth Upham Yates, and New York's Emily Howland filled pulpits at white churches, while Nebraska's Clara Bewick Colby went to Bethel, a black church. Rev. Dr. Anna Howard Shaw attracted so many worshipers at a theater that the doors were closed long before the service started.

Women's rights supporters introduced suffrage bills at every legislative session after 1895, although they did not expect them to pass. In fact, they could not achieve one of the major goals of the Women's Christian Temperance Union (WCTU)—raising the "age of consent," that is, the minimum age of a "woman" with whom a man can say he has had consensual sex. At the time in Georgia, that age was 10. A 1900 bill to raise it to 12 failed by six votes, with 71 ayes and 77 noes. The bill's sponsor, C. S. Reid, mused that his colleagues may have voted against it because they thought 12 was too low, though none of them offered an amendment to raise it. The age remained 10 until 1918, when it finally was raised to 14.

Another goal of the movement was hiring "matrons" for female penal institutions. Atlanta finally hired a female guard in August 1901 after the WCTU agreed to pay her salary. In December the police commissioner reported that she was invaluable.

As the century turned, Georgia women were allowed to practice medicine but not law; they were also prohibited from serving as notaries. Rights activists adopted a petition to the legislature in 1900 that did not bother to mention the right to vote. Rather, they requested that

- the University of Georgia be opened to women
- women become members of boards of education
- women physicians be placed on the staff of the state insane asylum
- the "age of protection" (or consent) be raised from 10 to 18 years
- girls of 18 be permitted to enter the textile department of the State Technological School. (Ibid., 4:584)

Three years later women posted placards at polls reading, "Taxpaying women should be allowed to vote at this bond election." They also began distributing information at the state fair and holding annual conventions. Georgia's

FOUNDING OF THE GIRL SCOUTS BY JULIETTE GORDON LOW

The Girl Scouts of America (GSA), founded in 1912, was the creation of JULIETTE GORDON LOW, an intelligent, committed woman who envisioned turning American girls and young women of all social classes into outdoor-loving, confident, and active citizens. By the 1990s the GSA claimed almost 4 million members.

Raised in privilege, Low led a lonely life, suffering from severe deafness and an unhappy marriage. A lifelong devotion to young people and a serendipitous meeting with Britain's Sir Robert Baden-Powell, founder of the Boy Scouts, and his sister, Agnes Powell, helped Low find a purpose in life.

Transplanting Agnes Powell's English Girl Guide model to American soil became Low's happy occupation at age 51. The friendship and guidance of the dynamic brother and sister proved invaluable. The carriage house behind Low's Savannah home became the first meeting place for two small girl scout troops, where they combined fun, outdoor activity, and leadership training. Through teaching girls how to conduct a business meeting, chop wood for campfires, or volunteer in the community, Low hoped to produce healthy, responsible citizens. Athletic activities and a snappy khaki uniform drew additional youngsters to her doorstep. The enthusiastic local response inspired her to found a national organization.

The early GSA membership was diverse but not integrated. There were Scout troops for black, Hispanic, and disabled girls in the early years, but according to the convention of the day, they met separately from their white, able-bodied counterparts in most cases. In the 1920s, as Low struggled with deafness and the cancer that would cause her death in 1927, she reached out to the world, bringing the World Camp of the Girl Scouts to New York in 1926. As a world traveler, she appreciated the value

Juliette Gordon Low, founder of the Girl Scouts of America. (© Bettmann/CORBIS)

of international friendships. Low felt that sponsoring exchange visits for Girl Scouts from many countries would serve as a building block for world peace.

In the 1930s a green uniform replaced the khaki uniform, and the organization found a commercial baker to produce the now famous Girl Scout Cookies. The organization integrated, and through each decade since its founding it has developed programs to address social issues of the day. Thus it remains a still-growing, viable, worthwhile testament to the vision of Juliette Gordon Low.

—JoEllen Broome

Prohibition party endorsed suffrage in 1908, and an Atlanta study showed that independent women in that city paid more than $13 million in property taxes. Nevertheless, the state legislature remained hostile to extending suffrage.

The tide began to turn in 1912, when REBECCA LATIMER FELTON joined her sister, Mary Latimer McLendon, in the suffrage movement. Together and with the help of attorney Leonard

Grossman, they successfully urged the legislature to pass a bill allowing women to become notaries. After 1916 testimony by West Virginia attorney Georgia McIntyre Wheeler, the legislature finally authorized women to practice law.

Several auxiliaries revitalized the movement in 1913 and 1914: Grossman led the Men's League; Ruth Buckholz presided over the Young People's Suffrage Association; educator Frances Smith

Whiteside started the Woman Suffrage League of Atlanta; and Emily C. McDougald headed the Equal Suffrage Party. The Equal Suffrage Party reached beyond Atlanta, to Columbia and Columbus, as well as Albany, Augusta, Athens, and Savannah.

Many of the newer suffragists went to the large voting rights parade in 1913 in Washington, D.C., where they carried a flag made for the 1895 national convention in Atlanta. That same year, the *Atlanta Constitution* offered Mary McLendon a regular column for suffrage news. In 1914 alone, suffragists held 275 meetings in Athens, Atlanta, Bainbridge, Decatur, and Macon. Two years later, Georgia suffragists held their first parade. Eleanor Raoul led it, on horseback, while Mrs. Loring Raoul drove a little yellow car that once belonged to national leader Anna Howard Shaw. McLendon rode with her in the car, which had special significance. To protest again taxation without representation, Shaw had refused to pay taxes on the car, so the government repossessed it. The car was then bought by Miss Sallie Fannie Gleaton of Conyers, who walked behind it in the parade.

At the Grand Opera House suffragists also sponsored the motion picture *Your Girl and Mine*, based on a play about suffrage. The Rome branch of the movement began publishing the *Woman's Magazine*, while Atlanta women gathered 10,000 petitions for municipal suffrage in 1916, and suffrage leaders engaged in Georgia's first "street speaking."

Yet many Georgia women opposed suffrage. Unlike the WCTU in most states, the Georgia branch never supported the vote for women, and it was only after a long internal conflict that Georgia's General Federation of Women's Clubs (GFWC) endorsed it at a raucous 1919 meeting in Columbus.

When the United States entered World War I in 1917, many Georgia women supported the war effort. Darien's Mildred Smith (later Clark) volunteered as a nurse in France. Decades later, after testimony from people whose lives Smith had saved, the French government awarded her its Legion of Honor. Countless other women volunteered for the Red Cross, sold Liberty Bonds, and worked in other ways, convincing many men that they merited the vote. The Georgia Parent Teacher Association (PTA) endorsed suffrage in 1918, but most important, prosuffrage candidate William J. Harris was elected to the U.S. Senate in November 1918.

As in other southern states at this time, in Georgia the vast majority of voters were Democrats. With the behind-the-scenes influence of the Latimer sisters, Atlanta's Democratic Executive Committee authorized women to vote in the 1919 primary. Nearly 4,000 women paid a $1 poll tax to vote. The tax clearly was designed to exclude black women, who were likely to be Republicans as well as too poor to pay it.

In 1919 Congress passed the 19th Amendment, granting women suffrage, and sent it to the states for ratification. Suffragists in Georgia had little hope for ratification by their legislature. In the 25 years of the suffrage movement there, they had received only two legislative hearings, and their bills had never made it out of committee to the full legislature. Thus, rather than ratification, the suffragists' goal was to avoid a resolution of rejection.

They were surprised when several legislators led passionate efforts to ratify the amendment in response to the prosuffrage *Atlanta Constitution* and the Democratic leadership, including Gov. Hugh Dorsey. Pres. Woodrow Wilson sent a telegram urging support of the amendment, but most legislators denounced him for meddling. As suffragists feared, the House not only voted against ratification, it also adopted a resolution of rejection, by a 132–34 vote. The Senate took no action.

In August 1920 Tennessee became the last state needed for ratification, and in November women voted in every state except Georgia and Mississippi. These states required voters to register six months before going to the polls, and because women were not allowed to register in May, they were not allowed to vote in the fall.

Mary McLendon made extraordinary efforts to vote in the September Democratic primary, appealing to local and national officials. She noted that war veterans were allowed to ignore the voter registration deadline, but no official was willing to allow the same for women.

1920S THROUGH WORLD WAR II ERA (1920–1950)

In 1921 the Georgia League of Women Voters, which had been founded the preceding year, convinced the legislature to adopt an act removing women's legal disabilities (except for sitting on juries, which remained a male privilege). To build coalitions, league president Annie Wright of Augusta hired the GFWC's Mrs. Z. L. Fitzpatrick, who had once "violently opposed" suffrage, to travel the state, "urging women to get out and vote and to nominate women" for public office. (Harper 1922, 6:136, 142n) Macon antisuffragists, however, remained obdurate. They not only refused to vote, they also funded Maryland's attempt to reject the 19th Amendment.

In this generally antifeminist atmosphere, it is ironic that Georgia would send the first female senator to Washington. Following the death of Sen. Thomas Watson, the governor appointed Rebecca Latimer Felton ad interim, until an election could be held. When Congress convened on November 21, 1922, she was sworn in, made a brief speech, and resigned.

During the 1920s Georgia continued to develop educational facilities for women. Berry College opened its doors in 1926 as a junior college. The school was the culmination of Martha Berry's work, begun in 1902, when she turned her family plantation into a work-study opportunity for poor rural boys, who so desperately wanted to attend that she sometimes had to turn down as many as 5,000 applications annually. In 1909 she added a girls' school. Berry was voted one of the 12 greatest American women in a 1931 national poll, and in 1937 she became the first woman on the Georgia Board of Regents.

Wesleyan College, which dropped "Female" from its name in 1917, moved to a new Macon campus in 1928. In this era its most famous alumnae, China's Soong sisters, were making names for themselves internationally. Ch'ing-ling married Sun Yat-sen and helped overthrow the Manchu dynasty; as Madame Chiang Kai-shek, Mei-ling would be one of the world's most powerful women from the 1930s through the 1950s.

The Great Depression that affected most states following the 1929 stock market crash hit Georgia earlier; its principal crop, cotton, was devastated by boll weevils in the early 1920s. Impoverished Georgians suffered genuine need by the late 1920s, and diseases caused by malnutrition, including beri-beri and pellagra, appeared. The administration of Franklin Roosevelt addressed the effects of the Depression with New Deal programs in the 1930s, but Georgia politicians refused to accept federal aid.

In such circumstances, even well-credentialed women could not expect to rise in business or the professions, but some managed to do so as authors. Among them were Pulitzer Prize winners Caroline Miller and the extraordinary MARGARET MITCHELL. In the 1940s Georgia produced the acclaimed CARSON MCCULLERS and the courageous LILLIAN SMITH, whose opposition to segregation made her a target of arsonists.

The 1940s brought World War II to Georgia, as its powerful congressional delegation arranged to have a number of military bases established there, including Fort Oglethorpe, the

THE PHENOMENON OF *GONE WITH THE WIND*

The novel *Gone with the Wind* became a cultural phenomenon shortly after its release. Six months after its publication in 1936, Margaret Mitchell's book had sold 1 million copies, and in 1939 Hollywood staged a lavish production of it. The Atlanta premiere of the film was celebrated as a grand event, with governors from nearby states in attendance and Confederate flags flying.

The story that was so embraced by the public took place in the 1860s—before, during, and after the Civil War—and focuses on Scarlett O'Hara as she adapts to the ever-changing political and social climate of the South. On the most basic level, *Gone with the Wind* chronicled the fundamental yearnings of the antebellum South. The saga depicted joy and hardships, finally painting Scarlett as a survivor.

Gone with the Wind was not, however, without criticism. It was panned for racist portrayals of African American characters with no apparent desire for freedom and roles limited to mammies and field hands. Disturbed by the public's acceptance of *Gone with the Wind*, in 2001 Alice Randall decided to write a parody called *The Wind Done Gone*. Her story, told from the point of view of Scarlett's mulatto half-sister, Cynara, is an attempt to expose the flaws of the original. Despite the controversy surrounding it, *Gone with the Wind* remains a cultural phenomenon and continues to entertain readers and viewers into the 21st century.

—Courtney Garnaas

third training camp of the Women's Army Corps (WAC). Begun near Macon in 1943, it was the only WAC facility commanded by a woman, Elizabeth Strayhorn. Also of note, the corps was the only female military unit to accept black women from the start.

Hundreds of thousands of men passed through training camps in Georgia, sometimes meeting and marrying local women; many women came south with the men. Northern newcomers in particular introduced new attitudes to Georgia, and Georgians who served elsewhere learned of different ways of life. Federal money that male politicians had refused to accept in the 1930s was spent in the 1940s on military needs, greatly transforming the state's economy.

In 1940 Georgia elected its first congresswoman, Florence Reville Gibbs, who completed the last three months of her dead husband's term. Six years later, HELEN DOUGLAS MANKIN was elected to Congress to fill the vacancy created by the resignation of Robert Ramspeck. The most unusual wartime milestone, however, was Atlanta's choice of a woman, Ira Jarrell, as its school superintendent in 1944. Although it was a time of great teacher shortages, no other similarly large system was headed by a female. Moreover, Jarrell atttained this top position following longtime leadership of the teachers' union. She held the post until her retirement in 1960.

POSTWAR AND CONTEMPORARY ERAS (1950–present)

Georgia women reached few milestones in the 1950s, but subsequent decades would be different. In 1961 Charlayne Hunter became the first black to enroll at the University of Georgia. As Charlayne Hunter-Gault, she would go on to have a long career in print and broadcast journalism. In 1973 the headlines would speak of *Roe v. Wade*, the U.S. Supreme Court decision on abortion that eclipsed *Doe v. Bolton*, a concurrent Georgia case. "Roe" and "Doe" were both anonymous women seeking to terminate pregnancies. "Roe" originated in Texas and was won by attorney Sarah Weddington; "Doe" was won by Margie Pitts Hames. Both women were barely out of law school when they argued these landmark cases before the nation's highest (and at the time all-male) court.

Female professors won two major cases in the 1980s, when the Georgia Board of Regents was ordered to pay more than $86,000 to six women who had not been promoted on an equal basis with men at Georgia Southwestern College. In a

Charlayne Hunter and the Integration of the University of Georgia

On January 9, 1961, Charlayne Hunter faced crowds of students and reporters as she became the first black to attend the University of Georgia in Athens. Firecrackers, Confederate flags, and taunts created a menacing atmosphere as she attended classes. Violence erupted, and the police were forced to use teargas to disperse a crowd hurling rocks at her dormitory. Hunter was suspended—for her safety—and escorted to Atlanta. Her stay there was short, as a court order was issued demanding that she be readmitted a few days after her suspension.

The university was quieter when she returned, as many students had accepted the situation, and university officials announced that further rioting would result in suspensions. Hunter was sent letters from well wishers around the world, and other students attempted to strike up friendships. During the second week of classes, the crowds following her dwindled, and life acquired a degree of normalcy.

In June 1963 Hunter received a degree in journalism and later achieved renown as a reporter at the *New York Times*. She followed her tenure at the *Times* with a broadcast career that includes work with PBS and CNN.

—D. Lea Stone

University of Georgia case, the same judge sentenced a male professor to jail for contempt after he refused to explain why a faculty committee had not granted tenure to a woman.

In 1983 Georgia native ALICE WALKER, author of *The Color Purple,* became the first African American woman to win the Pulitzer Prize in literature, which was first awarded in 1918. Olive Ann Burns's best-selling *Cold Sassy Tree* (1984) featured a Georgia family in the 1920s, and Fannie Flagg's wildly popular *Fried Green Tomatoes* (1987) was set in Juliette, near Macon.

A string of Georgia-based novels followed in the 1990s, including Susie Mee's *The Girl Who Loved Elvis* (1993), Linda Brown's *Crossing over Jordan* (1995), Tina McElroy Ansa's *The Hand I*

TIMELINE

United States Events

1620 Settlement of Plymouth Colony

1776 United States declares independence

1861–65 U.S. Civil War

1914–18 World War I

1920 Ratification of the 19th Amendment

1929–39 Great Depression

1939–45 World War II

1975 Vietnam War ends

Georgia Events

1733 The British establish a colony in Savannah.

1797 Catherine Littlefield Greene collaborates with Eli Whitney in developing the cotton gin.

1836 Georgia Female College is chartered in Macon.

1861 The Georgia legislature permits married women to deposit money in banks under their own names.

1881 Sophia B. Packard and Harriet E. Giles found Spelman College.

1890 The Howard family organizes the Georgia suffrage movement.

1912 Juliette Gordon Low founds the American Girl Scouts.

1919 The Georgia legislature adopts a resolution rejecting the 19th Amendment.

1936 Margaret Mitchell publishes *Gone with the Wind.*

1940 Florence Reville Gibbs is elected Georgia's first congresswoman.

1961 Charlayne Hunter becomes the first black to enroll at the University of Georgia.

1983 Alice Walker becomes the first African American woman to win a Pulitzer Prize.

1992 Cynthia McKinney becomes Georgia's first African American congresswoman.

2003 Two women take statewide positions: Kathy Cox as superintendent of public education and Angela Elizabeth Speir as public service commissioner.

Alice Walker speaking at a voter registration rally. (© Steve Jennings/Corbis)

Fan With (1996), and Janice Daugharty's *Like a Sister* (1999). Perhaps the most popular novel was Bailey White's *Mama Makes Up Her Mind and Other Dangers of Southern Living* (1993). White frequently read her work on public radio. Celestine Sibley, who wrote for the *Atlanta Journal-Constitution* for 55 years, was honored by the National Society of Newspaper Columnists in 1999, just weeks before her death at 85. She was only the second woman so honored.

CYNTHIA McKINNEY, elected in 1992 to the House of Representatives, was Georgia's first African American congresswoman. Unlike most states, Georgia elected women, black and white, to the House of Representatives before electing any to statewide office. In 1995 Linda Schrenko became Georgia's superintendent of education; she also was the first Republican woman elected to any office of note. (All of Georgia's congress-women were Democrats.) The second woman elected statewide was Secretary of State Cathy Cox, a Democrat who won that office in 1998.

In the 2002 Democratic primary, attorney Denise Majette upset Representative McKinney and went on to win McKinney's U.S. House seat. In 2003 two Republican women took statewide positions: Kathy Cox as superintendent of public education and Angela Elizabeth Speir as public service commissioner.

—Doris Weatherford

PROMINENT WOMEN

DOROTHY BOLDEN (1923–)

The work of Dorothy Lee Bolden of Atlanta, Georgia, aided domestics throughout the United States by upgrading their training, job placement, wages, and working conditions. The daughter of a cook and a chauffeur, Bolden washed diapers and cleaned houses for extra cash as a child. She attended school until age 14, when she quit to earn a living.

After marriage at age 18, to support six children Bolden continued working at various jobs, at a linen supply house, a bus station, Sears Roebuck, and Railroad Express, but she regularly quit salaried positions to work as a maid. Under the influence of her neighbor, Dr. Martin Luther King, Jr., she supported the civil rights movement and joined protests against the substandard educations black children received.

In 1968 Bolden formed the National Domestic Workers Union (NDWU) and began recruiting members from the Atlanta area. Among the services she offered maids were job counseling, brokered bargaining with employers, and improved safety and working conditions. In the 1970s she advised the Department of Health, Education, and Welfare; served the Legal Aid Society and League of Women Voters; and used her influence to drum up support for presidents Richard Nixon, Gerald Ford, and Jimmy Carter on labor issues. For her success in bringing dignity to maid's work, in 1975 Georgia governor George Busbee named her to the state Commission on the Status of Women.

ROSALYNN CARTER (1927–)

Rosalynn Smith Carter of Plains, Georgia, earned the nickname "Steel Magnolia" for the support she lent to her husband's difficult 1976 campaign against better-known candidates. She attended Georgia Southwestern College at Americus and worked as a seamstress, beautician, and bookkeeper for a farm supply company. She married Jimmy Carter in 1946. As Georgia's first lady during the 1970s, she supported the Regional Hospital in Atlanta, chaired the Georgia Special Olympics, and served on a state commission on emotional and mental disabilities.

During her residency in the White House (1977–1981), Carter served as a roving goodwill ambassador, lobbied for full health insurance coverage, and on state visits to foreign lands advocated for human rights and better health care for women. She labored for the Equal Rights Amendment, aid to refugees and the elderly, and reform of mental health assistance, including the break-up of large mental institutions into smaller, more personal group homes and increased federal funding for community mental health programs. She also encouraged her husband to appoint more women to public office. Carter discussed her involvement in government in her autobiography, *First Lady from Plains* (1984). After leaving the White House, Carter remained a champion of volunteerism. Both Carters are spokespersons for Habitat for Humanity and devote their spare time to fund-raising and building homes for the poor.

ELLEN CRAFT (ca. 1826–ca. 1897)

Born to a black slave and her white owner, Ellen Smith Craft of Clinton, Georgia, was separated from her mother when, to spare Craft's white mistress embarrassment, the master presented Ellen as a wedding gift to his daughter, Ellen's half-sister. Ellen married a slave, William Craft, who helped her escape slavery at age 22, so their children could be born free. To reach the North, William posed as her slave as she passed for a white male slaveowner.

Fearing capture under the Fugitive Slave Act of 1850, the Crafts fled to England, where Ellen promoted the British and Foreign Freedmen's Aid Society. In 1860, the couple recounted their flight from slavery in *Running a Thousand Miles for Freedom.* Late in the 1860s, they returned to farmland near Savannah and opened an industrial school.

REBECCA LATIMER FELTON (1835–1930)

Writer and reformer Rebecca Ann Latimer Felton of DeKalb County, Georgia, was the first woman to serve in the U.S. Senate. After her studies at Madison Female College, she married Dr. William Harrell Felton, an agrarian populist. Felton aided her husband as a writer and speaker and became an important political figure in her own right. For the *Atlanta Journal,* which she founded, she penned thrice-weekly editorials denouncing the mistreatment of prison work gangs and championing temperance, education for women, and women's rights. Increasingly conservative and racist as she aged, Felton published *My Memoirs of Georgia Politics* (1911).

Felton was active in numerous political causes and volunteer efforts. She served on the board of female managers of the 1893 Chicago World's Columbian Exposition, chaired the woman's executive board of the Cotton States and International Exposition in Atlanta (1894–1895), and was a member of the agricultural board of the St. Louis Exposition. In 1919 she published *Days of My Youth,* a memoir about growing up in the South. Three years later, she received an ad interim appointment to the U.S. Senate after the death of Sen. Thomas E. Watson. She attended one day before Watson's successor took his seat. At her death in 1930, the Senate adjourned early as a show of respect for its first female colleague.

NANCY MORGAN HART (1735–1830)

The only Georgia female to have a county named for her, Anne "Nancy" Morgan Hart was born in Orange County, North Carolina. Muscular and tall, she mastered musketry as well as midwifery,

both assets to women on the frontier. After marrying Benjamin Hart at age 36, she settled in Georgia on the Wilkes River. When the Revolutionary War began, she refused to retreat with noncombatants. Under the guns of six British soldiers, Hart pretended to cook a turkey dinner while intoxicating the men with corn liquor. She seized their weapons, shot the first man to menace her, and held the men for hanging.

Hart joined the county militia as a spy for Gen. Elijah Clarke, communicating with patriots by blowing into a conch shell. She also navigated the Savannah River on a handmade raft and masqueraded as a witless male in the surveillance preceding the battle of Kettle Creek. For her exploits Cherokees named her Hart Wahatchee (War Woman).

LUGENIA BURNS HOPE (1871–1947)

Activist, speaker, and reformer Lugenia Burns Hope of St. Louis, Missouri, fought racism through her work and association with a number of clubs and organizations. After attending the Chicago Art Institute, Chicago School of Design, and Chicago Business College, all between 1890 and 1893, she volunteered for settlement work at Hull House. Following marriage at age 26 to John Hope, she bore two sons and involved herself in community affairs while teaching physical education and arts and crafts at Roger Williams University.

After settling in Atlanta in 1906, Hope worked at Morehouse College and Atlanta University and joined the NAACP, Urban League, Southern Regional Council, and the Association of Southern Women for the Prevention of Lynching. She cofounded the Neighborhood Union, the city's first woman-operated social welfare agency for blacks, and helped the poor with recreation, education, medical treatment, and community opportunities. Her methods influenced social programs in Cape Verde and Haiti. She became a polished orator for the National Council of Negro Women, an aide to the National Youth Administration, and an impetus to the National Association of Colored Graduate Nurses and the Hostess House Program for Black Soldiers. In 1996, she was named among the Georgia Women of Achievement.

JULIETTE GORDON LOW (1860–1927)

The founder of the Girl Scouts of America, Juliette Gordon "Daisy" Low of Savannah, Georgia, overcame the isolation caused by a severe hearing loss by organizing girls to develop their interests and perform public service. Born to wealth, she suffered malnutrition and life-threatening illness during the Civil War. A freak accident on her wedding day left her deaf, and her marriage to William Low in 1886 proved unhappy. He died in 1905, and she speant years in court trying to retrieve property that he left to his mistress.

Low spent much of her time in Britain, where she cultivated a friendship with Robert Baden-Powell, founder of the Boy Scouts, and his sister, Agnes Powell, who established the female counterpart to the Boy Scouts, called Girl Guides. In 1911 Low convened 12 Girl Guides at her home in Glenlyon, Scotland, and later expanded the concept to girls living in London's poorest districts. In 1912 she founded the first Girl Scouts of America patrol in Savannah and initiated the Girl Scout handbook, *How Girls Can Help Their Country*. To encourage such projects as hiking, bee-keeping, and fire making, she embroidered merit badges and spread the concept of girl scouting across the country. At the beginning of World War I, 10,000 Girl Scouts volunteered in hospitals, factory child-care centers, and war bond drives.

In 1919 Low joined Baden-Powell in establishing the International Council of Girl Guides and Girl Scouts. She battled a lawsuit that the Boy Scouts of America launched against their female counterparts and discovered a fellow supporter in first lady Lou Hoover. While fighting cancer Low superintended the first World Camp of Girl Scouts in Pleasantville, New York. She was buried in her Girl Scout uniform.

HELEN DOUGLAS MANKIN (1894–1956)

Attorney and politician Helen Douglas Mankin of Atlanta, Georgia, attempted to restore equity to state politics and to involve more blacks in decision making. A graduate of the Washington Seminary in 1913, she completed Rockford College in Illinois in 1917 and earned a law degree from the Atlanta Law School at age 26. During World War I she volunteered for service with the Medical Women's National Association and drove an ambulance for the French army. After returning to private practice, she offered pro bono services to poor blacks, keeping her office solvent by lecturing at her alma mater. In 1927 Douglas married Guy M. Mankin.

In 1937, after working for the Georgia Child Labor Commission, Mankin was elected to the Georgia state legislature, where she urged prison reform and an investigation into malfeasance in the highway department. At age 50, she advanced to the U.S. House of Representatives to complete the term of Robert Ramspeck. There she opposed poll taxes and funding for the House on Un-American Activities Committee. She served 11 months in Congress, but was not reelected. She continued the practice of law until her death at age 60 in an automobile accident.

CARSON MCCULLERS (1917–1967)

A creator of alienated fictional characters, Lula Carson Smith McCullers of Columbus, Georgia, battled her own pain and loneliness through writing. Despite being a lover of the outdoors in childhood, she intended to become a concert pianist. She entered the Juilliard School of Music and studied creative writing at night at Columbia University and New York University. She earned money for tuition by working as a typist, waitress, dog-walker, bookkeeper, and accompanist for a ballet class.

Her writing career took shape during her studies at New York University and included publishing short stories in *Story* magazine. She returned to Georgia, and in 1937 she married Reeves McCullers, a soldier stationed at Fort Benning. They settled at Fort Bragg, North Carolina, while she completed *The Heart Is a Lonely Hunter* (1940), which won her the Houghton Mifflin Fiction Fellowship, a $1,200 purse, and instant fame. (The novel was made into a film in 1968.)

A part of the Southern Literary Renaissance, McCullers lived among outstanding American writers at the Bread Loaf writers' colony in Vermont and composed short stories for *Vogue*. Among her other contributions are *Reflections in a Golden Eye* (1941) and *The Member of the Wedding* (1946), considered her masterpiece, which she adapted for the Broadway stage. Her marriage ended when Reeves McCullers tried to convince her to join him in a double suicide and subsequently killed himself, in 1953. Afflicted by a stroke, paralysis, and alcoholism, McCullers was confined to a wheelchair toward the end of her life.

CYNTHIA MCKINNEY (1955–)

The first African American female to serve in Georgia's congressional delegation, Cynthia Ann McKinney of Atlanta, Georgia, championed causes on behalf of blacks, the poor, and working mothers. From her father, Billy McKinney, a participant in the civil rights movement, McKinney learned strategies for bringing about social change, especially an end to segregation. The young McKinney attended a Catholic parochial school before heading to the University of Southern California. Stunned by the hatred of Ku Klux Klansmen during a protest in Alabama against the imprisonment of a retarded black man, she determined to enter politics. In preparation she completed graduate study in international relations at Tufts University and taught at Spelman College, Clark Atlanta University, and Agnes Scott College. In 1987, she was elected to the Georgia House of Representatives.

An independent on moral and ethical issues, she denounced U.S. involvement in the Persian Gulf War and fought for new district lines in Georgia to ensure more black representation. Elected to Congress in 1992, she served on the agriculture and international relations committees, opposed the North American Free Trade Agreement, and supported the environmental cleanup of industrial sites in Augusta. In 2001 she denounced Pentagon patronage of sweatshops in Nicaragua. McKinney lost her congressional seat in 2002.

MARGARET MITCHELL (1900–1949)

Journalist Margaret Munnerlyn Mitchell of Atlanta wrote *Gone with the Wind* (1936), one of the world's most popular novels. The daughter of activists in the suffragist movement and in the Atlanta Historical Society, she absorbed in childhood insight into women's rights and southern history, the powerful themes that permeate her writing. After studying at the Woodberry School and the Washington Seminary, she became a reporter for the *Atlanta Journal* and violated the code of Georgia's segregated society by supporting black charities. In 1922 she married Berrien "Red" Kinnard Upshaw, but the marriage was annulled two years later. In 1925 she married John Marsh.

For her masterful historical romance, Mitchell studied sources at the public library to flesh out the 1,000-page story of Georgian survivors of the Civil War and Reconstruction. Within three months of publication, readers had snapped up a half-million copies of *Gone with the Wind*. Mitchell won a Pulitzer Prize and multiple awards and commendations for lifting the country's spirits from the Great Depression. In 1939 MGM premiered the film version of *Gone with the Wind* in Atlanta, with Mitchell as the studio's special guest.

Mitchell ignored readers' demands for a sequel to end speculation about the fictional heroine Scarlett O'Hara. Instead, she worked toward developing a Civil War reference center at the Margaret Mitchell Public Library in Fayetteville, Georgia, and supporting CARE and the Red Cross during World War II. Her sudden death from a collision with a taxi on Peachtree Street added to her mystique.

JESSYE NORMAN (1945–)

Soprano Jessye Norman of Augusta developed a signature style and mastered a wide variety of music. Like many black vocalists, she got her start in church choirs in early childhood and imitated grand opera on the radio. After entering the Marion Anderson singing contest in Philadelphia, at age 16 she earned a scholarship to Howard University and completed her training at Baltimore's Peabody Conservatory and the University of Michigan.

At age 23, Norman won first place at the International Music Competition in Munich and toured the Caribbean and Latin America. She appeared in Wagner's *Tannhäuser*, the beginning of her success in Europe. Following her debut in 1972 at La Scala Opera House in Milan in Verdi's *Aida*, she ventured back to the United States to sing at the Hollywood Bowl. After virtuoso recitals and performances at the Royal Opera House, Covent Garden, and stages across Europe, she withdrew to London to develop her voice.

In 1980 Norman returned to full-time singing, debuting with the Metropolitan Opera. During three decades, she has sung opera, jazz, and black spirituals around the world. Norman's success brought her honorary doctorates, the title of Musical America's Musician of the Year 1982,

three Grammy awards, and a commendation from New York's Associated Black Charities.

FLANNERY O'CONNOR (1925–1964)

An innovative symbolist author of southern gothic fiction, Flannery O'Connor of Savannah, Georgia, made her reputation by examining ugly characters who experience grim comeuppance and sudden epiphanies. Having studied at parochial schools, O'Connor was grounded in a strict Catholicism. She went on to earn a sociology degree at Georgia State College for Women in 1945 and a master's in fine art from the University of Iowa in 1947. O'Connor read widely from the Bible, St. Augustine, Thomas Aquinas, and Martin Buber. She suffered from the crippling effects of lupus, which struck her at age 25.

Deliberately imitating the deft imagery of Joseph Conrad and Henry James, O'Connor published her first stories in *Accent* and studied with writers at the Yaddo colony before deciding to reside at the home of friends in Ridgefield, Connecticut, to write in solitude. O'Connor's writings in *Critic, Harper's,* the *Kenyon Review, New World Writing*, and the *Sewanee Review* earned her an O. Henry Award and a cult following for her quirky stories, in particular "A Good Man Is Hard to Find" and "The Displaced Person." In hopes of a cure for her failing body, O'Connor made a pilgrimage to Lourdes shortly before her death at 39. Her posthumous collections include *Everything That Rises Must Converge* (1965), *Mystery and Manners* (1969), and *The Habit of Being* (1979).

MA RAINEY (GERTRUDE PRIDGETT) (1886–1939)

Gertrude Malissa Pridgett Rainey of Columbus, Georgia, transformed herself into jazz legend Ma Rainey, "Mother of the Blues." The daughter of minstrels, she began performing at the still-extant Springer Opera House at age 14. Four years later she and her husband, William Rainey, formed a cabaret and tent show duo billed as Ma and Pa Rainey. After their parting, she toured with her own band, the Georgia Smart Set.

A folk sensation during the 1920s, Rainey performed genuine, rural southern blues that exploited themes of bawdy sex, disloyal lovers, and unrequited love. She worked with Louis Armstrong and recorded "See See Rider," an African American classic. "Bo-Weevil Blues" was her signature tune. After retirement at age 39, Rainey returned to Columbus to manage the Lyric Theater and the Airdome.

LILLIAN SMITH (1897–1966)

Novelist Lillian Eugenia Smith of Jasper, Florida, upbraided the South for segregation. The daughter of a merchant, she learned both compassion and intolerance from her mother. At one point her family took in a foster child, until they discovered that she was part-black. Their rejection of the child fueled Smith's outrage, which she later vented in *Killers of the Dream* (1949).

The Smith family moved to Clayton, Georgia, in 1915. She left Piedmont College at the end of her freshman year to assist her father in operating a hotel in Daytona Beach, Florida. She studied piano at Baltimore's Peabody Conservatory and, during World War I, enlisted in the Student Nursing Corps. After a year of teaching school in rural Georgia, she became a missionary teacher in Huchow, China.

The split personality of women who were southern Christians as well as hate-mongering racists troubled Smith, setting her on a mission to fight such hypocrisy. While managing the Laurel Falls Camp, a family business in Clayton, she taught female campers to oppose and work against the racial caste system. In 1944 Smith published *Strange Fruit*, a story of interracial love that was suppressed in New England for alleged obscenity. Her writings deal openly with sexual desire, masturbation, and homosexuality. With lecture fees and book royalties, Smith was able to close the camp and devote herself to literature and activism. Twice during the 1950s, arsonists targeted her home. Undeterred by the loss of her manuscripts, she supported Martin Luther King, Jr., and worked with the Congress of Racial Equality (CORE). In 1964, two years before her death from breast cancer, she published *Our Faces, Our Words,* a salute to nonviolent activism.

ALICE WALKER (1944–)

A humanist, feminist, and literary lion, Alice Malsenior Walker of Eatonton, Georgia, learned compassion in the South. Born to a large family of sharecroppers, in her childhood she lost the sight in one eye to a BB fired by her brother. She learned storytelling from her mother, a domestic worker, and battled depression through expressive writing. After studying English at Spelman College in Atlanta and Sarah Lawrence College in New York, she joined the civil rights movement and was inspired by hearing Martin Luther King, Jr., deliver his "I Have a Dream" speech.

Walker began her career as a case worker for the New York City Department of Social Services, but later became a contributing editor of *Ms.* magazine as well as an essayist, short fiction writer, and novelist. She taught at Tougaloo College and Radcliffe Institute, and she initiated women's studies at Wellesley. The publication of *The Color Purple* (1982) and her involvement in the 1983 film version increased Walker's name recognition. As the first black female to earn a Pulitzer Prize, she used her prestige and influence to revive interest in the writings of Zora Neale Hurston.

—Mary Ellen Snodgrass

PROMINENT SITES

Bulloch Hall

180 Bulloch Avenue

Roswell, GA 30075

Telephone: (770) 992 1731

Web: http://www.cvb.roswell.ga.us/attractions3a.html

Built in 1840, Bulloch Hall was the childhood home of Martha Bulloch, who married Theodore Roosevelt, Sr., on December 22, 1853; their son Theodore Roosevelt, Jr., was the 26th president of the United States. The home and grounds have been restored, providing a glimpse into mid-19th-century life. An exhibit in the home focuses on the Bulloch and Roosevelt families.

Flannery O'Connor Childhood Home Foundation

207 East Charlton Street

Savannah, GA 31401

Telephone: (912) 223 6014

Web: http://www.llp.armstrong.edu/flannery/
    Fndtn.html

The childhood home of Flannery O'Connor was occupied by her family from 1925 to 1938. The building is now a memorial to O'Connor and a literary center for Savannah. The first floor of the house is open to the public on weekends. The living room has been restored to its appearance ca. 1930.

Georgia Capitol Museum

431 State Capitol

Atlanta, GA 30334

Telephone: (404) 651 6996

Web: http://www.sos.state.ga.us/museum/default.htm

The state capitol contains several statues honoring women of Georgia. The Georgia Hall of Fame has busts of Juliette Gordon Low, the founder of the Girl Scouts of America, and Margaret Mitchell, the journalist and author of *Gone with the Wind*. The Mary Latimere McLendon Fountain is located in the south wing on the main floor of the building. The Women's Christian Temperance Union dedicated the fountain to McLendon (1840–1921), the "Mother of Suffrage in Georgia," in 1923.

Georgia Music Hall of Fame Museum

200 Martin Luther King, Jr. Boulevard

Macon, GA 31201

Telephone: (888) GA ROCKS

Web: http://www.gamusichall.com

Honorees in the Georgia Music Hall of Fame include Brenda Lee, Gladys Knight, Lena Horne, and Gertrude "Ma" Rainey. *Tune Town*, the museum's permanent exhibit, is designed like a small Georgia town with each building featuring a different genre of music created by native Georgians.

Georgia Women of Achievement

PO Box 5851

Atlanta, GA 31107

Telephone: (404) 653 0800

Web: http://www.gawomen.org

This organization was founded in 1990 in response to a 1988 speech by former first lady Rosalynn Carter in which she proposed that the role of women in Georgia be formally recognized. March 1992 marked the first induction ceremony, which honored Flannery O'Connor, Juliette Gordon Low, Martha McChesney Berry, Lucy Craft Laney, and Sara Branham Matthews. There were 38 inductees as of early 2003.

Hammonds House Galleries and Resource Center of African American Art

503 Peeples Street

Atlanta, GA 30310

Telephone: (404) 752 8730

Web: http://www.hammondshouse.org

Georgia's only independent fine art museum is dedicated to presenting art by people of African descent. Elizabeth Catlett is one of the artists featured in the permanent collection.

Juliette Gordon Low Girl Scout National Center

142 Bull Street

Savannah, GA 31401

Telephone: (912) 233 4501

Web: http://www.girlscouts.org/about/birthplace/
    index.html

Juliette Gordon Low, founder of the Girl Scouts of America in 1912, was born at this home in 1860. It has been restored to its appearance in the 1880s, using original and period-specific furnishings, and displays artifacts belonging to Juliet and the Gordon family, including artwork created by her.

Margaret Mitchell House and Museum

990 Peachtree Street

Atlanta, GA 30309

Telephone: (404) 247 7015

Web: http://www.gwtw.org

Margaret Mitchell lived in Apartment 1 of the house at 990 Peachtree Street from 1925 to 1932 with her husband. She wrote the majority of the Pulitzer Prize–winning *Gone with the Wind* at the home. Three buildings comprise the complex: a visitor center, the house, and a small museum dedicated to original memorabilia from the movie version of *Gone with the Wind*. Mitchell's apartment, for which there are guided tours, has been restored with original and period-specific furniture, and an exhibit features her letters.

Martha Berry Museum and Oak Hill

PO Box 490189

Mount Berry, GA 30149

Telephone: (800) 220 5504

Web: http://www.berry.edu/oakhill

Martha Berry, born into a wealthy, traditional family, did not follow her contemporaries into the life of marriage and children expected of women of her social status. Instead, in 1902 she opened the Boys Industrial School, a boarding school, and in 1909 she opened a similar school for girls. Both operated under the umbrella of the Berry Schools. The campus of the complex includes a museum that tells the story of Berry's life as well as that of her former home, Oak Hill, which is open for tours.

Myrtle Hill Cemetery

South Broad Street

Rome, GA 30161

Telephone, Rome Cemetery Commission: (706) 236 4534

Web: http://roadsidegeorgia.com/site/myrtlehill.html

The cemetery dates back to the state's Confederate era. The Rome Camp of Sons of Confederate Veterans presented a memorial to Confederate women, as a gift to Rome, Georgia, in 1910. Its original location was on Broad Street, in downtown Rome, but the memorial was moved to its current location in the cemetery in 1952. The memorial depicts a woman nursing a wounded soldier, as well as a woman telling her daughter that her father has died in battle. The first wife of Pres. Woodrow Wilson, Ellen Axson Wilson, was buried in the cemetery in 1914. She was a native of Rome.

RESOURCES

FURTHER READING

HISTORY

Alexander, Adele Logan. *Ambiguous Lives: Free Women of Color in Rural Georgia, 1789–1879*. Fayetteville: University of Arkansas Press, 1991.

Anthony, Susan B., and Ida Husted Harper. *History of Woman Suffrage*. Vol. 4. Indianapolis, Ind.: Hollenbeck Press, 1902.

Bayor, Ronald H. *Race and the Shaping of Twentieth-Century Atlanta*. Chapel Hill: University of North Carolina Press, 1996.

Bernhard, Virginia, ed. *Southern Women: Histories and Identities*. Columbia: University of Missouri Press, 1992.

Boatwright, Eleanor Miot. *Status of Women in Georgia, 1783–1860*. Brooklyn, N.Y.: Carlson Publishing, 1994.

Bradbury, John. *Renaissance in the South: A Critical History of the Literature, 1920–1960*. Chapel Hill: University of North Carolina Press, 1963.

Coleman, Kenneth, ed. *A History of Georgia*. 2nd ed. Athens: University of Georgia Press, 1991.

Coryell, Janet L., ed. *Negotiating Boundaries of Southern Womanhood: Dealing with the Powers That Be*. Columbia: University of Missouri Press, 2000.

Cott, Nancy F., ed. *Root of Bitterness: Documents of the Social History of American Women*. 2nd ed. Boston: Northeastern University Press, 1996.

Coulter, E. Merton. *Georgia: A Short History*. Rev. ed. Chapel Hill: University of North Carolina Press, 1960.

Cunningham, H. H. *Doctors in Gray: The Confederate Medical Service*. Baton Rouge: Louisiana State University Press, 1993.

Deaton, Thomas M. *Bedspreads to Broadloom: The Story of the Tufted Carpet Industry*. Acton, Mass.: Tapestry Press, 1993.

Denney, Robert E. *Civil War Medicine: Care and Comfort of the Wounded*. New York: Sterling Publishing, 1995.

Dyer, Thomas G. *Secret Yankees: The Union Circle in Confederate Atlanta*. Baltimore, Md.: Johns Hopkins University Press, 1999.

Ehle, John. *Trail of Tears: The Rise and Fall of the Cherokee Nation*. New York: Doubleday, 1988.

Farnham, Christie Anne, ed. *Women of the American South: A Multicultural Reader*. New York: New York University Press, 1997.

Ferguson, Karen. *Black Politics in New Deal Atlanta*. Chapel Hill: University of North Carolina Press, 2002.

Georgia Writers' Project. *Georgia: A Guide to Its Towns and Countryside*. Atlanta, Ga.: Tupper and Love, 1954.

Green, Harry Clinton, and Mary Wolcott Green. *Pioneer Mothers of America*. 3 vols. New York: G. P. Putnam's Sons, 1912.

Hall, Leslie. *Land and Allegiance in Revolutionary Georgia*. Athens: University of Georgia Press, 2001.

Harper, Ida Husted. *History of Woman Suffrage*. Vol. 6. New York: J. J. Little & Ives, 1922.

Hughes, Langston, and Milton Meltzer. *A Pictorial History of the Negro in America*. New York: Crown, 1968.

Hunter, Tera W. *To 'joy my Freedom: Southern Black Women's Lives and Labors after the Civil War*. Cambridge, Mass.: Harvard University Press, 1997.

Jones, Charles C., Jr. *Antiquities of the Southern Indians, Particularly of the Georgia Tribes*. 1873. Reprint, Tuscaloosa: University of Alabama Press, 1999.

Ketchin, Susan. *The Christ-Haunted Landscape: Faith and Doubt in Southern Fiction*. Jackson: University Press of Mississippi, 1994.

King, Spencer B., Jr. *Georgia Voices: A Documentary History to 1872*. Athens: University of Georgia Press, 1966.

Kumar, Krishna, ed. *Women and Civil War: Impact, Organizations, and Action*. Boulder, Colo.: Lynne Rienner Publishers, 2001.

Lanning, John Tate. *The Spanish Missions of Georgia*. Chapel Hill: University of North Carolina Press, 1935.

Lockley, Timothy James. *Lines in the Sand: Race and Class in Low Country Georgia, 1750–1860*. Athens: University of Georgia Press, 2001.

Lovell, Caroline Couper. *The Golden Isles of Georgia*. Atlanta, Ga.: Cherokee Publishing, 1970.

Manson Myers, Robert. *Children of Pride: A True Story of Georgia during Civil War*. New Haven, Conn.: Yale University Press, 1987.

Martin, Harold H. *Georgia: A Bicentennial History*. New York: W. W. Norton, 1977.

McCall, Hugh. *The History of Georgia.* 1811. Reprint, Atlanta, Ga.: Cherokee Publishing, 1969.

McGough, Lucy S. *The Legal Status of Homemakers in Georgia.* Washington, D.C.: Homemakers Committee, National Commission on the Observance of International Women's Year/USGPO, 1977.

Millard, Janet M. *A Woman's Place: Fifty-two Women of Cobb County, Georgia, 1850–1981.* Marietta, Ga.: Cobb Marietta Girls Club, 1981.

Nicholson, Mrs. Madison G. *Ladies' Garden Club, Athens, Georgia: America's First Garden Club.* 85th anniversary ed. Athens, Ga.: The Print Shop, 1976.

Paquette, Robert Louis, and Louis A. Ferleger, eds. *Slavery, Secession, and Southern History.* Charlottesville: University Press of Virginia, 2000.

Perdue, Theda. "Cherokee Women and the Trail of Tears." *Journal of Women's History* (spring 1989): 14–30.

Reed, Ruth. *The Negro Women of Gainesville, Georgia.* Athens: University of Georgia Press, 1921.

Roth, Darlene R. *Atlanta Women from Myth to Modern Times: A Century of History.* Atlanta, Ga.: Atlanta Historical Society, 1980.

Roth, Darlene R. *Matronage: Patterns in Women's Organizations, Atlanta, Georgia, 1890–1940.* Brooklyn, N.Y.: Carlson Publishing, 1994.

Sawyer, Gordon. *Northeast Georgia: A History.* Charleston, S.C.: Arcadia Press, 2001.

Taylor, A. Elizabeth. *The Last Phase of the Woman Suffrage Movement in Georgia.* Savannah: Georgia Historical Society, 1959.

Tuck, Stephen G. N. *Beyond Atlanta: The Struggle for Racial Equality in Georgia, 1940–1980.* Athens: University of Georgia Press, 2001.

Whites, LeeAnn. *The Civil War as a Crisis in Gender: Augusta, Georgia, 1860–1890.* Athens: University of Georgia Press, 1995.

Wood, Betty. *Gender, Race, and Rank in a Revolutionary Age: The Georgia Lowcountry, 1750–1820.* Athens: University of Georgia Press, 2000.

BIOGRAPHIES AND AUTOBIOGRAPHIES

Andrews, Eliza Frances. *Journal of a Georgia Woman, 1870–1872.* Edited by S. Kittrell Rushing. Knoxville: University of Tennessee Press, 2002.

Auchincloss, Louis. *Pioneers and Caretakers: A Study of Nine American Women Novelists.* Boston: G. K. Hall, 1985.

Bailey, Cornelia. *God, Dr. Buzzard, and the Bolito Man: A Saltwater Geechee Talks about Life on Sapelo Island.* New York: Doubleday, 2000.

Bland, Sidney R. "Lugenia Burns Hope: Black Southern Reformer." *Journal of Southern History* (November 1990).

Burge, Dolly Lunt. *The Diary of Dolly Lunt Burge, 1848–1879.* Edited by Christine Jacobson Carter. Athens: University of Georgia Press, 1997.

Byers, Tracy. *Martha Berry, The Sunday Lady of Possum Trot.* New York: G. P. Putnam's Sons, 1932.

Clayton, Sarah Conley. *Requiem for a Lost City: A Memoir of Civil War Atlanta and the Old South.* Macon, Ga.: Mercer University Press, 1999.

Craft, William. *Running a Thousand Miles for Freedom: The Escape of William and Ellen Craft from Slavery.* 1860. Reprint, Baton Rouge: Louisiana State University Press, 1999.

Felton, Rebecca Latimer. *Country Life in Georgia in the Days of My Youth.* 1919. Reprint, New York: Arno Press, 1980.

Gay, Mary Ann Harris. *Life in Dixie during the War.* 1894. Reprint, Macon, Ga.: Mercer University Press, 2000.

Giannone, Richard. *Flannery O'Connor, Hermit Novelist.* Urbana: University of Illinois Press, 2000.

Gordon, Peter. *The Journal of Peter Gordon, 1732–1735.* Edited by E. Merton Coulter. Athens: University of Georgia Press, 1963.

Hanson, Elizabeth I. *Margaret Mitchell.* Boston: Twayne Publishers, 1990.

Hawkins, Regina Trice. *Hazel Jane Raines, Pioneer Lady of Flight.* Macon, Ga.: Mercer University Press, 1996.

Howard, Jane. "For Juliette Gordon Low's Girls, a Sparkling Diamond Jubilee." *Smithsonian*, October 1987, 46–56.

Hunter-Gault, Charlayne. *In My Place.* New York: Farrar, Straus & Giroux, 1992.

Inge, Tonette Bond, ed. *Southern Women Writers: The New Generation.* Tuscaloosa: University of Alabama Press, 1990.

Johnson, Charles J. *Mary Telfair: The Life and Legacy of a Nineteenth-Century Woman.* Savannah, Ga.: Frederic C. Beil, 2001.

Kytle, Elizabeth. *Willie Mae*. Athens: University of Georgia Press, 1993.

Lauret, Maria. *Alice Walker*. New York: St. Martin's Press, 2000.

Le Guin, Magnolia Wynn. *A Home-Concealed Woman: The Diaries of Magnolia Wynn Le Guin, 1901–1913*. Athens: University of Georgia Press, 1990.

McCaskill, Barbara. "'Yours Very Truly': Ellen Craft, The Fugitive as Text and Artifact." *African American Review* (winter 1994): 509–529.

McCullers, Carson. *Illumination and Night Glare: The Unfinished Autobiography of Carson McCullers*. Madison: University of Wisconsin Press, 1999.

Nasstrom, Kathryn L. *Everybody's Grandmother and Nobody's Fool: Frances Freeborn Pauley and the Struggle for Social Justice*. Ithaca, N.Y.: Cornell University Press, 2000.

O'Dell, Darlene. *Sites of Southern Memory: The Autobiographies of Katharine Du Pre Lumpkin, Lillian Smith, and Pauli Murray*. Charlottesville: University of Virginia Press, 2001.

Parsons, Sara Mitchell. *From Southern Wrongs to Civil Rights: The Memoir of a White Civil Rights Activist*. Tuscaloosa: University of Alabama Press, 2000.

Pember, Phoebe Yates. *A Southern Woman's Story: Life in Confederate Richmond*. 1879. Reprint, Wilmington, N.C.: Broadfoot Publishing, 1991.

Press, Petra. *Coretta Scott King: An Unauthorized Biography*. Des Plaines, Ill.: Heinemann Library, 1999.

Pyron, Darden Asbury. *Southern Daughter: The Life of Margaret Mitchell*. New York: Oxford University Press, 1991.

Roberson, Elizabeth Whitley. *Tiny Broadwick: The First Lady of Parachuting*. Gretna, La.: Pelican Publishing, 2001.

Robinson, Beverly J. *Aunt (ant) Phyllis*. Berkeley, Calif.: Regent Press, 1989.

Rouse, Jacqueline Anne. *Lugenia Burns Hope, Black Southern Reformer*. Athens: University of Georgia Press, 1989.

Rushmore, Robert. *Fanny Kemble*. New York: Crowell-Collier Press, 1970.

Russell, Ina Dillard. *Roots and Ever Green: The Selected Letters of Ina Dillard Russell*. Athens: University of Georgia Press, 1999.

Savigneau, Josyane. *Carson McCullers, A Life*. Translated by Joan E. Howard. Boston: Houghton Mifflin, 2001.

Shultz, Gladys Denny. *Lady from Savannah: The Life of Juliette Low*. Philadelphia: Lippincott, 1958.

Spritzer, Lorraine Nelson. *The Belle of Ashby Street: Helen Douglas Mankin and Georgia Politics*. Athens: University of Georgia Press, 1982.

Spritzer, Lorraine Nelson. *Grace Towns Hamilton and the Politics of Southern Change*. Athens: University of Georgia Press, 1997.

Stewart-Baxter, Derrick. *Ma Rainey and the Classic Blues Singers*. New York: Stein and Day, 1970.

Thomas, Ella Gertrude Clanton. *The Secret Eye: The Journal of Ella Gertrude Clanton Thomas, 1848–1889*. Edited by Virginia Ingraham Burr. Chapel Hill: University of North Carolina Press, 1990.

Trillin, Calvin. *An Education in Georgia: The Integration of Charlayne Hunter and Hamilton Holmes*. Athens: University of Georgia Press, 1991.

Wright, Constance. *Fanny Kemble and the Lovely Land*. New York: Dodd, Mead, 1972.

USEFUL WEB SITES

"Helen Douglas Mankin," Women in Congress
http://bioguide.congress.gov/congresswomen/index.asp
Jewish Women's Archive
http://www.jwa.org
"Lugenia Burns Hope," Georgia Women of Achievement
http://www.gawomen.org/honorees/hopel.htm
"Mother of the Carpet Capitol," Historic High Country Travel Association
http://georgiahighcountry.org/legends02.html
"Nancy Morgan Hart," Georgia Women of Achievement
http://www.gawomen.org/honorees/long/hartn_long.htm
"Nancy Morgan Hart, Revolutionary Heroine," National Society of the Daughters of the American Revolution
http://www.rootsweb.com/~kyhender/Articles/hart.htm

SELECTED ORGANIZATIONS AND INSTITUTIONS

Agnes Scott College Women's Studies
141 East College Avenue
Decatur, GA 30030
Telephone: (404) 471 6285
Web: http://www.agnesscott.edu/academics
Integrates liberal arts education with an examination of women's experience and feminist theory.

Augusta State University Women's Studies
2300 Walton Way
Augusta, GA 30904
Telephone: (706) 737 1400
Web: http://www.aug.edu/womens_studies
Offers the study of women's cultures, contributions, and perspectives from an interdisciplinary standpoint.

Center for the Study of Women, Science, and Technology
Georgia Institute of Technology
Atlanta, GA 30332
Telephone: (404) 894 1818
Links issues in the study of science and technology with those of gender, culture, and society.

Emory University Institute for Women's Studies
S301 Callaway Center
Atlanta, GA 30322
Telephone: (404) 727 0096
Web: http://www.emory.edu/WOMENS_STUDIES
Offers a doctoral program and an undergraduate major and minor in women's studies.

Georgia Department of Archives and History
330 Capitol Avenue Southeast
Atlanta, GA 30334
Telephone: (404) 656 2393
Web: http://www.sos.state.ga.us/archives
Identifies and preserves Georgia's most valuable historical documents.

Georgia Historical Society
501 Whitaker Street
Savannah, GA 31401
Telephone: (912) 651 2125
Web: http://www.georgiahistory.com
Works to collect, preserve, and share Georgian history through educational outreach programs and research services. Maintains a manuscript library.

Georgia Women's Collection Project
William Russell Pullen Library
Georgia State University
100 Decatur Street Southeast
Atlanta, GA 30303–3202
Telephone: (404) 651 2172
Web: http://www.library.gsu.edu/spcoll/women/index.htm
Collects, preserves, and makes available primary and secondary source material of or related to 20th-century women in Georgia.

Robert W. Woodruff Library
Emory University
540 Asbury Circle
Atlanta, GA 30322–2870
Telephone: (404) 727 6887
Web: http://web.library.emory.edu/libraries/woodruff
Maintains an online listing of manuscript sources on women's history.

University of Georgia
Main Library
Athens, GA 30602–1641
Telephone: (706) 542 3251
Web: http://www.libs.uga.edu
Offers an online gateway to the library catalog for all University of Georgia campuses.

University of Georgia Women's Studies Program
1200 South Lumpkin Street
Athens, GA 30602–3647
Telephone: (706) 542 2846
Web: http://www.uga.edu/~wsp/department_info/index.html
Offers graduate and undergraduate programs in women's studies.

Women's Studies Institute
Georgia State University
611 General Classroom Building
University Plaza
Atlanta, GA 30303–3083
Telephone: (404) 651 4633
Web: http://www.gsu.edu/~wwwwsi
Provides a sound liberal education with options for intensive study focusing on the intersections of race, class, gender, ethnicity, sexuality, religion, and culture.

HAWAII

Every night when she cooked supper, she'd been slipping excerpts from the Diamond Sutra,
written on tiny strips of rice paper, into her husband's food.
Already, her diligence had begun to pay—just as it had when she'd chanted
Henry himself through the Invasion of Okinawa. In those days, he'd been engaged to Flora, her
younger sister. But Flora had been worse than no help at all. After she was diagnosed with that
blood disease all she did was lie in bed all day and listen to love songs . . .
Flora had looked in her coffin . . . like a sleeping child. Flora would not be a fierce ghost. . . .
She'd passed on before the bonds of wedlock could cure her hankering for romance.
—Sylvia Watanabe, Talking to the Dead and Other Stories, 1992

Hawaii's traditions are vastly different from those of the mainland United States. In its indigenous culture class mattered more than gender, but gender-based taboos were real and severe. These mores changed rapidly: in less than a century, Hawaii has become a model of diversity and egalitarianism. The first state to legalize abortion and the first to ratify the Equal Rights Amendment, Hawaii was also earlier than most states to elect women to its legislature, to Congress, and as governor.

PREHISTORY

(Prehistory–1778)

The peoples who settled the Hawaiian Islands came originally from Southeast Asia and gradually spread east, first to the islands of present-day Melanesia and then to Tonga, Samoa, and Tahiti. Polynesians reached Hawaii around 400 A.D. Although sporadic contact with Tahiti continued for centuries, the culture that developed on Hawaii was unique, moving beyond the subsistence of early Polynesians to a richly ceremonial religious, cultural, and political life.

By the 14th century chiefs, or *alii*, had gained total control over the population; the *alii* owned the land and effectively owned the people who worked it. Society was governed by a strict set of laws and taboos, which the *alii* administered.

Women could be executed for eating with men, or eating foods reserved for men, including pork, bananas, and coconuts.

The gentle climate, plentiful plant and animal life, as well as abundant seafood gave Hawaiian women an easier life than women faced in harsher climates. They had no need for elaborate shelter or clothing; in fact, Hawaii was so temperate and predictable that the indigenous people had no word for weather. Hawaiian women gathered and prepared food, especially seafood and the starch staple, poi, and they

State Population (2000): 1,211,537
Female Population (2000): 602,866
Women in State Legislature (2003): 27.6%
Female College Enrollment (1999): 35,000 (55.6% of total)
Privately Held Women-owned Businesses (1997): 25,807
First Year of Full Suffrage: 1920

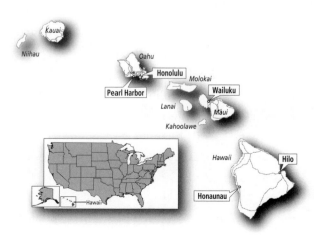

developed great skill at fabricating quilts and crafting useful and decorative items from leaf fibers and feathers. But they also had time to amuse themselves, making leis, necklaces of fresh flowers; chatting; and singing. British traveler Isabella Bird observed that the Hawaiian men seemed to do most of the child care. She also noted that, "Native women never need help [from men], as they are as strong, fearless, and active as the men, and rival them in swimming and other athletic sports." (Bird 1875, 66)

WHITE EXPLORATION TO AMERICAN ANNEXATION
(1778–1900)

Britain's Capt. James Cook was the first known European to sight the Hawaiian Islands; he made his discovery on January 20, 1778, and named them the Sandwich Islands for his patron, the earl of Sandwich. Cook's expedition changed Hawaii forever. Gradually Hawaii became a major way station for American whalers and for merchants plying the China trade. The whites brought with them diseases that over the course of 75 years ravaged the population. At the time of European contact the indigenous population numbered between 300,000 and 1 million; by 1850 it had fallen to about 85,000. In 1804 alone, an epidemic, probably cholera or bubonic plague, killed 150,000 indigenous women and men.

In 1810 Hawaiian warrior chief Kamehameha united the islands and founded the kingdom of Hawaii. On his death in 1819 his widow, KAAHUMANU, became *kuhina nui*, or co-sovereign, with his son Liholiho, who reigned as Kamehameha II. When Liholiho died in 1824, Kaahumanu continued as *kuhina nui* for his young son Kauikeaouli (Kamehameha III). Kaahumanu was the first of a series of influential royal women who helped shape Hawaii in the 19th century.

At Kaahumanu's insistence, Liholiho abolished the ancient taboos. When American missionaries arrived in 1820, Kaahumanu embraced Christianity and moved to westernize Hawaiian society. She built schools and churches; introduced a modern legal code, including jury trials; and attempted to impose a western moral code.

American missionaries transformed Hawaiian society and undermined the old social order, supporting and spreading American civilization and social organization as well as Christianity. Women missionaries, in particular, frowned on what they thought were licentious customs. The future of Hawaii's indigenous people, they believed, was in instilling in Hawaiian women habits that were "above those which are natural to their race." Hawaiian girls were placed in boarding schools to avoid what missionaries deemed the "evil and impure surrounding" of families. There they were taught "industrious and housewifely habits" and urged to dress and behave as westerners. (Ibid., 166, 198) Missionaries were most concerned with abolishing the sexual freedom of indigenous women, and even succeeded in forbidding women from dancing the hula. Gradually, women's rights were restricted, and in 1850 the kingdom adopted a constitution establishing the Hawaiian legislature—and only men could vote.

American missionaries were soon joined by planters eager to exploit the country's rich agricultural potential. By midcentury, sugar had become the mainstay of the economy, and growers imported first Chinese and, after 1880, Japanese laborers to work on their plantations. The vast majority of these immigrant workers were men, but the women who did come often worked alongside their husbands. Some brought their newborns to the cane fields, leaving the infants in cradles made of sacks while they stripped the cane their husbands cut.

Kamehameha III died in 1854 and was succeeded by his nephew, Alexander Liholiho, as Kamehameha IV. In 1856 the young king married Emma Rooke (later QUEEN EMMA KALELEONALANI). Initially many Hawaiians opposed the match

THE FOLIO

By the mid-1850s the call for women's rights sounded at Seneca Falls, New York, in 1848, had spread west across the Great Plains and the Pacific Ocean to the islands of Hawaii. In 1855 The Folio, a four-page woman's newspaper, was published in Honolulu. Not only was it the first woman's newspaper in Hawaii, but, reportedly, the first feminist publication west of the Rockies.

The Folio emerged from a movement that began when American missionaries from the East Coast of the United States arrived in the kingdom of Hawaii in the 1820s. They brought with them not just Christianity, mainland morals, and a spirit of reform, but also the printing press. In 1834 Hawaii published its first newspaper. By the 1840s a nonmissionary woman from Boston, Elizabeth Jarves, was in charge of publishing the Polynesian, a newspaper founded by her husband, James, which served as the official publication of the Hawaiian government.

One of the apparent goals of The Folio was to foster civic excitement among women. The trustees of the Honolulu Sailors' Home Society, a reform organization dedicated to temperance for seamen, had established a Committee of Ladies to raise money, through fund-raising fairs, to complete construction on a new boardinghouse for visiting sailors. Notices for the fair and requests for articles for what appears to be the first issue of The Folio went out in established reform publications, such as the Friend. When The Folio appeared at a fund-raising fair in Honolulu in November 1855, it was filled with writing about the familiar 19th-century ideals of reform, abolition, temperance, and education for women. One of the most strident articles issued a "call to arms," decrying women's lack of property rights and urging all toward a new era of women's emancipation.

Although the articles in The Folio were written anonymously, historians believe the newspaper was the creation of a small group of reformers—Rev. Samuel C. and Julia Damon, Henry and Catherine Whitney, W. L. and Catherine Lee, Elisha H. Allen, and Charles Gordon Hopkins. Most were involved with larger publications, including the Friend and the Polynesian. Helen Chapin, a newspaper scholar, believes that Catherine Whitney was the editor and main author of much of The Folio; it is likely she learned about the business from her husband, Henry, an editor at the Polynesian and founder of the Pacific Commercial Advertiser.

The promised second edition of The Folio never appeared, though its premiere issue was reprinted in the Friend. Twenty-five years elapsed before another woman's newspaper appeared in Hawaii—The Spirit of the Fair, another single-issue newspaper, was published in 1880.

—Laura J. Lambert

because Rooke was one-quarter Caucasian, but the new queen eventually became extremely popular, respected for charity work and for bringing health care to the indigenous population. She continued her work after her husband and their only child died. By 1874 she was so popular that riots broke out when the legislature selected David Kalakaua rather than Emma as sovereign.

As the century progressed American business interests gained control of the Hawaiian government. In 1887 they forced through the Bayonet Constitution, which reduced the monarch to a ceremonial role and disenfranchised most indigenous Hawaiians through income and property requirements. When QUEEN LYDIA KAMA'KAEHA LILI'UOKALANI acceded to the throne in 1891, she attempted to repudiate the constitution and return control of government to the monarchy in an effort to curb American domination. In response, a small group of white businessmen overthrew the monarchy in 1893 and declared the Republic of Hawaii. A royalist uprising in 1895 resulted in Lili'uokalani's arrest and confinement; when she was released the following year, she waged an unsuccessful battle to prevent American annexation of Hawaii.

Most Hawaiians did not support the Republic. Protest groups included Hui Kalai'aina, with up to 20,000 members, and Hui Aloha 'Aina for Women, with about 11,000 members. Despite popular opposition and Washington's acknowledgment that the overthrow of Lili'uokalani was

Hawaii's Queen Lili'uokalani. (AP/Wide World Photos)

illegal, on June 14, 1900, Pres. William McKinley signed the Organic Act, formally creating the Territory of Hawaii. The act specifically forbade the Hawaiian legislature to extend suffrage.

FROM ANNEXATION TO STATEHOOD (1900–1959)

Following annexation, women in Hawaii organized to preserve their heritage and achieve the vote. The Daughters of Hawaii began in 1903 with seven women who were daughters of American missionaries and had grown up in Hawaii. They felt strongly about their citizenship in the Hawaiian kingdom, regretted the business interests' takeover, and were determined to perpetuate the memory and spirit of old Hawaii. Membership was not restricted by the era's usual standard of race, but instead was limited to women directly descended from a person who lived in Hawaii prior to 1880.

By the time Honolulu women organized Hawaii's first suffrage society in 1912, they had strong support for their cause; that year all legislative candidates backed women's suffrage. In 1915 Hawaii's Democratic and Republican parties also formally endorsed suffrage. But the Hawaiian territorial legislature could not act without approval from Washington, and three years would pass before Pres. Woodrow Wilson signed the needed legislation

Gov. C. J. McCarthy recommended a suffrage bill early in the 1919 legislative session. The state Senate quickly passed it, but the House of Representatives, under the influence of the conservative business oligarchy that ran Hawaii, substituted a bill referring the question to the all-male electorate. Senators refused to accept the substitute, and the session ended in deadlock.

In response, suffragists formed the Hawaii Suffrage Association to bring pressure on lawmakers. Before the Hawaiian legislature could act, on June 4, 1919, the U.S. Congress passed and sent to the states for ratification the 19th Amendment that enfranchised all American women, including those of territories.

Hawaii elected its first woman to the territorial legislature in 1924—earlier than most states. ROSALIE KELI'INOI immediately promoted a bill allowing women to retain control of their property after marriage, legislation that most states had enacted decades earlier. Nine years later Pres. Franklin Roosevelt appointed Hawaii's first female judge, Carrick Hume Buck.

Pilot Cornelia Fort was in the air over Oahu when the Japanese bombed Pearl Harbor on December 7, 1941. Less than six hours later martial law was imposed and constitutional protections were suspended. At least 1,441 Hawaiians of Japanese ancestry were imprisoned in internment camps.

Hundreds of thousands of soldiers and sailors passed through Hawaii during the war, including members of the Army Nurse Corps and the Women's Army Corps. Many women in the Navy

EARLY-20TH-CENTURY WOMEN'S WORK

Hawaiian women emerged from the traditional workplace of the home and began to enter the public workforce at the turn of the 20th century, just after the United States annexed the islands as a territory. As an island culture struggling with the beginnings of urbanization, Hawaii had few industries, which limited job opportunities for women as well as men. However, the beginnings of tourism in Hawaii opened doors for women workers, as did the manufacturing and export of traditional Hawaiian goods—sugar, pineapples, and leis.

Women's entrance into the workforce included both indigenous Hawaiians, island-born women of European ancestry, and immigrant women, including first-generation Japanese women who often came to Hawaii as picture brides. By 1910 approximately one-third of working Japanese women were employed by the sugar factories. They performed arduous work—weeding fields, stripping and cutting sugarcane—for a mere 50 cents per day, which was only two-thirds of what their male counterparts earned. By the 1920s, however, the number of women working in the sugar industry had decreased, in part because second-generation Japanese—called nisei—often preferred to work in the pineapple factories.

Hawaii's commercial pineapple industry began in 1903. Although men were often regular, year-round workers, great numbers of women were hired during the late spring and summer, when the pineapples ripened. Indeed, the pineapple industry was one of the primary employers of women in the early 20th century. At the height of the season, pineapple factories ran two or three shifts each day. Women cut and sliced pineapples, packed them into cans, and served as managers of operations.

Women who did not find work in sugarcane fields or factories often turned to making flower leis. Using flowers found in their own gardens or neighborhoods, these women would string leis to be sold at the harbor, for arriving and departing tourists. In 1912 leis sold for 25 cents. On a good day, women could earn $9. The lei industry grew in conjunction with tourism, with huge increases beginning in the late 1920s, when luxury cruises were introduced to Hawaii, and in the 1950s, with airline travel.

As tourism continued to grow, the demand for women in other service sector jobs—such as hotel workers, greeters, maids and waitresses—grew in tandem. Today, although women in Hawaii now enjoy their choice of many professions, tourism is still a dominant employer.

—Laura J. Lambert

Nurse Corps were based in Hawaii from the beginning, and near the end of the war, the navy also sent its all-female WAVES to perform the many tasks involved in supplying the Pacific front.

After the war Hawaiians elected strong statehood advocates as their nonvoting delegate to Congress, including MARY ELIZABETH FARRINGTON. Nevertheless, more than a decade was needed to overcome objections from southern congressmen who did not want to admit a state with a nonwhite majority. The key to getting past such racism came from military strategists, who argued that statehood would strengthen the U.S. hold on this vital area in the Pacific. After approval by both houses of Congress and President Eisenhower in March 1959, Hawaii residents voted for statehood in June, and Hawaii became the 50th state on August 21 of that year.

STATEHOOD TO PRESENT
(1959–present)

Life in Hawaii changed rapidly after statehood. Tourism grew dramatically, and many working-class Hawaiian women found unionized jobs in the burgeoning hospitality industry. The population continued to increase, but old Hawaii faded; the 1960 census showed just 12,000 Hawaiians of indigenous descent, less than 2% of the population. Many feared that with the decline and assimilation of the indigenous population, Hawaiian culture would be destroyed; in the 1960s and 1970s a movement developed to preserve and revive Hawaii's heritage.

Many women were leaders of this revival. Gladys Kamakakuokalani Ainoa Brandt, for example, led the movement to revive the hula. Helene Hale, the first woman to be elected chair of the

HAWAIIAN WOMEN AND THE HULA

Women have always been important in the hula dance tradition of Hawaii's indigenous people. In the hula a sung poetic text is the basis for illustrative hand and arm gestures, which are choreographed in combination with named rhythmic foot and leg movements. The epic myth about Pele, the volcano goddess, relates how favored sister, Hi'iaka, learned the hula from best friend, Hopoe. Many hula schools consider this episode to mark the origins of hula. Artists' renditions and early photographs show both men and women performers, but images of women became important marketing tools as the Hawaiian tourist industry emerged.

By the 1930s such featured hula dancers as Aggie Auld, Kahala and Odetta Bray, Winona Love, Tootsey Notley, and Jenny Woodd gained marquee name recognition; numerous other women dancers populated chorus lines in showrooms and Hollywood films like *Waikiki Wedding* (1937) and *Song of the Islands* (1942). Tourist preferences for westernized Hawaiian music with English-language lyrics contributed to a decline of interest in older traditional styles of hula. By the early 1970s knowledge of traditional hula ritual practices was concentrated in a small group of mostly elderly women, including Eleanor Hiram Hoke, Edith Kanaka'ole, 'Iolani Luahine, Lokalia Montgomery, Mary Kawena Puku'i, and Kau'i Zuttermeister.

The early 1970s also witnessed a vibrant cultural renaissance among a new generation of Hawaiians, a reclaiming of practices nearly submerged under Americanization. One teacher, Maiki Aiu Lake, was unprecedented in opening classes to train hula teachers. Between 1972 and her untimely death in 1984, she taught and graduated 42 students with the title kumu hula—hula master. Many of these masters now direct award-winning hula schools that dominate hula competitions, which have become high-profile venues of prestige.

A grassroots project, undertaken by the nonprofit Kalihi-Palama Culture and Arts Society to document hula teachers active since World War II, led to the 1984 publication of *Nana I Na Loea Hula* (Look to the Hula Resources), in which 60 of 78 profiles are of women. Among the next generation of hula teachers are many daughters of well-known teachers who will carry their mothers' hula legacies into the future.

—Amy Ku'uleialoha Stillman

Hawaii County board of supervisors in 1962, began a local hula festival in Hilo in 1964. Hawaiian-language music enjoyed a revival, and in 1978 a constitutional convention promoted Hawaiian culture by creating the Office of Hawaiian Affairs and mandating that the schools teach Hawaiian language, culture, and history.

A report on the legal status of women at statehood showed exceptional gender equity in such issues as child custody and inheritance, with divorce much easier than in most states at that time. A woman could obtain a divorce if her husband "neglects or refuses to provide suitable maintenance for his wife during a continuous period of 60 days or more."

The Hawaiian government remained liberal on women's issues through the end of the 20th century. It was the first state to legalize abortion in 1970—three years before the U.S. Supreme Court decision in *Roe v. Wade*—and in 1972 Hawaii was the first state to ratify the Equal Rights Amendment. Beginning in 1974, Hawaiian employers were required to prepay health insurance for all workers, as well as provide generous workers' compensation benefits. The result was that a 2000 study showed only 7.5% of Hawaii's women were uninsured, the lowest rate in the nation.

Following statehood, women quickly assumed leadership positions in government. In 1964 PATSY MINK became the first nonwhite woman elected to the U.S. Congress; in 1956 she had been the first Asian American woman in the territorial legislature. Mink's legislative work had tremendous impact on all American women: she was the coauthor of Title IX of the 1972 Educational Equity Act, which mandated gender equality in school spending, including athletic departments.

Hawaiian women continued to set electoral precedents during the 20th century's last quarter. Jean Sadako King was elected as the state's first female lieutenant governor in 1978; she served until 1982, when she lost the gubernatorial race.

Governor-elect Linda Lingle at a news conference on November 27, 2002. (AP/Wide World Photos)

Eileen Anderson was mayor of Honolulu from 1981 to 1985, and in 1987 PATRICIA FUKUDA SAIKI was elected to the U.S. House of Representatives; she was the first Republican to be elected to Congress since statehood. JoAnn Yukimura served as county mayor of Kauai for six years. She was succeeded in office by Maryanne W. Kusaka. In the judiciary Paula A. Nakayama became the first woman on the Hawaii supreme court when she began her ten-year term in April 1993.

In the 2002 election Hawaiians elected the state's first female governor, Republican Linda C. Lingle of Maui. She ran against Democrat Mazie K. Hirono, who had served as lieutenant governor since 1994. Although Hawaii had no women in the 108th Congress (2003–2005), its 28% female representation in the state legislature was higher than that of most states.

—Doris Weatherford

TIMELINE

United States Events		Hawaii Events
	1600	
1620 Settlement of Plymouth Colony		
	1700	
1776 United States declares independence		
		1778 British Capt. James Cook lands in the Hawaiian Islands.
	1800	1810 Kamehameha I unites the Hawaiian Islands.
		1819–32 Kaahumanu reigns as co-sovereign.
		1820 American missionaries arrive in Hawaii.
1861–65 U.S. Civil War		1887 American business interests force Hawaii to adopt the Bayonet Constitution.
		1893 American business interests depose Queen Lydia Kama'kaeha Lili'uokalani.
		1895 Royalist uprising fails.
	1900	1900 Hawaii becomes a U.S. territory.
		1903 Daughters of Hawaii are formed.
		1912 Honolulu women organize Hawaii's first suffrage society.
1914–18 World War I		
1920 Ratification of the 19th Amendment		
		1924 Rosalie Keli'inoi becomes the first woman elected to the territorial legislature.
1929–39 Great Depression		1934 Pres. Franklin D. Roosevelt appoints Hawaii's first female judge, Carrick Hume Buck.
1939–45 World War II		1959 Hawaii becomes a state.
		1964 Patsy Mink becomes the first nonwhite woman elected to U.S. Congress.
		1970 Hawaii is first state to legalize abortion.
		1972 Hawaii is first state to ratify the Equal Rights Amendment.
1975 Vietnam War ends		1978 Jean Sadako King is elected as Hawaii's first female lieutenant governor.
	2000	2002 Linda C. Lingle is elected Hawaii's first female governor.

PROMINENT WOMEN

BERNICE PAUAHI BISHOP (1831–1884)

Beloved philanthopist Princess Bernice Pauahi Paki Bishop was a strong supporter of education for indigenous Hawaiians. She was the last of the royal Hawaiian dynasty, founded by her great-grandfather, Kamehameha I the Great, at the unification of the Hawaiian Islands in 1810. The daughter of Konia and Paki, she grew up with adoptive sister Lydia Lili'uokalani, Hawaii's last queen, and studied in the Chiefs' Children's School, a mission school for royalty. At age 19, against the objections of her family, she married merchant and banker Charles Reed Bishop.

The sole heir to vast family properties after the death of her sister, Ruth Ke'elikolani, Bishop was the island's largest landholder. Having no children of her own, she determined to provide for the education of all indigenous children. Her will provided for the establishment of the Kamehameha Schools for Boys and Girls, which opened the boys' facility in 1887 and the girls' school seven years later. The Kamehameha Schools is the largest private charitable trust in the United States.

MARY FARRINGTON (1898–1984)

Mary Elizabeth Pruett Farrington of Tokyo, Japan, was a successful journalist and publisher who supported Hawaiian statehood. The daughter of missionaries, she attended Tokyo Foreign School in Japan, and schools in Tennessee, Texas, and California. She graduated from Ward-Belmont Junior College in Nashville in 1916 and from the University of Wisconsin at Madison in 1918. She left her job on the staff of the *Wisconsin State Journal* to report legislative news from Washington, D.C., to midwestern papers. After establishing the Washington Press Service in 1920 and marrying, she headed the League of Republican Women in Washington and the National Federation of Women's Clubs. In 1948 she founded the *Washington Newsletter*, which she also edited.

At the death of her husband, publisher Joseph Rider Farrington in 1954, Mary Farrington served out the last two years of his term as Hawaiian territorial representative to the U.S. Congress. Like her husband, she was an outspoken supporter of statehood for Hawaii and defended the territory against charges of communist infiltration. After losing the 1956 campaign for reelection, she returned to journalism and headed the *Honolulu Star-Bulletin, Hilo Tribune-Herald*, the Honolulu Lithograph Company, and the Hawaiian Broadcasting System. In 1969 she accepted a presidential appointment to the Department of Interior's Office of the Territories.

KAAHUMANU (ca. 1772–1832)

Queen Kaahumanu of Hana, Maui, was coruler of Hawaii from 1819 to 1832. Of royal birth, she married Kamehameha I when she was 10; he was 30 years her senior. As his favorite wife, she supported union of the island chain, encouraged westernization, and shared government duties with her husband. After his death, as cosovereign, she pushed Kamehameha II to abolish taboos, such as those forbidding women to eat with men, and encouraged reforms that elevated women's position in society. Following the death of Kamehameha II in 1824, she became coregent for Kamehameha III and ruled in his name. A friend to New England missionaries, Kaahumanu was baptized in 1825 under the western name of Elisabeta after England's Queen Elizabeth I. During her reign, she promoted Christianity, introduced codified law on the islands, built schools, and encouraged indigenous crafts.

EMMA KALELEONALANI (1836–1885)

Queen Emma Kaleleonalani Rooke of Honolulu earned indigenous Hawaiians' respect and love for her humanitarianism. Daughter of Chief George Nae'a and Fanny Kekelaokalani, niece of Kamehameha I the Great, she was adopted by Grace and T. C. Rooke, the court physician, and was taught both English and indigenous languages and traditions at the Chiefs' Children's School. As the wife of Kamehameha IV (reigned 1854–1863), Kaleleonalani established the Queen's Hospital to help indigenous people when they fell ill of diseases brought to the islands by Europeans.

Following the death of her husband and four-year-old son, Queen Emma poured her energies into charity work. She founded schools in Honolulu and on Maui and supported St. Andrews Cathedral with money she acquired from England's Queen Victoria. After King Lunalilo died in 1874, Queen Emma campaigned unsuccessfully against David Kalakaua for the throne.

QUEEN KAPI'OLANI (1834–1899)

Queen Kapi'olani, wife of King David Kalakaua (reigned 1874–1891), fought European diseases that decimated the indigenous Hawaiian population. Descended from the Kauai royal line, she assisted her husband in sparking a cultural renaissance on the islands and wrote a love song for him, "Ipo Lei Manu," about a gentle lover. She was crowned queen in 1883. The queen helped found a home for children of people with leprosy and campaigned for Kapi'olani Maternity Home and Home for Leper Girls. A medical center treating women and children opened in 1890 under her name.

ROSALIE KELI'INOI (1875–1952)

Rosalie Enos Keli'inoi of Wailuku, Maui, was Hawaii's first female legislator. The daughter of a Portuguese merchant and rancher and a Hawaiian mother, she studied at St. Anthony's School for Girls before marrying bartender Thomas Lyons in 1893. She had seven children with him. From her second husband, Samuel Keli'inoi, she gained an understanding of politics. In 1925, a year after her election to the territorial legislature, she sponsored the law granting women property rights. Keli'inoi also promoted Hawaiian culture and supported funding for programs to boost well-being in pregnant women and infants. She also backed the purchase of Hulihe'e Palace and grounds, the former vacation home of Queen Emma Kaleleonalani in Kailua, Kona, which became a cultural museum of island furniture and Hawaiiana.

QUEEN LILI'UOKALANI (1838–1917)

Lydia Kamaka'eha Lili'uokalani, Hawaii's last queen, was born to two indigenous high chiefs. As was customary she was not raised by her parents but grew up the adoptive sister of Bernice Pauahi Bishop. In 1862 she married John Owen Dominis. She became queen following the death of her brother, King David Kalakaua, in 1891. Lili'uokalani opposed the domination of Hawaii by U.S. business interests and attempted a series of reforms designed to return control of government to the monarchy. In 1893 she was deposed in an American-backed coup. She exited peacefully to avoid bloodshed, but campaigned for the return of island sovereignty under a stronger constitution. Following a royalist uprising in 1895, she was charged with treason and placed under house arrest until she agreed to abdicate formally. For the next three years she fought U.S. annexation of the islands.

Lili'uokalani was also a talented songwriter, composing some 160 original songs, ballads, and chants that incorporated both western and island traditions. In 1897 she compiled 110 of her melodies into a manuscript, *The Queen's Songbook*, which was published in 1999. The most familiar of her songs was "Aloha Oe."

PATSY MINK (1928–2002)

Japanese American legislator Patsy Takemoto Mink of Maui was the first woman of color and first Asian American woman elected to the U.S. Congress. She attended Kaunoa English Standard School and developed an interest in politics during World War II. Mink had intended to go to medical school following her graduation from high school, but was not accepted at any of the schools to which she applied because of her gender and race. Instead, she went to law school at the University of Chicago, from which she graduated in 1951. She married John Mink, a geology graduate student, the same year. Because she had difficulty finding an office that would hire an Asian American female, she returned to Hawaii and opened her own practice, specializing in criminal defense, divorce, and adoption cases. She also became involved in Democratic party politics. In 1956 she was elected to the Territorial House of Representatives.

In 1964 Mink won election to the U.S. Congress, where she acquired a reputation for uncompromisingly liberal views, particularly on civil rights, the rights of women and children, and education. In 1976 Pres. Jimmy Carter appointed her to an environmental supervision post, which she resigned to take the presidency of Americans for Democratic Action, a liberal lobby. Returned by the voters to the U.S. House of Representatives in 1990, she supported Headstart, increased funding for schools, and birth control programs.

PATRICIA FUKUDA SAIKI (1930–)

A strong Republican party organizer, Patricia Fukuda Saiki of Hilo challenged the male network in her party and supported Asian American causes. She received her bachelor's degree from the University of Hawaii at Manoa in 1952. At age 38 she was elected to a term in the state House of Representatives and followed with two terms in the state Senate. After election to the U.S. House of Representatives in 1986, she became the first Republican representing Hawaii since it gained statehood. Saiki championed unpopular legislation, particularly compensation for Japanese Americans interned during World War II. She was not a candidate for reelection in 1990 but was an unsuccessful nominee for the Senate that year. She lost the gubernatorial election in 1994.

—Mary Ellen Snodgrass

PROMINENT SITES

Bernice Pauahi Bishop Museum
The State Museum of Natural and Cultural History
1525 Bernice Street
Honolulu, HI 96817
Telephone: (808) 847 3511
Web: http://www.bishopmuseum.org
The museum was founded in 1889 by Charles Bishop in honor of his late wife, Princess Bernice Pauahi Bishop, the last descendent of the royal Kamehameha family. It originally housed a large collection of Hawaiian artifacts and royal family heirlooms, including the royal carriage of the last ruling monarch, Queen Lili'uokalani. It presently exhibits material that celebrates the importance of the hula in Hawaiian culture.

Holo-holo-ku Heiau (Run Run Stand Fast Heiau)
0.1 mile up Route 580 off Highway 56
Island of Kauai
Web: http://www.kauai-hawaii.com/coconut/
　holoholoku_h.html
A *heiau* is a site where Hawaiians honored their gods before royalty became Christians in the 19th century. A cemetery was built over the site in the 1890s, but the Kauai Historical Society and the Bishop Museum have restored parts of *heiau*. The Royal Birthstones are still there. Women of royal blood were required to reach the stones before giving birth to ensure the child's royal status.

Maui Historical Society, Bailey House Museum
2375-A Main Street
Wailuku, HI 96793
Telephone: (808) 244 3326
Web: http://www.mauimuseum.org/index.html
The Bailey House was the home of Edward Bailey and his wife. They were missionaries from Massachusetts who ran a female boarding school. There, removed from what missionaries thought were the impure influences of their families, indigenous girls were taught Christianity and encouraged to adopt western mores.

Puuhonnua O Honaunau National Park
PO Box 128
Honaunau, HI 96726
Telephone: (808) 328 2326
Web: http://www.gorp.com/gorp/resource/
　us_nhp/hi_puuho.htm
The Puuhonnua O Honaunau (place of refuge) was established early in the 15th century. The sacred spot gave sanctuary to women and children during times of war, as well as to breakers of religious law. Priests at the site could absolve the lawbreakers. The park has archaeological sites including some coastal village sites.

Queen Emma Summer Palace
2913 Pali Highway
Honolulu, HI 96817
Telephone: (808) 595 6291
Web: http://www.daughtersofhawaii.org/
　hanaiakamalama
The Queen Emma Summer Palace, originally named *Hanaiakamalama*, was Queen Emma's private mountain retreat outside Honolulu. It is now maintained by the Daughters of Hawaii as a museum of Queen Emma's life, reflecting her Hawaiian and English heritage through the display of rare artifacts. It also features beautiful gardens.

Ramsay Museum
1128 Smith Street
Honolulu, HI 96817
Web: http://www.ramsaymuseum.org/RAMSAY.HTML
The museum has a permanent exhibit of quill and ink drawings by Ramsay, who uses only one name. A skylight in the museum is also decorated with Ramsay's drawing tools. She is an internationally known artist, and Hawaii's first member of the National Society of Illustrators. The museum has been host to more than 200 temporary exhibits featuring Hawaiian artists.

RESOURCES

FURTHER READING

HISTORY

Anthony, Susan B., and Ida Husted Harper. *History of Woman Suffrage.* Vol. 4. Indianapolis, Ind.: Hollenbeck Press, 1902.

Bird, Isabella. *Six Months in the Sandwich Islands.* 1875. Reprint, Honolulu: Mutual Publishing, 1998.

Chinen, Joyce N., Kathleen O. Kane, and Ida M. Yoshinaga, eds. *Women in Hawaii: Sites, Identities, and Voices.* Honolulu: University of Hawaii Press, 1997.

Dale, Laura. *Hawaii, the 50th State.* Washington, D.C.: USGPO, 1959.

Daughters of Hawaii. *Treasures of the Hawaiian Kingdom.* Honolulu, Hawaii: Tongg Publishing, 1989.

Drury, Clifford. *First White Women Over the Rockies.* 3 vols. Glendale, Calif.: A. H. Clarke, 1963–1966.

Harper, Ida Husted. *History of Woman Suffrage.* Vols. 5–6. New York: J. J. Little & Ives, 1922.

"The Hawaiian Monarchy." *Honolulu Star-Bulletin,* 16 June 1999.

Hyatt, Shirley. *By Square-Rigger to Honolulu.* Honolulu, Hawaii: Friends of the Falls of Clyde, 1983.

Judd, Laura Fish. *Honolulu: Sketches of Life in the Hawaiian Islands from 1828 to 1861.* 1880. Reprint, edited by Dale L. Morgan. Chicago: Lakeside Press, 1966.

Kirch, Patrick Vinton. *Feathered Gods and Fishhooks: An Introduction to Hawaiian Archeology and Prehistory.* Honolulu: University of Hawaii Press, 1999.

Kwon, Brenda L. *Beyond Keeaumoku: Koreans, Nationalism, and Local Culture in Hawai'i.* New York: Garland Publishing, 1999.

Lebra, Joyce Chapman. *Women's Voices in Hawaii.* Niwot: University Press of Colorado, 1991.

Manning, Caroline. *The Employment of Women in the Pineapple Canneries of Hawaii.* Washington, D.C.: USGPO, 1930.

Matsuda, Mari J., ed. *Called from Within: Early Women Lawyers of Hawai'i.* Honolulu: University of Hawaii Press, 1992.

Merry, Sally Engle. *Colonizing Hawaii: The Cultural Power of Law.* Princeton, N.J.: Princeton University Press, 2000.

Mrantz, Maxine. *Women of Old Hawaii.* Honolulu, Hawaii: Aloha Graphics and Sales, 1975.

Nunes, Shiho S. *The Shishu Ladies of Hilo: Japanese Embroidery in Hawai'i.* Honolulu: University of Hawaii Press, 1999.

Patterson, Wayne. *The Ilse: First-generation Korean Immigrants in Hawaii, 1903–1973.* Honolulu: University of Hawaii Press, 2000.

Saiki, Patsy Sumie. *Japanese Women in Hawaii: The First 100 Years.* Honolulu, Hawaii: Kisaku, 1985.

Sauvin, Georges. *A Tree in Bud: The Hawaiian Kingdom, 1889–1893.* Honolulu: University of Hawaii Press, 1987.

Stanton, Elizabeth Cady, Susan B. Anthony, and Matilda Joslyn Gage. *History of Woman Suffrage.* Vols. 1–3. Rochester, N.Y.: Charles Mann Printing, 1886.

Van Sant, John E. *Pacific Pioneers: Japanese Journeys to America and Hawaii, 1850–80.* Urbana: University of Illinois Press, 2000.

Watts, Margit Misangyi. *High Tea at Halekulani: Feminist Theory and American Clubwomen.* Brooklyn, N.Y.: Carlson Publishing, 1993.

Young, Kanalu G. Terry. *Rethinking the Native Hawaiian Past.* New York: Garland Publishing, 1998.

Young, Nancy Foon, and Judy R. Parrish, eds. *Montage: An Ethnic History of Women in Hawaii.* Honolulu, Hawaii: State Commission on the Status of Women, 1977.

Zwiep, Mary. *Pilgrim Path: The First Company of Women Missionaries to Hawaii.* Madison: University of Wisconsin Press, 1991.

AUTOBIOGRAPHY AND BIOGRAPHY

Allen, Helena G. *The Betrayal of Liliuokalani, Last Queen of Hawaii, 1838–1917.* Glendale, Calif.: A. H. Clark, 1982.

Davidson, Sue. *A Heart in Politics: Jeannette Rankin and Patsy T. Mink.* Seattle, Wash.: Seal Press, 1994.

Gale Research. *Notable Asian Americans.* Detroit, Mich., 1995.

Kanahele, George S. *Emma: Hawaii's Remarkable Queen.* Honolulu, Hawaii: Queen Emma Foundation, 1999.

Kingston, Maxine Hong. *Hawaii One Summer.* Honolulu: University of Hawaii Press, 1998.

Mellen, Kathleen Dickenson. *The Magnificent Matriarch, Kaahumanu, Queen of Hawaii.* New York: Hastings House, 1952.

Peterson, Barbara Bennett, ed. *Notable Women of Hawaii.* Honolulu: University of Hawaii Press, 1984.

Sobrero, Gina. *An Italian Baroness in Hawai'i: The Travel Diary of Gina Sobrero, Bride of Robert Wilcox, 1887.* Honolulu: Hawaiian Historical Society, 1991.

Yardley, Maili. *Queen Kapiolani.* Honolulu, Hawaii: Topgallant Publishing, 1985.

USEFUL WEB SITES

Bishop Museum
http://www.bishopmuseum.org/history.html
"The Folio of 1855—A Plea For Women's Rights"
http://www.hawaiianhistory.org/moments/folio.html
"Hawaii's Story by Hawaii's Queen," A Celebration of Women Writers
http://digital.library.upenn.edu/women/liliuokalani/hawaii/hawaii.html
Hawaii State Commission on the Status of Women
http://www.state.hi.us/hscsw
Hawaii Women's Heritage Project
http://www.soc.hawaii.edu/hwhp
"History of the Hawaiian Monarch"
http://www.aloha.net/~rodney/page11.html
'Iolani Palace
http://www.iolanipalace.org
"Mary Elizabeth Pruett Farrington," Women in Congress
http://bioguide.gov/congresswomen/index.asp
"The Royal Family of Hawaii"
http://www.royalty.nu/America/Hawaii.html
"Occupations," University of Hawaii, Manoa—Center for Oral History
http://www2.soc.hawaii.edu/css/oral_hist/occupa.html

SELECTED ORGANIZATIONS AND INSTITUTIONS

The Hawaiian Collection
University of Hawaii at Manoa Library
2550 The Mall
Honolulu, HI 96822
Telephone: (808) 956 8264

Web: http://www2.hawaii.edu/~speccoll/hawaii.html
A comprehensive collection of retrospective and current materials pertaining to Hawaii, the library offers more than 133,500 volumes relating to Hawaiian history, culture, art, and science.

Hawaiian Historical Society
560 Kawaiaha'o Street
Honolulu, HI 96813
Telephone: (808) 537 6271
Web: http://www.hawaiianhistory.org/index.html
The society's library includes a research collection of printed and manuscript material for use by scholars, historians, and others in the community interested in the history of Hawaii and the Pacific Island area.

Hawaii State Archives
Kekauluohi Building
Iolani Palace Grounds
Honolulu, HI 96813
Telephone: (808) 586 0329
Web: http://www.state.hi.us/dags/archives
Collections include government records from the monarchy to the current legislative session, private collections of individuals and organizations, historical photographs, maps, and library collections specializing in Hawaiian history, culture, and Pacific voyages.

University of Hawaii–Manoa Library
2550 McCarthy Mall
Honolulu, HI 96822
Telephone: (808) 956 7205
Web: http://libweb.hawaii.edu/uhmlib/index.htm
Online gateway to a directory and library catalog.

University of Hawaii–Manoa Women's Studies Program
College of Social Sciences
University of Hawaii at Manoa
Social Sciences Building 722
2424 Maile Way
Honolulu, HI 96822
Telephone: (808) 956 7464
Web: http://www2.soc.hawaii.edu/ws
Aims to expand and challenge the existing curriculum and to provide an intellectual home for the majority of female students on the university's campus.

IDAHO

Beside our house, painted the same umber red as other shacks built by local loggers on company land, flowed the water from the spring, and from its constant source we took our water. . . . A narrow footbridge crossed the spring to the path leading to the outhouse. . . . Beyond the outhouse the trees grew dense, and the little building seemed the last safe place before the forest closed in.
—Kim Barnes, *In the Wilderness: Coming of Age in Unknown Country,* 1996.

When Idaho became a territory in 1863, men outnumbered women by 30 to 1. Historically, a shortage of women on the frontier was beneficial to the political status of women. Men encouraged women to move to new territories by offering them more freedom and opportunity than was typical in the rest of the country. Idaho exemplified this trend by being the fifth state to grant women the right to vote. While early records exhibit a relatively high level of gender equality, Idaho's contemporary record on women's issues and achievements is diminished relative to other states.

banged in front and sometimes tied at the back." Their skirts were "never short, and they liked bright shawls, wearing them pulled over their heads so their faces were half hidden." (Federal Writers' Project 1937, 353)

After the introduction of horses to North America by the Spanish, the Shoshone hunted

State Population (2000): 1,293,953

Female Population (2000): 645,293

Women in State Legislature (2003): 25.7%

Female College Enrollment (1999): 36,000 (55.4% of total)

Privately Held Women-owned Businesses (1997): 25,763

First Year of Full Suffrage: 1896

PREHISTORY TO TERRITORIAL STATUS
(Prehistory–1863)

Idaho's two major Native American groups were the Shoshone in the south and the Nez Percé in the north. Some Paiutes, who were centered in Nevada, also lived at the southern fringe of the area. The Paiutes, the poorest of western tribes, had no permanent villages. Within Idaho's major groups were various seminomadic clans, members of which traveled between seasonal sources of food when the weather allowed. They camped in tepees in the summer and lived in semipermanent housing in the winter.

Rivers and their annual spring runs of salmon were especially important to the Nez Percé. Women dried the fish, gathered berries and nuts, and dug camas bulbs, which provided a starchy, onionlike vegetable for their meals. The women were described by whites as having "long hair, sometimes

buffalo and developed an economy similar to that of Native Americans of the Plains, who lived a nomadic lifestyle. Shoshone men and women exhibited their relative equality by wearing similar clothing made by women, which elicited praise from many observers. Early explorer Meriwether Lewis called their ceremonial robes, which were made of otter and ermine fur, "the most elegant Indian garment" that he had encountered. (Federal Writers' Project 1937, 353)

As in most tribes, women owned tepees and any articles that they made, and both women and men functioned as healers and spiritual advisers. Shoshone women were free to make their own marital choices, and many accepted white men—especially French Canadians—as partners.

The lifestyle of the native women prepared them well for becoming guides and interpreters to the expeditions of whites that came through Idaho. SACAGAWEA, perhaps the most famous, was a guide to the Lewis and Clark Expedition. Other women did the same, especially MARIE DORION, whose trip from Missouri to the Pacific was longer and much more difficult than that of Sacagawea.

In 1824 a British settlement led by Alexander Ross brought hundreds of nonwhite newcomers to the territory, including women from 11 different tribes. Peter Skene Ogden, who replaced Ross, was married to an Indian woman named Julia Rivet. Her wilderness skills were said to be equal to her husband's; she and their young children traveled with him on numerous ventures.

The first white woman to settle in Idaho was Eliza Hart Spalding, who had married Henry Spalding in the chapel of Ohio's Western Reserve College in 1833. The Spaldings moved to Cincinnati's Lane Theological Seminary, one of the country's most liberal educational institutions at the time. There Eliza not only ran a student boardinghouse to support her husband, Henry, but also learned Greek and attended lectures by

the seminary's president, Rev. Lyman Beecher, father of Harriet Beecher Stowe.

At an earlier time Henry Spalding had known a young woman named Narcissa Prentiss and had proposed to her, but had been rejected. The American Board for Foreign Missions selected Prentiss and Dr. Marcus Whitman, the man she did choose as her husband, as well as the Spaldings, to be the first American missionary couples to serve Native Americans in the Far West. During their 1836 trip west, Narcissa Whitman and Eliza Spalding became the first white women to cross the Continental Divide. While the Whitmans settled near Walla Walla, Washington, the Spaldings lived near what became the Idaho town of Lewiston.

The Spaldings emphasized practical, agrarian arts that would help the Nez Percé adjust to a changing world. In addition to the usual mission school, they also built mills for sawing lumber and grinding corn and even imported a printing press. Idaho's first white child, born in 1837, was named for her mother, and Eliza Spalding went on to have three more children. While raising her children, she taught domestic skills to Nez Percé women and painted pictures of biblical scenes for the classes she taught. The mission board soon sent six other women to expand its work in the region. One of them was Sarah Smith, who established a mission with her husband Asa Smith on the Clearwater River.

More and more whites came into the area in the 1840s, which upset Native Americans. The Nez Percé, however, so admired Eliza Spalding that they protected her and her children when Cayuse killed the Whitmans in 1847. Henry Spalding was absent at the time but when he returned, he and his family relocated to Oregon. Eliza died there of tuberculosis in 1851. Her family eventually returned to Idaho.

Jesuits also established missions during this time, but they brought no Catholic women and had a far smaller long-term effect than the Mormons, who began their first mission in 1855. Church elders headquartered at Salt Lake encouraged the missionaries, most of whom were single, to marry Native American women and thus further the faith, but the intended brides seem to have found Mormon men undesirable. Idaho's residents were accustomed to a matrilineal society in which women had appreciable freedom. In contrast to the Native American woman's willingness to wed French men, none appears to have married a Mormon. The conversion-through-marriage approach was such a failure that the mission was abandoned.

When the Mormons began colonizing the area again in 1860, they sent a wagon train filled with both men and women. These settlers established Franklin, Idaho's oldest town, and other settlers soon followed. Eventually Idaho would have a greater percentage of Mormons in its population than any state except Utah. Although Mormonism offered no leadership positions to women, its communal, protective life-style had appeal for some. Scandinavian and English women, in particular, traveled thousands of miles to marry Mormons and spread the faith in southern Idaho.

During this period many men came to Idaho lured by the promise of gold. In 1849 alone, 20,000 people headed west on the Oregon Trail to California or Alaska, and gold strikes in Idaho during the next decades brought more men. Women also mined occasionally, but more of them worked in boardinghouses and brothels. A number of the brothels were made up of Chinese women who were kept like slaves for Chinese miners, men who were only a step above slavery themselves.

As whites panned their rivers and plowed their land, initially hospitable Native Americans resisted, which invited retaliation. In January 1863 cavalrymen killed approximately 400 Shoshone, many of them women and children, in what is termed the battle of Bear River.

In response to both the Civil War and Native American uprisings, Congress established the Idaho Territory on March 4, 1863. Its borders, however, would not be finalized until the end of the decade. At this time Idaho included all of Montana, most of Wyoming, and parts of other future states. The name of the new territory also caused appreciable debate in Congress, and some records indicate that it was Luzena Wallace who named the state of Idaho. A North Carolina native, she would become Idaho's first first lady when her husband was appointed territorial governor by his friend, Pres. Abraham Lincoln.

This vast new territory—larger than the current size of Texas—had a nonnative population of 30,559 men and 1,089 women.

TERRITORIAL STATUS TO STATEHOOD (1863–1890)

The Civil War, raging thousands of miles away, meant little to the people of the large Idaho territory. In 1863 wagon trains from Arkansas and Missouri transported women to Idaho, eager to escape the strife in their home states. When the wagons stopped at Boise, the unmarried women were inundated with immediate marriage proposals. Most settled there, and Boise became the capital city in 1865. The following year telegraph lines brought the communication age to Idaho, sooner than to other frontiers. However, it was not until 1874 that railroads would reach Idaho. Instead, the 1870s regressed to frontier warfare.

The Nez Percé made their dramatic last stand during five months of 1877. The Spaldings had converted the Nez Percé Chief Joseph, whose tribe had a long history of accommodation to whites, but when trespassers on reservation land found gold, Gen. Oliver O. Howard gave the Nez Percé 30 days to vacate. With their livestock, some 800 attempted to comply, but rain-swollen rivers forced them to change routes repeatedly, while the army continued to bear down upon them. While trying to flee to Canada, they held off the professional soldiers in 18 skirmishes. In the battle of Big Hole River, for example, 70 Nez Percé died; the majority were women and children. Just 40 miles short of their Canadian goal, the U.S. Army attacked again at Bear Paw Mountain. After traveling 1,500 miles, Chief Joseph announced that he would no longer fight, and his once-proud tribe was taken captive. Only 87 men, 184 women, and 147 children remained alive, and many of them would die in exile in Oklahoma.

Just months after the Nez Percé defeat, the military switched its attention to what is termed the 1878 Bannock War in southern Idaho. Bannocks were a Paiute clan, and Nevada's Sarah Winnemucca, a Paiute, played a significant role in this conflict as a scout and diplomat. She spoke English, Spanish, and three Native American

Two Nez Percé women in ceremonial dress, ca. 1890, less than 20 years after the Nez Percé were dispersed from their Idaho reservation. (MSCUA, Univ. of Wash. Libraries, L92-86.74)

languages and would go on to national fame as an advocate for the Native American cause.

Idaho's Indian wars ended by a final conflict with the remote people called Sheepeaters, and the 1880s would be the transition decade to statehood. Although the territory had been created in 1863, Idaho lacked any legal code for three years after, because the San Francisco printer refused to release the law books until his fee was paid. In some respects Idaho was an unruly place, where some women supported themselves as "hurdy-gurdy girls" in saloons. Not typically prostitutes, these women charged men for dancing, a fee of 50 cents per dance, plus a 50-cent drink. They were the very antitheses of Mormon women, who also lived in the area. As a result, Idaho developed two highly distinct cultures in close proximity.

Although most Idahoans were tolerant of these different cultures, when Congress made polygamy illegal in 1882, Idaho's federal marshal set about enforcing this law. Historians estimate that no more than 3% of Idaho's Mormons were polygamists, but hundreds of arrest warrants were issued and many Mormon men went into hiding, leaving their women with considerable economic responsibilities. Law enforcement officials ignored the violence associated with this gun-and-saloon culture and focused instead on the validity of Mormon marriages.

Other Idaho minorities included the Basques from northern Spain. Basque men were recruited as shepherds, and after establishing themselves, they typically arranged marriages to Basque women by mail. By 1870 Idaho also had more than 4,000 Chinese residents, who were mostly men imported in groups for dangerous jobs in mines and on railroad constructions. Almost all left their wives in China, where women might live for decades without knowing whether or not their husbands would return. The few Chinese women who did come nearly always were brought to the United States as sexual slaves. If they survived,

POLLY BEMIS: PIONEER FROM CHINA

Polly Bemis was a Chinese pioneer woman who lived in Idaho for more than 60 years. Her story has intrigued and inspired succeeding generations, because she conquered adversity and enjoyed a happy, productive life. Born in northern China in 1853, sold by her starving parents, smuggled into the United States, and sold for $2,500 to a Chinese man whose concubine she became, Polly arrived in mountainous Warren, Idaho, in 1872. A romanticized version of the story of her life states that Charlie Bemis later "won her in a poker game," but Polly denied this claim before she died.

The 1880 census lists Polly as a widow, sharing a house with Bemis. While her Chinese first name is unknown, her August 1894 marriage certificate named her "Polly Nathoy." Although some people have called her "Lalu" in books and film, there is currently no evidence of that name. From Warren the couple moved down to the Salmon River where Bemis had a mining claim. There Polly raised fruits and vegetables and kept chickens for eggs, while her husband hunted animals for meat. Being a Chinese woman married to a Caucasian man, she fascinated the miners and tourists who visited their remote home. Her story, publicized in newspapers and in a national magazine, made her a minor celebrity during her lifetime. Despite her marriage to an American, she would never become a U.S. citizen since, prior to 1943, U.S. law denied citizenship to emigrants from Asia.

In August 1922 fire destroyed the Bemis home. A neighbor helped save Charlie Bemis, who was then bedridden, and the couple stayed there. Bemis died in October and was buried at the neighbor's ranch. Polly lived in Warren until her home was rebuilt in 1924. In August 1933 she became very ill and died that November in the Grangeville, Idaho, hospital at age 80. Her home is now a museum and is listed on the National Register of Historic Places. Her remains, exhumed from the Grangeville cemetery, rest nearby.

—Priscilla Wegars

Excerpt from Priscilla Wegars, "Polly Bemis: Lurid Life or Literary Legend?" In *Wild Women of the Old West*, edited by Richard W. Etulain and Glenda Riley. Golden, Colo.: Fulcrum, 2003.

some of these women could eventually manage to create good lives for themselves.

When Idaho prepared for statehood, suffrage leader Abigail Scott Duniway of Oregon appealed to both the 1887 territorial legislature and the 1889 state constitutional convention to include women. Duniway's newspaper, *The New Northwest,* had many subscribers in Idaho, and Boise's *Daily Statesman* publishers, Mr. and Mrs. Milton Kelly, also supported suffrage. Although most politicians said they agreed, they were not prepared to take on the issue at a time when Congress had repealed women's suffrage in Utah. On July 3, 1890, Idaho became the 43rd state without women as full citizens.

PROGRESSIVE ERA
(1890–1920)

Women met in a country schoolhouse at Hagerman, Idaho, in 1893 to organize a suffrage society. The teacher who offered her classroom, Elizabeth Ingram, was elected president, and Helen Young, Idaho's first female attorney, was an officer. They set to work lobbying the political parties to include suffrage in their platforms. Liberal Republican William E. Borah, who later would become Idaho's U.S. senator, introduced the suffrage plank at the 1894 state convention, and within two years, all four of Idaho's political parties had endorsed the vote for women.

The national suffrage association sent Emma Smith DeVoe of Illinois, who lined up legislative sponsors, and by an overwhelming margin, the issue was put on the 1896 ballot. DeVoe consciously kept the campaign low-key, holding no rallies or parades, and instead choosing the more demure strategy of selling a cookbook to raise funds. By the time that the liquor and gambling interests—typical opponents of women's suffrage in many states—were aware of her motives, she had signed up 2,000 dues-paying members of the suffrage association, which in political terms was a considerable number in a population of less than 90,000.

With support from Laura Johns of Kansas, Mary C. C. Bradford of Colorado, and national suffrage president Carrie Chapman Catt, Idaho women opened a headquarters at Boise. They recruited women in every county to work the polls, and did such a good job of publicity that 62 of the state's 65 newspapers advocated suffrage, which won by 12,126 to 6,282 votes. The women carried every county in the state except Custer, where pioneer western suffragist Abigail Scott Duniway had once lived.

Some conservative opponents, however, went to court, arguing that the measure required a majority of all electors, rather than the majority who actually voted on the issue. William Borah and other attorneys defended the women's victory before the Idaho supreme court, and for the first time in the history of the suffrage movement, a court gave women their legitimate win. Unlike Washington and other states where courts threw out suffrage victories on technicalities, Idaho's judiciary ruled that the voters' will should prevail.

In the 1898 election Republican Clara Campbell, Democrat Hattie Noble, and Populist Mary Allen Wright were elected to the legislature. Four women won elections as county treasurers; 15 won races for county school superintendents, and Permeal Jane French won the statewide election for superintendent of public instruction. Idaho was thus the second state to elect a woman to statewide office, following only North Dakota. By 1900 three women served as deputy sheriffs. Women also were appointed to the board of regents for the state university, which had been open to female students since its 1891 opening.

But things began to change with the 1900 legislature, which passed a bill exempting women from jury service. Eunice Pond Athey, secretary of the state suffrage association, wrote, "[W]hile the ostensible object was to relieve them [women] of an onerous duty, the real one was to protect the gamblers and other law-breakers to whom women jurors show no favor." (Anthony and Harper 1902, 4:596) Although Gov. Frank W. Hunt vetoed the bill as women requested, it was an indication of things to come, because the 20th century would prove more conservative than the 19th century had. Only three more women were elected to the legislature during the next 20 years.

Like unenfranchised women in other states, Idaho women worked for the goals of the General Federation of Women's Clubs. Idaho had about 15 such clubs, which achieved appreciable local success, especially in establishing libraries. During World War I Idaho women joined others across the nation in war-support activities such as knitting and food conservation. Some women worked at nontraditional jobs, including working for the railroad in Pocatello. Approximately 150 women there did everything from running drill presses and lathes to cleaning cars.

In 1920, when the 19th Amendment that granted all American women the vote went to the states for ratification, Idaho women had been voting for 24 years. The Idaho House of Representatives ratified the amendment unanimously, and the ratification passed the Senate, although six senators voted against their female constituents.

1920s THROUGH WORLD WAR II ERA (1920–1950)

Of the many innovations of the 1920s, electricity and automobiles may have been the most important. For rural women these modern advances were especially transforming. Electrical appliances made housework infinitely easier and quicker, giving women time for activities beyond the menial ones. Cars also were liberating for rural women, who traditionally had limited access to transportation. Farm women, in general, began driving sooner than women from the city, and Idaho did not require a driver's license until 1935.

Middle-class tourism began with cars, and in 1931 Sister Alfreda Elsensohn, a retired Benedictine nun, took advantage of this trend. She founded a museum in the north-central Idaho town of Cottonwood in order to display Idaho artifacts. Other exceptional women of the era include horsewoman KITTY WILKINS, reputedly a millionaire from the sale of thoroughbreds, and Emma Yearian, a successful sheep rancher who was elected to the legislature in 1930.

As in other states, the Great Depression seriously affected Idaho. By 1933 incomes had plummeted by 50%. The state was so needy during these times that it would rank fifth on a list of federal expenditures per person. Most of this money, however, was spent in supporting jobs for men.

It was not until World War II that Idaho women were paid well for their work. Thousands were employed at Pocatello's Farragut Naval Training Station. Unmarried women lived in dormitories that were among the 776 buildings constructed there. Farragut, the largest such inland facility, was big enough that it was briefly Idaho's

---

LIFE IN THE MINIDOKA JAPANESE INTERNMENT CAMP

On February 18, 1942, just months after Japan bombed Hawaii's Pearl Harbor, Pres. Franklin D. Roosevelt signed Executive Order 9066, which called for the removal of 112,000 Japanese Americans from the West Coast. With wartime hysteria and distrust at a peak, men, women, and children of Japanese descent were forced to leave homes and jobs and report to internment camps throughout the United States. Among the ten major camps located in the interior West was Minidoka Relocation Center, situated on 33,000 desolate acres of land in south-central Idaho.

The Minidoka camp contained two elementary schools, a high school, a library, a 196-bed hospital, fire stations, a three-mile barracks area, and various warehouse-like buildings. Internee Tama Tokuda writes of her family's arrival at Minidoka:

As we climbed down from the buses with our name tags, clutching our only worldly possessions, we were greeted by friends who had preceded us, their faces and heads tied with white rags and handkerchiefs to ward off the fine dust that swirled around us. We were led to an unfinished tar-papered barrack where we hung up blankets between the families that were going to share the first night together.

Living conditions were cramped. In the Relocation Center Diary, Arthur Klienkopf, Superintendent of Education–Minidoka Relocation Center, writes:

There were six apartments which housed 20 people. There was a family of 9 in a one-room apartment, size 20ft x 20ft. . . . there were 16 families of 8 or 9 persons living in those one room apartments. Blankets suspended from the ceiling served as partitions. . . .

Minidoka weather ranged from –21°F in the winter of 1942 to 104°F in the summer of the same year. The August 1942 diary of internee Toku Shimomura reads:

I boiled in the 110 degree heat and found it difficult to function. Lunch was stew and rice pudding. Supper was macaroni and chocolate pudding. . . . What a view! I have never seen such a dust storm. I stayed in my room and looked out the window. It was so dark we were all afraid to move. Pessimistic words came out of everyone's mouth. We were sent to such a harsh place.

Despite the harsh conditions, Minidoka was considered to be one of the better camps, with lighter security and more activities available for internees. The internees formed bands, choirs, orchestras, sports teams, and a local paper, *The Minidoka Irrigator*.

On December 18, 1944, the War Relocation Authority announced all internment camps would close by the end of 1945. The following January, nearly three years after Executive Order 9066 was issued, Minidoka internees returned to the West Coast. And finally, on October 23, 1945, the Minidoka Relocation Center closed.

—Courtney Garnaas

Excerpts from: Tama Tokuda, "A Journey Back to the Beginning of an Emotional Relationship." *International Examiner*, 6 November 1985, 4.
"Toku Shimomura's Diary: A Chronology of Japanese American Internment."
http://www.microsoft.com/mscorp/artcollection/exhibitions/sep_dec/roger4.htm
Arthur Klienkopf, Relocation Center Diary.
http://www.friendsofminidoka.org/history/ww2internment.asp

largest city. Almost 300,000 sailors attended classes there, many of them taught by the WAVES, the pioneering U.S. Navy female branch. Other women who came to Idaho during the war were not there by choice: about 10,000 Japanese Americans were interned at several different camps in Idaho, including many women who were held at the Minidoka Relocation Area in southern Idaho.

POSTWAR AND CONTEMPORARY ERAS (1950–present)

It was during the postwar years that Idaho had its only long-term congresswoman, GRACIE PFOST, who devoted her entire life to public service. She served as a member of the House of Representatives from 1953 to 1962.

While feminism surged in the rest of the nation in the late 1960s and 1970s, Idaho's movement regressed. In the 1971 case of *Reed v. Reed*, Idaho's attorney general went all the way to the U.S. Supreme Court defending a law that gave male family members automatic preference over females as executors of estates. The Court, however, struck down Idaho's law as unconstitutional. Later in the decade, in 1977, Idaho's legislators rescinded their ratification of the Equal Rights Amendment (ERA), which was an extremely rare thing for a legislature to do.

AMY TRICE AND THE KOOTENAI TRIBE

In 1974 Amy Trice, the chairperson of the Kootenai in Idaho, declared war on the United States. In the spirit of the Indian Rights movement then under way in various parts of the country, Trice was determined to protest against what many considered to be the unfairness and neglect of the Kootenai by the federal government.

As late as the 1930s, the impoverished Kootenai people lived in tepees near Bonners Ferry, Idaho. At the time a local physician persuaded the government to build 18 houses for the small tribe. By the 1970s however, conditions for the 65-member Kootenai tribe had barely improved. There were no jobs available, only a few houses remained, elders were sick, and the future was bleak for the tribe's children. Additionally, the federal Bureau of Indian Affairs would not help, saying that the small size of the tribe disqualified it for assistance.

On September 20, 1974, after consulting with her people, Amy Trice and the Kootenai declared war on the United States. In an interview with the Public Broadcasting System (PBS) in 1989, Trice said it was not a "full-scale blood and gut war, but a war with the mind, with the pen." To raise money the tribe printed Kootenai Nation War Bonds, and members placed a toll-booth on the state highway near Bonners Ferry, where young people solicited donations for the Kootenai cause from travelers. This activity attracted TV reporters, and shortly thereafter the state police, concerned with potential

violence, began monitoring the Kootenai. One night, the police mounted a spotlight on the tribal office door. An elder Kootenai woman, determined to give the police the show they were seeking, undid her braids and danced while boys drummed and sang. "Word got out that we were on the warpath. . . . All we had was just a fly-swatter!"

The notoriety brought results. The commissioner of Indian affairs went to Idaho and negotiated Amy Trice's war demands. With the help of grants and loans, the road on the tribe's land was improved and housing structures were built. Trice said:

> The first batch of 13 houses were beautifully built and nice. We have a home now, and [land] on which the houses and [new] center are located. It's not a gift. Some people think, "Those Indians have everything free, they get monthly checks." We don't get monthly checks. We pay for our homes. We paid for these. We borrow and we work just like anyone else. If given the chance we pay our debts back.

Since 1974 the Kootenai tribe's lands have grown from 12 acres to 3,985 acres, and their membership has grown to 164. The tribe operates a medical center, a tribal school, a sturgeon fish hatchery, a hotel, and a casino. Amy Trice's son, Gary Aitken, succeeded his mother as tribal chairperson.

—Susan M. Stacy

Excerpt from Susan M. Stacy, *A Companion Book to Idaho Public Television's "Proceeding on through a Beautiful Country."* Boise: Idaho Educational Public Broadcasting Foundation, 1990.

Republican Helen Chenoweth, the second woman from Idaho to be elected to the U.S. House of Representatives, with Sen. Larry Craig in a GOP victory celebration on election night, 1996. (AP/Wide World Photos)

In 1992 Idaho had its first woman on the state supreme court, when Linda Copple Trout was appointed. She rose to the position of chief justice in 1997. In 1994 Idaho elected its second female member of Congress, Republican HELEN CHENOWETH. A constitutional scholar, she was the target of harsh criticism for her extreme antienvironmental and progun views. She also opposed organized feminism and insisted on being called "congressman." She won reelection in 1998, but in October 2000, she announced her return to private life.

Linda Pall, a city council member in the university town of Moscow, was the Democratic nominee to replace her, but she lost to Republican Butch Otter. Idaho's top leadership was, as of 2003, all male, except for State Superintendent of Public Instruction Marilyn Howard.

—Doris Weatherford

TIMELINE

United States Events		Idaho Events
	1600	
1620 Settlement of Plymouth Colony		
	1700	
1776 United States declares independence		
	1800	
		1805 Sacagawea joins Lewis and Clark expedition, which travels through Idaho.
		1814 Marie Dorion becomes the first woman to escort white men all the way to the Pacific.
		1836 Eliza Spalding becomes the first white woman to settle in Idaho.
1861–65 U.S. Civil War		1863 Idaho gains territorial status.
		1877 The last stance of the Nez Percé, under Chief Joseph.
		1890 Idaho gains statehood.
		1893 Elizabeth Ingram, Helen Young, and others form state suffrage society.
		1896 Women win the right to vote.
1914–18 World War I	**1900**	
1920 Ratification of the 19th Amendment		1920 Idaho ratifies the 19th Amendment.
1929–39 Great Depression		
1939–45 World War II		
		1953–62 Gracie Pfost, Idaho's longest term member of U.S. Congress, serves as Idaho's representative.
		1974 Kootenai tribal chairperson Amy Trice declares war on U.S. government to call attention to the tribe's problems.
1975 Vietnam War ends		1977 Idaho rescinds its ratification of the Equal Rights Amendment.
		1992 Linda Copple Trout is first woman appointed to state supreme court.
		1994 Helen Chenoweth becomes second woman elected to Congress.
		1997 Trout becomes chief justice of state supreme court.
	2000	2003 Superintendent of Public Instruction Marilyn Howard is the only woman in a top state position.

PROMINENT WOMEN

HELEN CHENOWETH (1938–)

A successful grassroots organizer, U.S. congress-woman Helen Chenoweth of Topeka, Kansas, earned a reputation for demanding accountability in government. She grew up in Burlingame, Kansas, an agrarian community. During World War II, her parents moved the family to Culver City, California. A graduate of Whitworth College in Spokane, Washington, and the University of Minnesota, she entered politics as the manager of congressional campaigns. At age 26, she opened a legal and medical management consulting firm, for which she lectured at the University of Idaho's School of Law and recruited doctors for the state's rural areas. From 1975 to 1977 she was executive director of the Idaho Republican party. Until 1978 she served as Congressman Steve Symms's chief of staff. She established Consulting Associates Incorporated, a Washington, D.C., lobby for the environment, energy, and natural resources.

From a landslide at the polls in November 1994, Chenoweth initiated the first of three terms in the U.S. House of Representatives, where she served as committeewoman in agriculture, resources, and veterans' affairs. Although outspokenly supportive of the evangelical movement and opposed to abortion, the protection of endangered species, and gun control, she presented herself as typical of Idaho's mainstream. Because she supported right-wing militias, the *Idaho Statesman* named her the "poster child" for militant conservative groups.

MARIE DORION (ca. 1786–1850)

Also called Marie of the Iowas, L'Aguivoise, or Dorion Woman, pioneer Marie Aioe Dorion earned the name "Madonna of the Oregon Trail" for being the first woman and mother to travel the route. At age 20, she married trading-post operator Pierre Dorion, Jr., of Yankton Sioux and French Canadian parentage, who harvested pelts for Manuel Lisa from St. Louis, Missouri, to the upper Dakotas. While working for fur magnate John Jacob Astor in March 1811, Pierre brought Marie and their two small sons, Jean Baptiste and Paul, ages five and two, on an extensive expedition, for which she served as guide, interpreter, and ambassador to local tribes. Two months before the party reached Astoria, Oregon, in February 1812, she gave birth to a third son, who died eight days later.

On the return trip, near the Boise River on January 10, 1814, Marie and her two sons were the only expedition members to survive Native American attacks. The rest of that winter, the trio was stranded in the Blue Mountains. To survive she slaughtered her horses, made camp under their hides spread over cedar boughs, smoked the meat, and snared mice and squirrels for additional food. Through a spring blizzard she and her sons walked for 15 days the 250 miles to eastern Washington to reunite with the Astor party.

Marie Dorion quit the expedition and moved north to Fort Okanogan, where she married Louis Joseph Venier, a trapper later killed by Native Americans. Her third husband, Jean Baptiste Toupin, was an interpreter at Walla Walla, Washington. Marie and her family were the first to settle French Prairie in the Willamette Valley, where she lived out the last 12 years of her life. Her oldest boy, Baptiste Dorion, interpreted for the Hudson's Bay Company. Her other son, Paul, accompanied historian Francis Parkman on his western expedition.

PERMEAL JANE FRENCH (1867–1954)

University administrator and politician Permeal Jane French was Idaho's first female electee in statewide office and the second woman in the nation to win a statewide election. Born to Irish Catholics in Idaho City, she earned a degree from the College of Notre Dame and taught public school in Idaho before completing postgraduate degrees from the University of Idaho and George Washington University. In 1898 she garnered the support of women's clubs when she successfully ran for a four-year term as superintendent of public instruction. This election made her the first Idaho woman elected to statewide office and the second in the country to do so. For state students, she produced worthy innovations, beginning with a uniform course outline and a statewide eighth-grade examination.

Five years later French was appointed the first dean of women at the University of Idaho. She added women's residence halls to the campus and, during the Great Depression, traveled the state to speak on the need for educating daughters as well as sons. In 1924 she built the Blue Bucket Inn, the school's first student center. At age 69, she retired to Seattle, Washington.

GRACIE PFOST (1906–1965)

Called "Idaho's First Lady of Politics," Democrat Gracie Bowers Pfost of Harrison, Arkansas, was the first woman in Idaho to serve in the U.S. Congress. Her family settled in the Boise Valley when she was five. She attended local schools and graduated in 1926 from Links Business University before working as a realtor and a chemist in the dairy industry. In 1923 she wed John Walter Pfost, who encouraged his wife's political career, which included multiple terms as deputy county clerk, auditor, recorder, and treasurer for Canyon County.

After a failed run for Congress, at age 47 Pfost applied her skill as a populist orator to win the first of five consecutive terms in the U.S. House of Representatives in 1952. As a legislator and committee member on issues of interior

affairs, irrigation and reclamation, post office and civil service, and mines and public lands, she promoted agriculture, mining of lead and zinc, and timber rights as well as lower taxes, federal aid to education, and greater social security coverage. For championing a dam at Hell's Canyon during the creation of the Wilderness Act, she earned the nickname "Hell's Belle." She also worked hard against the anticommunist ideology that characterized the House of Representatives in the early 1950s, walking out of a committee hearing in which witnesses were not allowed to defend themselves.

In 1962 Pfost ran unsuccessfully against Len B. Jordan for the U.S. Senate. The next year Pres. John F. Kennedy named her to the Federal Housing Administration to head Public Housing for the Elderly, a job she held for the last two years of her life. Pfost's volunteer service included women's clubs, Girl Scouts, Chamber of Commerce, and the Idaho Real Estate Board. On August 11, 1965, she died of Hodgkin's Disease near Baltimore, Maryland.

SACAGAWEA (ca. 1784–ca. 1812)

An interpreter and ambassador to Native American tribes during the Lewis and Clark Expedition in 1805, Sacagawea—also called Sacajawea, Sakakagawea, "Owl Woman," or "Bird Girl"—became the most honored female Native American in history. Born to a Lemhi Shoshone family near central Idaho, she was kidnapped at age 13 and enslaved by the Hidatsa Indians, who murdered and scalped her mother. At her captors' village in North Dakota, around age 20, she became the second of the two wives of Toussaint Charbonneau, a Sioux French Canadian trader who either bought her or won her at gambling. She gave birth to their son, Jean Baptiste "Pompey" Charbonneau, two months before the federal exploratory party set out in eight canoes from Fort Mandan for the Pacific Coast on April 7, 1805.

In addition to translating both Shoshone and Sioux and negotiating in sign language, Sacagawea established the party's friendly intentions by carrying her son on her back. She proved useful in numerous incidents on the way west, including cooking, sewing, trading for horses, and introducing the party to edible and medicinal roots and herbs.

In August 1805 she reunited with her brother Cameahwait, who had become a chief among Idaho's Shoshone. She spent the winter with her family in Idaho, while Shoshone men escorted the expedition to the Pacific. Sacagawea returned with them to North Dakota the following year. The rest of her life is unclear. She appears to have reared her son alone and probably died at age 28 of fever shortly after the birth of a daughter, Lizette. One version of her life story describes her reuniting with her tribe in Wyoming and dying at age 100. In 2000 New Mexican sculptor Glenna Goodacre created a U.S. dollar coin honoring Sacagawea.

LAUREL THATCHER ULRICH (1938–)

Author and feminist historian Laurel Thatcher Ulrich of Sugar City, Idaho, won the Bancroft Prize and Pulitzer Prize for incisive studies of colonial American women. Educated at the University of Utah (B.A. in 1960), Simmons College (M.A. in 1971), and the University of New Hampshire (Ph.D. in 1980), she taught English and history while rearing five children and supporting the Mormon Relief Society, a benevolent outreach of church women. At age 42, she joined the history staff at the University of New Hampshire.

Ulrich began publishing with a coauthored text, *A Beginner's Boston* (1970), and contributed articles to *Feminist Studies, Ensign,* and *Dialogue* publications. In a painstaking refutation of stereotypes about colonial New England, she combed court records, diaries, and legal papers for data to incorporate in *Good Wives: Image and Reality in the Lives of Women in Early New England,*

1650–1750 (1982), which characterized women's roles in the economy, agriculture, fiber work, child-rearing and education, and religion. She won a MacArthur genius grant in 1974 and later attained fame for authoring *A Midwife's Tale: The Life of Martha Ballard, Based on Her Diary, 1785–1812* (1990), a commentary on a Maine midwife and herbalist interlaced with citations from Ballard's diary. Because of her feminist stance on ordaining women as priests, in 1993 the male Mormon hierarchy refused to invite her to address a conclave of Mormon women. In 2001 Ulrich produced *The Age of Homespun: Objects and Stories in the Creation of an American Myth* (2001). She became Phillips Professor of Early American History at Harvard University and director of the Charles Warren Center for Studies in American History.

KITTY WILKINS (1857–1936)

Called the "Idaho Horse Queen," Kitty Wilkins was a frontierswoman, rancher, and horse dealer. A settler of Mountain Home, Idaho, a crossroads of the American West, in the 1890s she built up commerce on the Oregon Trail in the years following Idaho's admission to the Union. She established a livestock business respected as far east as the Mississippi River. Her skill at breeding saddle horses resulted in a herd of 4,000 steeds that supplied combat animals to the U.S. Cavalry.

Although Wilkins was known to ride sidesaddle in an elegant upswept hairdo and equestrian outfits, at her ranch at Glenn's Ferry she rejected a traditional female role. She trained her own colts and personally escorted them to market by boxcar, from which she auctioned them off to buyers in rail yards. After the outbreak of World War I, she shipped thousands of horses from Idaho's Bruneau Desert to combat zones in Europe. As a result of her success in husbandry and breeding, Mountain Home earned a reputation as the West's horse capital.

—Mary Ellen Snodgrass

PROMINENT SITES

1870 Idaho State Penitentiary
2445 Old Penitentiary Road
Boise, ID 83712
Telephone: (208) 368 6080
This penitentiary opened in 1870 and is on the National Registry of Historic Places. The first female inmate was seven months pregnant and was forced to live with male prisoners because the officials did not anticipate that women would be sent to jail. This woman's story, along with those of the other female inmates, is chronicled in the tour of the museum.

Historical Museum at St. Gertrude's
Monastery of St. Gertrude
Cottonwood, ID 83522–9408
Telephone: (208) 962 3224
Web: http://www.stgertrudes.org
The 70-year-old museum is one of the oldest in the West. It celebrates the heritage of north-central Idaho, including that of many of the women important in the area's history, such as Frances Zaunmiller-Wisner, the proprietor of Campbell's Ferry in the Salmon River Wilderness starting in 1942, and Polly Bemis, a Chinese slave who was brought to the area in 1872.

Idaho Black History Museum
Julia Davis Park
508 North Julia Davis Drive
Boise, ID 83702
Telephone: (208) 433 0017
Web: http://www.ibhm.org/Home.htm
This small museum presents a series of temporary exhibits every year, many of which include subject matter relating to the history of women in Idaho. Also, every year, from February to March, the museum presents an exhibit on women's history.

Idaho Highway Historical Marker Guide
Idaho Transportation Department
Office of Public Affairs
PO Box 7129
Boise, ID 83707
Web: http://www2.state.id.us/itd/hmg/HMGindex.htm
Women who are honored with markers on this highway circuit include the following: Emma Edwards, the only woman to design a state seal in America; Sacagawea, who acted as a guide to the Lewis and Clark expedition; and Marie Dorion, the only woman to join the 3,500-mile Wilson Price Expedition of 1811 and the first woman to travel the Oregon Trail.

Idaho Historical Museum
610 North Julia Davis Drive
Boise, ID 83702
Telephone: (208) 334 2120
Web: http://www.idahohistory.net/museum.html
The museum hosts many exhibits each March celebrating Women's History Month. An *Idaho Suffragette* exhibit is displayed the majority of the time, and the museum offers exhibits on the Native Americans who lived in what is now Idaho as well as on the Chinese and Basque populations throughout the state's history. The museum is operated by the Idaho Historical Society.

Lemhi County Historical Museum
210 Main Street
Salmon, ID 83467
Telephone: (208) 756 3342
Web: http://sacajaweahome.com/boardnmuseum.htm
Lemhi County is the birthplace of Sacagawea, the guide who led Lewis and Clark on their expedition to the West Coast of North America. The museum possesses some artifacts from Lewis and Clark's expedition, as well as belongings of Sacagawea's descendants. There are books about Sacagawea for visitors to browse through as well.

Nez Percé National Historic Park
39063 U.S. Highway 95
Spalding, ID 83540
Telephone: (208) 843 2261
The visitor center is located in Spalding, where missionary husband and wife team Henry and Eliza Spalding created the first mission to the Nez Percé in November 1836. Eliza, along with fellow missionary Narcissa Whitman, was the first white woman to cross the Rocky Mountains.

Oasis Bordello Museum
605 Cedar Street
Wallace, ID 83873
Telephone: (208) 753 0801
Web: http://www.imbris.net/~mrmayfield
There is a 20-minute tour of the upper rooms of this bordello. The Oasis was one of five brothels that operated until 1973 on Main Street without hindrance.

RESOURCES

FURTHER READING

HISTORY

Anthony, Susan B., and Ida Husted Harper. *History of Woman Suffrage*. Vol. 4. Indianapolis, Ind.: Hollenbeck Press, 1902.

Butruille, Susan G. *Women's Voices from the Oregon Trail: The Times That Tried Women's Souls, and a Guide to Women's History Along the Oregon Trail*. 2nd ed. Boise, Idaho: Tamarack Books, 1994.

Carlson, Laurie M. *On Sidesaddles to Heaven: The Women of the Rocky Mountain Mission*. Caldwell, Idaho: Caxton Printers, 1998.

Cook, Linda J. *The Legal Status of Homemakers in Idaho*. Washington, D.C.: Homemakers Committee, National Commission on the Observance of International Women's Year, USGPO, 1977.

Coulter, Anne Hendren. *Hidden Lives and Unhistoric Acts*. Boise, Idaho: West Shore Press, 1999.

Drury, Clifford. *First White Women over the Rockies*. 3 vols. Glendale, Calif.: A. H. Clarke, 1963–1966.

Federal Writers' Project. *Idaho: A Guide in Words and Pictures*. 1937. Reprint, New York: Oxford University Press, 1950.

Garrison, Ruth. *Elder Tales: Spirited Women Over Sixty Tell Their Stories*. Boise: Historic Idaho, 2000.

James, Caroline. *Nez Percé Women in Transition, 1877–1990*. Moscow: University of Idaho Press, 1996.

Penson-Ward, Betty. *Who's Who of Idaho Women of the Past: A Reference Dictionary*. Wilder: Idaho Commission on Women's Programs, 1981.

Penson-Ward, Betty. *Idaho Women in History: Big and Little Biographies and Other Gender Stories*. Boise, Idaho: Legendary Publishing, 1991.

Peterson, F. Ross. *Idaho: A Bicentennial History*. New York: W. W. Norton, 1976.

Schwantes, Charles. *In Mountain Shadow: A History of Idaho*. Lincoln: University of Nebraska Press, 1991.

Simpson, Claude, and Catherine Simpson. *North of the Narrows: Men and Women of the Upper Priest Lake Country, Idaho*. Moscow: University of Idaho Press, 1981.

Stacy, Susan M. *Conversations, A Companion Book to Idaho Public Television's "Proceeding on through a Beautiful Country."* Boise: Idaho Educational Public Broadcasting Foundation, 1990.

Swetnam, Susan Hendricks. *Lives of the Saints in Southeast Idaho*. Moscow: University of Idaho Press, 1991.

Wells, B. B. *America and Woman Suffrage: Wyoming, Colorado, Utah, Idaho*. London: W. & G. Baird, 1909.

BIOGRAPHY AND AUTOBIOGRAPHY

Anderson, Nancy F. *Lora Webb Nichols: Homesteader's Daughter, Miner's Bride*. Caldwell, Idaho: Caxton Printers, 1995.

Barnes, Kim. *In the Wilderness: Coming of Age in Unknown Country*. New York: Doubleday, 1996.

Barnes, Kim. *Hungry for the World: A Memoir*. New York: Villard, 2000.

Bragg, L. E. *More than Petticoats: Remarkable Idaho Women*. Guilford, Conn.: Two Dot, 2001.

Bussard, June Elizabeth. *Skinny Scotty: The Adventurous Life of Rosa Ellen Scott*. Grass Valley, Calif.: J & J Books, 1996.

Easum, Dick D'. *Dowager of Discipline: The Life of Dean of Women Permeal French*. Moscow: University of Idaho Press, 1981.

Ewart, Sara E. "Evolution of an Environmentalist." *Montana: The Magazine of Western History*, 1 April 2001, 36.

Freeman-Toole, T. Louise. *Standing up to the Rock*. Lincoln: University of Nebraska Press, 2001.

Furey-Werhan, Carol. *Haven in the Wilderness: The Story of Frances Zaunmiller Wisner of Campbell's Ferry, Idaho*. Parks, Ariz.: n.p., 1996.

Goode, Stephen. "The Lady Is Definitely Not Politically Correct." *Insight on the News*, 11 December 11 1995, 16–17.

Hunsaker, Joyce Badgley. *Sacagawea Speaks: Beyond the Shining Mountains with Lewis and Clark*. Guilford, Conn.: Two Dot, 2001.

Maguire, James H. *Mary Hallock Foote*. Boise, Idaho: Boise State College, 1972.

Miller, Darlis A. *Mary Hallock Foote: Author-Illustrator of the American West*. Norman: University of Oklahoma Press, 2002.

Morrill, Allen Conrad. *Out of the Blanket: The Story of Sue and Kate McBeth, Missionaries to the Nez Percés*. Moscow: University of Idaho Press, 1978.

Peavey, Diane Josephy. *Bitterbrush Country: Living on the Edge of the Land.* Golden, Colo.: Fulcrum Publishers, 2001.

Rauber, Paul. "Eco-thug: Helen Chenoweth." *Sierra,* May–June 1996, 28.

Rosin, Hanna. "Invasion of the Church Ladies." *New Republic,* 24 April 1995, 20–25.

Seymour, Flora Warren. *Sacagawea, American Pathfinder.* New York: Aladdin Books, 1991.

Shipps, Jan. "Dangerous History: Laurel Ulrich and Her Mormon Sisters." *Christian Century,* 20 October 1993, 1012–1015.

Stuttaford, Genevieve. "A Midwife's Tale: The Life of Martha Ballard Based on Her Diary, 1785–1812." *Publishers Weekly,* 26 January 1990, 409.

Swetnam, Susan Hendricks. *Home Mountains: Reflections from a Western Middle Age.* Pullman: Washington State University Press, 2000.

"UI Professor Presents Women's History Month," *University of Idaho News Digest,* 4 March 1998.

Ulrich, Laurel Thatcher. "An Epiphany in a Broom Closet." *Weber Studies,* (Winter 1993).

Wallner, Rosemary. *Sacagawea, 1788–1812.* Mankato, Idaho: Blue Earth Books, 2003.

Wegars, Priscilla. "Polly Bemis: Lurid Life or Literary Legend?" In *Wild Women of the Old West.* Edited by Richard Etulain and Glenda Riley. Golden, Colo.: Fulcrum, 2003.

White, Alana. *Sacagawea: Westward with Lewis and Clark.* Springfield, N.J.: Enslow, 1997.

USEFUL WEB SITES

"Gracie Bowers Pfost," University of Idaho
http://www.lib.uidaho.edu/special-collections/Manuscripts/mg044.htm

"Idaho Women: Permeal Jane French," Mike Crapo, U.S. Representative Web Site
http://www.senate.gov/~crapo/idaho/women/IWPermealFrench.htm

"Pfost, Gracie Bowers, 1906–1965," Biographical Dictionary of the United States Congress
http://bioguide.congress.gov/congresswomen/index.asp

Shirley, Gayle C. "Madame Marie Dorion: Madonna of the Oregon Trail"
http://www.eastoregonian.com/petticoats/petticoats.html

University of Idaho Library online gateway
http://www.lib.uidaho.edu

SELECTED ORGANIZATIONS AND INSTITUTIONS

Idaho State Historical Society
1109 Main Street, Suite 250
Boise, ID 83702
Telephone: (208) 334 2682
Web: http://www.idahohistory.net
The society manages a historical library, museum, historic sites, and other projects. Two of the society's publications, "Idaho Yesterdays" and "TimeLine," are available online.

Idaho Women's Commission
PO Box 8915
Moscow, ID 83843
Telephone: (208) 885 3758
Web: http://www.state.id.us/women
A state agency, the commission uses educational and informational publications and other efforts to work toward equal opportunities for women.

Pioneer Women of the West, Special Collections and Archives
University of Idaho Library
University Avenue
Moscow, ID 83844–2350
Telephone: (208) 885 6584
Web: http://www.lib.uidaho.edu/special-collections/women.htm
Online access to special collections about Idaho women's history.

University of Idaho Women's Studies Program
University of Idaho
College of Letters and Science
675 Perimeter Drive
Moscow, ID 83844
Telephone: (208) 885 7866
Web: http://www.uidaho.edu/LS/WomSt
The program offers a minor in women's studies through an interdisciplinary program that uses gender to examine such cultural variables as class, ethnicity, nationality, sexual identity, and age.

ILLINOIS

The morning light in my new bedroom was not so different from . . . Lake Bascom,
but Meander's morning smell was a shock. The live steers and hogs waiting for the move to Bishop
Meat fouled the Meander stockyards . . . so far from anything I imagined about death . . .
I never wished to move back to Meander, but make no mistake: life on the farm was no idyll.
The day we arrived, snow fell out of a concrete sky. . . . Nancy and I needed only one morning of
waiting for the school bus to learn how hard the wind blew across those wide-open fields . . .
—Elizabeth Evans, *The Blue Hour*, 1994

Illinois has had many milestones for women. It was the first state to elect a black woman to the U.S. Senate. Its largest city, Chicago, was the first major city in the United States to elect a female mayor and the first city to hire a female superintendent for its school system.

State Population (2000): 12,419,293

Female Population (2000): 6,338,957

Women in State Legislature (2003): 27.1%

Female College Enrollment (1999): 412,000 (56.2% of total)

Privately Held Women-owned Businesses (1997): 239,725

First Year of Full Suffrage: 1920

PREHISTORY

(Prehistory–1673)

Illinois was once inhabited by indigenous peoples often referred to as Mound Builders. These prehistoric humans built some 10,000 mounds in what would become Illinois; some of the mounds had everyday uses, others were used for sacred functions. The mounds contain pottery and amulets, as well as evidence of textiles, which were probably woven by women. Artifacts suggest the existence of a vast trade network—with copper from Minnesota, obsidian from Montana, and shells from the Gulf of Mexico.

For unexplained reasons the Mound Builders disappeared about 1000 A.D.; the social and trading organization of peoples living in the area when whites arrived had become less sophisticated. The Illinois Confederacy consisted of six tribes, the best known of which were the Peoria and the Kaskaskia. They spoke variants of the Algonquian language, while the Miami, who centered in Ohio but sometimes lived south of what would become Chicago, were Iroquois speakers. They all built communal log lodges that housed up to a dozen families, and some of their villages were quite large.

361

Women were the primary farmers, raising corn, beans, and pumpkins, which they sun-dried. They gathered an abundance of wild foods, including mulberries, plums, pawpaws, and persimmons, as well as walnuts and hazel-nuts. Women also dug roots for medicine and food. Like many Native American tribes, they kept war captives, especially women and chil-dren, as slaves. Men often preferred to die rather than be captured, as reported by the *De Gannes Memoir* (ca. 1695): "Male captives were tortured by fire, their bodies cut open, and their hearts eaten raw. Mothers then hastened to dip the feet of their male children in the blood of the thoracic cavity." (Federal Writers' Project 1939, 18)

Given the higher death rate of men, Illinois tribes, like others in the Americas, were sometimes polygamous. Men were in short supply, and sisters not uncommonly married the same man and would share household responsibilities.

Early white explorers and adventurers also commented on how hard Native American women worked. According to Henri Joutel, who explored villages along the Illinois River in 1687: "The men have no other business but going to the war and hunting, and the women must fetch the game when they have killed it, which sometimes they are to carry very far to their dwelling." (Jablow 1974, 107) Women then butchered, smoked or dried the meat, and stored it in pits. They tanned hides from which they made bedding and garments, including footwear.

As East Coast whites pushed the Native Americans of the Atlantic Coast west, other tribes entered Illinois; by the time of major white settle-ment in Illinois, these relative newcomers had been in the area for about a century. The most notable were the Sac (or Sauk) and their kin, the Fox. Women of these tribes trained boys in mili-tarism; if a sentinel fell asleep, for instance, the women publicly flogged him.

WHITE EXPLORATION TO U.S. ACQUISITION (1673–1818)

Jesuit priest Jacques Marquette and fur trader Louis Joliet came from Michigan's French fur-trading set-tlement in 1673, paddling their canoe down the Mississippi River to Kaskaskia, in the southwestern part of present-day Illinois. They continued their voyage, but Marquette returned to Kaskaskia the next year.

Michel Ako, a native of France, visited Illinois in 1678—a year earlier than René-Robert Cavelier de LaSalle, who traveled the Kankakee and Illinois Rivers in 1679 to Lake Peoria. Family settlement would wait until Henri Tonti arrived in 1691. A Sicilian, Tonti led French Canadian settlers to Illinois in the 1690s; Ako had returned by March 20, 1695, when the first entry was made in the reg-ister of baptisms of the Mission of Illinois: "I, James Gravier, of the Society of Jesus, baptized Peter Ako, newly born of P. Michel Ako, Godfather was D. de Hautchy, Godmother Mary Arami, Mary Jane grandmother of the child." (Breese 1884, 142) The (unnamed) mother was likely a Native American; later records similarly lacked information on women, especially those of the lower classes. Occasionally, though, priests detailed weddings and baptisms of the wealthy, including information on attendants and ancestors.

Father Francois Pinet opened a Jesuit mission called Guardian Angel at Chicago in 1696, but it was relocated to Kaskaskia and Cahokia in 1699. These now-obscure towns, across the Mississippi from Missouri, would be the center of Illinois life for more than a century. Much later, after American settlement, the area was called the American Bottom; it is river-bottom land, and its delta economy would cause its residents to iden-tify with the Deep South.

In Illinois, as elsewhere, many French men married Native American women. Even when mar-riages were common law and even if a trader had more than one family, he invariably treated all his

IKONETA: THE ILLINOIS *BERDACHE*

In 1673 French expeditionists in what would become Illinois came into contact with the Illini tribe. Members of the expedition team led by Jacques Marquette (1637–1675) left behind numerous written records detailing their observations of daily life in Illini society. Marquette, in particular, paid careful attention to the curious appearance and behaviors of the men that the Illini referred to as *ikoneta*, male members of the Illini tribe who dressed and behaved like the females. Marquette adopted the French term *berdache* (kept boy or male prostitute) to describe the *ikoneta* in his journals.

The berdache phenomenon was more complicated than simple cross-dressing, as it entailed not only women's clothing, but also the complete assumption of women's social occupations and restrictions, as well as the pursuit of sexual relationships with both men and women. The Illini considered the *berdache* subculture to be a synthesis of male and female behaviors in a single "two-spirited" individual. Thus, rather than acting as a deviant member of the traditional male-female gender dichotomy, the *berdache* occupied a separate gender space in Illini society.

Marquette and his men were particularly interested in the cultural practices surrounding the development of the *berdache* identity. Upon closer investigation, the expedition team found that those Illini destined to live as *berdaches* began their way of life as children. If boys were observed to take more interest in domestic activities than in warfare, the Illini raised them as women. The boys continued to dress and act as women until the onset of puberty, when they underwent the dream fast—a ceremony and rite of passage in which young men were thought to have confirmed their destiny as adult *berdaches*.

As adults, *berdaches* were confined to a status system reserved for women. Like Illini women, *berdaches* were prohibited from picking up the bow and arrow in raids or on hunts because these were considered symbols of masculinity and virility. However, many Illini *berdaches* created a separate role for themselves by becoming shamans, or spiritual mediators. *Berdaches* were particularly inclined to this role because of their common association with manitous (shape-shifters). The Illini believed that *berdaches* were able to move between the male and female realms to create their own identity, and as such were more adept at spiritual mediation. As shamans, *ikonetas* continued to occupy two worlds, maneuvering between spiritual and physical realities.

—Catherine Griffis

---

children as legitimate. One of Kaskaskia's earliest families, for example, "was founded by the daughter of the Kaskaskia chief, Rouensa. She married a French woodsman named Accoult. . . .When he died, she married another Frenchman. . . . She bore seven children and when she died . . . was buried under her pew in the Kaskaskia church." (Brownell 1958, 63)

French Canadian women arrived in the early 1700s, and Kaskaskia, Cahokia, and the later Prairie du Rocher and Renault soon were French-speaking villages looking much like those in Quebec. Homes were built with upright logs and a plastered exterior, an appearance quite different from the American log cabin: the roof was steep, many had gables, and most had a porch on all four sides. Affluent families brought fine furniture up the Mississippi from New Orleans, especially after Fort Chartres opened in 1720 at Prairie du Rocher. The fort was quite grand, featuring an arched gateway 15 feet high and 2 feet thick.

The commandant of Illinois in the 1740s was Alphonse de La Buissoniere; his position was achieved, in part, by his wife's connections. The relatively high status of women is reflected in the Fort Chartres deed: both signed it, and she used her maiden name, Therese Trudeau. Women with less social rank also acted independently. In 1724, for instance, a royal notary complied an estate inventory for Marie Maurice Medard, whose husband, Pierre Etevenard dit Beausoleil, had been killed by the Fox. She inherited without question two major tracts of land.

Another official created a 1733 boundary between land claimed by Agnes Philippe Chassin and a nobleman who had been harassing her.

Madame Chassin's father was French Canadian; her mother was Marie Rouensa, the daughter of a Kaskaskia chief. Her husband, Nicholas Chassin, was the sutler, or civilian storekeeper, at Fort Chartres; in 1729 he had gone to Louisiana for supplies and never returned.

Three decades later Philip Pittman noted the area's multiracial aspect: "The land was purchased of the savages by a few Canadians, some of whom married women of the Kaoquias nation, and others brought their wives from Canada." (Angle 1968, 45) Pittman was exploring because Britain had just acquired the land in the French and Indian War. Without any appreciable local fighting, the French surrendered Fort Chartres and the British took over in 1765.

Just a decade after the British took over, the American Revolution began. In 1778, Virginian George Rogers Clark led troops all the way to western Illinois, where they captured Cahokia and Kaskaskia. The British abandoned Fort Chartres and within a few decades its once proud walls had collapsed into wilderness

Congress made Illinois part of the Northwest Territory in 1787, in an act that also forbade slavery in the territory. For many decades, however, residents would ignore the new government, and Illinois continued to be much more European than American. Nor did many Americans settle in the area. One of the few exceptions was Catharine Lemen, who came with her husband and two children in 1786; she would have ten children in the wilderness of eastern Illinois.

The United States did not build a fort in the Illinois Territory until 1803, 20 years after Britain ceded the land in 1783. That fort, Fort Dearborn, would become the great city of Chicago. Chicago's first white woman arrived in 1803 with the fort's opening; the widow of a British officer killed in 1794, she came with her second husband, American John Kinzie. Mrs. Kinzie reared seven children, including a daughter who soon married Lt. Lina J.

Helm of Kentucky. A daughter-in-law, Augusta Magill Kinzie, later was a much-published novelist.

Rebecca Wells, the niece of federal Indian agent William Wells, soon came from Kentucky. Her expert marksmanship helped to captivate Fort Dearborn's commander, Capt. Nathan Heald, and they married in 1811. When the War of 1812 began, 9 young women and their 18 children lived in Fort Dearborn. They learned of the war when a runner from Detroit brought orders that the 93 whites were to head for either Detroit or Fort Wayne, Indiana.

The war ended in 1815; Fort Dearborn, which had been damaged in the fighting, was rebuilt in 1816. Probably because of widespread publicity of the danger U.S. citizens faced in the area, Illinois became a state sooner than it should have. In 1818 the population was still short of the 60,000 required by the Northwest Ordinance for consideration for statehood. At that time, however, governors also functioned as military leaders, and, because men had more confidence in leaders they elected, Illinois became the nation's 21st state on December 3 of that year.

STATEHOOD THROUGH CIVIL WAR ERA (1818–1875)

After more than a century of primarily French influence, Illinois became Anglicized with statehood. Because Illinois bordered the slave states of Kentucky and Missouri, it began attracting both free and runaway blacks by the 1830s. "Free Frank" McWhorter and his wife, Lucy, for example, moved to Pike County after their Kentucky master allowed them to keep their earnings from after-hours work and purchase their freedom. Lucy had borne at least two sons who were grown by then, and the hardworking family bought 800 acres on which they founded the mixed-race town of New Philadelphia.

Even more striking is the experience of the Coopers, who settled in Cass County in 1821;

Mrs. Cooper was white and Mr. Cooper was black, but neighbors apparently accepted them. Their case is rare, however, and Cass County is an appreciable distance from American Bottom, where Elijah Lovejoy and his bride, Celia Ann French, found Alton as conservative as the Deep South. He had been harassed for publishing an abolitionist newspaper in Missouri, and they had moved in hope of finding a more broadminded place to live soon after their 1835 marriage, but Alton men welcomed them by pushing his printing press into the Mississippi.

The Ohio Anti-Slavery Society provided another press, but wild rumors spread about Elijah's supposed desire for a black wife. Celia had to defend more than her reputation: she also had to fight men who were attempting to drag him from their home, swearing they would have to take her first. The mob slunk off, but in November 1837, Alton residents set fire to the press building; when Elijah ran to it, they killed him.

Mormons also met violence in Illinois, but the first few years after their 1839 arrival were hopeful. Following their prophet Joseph Smith and his wife, Emma Hale Smith, Mormons from western New York established the town of Nauvoo. For the first half of the 1840s, it was larger than Chicago and, because Mormons led a disciplined communal life, it may have been the best governed of any frontier city. While bearing nine children Emma Smith led the Female Relief Society (begun in 1842). Many consider this group to be the first major organization of women controlled by women; it saw to the needs of newcomers, many from Europe.

As the news began to circulate about Smith's advocacy of Old Testament polygamy, however, local men began to attack Mormons. Joseph and Hyrum Smith were jailed at Carthage and, on June 27, 1844, a mob killed them. Virtual civil war broke out, and terrified Hancock County women lived with threats of assault and arson from non-Mormon men. When church leaders surrendered

late in 1845, some 2,000 people began their move to Utah, interrupted by a long sojourn in Iowa. As Nauvoo became a ghost town, Emma Smith was one of the few who stayed. Although she remained a Mormon, her second husband was a non-Mormon. She continued to deny that Joseph Smith had other wives, although some assert that he had married as many as 50 women.

Mormons were not the only unconventional sect in Illinois. The state's most famous utopian colony was at Bishop Hill, where Swedes settled in 1846. They followed Erik Jansson and his wife, Maja Stina Larsdotter, from Uppsala. The Janssonists' first winter was hard, with 96 deaths, but the 1,500-member commune soon prospered. Women joined men in erecting brick buildings, in which women manufactured linen and brooms. After his wife died in 1849, Jansson quickly remarried and then died in 1850 in a fight over a female cousin.

In 1855 the first women's rights society in the state was established at Earlville. Susan Hoxie Richardson, a cousin of Susan B. Anthony, led it; Octavia Grover was secretary. Ohio's Hannah Tracy Cutler and Frances Gage spoke on women's rights in an 1860 tour, sometimes joined by Dr. Ellen B. Ferguson and Rev. and Mrs. Harrison of Earlville. Catherine Waite and her husband, a judge, also were part of this movement to change laws on married women's property rights. The society's work, however, soon took second place to the antislavery cause.

In 1860 Springfield's Abraham Lincoln won the presidential election; the Civil War then absorbed all reformist energy. More than 250,000 Illinois men joined the military, and its women were among the Union's most outstanding. Mary Todd Lincoln was the most famous, but Mary Ashton Rice Livermore, Mary Ann Bickerdyke, and others were vital to victory.

Huge hospitals arose at Mound City and Cairo, where the Mississippi and Ohio Rivers meet, to handle tens of thousands of wounded men. The Sisters of the Holy Cross were among the nurses; their work did much to counter the era's prejudice against Roman Catholics. Other women worked on dangerously overcrowded hospital ships, and some faced the dangers of battlefields in the South.

The soldier Jennie Hodgers spent a lifetime posing as Albert Cashiers. Born in Ireland, she enlisted under that name in Belvidere in 1862 and served in combat, including the siege of Vicksburg. Although many women on both sides disguised themselves as men to fight, none did so as successfully. She served until the war ended, collected a pension, and lived out her life as Albert Cashiers in Saunemin. Her gender was discovered only when she was hospitalized shortly before her 1915 death.

Julia Dent Grant of Galena was nearly captured by Confederates in 1862, when she was in Mississippi with her husband, Gen. Ulysses S. Grant. His aides often wanted her nearby, however, because Grant avoided alcohol when his wife was in camp.

Another Galena resident who went to war was Clarissa Geer Hobbs, who accompanied her husband, James, so early that systems had not yet been devised for assigning women as nurses. Instead, a recruiting officer at Dubuque, on the border between Illinois and Iowa, signed up the insistent Hobbs as a soldier; she drew rations and was issued two blankets.

Ultimately Hobbs did the nursing that the era assumed was innate to women, but because nursing was not yet professionalized, women had to develop skills on their own. In addition, temporary hospitals were often chaotic and dangerous, and more than one nurse carried a pistol for protection from out-of-control patients and alcoholic physicians.

Tens of thousands of other women ran farms and businesses when their men were drafted, and in all of these experiences, women developed new skills. At the war's end women in general would be much stronger, more confident, and more insistent on fairness. Future Illinois suffragist Elizabeth Boynton Harbert—who held a doctorate from Ohio Wesleyan University—said of the war: "That historic 'first gun' not only jarred loose every rivet in the manacles of 4,000,000 slaves, but when the smoke of the cannonading had lifted, the entire horizon of woman was broadened."(Stanton, Anthony, and Gage 1886, 3:582)

MYRA COLBY BRADWELL was one of the state's first women to move into the broader professional sphere. During the Civil War she had worked for the U.S. Sanitary Commission and, in 1868, began her long fight for female lawyers. With support from her attorney husband, she published the *Chicago Legal News*, a nationally read weekly. Bradwell passed the state bar exam in 1869, but the Illinois supreme court refused to grant her a license on the grounds of gender.

Indeed, the women's rights movement regrouped during this era. The Woman's College at Evanston, opened in 1871, was the first institution of higher education granted a charter by the Illinois legislature. The college was unusual, however, in having only women on its board of trustees; also unusual was the trustees' election of FRANCES WILLARD as president of the college. Chicago's Jennie Fowler Willing earned its first master's degree and preached the baccalaureate sermon; Willing, a Methodist, was the state's first woman licensed as a preacher in 1873.

The year 1868 also saw the formation of Sorosis, a Chicago professional women's club akin to New York's Sorosis, which had also been established in 1868. Delia Waterman was president; the club's news organ, *Chicago Sorosis*, was edited by Agnes Knowlton, Cynthia Leonard, and Mary L. Walker. Walker also published *The Agitator* with Mary Livermore; Charlotte Clark briefly issued *The Inland Monthly*.

BRADWELL V. ILLINOIS

Myra Colby Bradwell fought for the right of American women to become lawyers, taking her case to the 1873 Supreme Court in *Bradwell v. Illinois*. However, the Supreme Court decided against Bradwell, declaring that the decision on women's admission to the bar was within the purview of the individual states. This decision ultimately hindered women's entrance into professional occupations and prolonged their battle for equal rights.

Bradwell had passed the Illinois bar exam in 1869, but was denied permission by the state supreme court to practice law because of her gender. The court first based its decision on the legal concept of coverture, which defined women as lacking independent recognition after marriage. The court further argued that because politics was a traditionally male-dominated occupation and women's suffrage was yet to be granted, women could not fulfill legal occupations. Complicating the ruling was the decision of the state of Iowa to admit Arabella Mansfield to its bar in 1869. This difference between the states created the opportunity for Bradwell's appeal.

Bradwell appealed her case to the U.S. Supreme Court in 1872. Her argument had two points. First, because Iowa granted permission for a woman to join the bar, then women's entrance to the profession should be permissible in all states. Bradwell's argument was also based on the 14th Amendment, through which Bradwell's lawyer argued that as citizens, women have a federally protected privilege to practice any chosen profession.

In addition to finding that admission to the state bar belonged to each state, the justices argued that "the paramount destiny and mission of women are to fulfill the noble and benign offices of wife and mother. This is the law of the creator." The effects of this decision extended beyond Bradwell. By denying her claim, the federal government refused to address the role of women in professional occupations, thus forcing women to adopt a state-based strategy in their battle for equal rights.

—Jennifer Searcy

In September of that busy year, the Illinois Equal Suffrage Association (ESA) began in Chicago's Library Hall. Mary Livermore was elected president, while Dr. Mary Safford and Kate Doggett were named delegates to the Woman's Industrial Congress in Berlin. A physician, Safford later moved to Tarpon Springs, Florida; Doggett led the Association for the Advancement of Women, which evolved into the American Association of University Women.

The 1870 suffrage convention was held at the Springfield Opera House during a revision of the state constitution that took place in the state capitol. The constitution's writers also heard from opponents, including 380 Peoria women who signed an antisuffrage petition.

Catharine V. Waite attempted to vote in Hyde Park's 1871 municipal election, joining women in about a dozen states who tested the gender-neutral language of the 15th Amendment to the U.S. Constitution, which ensured the vote for black men. When a Cook County official refused to register Waite, she sued; her husband, Judge Charles B. Waite, argued the case, but his judicial colleagues were not moved.

The 1871 Chicago fire killed approximately 300 and left 75,000 homeless, many recent immigrants with no family to take them in. Among the buildings burned was the Woman's Hospital Medical College, which Dr. Mary Harris Thompson had begun the previous year. Thompson had earned her degree in 1863 from New England Female College of Medicine, and, after working for the Civil War's Sanitary Commission, she organized the Chicago Hospital for Women and Children in 1865; five years later, she expanded it into a teaching hospital.

The college was four days into its second year when it burned, but Dr. Thompson quickly raised $25,000 to rebuild. The hospital cared for patients until shortly before Thompson's death in 1895. By then the hospital had been absorbed by Northwestern University. Thompson never married and initially faced considerable hostility from male colleagues, but in 1881 they elected her vice president of the Chicago Medical Society. Also a pioneer surgeon, she invented a specialized needle for abdominal surgery.

The 1872 Illinois ESA convention was held in Bloomington, and again some women went on to the legislative session, where Susan B. Anthony led them in lobbying for what was termed the Alta Hulett bill. While the courts continued to consider Myra Bradwell's appeal of her 1869 exclusion from the bar, Alta Hulett had drafted a bill that would allow women to practice law. The Illinois legislature passed the bill and the governor signed it, but the new state law made no difference to the U.S. Supreme Court, which handed women's rights advocates a major defeat in *Bradwell v. Illinois* (1873). In that decision the Court declared that states were free to exclude women from the practice of law.

Illinois attorneys had had their attention concentrated by the Hulett bill and by discussion of similar cases in Iowa and Missouri. As Myra Bradwell continued to publish the *Chicago Legal News*, the bar association offered her honorary membership; Alta Hulett's unmarried status helped her. After reading law in Rockford as a teenager, Hulett had made the highest score among 28 bar examination applicants. She was licensed on June 6, 1873, two days after her 19th birthday.

Others soon followed, including M. Fredrica Perry and Ellen A. Martin, University of Michigan graduates who practiced together in Chicago; Martin later organized the Chicago Political Equality League and the National Woman Lawyers' League. Marietta B. R. Shay graduated from a Bloomington law school in 1879 and wrote a book on common-law pleading.

Unnoticed in national publicity, however, was Ada H. Kepsey of Effingham, a small town near Champaign. After working with her attorney husband, she graduated from Chicago's Union Law School in 1870—between Myra Bradwell's 1869 bar examination and Alta Hulett's 1872 bill. A local judge had simply ignored his superiors when he admitted Kepsey to the bar in November 1870.

During these legal pleadings and political measures, Myra Bradwell's husband had been elected to the legislature, and he successfully sponsored bills to allow male voters to elect women to school offices. In November 1873 ten counties chose women as county school superintendent, well ahead of other states. As voters probably intended, many of these women did commendable jobs of instituting efficiency and straightening out incomplete and probably corrupt records; in Knox County, the $182,423.22 budget was perfectly balanced for the first time in years.

SUFFRAGE AND PROGRESSIVE ERAS (1875–1920)

Dr. Sarah Hackett Stevenson, an Ogle County native and the 1874 valedictorian of Dr. Mary Thompson's medical school, wrote *Boys and Girls in Biology* (1875), a text for high school students. It was based on her work in London with Thomas Huxley, a pioneer in the theory of evolution. In 1876 the Illinois Medical Society chose Stevenson as its delegate to the American Medical Association's convention in Philadelphia, where she became the AMA's first female member.

Two hundred women were charter members of the Illinois Charities Aid Association in 1877, and many women wrote for its publication, *Illinois Social Science Journal*. The president was Evanston's Elizabeth Boynton Harbert, who also presided over the ESA and edited the women's section of a national magazine, *Inter-Ocean*.

Chicago became one of the most polyglot cities in the world as immigrants poured in during the late 19th century. The most unusual women among them were Czech, then called Cechs or Bohemians; the first to come, in the late 1860s, were skilled cigar makers. They left their husbands and children in Bohemia while they established themselves in the United States. More likely than other women to seek careers, by 1915 the Chicago directory of Bohemians listed 19 female and 36 male physicians.

Most of the millions of immigrants were unskilled and poor. Inspired by London's Toynbee Hall (and unaware of New York City's 1887 University Settlement House) JANE ADDAMS and Ellen Gates Starr began a settlement house for immigrants in 1889. Chicago's Hull House, which became the world's most well-known laboratory for improving the lives of ordinary people through modern social science, had social workers who assisted newcomers with the complexities of immigration law, finding jobs and learning skills, and the adjustment to a new language and cultural standards. Hull House also offered lawyers to handle problems with landlords, employers, and other legal issues. Its courses in health, nutrition, and other topics were mostly aimed at women and girls, but males also participated in music, art, and theater.

Dozens of women and men lived and worked at Hull House. Among the most noted were economist Edith Abbott and her sister, sociologist Grace Abbott. Dr. ALICE HAMILTON and JULIA LATHROP pioneered new fields based on their youthful Hull House experience, while Kentucky's SOPHONISBA BRECKINRIDGE did the same. Emily Balch of Massachusetts would follow Addams as the second American woman to win the Nobel Peace Prize.

In 1891, almost two decades after Illinois began allowing men to elect women to school offices, the law was changed so that women could vote for school officials themselves. The bill was badly drafted, however, and some women were rejected by ill-informed poll officials. Unclear language also meant that women spent years in court trying to determine if they had the right to vote on school-related issues and taxes or merely for

Jane Addams in 1935 with young visitors to Hull House, which she founded in 1889. Hull House is still in operation, offering a wide range of community services in several facilities throughout Chicago. (AP/Wide World Photos)

school board members and county superintendents. An additional complication was that mayors appointed school boards in large cities, leaving Chicago women voteless—but with female representation on the board. By 1900 all the state's principal cities had women on their school boards—earlier than in most states.

The University of Illinois had begun admitting women in 1870; the private University of Chicago was coeducational from its 1891 beginning. It had an unusual dean of women in Alice Freeman Palmer, a superb academician who had been president of Wellesley College in Massachusetts at age 27. She had to resign when she married in 1887—but Chicago was so much more open to new ideas than Wellesley that it allowed her to create her own schedule; much like a modern consultant, she maintained her Boston home and traveled to

Chicago by train. With her assistant, Marion Talbot, Palmer implemented a modern curriculum, especially in the social sciences, and a system of student residences that featured female mentors.

Chicago's big year in history came in 1892–1893. Having won the bid for the World's Fair that commemorated the 400th anniversary of Columbus's 1492 voyage, Chicago played host to 21 million visitors for a year, from Columbus Day 1892 to 1893. Women's activities focused on May of 1893, when the World's Congress of Representative Women brought 150,000 women from 27 nations to the city. No other event in American history provided women with so many opportunities to meet and exchange ideas and

strategies; a number of organizations grew out of the Congress, including the National Council of Jewish Women and the group that evolved into the American Nurses Association.

The biggest controversy was the supervisory board's reluctance to allow black women to participate. Mississippi native Ida B. Wells (later Wells-Barnett) led the protest, and black women ultimately won a small space that they used for an exhibit, *Evidences of the Advancement of Colored Women of the United States*. About a dozen black women were included as speakers—but not Wells.

Illinois had a black women's group; the Autumn Leaf Club, begun in Galesburg in 1890. The fair prompted the organization of more

THE CHICAGO'S WORLD'S FAIR

The 1893 Chicago World's Fair was held to mark the 400th anniversary of Columbus's voyage to the Americas and to celebrate the technological, cultural, and commercial achievements of the United States. Women took the opportunity provided by the fair to present to the public the changing definition of womanhood in the late 19th century.

Although the Chicago World's Fair was arranged by an all-male governing organization, women petitioned for an active role in its planning. Congress authorized the creation of a separate Board of Lady Managers in 1890. Composed of two female representatives from each state, the board representatives tended to be from prominent families or those with roots in the voluntary association movement. Thus, for the most part, involvement of women in the fair was limited to those who were white and of the upper or middle class.

The Board of Lady Managers was led by Bertha Palmer, wife of prominent Chicago real estate tycoon Potter Palmer. Through her leadership the Board of Lady Managers created a venue for exhibits that celebrated female accomplishments in areas like the sciences and the arts. These exhibitions were housed in the Women's Building, a separate venue that was designed by female architect Sophia Hayden and emphasized the popular concept of women's special but separate role in the late 19th century. The Women's Building featured a Gallery of Honor that

displayed works of female artists, including Mary Cassatt. An Invention Room highlighted female inventors, and the Science Room celebrated the achievements of women like astronomer Maria Mitchell. The Women's Building also displayed hundreds of books by female authors, and among many Illinois novelists was Emma Altgeld, whose husband became governor while the fair was in progress. She displayed *Sarah's Choice; or, The Norton Family* (1887). The ESA's Elizabeth Boynton Harbert sent two novels, *Out of Her Sphere* (1871) and *Amore* (1892). Carolyn Corbin—who was both a founder of the Association for the Advancement of Women and president of the Illinois Association Opposed to Woman Suffrage—also displayed two novels. Eva Munson Smith compiled 150 musical compositions by 50 women in *Woman in Sacred Song*.

African American women were denied an active role by the board. As a settlement of the controversy over this, a few black women were given token appointments and allowed a small exhibit, but white female representatives were the interpreters of the role of African Americans, thereby alienating black women and diminishing their accomplishments. Overall the Chicago's World Fair provided women with a public arena to highlight their achievements and advocate for their equality, but one in which traditional concepts of race and class still held sway.

—Jennifer Searcy

societies for black women: the Ida B. Wells Club was begun in late 1893 when the Tourgee Club, a black men's group, "invited Miss Ida B. Wells, who had just returned from England, to be hostess and speaker for the club's 'ladies day.'" Women soon decided to form their own organization; they elected Wells president, with Elizabeth Lindsay Davis as secretary. One of their first goals was raising money "to prosecute a policeman for killing an innocent colored man." (Elizabeth Davis 1997, 27)

The next year Davis founded Chicago's Phillis Wheatley Club. It ran a day nursery and taught sewing—but also undertook political action, including closing down a disreputable saloon. She organized the Peoria Woman's Aid Club in 1899, while other women began both the Springfield Colored Woman's Club and Evanston's Julia Gaston Club.

The Illinois branch of the General Federation of Woman's Clubs (GFWC) began in 1894, four years after the GFWC began nationally. FANNIE BARRIER WILLIAMS, a well-educated black woman whose speeches at the Columbian Exposition were witty and eloquent, set about integrating it, and although she encountered some resistance, the Chicago Woman's Club admitted blacks sooner than most GFWC affiliates. The Illinois GFWC also was more politically astute than most, and—even though it would not endorse suffrage for another decade—the club made an immediate difference in the 1894 election.

One issue left unclear in the 1891 school suffrage bill was women's eligibility to vote for and be candidates for the elected trustees of the University of Illinois. Attorney Catharine Waugh McCullough ignored a negative opinion from the state's attorney general when she led about 50 women to the 1894 Cook County Democratic convention, with the goal of having a woman nominated for the post of university trustee. The Democratic men responded, nominating Julia

Holmes Smith. A dean at the private National Medical College, Dr. Smith was the only woman in the world to hold such a position at a coeducational institution.

Republicans were forced to follow at their convention, where they nominated Lucy L. Flower, a philanthropist and former president of the Chicago Woman's Club. The Prohibitionists went further and nominated women for two trustee slots; one was professor Rena Michaels Atchinson, who was also secretary of the ESA. Alarmed, the incumbent trustees publicized the attorney general's negative view, but McCullough answered with her own well-publicized brief, and "women went right on voting." (Anthony and Harper 1902, 4:606)

Both Democrat Smith and Prohibitionist Atchinson ran ahead of the men on their parties' tickets, but voting was done along party lines and Republican Flowers won. When a vacancy occurred shortly before she took her seat, however, Democratic governor John Peter Altgeld appointed Smith. Thus, the board of trustees of the University of Illinois had two women members decades prior to any other state university or college. Indeed, many states still excluded women entirely from their most prestigious state university.

Repeated attempts to expand suffrage nonetheless failed in the legislature, and to bring attention to the issue, state senator Miles B. Castle filed an 1898 bill to exempt voteless women from taxation. Lena Morrow spent much of 1898 speaking to men in labor unions; she obtained 25,000 petition signatures from union men in favor of granting women the vote. In addition, Mary Kenny (later O'Sullivan) and Florence Kelley also were important labor leaders and suffragists in this era. They lobbied through a precedent-setting Factory Inspection Law, and Governor Altgeld appointed Kelley as the nation's first factory inspector.

Margaret Haley (who later founded the American Federation of Teachers) and Catherine Goggin were among the teachers who went unpaid in 1899 and 1900, when Chicago experienced an unexplained decline in revenues. On their own, they began searching public records and found that money was short because some of the state's largest corporations had not paid taxes. The two presented their research to the 4,000-member Chicago Teachers' Federation and then followed up with the tax assessment board. When that body refused to act, the Teachers' Federation sued, and the case went to the Illinois supreme court. The court sided with business, refusing to grant the teachers an injunction.

Another 1901 case was more successful: Mary Murphy sued the Chicago school board when she was automatically dismissed from her teaching job at marriage. The court agreed that marriage is not misconduct and therefore was not a firing offense under the board's written grounds for dismissal.

The Woman's Club of Chicago's Frederick Douglass Center formed in 1904, and FANNIE BARRIER WILLIAMS would be its most active president. According to Elizabeth Lindsay Davis, however, the center was founded by Rev. Celia Parker Wooley, a white woman "who left her home and came with her husband to live among colored people." (Elizabeth Davis 1997, 36) A Unitarian minister, Wooley's novels were among those displayed at the Columbian Exposition.

Black women also supported an orphanage founded by Amanda Berry Smith, while the Phillis Wheatley Club worked on other social needs.

A problem that was assuming alarming proportions [was] that of colored women coming into the city, many of them from the best families in other States, and finding it impossible to secure a congenial environment. . . . Many of these girls were going astray by being led unawares into disreputable . . . employment because of lack of the protection that strange girls of the other Races enjoy. (Ibid., 16)

African American club women did not limit their work to their own race: records show financial contributions to the mostly white Equal Suffrage Association and to the later League of Women Voters. Black women's clubs also contributed money for the building of a monument to educator Ella Flagg Young, who became America's first female superintendent of schools in 1909 and the first female leader of the National Education Association in 1910.

The Women's Trade Union League (WTUL), founded in 1903, was an unusual coalition of working-class women and their upper-class supporters. Margaret Drier Robins, a wealthy woman who devoted her life to the poor, was the Chicago WTUL's first president; she also edited *Life and Labor*. Unlike most women of the upper classes, Robins commanded great respect from blue-collar men, who elected her to the executive committee of the Chicago branch of the American Federation of Labor in 1906—an exceptional achievement for a woman even today and virtually unheard of for a nonemployed woman.

Hull House's Mary McDowell was WTUL president in 1910, when some 40,000 Chicago workers went on strike. Most were women who sewed men's garments, and although many male members of the United Garment Workers crossed their picket lines, the women stayed out for 16 weeks. The loss of pay was a painful sacrifice for many young immigrant women—most of whom not only supported themselves, but often entire families overseas. The strikers spoke so many languages, in fact, that 16 union halls were needed to conduct meetings.

With intervention from Hull House, employers largely agreed to the women's demands. Some of the workers went on to careers as union leaders, among them AGNES NESTOR and Bessie Abramovitz, an 18-year-old immigrant whose objection to a pay cut at the elite men's clothier Hart, Schaffner & Marx sparked the strike.

The strike energized the ESA and brought working women into what had been primarily an organization of middle-class housewives. The Chicago Men's Equal Suffrage League began in 1909 with former senator Thomas McMillan at the helm. With links to the WTUL, the Teachers' Federation, the prestigious Chicago Woman's Club, and Ellen Martin's Chicago Political Equality League, the Illinois ESA soon had 200,000 members.

After 1910 the ESA had a permanent headquarters on Chicago's Michigan Avenue as well as two paid lobbyists in Springfield. They drafted a complex bill to allow women to vote on all offices not named in the state constitution, an astute strategy that both avoided the need for constitutional amendments that had to be submitted to the all-male electorate and also made legislators more apt to vote for the bill because it could not hurt them personally, as women were forgoing the right to vote in their races. The highest office for which women could vote was U.S. president, so the model became known as presidential suffrage—but, in fact, if the bill passed, Illinois women would be able to vote in many races.

Grace Wilbur Trout led lobbying, and, in the spring of 1913 suffrage was affirmed by both the state House of Representatives and the Senate. Antisuffragists stormed the governor's office in hopes of a veto, but the governor signed the bill on June 26, 1913. Chicago women celebrated in an automobile parade down Michigan Avenue. As feared, however, opponents went to court, and the ESA had to hire constitutional experts to research, testify, and argue. The ESA was nearly bankrupt, but newspaper publisher William Randolph Hearst paid the cost of a special suffrage edition of his *Chicago Examiner* and donated the proceeds to the ESA.

While the case was being heard, municipal elections were held in April 1914. To demonstrate that women truly wanted the vote, the ESA led massive voter registration efforts; more than 200,000 women registered in Chicago alone. Fifteen thousand marched in a May parade, and on June 13, 1914, the Illinois General Federation of Women's Clubs finally endorsed suffrage. Suffragists won their court case on the same day.

Also in 1914 Chicago's 28-year-old Margaret Anderson began *Little Review*. She featured then unknown writers, including Robert Frost, Emma Goldman, Ernest Hemingway, Amy Lowell, and Gertrude Stein. Anderson moved the magazine to New York City in 1917, where she would be arrested for obscenity when she published James Joyce's *Ulysses* in 1921.

In 1915, during World War I, 42 leaders of the Woman's Peace Party, many of them Hull House women, sailed across the Atlantic Ocean. They risked torpedoes from new German U-boats to attend the International Congress of Women at The Hague; some traveled as far as Russia to urge an end to the war. Once the United States entered the war in 1917, most women supported the conflict. ESA president Grace Wilbur Trout was appointed to the executive committee of the Woman's Council of National Defense, and Illinois women sold Liberty Bonds and performed other war work. Some got jobs in unconventional areas like driving streetcars and delivering mail. Dr. Mary F. Warning was credited for doing "more in Chicago than any other woman to put things over for the Red Cross." She led other African American women who "met and served all the colored troops passing through Chicago." (Ibid., 63)

Illinois suffragists lobbied their congressmen throughout the war, and it would be one of relatively few large states in which the entire delegation voted for the 19th Amendment to the U.S. Constitution that granted the vote to all American women. It passed out of Congress on June 4, 1919, and on June 10, Illinois, Wisconsin, and Michigan were the first three states to ratify.

The Illinois Senate vote was unanimous, and only three House members voted against it. The suffrage association transformed itself into the League of Women Voters, with Mrs. H. W. Cheney of Chicago as president. Long after the 1855 start of the state's first women's rights organization, Illinois women finally could look forward to full voting rights in 1920.

1920s THROUGH WORLD WAR II ERA (1920–1950)

Only Montana and Oklahoma elected a woman to Congress earlier than Illinois. The state's voters sent Winnifred Sprague Mason Huck to Washington, D.C., in 1922. In 1924 the first presidential election in which all American women could vote, the Prohibition party nominated WCTU lecturer Marie C. Brehm of Chicago for vice president of the United States. Because Prohibition already was in effect, however, the party essentially had no platform and did not attract as many voters as in the past.

Another Chicagoan set a national precedent in 1926, when attorney Violette Neatly Anderson became the first black woman to argue before the U.S. Supreme Court. Born in England in 1882, she was in her mid-forties when the Cook County prosecutor's office sent her to represent Illinois before the nation's highest court.

Suffrage leader RUTH HANNA MCCORMICK won her 1928 U.S. House race, making Illinois the first state to twice elect women to Congress. The Chicago Symphony Orchestra set a 1932 milestone by performing a work by African American composer Florence Price of Arkansas.

For most people, however, 1932 was the nadir of the Great Depression. Major Illinois corporations fired half or more of their employees, and many people were evicted from their homes for nonpayment of rent. The Red Cross set up soup kitchens that literally prevented starvation, especially in Chicago. Teachers were paid in scrip that stores might or might not accept, and even urban professional women began planting gardens and canning bargain foods.

Half of Illinois families accepted government assistance at some point, but most jobs offered through these aid programs were for men. The New Deal's Civilian Conservation Corps, for example, sent 100,000 young men from urban areas of Illinois to Michigan and other states, where they worked in forest and park projects, but no such program existed for young women.

When Europe again erupted in war, the effect was the same as it had been in 1917—women who could not get a job of any sort in 1939 were recruited in 1941. They were most likely to be hired in the dangerous munitions industry, where managers had discovered in World War I that women were more careful than men at handling explosives.

The Rock Island arsenal and plants at Joliet and Carbondale supplied much of the army's ammunition, ranging from rifle bullets to bombs. Indeed, some of the construction of the atomic bombs, which ended the war in the Pacific when they were dropped on Japan, took place under the football field at the University of Chicago—and women with expertise in science and math worked on the highly secret project.

Two Illinois women served in Congress during the war. Republican Jessie Sumner, a Milford judge, defeated a Democratic incumbent in 1938. So isolationist that she tried to postpone the D-Day invasion of Nazi-occupied France, she attacked popular generals and voted against veterans' benefits. Her rural constituents reelected Sumner until she retired in 1946 to become a bank president.

Emily Taft Douglas was an internationalist who chaired the Illinois League of Women Voters. Her husband, University of Chicago economist Paul Douglas, was so dedicated to defeating fascism that he joined the Marines at age 50. Despite strong opposition from the *Chicago Tribune*, Douglas defeated the isolationist incumbent in

1944. She sat on the prestigious House Foreign Affairs Committee, where her work was critical in the establishment of the United Nations. The war was over by the 1946 election, and voters tired of the sacrifices it required ousted her. When she returned to the nation's capital in 1948, it was as the wife of Sen. Paul Douglas—a role that many found more appropriate for postwar women.

POSTWAR AND CONTEMPORARY ERAS
(1950–present)

Poet GWENDOLYN BROOKS, a lifelong Chicagoan, won the Pulitzer Prize in 1950. Another Chicago writer, Lorraine Hansberry, moved east. Her *Raisin in the Sun* (1959) won the New York Drama Critics Circle Award and was the first play by an African American woman to be staged on Broadway. She died just six years later at age 35. A third writer, Esther Friedman Lederer, began writing for the *Chicago Sun-Times* in 1955 as "Ann Landers." An Iowa native, her advice column would affect American behavior and mores for much of the second half of the 20th century.

In the 1950 election Illinois sent a fifth woman to Congress. Republican Marguerite Stitt Church of Evanston replaced her husband, who died during a House committee meeting. Unlike many widows, however, she was returned to office by the voters for the next 12 years. She served on the Foreign Affairs Committee and traveled widely, especially in Asia, retiring at age 70.

IRNA PHILLIPS, INVENTOR OF THE SOAP OPERA

Nearly every soap opera on daytime television can be traced to Irna Phillips (1901–1973), the legendary radio and television writer credited with creating the genre in 1930. From its beginnings on radio, the soap opera grew to become one of the most popular and profitable genres on television, making Phillips one of the earliest women among the ranks of men to have shaped what television is today.

Many point to Phillips's difficult childhood as the root of her creative success and her elaborate and emotional storytelling abilities. Born into relative poverty, the youngest of ten children, Phillips was admittedly a lonely adolescent. She survived by reading extensively, filling her world with imaginary characters that lived full, vivid, and dramatic lives. Her successes at school took her, first, to Northwestern University, then to the University of Illinois, where she pursued acting until a teacher suggested that her looks would hamper a career on stage or film. After several years of teaching in Missouri and Ohio, Phillips returned to Chicago in 1930, ending up at WGN studios, where she read poetry on a modest show called *Thought for the Day.*

After two weeks on the job, Phillips was asked to create a serial drama about a family. On October 20, 1930, Phillips debuted the first-ever soap opera, *Painted Dreams,* told solely in the voices of women. For two years, she wrote the script and, with one other actress, performed each of the six roles.

Painted Dreams opened the door for soap operas to come, starting with *Today's Children,* which Phillips created for WGN's rival, WMAQ. Within ten years, Phillips had five soap operas on the air, all of which included the cliffhanger, dramatic music, a bias toward the middle and upper classes, and plots that unfolded slowly. Hospital dramas also made a debut at this time.

At the height of her radio soap career, Phillips was writing the equivalent of 40 novels per year. She kept her writing fresh by incorporating current issues. During World War II she used soaps to sell war bonds, and in 1941 developed *Women Alone,* a short-lived soap that spoke to the wives of soldiers abroad. This dedication to addressing social issues continued when soaps made the leap to television in 1952. Indeed, Phillips's *Another World* was the first show to incorporate abortion in its plot (1964); she later wrote scripts that encompassed the Vietnam War, homosexuality, prostitution, child abuse, and interracial relationships.

Although Phillips died in 1973 in her hometown of Chicago, her legacy has been carried on by her proteges, Agnes Nixon and William Bell. Together with Phillips, they developed soaps that have become household names: *Guiding Light, As the World Turns, All My Children, The Young and the Restless,* and *Days of Our Lives.*

—Laura J. Lambert

TIMELINE

United States Events		Illinois Events
	1600	
1620 Settlement of Plymouth Colony		
		1673 Jacques Marquette, a Jesuit priest, and Louis Joliet, a fur trader, are the first white settlers in Illinois.
	1700	
1776 United States declares independence		
		1787 Northwest Ordinance makes Illinois part of the Northwest Territory.
	1800	
		1818 Illinois achieves statehood.
1861–65 U.S. Civil War		1871 Great Chicago Fire.
		1873 Ten Illinois counties elect women as school superintendents.
		1889 Jane Addams and Ellen Gates Starr found Hull House in Chicago.
	1900	
		1913 Illinois women win the right to vote in presidential elections as well as elections for several state offices.
1914–18 World War I		1919 Illinois ratifies the 19th Amendment.
1920 Ratification of the 19th Amendment		1922 Winnifred Mason Huck is the first Illinois woman to serve in the U.S. House of Representatives.
1929–39 Great Depression		
1939–45 World War II		
1975 Vietnam War ends		
		1979 Jane Byrne elected mayor of Chicago; she becomes first female mayor of a major U.S. city.
		1990 Dawn Netsch elected state comptroller—the first Illinois woman to hold a statewide office.
		1992 Carol Moseley-Braun becomes first black woman elected to the U.S. Senate.
	2000	
		2003 Lisa Madigan is elected state attorney general.

served only one term, during which she never spoke on the House floor.

The women of Ellisville, a farm town near Peoria, also kept quiet. Women gained control of all the town's offices by keeping their plans for a write-in slate secret from the men, including incumbents who were their husbands. Mayor Tille Forneris, who served throughout the 1960s, said they were tired of male apathy. While the women were in office, the sewage system was repaired and other improvements were made.

The 1960s also brought a different sort of congresswoman. Charlotte Thompson Reid of Aurora was a Republican who had a career in radio. Many midwestern listeners knew her as "Annette King," a singer on a morning show broadcast from Chicago. Elected in 1962, she served until 1971, when Pres. Richard Nixon appointed her to the Federal Communications Commission.

Illinois had no women in Congress when the Equal Rights Amendment (ERA) passed in 1972. Many states ratified quickly, but that the ERA never won final ratification is, in great part, the doing of an Illinois woman: Republican party activist Phyllis Schlafly of Alton. Schlafly took her crusade nationwide, where she met enough success that the ERA won only 35 of the necessary 38 states. Her most effective argument against the ERA probably was that women, like men, would be subject to the military draft. Too conservative even for her rural district of traditional white voters, she had lost congressional races in 1952, 1960, and 1970. Schlafly later formed the Eagle Forum, which promoted increased military spending and opposed gun control and gay rights.

While the ERA was debated, millions of women began to use birth control pills, which were first prescribed in 1960. The Roman Catholic Church opposed birth control; Chicago had been largely Catholic since the great immigration waves of the 19th century. Attendance at Catholic mass dropped 20% in the 1960s, but the number of

Edna Oakes Simpson of Carrollton, who also replaced her deceased husband, entered the House in 1959. Her rural district north of Alton was so thoroughly Republican that she won the election without making any campaign appearances; she women who became nuns declined much more dramatically: by 1969, five sisters left Illinois religious orders for every one who entered, forcing many parochial schools to close.

The U.S. Supreme Court ruled in 1973 that states could not completely outlaw abortions. Illinois's ban on the use of Medicaid funds for abortions became a national test case; when *Harris v. McRae* finally reached the U.S. Supreme Court in 1980, the Court upheld the ban except when an abortion was necessary to save a woman's life.

Democrat Cardiss Collins won a special election to replace her Chicago congressman husband when he was killed in a 1973 plane crash, but she was no typical widow. The nation's second African American congresswoman, she sponsored legislation to benefit women and minorities. Representative Collins was consistently reelected by huge margins for more than two decades. International attention again focused on Chicago in 1979, when it became the first major U.S. city to elect a woman, JANE BYRNE, as mayor.

The Rockford area elected Republican Lynn Morley Martin to Congress in 1980, the year that Illinois native Ronald Reagan won the presidency. She rose quickly on the House Budget Committee, but lost a 1990 race for the U.S. Senate by a wide margin. Pres. George H. W. Bush then appointed Martin to head the Department of Labor.

Although Illinois had sent women to Congress since the 1920s, it was slow to elect them to statewide executive office. The first woman was elected only in 1990: Democrat Dawn Clark Netsch became comptroller that year, but lost her 1994 race for the governor's office by a wide margin. Republican Loleta Didrickson replaced Netsch as comptroller in 1994, while Judy Baar Topinka, also a Republican, was elected treasurer.

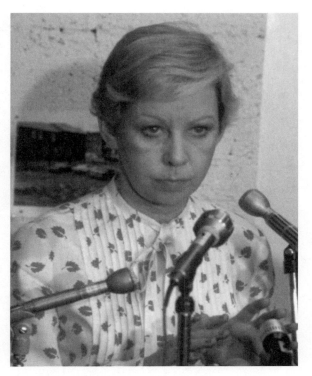

Jane Byrne giving a press conference during her successful campaign for mayor of Chicago in 1979. Byrne was the first woman elected as mayor of a major U.S. city. (AP/Wide World Photos)

Republican Corinne Wood won the lieutenant governorship in 1998. In 1992 Illinois became the first state to elect a black woman, CAROL MOSELEY-BRAUN, to the U.S. Senate.

During the last years of Moseley-Braun's term, the state's 22-member House delegation was the nation's largest without women. Two congressional districts, however, elected women in 1998, and both Republican Judy Biggert and Democrat Jan Schakowsky were reelected in 2000. In 2002 the U.S. Postal Service issued a stamp to honor *Chicago Defender* journalist Ethel Payne, who was known in the civil rights era of the 1950s and 1960s as "the first lady of the black press," and in 2003 voters elected Democrat Lisa Madigan as the state's attorney general.

—Doris Weatherford

PROMINENT WOMEN

JANE ADDAMS (1860–1935)

Social activist and suffragist Laura Jane Addams was the first American woman to be awarded a Nobel Prize. Born in Cedarville, Illinois, she was the daughter of a Quaker building magnate and abolitionist who was dedicated to benevolence and humanitarianism. She graduated in 1882 from Rockford Female Seminary as valedictorian of her class. She studied medicine for a year at Woman's Medical College of Pennsylvania but did not finish. Health problems kept her at home for several years; after recovering, she traveled in Europe from 1883 to 1885, and then resided in Maryland for several years.

During another trip to Europe in 1889, she visited Toynbee Hall, a London settlement house. Aided by colleague Ellen Gates Starr, Addams devoted herself to organizing a similar training center, soup kitchen, and child development complex in Chicago's slums. Hull House opened in September 1889, providing aid to immigrants and the disadvantaged through English classes, child care, and legal services, resources not otherwise available to immigrants and the poor. Addams developed into an expert fundraiser while also lobbying for world peace, a juvenile justice system, equal housing, safe workplaces, and eight-hour workdays. Her establishment of the National Federation of Settlements and support of the American Civil Liberties Union and National Conference of Social Work place her at the forefront of the early-20th-century American reform movement. She was awarded the Nobel Peace Prize, the first American woman so honored, in 1931 for her efforts.

MARGARET AYER BARNES (1886–1967)

Versatile author and educator Margaret Ayer Barnes of Chicago enjoyed success in drama and short and long fiction. After graduating from Bryn Mawr College in Pennsylvania in 1920, she joined the staff as alumnae director and advanced educational opportunities for women with the creation of the Working Woman's College. She published short fiction in *Pictorial Review* and collected her stories in *Prevailing Winds* (1928). Paralysis from a spinal injury in 1929 forced her to give up activism in favor of full-time writing.

In a later stage of her career, Barnes produced a play based on Edith Wharton's *Age of Innocence* and wrote two successful dramas, *Jenny* (1929) and *Dishonored Lady* (1930), the subject of a film starring Hedy Lamarr. Barnes was awarded two honorary degrees and, for her best-selling novel of manners, *Years of Grace* (1930), was awarded a Pulitzer Prize. The novel depicts a Chicago trendsetter in an era of moral change. She followed with *Edna, His Wife* (1935), the fictional portrait of a woman ill-suited for the upper class, and *Wisdom's Gate* (1938), a melodrama of divorce, infidelity, and reconciliation.

MYRA COLBY BRADWELL (1831–1894)

Attorney, suffragist, and publisher Myra R. Colby Bradwell of Manchester, Vermont, was the first to challenge gender discrimination in the legal profession. After her education in Wisconsin and Illinois public schools, she became a teacher. At age 23, she moved to Chicago, where her husband, James Bradwell, whom she married in 1852, practiced law and served as a judge. During the 1860s she volunteered with the Sanitary Commission and post–Civil War charities for veterans, widows, and orphans.

In 1868 Bradwell began publishing the *Chicago Legal News*, which printed statutes, court rulings, zoning laws, railroad regulations, and articles on legal reforms. She also sold legal forms and law office supplies. In 1869 she passed the bar examination but was denied admittance because of her gender. She co-organized the Chicago branch of the American Woman Suffrage Association and successfully campaigned for rights for married women in Illinois, including guardianship of children, appointment as notaries, and participation in school offices. After representing Illinois at the Philadelphia Centennial Exposition, she helped secure the 1893 World's Columbian Exposition for Chicago.

For several decades, Bradwell sought a license to practice law, but could not win her case; in 1873, an appeal to the U.S. Supreme Court (*Bradwell v. Illinois*) was unsuccessful. In 1890 the Illinois supreme court reversed previous rulings and granted her a license. She was an officer of the Illinois Bar Association for four terms. In 1892 Bradwell won the privilege of presenting cases before the U.S. Supreme Court. At her death, her daughter, Bessie Bradwell Helmer, took over her mother's publishing house and legal practice.

SOPHONISBA BRECKINRIDGE (1866–1948)

Activist and educator Sophonisba Preston Breckinridge of Lexington, Kentucky, was a key contributor to the development of social work in the United States. The daughter of a U.S. congressman, she learned about abolitionism and public service from her parents. After graduating from Wellesley College in 1888 and teaching high school math in Washington, D.C., she completed a doctorate in political science and economics at the University of Chicago in 1901, becoming the world's first female with that degree. She graduated from the University of Chicago Law School in 1904. While assisting Jane Addams and Ellen Gates Starr with settlement work at Hull House, she coauthored *The Delinquent Child and the Home* (1912), the first of many works on women, marriage, juvenile delinquency, the immigrant underclass, and civil rights.

While a full professor at the University of Chicago, Breckinridge championed women's suffrage and civil rights and held positions of authority in the American Association of University Women, the National Association for the Advancement of Colored People, Woman's Peace Party, Children's Bureau, and the Women's International League for Peace and Freedom. She wrote many articles about and did research in social work while teaching at the Chicago School of Civics and Philanthropy, progressing to the post of dean of research. In 1933 Pres. Franklin D. Roosevelt appointed her the first female delegate to the Pan-American Congress in Uruguay.

GWENDOLYN BROOKS (1917–2000)

Poet Gwendolyn Elizabeth Brooks of Topeka, Kansas, was the first African American to win a Pulitzer Prize, be awarded a Guggenheim Fellowship, and garner an American Academy of the Arts and Letters grant in literature. While attending Englewood High in Chicago, she read the major poets of the day, studied their methods, and attended readings by Langston Hughes and James Weldon Johnson. By 1935 she was submitting verse to *American Childhood, Chicago Defender,* and *Hyde Parker.*

She earned a degree from Wilson Junior College in 1936 and subsequently taught at Chicago Teacher's College. In 1945 she published an anthology, *A Street in Bronzeville* (1945), a collection of lyric portraits that garnered her grants from the American Academy of Arts and Letters and the National Institute of Arts and Letters, two Guggenheim fellowships, and a Midwestern Writers' Conference poetry award.

Brooks began focusing on women's lives and wrote *Annie Allen* (1949), which earned a Eunice Tietjens prize and the Pulitzer Prize for poetry. She followed with autobiographical fiction, *Maud Martha* (1953), and wrote children's poems for *Bronzeville Boys and Girls* (1956). During the civil rights struggle of the 1950s and 1960s, she completed *The Bean Eaters* (1960), *Selected Poems* (1963), and *In the Mecca* (1968), a bitter urban satire. At age 51, she was named poet laureate of Illinois. She entered her most productive era in 1969, publishing six poetry collections by 1971. After writing an autobiography, *The World of Gwendolyn Brooks* (1971), she abandoned white publishing houses and produced nine volumes for black publishers, ending with *Say That the River Turns: The Impact of Gwendolyn Brooks* (1987). She was appointed the 1973 poetry consultant of the Library of Congress and was awarded a Frost Medal, along with senior fellowship in literature from the National Endowment for the Arts.

JANE BYRNE (1934–)

A native of Chicago, Jane Margaret Burke Byrne surprised seasoned politicians by her election as the first female mayor of the city. Byrne was educated at Saint Scholastica High School and Barat College in Lake Forest, Illinois. In widowhood, she applied her energies to the presidential campaign of John F. Kennedy. From postgraduate work at the University of Illinois, she moved into politics in the office of Mayor Richard Daley and was appointed manager of the Head Start program and the Chicago Committee on Urban Opportunity. As commissioner of consumer affairs, Byrne was Daley's first female Cabinet member.

A champion of consumer protection, Byrne won a plum position on the Democratic National Committee in 1972 and cochaired the Cook County Democratic Central Committee. Byrne accused Daley's successor, Michael A. Bilandic, of corruption and disregard for the public good, an accusation for which Bilandic dismissed her from her position in his administration. Byrne ran for mayor, and in 1979 won a landslide victory. In her inaugural address, she promised to combat the spreading "blight of boarded-up buildings, burned-out homes, and dying commercial areas." Her administration saw civic improvements, especially in transportation, but was marred by enough internal dissension that she lost her reelection bid.

HILLARY RODHAM CLINTON (1947–)

Attorney and politician Hillary Diane Rodham Clinton of Park Ridge, Illinois, was the first U.S. president's wife to further her career in the U.S. Senate. She earned a bachelor's degree from Wellesley and a law degree from Yale (1972), joined the staff of the Children's Defense Fund, and used her skills to pursue children's rights and education reform. In 1974 she taught at the University of Arkansas. After marrying Bill Clinton in 1975, she lived in Little Rock and joined the faculty of the University of Arkansas Law School. Shortly thereafter, in 1976, she joined the Rose Law Firm while her husband pursued a political career as attorney general and governor. While serving Arkansas as first lady, she was named partner at the Rose Law Firm—the first female to achieve that position— coestablished the Arkansas Advocates for Children and Families, and chaired the Arkansas Education Standards Committee.

During her tumultuous residence in the White House, Hillary Clinton influenced her husband's domestic policymaking and led the Task Force on National Health Care, a failed reform initiative intended to broaden the accessibility of medical treatment and prescription drugs. In 1995 she spoke at the United Nations International Conference on Women in Beijing; followed by a goodwill tour of Pakistan and India; and published *It Takes a Village: And Other Lessons Children Teach Us* (1998), a prochild overview of family responsibility. In 2000 she established residence in New York and successfully ran for the U.S. Senate, sparking speculation that she planned to run for president. She was the first former first lady to be elected to the Senate and the first woman elected statewide in New York.

KATHERINE DUNHAM (1909–)

Dancer, anthropologist, and activist Katherine Dunham of Joliet, Illinois, is often called the Matriarch of Black Dance. Trained in cultural anthropology, and with bachelor's, master's, and doctorate degrees from the University of Chicago, she taught dance and joined a troupe, the Ballets Negre, which performed at the city's Beaux Arts Ball. After supervising her own company, the Negro Dance Group, in 1938 she researched peasant dance in Haiti and Jamaica on a Rosenwald Foundation grant and wrote three books about her initiation into voodoo ritual. She was appointed dance director for the Federal Theatre Project, while in that position she staged the revue *L'Ag'Ya*.

Already respected in the arts, Dunham showcased African American talent and style in New York City. She plotted original choreography on Broadway for the musical *Cabin in the Sky* (1940) and *Carib Song* (1944) and for the film *Stormy Weather* (1943). Her decade of administration and teaching at the Performing Arts Training Center in St. Louis and at the Dunham School of Dance and Theatre in New York City shaped a generation of black dance performance; among her influences were indigenous Caribbean dance, folk ceremony, and structured movement of all kinds from modern kinetics to classical ballet. After years of touring Europe, Australia, Asia, and Mexico with her dance troupe, she issued an autobiography, *A Touch of Innocence* (1959). In her eighties, she established a medical center for the poor and undertook a 47-day fast protesting the U.S. denial of entry to Haitian refugees. She initiated the Katherine Dunham Legacy Project for the Library of Congress, which archives her work along with that of Martha Graham.

BETTY FRIEDAN (1921–)

The grand dame of modern feminism, Betty Naomi Goldstein Friedan of Peoria, Illinois, set the tone and direction of the women's movement in the 1960s. She earned a psychology degree from Smith College in 1942, where she was class valedictorian, and a graduate degree at the University of California at Berkeley. In 1947 she married Carl Friedan; they divorced in 1969. Disillusioned with the lack of opportunities for women, she surveyed and interviewed numerous people before compiling *The Feminine Mystique* (1963), a sociological classic characterizing female discontent as the result of limited life choices.

Rocketed to instant recognition, Friedan was interviewed for various print media and made public appearances to articulate women's frustrations. In 1966 she cofounded the National Organization of Women and established the National Women's Strike for Equality, the National Women's Political Caucus, and the first National Abortion Rights Action League. She staged sit-ins against gender discrimination, published articles supporting the Equal Rights Amendment, gave speeches decrying sexual exploitation in print and film, and summarized her life's work in *It Changed My Life: Writings on the Women's Movement* (1976) and *The Second Stage* (1981), a controversial reflection on women's progress toward full liberation. Her memoir, *Life So Far,* was published in 2000.

ALICE HAMILTON (1869–1970)

Native New Yorker Dr. Alice Hamilton, a pioneer of industrial toxicology, became the first female professor at Harvard University. As a girl she had enjoyed the comforts of her grandmother's Fort Wayne, Indiana, mansion, where she and her sister, mythologist Edith Hamilton, were privately tutored in the humanities and arts. After studying at Miss Porter's School in Connecticut, Alice completed her training at the Fort Wayne College of Medicine and graduated from the University of Michigan Medical School in 1893; she interned in Minneapolis and Boston and then went to work in an Ann Arbor, Michigan, bacteriology lab.

After subsequent coursework at Johns Hopkins Medical School, in 1898 Dr. Hamilton was appointed professor of pathology at Northwestern University. She aided social reformer Jane Addams as resident physician at Hull House, a settlement house in the Chicago slums. Dr. Hamilton deepened and widened her knowledge of the latest theories on microbiology at the Pasteur Institute in Paris before working at the Memorial Institute for Infectious Disease and publishing a monograph connecting the housefly with the spread of typhoid. She defended immigrant workers and factory laborers by demanding safe workplace legislation, workers' compensation, health insurance, and factory inspections. In 1908 she was appointed to the Illinois Commission of Occupational Diseases and as an inspector for the U.S. Bureau of Labor. At her direction, companies reduced worker injury from contact with aniline dye, arsenic, carbon monoxide, and lead. In 1919 she became the first female professor at Harvard Medical School. She published *Industrial Poisons in the United States* (1925) and *Industrial Toxicology* (1934), two respected texts, and continued to be active in social issues until her death in 1970.

JULIA LATHROP (1858–1932)

Julia Clifford Lathrop of Rockford, Illinois, a suffragist and a social worker at Jane Addams's Hull House in the Chicago slums, was the first woman appointed to head a federal bureau. Educated at Rockford Seminary (1876–1877), she then transferred to Vassar, where she received her bachelor's degree in 1880. She donated her

time as the first woman serving on the Illinois Board of Charities. She initiated and improved programs for and treatment of the mentally ill by inspecting institutions and publicizing the incarceration of the insane in workhouses. Her reform efforts included employment of the first female doctors at state hospitals and the establishment of the first U.S. juvenile court. In 1890 she joined Jane Addams at Hull House.

Lathrop built a treatment center for psychopaths and in 1903 launched graduate courses in social work at the University of Chicago; these courses ultimately developed into the Institute of Social Science. She wrote professional monographs, lobbied for orphan resettlement after World War I, and presided over the National Conference of Social Work. Pres. William Howard Taft appointed her to head the newly created Children's Bureau of the Department of Commerce and Labor in 1912. There, she investigated high infant mortality and delinquency rates, malnutrition, and illegitimacy; she campaigned for women's pensions, registration of births, and curtailment of child labor. After women secured the vote in 1920, she organized the Illinois chapter of the League of Women Voters, and served on the Child Welfare Committee of the League of Nations.

RUTH HANNA MCCORMICK (1880–1944)

Congresswoman Ruth Hanna McCormick of Cleveland, Ohio, was the first chair of the Women's Executive Committee of the Republican National Committee. The granddaughter of a coal merchant, daughter of a politician, and niece of a historian, she was well educated at private schools and concluded her training at Miss Porter's School in Connecticut. Against her parents' wishes, she did not attend college. Until her 1903 marriage to Joseph Medill McCormick, a U.S. representative and publisher of the *Chicago Tribune*, she worked in her father's campaigns.

Drawn to liberal causes, she supported settlement houses and the Women's Trade Union League and lobbied the Illinois legislature to establish a minimum wage, to ensure women's right to vote, and to prohibit child labor.

McCormick helped to establish the Progressive party and supported her husband during a successful run for the U.S. Senate. In her forties, she developed antiliberal leanings, organized Republican women's clubs, and opposed the League of Women Voters, an organization that encouraged women to participate in public forums and to run for office. In 1925 she replaced her husband in Congress after his death; in 1928 she was elected to the Illinois legislature. During the Great Depression, she ran her own radio station and published the Rockford Consolidated Newspapers. She remarried, involved herself in ranching and breeding cattle and sheep, and founded the Sandia School for Girls in Albuquerque, New Mexico.

CAROL MOSELEY-BRAUN (1947–)

Politician and diplomat Carol Moseley-Braun of Chicago was the first African American woman elected to the U.S. Senate. Committed from girlhood to community spirit and racial justice, she launched a one-girl restaurant sit-in and marched with Martin Luther King, Jr., in a crusade for open housing. After graduating from the University of Illinois in 1969 and earning a degree from the University of Chicago Law School in 1972, she practiced law as assistant U.S. attorney. She won a seat in the Illinois House of Representatives, where, as legislative floor leader, she battled for welfare reform, equal education and health care, and gun control.

From Cook County recorder of deeds (1988–1992) to U.S. senator (1992–1998) Moseley-Braun gained political savvy and experience, facing off against southern conservative Sen. Jesse Helms, who ridiculed her publicly. She worked for numerous civil rights and women's causes, particularly child care, hiring of women and minorities, and reproductive rights. She lost her seat in 1998 after coming under criticism for poor decisions in the spending of campaign funds and accusations that she promoted legislation that favored her corporate sponsors. Moseley-Braun was confirmed as ambassador to New Zealand and Samoa the following year. When her tenure as ambassador ended in 2001, she took consulting work and taught political science in Atlanta at Morris Brown College. In 2003 she explored a possible run for the presidency.

AGNES NESTOR (1880–1948)

The first female to lead a major union, Agnes Nestor of Grand Rapids, Michigan, developed from shop girl to labor leader and advocate for women's causes. Educated in parochial schools, she embraced the unionism of her father, an Irish machinist. In 1897 she moved with her family to Chicago, where she began working in a glove factory, and she joined organized male workers in a successful strike. In 1902 she led female glove sewers to form their own local, the nucleus of the International Glove Workers Union. For decades she held offices in the union and furthered the Chicago Women's Trade Union League as president and member of the executive board. She applied her early labor experience to organizing other needle trade unions and assisting striking garment workers.

In addition to labor organization, Nestor's crusades expanded to women's issues, notably maternity health benefits, a minimum wage, and women's suffrage. She lobbied the Illinois legislature against child labor and for a ten-hour workday. She served on the National Commission on Vocational Education and the U.S. Council of National Defense, commitments that garnered her an honorary doctorate from Loyola University.

CAROL SHIELDS (1935–)

Author Carol Shields of Oak Park, Illinois, moved gradually to fame as a chronicler of everyday triumphs. The daughter of a candy manufacturer, she completed college at Hanover and studied in England and at the University of Ottawa where she received her master's degree. After marrying Donald Hugh Shields, a professor, in 1957, she resided in Vancouver while rearing a son and four daughters. The rise of feminism in the 1960s turned her attention to inequities in society and literature and fueled her early poems. After beginning graduate study at the University of Ottawa, she issued her first poetry anthology in 1972.

Four years later Shields began editing the *Canadian Slavonic Papers* at home while researching a thesis and writing a novel, *Small Ceremonies* (1976), the first of four novels with unassuming protagonists. While teaching at the University of Manitoba, she published a short story collection, *Various Miracles* (1985), and ventured into fictional romance with *The Republic of Love* (1992). Critical opinion rose in response to *The Stone Diaries* (1993), a compelling study of an average woman, which won the Pulitzer Prize, the Governor General's Award, and the National Book Critics Circle Award. She received the Orange Prize for *Larry's Party* (1997), an examination of an unpromising life. She later was awarded the Chevalier de l'Ordre des Arts et des Lettres, a Guggenheim fellowship, and was nominated for the Booker Prize. She has also been granted honorary degrees from 11 Canadian universities. Her novel, *Unless*, was published in 2002.

FRANCES WILLARD (1839–1898)

The first woman to head a U.S. college, Frances Elizabeth Caroline Willard was a founder of the World Women's Christian Temperance Union. Born to a farmer and a schoolteacher in Churchville, New York, she was educated at the Northwestern Female Academy in Evanston, where she graduated first in her class in 1859. While teaching school, she became an officer of the American Methodist Ladies Centennial Association. In 1871 she began serving as president of the new Woman's College at Evanston; when the college became a part of Northwestern University in 1873, Willard was named the first dean of women.

Mounting interest in social reform turned Willard's attention from education to temperance. As cofounder and president of the Women's Christian Temperance Union (WCTU) in 1874 and editor of its journal, *Our Union*, she dedicated the rest of her life to improving opportunities for women. Her campaigns included demands for more women in police work, an end to prostitution, economic independence for women, prison reform, and suffrage, beginning with giving women the vote on matters affecting the home and family. Her vigor and idealism boosted the WCTU to the height of its popularity in the late 19th century, when it was the nation's largest women's organization. *Glimpses of Fifty Years*, her autobiography, was published in 1889.

FANNIE BARRIER WILLIAMS (1855–1944)

Civil rights activist Fannie Barrier Williams supported black women by cofounding the National League of Colored Women. Born in Brockport, New York, she graduated from the Brockport Normal School in 1870—the first African American to graduate from that institution—and taught in southern freedmen's schools. She studied at the New England Conservatory of Music and the School of Fine Arts in Washington, D.C., where she met her future husband, whom she married in 1887. They moved to Chicago and opened a law office; she helped him to raise funds to establish the Frederick Douglass Center, a multiracial settlement house, and to open a racially integrated nursing school at Provident Hospital.

In 1893, at Chicago's Columbian Exposition, Williams addressed the World's Congress of Representative Women, on the progress of black women since emancipation, and the World's Parliament of Religions, the beginning of her career as a lecturer and social reformer. While writing for the *Chicago Record-Herald, Woman's Era,* and *New York Age,* she advanced the cause of black women by championing their character and achievement and publicizing the benefits of employing them in white-owned businesses. In 1894 she confronted the racism of the upper classes by becoming the first black member in the Chicago Woman's Club. In 1924 she was appointed as the first black board member of the Chicago library system.

OPRAH WINFREY (1954–)

Recognized by her first name alone, Oprah Gail Winfrey developed the TV talk show into a platform for moral and social change, family unity, and public literacy. A native of Kosciusko, Mississippi, she spent her early childhood on her grandmother's farm, then lived with her mother in Milwaukee. To escape abuse by a male cousin, she spent her teens in Nashville, Tennessee, with her father and excelled at drama and speech in public schools. From broadcasting news on radio and further training in speech at Tennessee State University, she advanced to coanchor of evening news for WTVF-TV in Nashville and TJZ-TV in Baltimore, Maryland.

At age 23, Winfrey began hosting a talk radio broadcast, which was the beginning of her rise to stardom, on *A.M. Chicago.* A month later *A.M. Chicago,* a forum for discussing current issues and events, was the leader in its time slot. In 1985 she debuted *The Oprah Winfrey Show,* a nationally syndicated television program that has won a total of 35 Emmys and the devotion of millions of fans. Also in 1985 she played a brutalized prison inmate in the film *The Color Purple,* a classic that brought nominations for a Golden Globe and an Oscar. Subsequent screen appearances include a role in *Native Son* and a starring role in *Beloved* (1998), the story of a former Kentuckian retrieved from slavery by the Underground Railroad. She has used her fame and wealth to aid others, notably the child welfare program at Chicago's Cabrini-Green housing project and Atlanta's Morehouse College. As the first woman to produce a talk show and to own a television studio, Harpo Productions, she has been named Entertainer of the Year and in 1994 was inducted into the National Women's Hall of Fame. In 2003 *Forbes* magazine included Winfrey on its annual billionaire list: Winfrey was the first African American woman to become a billionaire.

—Mary Ellen Snodgrass

PROMINENT SITES

Bertha Van Hoosen, M.D., Historic Marker
South Lobby
Fine Arts Building
410 South Michigan Avenue
Chicago, IL 60605
The historic marker at this site reads "At this site on November 18, 1915, was founded the American Medical Women's Association, dedicated to the support of women physicians and women's health. As its founder and first president, Bertha Van Hoosen, M.D., demonstrated her dedication to the women's medical movement and her lifetime commitment to humanity as a physician whose compassion for people equaled her comprehension of science." Always at the forefront of medical practice, Dr. Van Hoosen's involvement in medical technology included the development of "twilight sleep," a pain reliever used in childbirth.

DuSable Museum of African American History
740 East 56th Place
Chicago, IL 60637
Telephone: (773) 947 0600
Web: http://www.dusablemuseum.org
Dr. Margaret Goss Burroughs founded the DuSable Museum in 1961 with a $10 charter. It is the oldest nonprofit organization solely dedicated to preserving and sharing with others the history and culture of African Americans. It offers a vast collection of artifacts, books, photos, art objects, and memorabilia.

International Museum of Surgical Science
1524 North Lake Shore Drive
Chicago, IL 60610
Telephone: (312) 642 6502
Web: http://www.imss.org/html/frames.html
The museum, located in a landmark mansion, exhibits artifacts used in surgical operations over the last 4,000 years. A statue of Marie Curie honors her contributions to humanity. The museum also holds letters written by Florence Nightingale. A small nursing exhibit is primarily dedicated to the history of midwifery.

Jane Addams' Hull-House Museum
University of Illinois–Chicago
800 South Halsted
Chicago, IL 60607–7017

Telephone: (312) 413 5353
Web: http://www.uic.edu/jaddams/hull/hull_house.html
The Hull Mansion was built in 1856; Jane Addams (1860–1935) began occupying it in 1889 when she and Ellen Gates Starr founded the Hull-House Settlement. The home has been restored to its appearance at the early days of the settlement with original furnishings, paintings, and photos. Exhibitions are mounted throughout the museum.

Mexican Fine Arts Center Museum
1852 West 19th Street
Chicago, IL 60608
Telephone: (312) 738 1503
Web: http://www.mfacmchicago.org
The museum celebrates both Mexicans and Mexican Americans. The permanent collection includes paintings by Leonora Carrington, Sarah Jimenez Vernis, and Ester Hernandez.

Mother Jones Burial Plot
Union Miners' Cemetery
Mount Olive, IL 62069
28 East Jackson
Chicago, IL 60604
Telephone: (312) 663 4107
Web: http://www.kentlaw.edu/ilhs/minecem.htm
Mary Harris Jones was a famous leader of the labor movement, described by a U.S. district attorney in 1902 as "the most dangerous woman in America." She asked to be buried among "her boys" upon her death; "her boys" were killed during the Virden Riot in 1898, which occurred when men tried to prevent a train carrying 180 strikebreakers from getting to the mines. Her grave is marked with a granite obelisk on which a large medallion bearing her likeness is guarded by larger-than-life bronze statues of coal miners. The cemetery is the only one in America owned by a union organization.

Museum of Broadcast Communications
Chicago Cultural Center
78 East Washington Street
Chicago, IL 60602
Telephone: (312) 629 6000
Web: http://www.museum.tv/contact_us.shtml

The museum opened in 1987 to honor the achievements of the broadcasting community. Visitors can use the A. C. Nielsen Research Center to explore its 10,000 TV shows, 50,000 hours of radio, 9,000 commercials, and 2,500 newscasts. Women honored include Susan Stamburg, who became anchor of National Public Radio's *All Things Considered* in 1972, and she was the first woman to host a nightly news show regularly; singer Kate Smith, who was also host of the popular show the *Kate Smith Hour;* and Yvonne Daniels, known as the "First lady of Chicago Radio," who was a host for WSDM/Chicago, the first all-female radio station from 1967 to 1973.

Perry County Jail Museum

Perry County Historical Society
108 West Jackson Street
Pinckneyville, IL 62274
Telephone: (618) 357 2225
Web: http://www.fnbpville.com/perrycounty.html
The historical society is dedicated to presenting local history, maintaining local genealogy records, and educating the community. The museum is housed in the former Perry County Jail, which was operational between 1871 and 1988. The front of the building was an eight-room home. The county sheriff lived in seven rooms, and the eighth, a bedroom above the kitchen, was used as the women's cell. Artifacts from the county that were primarily used by women, including cooking and sewing implements, are displayed in the room. A cellblock was attached to the building that could house 16 men.

Wilmette Historical Museum

609 Ridge Road
Wilmette, IL 60091
Telephone: (847) 853 7666
Web: http://www.wilmettehistory.org
The museum is dedicated to exploring and celebrating the history of Wilmette people from the earliest Native Americans to its present residents. The research library is open to the public and includes photos, newspapers, books, maps, oral history tapes, and archival materials. The permanent collection includes artifacts, fine art, and a costume collection. A portrait of Archange Ouilmette, an early resident, is on permanent display. Ouilmette was a major landowner in the area and the site of her cabin is included on a walking tour.

RESOURCES

FURTHER READING

HISTORY

Angle, Paul M. *Prairie State: Impressions of Illinois, 1673–1967, By Travelers and Other Observers.* Chicago: University of Chicago Press, 1968.

Anthony, Susan B., and Ida Husted Harper. *History of Woman Suffrage.* Vol. 4. Indianapolis, Ind.: Hollenbeck Press, 1902.

Breckinridge, Sophonisba Preston. *Women in the Twentieth Century; A Study of Their Political, Social and Economic Activities.* 1933. Reprint, New York: Arno Press, 1972.

Breese, Sidney. *The Early History of Illinois.* Chicago: E. B. Myers, 1884.

Brownell, Baker. *The Other Illinois.* New York: Duell, Sloan and Pearce, 1958.

Buck, Solon Justus. *Illinois in 1818: Centennial History of Illinois.* 2nd rev. ed. Urbana: University of Illinois Press, 1967.

Carrier, Lois A. *Illinois: Crossroads of a Continent.* Urbana: University of Illinois Press, 1993.

Cott, Nancy F., ed. *Root of Bitterness: Documents of the Social History of American Women.* 2nd ed. Boston: Northeastern University Press, 1996.

Curry, Lynne. *Modern Mothers in the Heartland: Gender, Health, and Progress in Illinois, 1900–1930.* Columbus: Ohio State University Press, 1999.

Davis, Elizabeth Lindsay. *The Story of the Illinois Federation of Colored Women's Clubs.* New York: G. K. Hall, 1997.

Davis, James Edward. *Frontier Illinois.* Bloomington: Indiana University Press, 1998.

Drell, Adrienne, ed. *20th Century Chicago: 100 Years, 100 Voices.* Chicago: Sports Publishing, 1999.

Ekberg, Carl J. *French Roots in the Illinois Country: The Mississippi Frontier in Colonial Times.* Urbana: University of Illinois Press, 1998.

Federal Writers' Project. *Illinois: A Descriptive and Historical Guide.* 1939. Reprint, St. Clair Shores, Mich.: Scholarly Press, 1976.

Ford, Thomas. *A History of Illinois: From Its Commencement As a State in 1818 to 1847.* 1854. Reprint, Urbana: University of Illinois Press, 1995.

Gallagher, Bernice E. *Illinois Women Novelists in the Nineteenth Century: An Analysis and Annotated Bibliography.* Urbana: University of Illinois Press, 1994.

Goodwin, Joanne L. *Gender and the Politics of Welfare Reform: Mothers' Pensions in Chicago, 1911–1929.* Chicago: University of Chicago Press, 1997.

Gussow, Zachary. *The Sac, Fox, and Iowa Indians.* New York: Garland Publishing, 1974.

Hampshire, Annette P. *Mormonism in Conflict: The Nauvoo Years.* New York: E. Mellen Press, 1985.

Harper, Ida Husted. *History of Woman Suffrage.* Vol. 6. New York: J. J. Little & Ives, 1902.

Hendricks, Wanda A. *Gender, Race, and Politics in the Midwest: Black Club Women in Illinois.* Bloomington: Indiana University Press, 1998.

Hicken, Victor. *Illinois in the Civil War.* 2nd ed. Urbana: University of Illinois Press, 1991.

Illinois Commission on the Status of Women. *Final Report of the Governor's Commission on the Status of Women in Illinois.* Chicago: Governor's Commission, 1998.

Jablow, Joseph. *Illinois, Kickapoo and Potawatomi Indians.* New York: Garland Publishing, 1974.

Jacobs, Sue-Ellen, Wesley Thomas, and Sabine Lang, eds. *Two-Spirit People: Native American Gender Identity, Sexuality, and Spirituality.* Urbana: University of Illinois Press, 1997.

Jensen, Richard J. *Illinois: A Bicentennial History.* New York: W. W. Norton, 1978.

Knupfer, Anne Meis. *Toward a Tenderer Humanity and a Nobler Womanhood: African American Women's Clubs in Turn-of-the-Century Chicago.* New York: New York University Press, 1996.

Lightner, David L., ed. *Asylum, Prison, and Poorhouse: The Writings and Reform Work of Dorothea Dix in Illinois.* Carbondale: Southern Illinois University Press, 1999.

Mason, Edward G. *Chapters from Illinois History.* Chicago: Herbert S. Stone & Co., 1901.

Nardini, Gloria. *Che Bella Figura!: The Power of Performance in an Italian Ladies' Club in Chicago.* Albany: State University of New York Press, 1999.

O'Dell, Cary. *Women Pioneers in Television: Biographies of Fifteen Industry Leaders.* Jefferson, N.C.: McFarland, 1997.

Rabinovitz, Lauren. *For the Love of Pleasure: Women, Movies, and Culture in Turn-of-the-Century Chicago.* New Brunswick, N.J.: Rutgers University Press, 1998.

Russo, Gus. *The Outfit: The Role of Chicago's Underworld in the Shaping of Modern America.* New York: Bloomsbury, 2001.

Rydell, Robert W. *All the World's a Fair: Visions of Empire at American International Expositions, 1876–1916.* Chicago: University of Chicago Press, 1984.

Sawyers, June Skinner. *Chicago Sketches: Urban Tales, Stories and Legends from Chicago History.* Chicago: Wild Onion Books, 1995.

Scott, Anne Firor. *Natural Allies: Women's Associations in American History.* Urbana: University of Illinois Press, 1991.

Stanton, Elizabeth Cady, Susan B. Anthony, and Matilda Joslyn Gage. *History of Woman Suffrage.* Vols. 1–3. Rochester, N.Y.: Charles Mann Printing, 1886.

Stebner, Eleanor J. *The Women of Hull House: A Study in Spirituality, Vocation, and Friendship.* Albany: State University of New York Press, 1997.

Stowell, Daniel W., ed. *In Tender Consideration: Women, Families, and the Law in Abraham Lincoln's Illinois.* Urbana: University of Illinois Press, 2002.

Weimann, Jeanne Madeline. *The Fair Women.* Chicago: Academy Chicago, 1981.

BIOGRAPHY AND AUTOBIOGRAPHY

Addams, Jane. *Twenty Years at Hull-House.* 1910. Reprint, New York: Signet Classic, 1999.

Addams, Jane. *My Friend, Julia Lathrop.* 1935. Reprint, New York: Arno Press, 1974.

Bowen, Louise de Koven. *Growing Up With a City.* 1926. Reprint, Urbana: University of Illinois Press, 2002.

Byrne, Jane. *My Chicago.* New York: W. W. Norton, 1992.

Clinton, Hillary Rodham. *The Unique Voice of Hillary Rodham Clinton: A Portrait in Her Own Words.* Edited by Claire G. Osborne. New York: Avon Books, 1997.

Costin, Lela B. *Two Sisters for Social Justice: A Biography of Grace and Edith Abbott.* Urbana: University of Illinois Press, 1983.

Davis, Allen Freeman. *American Heroine: The Life and Legend of Jane Addams.* Chicago: Ivan Dee, 2000.

Elshtain, Jean Bethke. *Jane Addams and the Dream of American Democracy: A Life.* New York: Basic Books, 2002.

Farnham, Eliza W. *Life in Prairie Land.* New York: Harper & Brothers, 1846.

Friedan, Betty. *Life So Far.* New York: Simon & Schuster, 2000.

Friedman, Jane M. *America's First Woman Lawyer: The Biography of Myra Bradwell.* Buffalo, N.Y.: Prometheus Books, 1993.

Haskins, James. *Katherine Dunham.* New York: Coward, McCann & Geoghegan, 1982.

Israel, Adrienne M. *Amanda Berry Smith: From Washerwoman to Evangelist.* Lanham, Md.: Scarecrow Press, 1998.

James, Marie. *Orphan Girl: The Memoir of a Chicago Bag Lady.* Chicago: Cornerstone Press, 1998.

Lightner, David L., ed. *Asylum, Prison, and Poorhouse: The Writings of Dorothea Dix in Illinois.* Carbondale: Southern Illinois University Press, 1999.

Linn, James Weber. *Jane Addams: A Biography.* Urbana: University of Illinois Press, 2000.

Livermore, Mary Ashton Rice. *Story of My Life: Or, The Sunshine and Shadow of Seventy Years.* 1897. Reprint, New York: Arno Press, 1974.

Lunin Schultz, Rima, and Adele Hast, eds. *Women Building Chicago, 1790–1990: A Biographical Dictionary.* Bloomington: Indiana University Press, 2001.

Miller, Kristie. *Ruth Hanna McCormick: A Life in Politics, 1880–1944.* Albuquerque: University of New Mexico Press, 1992.

Nestor, Agnes. *Woman's Labor Leader, an Autobiography.* Rockford, Ill.: Bellevue Books, 1954.

Rendleman, Edith Bradley. *All Anybody Ever Wanted of Me Was to Work: The Memoirs of Edith Bradley Rendleman.* Carbondale: Southern Illinois University Press, 1996.

Sapinsley, Barbara. *The Private War of Mrs. Packard.* New York: Kodansha International, 1995.

Sicherman, Barbara. *Alice Hamilton, A Life in Letters*. Cambridge, Mass.: Harvard University Press, 1984.

Tillson, Christiana Holmes. *A Woman's Story of Pioneer Illinois*. 1919. Reprint, Carbondale: Southern Illinois University Press, 1995.

Tucker, Cynthia Grant. *Healer in Harm's Way: Mary Collson, A Clergywoman in Christian Science*. 2nd ed. Knoxville: University of Tennessee Press, 1994.

Wieck, David Thoreau. *Woman from Spillertown: A Memoir of Agnes Burns Wieck*. Carbondale: Southern Illinois University Press, 1992.

Willard, Frances Elizabeth. *A Wheel Within a Wheel: How I Learned to Ride the Bicycle with Some Reflections by the Way*. 1895. Reprint, Bedford, Mass.: Applewood Books, 1997.

Winfrey, Oprah. *Oprah Winfrey Speaks: Insight From the World's Most Influential Voice*. Edited by Janet Lowe. New York: Wiley, 1998.

USEFUL WEB SITES

"Ahead of Their Time: A Brief History of Women's Suffrage in Illinois," Illinois State Archives
http://alexia.lis.uiuc.edu/~sorensen/suff.html

"Urban Experience in Chicago: Hull House and Its Neighborhoods 1889–1963," University of Illinois at Chicago: Jane Addams Hull House Museum
http://www.uic.edu/jaddams/hull/urbanexp

SELECTED ORGANIZATIONS AND INSTITUTIONS

DePaul University Women's Studies Program
990 West Fullerton Avenue, Suite 2300
Chicago, IL 60614
Telephone: (773) 325 4500
Web: http://condor.depaul.edu/~wms
Interdisciplinary program focusing on women's accomplishments, conditions, and contributions within their cultural and cross-cultural contexts.

Illinois State Archives
Norton Building
Capitol Complex
Springfield, IL 62756
Telephone: (217) 782 4682
Web: http://www.cyberdriveillinois.com/departments/archives/archives.html
Depository of public records of Illinois state and local government agencies. Does not include manuscript, newspaper, or other nonofficial sources.

Illinois State Historical Library
Illinois Historic Preservation Agency
1 Old State Capitol Plaza
Springfield, IL 62701
Telephone: (217) 524 7216
Web: http://www.state.il.us/hpa/lib/default.htm
A public, noncirculating research facility that contains material on all aspects of Illinois history. Includes an online catalog that features information on state and local women's history.

Loyola University–Chicago Women's Studies Program
Lake Shore Campus, Sullivan 200
6525 North Sheridan Road
Chicago, IL 60626
Telephone: (773) 508 2934
Web: http://www.luc.edu/depts/women_stu
The first women's studies program at a Jesuit institution, the program works to integrate knowledge about women, gender, and sexuality into scholarship across the disciplines.

Northwestern University Gender Studies
1859 Sheridan Road
Kresge Hall 124
Evanston, IL 60208
Telephone: (847) 491 5871
Web: http://www.genderstudies.northwestern.edu
Program committed to exploring new avenues of interdisciplinary scholarship in the study of gender and sexuality and to developing a cutting-edge perspective on race and internationalism.

Northwestern University Library
1970 Campus Drive
Evanston, IL 60208–2300
Telephone: (847) 491 7658
Web: http://www.library.northwestern.edu
Online gateway to Northwestern's catalog as well as Chicago area and statewide catalogs.

University of Chicago Center for Gender Studies
5733 South University Avenue
Chicago, IL 60637
Telephone: (773) 702 9936

Web: http://humanities.uchicago.edu/orgs/cgs
Consolidates work on gender and sexuality, and in feminist, gay and lesbian, and queer studies.

University of Illinois–Springfield Women's Studies
College of Liberal Arts and Sciences
Springfield, IL 62794
Telephone: (217) 786 6962
Web: http://www.uis.edu/womensstudies
An interdisciplinary program that combines the substance and methodologies of many disciplines to study women and gender.

University of Illinois at Urbana–Champaign Women's Studies
911 South Sixth Street, MC 494
Champaign, IL 61820
Telephone: (217) 333 2990

Web: http://www.womstd.uiuc.edu
Works to provide an educational environment that promotes an awareness of and appreciation for differences created by gender, race, ethnicity, class, global location, and sexual orientation.

Women's Studies Library at University of Illinois at Urbana–Champaign
Room 415, Main Library
1408 West Gregory Drive
Urbana, IL 61801
Telephone: (217) 333 7998
Web: http://door.library.uiuc.edu/wst
Online database of the collection's indexes, abstracts, general and specialized bibliographies, catalogs, guides, directories, CDs, United Nations documents, selected monographs and serials, and more.